PROGRAMMING FUNDAMENTALS
USING JAVA

PROGRAMMING FUNDAMENTALS USING JAVA

A Game Application Approach

William McAllister and S. Jane Fritz

St Joseph's College, New York

MERCURY LEARNING AND INFORMATION

Dulles, Virginia
Boston, Massachusetts
New Delhi

Publisher: David Pallai

MERCURY LEARNING AND INFORMATION
22841 Quicksilver Drive
Dulles, VA 20166
info@merclearning.com
www.merclearning.com
1-800-758-3756

This book is printed on acid-free paper.

W. McAllister and S. Jane Fritz.
Programming Fundamentals Using Java: A Game Application Approach.
ISBN: 978-1-938549-76-2

The publisher recognizes and respects all marks used by companies, manufacturers, and developers as a means to distinguish their products. All brand names and product names mentioned in this book are trademarks or service marks of their respective companies. Any omission or misuse (of any kind) of service marks or trademarks, etc. is not an attempt to infringe on the property of others.

Library of Congress Control Number: 2014941166

14151632 Printed in the United States of America
This book is printed on acid-free paper.

Our titles are available for adoption, license, or bulk purchase by institutions, corporations, etc.
For additional information, please contact the Customer Service Dept. at 1-800-758-3756 (toll free). Digital versions of our titles are available at: www.authorcloudware.com

To the memory of my mother Alma, who cherished in me something she was not afforded - a formal education.

—Bill McAllister

To all those who have taught me by example that "if you can dream it, you can do it," with gratitude.

—S. Jane Fritz

To our students, whose enthusiasm for learning has always inspired us to pursue improved teaching techniques.

—Bill McAllister
—S. Jane Fritz

Contents

Preface		xv
Acknowledgments		xxiii
Credits		xxv

Chapter 1 Introduction   **1**

1.1	The Computer System	2
1.2	A Brief History of Computing	5
	1.2.1 Early Computing Devices	6
	1.2.2 Computers Become a Reality	7
	1.2.3 Computer Generations	9
	1.2.4 More Notable Contributions	11
	1.2.5 Smaller, Faster, Cheaper Computers	12
1.3	Specifying a Program	13
	1.3.1 Specifying a Game Program	15
1.4	Sample Student Games	17
1.5	Java and Platform Independence	17
	1.5.1 The Java Application Programming Interface	19
1.6	Object Oriented Programming Languages	21
1.7	Integrated Development Environments and the Program Development Process	22
	1.7.1 Mobile-Device Application Development Environments	25
1.8.	Our Game Development Environment: A First Look	26
	1.8.1 The Game Window	26
	1.8.2 The Game Board Coordinate System	27
	1.8.3 Installing and Incorporating the Game Package into a Program	28

	1.8.4 Creating and Displaying a Game Window and Its Title	28
	1.8.5 Changing the Game Board's Size	29
1.9	Representing Information in Memory	30
	1.9.1 Representing Character Data	30
	1.9.2 Representing Translated Instructions	31
	1.9.3 Representing Numeric Data	32
1.10	Chapter Summary	34

Chapter 2 Variables, Input/Output, and Calculations — **39**

2.1	The Java Application Program Template	40
2.2	Variables	41
2.3	Primitive Variables	42
2.4	System Console Output	44
	2.4.1 String Output	44
	2.4.2 The Concatenation Operator and Annotated Numeric Output	44
	2.4.3 Escape Sequences	45
2.5	String Objects and Reference Variables	48
2.6	Calculations and the `Math` Class	50
	2.6.1 Arithmetic Calculations and the Rules of Precedence	50
	2.6.2 The Assignment Operator and Assignment Statements	53
	2.6.3 Promotion and Casting	54
	2.6.4 The `Math` Class	56
2.7	Dialog Box Output and Input	58
	2.7.1 Message Dialog Boxes	59
	2.7.2 Input Dialog Boxes	60
	2.7.3 Parsing Stings Into Numerics	60
2.8	Graphical Text Output	64
	2.8.1 The `drawString` Method	64
	2.8.2 The `draw` Call Back Method	65
	2.8.3 The `setFont` Method: A First Look	67
2.9	The Counting Algorithm	67
	2.9.1 A Counting Application: Displaying a Game's Time	68
2.10	Formatting Numeric Output: A First Pass	70
2.11	Chapter Summary	71

Chapter 3 Methods, Classes, and Objects: A First Look — **75**

3.1	Methods We Write	76
	3.1.1 Syntax of a Method	76
3.2	Information Passing	79
	3.2.1 Parameters and Arguments	79
	3.2.2 Scope and Side Effects of Value Parameters	82
	3.2.3 Returned Values	84
	3.2.4 Class-level Variables	85

3.3 The API Graphics Class   89

    3.3.1 Changing the Drawing Color   89

    3.3.2 Drawing Lines, Rectangles, Ovals, and Circles   90

3.4 Object Oriented Programming   93

    3.4.1 What Are Classes and Objects?   93

3.5 Defining Classes and Creating Objects   94

    3.5.1 Specifying a Class: Unified Modeling Language Diagrams   94

    3.5.2 The Class Code Template   95

    3.5.3 Creating Objects   96

    3.5.4 Displaying an Object   98

    3.5.5 Designing a Graphical Object   100

3.6 Adding Methods to Classes   102

    3.6.1 The `show` Method   103

    3.6.2 Constructors and the Keyword `this`   107

    3.6.3 Private Access and the `set/get` Methods   109

    3.6.4 The `toString` and `input` Methods   116

3.7 Overloading Constructors   121

3.8 Passing Objects To and From Worker Methods   125

3.9 Chapter Summary   128

Chapter 4 Boolean Expressions, Making Decisions, and Disk Input and Output   **137**

4.1 Alternatives to Sequential Execution   138

4.2 Boolean Expressions   138

    4.2.1 Simple Boolean Expressions   139

    4.2.2 Compound Boolean Expressions   140

    4.2.3 Comparing String Objects   143

4.3 The `if` Statement   144

4.4 The `if-else` Statement   150

4.5 Nested `if` Statements   158

4.6 The `switch` Statement   160

4.7 Console Input and the `Scanner` Class   169

4.8 Disk Input and Output: A First Look   172

    4.8.1 Sequential Text File Input   173

    4.8.2 Determining the Existence of a File   175

    4.8.3 Sequential Text File Output   175

    4.8.4 Appending Data to an Existing Text File   179

    4.8.5 Deleting, Modifying, and Adding File Data Items   179

4.9 Exceptions: A First Pass   179

4.10 Chapter Summary   185

Chapter 5 Repeating Statements: Loops   **191**

5.1 A Second Alternative to Sequential Execution   192

5.2 The `for` Statement   193

    5.2.1 Syntax of the `for` Statement   193

    5.2.2 A `for` Loop Application   197

    5.2.3 The Totaling and Averaging Algorithms   200

5.3 Formatting Numeric Output: A Second Pass   202

    5.3.1 Currency Formatting   202

    5.3.2 The `DecimalFormat` Class: A Second Look   204

5.4 Nesting `for` Loops   208

5.5 The `while` Statement   212

    5.5.1 Syntax of the `while` Statement   212

    5.5.2 Sentinel Loops   214

    5.5.3 Detecting an End of File   217

5.6 The `do-while` Statement   219

    5.6.1 Syntax of the `do-while` Statement   219

5.7 The `break` and `continue` Statements   221

5.8 Which Loop Statement to Use   222

5.9 The `Random` Class   224

5.10 The Enhanced `for` Statement   228

5.11 Chapter Summary   229

Chapter 6 Arrays   **235**

6.1 The Origin of Arrays   236

6.2 The Concept of Arrays   236

6.3 Declaring Arrays   238

    6.3.1 Dynamic Allocation of Arrays   239

6.4 Arrays and Loops   241

6.5 Arrays of Objects   243

    6.5.1 Processing an Array's Objects   245

6.6 Passing Arrays Between Methods   250

    6.6.1 Passing Arrays of Primitives to a Worker Method   251

    6.6.2 Passing Arrays of Objects to a Worker Method   253

    6.6.3 Returning an Array from a Worker Method   257

6.7 Parallel Arrays   258

6.8 Common Array Algorithms   265

    6.8.1 Searching   266

    6.8.2 Minimums and Maximums   267

    6.8.3 Sorting   269

6.9 Application Programming Interface Array Support   278

    6.9.1 The `arraycopy` Method   278

    6.9.2 The `Arrays` Class   279

6.10 Multidimensional Arrays   283

    6.10.1 Two-Dimensional Arrays   284

6.11	Deleting, Modifying, and Adding Disk File Items	286
6.12	Chapter Summary	290

Chapter 7 Methods, Classes, and Objects: A Second Look — 297

7.1	Static Data Members	298
7.2	Methods Invoking Methods Within their Class	301
7.3	Comparing Objects	303
	7.3.1 Shallow Comparisons	304
	7.3.2 Deep Comparisons	305
7.4	Copying and Cloning Objects	306
	7.4.1 Shallow Copies	307
	7.4.2 Deep Copies and Clones	308
7.5	The `String` Class: A Second Look	318
	7.5.1 Creating Strings from Primitive Values	318
	7.5.2 Converting Strings to Characters	319
	7.5.3 Processing Strings	319
7.6	The `Wrapper` Classes: A Second Look	322
	7.6.1 Wrapper Class Objects	322
	7.6.2 Autoboxing and Unboxing	324
	7.6.3 Wrapper Class Constants	326
	7.6.4 The `Character` Wrapper Class	326
7.7	Aggregation	328
7.8	Inner Classes	337
7.9	Processing Large Numbers	340
7.10	Enumerated Types	343
7.11	Chapter Summary	347

Chapter 8 Inheritance

8.1	The Concept of Inheritance	354
8.2	The UML Diagrams and Language Inheritance	355
8.3	Implementing Inheritance	357
	8.3.1 Constructors and Inherited Method Invocations	360
	8.3.2 Overriding Methods	364
	8.3.3 Extending Inherited Data Members	368
8.4	Using Inheritance in the Design Process	372
	8.4.1 Abstract Classes	372
	8.4.2 Designing Parent Methods to Invoke Child Methods	381
	8.4.3 Abstract Parent Methods	382
	8.4.4 Final Classes	383
	8.4.5 Protected Data Members	383
	8.4.6 Making a Class Inheritance Ready: Best Practices	384
8.5	Polymorphism	385
	8.5.1 Parent and Child References	385
	8.5.2 Polymorphic Invocations	387

8.5.3 Polymorphic Arrays   390

8.5.4 Polymorphism's Role in Parameter Passing   392

8.5.5 The Methods `getClass` and `getName` and the `instanceof` Operator   393

8.6 Interfaces   398

    8.6.1 Adapter Classes   405

8.7 Serializing Objects   406

8.8 Chapter Summary   411

Chapter 9 Recursion   **417**

9.1 What is Recursion?   418

9.2 Understanding a Recursive Method's Execution Path   421

9.3 Formulating and Implementing Recursive Algorithms   423

    9.3.1 The Base Case, Reduced Problem, and General Solution   423

    9.3.2 Implementing Recursive Algorithms   425

    9.3.3 Practice Problems   428

9.4 A Recursion Case Study: The Towers of Hanoi   429

9.5 Problems With Recursion   435

    9.5.1 When to Use Recursion   437

    9.5.2 Dynamic Programming   440

9.6 Chapter Summary   444

Chapter 10 Exceptions: A Second Pass   **449**

10.1 An Overview   450

10.2 Java's Exception Classes and Exception Objects   451

10.3 Processing Thrown Exceptions   453

    10.3.1 Nonerror Checking Use of Exceptions   459

    10.3.2 The `finally` Clause   461

10.4 The `throw` Statement and Error Messages   464

10.5 Defining and Exception Classes   472

10.6 Chapter Summary   475

Chapter 11 Graphical User Interfaces   **479**

11.1 Overview   480

11.2 Enhancing Dialog Boxes   482

11.3 Creating a Graphical User Interface for an Application   487

    11.3.1 The Content Pane   488

    11.3.2 Creating and Displaying a Program Window   488

    11.3.3 Adding GUI Components to a Window   492

11.4 Event Processing   500

    11.4.1 Implementing Event Handler Methods   501

    11.4.2 Registering the Event Handler   503

    11.4.3 Paint Events, `JPanels` and Two-Dimensional Graphics   509

    11.4.4 Mouse, Keyboard, and Timer Events   512

11.5 Layout Managers   522

    11.5.1 Designating the Layout Manager   523

    11.5.2 Border Layout   524

    11.5.3 Flow Layout   527

    11.5.4 Grid Layout   529

11.6 Applets   531

    11.6.1 Developing an Applet   532

    11.6.2 HTML Document Basics   534

    11.6.3 The Applet Execution Path   535

    11.6.4 Incorporating GUIs and Two-Dimensional
          Graphics into Applets   536

    11.6.5 Portability and Security Issues   543

11.7 Chapter Summary   544

Chapter 12 Graphical User Interfaces: A Second Look   **549**

12.1 Borders, Check Boxes, and Radio Buttons   550

    12.1.1 Borders   550

    12.1.2 Check Boxes   551

    12.1.3 Radio Buttons   555

12.2 Combo Boxes and Lists   563

12.3 Menus   572

    12.3.1 Drop-Down Menus   572

    12.3.2 Pop-Up Menus   581

12.4 File Chooser and Color Chooser Dialog Boxes   585

    12.4.1 File-Chooser Dialog Box   585

    12.4.2 Color-Chooser Dialog Box   587

12.5 Chapter Summary   590

Chapter 13 Generics and the API Collections Framework   **595**

13.1 Overview   596

13.2 Generic Methods   596

    13.2.1 Overloading Generic Methods   600

    13.2.2 Arrays as Generic Parameters and Returned Values   603

    13.2.3 Copying a Generic Array   606

    13.2.4 Operating on Generic Objects   608

13.3 Generic Classes   611

    13.3.1 Generic Data Structure Classes   615

13.4 The API Collections Framework   621

    13.4.1 Framework Interfaces   622

    13.4.2 Framework Algorithms: The `Collections` Class   622

    13.4.3 The `LinkedList` and `ArrayList` Classes   623

    13.4.4 The `HashSet`, `TreeSet`, and `LinkedSet` Classes   630

      13.4.5   The `ArrayDeque` and `PriorityQueue` Classes   630

      13.4.6   The `HashMap`, `TreeMap`, and `LinkedHashMap` Classes   633

  13.5 Chapter Summary   637

Chapter 14 Multithreading and Concurrency   **643**

  14.1 Overview   644

  14.2 Creating and Initiating Threads   645

  14.3 Thread States   649

      14.3.1   The New, Runnable, and Terminated States   649

      14.3.2   The Blocked, Waiting, and Timed Waiting States   651

  14.4 The Producer and Consumer Problem   652

  14.5 Solutions to the Producer and Consumer Problem   660

      14.5.1   Synchronizing a Buffer Class: Synchronized Methods   660

      14.5.2   The API `ArrayBlockingQueue` Class   668

  14.6 The Synchronized Statement   673

  14.7 Chapter Summary   677

Appendix A   Description of the Game Environment   **683**

Appendix B   Using the Game Environment Package   **691**

Appendix C   ASCII Table   **693**

Appendix D   Java Key Words   **697**

Appendix E   Java Operators and Their Relative Precedence   **699**

Appendix F   Glossary of Programming Terms   **701**

Appendix G   Using the Online API Documentation   **709**

Appendix H   Solutions to Selected Knowledge Exercises   **713**

Index   **725**

Preface

This is a Java textbook for beginning programmers that uses game programming as a central pedagogical tool to improve student engagement, learning outcomes, and retention. Game programming is incorporated into the text in a way that does not compromise the amount of material traditionally covered in a basic or advanced programming course and permits instructors who are not familiar with game programming and computer graphics concepts to realize the verified pedagogical advantages of game programming.

The book's DVD includes a game environment that is easily integrated into projects created with the popular Java Development Environments, including Eclipse, NetBeans, and JCreator in a student-friendly way and also includes a set of executable student games to pique their interest by giving them a glimpse into their future capabilities. The material presented in the book is in full compliance with the 2013 ACM/IEEE computer science curriculum guidelines and provides an in-depth discussion of graphical user interfaces (GUIs). It has been used to teach programming to students whose majors are within and outside of the computing fields.

Features

We use an objects-early approach to learning Java in that the defining and implementation of classes is introduced in the middle of Chapter 3. In preparation for this material, the terms object and class are introduced in Chapter 1 in the context of game piece objects and reinforced in Chapter 2 by continually referring to strings as string objects and differentiating between the primitive types and the `String` class. In addition, the concept of a reference variable is introduced within the concept of string objects in Chapter 2, and students become familiar with the idea that classes contain data members and methods via the chapter's discussion of the `Math` class, dialog boxes, and the formatting of numeric values. All of this facilitates the discussion in Chapter 3 of the definition and implementation of methods and classes and the declaration of objects.

The pedagogical tool, game programming, makes the concepts of object-oriented programming more tangible and more interesting to the student. For example, objects are output by drawing them at their current location rather than outputting their (x, y) coordinates to the system console. The functionality of `set` and `get` methods and the counting algorithm is illustrated by using them to relocate and animate game piece objects and keep a game's score. Decision statements are used to reflect animated game pieces, detect collisions between them, and to decide when a game is over, and loops are used to draw checkerboard squares and checkers. Because of this new pedagogical approach, student smiles have replaced frowns, enthusiasm has replaced complacency, and "teach us this" has replaced "do we have to know that?" Our classrooms have been transformed from a lecture-based venue to a highly engaged interactive learning environment.

Throughout the book, after a concept is introduced and discussed, its use is illustrated in a succinctly composed working program, and the parts of the program that utilize the new concepts are fully discussed.

Use of the Book

The material in this book can be covered within two courses: a basic programming course followed by an advanced programming course. The basic programming course would normally cover the first seven chapters supplemented with selected materials from Chapters 8 and 10. The remainder of the material would be covered in the advanced course. Alternately, the advanced topics can be incorporated into several other courses such as the use of the GUI chapters in a Web-page-building course, the use of the recursion, generics, and the Application Programming Interface (API) and Collections Framework chapters in a data-structures course, and the multitasking and concurrency chapter in an operating-system course.

The book is written in a way that it and its associated resources could not only be used at the college level, but also at the high school level or used in a self-instructional mode.

Chapter Overviews

Chapter 1: Introduction

This chapter includes a brief history of computer science and topics that are fundamental to an understanding of the concepts presented in the remainder of the textbook. These topics include an overview of the computer system and the representation of data in memory, the programming process and the role of an IDE in that process, platform independence and how Java achieves it, as well as an overview of object-oriented programming and the Application Programming Interface (API). Readers are asked to execute several student-written games contained on the book's DVD, which usually peaks their interest, as does the brief description of the game environment included in this chapter.

Chapter 2: Variables, Input/Output, and Calculations

Primitive variables, dialog box input, performing calculations, and performing output to dialog boxes, the system console, and to the game-board window are discussed in this chapter. The declaration of objects and the topic of reference variables are introduced within the context of the declaration of `String` objects, as are the topics of classes and methods within the chapter's discussion of the `Math` class, the formatting of text and numeric output, and graphical text output.

Chapter 3: Methods, Classes, and Objects: A First Look

The foundational object oriented programming concepts used in the next three chapters are discussed in this chapter. It begins with the techniques used to write methods and pass information via value parameters and return statements, and the `Graphic` class's two-dimensional shape-drawing methods are used in the discussion of parameter passing. The techniques used to specify and write classes are then discussed via a progressively developed game piece class's UML diagram and the progressive implementation of its data members, constructors, and methods. The motivation for `set` and `get` methods, and the `toString`, `input`, and `show` methods are discussed and these methods are implemented. Throughout the chapter, sketches are used to illustrate the reference variable and data-member memory model, and the chapter concludes with a graphical application that utilizes the learned concepts.

Chapter 4: Boolean Expressions, Making Decisions, and Disk Input and Output

This chapter begins a two-chapter sequence on control of flow. After a discussion of Boolean expressions and relational and logic operators, the students are introduced to Java's `if`, `if-else`, and `switch` statements. Their use is illustrated within a graphical context to reflect animated objects, detect when they collide, and to decide which direction to move them in response to a keystroke input. Disk text file I/O is also introduced in this class, which is preceded by a discussion of input using the scanner class and followed by an introduction to the concept and processing of thrown exceptions. The chapter concludes with a graphical application that utilizes the learned concepts.

Chapter 5: Repeating Statements: Loops

The `for`, `while`, `do-while`, and enhanced for loops are presented in this chapter, as are the concepts of counting loops, sentinel loops, and nested loops. The role that the `break` and `continue` statements play in repetition constructs is discussed, and Chapter 2's discussion of the formatting of numeric information and the generation of pseudorandom numbers is extended via a discussion of currency formatting and the API `DecimalFormat` and `Random` classes. The chapter concludes with a discussion of which loop construct to use for a particular application, and uses a graphical guessing game application and an application that draws a checker board to illustrate these learned concepts.

Chapter 6: Arrays

We placed this chapter after the loops chapter in an effort to immediately reinforce the student's understanding of loops via a discussion of the role loops play in the processing of arrays and the implementation of that processing. The chapter begins with a discussion of the concept of an array and arrays of primitive variables, and it illustrates the primitive array memory model. It then extends these concepts to arrays of reference variables and the objects they reference, and it discusses the passing of arrays to and from methods and illustrates the memory model used to accomplish this. The concept of parallel arrays is discussed as well as the array copying, sorting, minimum, and maximum algorithms and the API implementations of these algorithms. The chapter also discusses multidimensional arrays and the role arrays play in the addition, and deletion of information contained in disk files. The learned concepts are illustrated within graphical applications that use arrays of game piece objects to display an animated parade and to sort and locate particular game piece objects.

Chapter 7: Methods, Classes, and Objects: A Second Look

This chapter extends the object oriented programming concepts discussed in Chapter 3 and serves as the OOP foundation on which the remaining chapters of the text are built. It begins with a discussion of static data members, shallow and deep copying and comparisons, and the cloning of objects. The concept of aggregation and its implementation is then discussed, as are inner classes and their methods and the autoboxing feature of the wrapper classes. The processing of large numeric values is also covered in this chapter, as well as enumerated types and the methods of the `String` class. The learned concepts are illustrated within graphical applications that clone objects, use aggregated game piece objects, parse words from sentences, and perform calculations on large numbers.

Chapter 8: Inheritance

In this chapter, the terminology and concept of inheritance are discussed, as is the way this concept is used in the design and implementation phases of a software project to reduce the time and effort required to complete the project. The topics of extended classes, overriding methods, sub and super classes invoking each other's methods, and the role of abstract and final classes and methods in the design process are also discussed. All of these topics lead into a discussion of polymorphism and polymorphic arrays and the role of polymorphism in the design process. The chapter concludes with a discussion of interface and adapter classes and the serialization of objects. These learned concepts are illustrated in an evolving series of graphical applications that begin with the inheritance of a boat's hull and ends with a polymorphic display of all of the types of boats in a boat dealer's inventory.

Chapter 9 Recursion

This chapter begins by explaining the concept of recursion and recursive methods and a methodology for formulating and implementing recursive algorithms correctly. It then illustrates the use of the methodology in the discovery and implementations of several recursive algorithms, including the Towers of Hanoi. As students progress through the discovery and implementation of these algorithms, they develop the ability to think recursively and to extend the methodology to the discovery and implementation of other recursive algorithms. The chapter concludes with a discussion of the runtime problems associated with recursive algorithms, the role of dynamic programming in the implementation process, and when it is appropriate or efficient to use recursion in the programs we write. The learned concepts are illustrated in applications that compute the terms of the Fibonacci sequence, draw a Sierpinsky fractal, and solve the Towers of Hanoi problem.

Chapter 10: Exceptions: A Second Pass

Chapter 4's discussion of catching exceptions thrown from methods we invoke is expanded upon in this chapter, which discusses the *throwing* of exception objects from methods we write. The impact that this has on a method's reusability is discussed and illustrated, as is the ability to create and process exception error messages. In addition, the motivation for creating new exception classes is discussed, as well as the techniques for implementing these classes and using the concept of an exception in a non-error checking mode. The learned concepts are illustrated in several applications that include the use of exceptions in a graphical application to keep a game piece on a game board.

Chapter 11: Graphical User Interfaces

This chapter presents methods used to display enhanced dialog boxes and the fundamental techniques used to incorporate a graphical user interface (GUI) into an application and a Web-based applet program. These techniques include the building of an interface that contains two-dimensional shapes and text fields, labels and button components, and the sizing and positioning of these components within the interface with and without the use of a layout manager. The techniques used to write and register event-handler methods that respond to the program user's interaction with these interfaces via mouse actions and keystrokes, and respond to the expiration of timer intervals are also discussed. The chapter concludes with a discussion of the implementation of Java applets, the downloading and execution of these programs by a Web browser, and the security issues associated with applets. The learned concepts are illustrated in several applications that use GUIs, a functional applet, and game applications built without the use of the book's game environment.

Chapter 12: Graphical User Interfaces: A Second Look

The GUI components discussed in Chapter 11 are expanded upon in this chapter to include radio buttons, check boxes, combo boxes, lists, and drop-down and pop-up menus. The chapter also includes a discussion of the use of API dialog boxes that facilitate the specification of a file path to be used in a file I/O operation and the selection of a color to be used in a graphical application. These learned concepts are illustrated in an evolving series of GUI applications that solicit a meal choice from the program user and an application that permits the user to select the background color of the application's window.

Chapter 13: Generics and the API Collections Framework

This chapter begins by introducing the concept of generics and its role in extending the reusability of the methods and classes we write. It discusses the techniques used to implement a generic method that can be passed any type of object and a generic class whose data members' types can be specified when an instance of the class is created. The chapter concludes with a discussion of the API Collections Framework, which contains a set of generically implemented data structure classes, generic methods that operate on the data stored in these classes, and a set of generic interfaces associated with these classes. These learned concepts are illustrated in a set of applications that implement generic methods and a generic data structure class, and applications that use two of the generic classes in the Collections Framework to store a data set.

Chapter 14: Multithreading and Concurrency

The terminology, concepts, advantages, implementation, and problems associated with multi-threaded programs are discussed in this chapter. After discussing the implementation of multithread applications in Java and the states in which a thread can exist during its lifecycle, our attention turns to the discovery of the problems, including the Producer-Consumer problem, associated with sharing data between threads. Armed with an understanding of these problems, the student is then introduced to the synchronized statement and synchronized methods used to avoid these problems. The chapter concludes with a discussion of the API class `ArrayBlockingQueue`, which is used to share data between threads in a problem-free (thread-safe) way. The learned concepts are illustrated in a set of multithreaded applications that share data in an unsafe and safe way and an application that uses an `ArrayBlockingQueue` instance to share data among threads.

Appendices of the Textbook

The eight appendices contain:

- A description of the game programming environment (Appendix A)
- Directions on how to incorporate the game environment into a programming project (Appendix B)

  Note: The book's DVD contains the game environment and predefined Eclipse, NetBeans, and JCreator project templates that have the game environment incorporated into them.

- An ASCII table that contains the decimal, octal, hexadecimal, and binary representation of each the characters defined in the table (Appendix C)
- A list of Java keywords (Appendix D)
- A list of all of the Java operators and their precedence (Appendix E)
- A glossary of programming terms (Appendix F)
- A brief description of how to use the API online documentation (Appendix G)
- Answers to the odd numbered Knowledge Exercises that appear at the end of each chapter to facilitate student self-instruction outside the classroom (Appendix H).

The Book's DVD

The DVD in the back of the book contains a table of contents and the following materials, arranged in separate folders:

- Samples of student-written games in an executable format with instruction on how to run them
- The game environment

  o Eclipse, NetBeans, and JCreator template projects with the environment incorporated into them and instructions on how to use them to begin a new project without altering the system's CLASSPATH variable

  o A description of the environment and its call back methods used to draw and animate objects and respond to mouse, keyboard, and timer events

  o The environment's classes and methods in the form of class files, a jar file, and an importable package

- The source files for all of the applications presented in the text
- All of the book's figures
- All of the book's appendices

The Instructor's DVD *(available upon adoption to instructors)*

The DVD contains a table of contents and the following materials, arranged in separate folders:

- Answers to all of the knowledge exercises that appear at the end of each chapter
- Microsoft PowerPoint lecture slides for each chapter
- The source files for all of the applications presented in the text
- All of the book's figures
- Samples of student-written games in an executable format with instruction on how to run them

Digital Versions

Digital versions of this text and its resources are available on the publisher's electronic delivery site, *www.authorcloudware.com,* as well as other popular e-vendor sites.

W. McAllister
S. Jane Fritz
Patchogue, NY
August, 2014

Acknowledgments

We would like to thank three of our students who graciously granted us permission to include their game projects on the DVD that accompanies this book: Arielle Gulino, Andrew Zaech, and Ryan McAllister. We also thank all of our students whose enthusiasm for the incorporation of game programming into our pedagogy was the inspiration for the preparation of this book.

We would also like to thank the administration of St. Joseph's College and the members of the Promotions and Awards Committee for granting Bill a sabbatical, which was dedicated to the preparation of this manuscript, as well as our colleagues, and the entire St. Joseph's College Community who offered encouragement and support during its preparation.

We also thank David Pallai, the publisher and founder of Mercury Learning and Information for establishing and managing a publishing company that produces a high-quality product at an affordable cost, and his production team for guiding us through the development and production process, specifically Jennifer Blaney and Meg Salvia.

Finally, we would like to thank our families and friends for their endless patience when we were too busy to be ourselves.

To the Students

It is our hope that the approach to the material in this book will challenge you, engage you, and inspire you to continue your study of computer science and to enjoy a rewarding career by immersing yourself in this area of national need.

Credits

Chapter 1

Figure 1.16 Grace Hopper (http://www.history.navy.mil/photos/pers-us/uspers-h/g-hoppr.htm)

Figure 1.17 Grace Hopper's Bug (http://www.history.navy.mil/photos/pers-us/uspers-h/g-hoppr.htm)

Figure 17.18 Steve Jobs, by Kees de Vos from The Hague, The Netherlands [CC-BY-SA-2.0 (http://creativecommons.org/licenses/by-sa/2.0)], via Wikimedia Commons, (http://upload.wikimedia.org/wikipedia/commons/5/54/Steve_Jobs.jpg)

Figure 1.19 Bill Gates, by Matthew YoheAido2002 at en.wikipedia [CC-BY-3.0 (http://creative-commons.org/licenses/by/3.0)], from Wikimedia Com, (http://upload.wikimedia.org/wikipedia/commons/7/7f/Bill_Gates_2004_cr.jpg)

Figure 1.20 Vinton Cerf and Robert Kahn (http://georgewbush-whitehouse.archives.gov/ask/20051109-2.html)

Figure 1.21 Donald Knuth (Case Alumni Association and Foundation 2010, Flicker and (http://www.casealum.org/view.image?Id=1818)

Figure 1.22 Tim Berners-Lee, Courtesy of World Wide Web Consortium, Massachusetts Institute of Technology (www.w3.org/People/Berners-Lee)

Chapter 3

Green tea cup on windowsill © GoodMood Photo/Shutterstock.com, Image ID: 158310728

Chapter 4

Two Game Figurines © Melanie Kintz, Mellimage/Shutterstock.com, Image ID: 70027117

Chapter 5

Loops of a scaring roller coaster © Marcio Jose Bastos Silva /Shutterstock.com, Image ID: 97819241

Chapter 8

Boats on phewa-lake-nepal © Worapan Kong /ShutterStock.com, Image ID: 132349601

Chapter 9

Nested Traditional Matryoschka Dolls © PiXXart/Shutterstock.com, Image ID: 112054022

Chapter 10

Construction site © Victor Correia/ShutterStock.com, Image ID: 113180041

Chapter 11

Pocket sliding fifteen puzzle game © Coprid/ShutterStock.com, Image ID: 81197962

Chapter 12

Vector Retro Menu Design © Yienkeat /ShutterStock.com, Image ID: 108289445

Chapter 13

Collection of spaceship, planets and stars © Motuwe/ Shutterstock.com, Image ID: 140336917

Chapter 14

Maze Game with Solution © VOOK /ShutterStock.com, Image ID: 95912809

INTRODUCTION

1.1   *The Computer System* *2*

1.2   *A Brief History of Computing* *5*

1.3   *Specifying a Program* *13*

1.4   *Sample Student Games* *17*

1.5   *Java and Platform Independence* *17*

1.6   *Object-Oriented Programming Languages* *21*

1.7   *Integrated Development Environments
       and the Program Development Process.* *22*

1.8   *Our Game Development Environment: A First Look* . . . *26*

1.9   *Representing Information in Memory.* *30*

1.10 *Chapter Summary* *34*

In this chapter

This chapter presents topics that are fundamental to computing and the programming process and discusses tools that programmers use to write programs. Because the focus of this text is on learning to program, an understanding of these concepts and tools is essential. The topics include a brief history of computing, which will highlight some of the important contributions to the field and facilitate an understanding of the modern computer system as well as how data is stored. The tools discussed in the chapter are used to develop an unambiguous description of a program and to minimize the effort required to transform this description into a functional program that can run on any computer system or mobile device.

After successfully completing this chapter, you should:

- Understand the hardware and software components of a computer system
- Gain an appreciation for the history and evolution of computing
- Be able to specify simple programs and games
- Have used some examples of student-written game programs
- Understand why Java programs can be run on any computer system
- Be familiar with the concept of objects, classes, and the object-oriented programming paradigm
- Understand the programming process and the role of Integrated Development Environment programs in this process
- Be familiar with the features of the game-development tool on the DVD that accompanies this textbook
- Understand how data is represented inside computer systems

1.1 THE COMPUTER SYSTEM

Over the last twenty years, computers and the use of the Internet have become part of our everyday lives. Daily communication that was performed using postal systems and telephone conversations are now performed more efficiently using computer-based e-mails and text messaging. Much of the information gathering we performed in libraries is now done from the comfort of our homes using a computer attached to the Internet, as is much of the shopping we do. As a result, the number of computers available in the world continues to grow (Figure 1.1).

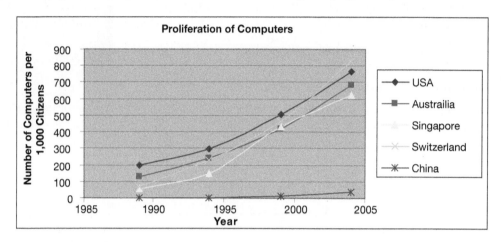

Figure 1.1
Growth in the number of computers per capita over a fifteen-year period.

In many of the developed countries of the world there is now one computer, or more accurately, one computer system for every citizen in the country. Although many of these people would say that they use a computer every day, they really should say that they use a computer system every day.

As shown in Figure 1.2, a computer system is comprised of two major components: software and hardware. As its name implies, hardware is the hard, or tangible, part of the computer system. It is the collection of electronic circuits, mechanical devices, and enclosures manufactured in a factory. When we purchase a computer system and look into the box it comes in, what we see is the hardware.

However, the box also contains software, but, as its name implies, it is the soft, or less-tangible portion of the computer system, and so it is not as easy to detect. Software, or programs, consists

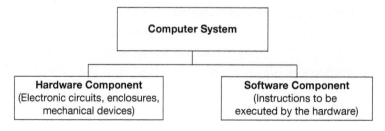

Figure 1.2
The two major components of a computer system.

of sequences of instructions written by programmers to perform specific tasks. These instructions are executed by the computer system's hardware, and both components are essential to a computer system. A computer system that contained only hardware would have no instructions to execute, so it would do nothing but consume electrical power. A computer system that contained only software would not be able to execute the program's instructions.

The software of a computer system is comprised of two major subcomponents: operating system software and application software (Figure 1.3). Microsoft Windows, Apple OS, and Linux are all examples of operating system programs. This set of programs contains instructions to manage the hardware resources of the computer system and provides an interface, usually a point-and-click interface, through which the user interacts with the computer system. In addition, most application software interacts with the hardware through various groups of operating system instructions.

Although nonoperating system software can be categorized in several groupings, we will consider all nonoperating system software to be collected into one group, application software, as shown in Figure 1.3. In this textbook, we will learn how to write application software using the programming language Java.

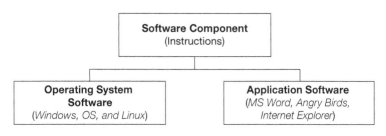

Figure 1.3
Computer software subcomponents.

The hardware of the computer system can be divided into three main categories, or subcomponents, based on the function they perform. Hardware that communicates with humans and other computer systems is grouped into the category input/output (I/O) devices. Hardware used to store information inside the computer system is grouped into the category storage devices. Finally, all other functions performed by the hardware are part of a category named the central processing unit (CPU).

Figure 1.4 shows the standard conceptual arrangement of the three hardware categories with the CPU at the center of the arrangement. The storage devices are shown on the right and bottom of the figure and are divided into two types of devices: backing storage, often referred to as secondary storage, and random access memory (RAM), also called main memory. With the exception of backing storage, each of the hardware components has been assigned an acronym, which is shown parenthetically below the name of the component in Figure 1.4. For brevity, the components are most often referred to using their acronyms: I/O devices, CPU, and RAM (pronounced as "ram").

The arrows into and out of the I/O devices at the top left of Figure 1.4 indicate the flow of information entering (input) and leaving (output) the computer system. The other arrows in the

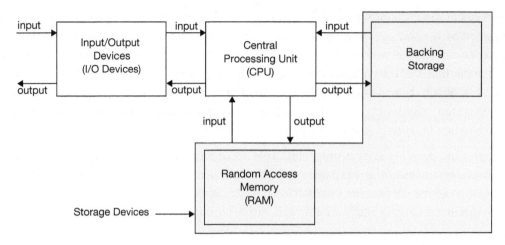

Figure 1.4
Arrangement of the hardware subcomponents of a computer system.

figure represent the flow of information among the computer-system components. The central processing unit can receive information from (arrows labeled "input") and send information to (arrows labeled "output") the other system components. The flow of information is always relative to the CPU. Information sent to the CPU is considered input, and information sent from the CPU is considered output.

Hardware that communicates with humans and other computer systems is grouped into the component I/O devices. These devices are the interface between the computer system and the rest of the world. Input devices send information into the system. Examples of input devices include a keyboard, a touch screen, a mouse, a microphone, a digitizer, and a modem. Output devices send information out from the system. Examples of output devices include a monitor, a printer, a speaker, and a modem. A modem is both an input and output device and is normally used to transfer information between computer systems.

Hardware devices that have the ability to store and recall information are grouped into the component storage services. All but one of these devices fall into the subcomponent backing storage, shown on the top right side of Figure 1.4. Examples of storage devices include hard drives, flash drives, subscriber identification module (SIM) cards, CD drives, and magnetic tape drives. One storage device, random access memory (RAM) is depicted separately at the bottom of Figure 1.4. One difference between this storage device and all of the other storage devices is its speed. It can access information, meaning store and recall information, faster than any other storage device. Its information-access speed approaches the speed at which the CPU can transfer information.

Programs run faster when their instructions are stored in RAM, so it is an advantage to have a high-capacity RAM in a computer system. Unfortunately, the materials and manufacturing process used to achieve RAM's speed make it the most expensive type of storage. To make computer systems affordable, backing-storage devices are added to the system. When a program is in execution, the operating system software attempts to transfer the program's instructions and the data the instruction processes from backing storage to RAM before this information is needed by the CPU.

Another reason for adding backing storage, or secondary storage, to a computer system is the fact that RAM is volatile, which means that it only retains its memory when it is attached to an electrical power source: no electricity, no memory. All backing-storage devices are nonvolatile, which means that the information they store is not lost when they are detached from a power source. As a result, these devices can be used to archive program instructions and data within the computer system when it is powered down (e.g., hard drives), and can be used to manually transport information between computer systems (e.g., flash drives).

The I/O and storage components of the computer system give us the ability to transfer information into and out of the computer system and the ability to store and recall that information. The CPU depicted in the center of Figure 1.4 gives us the ability to process the information, and so it is aptly named the central processing unit. If we were inclined to designate one of the computer-system components as the brain of the system, we would probably bestow that title on the CPU. However, despite the remarkable tasks that computers perform, the CPU's electronic circuits only perform five very basic processing operations:

1. Transfer information (i.e., instructions and data) to and from the other components of the computer system and interpret instructions
2. Store a very small amount of information, e.g., one instruction and sixteen pieces of data
3. Perform arithmetic operations such as addition, subtraction, multiplication, and division
4. Perform logic operations involving relational operators (such as $10 < 6$, and $a >= 12$) and logical operators (such as A AND B, and A OR B)
5. Execute instructions in the order in which they are written or skip some instructions based on the truth value of a logic operation

The magic here is that all of the remarkable tasks that computers do have been expressed as a sequence of these five basic processing operations. A step-by-step sequence of these operations to perform a particular task is called an **algorithm**. The most difficult part of a programmer's job is to develop, or discover, algorithms. Once an algorithm is discovered, it is written into a programming language and verified via a testing process.

Definition

An **algorithm** is a step-by-step sequence of the five processing operations a computer system can execute to solve a problem or perform a particular task.

A **computer program** is an algorithm written in a programming language.

■1.2■ A BRIEF HISTORY OF COMPUTING

Long before our modern computers existed, people had the need to count or compute. As a matter of fact, the early meaning of the term computer referred not to a machine but to a person who performed calculations. In this section, we will see the amazing development of the revolutionary machines that have changed the way we learn, teach, shop, do research, and are entertained.

1.2.1 Early Computing Devices[1]

If computers are really such an important part of our lives today, you might wonder and ask the question: Who invented the computer?

Although this is a simple question, it does not have a simple answer such as Thomas Edison invented the light bulb or Alexander Graham Bell invented the telephone. One reason for this complexity is that computers evolved over thousands of years, and many people from different cultures and diverse fields such as mathematics, physics, engineering, business, and even textile design were involved in laying the foundation for the modern electronic computer.

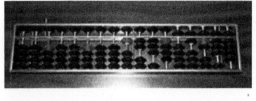

Figure 1.5
The abacus.

The roots of computing dates from about 50,000 to 30,000 BC when people counted their sheep and other possessions using their fingers, stones, or notches on sticks. The first computing device, the abacus, was introduced in China around 2,600 BC and used pebbles or stones. A later version of the abacus (shown in Figure 1.5) used beads that could be moved on a wire frame to perform basic counting and arithmetic functions. These were widely used in Europe and Asia, and some of these devices are still in use today.[2]

Figure 1.6
A typical modern slide rule.

It was not until the seventeenth century that there were other notable attempts at building computing devices. Napier's bones and the slide rule (Figure 1.6) were two of these devices.

Blaise Pascal (Figure 1.7), at the age of 18, built a mechanical calculator called the Pascaline to perform basic addition and multiplication.

Because manufacturing technology was not yet well developed, these devices had to be carved or forged by hand, which required tedious work. Although it would seem likely that the development of computing devices would continue at a more rapid pace, very little progress was made from the seventeenth century until the 1800s, and we might ask why. Perhaps it was because this was a time of war, colonization, and the struggle for survival in much of the world. (If you think about the United States, for example, from 1776 through the 1800s, building a calculator was not considered a priority at that time.)

Figure 1.7
Blaise Pascal: philosopher, mathematician, inventor.

In 1801, Joseph Marie Jacquard, a textile designer, discovered that he could program his weaving loom (Figure 1.8) to create intricate patterns in the fabric, by storing the instructions on punched cards or paper tape. These binary instructions directed the loom to raise or lower certain threads depending upon whether or not a hole was punched on the tape. Later on, this concept would develop into the idea of creating a stored program computer based on binary instructions; it would be implemented in the twentieth century using punched cards for computer input.

Figure 1.8
A Jacquard Loom.

1.2.2 Computers Become a Reality

Charles Babbage, a mathematician working in England around 1822, designed the prototype of a machine, known as the Difference Engine, to compile mathematical tables. It was a large hand-cranked machine built of metal wheels and gears and although he continued to add refinements to it, he never fully completed it. By 1837, Babbage took his ideas one step further and designed a more complex Analytical Engine Figure 1.9), which he envisioned to be a general purpose computational machine and which had many characteristics in common with modern computers. He designed it to be steam powered, which would not make it portable, but would automate mathematical calculations. Due to the limitations of available technology, it was not completed in his lifetime, but it has recently been completed and works as he described it. Charles Babbage has been called the father of the computer for his innovative work on the first mechanical computer.

Lady Ada Augusta Byron Lovelace (Figure 1.10), the daughter of the poet Lord Byron, became intrigued with Babbage's work and began to write instructions, or what we now call programs, for his machine. She is known today as the first programmer, and the programming language used for U.S. government applications is named Ada in her honor. Ada was unique in being a well-educated woman, skilled in mathematics, at a time when women had little formal or advanced schooling. She was able to perform the advanced mathematical and engineering design functions required for programming a theoretical computer that was not yet completely operational.

In the 1890s, in the United States, Herman Hollerith was working on a mechanical calculator and was asked by the government to design a machine that could record and store census data. The population was growing so fast that hand calculation could not keep pace with the growing volume of data: by the time the data was tabulated it was outdated and the next census had begun. Hollerith used punched cards to input the data to his new machine (Figure 1.11), which successfully compiled and tabulated even greater amounts of data in record time. Following this success, he founded a company with Thomas Watson, which later became known for computing, the International Business Machine Corporation (IBM).

Figure 1.9
Charles Babbage's Analytical Engine.

Figure 1.10
Lady Ada Augusta Byron Lovelace, the first programmer.

Figure 1.11
Hollerith's electric tabulating machine.

Figure 1.12
Alan Turing, father of theoretical computer science.

In the 1900s, the demand for recording and processing large amounts of data continued to increase, and there were numerous attempts to design more advanced computing machines. The need came from businesses as well as the military. Large universities and mathematicians throughout the world began to design and build these early computing machines. Around 1939–1942, the Atanasoff-Berry computer (ABC) was built by Dr. John V. Atanasoff and Clifford Berry at Iowa State University. It was the first electronic digital computer. At about the same time, Konrad Zuse, working in Germany, built the first fully programmable computer, the Z3.

Also in the early 1940s, the Colossus was built with the assistance of the brilliant British mathematician Alan Turing (Figure 1.12). It was designed as a code-breaking machine that could decipher the German codes created with the Enigma encoding machine. Turing's contribution to breaking the German codes helped to defeat Hitler in World War II. Turing also explored Artificial Intelligence (Google "Turing Test" for specific details), and he is highly regarded as the father of theoretical computer science, laying a foundation upon which to build advanced computing machines.

In 1944, the Harvard Mark I was designed and built through the efforts of Howard Aiken working with Grace Hopper. Built at Harvard University by IBM, the Mark I was the first electromechanical computer, and it was used to produce mathematical tables. It could be programmed using paper tape.

The first electronic general purpose digital computer, the Electronic Numerical Integrator and Computer (ENIAC) was built at the University of Pennsylvania in 1946 by John Mauchly and J. Presper Eckert. This computer weighed 30 tons and had over 18,000 vacuum tubes and thousands of electronic relays (Figure 1.13). It filled a large room that was required to be air conditioned because of the heat this machine generated. It could add or subtract 5,000 times a second, a thousand times faster than any other machine at that time. It also had modules to multiply, divide, and calculate square roots.

(a) Replacing vacuum tubes.

(b) Programming the ENIAC.

U.S. Army photos.

Figure 1.13
Troubleshooting the ENIAC.

U.S. Army photo   U.S Army photo

Figure 1.14
First programmers of the ENIAC.

Most of the ENIAC's programming was done by six women, including those shown in Figure 1.14.

John von Neumann (Figure 1.15) proposed modifications to the ENIAC, which included using binary instead of decimal numbers. His design for a stored program binary computer where both the program and the data could be stored in the computer's memory became known as the von Neumann architecture, which is still in use today. In 1945, he proposed the design for the Electronic Discrete Variable Automatic Computer (EDVAC) and later worked on the Institute for Advanced Study (IAS) computer in Princeton. He is often called the father of the modern computer and game theory.

Figure 1.15
John von Neumann, father of the modern computer and game theory.

Computer Generations[3]

The computers that followed are usually grouped into generations, each characterized by a specific component or technology. The dates are approximate.

First-Generation (1937–1946): *Vacuum Tubes*

These very large computers used thousands of vacuum tubes, generated a lot of heat, and were fairly unreliable. Memory storage was on magnetic drums, input was performed using punched cards or paper tape, and output was displayed on paper printouts. Computers of this generation could only perform a single task, lacked an operating system, and were programmed using a sequence of ones and zeros known as machine language. First-generation machines include the ENIAC, Electronic Delay Storage Automatic Calculator (EDSAC), and EDVAC computers.

Second-Generation (1947–1963): *Transistors*

This generation of computers used transistors, which were much more reliable than the vacuum tubes they replaced. Transistors were also smaller, cheaper, and consumed less electrical power. Machine language was replaced with assembly language, which was a more English-like language, and higher-level languages such as Common Business Oriented Language (COBOL) and Formula Translation (FORTRAN) were developed for this generation of computers. In 1951, the universal automatic computer (UNIVAC 1) was introduced as the first commercial computer. In 1953, the IBM 650 and 700 series computers were introduced. Operating systems were designed for these machines, and over 100 computer-programming languages were developed during this generation. Storage media such as magnetic tape and disks were in use, and printers were available for output.

Third-Generation (1964–1971): *Integrated Circuits (IC) or "chips"*

Transistors were miniaturized and placed on chips and integrated circuits (IC), developed by Jack Kilby and Robert Noyce. This invention resulted in smaller, more powerful, more reliable, and cheaper computers. Users could now interact with computers through keyboards and monitors instead of punched cards and printouts. Operating systems monitored memory usage and controlled the scheduling of multiple applications that could share the system resources.

Fourth-Generation (1971-present): *Microprocessors and Very Large Scale Integration (VLSI)*

Very-large-scale integration (VLSI) resulted in thousands of computer circuits being reduced to fit on a chip, reducing the room-size computers of the first generation to something that could fit in your hand. Components of the computer, from the central processing unit and memory to input/output controls, could now be located on a single microprocessor chip. In addition to their small size, computers became affordable for individuals, and in 1977, the personal computer (PC) became available from three companies: Apple, Tandy/Radio Shack, and Commodore. In 1980, Microsoft released its disk operating system (MS-DOS), and in 1981, IBM introduced the PC for home and office use. Three years later, Apple introduced the Macintosh computer with its icon-driven interface. In 1985, Microsoft released the Windows operating system. Fourth-generation computers also used graphical user interfaces (GUI, pronounced "gooey") and provided a mouse for ease of use. Object-oriented languages, such as Java, were developed for more efficient software development. These smaller, more reliable and powerful computers could now be linked together, resulting in the growth of networks and the Internet.

Fifth-Generation (Present and Beyond): *Artificial Intelligence, Parallel Processing, Quantum Computing*

Fifth-generation computing devices are characterized by artificial intelligence and the advancement of devices that will respond to natural language and be capable of learning. Although these features are still in the early stages of development, some applications such as voice recognition are currently available. The use of parallel processing, quantum computing, and nanotechnology will help to achieve these advances and will change computing in the future.

1.2.4 More Notable Contributions

In addition to the achievements already mentioned, there were many others who made notable contributions to the computing field. The names and contributions of a few of these innovators follow, and you are invited to continue to add to the list.

Admiral Grace Murray Hopper (Figure 1.16) was a pioneer in the field of computing. She was one of the first programmers of the Harvard Mark I computer and is known for the development of the first compiler and assembly language. Her work in programming led to the development of the language COBOL, and she later worked on Ada.

Figure 1.16
Admiral Grace
Hopper.

She coined the term "debugging" when she removed a bug (or moth) from a computer's circuitry that was interrupting the flow of electricity, and taped it into her notebook (Figure 1.17).

Steve Jobs (Figure 1.18) and Steve Wozniak were the cofounders of Apple Computers. The Apple I was one of the three personal computers introduced in 1977 for home use. Together they developed the point-and-click approach to computing. In 1984, they introduced the MAC OS that developed into the modern graphical user interface, which today is standard on modern computers. Steve Jobs is also a cofounder of Pixar Animation and has been described as the father of the digital revolution.

Bill Gates (Figure 1.19) and Paul Allen cofounded Microsoft, one of the largest U.S. corporations, and supplied the disk operating system (DOS) to IBM to run on its PCs. In 1985, Microsoft developed a graphical operating system known as Windows, which is the operating system used on over 80% of today's computers.

James Gosling is credited with the development of the object-oriented programming language known as Java. He is called the father of Java programming.

Bob Metcalfe and David Boggs invented the Ethernet, the technology upon which local computer area networks are based.

Vinton Cerf (Figure 1.20a) and Robert Kahn (Figure 1.20b) are considered to be the fathers of the Internet and the Transmission Control Protocol/Internet Protocol (TCP/IP) upon which the

Figure 1.17
Grace Hopper's first recorded computer "bug."

Figure 1.18
Steve Jobs, cofounder of
Apple Computer.

Figure 1.19
Bill Gates, cofounder of
Microsoft Corporation.

(a)   (b)

Figure 1.20
Vinton Cerf and Robert Kahn, inventors of the Internet.

Figure 1.21
Donald Knuth, father
of the analysis of
algorithms.

Figure 1.22
Tim Berners-Lee,
inventor of the World
Wide Web.

Internet is based. Vinton Cerf created the first commercial Internet e-mail system and is now Vice President and Chief Internet Evangelist for Google.

Donald Knuth (Figure 1.21), a computer scientist, mathematician, and Professor Emeritus at Stanford University, has been called the father of the analysis of algorithms. His multivolume set of books entitled *The Art of Computer Programming* is the classical reference for all programmers. He is also the developer of the text document (TEX) typesetting system for creating high-quality digital publications.

Tim Berners-Lee (Figure 1.22) is known as the inventor of the World Wide Web and continues to direct the Web's development as the director of The World Wide Web Consortium (W3C). He is also a director of the World Wide Web Foundation, which furthers the potential of the Web to benefit humanity.

1.2.5 Smaller, Faster, Cheaper Computers[4]

Computing has made more progress in 15 years than transportation has made in 2,000 years, having gotten smaller, faster, and cheaper during that time. Your cell phone today is about a million times cheaper, a thousand times more powerful, and a hundred thousand times smaller than the one computer that was used at MIT in 1965.

According to Ed Lazowska, chairman of the University of Washington's Computer Science and Engineering Department, if Detroit car makers could have paralleled the innovations that hardware and software manufacturers have realized for computers, today's cars would be tiny, powerful, and inexpensive. They would be as small as toasters, cost $200, travel 100,000 miles per hour, and would run 150,000 miles on a gallon of fuel. "In Roman times, people traveled along on horses or in carts at about 20 miles per day," he said. "In the early part of this century, the automobile allowed people to travel at 20 miles per hour. Today, supersonic military aircraft travel at about 20 miles per minute. That progress is about a factor of 1,000 in about 2,000 years," Lazowska wrote in an e-mail message.

Another analogy by Rick Decker and Stuart Hirshfield in *The Analytical Engine* states, "If automotive technology had progressed as fast as computer technology between 1960 and today, the car today would have an engine less than a tenth of an inch across, would get 120,000 miles per gallon, have a top speed of 240,000 miles per hour, and would cost $4.00."[5] Also, at a recent Computer Dealers Exhibition (COMDEX) meeting, Bill Gates is reported to have said that if GM had kept up with technology like the computer industry has, we would all be driving $25 cars that get 1,000 miles per gallon.

Computers and the programs that provide their instructions will continue to increase in speed, reliability, and functionality, limited only by human creativity.

1.3 SPECIFYING A PROGRAM

As discussed in Section 1.1, an increasingly large number of people own and use a computer as part of their everyday lives, yet a very low percentage of these computer users actually know how to write a computer program. In fact, if you understand the material in the first two sections of this textbook, you already know more about computer programming than most of the world's population. As a result, most programs are not written by the program users. Rather, they are written by a group of computer processionals most people would refer to as programmers, but more accurately, they should be called **software engineers**. A new program that does not meet the needs of the end user is not going to be well received, so it is important that there be a way to describe the requirements of a new program in a way that is understandable to the end users.

> **Definition**
>
> A **software engineer** is a computer professional who produces programs that are on time, within budget, are fault free, and satisfy the end users' needs.

The more formal techniques for describing the requirements of a new program are part of the discipline of systems analysis, which is a subset of software engineering. These formal techniques are all based on one specification of the arrangement of the components of the computer system shown Figure 1.4. They assume that the users' interaction with the program is via the input and output devices, so the simplest way for end users to define what task the program is to perform is to enter into conversation with a systems analyst aimed at defining the inputs to, and the outputs from, the program.

For example, suppose your friend Annie recently purchased a computer and is having trouble managing her money. Knowing you completed a course in computer programming, she comes to you for help. You and Annie enter into the following conversation, which typically involves the probative words who, what, why, where, when, and how:

Annie: I want to know *where* my money goes.

You: OK Annie, *what* bills do you pay each month?

Annie: Well, there's food, rent, electric, telephone, and clothing.

You: *How* much is each bill?

Annie: That's part of the problem; they change each month, and so does my income because I work on commission.

You: Well, do you know roughly *what* percent of your income is spent on each?

Annie: No, but I sure would like to know that. I have a feeling some months I'm spending too much of my income on food and clothing, which leaves me with no mad money.

You: *What* is mad money?

Annie: You know, money I can spend on anything I like other than these bills. I want to know *how* much that is each month. I am sure someone is taking my money.

You: Gee, Annie, you sound a little paranoid.

Annie: You'd be paranoid too if everyone was out to get you!

You (whispered): Why do I bother?

Based on this conversation, you know the two things Annie would like her computer system to determine and output are the amount of "mad money" (discretionary funds) she will have at the end of a month and the percent of her monthly income she spent on each of her five monthly bills. To determine this, she will have to input the amount of each of her five monthly bills and her income for that month. You have decided to include the month and year as two additional inputs to the program, so she will be able to save and distinguish one month's results from another. A simple description, or specification, for this program is shown below. It is a tabulation of the program inputs and outputs preceded by the name of the program and a brief statement that describes the overall task the program performs.

Program Specification

Program Name: *Annie's Money Manager*

Task:	To determine Annie's monthly discretionary funds and the distribution of her monthly expenses
Inputs (8):	Month and Year
	Income for the month
	Amount spent during the month on each of the following five items: food, rent, electric, telephone, and clothing
Outputs (6):	Percent of monthly income spent on each of these five items: food, rent, electric, telephone and clothing
	Amount of discretionary funds

Typically, the program specification is refined through an iterative process that involves its review by the end user and a subsequent conversation. This process could introduce more functionality into the specification of Annie's program. For example, it could also include the ability to output an annual report showing the values of the six outputs for any given year, or perhaps for a range of months. Obviously, this would expand the specification given above.

Given the specification of the program, the programmers' goal is to write a program that accepts the specified inputs and produces the desired outputs. The programmers may have to consult with other experts if it is unclear to them how to determine the outputs from the given inputs. For example, if the programmers assigned to write Annie's program did not know how to compute percentages, they would have to consult a mathematician.

1.3.1 Specifying a Game Program

The technique discussed to specify Annie's program is similar to that of specifying any program: conduct a brief conversation with the user and then tabulate the program's name, the task it performs, the inputs, and the outputs. This approach can also be used to specify a program that is used to play a game. In addition, the realization that all game programs share a common set of features can facilitate the specification process if the systems analysts include questions about these features in the conversations they have with the game's inventor.

For example, most games involve game objects (e.g., trucks, cars, and a frog). In addition, all games have an objective or a way to win the game (e.g., moving a frog object to the other side of a road without having it run over by a truck or a car). Most games also have other features in common. A list of common features to include in a game's specification conversation is given in Figure 1.23.

- Name of the game

- Objects (starships, trucks, sling shots, etc.) that will be part of the game

- Objective of the game

- Way to calculate the score of the game

- Time limits imposed on the game

- Game pieces (objects) that will be animated

- Game pieces controlled by the game player (the program's user)

- Input devices used to control the game objects

- Particular colors to include in the game

- Determining when the game ends

- Events that take place when the game ends

- Keeping track of the highest game score achieved and the name of the game player who achieved it

---

Figure 1.23
Common game features.

Armed with this checklist of common game features, a typical conversation with your friend Ryan (an aspiring game inventor who has not taken a programming course) could be:

You: Hi Ryan, what's up?

Ryan: I've got a great idea for a video game called Deep Space Delivery.

You: *What* is the objective of the game?

Ryan: To deliver as many supply packets as possible (picked up from a supply depot) to five different planets before time runs out.

You: *How* is a player's score calculated?

Ryan: The player gets one point for each packet delivered, and if the player delivers all of the packets at the depot before the time runs out, the player receives one point for each second of time remaining.

You: *What* is the time limit on the game, and *how many* packets will be in the depot?

Ryan: One minute and 30 packets.

You: Looks like the game pieces (objects) are the planets, the supply packets, and the supply ship. Is that correct?

Ryan: Yes, but don't forget to include the supply depot.

You: *How* will the player move the supply ship and pick up and drop off the packets?

Ryan: Using keys on the keyboard.

You: Will any of the other game pieces be moving?

Ryan: Yes, the planets will be moving and bouncing off the edges of the game board. Also, make one of the planets white and another red.

You: Would you want to keep track of the highest game score achieved and the name of the game player that achieved it?

Ryan: Yes, that's a good idea.

You: Sounds good Ryan. I'll write up a specification for the game for you to look over. Then, I'll write the program, and we'll split the profits. How's that sound?

Ryan: How about a 40% share for you?

Ryan (whispered): It's all my idea.

You: OK.

You (whispered): But I'm doing all the work.

Based on this conversation, the specification of Ryan's game is given below.

Program Specification

Program Name: *Deep Space Delivery*

Task:	A starship is to pick up supply packets at a supply depot and deliver as many supply packets as possible to five moving planets before time runs out. The player will receive one point per packet delivered and one point per second remaining on the game time after all packets are delivered.
Inputs (7):	The four cursor control keys (up, down, right, and left) used to control the position of the starship

The 'A' key, which is used to pick up a supply packet when the ship is at the supply depot

The 'Z' key, which is used to drop off a packet when the starship is at a planet

The game player's name input when the game is launched

Outputs (5): The time remaining in the game, in seconds, beginning from 60 seconds

The player's score

The message "Game Over" when the game time reaches zero, or when all packets are delivered

The highest score achieved and the name of the person who achieved it to be output to the game board and a disk file when the game time reaches zero

The details for more functionality could be added to the specification of Ryan's program. For example, the delivery of a packet to a faster moving planet could be awarded multiple points, multiple levels of difficulty could be added to the game, and the highest game score achieved with the name of the game player who achieved it could be announced at the beginning of the game.

1.4 SAMPLE STUDENT GAMES

We will soon be able to write a program that implements the specification of the Deep Space Delivery game presented in the preceding section. The game programs on the DVD that accompanies this textbook were specified and written by students enrolled in an introductory programming course. To run these programs, simply double click the "Sample Student Games" folder on the DVD and copy the subfolders onto your hard drive. Double click one of the subfolders and then double click the file with the .jar extension. Running these programs will give you a sense of what you will be able to accomplish after gaining an understanding of the material in the first five chapters of this textbook.

1.5 JAVA AND PLATFORM INDEPENDENCE

A computer system's platform is the CPU model and the operating system software it is running. For example, many PCs run on an Intel CPU/Windows platform, and Apple computers manufactured after the midpoint of 2011 run on an Intel CPU/OS X platform. As a result of the evolution of CPUs and operating system software that has taken place over the last 30 years, there are many different platforms in use today.

The variety of platforms has always been a problem for software developers because each platform has a language of its own, meaning that a platform can only execute a program that is written in its language. To produce a program that could run on two different platforms, the programmer either had to write the program twice, first in the language of one platform and then in the language of the other, or write the program in a more generic language (for example, C++) and then use two other programs to translate that program into the language of the individual platforms. In this case, the C++ program is referred to as source code, and the resulting translations of this source code are called executable modules or executables.

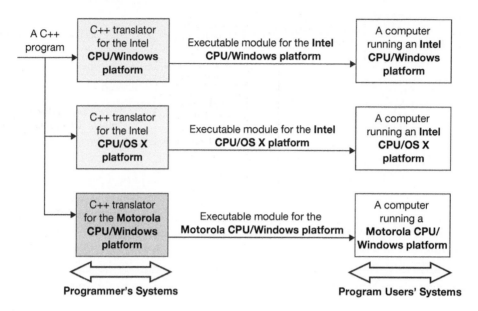

Figure 1.24
The C++ multiple-platform translation process.

When we consider the number of platforms that exist and the fact that writing in the language of a particular platform is a very tedious and time-consuming process, writing programs in a generic language is the most efficient and cost-effective approach. Figure 1.24 illustrates the use of this process to produce executable modules for three different platforms. The programmer would have to translate the program using three different translators to generate the three different executable modules.

During the early 1990s, the Internet was made commercially available to private individuals, which made it possible for them to share information between their computer systems. The idea that this information could be a program resident on one computer system (perhaps a program to display a Website) presented a fundamental problem. If the two computers were not running the same platform, the executable module downloaded from one platform (the host platform) would not run on the other (the client platform), and the Website would not be displayed on the client machine. Using the process illustrated in Figure 1.24 to produce a downloadable executable module for all platforms was an impractical solution because, for one thing, a program that was written today should be able to be run on the platforms of tomorrow. Fortunately, a team of computer scientists at Sun Microsystems lead by James Gosling had already come up with a more practical solution.

The team's idea was to change the process used to produce an executable module. Instead of the host machine producing the executable module, the client machine would produce it. The host machine would simply translate the program, written in a new programming language named Java, into a set of byte codes. Byte codes should be thought of as a pseudo-executable module for a virtual machine, named the Java Virtual Machine (JVM), which are not in the language of any platform in existence. Once generated, the byte codes could then be downloaded to any client machine, and the client machine would use a byte code translator program to translate the downloaded byte codes into the language of its platform. Figure 1.25 illustrates the Gosling team's new process.

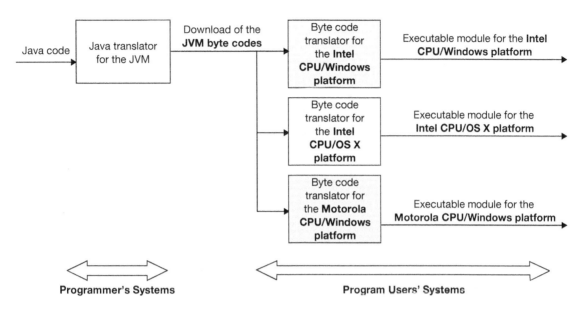

Figure 1.25
The Java multiple-platform translation process.

> **NOTE** *The grammatical rules for writing a program in the Java language were described by the Gosling team in the Java Language Specification (JLS), available online.*

To make this process work, Gosling's team assumed that the manufacturer of the client computer system would install a translator that translated Java byte codes into the language of their system's platform. Realizing that all future customers would want to attach their new computer to the Internet, computer manufacturers complied and proudly advertised their system as "Internet ready."

The fact that the same set of byte codes could be downloaded and used to produce an executable module on any platform that had a byte code translation program on it made Java programs platform independent. Programs written in Java or more accurately, the program's byte codes) could be downloaded, translated, and then executed on any platform that contained a platform-specific byte code translator.

1.5.1 The Java Application Programming Interface

In addition to providing a translator that translates Java programs into byte codes, the creators of Java also identified a group of data (e.g., the mathematical constant pi) and tasks (e.g., computing the square root of a given number) that were likely to be used in Java programs. A description of these data and tasks was then published as the Java Application Programming Interface (API) specification. If a Java programmer wanted to create a new window for a program, which normally most programmers want to do, it could be easily done by incorporating the API task that contained all of the Java byte codes necessary to display a window into that program.

For ease of use, the data and tasks that are similar were grouped together. These grouping are called packages, and within the packages there are subgroupings called **classes**. There are approximately

200 packages and 4,000 classes in the Java API. Most of these classes contain both data and the Java instructions to perform common tasks. A set of instructions to perform a task is called a method. The data and methods that are in the same class are said to be **members** of the class.

Definition
A **class** is made up of a group of related data members and member methods.
A **method** is a set of instructions used to perform a task.
Data members are the instance variables that contain the data values for the class.

Just as Java's creators assumed that the manufacturers of computer systems would install a translator that translated byte codes into the language of their system's platform, they also assumed that the manufacturers would install an implementation of the data and methods defined in the API specification. Once again, to advertise that their system was Internet ready, the manufacturers complied. Technically speaking, the byte code translator and the API implementation on the client machine (along with a memory manager) are called the Java Runtime Environment (JRE), and the JRE and the client system's operating system are considered an implementation of the Java Virtual Machine. Figure 1.26 gives the components of the Java Virtual Machine specific to a system running an Intel CPU/Windows platform.

Based on Gosling's team's idea, any programming language can achieve platform independence if the language designers provide a translator that translates the language into Java byte codes. The resulting translation will run on any computer system or mobile device that implements the Java Virtual Machine.

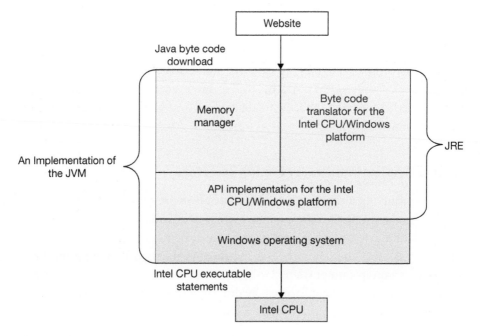

Figure 1.26
System-specific components of the Java Virtual Machine.

1.6 OBJECT-ORIENTED PROGRAMMING LANGUAGES

Just as related methods and data are grouped into classes in the API specification, they can also be grouped into classes that are defined within programs written using object-oriented programming (OOP) languages. Java, by design, is an OOP language. Grouping related methods and data inside a class that is defined in a Java program is more than a convenient way of arranging related data and methods. The real motivation for permitting this class grouping in object-oriented programming languages is that it is a good way of modeling the objects that the program will deal with.

As an example, consider a video game program that involves starship objects. Each starship object will have a name and a (x, y) location. In addition, as the game is played a new starship can be created, starships can be drawn on the monitor, and a starship's location can be changed. A good model for these starship objects would be to define a class named Starship (depicted as the blue rectangle in Figure 1.27). As shown in the figure, the class would have three data members (name, x, and y), and three member methods (create, draw, and move).

It is important to understand that a class is not itself an object, but rather it is a description of an object. From one class we can create an unlimited number of **objects** or instances of the class. A useful analogy is to consider classes we encounter in everyday life: a blueprint, a cookie cutter, a stencil, a pottery mold, a dress pattern, and the human genome pattern. From one blueprint we can create lots of houses, from one cookie cutter lots of cookies, from one stencil lots of pictures,

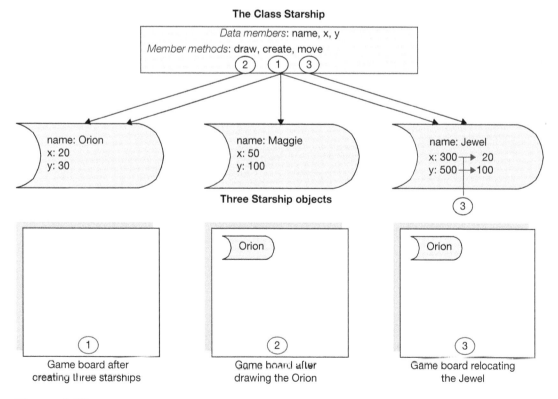

Figure 1.27
The Starship class, three Starship objects, and the use of the class's methods.

from one pottery mold lots of vases, from one pattern lots of dresses, and from one human genome pattern lots of people.

Definition

In an object-oriented programming language, a **class** is a template for an object, and an **object** is a particular instance of a class.

The Starship class would be a template for a starship object. Each time a starship enters the game, a new starship would be created from this template with a given name and initial (x, y) location using the class's create method. A starship's name and (x, y) location would be stored in its three data members, which each object created from the class Starship would contain. In addition, the tasks of drawing and relocating a starship would be performed by the Java instructions that make up the class's draw and move methods.

The center and bottom sections of Figure 1.27 depict the use of the Starship class's three member methods used in the following order:

1. The create method (indicated by the number 1 in the figure) was used to create or construct the three starship objects shown in the center of the figure: the Orion at (20, 30), the Maggie at (50, 100), and the Jewel at (300, 500). Notice that after they are created, each starship contains three data members to store the ship's name and its (x, y) location. Although these three starships have been created, they are not displayed on the game board shown at the lower left portion of the figure because the draw method has not been used.

2. The draw method (shown as number 2 in the figure) was used to display the starship Orion at its current location (20, 30), as depicted in the bottom center of the figure. The draw method has not operated on the other two starships, so, even though they exist, they do not appear on the game board. (Note: The origin is located at the upper left corner of the game board and positive y is downward.)

3. The move method (represented by the number 3 in the figure) was used to change the current location of the starship Jewel from (300, 500) to (20, 100) as depicted on the center right portion of the figure. As shown at the bottom right portion of the figure, it is not displayed because the draw method was not performed on it. After relocating the starship, if the draw task were performed on the Jewel, it would have been displayed directly below the Orion at (20, 100).

NOTE   *Each object contains the data members of its class and can be operated on by the class's methods.*

1.7 INTEGRATED DEVELOPMENT ENVIRONMENTS AND THE PROGRAM DEVELOPMENT PROCESS

An Integrated Development Environment (IDE) is a program to help programmers write programs. Usually they are language specific in that a particular IDE can be used to develop programs in one, and only one, programming language. For example, NetBeans and Eclipse are two popular

IDEs used to develop programs written in Java, and the IDE Microsoft Visual C++ can be used to develop programs written in the language C++. Many popular IDEs can be downloaded for free from the IDE's Website.

What these programs have in common is that they integrate a set of program development tools into one program. Examples of these tools are a text editor used to type, edit, save, and re-open the program's instructions, and a translator used to translate the program instructions into the language of the platform it is to run on. In the case of a Java IDE, this would be a translation from Java into Java byte codes. In addition, most IDEs have an autocomplete feature to facilitate the typing of the program and a grammar checker to help locate and correct grammatical errors in the program's instructions.

Armed with a good specification of a program and a good IDE, we are almost ready to begin the program development process, which is illustrated in Figure 1.28. Before we begin, we must read the program's task contained in its specification and discover a set of algorithms that perform the tasks. For example, how will we determine when a starship delivers a supply packet to a planet in Ryan's Deep Space Delivery program? As mentioned at the end of Section 1.1, this can be the most difficult part of writing a program, and most software engineers take an advanced course in algorithm discovery. We will illustrate the discovery process via the programming examples presented throughout this textbook.

After discovering the program's algorithms, we are ready to begin the program development process (Figure 1.28). Generally, the process begins with representing the algorithms as a set of program instructions (called code), translating the code, and then correcting the grammatical errors (called syntax errors in computer science). Once all of the syntax errors have been eliminated, the IDE's translator will produce an executable module that it then runs. In the case of Java, the IDE generates and then executes the Java byte codes on the Java Virtual Machine installed on the programmer's computer.

The programmer then changes roles from programmer to program user to test the program for correctness. To do this, the user (or tester) supplies the inputs to the program and examines the out-

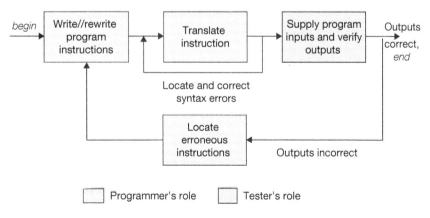

Figure 1.28
An overview of the program development process.

puts it produces. If the program produces the correct outputs for several well-chosen sets of inputs, the program is complete. If it does not, the tester changes back to the role of a programmer, locates the erroneous instruction(s), and the process is repeated beginning with rewriting those instructions.

One refinement to the process is necessary for anything other than a very, very small program because of the fact that we cannot effectively solve large problems. When we consider that we humans have visited the moon and that many of the more common operating systems consist of over a million lines of instructions, this statement leads us to a paradox: If we can't solve large problems, how did we do these things?

The answer lies in the 4,000 BC writings on a Chinese cave wall that explain that big things can be divided into little things, little things can be divided into nothing. Today's version of this is: divide and conquer. Just as the task of going to the moon was divided into hundreds of small problems whose solutions were integrated into the lunar mission, a large program is divided into many small parts, which can be combined to become the large program.

Object-oriented programming languages present several obvious dividing lines. Because the specification identifies the types of objects the program will deal with, the program is first divided into classes, one for each type of object. Then, within each class, the tasks to be performed on the class's objects are defined. Simple tasks become member methods, complex tasks are divided into several simple tasks (each of which also becomes a member method). Each method within a class is written and tested separately. Basically, each method is considered to be a small program, and it is developed using the process illustrated in Figure 1.28. Once all of the methods in a class are operating correctly, the methods in another class are developed using this divide-and-conquer concept. When all the classes are complete, they are integrated into the large program. Object-oriented programming languages make it easy to integrate the classes into the large program.

As an example, consider the development of the Starship class shown in Figure 1.27, which is part of a game program. Three methods (create, draw, and move) have to be developed using the process illustrated in Figure 1.28. Because we cannot draw or move a Starship that has not yet been created, the create method would be developed first. After the method is written and the syntax errors are found and corrected, we would write a few more lines of Java to test the method. This code is often referred to as **driver** code because it takes the method for a "test drive." It would use the method to construct a Starship object, perhaps Maggie in the center of Figure 1.27, and output its data members. If the name Maggie and position (50, 100) were output, we would conclude the create method was working. If not, we would examine the instructions that make up the create method, locate and correct the errors, and repeat the translation and test portion of the process.

NOTE	*Driver code is disposable Java instructions use to test a method. It normally does not become part of the final program's instructions.*

The next logical step would be to develop the draw method because, as we will see, it can be used in the testing of the move method. After the syntax errors are found and corrected, we would write a few more lines of Java driver code to test the method. The code would use the create method to construct a Starship object, perhaps Orion shown on the left side of Figure 1.27, and then use the draw method to display it on the game board. If it were displayed in its proper location with the name Orion on the side of the ship, we would conclude the draw method was working. If not, we would examine the instructions that make up the draw method, locate and correct the errors, and then repeat the translation and test portion of the process.

Next, we would develop the move method, write its code, translate the code and correct the syntax errors, and then write a few more lines of Java driver code to test it. The code would create a Starship object, perhaps Jewel at (300, 500), as shown on the right side of Figure 1.27, then use the move method to change its position to (20, 100) and the draw method to display it on the game board (monitor). If it were displayed in its new location (20, 100) with the name Jewel on the side of the ship, we would conclude the move method was working. If not, we would examine the instructions that make up the move method, locate and correct the errors, and repeat the translation and test portion of the process.

After completing the development of our Starship class in three manageable steps, we would eliminate the driver code and replace it with the instructions to use the Starship class and its methods in our game program.

1.7.1 Mobile-Device Application Development Environments

The level of miniaturization of the basic components of a computing system that has taken place in the last ten years has brought to the marketplace a variety of hand-held computing devices. These devices, often referred to as mobile devices, include smart phones, personal digital assistants (PDAs), and tablet devices.

The development of a program for a mobile device follows the same process as that used to develop a program for a non-mobile computing device discussed in this chapter. After a specification is written and the program's algorithms are discovered, an IDE is used to develop the specification into a functional program using the process shown in Figure 1.28. However, two problems arise when applying the development process to mobile-device applications. Because these devices have limited computing power, it is impractical to conduct the development process on them, so the process is conducted on a more powerful non-mobile computing system. In addition, the concept of platform independence has not been extended to mobile devices, so an executable module must be produced for each mobile-device platform.

Because a majority of mobile applications run on smartphones, and a great majority of smartphones run an Android-based platform, this section will conclude with an overview of the tools available for developing applications for any Android-based smartphone or tablet device. Although the details presented are specific to those devices, the concepts presented are typical of the tools employed to develop applications on most mobile devices.

Android device applications can be written in Java on a personal computer. The preferred IDE is Eclipse, which is a free download. Eclipse is preferred because two sets of tools that facilitate the development of an Android-device application are easily integrated into it. Both of these tools can be freely downloaded. The first of these, the Android Software Development Kit (SDK), can be downloaded from the Android developers' Website. The second set of tools, the Android Development Tools (ADT) Eclipse plug-in can be downloaded from the Eclipse Website. If your personal computer is running a Windows operating system, you can download the Eclipse IDE, the SDK, and the ADT as one bundle from the Android Developers Website, found at *http://developer.android.com/sdk/index. html*.

Some of the features the two sets of tools provide include:

- The latest version of the Android operating system
- Platform-dependent translators
- A set of emulators that run the translated code on a simulation of any Android-based mobile device including displaying its screen and emulating all of its I/O functionality
- The ability to upload developed applications to the Android Market (a Web-based store for free and purchased applications)

Using these tools and knowledge of Java, you will be able to develop and market applications for any Android device from the comfort of your own personal-computer system.

1.8 OUR GAME DEVELOPMENT ENVIRONMENT: A FIRST LOOK

In Section 1.4, you were asked to run several of the sample game programs contained on the DVD that accompanies this textbook. The DVD also contains a folder named Package that contains a Java package named `edu.sjcny.gpv1`. This package can be thought of as a game development addition to the API because it contains methods that perform tasks that are common to most game programs. Appendix A contains descriptions of the methods contained in this package.

The incorporation of this package, or game development environment, into a game program facilitates its development. The students who created all the sample game programs contained on the book's DVD incorporated it into their programs. In this section, we will describe how to easily create and display a game window using the methods in this package, how to incorporate the package into a game program, and how to change some of the game window's properties.

1.8.1 The Game Window

When incorporated into a Java program, two of the game environment's methods can be used to create and display the game window shown in Figure 1.29. The Pause and Start buttons on the right side of the game window can be used by the game player to pause the game and to start/restart the game. The directional buttons below them, or the keyboard keys, can be used to control the position of the game objects during the game.

The coral-colored area on left side of the game window, called the game board, is where the game objects appear. Like most windows, it can be dragged around by its title bar, minimized to the status bar, and redisplayed by clicking its icon on the status bar. It cannot be maximized, however, the programmer can change its size to accommodate the needs of a particular game. The default size of the game window is 622x535 pixels, which are closely spaced dots of color that make up the surface of a computer monitor.

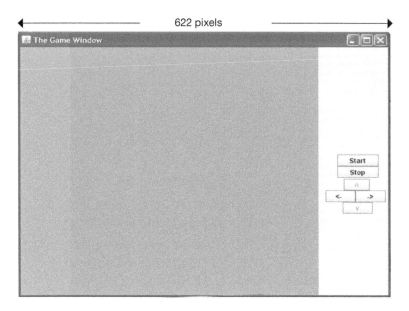

Figure 1.29
The game environment's window.

1.8.2 The Game Board Coordinate System

Figure 1.30 shows the game board coordinate system. Game objects are positioned on the game board by specifying their x and y game board coordinates. The system is a two-dimensional Cartesian system with its origin at the upper left corner of the game window. The positive x direction is to the right, and positive y direction is down. The units of the axis system are pixels.

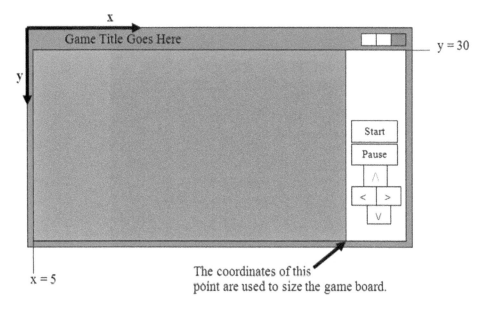

Figure 1.30
The game board coordinate system.

As shown on the upper right and lower left sides of Figure 1.30, the title bar of the window is 30 pixels high, and the left boundary of the window is 5 pixels wide. The coordinates of the lower right corner of the game board for the default window size are (500, 500). If the programmer decides that a larger or smaller game board is appropriate for the game being developed, the x and y coordinates of the lower right corner of the game board can be changed, which will be described in Section 1.8.5.

1.8.3 Installing and Incorporating the Game Package into a Program

Appendix B contains detailed instructions on how to incorporate the game package, which contains the game development environment, into a Java program. The simplest approach is to use one of the projects contained in the "IDE Specific Tools" subfolder on the DVD that accompanies this book. This subfolder contains an Eclipse, a NetBeans, and a JCreator project that has the game package already incorporated into them as well as the code described in the next section, which creates and displays the game window. When the projects are run, they display the game window shown in Figure 1.29. Game program specific code and classes can be added to them.

The JCreator and NetBeans projects on the DVD can be copied from the DVD and pasted into a folder, and then the project can be opened, modified, and run from within the IDEs. The Eclipse project must be imported into an Eclipse workspace folder using the Import feature available on the Eclipse File drop-down menu. After the Eclipse project is imported from the DVD, it can be opened, modified, and run from within Eclipse. Detailed instructions on the use of the DVD's three preexisting game projects are given in Appendix B.

As an alternative, the game package edu.sjcny.gpv1 in the "Game Environment" folder on the DVD can be added to any newly created Java project by following the procedures given in Appendix B, most of which do not include having to change the system's CLASSPATH variable. When these alternative approaches are used, the code described in the next section, which creates and displays the game window, must be added to the project's code.

1.8.4 Creating and Displaying a Game Window and Its Title

After you have incorporated (imported) the game package into your program, you can use the methods in the package to create and display the graphical window in which your game will run. The Java program shown in Figure 1.31 is a template, or starting point, for all of our graphical game application programs. When this program is run, the game window shown in Figure 1.29 is created and displayed.

As we will learn in Chapter 2, lines 2, 3, 7, 8, 10, and 11 are the minimum set of instructions that make up a Java application program. For that reason, many IDEs generate these instructions when a new programming application is created. The one exception is the phrase `extends DrawableAdapter`, which must be added to the end of line 2 if the game package is to be used in the program. Lines 1, 4, 5, and 9 complete the game program template.

```
1   import edu.sjcny.gpv1.*;
2   public class GameWindowDemo extends DrawableAdapter
3   {
4      static GameWindowDemo ga = new GameWindowDemo( );
5      static GameBoard gb = new GameBoard(ga, "The Game Window");
6
7      public static void main(String[] args)
8      {
9         showGameBoard(gb);
10     }
11 }
```

Figure 1.31
The Java instructions to create and display the game window.

The import statement on line 1 of Figure 1.31 makes the methods in the game package available to the program. Lines 4, 5, and 9 use these methods to create and display the game window shown in Figure 1.29. Each Java program is given a name, which is part of its specification. This program is named GameWindowDemo, which is typed on line 2 after the word class and typed two more times on line 4.

As previously mentioned, Figure 1.31 will be the template for all of our graphical game application programs. To adapt it to a particular game program, the new program's name would appear on lines 2 and 4, and the game's title and perhaps the name of its creator would appear at the end of line 5. For example, if a new game program's name was Project1, and the game was Frogger created by Bob, the changes to lines 2, 4, and 5 would be as highlighted below:

```
1   import edu.sjcny.gpv1.*;
2   public class Project1 extends DrawableAdapter
3   {
4      static Project1 ga = new Project1 ( );
5      static GameBoard gb = new GameBoard(ga, "Frogger, by Bob");
6
7      public static void main(String[] args)
8      {
9         showGameBoard(gb);
10     }
11 }
```

1.8.5 Changing the Game Board's Size

As mentioned in Section 1.8.1, the default size of the game window is 622x535 pixels. This was chosen to make the coordinates of the game board's lower right corner (500, 500). To change the game board's size, and thus the window size, we add the new coordinates of the game board's lower right corner to the end of line 5 of Figure 1.31. This is the line that constructs the window. For example, to obtain a game board whose lower right corner is located at (700, 650), we would change line 5 to:

```
static GameBoard gb = new GameBoard(ga, "The Game Window",700, 650);
```

The title bar of the window would still be 30 pixels high, and the left border of the window would still be 5 pixels wide, as shown in Figure 1.29, but the window's height and width would be increased to accommodate the larger game board.

1.9 REPRESENTING INFORMATION IN MEMORY

As discussed in Section 1.1, the memory component of the computer system has the ability to store and recall information, and that information could be the data that the program processes or the instructions that make up the program. The scheme used to store or represent the information in memory is dependent on the type of information being stored. Data is stored using a different scheme than translated program instructions. In addition, character data, which is data typed into a word processor or IDE, is stored differently than numeric data, which is data that will be used in arithmetic expressions.

There are three memory storage schemes used to represent three different types of information: (1) character data, (2) translated instructions, and (3) numeric data. All three of these schemes were designed around the basic hardware memory unit: a bit, which stands for *binary* dig*it*. Conceptually, a bit should be thought of as a single switch that can be turned on or off. All of memory uses this storage concept, and storage devices such as RAM, disks, flash drives, and tape drives may contain billions (giga) and even trillions (tera) of these bits.

For brevity, when a bit is turned on we say it is in state 1 (one), and when it is off we say it is in state 0 (zero). These should only be thought of as the numerics one and zero when the information stored is numeric data. Figure 1.32 depicts eight adjacent bits in on-off states and their briefer binary (1-0) depiction.

off on off off off off on off	01000010
on-off Depiction	**1-0 Depiction**

Figure 1.32
The state of eight adjacent on-off bits and their 1-0 depiction.

1.9.1 Representing Character Data

The scheme used to represent character data in memory is rather straightforward. A table[7] was composed in which each character to be represented was assigned a unique eight-bit pattern. For example, the character B was assigned the pattern 01000010, the lower-case version of this character, b, was assigned the pattern 01100010, and the character 1 was assigned the pattern 00110001.

The table is named the Extended American Standard Code for Information Interchange because it was an expansion of a table named the American Standard Code for Information Interchange, which represented characters using patterns of seven bits. The seven-bit table was assigned the acronym ASCII (pronounced "ask ee"), and the extended table is referred to as the Extended ASCII table. Both tables include all of the upper- and lower-case letters of the Modern

Latin (English) alphabet, the digits 0 to 9, a set of special characters (e.g., !, @, #, $, %, ^, etc.), and some control characters such as horizontal tab and line feed. Because there are 128 (2^7) unique ways to arrange 7 bits and 256 (2^8) unique ways to arrange 8 bits, adding the eighth bit to the Extended ASCII table doubled the size of the ASCII table.

The first 128 characters in the Extended ASCII table are given in Appendix C. The bit patterns in this table are used to represent character information on all computer systems when the alphabetic characters the system is processing are limited to the Modern Latin (English) alphabet. When this is the case, and we want to represent the letter B in storage, eight adjacent (or contiguous) bits of storage (called a **byte** of storage) are set to the Extended ASCII pattern for B: 01000010. If we fetched a byte of storage from an area of memory in which we knew that characters were stored, and that byte contained the pattern 01000010, we would know that the character B was stored there. We say that a keyboard is an ASCII keyboard if it generates this bit pattern when a capital B is struck, and a printer is an ASCII printer if it prints the character B when it receives this bit pattern.

Definition
Eight adjacent or contiguous bits are called a **byte** of storage

To accommodate the international exchange of information over the Internet, the Extended ASCII table was expanded to include unique bit patterns for the symbols used in the other alphabets of the world. To provide a unique bit pattern for each entry in this expanded table, named the UNICODE table, the number of bits assigned to each character was increased from 8 to 16 bits (2 bytes) per character. The first 256 entries in the UNICODE table are the characters in the Extended ASCII table, with the leftmost 8 bits of their 16-bit pattern set to 0 and the rightmost 8 bits set to their Extended ASCII table patterns. For example, because the Extended ASCII representation of B is 01000010, its UNICODE representation is 00000000 01000010. Characters processed by Java programs are stored in memory using their UNICODE table representations.

NOTE *Character data is represented in memory using either the Extended ASCII or UNICODE table.*

1.9.2 Representing Translated Instructions

The technique used to represent translated instructions in memory is the same technique used to represent characters in memory. A table is composed containing all of the possible translated instructions, and a unique bit pattern is assigned to each of them. For example, the bit pattern for the translated instruction to subtract two integers could be 01000000, and the bit pattern to divide two integers could be 01000010.

Unlike the Extended ASCII and UNICODE tables that are used by all computer systems to store characters, these translated instruction tables vary from one CPU to another. Not only do the bit patterns vary, but the number of bits used to represent a translated instruction also varies. The tables are platform dependent, which is the reason Java came into being. To determine the translated memory representation of a divide instruction on a particular platform, we have to look up the bit pattern for the divide instruction in the instruction table of the CPU of that platform.

For the Java Virtual Machine, each translated instruction is assigned an eight-bit pattern. Because the patterns consist of eight bits, or one byte, the patterns are called byte codes. Table 1.1 gives the Java byte codes for the translated integer arithmetic instructions: add, subtract, multiply, and divide. As indicated in this table, when the Java Virtual Machine receives a byte code of 01101100, it performs a divide operation.

Table 1.1
Java Byte Codes for Integer Arithmetic Instructions

Instruction	Java Byte Code
add	01100000
subtract	01100100
multiply	01101000
divide	01101100

Translated Java instructions are represented in memory using patterns of eight bits called byte codes.

1.9.3 Representing Numeric Data

Unlike the two previously described schemes, the scheme used to represent numeric data does not use a table because, for one thing, the table would be infinitely long. Rather, the scheme is based on the theory of numbers. All number systems have a base. Our number system's base is 10, which anthropologists speculate is due to the fact that we have ten fingers and ten toes. In number theory, the base of a number system determines the number of digits in the system. Because our number system is base 10, it has 10 digits (0 through 9). Conversely, the theory of numbers tells us that if a number system has 10 digits, its base is 10.

Armed with this knowledge of number systems, it was decided that numeric data would be represented in memory using a number system whose base is 2 because one bit can represent the system's two digits: 0 and 1*. Anthropologists would tell us that a base-2 number system would probably be our number system if we had two fingers. Because we do not have two fingers, we need to understand how to convert from base 2 to base 10 to interpret what base-10 number a bit pattern represents and how to convert numbers from base 10 to base 2 so we can store numbers in memory.

Numeric data (data that will be used in a mathematical expression) is represented in memory using a binary number system.

Fundamental to these conversions is the realization that digit position values in a base-2 number system are not the same as in our base-10 system. Starting from the right, the digit position values in our number system are the 1s position, the 10s position, the 100s position, etc.

---

*John von Neumann, often called the father of the modern computer, originally proposed this scheme.

These represent 10^0, 10^1, 10^2, etc. Extrapolating this to a base-2 system, the digit position values starting from the right are 2^0, 2^1, 2^2, etc. Figure 1.33 gives the first eight digit position values of the base-2 number system with their decimal (base 10) equivalent below them. Knowing the digit position values of the binary number system, we can now convert from base 2 to base 10, and base 10 to base 2.

2^7	2^6	2^5	2^4	2^3	2^2	2^1	2^0	
128	64	32	16	8	4	2	1	base-2 position values

Figure 1.33
First eight digit position values of the binary number system.

To convert a base-2 representation (e.g., 01000010) of an integer numeric value stored in memory to base 10, we simply write the bit pattern below the base-10 digit position values that are shown in Figure 1.33 and add the values that have a 1 under them. For example, for the bit pattern 01000010, the process would be:

128	64	32	16	8	4	2	1	base-2 position values
0	1	0	0	0	0	1	0	internal representation
	64					2		

Therefore, 01000010 represents the base-10 number 66 (64 + 2).

This conversion process implies that the bit pattern 11111111 represents the largest integer that can be represented using 8 bits, which is the base-10 number 255 (255 = 128 + 64 + 32 + 16 + 8 + 4 + 2 + 1). To represent integers larger than 255, more bytes of storage would be dedicated to each integer numeric value.

To convert a base-10 integer to its binary bit pattern to store the numeric value in memory, we begin by writing out the base-10 digit position values that are shown in Figure 1.33. Then starting on the left, we place a 1 under all of the position values that when added together give the base-10 number. The remaining position values are filled in with zeros.

To quickly determine which positions that should have a 1 placed under them, use the following algorithm until the right most position value is reached:

1. Let n (e.g., 66) be the base-10 integer value to be represented in memory
2. Start at the left most bit, b
3. Set v to b's position value (e.g., $v = 128$)
4. If $(n - v)$ is positive or equal to zero then:
   a. Place a 1 under b's position
   b. Set $n = (n - v)$
   Else place a 0 under b's position
5. Move b to the next bit to the right
6. Go to step 3

Table 1.2 illustrates the use of this algorithm to convert 66 to its 8-bit binary representation. Each row in the table represents an execution of steps 3 and 4 of the algorithm.

Table 1.2
Conversion of the Integer 66 to its 8-Bit Binary Representation

n	b	v	n − v	Binary Representation of n
66	7	128	−62	0
66	6	64	2	01
2	5	32	−30	010
2	4	16	−14	0100
2	3	8	−6	01000
2	2	4	−2	010000
2	1	2	0	0100001
0	0	1	−1	01000010

Before we conclude our discussion on how numeric data is stored in memory, we should comment on how negative integers and numbers with fractional parts, which are called real numbers in mathematics, are represented in memory. The short answer is that negative integers are represented using a scheme named twos complement form, and numbers with fractional parts are represented in a standardized[6] form analogous to scientific notation (as when 235.2374 is expressed as 2.352374×10^2). The details of these schemes are beyond the scope of this text, however, an understanding of the representation of positive integers as binary numbers discussed in this section is fundamental to an understanding these two representation schemes.

Finally, consider a byte of storage that contained the bit pattern 01000010. When we attempt to determine what is stored in this byte, a dilemma arises. If we look into the Extended ASCII table we would conclude the character B is stored there. We have also learned that this could also be the base-10 integer 66. It is also the byte code instruction to store an integer in RAM memory. To resolve these kinds of dilemmas, the language translator keeps track of the types of information that is stored in various parts of RAM. If we knew that the bit pattern 01000010 was in the area of RAM where characters are stored, then it represents character B.

1.10 CHAPTER SUMMARY

In this chapter, you learned about the hardware and software components of a computer system, how they are arranged, and how they interact with the user. The hardware components consist of the central processing unit, memory, and input/output devices. Main or RAM memory interacts with the CPU and stores the data and instructions that are about to be processed by the CPU. The backing store or secondary memory, such as a hard drive, stores data and instructions more permanently.

The modern computer was developed over centuries through the efforts of many people. It has become smaller, faster, cheaper, and more reliable as it evolved from a room-sized device to the small hand-held mobile and wearable devices common today.

Java is an object-oriented programming language that allows a programmer to represent and process real-world objects within application programs and computer games. Classes are the templates for creating objects, which contain both data and methods to operate on the data. All information contained in a computer is represented in binary as translated instructions, numeric data, and character data. Java programs are translated into byte codes, which can be executed by the Java Virtual Machine, making them platform independent and portable.

New programs are defined in a written specification, then the program's algorithms are discovered and an IDE is used to compose and test the program. Game programs are more easily composed by importing a game environment into the program, such as the one contained on the DVD that accompanies this textbook. Game environments supplement the Java API by providing methods that perform tasks common to most games, such creating an interactive game board on which the game objects can be drawn and moved.

The discovery of a program's algorithms is usually the most difficult part of producing a new program. Throughout this text, we will use game programming to illustrate the use of programming concepts and use game algorithms to introduce the reader to the algorithm discovery process.

Knowledge Exercises

1. Between 1989 and 2004, the number of computers per 1,000 U.S. citizens increased by a factor of approximately:
   a) 2   b) 4
   c) 8   d) 12

2. What is the difference between hardware and software?

3. Explain the difference between operating systems and application programs.

4. Which of the following characteristics are associated with RAM (main) memory?
   a) Nonvolatile   b) Very fast
   c) Very large capacity   d) Expensive

5. Which of the following characteristics are associated with backing (secondary) storage?
   a) Nonvolatile   b) Very fast
   c) Very large capacity   d) Expensive

6. Give three examples of:
   a) Input devices   b) Output devices
   c) Backing (secondary) storage devices

7. Some computer devices have a single use while others have multiple uses.
   a) Name a device that is only used for output.
   b) Name a device that is only used for input.
   c) What device can be used for both input and output?

8. Name and explain the function of each of the three major hardware components of a computer system.

9. How would you respond to a friend who asked you who invented the computer?

10. Examples of operating system programs include all of the following except:
   a) MAC OS
   b) Windows
   c) Java
   d) Linux

11. Volatile memory refers to memory that:
   a) Permanently stores data
   b) Loses its contents if power is interrupted
   c) Is added to the computer externally

12. Word processing, e-mailing, and searching the Web are all examples of using:
   a) Application software
   b) Systems software
   c) Programming
   d) None of the above

13. Which of these replaced vacuum tubes in second-generation computers?
   a) Paper tape
   b) The mouse
   c) Chips
   d) Transistors

14. Who developed assembly language, the first compiler, and the language COBOL?
   a) Alan Turing
   b) Ada Lovelace
   c) Grace Hopper
   d) John von Neumann

15. Name the person referred to by each of these titles or descriptions:
   a) First programmer
   b) Inventor of the Java programming language

16. Give the four features of a program that are identified in its specification.

17. What is meant by platform independence?

18. True or False: To achieve platform independence, Java byte codes are translated on the end user's computer system.

19. What is the difference between a class and an object?

20. In a video game, a paddle will be used to reflect a ball into a pile of 200 bricks.
   a) How many objects will be involved in the game? What are they?
   b) How many classes will be defined in the program? Name them.

21. Give the terms that are represented by the following acronyms:
   a) CPU
   b) RAM
   c) I/O
   d) IDE
   e) JVM
   f) API
   g) GUI

22. Which of these refers to the process of breaking a problem into smaller parts in order to solve or program it?
   a) Divide and conquer
   b) Platform independence
   c) Portability
   d) Translation

23. The upper left corner of the game environment's game board is located at the (x, y) pixel coordinates:

   a) (0, 0)   b) (500,500)
   c) (622,535)   d) (5, 30)

24. Which of these is not a component of a typical game program?

   a) Score   b) Time limits
   c) Napier's bones   d) Game piece objects

25. Name the three types of information represented in memory.

26. Write the 8-bit binary equivalent for each of these base-10 numeric values:

   a) 51   b) 77
   c) 115   d) 131
   e) 227   f) 254

27. Write the base-10 (decimal) equivalent number for each of these binary values:

   a) 01010011   b) 00101111
   c) 00000000

28. Give the 8-bit memory representation of the characters C and c.

Preprogramming Exercises

1. Think of a video game and conduct a conversation with yourself that includes the features common to most games that are tabulated in Figure 1.1.23. Based on that conversation, write a specification for the game that gives the game's name, the task or objective of the game, and a description of the inputs and outputs. The game must include at least two different types of game objects and one of the objects has to be controlled by the user via the cursor control keys and the game board directional buttons.

2. Logan is a teacher with 25 students in his class. Write a specification for a program that will show Logan the lowest, highest, and average class grades on an examination.

3. Using the template given in Figure 1.31 and the directions given in Section 1.8.5, write the line of code necessary to change the game window's size to 800x600 with the new title "My Great Game Window."

Enrichment

In the same way that computers and programming languages have evolved over time, game programs also have developed from very simple games to the present multiuser, interactive games. Search the Internet to discover some of the historical developments of computer games. Some of the questions you might research are:

- When and where the first games were developed
- What companies were created for developing games

- Who are the leaders today in the field of games
- How do today's games differ from the earliest computer games

(Be sure to record the sources of your information.)

References

Fullerton, Tracy, *Game Design Workshop*, 2nd ed. Burlington, MA: Morgan Kaufman Publishers, 2008.

Iverson, Jakob, and Michael Eierman. *Learning Mobile App Development*. Upper Saddle River, NJ: Addison-Wesley, 2013.

Lucci, Stephen, and Danny Kopec. *Artificial Intelligence in the 21st Century.* Dulles, VA: Mercury Learning and Information, 2013.

Swade, Doron. *Charles Babbage and his Calculating Machines*. London: Science Museum, 1998.

Endnotes

[1] http://en.wikipedia.org/wiki/History_of_computing

[2] http://www.computersciencelab.com/ComputerHistory/History.htm

[3] http://www.webopedia.com/DidYouKnow/Hardware_Software/2002/FiveGenerations.asp

[4] http://community.seattletimes.nwsource.com/archive/?date=19961124&slug=2361376

[5] Decker, Rick and Stuart Hirschfield. *The Analytical Engine. Belmont, CA. Wadsworth Publishing Company, 1992, p.17 (Now online: http://www.course.com/downloads/computerscience/aeonline/)*

[6] The standard is named IEEE 754-2008

[7] *http://docs.oracle.com/javase/specs/jvms/se7/html/jvms-7.html*

CHAPTER **2**

VARIABLES, INPUT/OUTPUT, AND CALCULATIONS

2.1 *The Java Application Program Template* *40*
2.2 *Variables* *41*
2.3 *Primitive Variables* *42*
2.4 *System Console Output* *44*
2.5 *String Objects and Reference Variables* *48*
2.6 *Calculations and the Math Class* *50*
2.7 *Dialog Box Output and Input* *58*
2.8 *Graphical Text Output* *64*
2.9 *The Counting Algorithm* *67*
2.10 *Formatting Numeric Output: a First Pass* *70*
2.11 *Chapter Summary* *71*

In this chapter

In this chapter, you will learn how to use the basic Java program template to develop a program that performs input, mathematical calculations, and output. Various methods to facilitate meaningful input and understandable output will be introduced, as will techniques for storing data in RAM memory and performing mathematical calculations that go beyond basic arithmetic operations. All these techniques are used in most programming applications.

After successfully completing this chapter you should:

- Understand the basic components of a Java program
- Recognize the difference between primitive and reference variables and how they store data
- Be able to declare and use variables in a program
- Perform input from a dialog box
- Perform output to a dialog box, as well as output to the system console and a graphical window
- Use arithmetic calculations and mathematical functions and constants in the Java Math class
- Perform basic formatting of numeric output
- Understand and be able to use the counting algorithm
- Apply these concepts to begin producing a computer game

2.1 THE JAVA APPLICATION PROGRAM TEMPLATE

If you were writing a letter to you friend Sally, it would probably begin with an opening salutation, for example, "Dear Sally," and end with a closing salutation, for example, "Sincerely," followed by your signature. Opening and closing salutations are usually considered to be a minimum template for any letter we compose. In between these salutations, we would put the text specific to the letter we are writing.

Similarly, most programming languages have templates for composing a program in that language. These templates begin and end with text specific to the language, and we write, or *code*, the instructions specific to the program we are composing inside the template. The minimum template for a Java program is depicted in the top half of Figure 2.1.

```
1 public class ProgramName
2 {
3    public static void main(String[] args)
4    {
5
6    }
7 }
```
Java Program Template
```
1 public class ProgramName
2 {
3    public static void main(String[] args)
4    {
5        System.out.println("Hello");
6    }
7 }
```
Java Program to Output the Word "Hello"

Figure 2.1
Template of a Java program and a program that outputs the word "Hello."

The phrase `ProgramName` on line 1 of this template is replaced with the name of the program being composed, and the instructions specific to the program are placed within the program's *code block,* within the braces that appear on lines 4 and 6. For example, in the bottom half of Figure 2.1 an instruction, or *executable* statement, has been added to line 5 of the template to produce a program that outputs the word "Hello."

NOTE   *All Java* **executable** *statements end with a semicolon.*

When a Java program is run, the first instruction to execute is always the first executable instruction coded after the open brace on line 4. In programming jargon this statement is said to be the program entry point, and all programming languages designate a location in the program template to be the program's entry (starting) point. By default, the program statements that follow the program entry point usually execute sequentially in the order they appear in the program.

If an Integrated Development Environment (IDE) is being used to compose a program, it will normally ask for the name of the program (or project). Then the IDE generates the code template with the phrase `ProgramName` on line 1 replaced with the program's name. In addition to the seven lines shown in the top of Figure 2.1, some IDEs add several other lines to the template, the most common of which is a statement on line 5 to output the phrase "Hello World." However, for the template to be grammatically correct, all IDEs will include the seven lines shown in the top portion of Figure 2.1.

2.2 VARIABLES

Most programs process data that is input to the program. For example, a program may compute the sum of two input bank deposits. To be processed, data must be stored in the memory of the computer system. All programming languages contain statements for defining *variables,* which are memory cells that can store one piece of data. Before a variable can be used in a Java program, it must first be declared. When a variable is defined, or declared in a program, the programmer assigns it a name and designates the type of information to be stored in the cell. For example, a variable named `deposit` could be used to store the amount of a deposit, in which case its type would be a number with a fractional part.

Definition
A **variable** is a named memory cell that can store a specific type of data.
Variables must be declared before they can be used.

In Java, valid variable names must begin with a letter and cannot contain spaces. After the first letter, the remaining characters can be letters, digits, or an underscore. They cannot be Java key words. (See Appendix D.) Variable names that do not follow these rules are invalid and are identified by the Java translator as syntax (grammatical) errors. Good coding style dictates that variables begin with a lowercase letter, and new words in the variable name begin with an uppercase letter. In addition, the name of the variable should be representative of the data item being stored in the memory cell yet be as brief as possible. For example, a variable used to store the balance of my savings account could be named `myBalance`.

Good choices for variable names make our programs more readable. The variables on the left side of Figure 2.2 are well composed: they are syntactically correct, use good naming conventions, and imply what they store. The variable names on the right side of the figure are not well composed, concise, or meaningful.

Well Composed	Poorly Composed
firstName	Fst
deposit1	theFirstOftheBankDeposits
myBalance	mb
Valid	**Invalid**
zipCode	zip Code
phoneNum	phone#
grade1	1stGrade

Figure 2.2
Variable names.

The information stored in a memory cell can change or vary during the execution of the program (which is why these storage cells are call variables). However, once designated, the *type* of the information stored in the memory cell (e.g., a number with a fractional part) cannot be changed.

In Java, there are two kinds of variables: **primitive** variables and **reference** variables. The type of data stored in primitive variables can be a single numeric data value, one character, or one Boolean truth value. Reference variables store RAM memory addresses. The grammar, or syntax, used to declare a primitive variable is the same grammar used to declare a reference variable. In the next section, we will discuss this syntax and the use of primitive variables in our programs. The use of reference variables will be discussed in Section 2.5.

Definition

Primitive variables store one numeric value, one character, or one truth value.

Reference variables store memory addresses.

2.3 PRIMITIVE VARIABLES

The Java statement used to declare a variable begins with the type of the information stored in the variable, said to be the variable's *type*, followed by the name of the variable. Like all Java statements, variable declaration statements end with a semicolon. Optionally, the declaration statement can also include the value to be initially stored in the variable. If the initial value is not specified within the variable declaration statement, the variable is set to a default value. Default values are dependent on the type of information stored in the variable. For example, the statements

```
double deposit;
double price = 5.21;
```

declare the variables named `deposit` and `price`, with `deposit` initialized to the default value 0.0 and `price` initialized to the value 5.21. The word `double` is a *keyword* in Java.

In programming languages, keywords are words that have special meaning to the translator that translates program statements into the language of the computer system. The keyword `double` means that the memory cell being defined will store a number with a fractional part and the size of the storage cell will be 8 bytes (64 bits). Table 2.1 gives the keywords used to specify the type of a primitive variable. The size of the storage cell implied by the use of the keywords is also given. As noted in the table, the keywords used to declare integer and real numeric types are different, and the size of the storage cell limits the numeric range and precision of the stored numeric value.

When storage is not at a premium, it is best to use the type `int` for integer variables because most programs deal with integers within the range -2,147,483,648 to +2,147,483,647. If a data item were beyond that range, it would not be properly represented in an `int` variable. For larger integer values, the type `long` should be used. Integer data beyond the range of the type `long` cannot be stored in a primitive variable. The Java API class `BigInteger` provides a remedy for this situation and will be discussed in Chapter 7, "Methods and Objects: A Second Look."

Table 2.1

Primitive Data Types

Data Type	Key Word	Cell Size (bytes)	Range and Precision
Integer Numeric	byte	1	-128 to +127
	short	2	-32,768 to +32,767
	int	4	-2,147,483,648 to +2,147,483,647
	long	8	-9,223, 372,036,854,775,808 to +9,223, 372,036,854,775,807
Real Numeric	float	4	±1.40129846432481707 E-45 to ±3.4028234663852886 E+38 *(7 digits of precision)*
	double	8	±4.94065645841246544 E-324 to ±1.797693134862157 E+308 *(15 digits of precision)*
Truth Value	boolean	1	true or false
One Character	char	2	Upper and lowercase keyboard characters and other entities (see Appendix C)

When storage is not at a premium, it is best to use the type `double` for variables that will store real numbers (numbers with fractional or decimal parts) because the range of the real numbers processed by a program is usually within the range of the type `double`. As is the case for large integers, Java provides an API class (`BigDouble`) for storing real numbers whose range exceeds that of a double. In addition, because numeric literals, (e.g., 1.5) are represented as type double, an `f` (for float) must be added to the end of an initial value in a float variable declaration to inform the translator that the loss of precision is acceptable:

```java
float change = 1.5f;
```

When the initial value of a character variable is specified, it is enclosed in single quotation marks, and the initial values of Boolean variables begin with a lowercase letter:

```java
char myFirstIntial = 'W';
boolean isRaining = false;
```

Multiple variables of the same type can be declared in a single Java statement. The variables are separated by commas, and the statement cannot include initial values:

```java
short n1, n2, n3;
boolean isRaining, isSnowing;
char letter1, letter2, digit1, digit2;
```

When initial values are not specified in a variable declaration statement, the variables are set to default values. The default value for the integer types (`byte`, `short`, `int`, and `long`) is zero, and the default value for the real types (`float` and `double`) is 0.0. For the Boolean type (`boolean`), the default value is `false`, and for the character type (`char`), it is `''`. The values `true` and `false` are Java keywords.

2.4 SYSTEM CONSOLE OUTPUT

The system console is a window that a program can use to communicate with the user of the program. When information flows from the program to the system-console window, we say that the program is performing output. Conversely, when the information flow is from the system-console window to the program, we say the program is performing input. For brevity, these information transfers are referred to as console input and console output, respectively, or more simply console I/O. In this section, we will discuss console output, and console input will be discussed in Chapter 4 "Boolean Expressions, Making Decisions, and Disk I/O."

The two Java statements used to perform output to the system console are:

```
System.out.print( );
System.out.println( );
```

Like all Java executable statements, they both end with a semicolon. The output item, which is referred to as an argument, is coded inside the statement's open and close parentheses. The only difference between these two statements is that the first one leaves the console's cursor at the end of the output item, and the second one positions it at the beginning of the next line.

2.4.1 String Output

Technically speaking, the item to be output must be a sequence of characters, which in programming languages is called a *string* (e.g., This is Console Output). In Java, strings can either be *string literals* or `String` objects. String objects will be discussed in Section 2.5.

String literals are strings enclosed in double quotes. To output *"This is Console Output"* we would code the string literal `"This is Console Output"` inside the parentheses of a console output statement. The following code fragment would display two lines of output:

```
System.out.println("This is Console Output");
System.out.print  ("from the program");
```

The first line would contain *This is Console Output*, and the second line would contain *from the program*. Because the second line is a `print` statement, the console's cursor would appear on the second line just after the word program.

2.4.2 The Concatenation Operator and Annotated Numeric Output

The concatenation operator, which is coded as a plus (+) sign, can be used to combine two strings into one. The statement

```
System.out.println("Hello" + "World");
```

produces the output *Hello World* to the system console. Before the output is performed, the first string literal, containing the word "Hello", is combined with the second string literal "World". The resulting string, "Hello World", is then output to the console. There is no limit to the number of string literals that can be combined using concatenation operators to produce the string argument output by the `print` and `println` methods. The statement

```
System.out.println("Hello" + "World," + " I'm Bill.");
```

produces the console output *Hello World, I'm Bill.*

To make the output of numeric data more meaningful and user-friendly, the output should always be identified or annotated. For example, the output *The price is $5.21* is much more informative than the output *5.21* The annotation *The price is $* can be included in the output using the concatenation operator.

```
System.out.println("The price is $" + price);
```

The Java translator interprets the plus sign used in this context as the concatenation operator because the item to its left is a string literal. It will fetch the contents of the variable `price`, convert it to a string, and then concatenate that string with the previous string literal. The resulting console output is "The price is $5.21."

Because there is no limit to the number of string literals that can be combined to produce the string argument of the `println` and `print` methods, the annotated contents of several variables can be output to the console using one console output statement. The console output *The price of the 10 items is $5.21.* is produced by the code fragment:

```
int quantity = 10;
double price = 5.21;
System.out.println( "The price of the " + quantity +
                    " items is $" + price + ".");
```

The indentation in the above `System.out.println` statement has been used to improve its readability. It prevents the statement from going beyond the eightieth column and is considered good programming practice.

2.4.3 Escape Sequences

It is often necessary to output strings containing characters that have special meaning to the Java translator. For example, a double quotation mark (") is meant either to begin or end a string literal, and a single quote (') is meant to begin or end a character literal. Suppose we wanted to output *Joe said, "Hello"* followed by a period. To be grammatically correct in English, the word Hello has quotes around it because it is something Joe said. However, the output statement

```
System.out.println("Joe said, "Hello".");
```

would result in a syntax error because a double quotation mark in Java is meant to be either the beginning or end of a string literal. Therefore, the translator would assume the quotation mark preceding the word `Hello` was meant to terminate the string literal, which began with the quotation mark preceding the word `Joe`. Under this assumption, the translator expects the next character to be a close parenthesis followed by a semicolon, or a concatenation operator. Instead, it finds the character H, which produces a syntax error.

To solve this problem, Java provides escape sequences, which are a sequence of two characters coded inside a string literal. The first character in the sequence is always the backslash (\) character. When the translator encounters a backslash inside a string literal, it always considers this to be the beginning of an escape sequence and effectively looks up the meaning of the escape sequence, given in Table 2.2. In other words, the backslash tells the translator to **escape** from its normal way of interpreting this backslash and the next character, and instead look into the table of escape sequences for the meaning of these two characters.

For example the escape sequence \" (coded inside a string literal) means don't interpret the quotation mark as the beginning or end of a string literal but output a quotation mark. Therefore, the syntactically correct way to output the sentence *Joe said, "Hello".* is:

```
System.out.printlin("Joe said, \"Hello\".");
```

Now the quotation mark preceding the H in Hello is part of the escape sequence to output a quotation mark. It is not interpreted as the close of the string literal, which began with the quotation mark preceding the word Joe. Another escape sequence is coded after the o in Hello for the same reason. Proceeding to the right in the string literal, the translator encounters the quotation mark that follows the period, which it correctly interprets as the close of the string literal.

Because a backslash inside a string literal is interpreted as the beginning of an escape sequence, one obvious question is "how would we output a backslash?" The answer is that there is an escape sequence for outputting a backslash, which is a double backslash. The statement

```
System.out.println("Down \\/    Up /\\");
produces the output:  Down V    Up ∧.
```

The escape sequence \' is used to output a single quotation mark, and the escape sequence \n causes the cursor to move to a new line before completing the output. The escape sequence \t tabs the cursor to the right; this is useful when you want output to appear in columns. A list of the escape sequences is shown in Table 2.2.

Table 2.2
Escape Sequences

Escape Sequence	Sequence Name	Meaning
\"	Double quote	Output the double quotation mark (") character
\\	Backslash	Output the backslash (\) character
\'	Single quote	Output the single quotation mark (') character
\b	Backspace	Move the cursor back one character position
\t	Horizontal tab	Move the cursor to the next horizontal tab position
\n	New line	Move the cursor to beginning of the next line
\r	Carriage return	Move the cursor to beginning of the current line
\f	New page (form feed)	Move the cursor to the top left of the next page

The application shown in Figure 2.3 illustrates the declaration and initialization of primitive variables and the use of string literals and escape sequences to output the data stored in these variables. The program's outputs are included in the figure after the program's code.

```
1    public class ConsoleOutput
2    {
3      public static void main(String[] args)
4      {
5        // Primitive variable declarations
6        int age = 21;
7        double weight = 185.25;
8        boolean isRaining = false;
9        char letter1 = 'A';
10
11       System.out.println("The Program's Output Appears Below");
12       System.out.println("\t\t\"Hello World!\"");
13       System.out.print("\nJohn is " + age + " years old");
14       System.out.println(" and weighs "  + weight + " pounds");
15       System.out.println("Today it is " + isRaining +
16                          " that it is raining\n");
17       System.out.println("The first letter of the alphabet is " +
18                          letter1);
19
20       System.out.println("1/2 + 1/4 = 3/4");//blank lines are ignored
21     }
22   }
```

Program Output

The Program's Output Appears Below
      "Hello World!"

John is 21 years old and weighs 185.25 pounds
Today it is false that it is raining

The first letter of the alphabet is A
1/2 + 1/4 = 3/4

Figure 2.3
The application **ConsoleOutput** and the output it produces.

  It is good coding style to declare all variables at the beginning of a program.

Lines 6-9 declare and initialize four different types of primitive variables. Lines 11 and 12 produce the first two lines of the program's output. Each statement contains one string literal. The string literal on line 12 begins with two tab escape sequences, which are used to center the second line of output under the first. In addition, Hello World! coded on line 12, is surrounded by two double-quote escape sequences, which produces the quotation marks on the second output line.

Lines 13–18 output the variables declared and initialized on lines 6-9. A new-line escape sequence begins the first string literal on line 13, which produces the blank line that precedes the third line of text output. Two concatenation operators are used on line 13 to combine the two string literals and the contents of the variable `age` after it is converted to a string. Line 14 uses similar operations to annotate the output of John's age and weight. The output displayed by lines 13 and 14 appear on the same line because line 13 uses a `print` rather than a `println` statement. As a result, the cursor is not advanced to the beginning of the next line after line 13 completes execution, which causes the output produced by line 14 to begin immediately after the word old. One subtlety on line 14 of the program is that its string literal begins with a space. This space becomes the space that separates the word *old* from the word and in the output produced by lines 13 and 14.

Lines 15-16 produce the next line of output, which contains the string version of the contents of the Boolean variable `isRaining`. They also produce the next blank line of output because the last string literal ends in a new-line escape sequence. The final two lines of output are produced by lines 17-18, which output the contents of the character variable `letter1`, and line 20, which outputs a single string literal.

Comments and Blank Lines

Line 5 of the program contains a single-line comment. A single-line comment begins with two forward slashes (//) and is terminated by a new line (`Enter`) keystroke. Comments are added to a program to improve the program's readability; they are ignored by the translator.

> It is good practice to include comments in your program to describe the portions that are not obvious to the reader.

A second comment appears at the end of line 20, stating blank lines (e.g., lines 10 and 19) in a program are ignored by the translator. It is good programming practice to separate major portions of a program with a blank line. This technique, like comments, improves the readability of a program. We will see more examples of the use of blank lines in a program later in this chapter.

2.5 STRING OBJECTS AND REFERENCE VARIABLES

As previously mentioned, in Java there are two kinds of variables: primitive variables and reference variables. Primitive variables store numeric, character, or Boolean data values. Reference variables store memory addresses. These addresses are the addresses of memory resident programming constructs called objects, and the contents of a reference variable is used to locate a particular object. We say they refer to an object, which is how they get their name, reference variables.

Suppose that we were writing a program and we wanted store the string `John` in memory. Based on what we have learned about primitive variables, we should declare a string variable, perhaps named `firstName`, and then initialize it to the string `"John"`. Unfortunately, Java does not contain string type variables, so the statement

```
string firstName = "John";  // error
```

is grammatically incorrect. However, there are `String` objects in Java. A `String` object can store a sequence of characters, and the address of the object can be stored in a reference variable. We begin by declaring a `String` reference variable that will store the address of our String object. Then we store the address of a newly created `String` object, containing the string "John" in the reference variable:

```
String firstName;
firstName = new String("John");
```

As we will learn in Chapter 3 "Methods, Classes and Objects: A First Look," this two-line grammar can be used to create objects in any class. For example, `Starship` objects, `Snowman` objects, or `Paddle` objects can be created simply by replacing the word `String` on both lines with the class names `Starship`, `Snowman`, or `Paddle`, and replacing the string "John" with something more relevant to these objects. The first line creates an uninitialized reference variable that, like uninitialized primitive variables, is set to a default value. The default value for reference variables is `null`. When the variable is a `String` reference variable, we say that the reference variable stores the `null` string.

 "String s contains the null string," means that s stores a `null` value.

Because strings are so commonly used in programs, Java provides a simplified one-line grammar for creating and initializing `String` objects:

```
String firstName = "John";
```

NOTE *The abbreviated grammar to declare a string* `String` *object is:*
String referenceVariableName = intialStringLiteralValue;

This one-line grammar can only be used to create `String` objects and is modeled on the grammar used to declare and initialize primitive variables. Although the grammar is very similar, we must keep in mind that unlike the primitive variable `age`, initialized to store the value 21 on line 6 of Figure 2.3, the reference variable `firstName` is not initialized to the string "John". Rather, the reference variable `firstName` stores the address of and refers to the `String` object that is initialized to the string "John". Figure 2.4 shows the statements used to allocate memory to primitive variables and objects/reference variables. The arrow in the figure indicates that the reference variable `firstName` refers, or points, to the object.

Figure 2.4
Memory allocated to primitive variables and objects/reference variables.

In addition to providing a simplified grammar for creating `String` objects, Java also provides a simplified grammar for outputting the strings contained inside these objects. Once again, it is modeled after the grammar used to output primitive variables. To output the string contained in a `String` object, we simply code the name of the variable that refers to the object. For example, the following code fragment produces the output *My name is John Smith, my age is 21* on the system console:

```
int age = 21;
String firstName = "John";
String lastName = "Smith";
System.out.print ("My name is "  + firstName  + " " + lastName);
System.out.println (", my age is "  +  age);
```

The differences between the way Java stores primitive data items and string data items can be ignored when writing variable declaration statements and output statements. As we will see in Chapter 3, these differences cannot be ignored for any other kind of object.

2.6 CALCULATIONS AND THE MATH CLASS

The first operational computers were used by mathematicians to compute the values of equations, which is how they obtained their name *computers*, and a significant portion of the processing that modern computers perform is still calculations. Java, like most programming languages, provides the ability to perform basic arithmetic calculations and provides additional features to perform more complex calculations. This section begins with a discussion of how to incorporate basic arithmetic calculations into a Java program and then discusses how to incorporate commonly used mathematical constants and functions into these calculations.

2.6.1 Arithmetic Calculations and the Rules of Precedence

Arithmetic calculations are performed in Java using arithmetic expressions. Arithmetic expressions consist of a series of operands separated by operators. In the simplest case, the operands are numeric constants, and the operators are the four arithmetic operators: add subtract, multiply, and divide. For example, $10 + 21 - 5$ is a simple arithmetic expression that evaluates to 26. Generally, simple arithmetic expressions are evaluated from left to right. The addition would therefore be performed before the subtraction.

The symbols used for the four arithmetic operators are given in Table 2.3. The third entry in the table, the modulo (or mod) operator, is used to find the remainder in division. For example, 14 % 3 evaluates to 2. All of the operators can be used with integer or real operands.

In addition to numeric constants, called numeric literals, operands can be the names of variables that store numeric values. When a memory cell name is used in an arithmetic expression, the value stored in the memory cell is fetched, substituted for the memory cell name, and the arithmetic expression is evaluated. For example, given the variable declarations:

```
int x = 10;
int y = 29;
int z = 5;
```

Table 2.3

The Java Symbols for the Arithmetic Operators (In Order of Precedence)

Arithmetic Operation	Java Symbol
multiply	*
divide	/
Modulo or mod	%
add	+
subtract	-

the arithmetic expression $x + y - z$ evaluates to 34. A mix of numeric literals and memory cell names can be used as the operands in any arithmetic expression, so the expression $x + 29 - z$ is a valid arithmetic expression that also evaluates to 34.

An arithmetic operation performed on two integers always results in an integer value, and an arithmetic operation performed on two real values always results in a real value. When one operand is an integer and the other is a real value, the result is always a real value, and the arithmetic is referred to as *mixed mode* arithmetic. Before mixed mode arithmetic is performed, the integer value is converted to a real value (e.g., 10 becomes 10.0).

Integer Division

When the two operands are integers and division is performed, the results are sometimes surprising. That is because the division of two integers always produces an integer result that is truncated and not rounded. For example, given the variable declarations

```
int x = 10;
int y = 29;
int z = 5;
```

the following arithmetic expressions would evaluate to the values on the far right side of each expression:

$x / z = 10 / 5 = 2$
$y / x = 29 / 10 = 2$ (0.9 lost, due to truncation)
$z / x = 5 / 10 = 0$ (the most surprising result, 0.5 is truncated to zero)

Precedence Rules

Consider the arithmetic expression $10 + 6 - 2$. The expression evaluates to 14 whether we perform the addition first (16-2) or the subtraction first (10+4). Similarly, the expression 10 * 6/2 evaluates to 30 whether we perform the multiplication first (60/2) or the division first (10*3). In both cases, the value of the expressions is independent of the order in which we apply the arithmetic operators. In general, if an expression contains just addition and subtraction operators, or contains just multiplication and division operators, then the evaluation of the expression is independent of the order in which we apply the arithmetic operators. Java considers these expressions to be simple arithmetic expressions and, as previously stated, they are evaluated from left to right.

This is not the case for arithmetic expressions that mix addition and/or subtraction operators with multiplication and/or division operators. Consider the expression 10 + 6 * 2, which performs addition and multiplication. If we perform the addition first, the expression evaluates to 32 (16 * 2), but if the multiplication is done first it evaluates to 22 (10 + 12). The arithmetic expression appears to be ambiguous. Fortunately, mathematicians have stipulated a way of resolving the ambiguity called the *rules of precedence*. These rules state that multiplication and division are performed before, or take precedence over, addition and subtraction. Using this rule, the expression 10 + 6 * 2 evaluates to 22.

Operators that are performed first, such as multiplication and division, are said to have higher precedence. Table 2.3 lists the arithmetic operators in high-to-low precedence order, with multiplication and division being the highest precedence operators in the table, and addition and subtraction the lowest. The expression 5 * 7 % 2 would evaluate to 1 because multiplication is of higher precedence than the mod operator. Java contains other operators, for example logic operators, and each Java operator has been assigned a precedence level. A complete list of Java operators and their assigned precedence level is given in Appendix E.

NOTE *Java evaluates arithmetic expressions using this mathematical rule of precedence: multiplication and division are performed before modulo (mod) operations, which are performed before addition and subtraction operations.*

If we wanted the addition or subtraction in an arithmetic expression to be performed before multiplication or division, we would use a set of parentheses to override the precedence rules. The expression (10 + 6) * 2 would evaluate to 32. To average the numbers 2, 4, and 6, we would write (2 + 4 + 6) / 3, which would evaluate to the correct average 4 = 12 / 3. (Without the parentheses, only the 6 would be divided by the 3 because the division operation would be performed first.)

NOTE *Parentheses override the rules of precedence.*

In summary, the parts of an arithmetic expression inside parentheses are evaluated first using the rules of precedence to determine the order of the operations. If the operators are of equal precedence, they are evaluated from left to right. The following example, which contains a set of nested parentheses and evaluates to 36, illustrates this process.

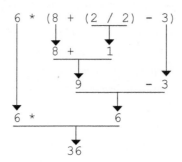

2.6.2 The Assignment Operator and Assignment Statements

In Section 2.3, we learned that a variable named `price` could be declared and initialized to the value 5.21 by coding:

```
double price = 5.21;
```

The equals (=) symbol used in this declaration is called the *assignment operator* because it assigns values to memory cells. In this case, the memory cell named `price` is assigned the value 5.21. Although the statement should be read as "double price *is assigned* 5.21," most programmers would read it as "double price *equals* 5.21," which is unfortunate because (as we will see) the operator does not represent the mathematical concept of equality. Rather, it represents the flow of the data value on its right side (in the above statement, 5.21) into the memory cell named on its left side, (in the above statement, `price`).

Assignment Statements

In addition to being used to initialize variables in a declaration statement, the assignment operator is also used in statements that reassign (actually overwrite) the contents of memory cells previously declared in a program. These statements are called assignment statements. For example, after the following two statements execute, the variable `price` stores the value 6.25.

```
double price = 5.21;
price = 6.25;
```

In addition to being a numeric literal, the entity on the right side of the assignment operator can be an arithmetic expression. For example:

```
answer =  x + 21 - z;
```

When this is the case, we should realize that the execution of the statement is performed in three steps:

1. *Fetch* the contents of the variables coded on the right side of the assignment operator from memory and substitute these values into the arithmetic expression
2. *Evaluate* the arithmetic expression considering parentheses and the rules of precedence
3. *Store* the value of the arithmetic expression in the memory cell coded on the left side of the assignment operator

In an assignment statement, the item on the left side of the assignment operator must be the name of a variable. The statement cannot be reversed by placing the name of the variable on the right side of the assignment operator. That is,

```
answer =  x + 21 -z;
```

is *not* the same as

```
x + 21 - z = answer;
```

The second expression will produce a syntax error. Armed with this understanding, the assignment statement (which is probably executed on a person's birthday)

```
age = age + 1;
```

will increase the value stored in the memory cell `age` by one. In addition, a mathematician would now understand that the assignment operator does not represent equality and would not run from this statement in horror proclaiming that nothing (in this case age) could be equal to itself plus one. Surveys of programs conducted in the 1970s indicate that 47% of the statements contained in programs are assignment statements, so this is an important concept to understand.

2.6.3 Promotion and Casting

Generally speaking, the type of the value being assigned to a variable should match the type of the variable. When this is not the case, the Java translator checks this to make sure that there is no chance that part of the value being assigned to the variable could be lost when the value is stored in the variable. For example, if a real number (e.g., 2.7) was assigned to an integer-type variable, the fractional part of the value (0.7) would be lost. As a result, the statement below produces the translation error "possible loss of precision," because it assigns a **double** value (2.7) to an integer memory cell.

```
int newValue = 2.7;
```

 Avoid assigning a numeric with a fractional part (e.g., types `float` and `double`) to **TIP** an integer type variable because it will generate a translation error.

This statement does not produce a syntax error because performing an arithmetic operation on two integers (21 / 10) always results in an integer (in this case, 21 / 10 = 2).

```
int newValue = 21/10;
```

The Java translator also checks assignment statements to determine if the value being assigned to the variable, coded on the left side of the assignment operator, is within the variable's range. As shown in the right column of Table 2.1, the range of the numeric values that can be stored in a numeric variable depends on its type. Within the four integer types, the type `long` has the largest numeric range, and within the real types, the type `double` has the largest range.

The progression shown in Figure 2.5 summarizes the valid assignments between types (those that will not result in a loss of precision and guarantees that the range of the variable being assigned is large enough to store the value assigned to it). A valid assignment is when the type of the variable being assigned is to the left of the type of the value being assigned to it (e.g., a `double` variable can be assigned `int` values). When this is the case, we say that the value has been promoted to the type of the variable.

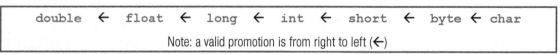

Figure 2.5
Valid promotions of numeric types.

Although the types of the variables used in the code fragment in the assignment statements below are not the same, they are valid because they follow the promotion order given in Figure 2.5.

```
byte aByte = 20;
char a = 'a';
```

```
int anInt;
double aDouble;
anInt = aByte;
anInt = a;
aDouble = aByte;
aDouble = anInt;
```

Mixed Mode Arithmetic Expressions

Mixed mode arithmetic expressions are expressions in which the operands are not of the same type. To evaluate the terms of these expressions, the operand whose type is further to the right in Figure 2.5 is promoted to the type of the other operand, the term is evaluated, and the resulting value is in the promoted type. For example, the following code fragment contains a mixed mode arithmetic expression:

```
double salary = 523.56;
float raise = 1.1f;
salary = 10 + salary * raise;
```

The arithmetic expression in the assignment statement contains an integer literal, a `double` variable, and a `float` variable. During the evaluation of this expression, the value stored in `raise` would be converted to a double, and then the multiplication operation would be performed. The result would be a double value. That value would then be added to the integer literal 10 after it was converted to double. The resulting double value would be assigned to the variable `salary`.

Casting

One use of the word casting is the process of turning an entity into something it is not. For example, a frail mild-mannered actor could be *cast* into the role of a professional wrestler. In computer science, the term is used to describe the process of changing the type of a value to another type.

Changing the type of a variable or numeric literal in mixed mode arithmetic expressions previously discussed is an example of automatic casting. Even when an arithmetic expression is not a mixed-mode expression, there are times when it is desirable to cast operands into other types before the expression is evaluated. For example, a value that is an integer variable could be cast into a real value before it is used in an arithmetic expression. This is a very common use of casting.

Consider the calculation of the ratio of two integer variables n1 and n2.

```
int n1 = 111;
int n2 = 10;
double ratio = n1 / n2;
```

The arithmetic expression will evaluate to an integer because both operands are integers. As a result, we will lose the factional part of the ratio, and the variable ratio will be assigned 11.0.

A situation that is more confusing is illustrated in the code fragment below. The integer denominator (100) is larger than the integer numerator (90). In this case, the variable `ratio` is always assigned 0.0.

```
int numberOfStudents = 100;
```

```
int numberPassing = 90;
double ratio = numberPassing / numberOfStudents;
```

To retain the factional part of a value calculated by dividing to integers, we change, or cast, the type of one of the operands into one of the real types (**double** or **float**). The syntax of this nonautomatic casting is to enclose the numeric type into which the operand is being cast inside of parentheses. The following fragment uses casting to change the fetched contents of the variable n1 into a double before the arithmetic operation is performed. The outer set of parentheses in the third statement is necessary because arithmetic operators take precedence over casting.

```
int n1 = 111;
int n2 = 10;
double ratio = ((double) n1) / n2;
```

After casting is performed, the arithmetic expression involves a double value (111.0) and an integer variable (n2): a mixed mode expression. Automatic casting then converts n2 to a double, and then the division is performed that produces a double (11.1). The value 11.1 is assigned to ratio. In this code fragment, ratio would be assigned the value 0.9.

```
int numberOfStudents = 100;
int numberPassing = 90;
double ratio = ((double) numberPassing) / numberOfStudents;
```

NOTE   *Arithmetic operators take precedence over nonautomatic casting.*

Another common use of casting is to inform the translator that you want to violate the promotion-only rules it imposes on assignment statements, shown in Figure 2.5. If we wanted the integer part of a double value to be assigned to an integer variable, we would use casting. The following statements assign the value 1 to the integer variable age:

```
double daysSinceBirth = 401.5;
int age = (int) daysSinceBirth / 365;
```

The mixed mode arithmetic in the second statement produces the value 1.1, which the casting converts to an integer (1) before it is assigned to the variable age. If the casting were left out of the second statement, it would not translate because it would be a violation of the promotion rules given in Figure 2.5. This use of casting informs the translator that we are intentionally violating these rules.

2.6.4 The Math Class

If we were to examine the code of applications written by several different programmers, we would quickly come to the realization that mathematical calculations, such as raising a number to a power or calculating the square root of a number, are performed in many programs. For example, a program that computes the radius of a circle given its area would divide the area by the constant PI, and then take the square root of the result. Obviously, the accuracy of the calculation is dependent on a precise value of PI. In addition, because the square root is not one of the mathematical operators available in most programming languages, the programmer would have to know the algorithm for computing the square root of a number using the math operators available in the programming language.

To facilitate the coding of programs that use common mathematical constants and calculations, Java, like most programming languages, provides precoded libraries containing these constants and mathematical functions. The constants are coded as initialized variables, and the mathematical functions are coded into subprograms. In Java, subprograms are called *methods*, and related methods and variables are collected into **classes**. As discussed in Section 1.5.1, the collection of the precoded classes available in Java is called the Java Application Programming Interface, or Java API. A complete description of the classes contained in the API, is available online. To locate this documentation, simply type "Java API Specification" into the search window of your browser.

The API class that contains mathematical constants and methods is called the Math class. Table 2.4 lists a mathematical constant and some of the most commonly used methods that are included in this class. The third column of the table gives a series of assignment statements that illustrate the use of the class's constants and methods. Notice that the name of the Math class followed by a dot precedes the name of the constant or method used in the statement. The angles used in the trigonometric functions that appear in the last three rows must be expressed in radians. The methods compute and return a value, which the coding examples in the rightmost column of the table assign to a variable.

Table 2.4
Commonly Used Math Class Constants and Methods

Constant or Method	Description	Coding Example
PI	The ratio of the circumference of a circle to its diameter (a `double`)	area = Math.PI * r * r;
abs	Computes and returns the absolute value of a number, n (returns the type it is sent)	nAbsolute = Math.abs(n);
pow	Computes and returns a number, n, raised to the power p (returns a `double`)	nToTheP = Math.pow(n, p);
sqrt	Computes and returns the square root of a number, n (returns a `double`)	rootN = Math.sqrt(n);
toRadians	Converts an angle, a, in degrees to radians (returns a `double`)	aRads = Math.toRadians(a);
sin	Computes and returns the sine of an angle, aRads, specified in *radians*	sinA = Math.sin(aRads);
cos	Computes and returns the cosine of an angle, aRads, specified in *radians*	cosA = Math.cos(aRads);
tan	Computes and returns the tangent of an angle, aRads, specified in *radians*	tanA = Math.tan(aRads);

The following code fragment calculates and outputs the sine of 45 degrees and 2 raised to the third power:

```
double angle = 45.0;
double angleInRadians = Math.toRadians(angle); //returns a double
double sineOfAngle = Math.sin(angleInRadians); //returns a double

System.out.println("The sine of " + angle + " is " + sineOfAngle);
System.out.println("2 cubed = " + Math.pow(2, 3));
```

Random Numbers

"A random number is a number generated by a process whose outcome is unpredictable and which cannot be subsequently reliably reproduced."[2] Random numbers are used in many computer applications such as game programs, encryption programs, and simulation programs. For example, flight simulator programs used to train pilots to react to air turbulence introduce turbulence into the flight at random times during the simulation.

The Math class contains a method named random that can be used to generate pseudorandom numbers. The numbers are not truly random because the sequence of numbers the method generates is based on the computer's real-time clock (i.e., the time of day) resolved to one millisecond, and therefore can be reliably reproduced.

The method returns a double in the range: $0.0 \leq$ randomNumber < 1.0. (The highest number generated by the method is always less than 1.0.) The following code fragment outputs two random numbers in that range. The specific numbers output would depend on the time of day the code fragment was executed.

```
double randomNumber;
randomNumber = Math.random();
System.out.println(randomNumber);
randomNumber = Math.random();
System.out.println(randomNumber);
```

The method can be used to generate numbers in the range: min $\leq$ randomNumber $<$ max using the assignment statements:

```
double randomNumber1 = min + Math.random() * (max - min);
int randomNumber2 = int(min + Math.random() * (max - min));
```

The second assignment statement uses casting to change the computed real number into an integer.

2.7 DIALOG BOX OUTPUT AND INPUT

Dialog boxes are a graphical way to communicate with the user of a Java program and offer an alternative to the console-based output produced by the println method in the System class. The *message dialog box* (Figure 2.6) is used to convey output to the user, and the **input dialog box** (Figure 2.7) is used to obtain input from the user. They are predefined graphical objects that automatically resize themselves to display the string argument sent to them. The string sent to a message dialog box is the text to be output to the user. In the case of an input dialog box, the string is an input prompt to be displayed to the user.

After a dialog box is displayed, the program execution is halted until the user clicks a button displayed in the box or strikes the return key. In the case of a graphics application, dialog boxes are normally used for all communication between the program and its user. Two methods in the class `JOptionPane`, `showMessageDialog`, and `showInputDialog` are used to display message (output) and input dialog boxes, respectively.

2.7.1 Message Dialog Boxes

The method `showMessageDialog` is a *static* method, as are the `Math` class's methods presented in Table 2.4 and its `random` method. As we will learn in Chapter 3, not all methods are static methods. When static methods are invoked, we must precede the name of the method with the name of its class followed by a dot. The `showMessageDialog` method and the `Math` class's `pow` method have another thing in common: they are both sent two arguments that are coded inside the parenthesis that follows the name of the method. For the `pow` method, we learned that these are the numbers to be raised to a power followed by the power to which to raise it.

In the case of the `showMessageDialog`, its two arguments describe the window to which the message box will be output followed by a string that contains the text of the output message. To output the message "Frogger, by George Smith," we would code

```
JOptionPane.showMessageDialog(null, "Frogger, by George Smith");
```

This would produce the message box shown in Figure 2.6(a). Coding `null` as the first argument causes the message dialog box to be displayed in the center of the monitor.

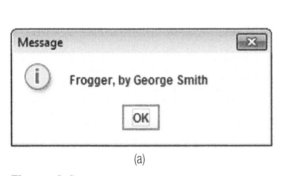

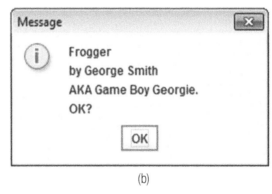

(a)   (b)

Figure 2.6
Two message dialog boxes.

The second argument, the string, can contain all of the elements and features of the string sent to the `println` method used to perform output to the console. As we have learned, the string can be a concatenation of a mix of string literals and numeric variables. Just as with console output, the string will be output on one line unless new-line escape sequences (\n) are included in the string. The width and height of the message box will expand to accommodate the string. For example, the statement

```
JOptionPane.showMessageDialog(null, "Frogger," + "\nby George Smith," +
                              "\nAKA Game Boy Georgie." + "\nOK?");
```
produces the output in Figure 2.6(b).

These features are especially useful in a very common use of a message box: to display a game's splash screen. A game splash screen is used to describe a game, its objective, and the manner in which the game pieces are controlled by the player. Usually, the name of the game and its creator (e.g., "Created by Game Boy Georgie") are also included.

2.7.2 Input Dialog Boxes

Input dialog boxes, which are displayed by the static method showInputDialog, are used to obtain input from the program's user (Figure 2.7). It is sent one argument, which the method displays as a prompt to the user. A text box is displayed below the prompt into which the user types the input. The box contains two buttons labeled "OK" and "Cancel." The string sent to the method can be a concatenation of a mix of string literals and variables, and the width and height of the input box is adjusted to accommodate the string and its embedded new-line escape sequences. Figure 2.7 shows the input dialog box produced by the statement

```
String s = JOptionPane.showInputDialog("Frogger has five " +
                                       "difficulty levels:" +
                                       "\n1 is the easiest," +
                                       "\n5 the most difficult," +
                                       "\nEnter your level");
```

Figure 2.7
An input dialog box before the user enters input.

If, in response to the displayed prompt, the user types into the text box and then clicks "OK" (or strikes the Enter key), the location of a String object that stores the user input text would be placed in the reference variable s. (For brevity, we would say that the InputDialogBox method "returns a string," when in fact it actually creates and returns the address of a String object.) If the user clicked "OK" or struck the Enter key without making an entry in the text box, the returned String object would contain the empty string (""). Finally, if the user clicked "Cancel," s would store the null string. (It would be set to null.)

2.7.3 Parsing Strings into Numerics

Most of us would agree that there is a fundamental difference between the string "one hundred seventy-six" and the number 176. For one thing, we would not try to add the string "one hundred seventy six" to the string "ten" to obtain "one hundred eighty six". Rather, if we read the question, "what is the sum of one hundred seventy-six and ten?" we would first convert the numbers to their numeric representations, 176 and 10, and then perform the addition. In computer science, the difference between strings and numerics goes deeper than that because even if we were told to add "176" and "10," we would still have to convert these two strings to their numeric representations before performing the addition.

 Operands in arithmetic expressions cannot be strings.

As discussed in Chapter 1, characters are stored using their Extended ASCII representation, and numerics are represented using their binary representation. Inside of String objects, the Extended ASCII representation is used. The difference between these two representations is shown below.

Extended ASCII Representation of 176	**Binary Representation of 176**
00110001 00110111 00110110	10110000
'1' '7' '6'	176

Because an input dialog box returns a string, when 176 is typed into its text box it returns the string "176", which must be converted to a numeric if it is to be used in an arithmetic expression. This conversion process is referred to as *parsing* strings into numerics. There is a set of classes in the API, called wrapper classes, which contain static methods to perform this conversion. The string to be converted to a numeric is sent to the method as an argument coded inside the open and close parentheses that follow the name of the method. The decision as to which class and method to use is based on the primitive numeric type the string is being converted to, as shown in Table 2.5.

Table 2.5
Numeric Wrapper Classes and Their Parsing Methods

To Convert a String to the Numeric Type	Use the Static Method	In the Wrapper Class
byte	parseByte	Byte
short	parseShort	Short
int	parseInt	Integer
long	parseLong	Long
float	parseFloat	Float
double	parseDouble	Double

To change the string literal "176" to its integer numeric representation, we would code:

```
int numericValue = Integer.parseInt("176");
```

To convert the string s to a numeric double, we would code:

```
double numericValue = Double.parseDouble(s);
```

Most often, the statements to accept a user input via an input dialog box, and the conversion of the returned string to a numeric, are coded one after the other.

```
String s =  JOPtionPane.showInputDiaog("Enter your age");
int age = Integer.parseInt(s);
s =  JOPtionPane.showInputDiaog("Enter your weight");
double weight = Double.parseDouble(s);
```

If the string sent to the wrapper class methods contains anything other than digits (i.e., the characters '0', '1', ..., '9'), a *runtime error* NumberFormatException occurs, and the program terminates. If the empty string is passed to the methods (the user clicked "OK" in an input dialog box without typing an input) or the null string is passed to methods (the user clicked "Cancel" without making an entry), the same runtime error occurs. We will learn how to deal with these errors at runtime to bring the program to a more informative conclusion in Chapter 4 and how to permit the user to correct the erroneous input in Chapter 5 "Repeating Statements: Loops."

NOTE   *A runtime error is an error that occurs while the program is in execution.*

The application shown in Figure 2.8 calculates the area of a circle given its radius, and it also calculates the radius of a circle given its area. The inputs to the program (a radius of 10 and an area

```
1   import javax.swing.JOptionPane;
2
3   public class AssignmentMathAndDialogIO
4   {
5      public static void main(String[] args)
6      {
7         String s;
8         double area, radius;
9
10        JOptionPane.showMessageDialog(null, "Circle area and radius" +
11                                           "\n calculation program");
12        s = JOptionPane.showInputDialog("To calculate an area," +
13                                           "\n    enter a radius");
14        radius = Double.parseDouble(s);
15        area = Math.PI * Math.pow(radius, 2);
16        JOptionPane.showMessageDialog(null, "The area of a circle" +
17                                           " whose radius = " +
18                                           radius + "\n is " + area);
19
20        s =JOptionPane.showInputDialog("To calculate a radius" +
21                                           "\n    enter an area");
22        area = Double.parseDouble(s);
23        radius = Math.sqrt(area / Math.PI);
24        JOptionPane.showMessageDialog(null, "The radius of a circle" +
25                                           " whose area = " +
26                                           area + "\nis " + radius);
27     }
28 }
```

Figure 2.8
The application AssignmentMathAndDialogIO.

of 200) and the corresponding outputs are show in Figure 2.9. The program demonstrates the use of assignment statements, parsing a string into a numeric, performing calculations, the use of the Math class, and dialog box I/O.

Line 1 of Figure 2.8 is an `import` statement. Import statements make API classes, and the constants and methods they contain, available to our programs. In this case, the class `JOption-Pane`, which contains the methods to perform dialog box input and output, is imported into the program. These methods are used to output the program's splash screen (lines 10–11) and to input the radius of a circle (lines 12–13). The new-line escape sequences (`\n`) in the strings sent to these methods produce a two-line message on the splash screen and a two-line input prompt, as shown at the top of Figure 2.9.

Line 14 parses the string representation of the input radius returned from the input dialog box into a double and assigns that double to the variable `radius`. Line 15 calculates the area of the circle. It uses the Math class's method `pow` to square the input radius and then multiplies that by the constant pi (`Math.PI`). Lines 16–18 output the radius and the computed area to a message dialog box (Figure 2.9c). The input radius and the calculated area are added to the output string with the use of the concatenation operator on line 18.

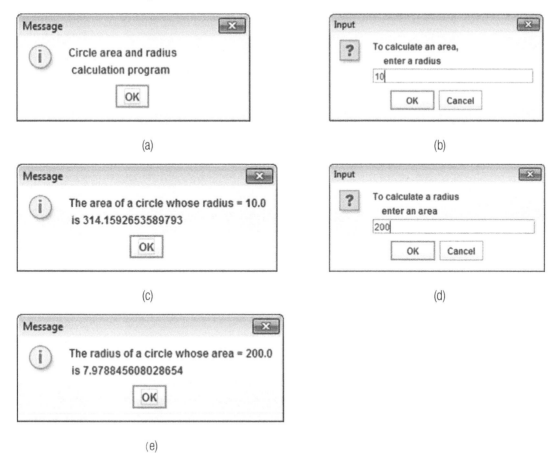

(a)

(b)

(c)

(d)

(e)

Figure 2.9
Input and resulting output from the application **AssignmentMathAndDialogIO**.

In a similar way, lines 20–26 accept an input area and compute the circle's radius. This calculation uses the Math class's `sqrt` method on line 23 to perform the calculation. The method accepts one argument, which in this case is the result of dividing the area by pi. The input to and output from this portion of the program is shown in Figure 2.9e.

2.8 GRAPHICAL TEXT OUTPUT

In Section 2.4, we invoked (or some would say "used" or "called") the `println` and `print` methods of the `PrintStream` class to perform text output to the system console. In this section, we will learn how to use the method `drawString` in the API `Graphics` class to perform text output to a graphics window. This type of output is called graphical text output. Unlike console output, we can specify the font type, size, and style (e.g., bold style) of graphical text output. In addition, we can output the text to any location in a graphics window. In game programming, text output is typically used to display the game's level of difficulty, the remaining time, the score, or other information on the game's status.

With this added capability come added responsibilities. For example, every time a graphics window that has been minimized is restored, the graphical text must be output again, or it will not be visible in the window. In fact, anything that appears in the window before it was minimized must be redrawn when the window is restored. One mechanism for doing this in graphics programs is to place the graphical output in a *call back* method. Our game environment contains several call back methods. In this section, we will learn how to use the call back method `draw`, the `Graphic` class's `drawString` method, and how to set the font type, size, and style of graphical text output.

2.8.1 The `drawString` Method

The `drawString` method is a part (member) of the API Graphics class and is used to output text to a graphical object (perhaps a window). When the method is invoked three arguments are passed to it. The first argument is the text to be output. The second and third arguments are the x and y coordinates where the text will be output. These coordinates locate the lower left position of the first character of text. Their origin is the upper left corner of the graphical object in which the text is to be displayed (e.g., our game board), with x positive to the right and y positive down.

To output the text "Hello World" to our game environment's game board, positioned with the lower left corner of the "H" at (200, 300), we would code:

```
g.drawString("Hello World", 200, 300);
```

Notice that the two characters `g.` precede the name of the method. This is because the method must draw its text on a `Graphics` object. In our case, the object g would have to be a `Graphics` object attached to our game board because we want the text to be drawn on the game board. As we will see in the next section, the attachment of the object g to our game board is performed for us by the game environment.

A method that operates on an object is called a nonstatic method. The syntax used to invoke these methods is the name of the object it is operating on, followed by a dot, followed by the name of the method and its argument list. We have used this syntax in Section 2.4 to invoke the `print` and `println` methods. They were invoked by proceeding their names with the Java pre-defined `PrintStream` object `System.out` followed by a dot. (As previously discussed, when we invoke static methods, we precede the method's name with the name of the method's class followed by a dot. For example, `Math.sqrt(9);`)

The simplest way to determine if a method is static or nonstatic is to click on its class name in the lower left window of the online Java API Specification then scroll down through the API documentation to the method's name. If the method is static, the word "static" will appear in the column to the left of the method's name. For example:

static double	sqrt(double a)
	Returns the correctly rounded positive square root of a `double` value

If the method is a nonstatic method, the word "static" will not appear in the column to the left of the methods name.

The remaining issue is determining where in our game application program we place the invocation to `drawString`. The short answer is in the `draw` call back method, which we will discuss next.

2.8.2 The `draw` Call Back Method

Figure 2.10 presents the Java application class `GraphicalTextOutput` that creates a game window object on line 7, which is displayed by line 11 when the `main` method executes. Lines 2–12 are identical to that of the game code template in Figure 1.31 except for the change in the application's class name (lines 4 and 6) and the title of the window (line 7). When the program is run, the window shown in Figure 2.11 appears on the monitor.

```
1    import edu.sjcny.gpv1.*;
2    import java.awt.Graphics;
3
4    public class GraphicalTextOutput extends DrawableAdapter
5    {
6       static GraphicalTextOutput ga = new GraphicalTextOutput( );
7       static GameBoard gb = new GameBoard(ga, "Graphical Text Output");
8
9       public static void main(String[] args)
10      {
11         showGameBoard(gb);
12      }
13
14      public void draw(Graphics g) //the drawing call back method
15      {
16         g.drawString("Hello World", 250, 220);
17
18      }
19   }
```

Figure 2.10
The application `GraphicalTextOutput`.

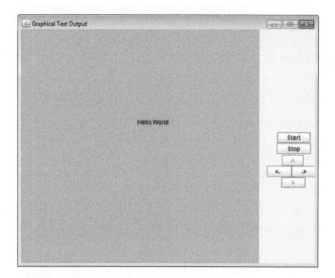

Figure 2.11
The output produced by the application `GraphicalTextOutput`.

Lines 14–18 is a coding of the game environment's draw call back method. The first line of the draw method, called the method's signature, must always be identical to the code on line 14, and it requires that the game environment be added (imported) to the program (line 1). The invocation to the drawString method has been coded on line 16, which, when executed, outputs the graphical text "Hello World" to our game board beginning at pixel location (250, 220). To use the drawString method the Graphics class must be imported into the program (line 2). But, when does it execute?

We have learned that the main method is invoked by the Java runtime environment causing its statements to execute, beginning with its first executable statement (the program entry point) and ending when the execution reaches the end of its code block, in this case, line 12. Thus, it would appear that line 11 would display the application's window, and then the program would end. But the draw method must have executed because the characters *Hello World* appear in the program's window (Figure 2.11). So again, we ask the question, "when does it execute?"

The answer is fundamental to why the method draw is referred to as a call back method. Line 11 in the main method invokes the method showGameBoard, which requests that the game environment display the game board window. Before the game environment displays the game's window, it invokes, or calls back, the draw method coded in the application, causing it to execute. When the draw method ends, the game environment completes the display of the game's window requested by the showGameBoard method. Thus, the application calls the game environment to display the game board window (line 11), and the game environment calls back the application's draw method to perform its drawings on the game board before the window is displayed. Specifically, the execution sequence is line 11 in the method main, the code of the showGameBoard method, the code at the beginning of a method in the game environment, the draw call back method lines 14-18), and finally, the remainder of the code in the game-environment method.

In fact, every time the program's window has to be redrawn (e.g., the window was minimized and then the window's icon on the status bar is clicked), the game environment's code invokes the `draw` method to redo its drawings on the game board. This can easily be verified by adding the statement

```
System.out.println("the draw method was invoked");
```

to the `draw` call back method. Then, every time the `draw` method is invoked, we will see an output on the system console.

> **NOTE** *Even though the main method containing the program's entry point ends its execution, a graphical program continues to execute until the program's graphical window (e.g., the gameboard window) is closed.*

2.8.3 The `setFont` Method: A First Look

Like the `drawString` method, the `setFont` method is a part (member) of the API `Graphics` class. It is used to change font type, style, and size. The output in Figure 2.11 used the default font values. Once changed, all subsequent graphical text output will use the new (or current) font type, style, and size until it is changed again. The method is passed one argument. The following code, when added to the `draw` method, changes the font type to Arial, the style to bold italic, and the font size to 16 points, and then outputs the text *The Font was Changed*. The syntax of the argument sent to the `setFont` method will be explained in Chapter 3.

```
g.setFont(new Font("Arial", Font.BOLD + Font.ITALIC, 16));
g.drawString("The Font was Changed", 150, 300);
```

2.9 THE COUNTING ALGORITHM

Counting is something that is done in most programs and is considered to be a fundamental algorithm in computer science. For example, in game programs it is used to count the number of seconds remaining in a game or the number of seconds since the game began. In the first case, the time starts at a designated amount of time and counts down to zero; in the second case, the time starts at zero and counts up. In both cases, the game's time is usually displayed on the game board. In this section, we will discuss the counting algorithm, and we will learn how to use it inside the game environment's call back method `timer1` to count seconds.

Most of us began to learn how to count by memorizing the integers beginning with 1. Our parents may have said to us, "say this: one, two, three, four." Most of us, on the first try, perhaps said "three, four," or "one, two, four," or some other erroneous sequence. Through repetition, eventually we memorized the sequence and extended it by recognizing that each new element is "one more."

Somewhere along our cognitive development path, we discovered the counting algorithm. In support of that is the realization that most people never memorized the integers from 1,242,518 to 1,243,589. However, most of us could recite that sequence of integers if asked to do so because we use the counting algorithm to determine the sequence. Below is the generalized counting algorithm that can be used to count forward or backward by any increment:

```
int count = aBeginningValue;
// repeat the next statement until count reaches the ending value
count = count + aCountingIncrement
```

For example, to count upward from 1 to 10 by 1s, we code:

```
int count = 1;
// repeat the next statement until count reaches 10
count = count + 1; // 1 becomes 2, 2 becomes 3, 3 becomes 4, …
```

To count backward by 5s, from 1,165 to 875, we code:

```
int count = 1165;
// repeat the next statement until count reaches 875
count = count  + -5; // 1165 becomes 1160, 1160 becomes 1155, …
```

Repeating statements is the topic of Chapter 5, so we will revisit the counting algorithm in that chapter. However, if we want to count seconds within a game program, the second line of the counting algorithm can be repeated by placing it inside a call back method named `timer1`. This method is invoked by the game environment once every second causing the statement to be repeated once a second.

2.9.1 A Counting Application: Displaying a Game's Time

The game environment has three timer call back methods named `timer1`, `timer2`, and `timer3`. Their signatures (first lines) are:

```
public void timer1( )
public void timer2( )
public void timer3( )
```

If you code these methods into your game program, they will be invoked every time their respective timers "tick." For example, the method `timer2` will be invoked every time `timer2` ticks. Because counting seconds is so common in games, by default `timer1` ticks every second. It begins ticking when the game window's `Start` button is clicked, pauses when the `Stop` button is clicked, and resumes ticking when the `Start` button is clicked. After a timer call back method ends its execution, the game environment invokes the `draw` call back method. The details of the other two timers, which are normally used to animate game objects, will be discussed in Chapter 6.

Figure 2.12 presents the graphical application `CountingSeconds` that illustrates the use of the counting algorithm to count upwards by one, starting from zero. The output produced by the program three seconds after the user clicks the `Start` button is shown in Figure 2.13.

The declaration of the counter variable `count` and its initialization to zero seconds is coded on line 8. (Note that the key word **static** is coded at the beginning of this line. The need for it will be explained in Chapter 3.) Declaring this variable on line 8 places it outside of the code blocks (the open and close braces) of all of the class's methods, which makes it makes available to *all* of the class's methods. Variables declared in this way are said to be *class level* variables.

```
1    import edu.sjcny.gpv1.*;
2    import java.awt.Graphics;
3    import java.awt.Font;
4    public class CountingSeconds extends DrawableAdapter
5    {
6      static CountingSeconds ga = new CountingSeconds( );
7      static GameBoard gb = new GameBoard(ga, "The Counting Algorithm");
8      static int count = 0;   // a class level variable
9
10     public static void main(String[] args)
11     {
12       showGameBoard(gb);
13     }
14
15     public void draw(Graphics g) // the drawing call back method
16     {
17       g.setFont(new Font("Arial", Font.BOLD, 18));
18       g.drawString("Your game time is: " + count, 10, 50);
19     }
20
21     public void timer1()
22     {
23       count = count + 1;
24     }
25   }
```

Figure 2.12
The application CountingSeconds.

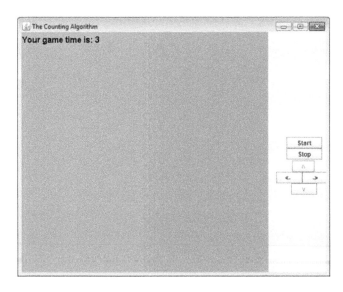

Figure 2.13
The output produced by the application CountingSeconds three seconds after the Start button is clicked.

The second line of the counting algorithm is coded on line 23 inside the `timer1` call back method (lines 21–24). Because timer1 ticks once a second (by default), line 23 is repeated every second, causing the counter variable `count` to count seconds. Each time the `timer1` method ends, the game environment invokes the `draw` method, which displays the new time on the game board by outputting the contents of the class-level variable `count` (line 18). The output appears in bold Arial 18 point font because line 17 invokes the *Graphic* class's `setFont` method to change the current font values. The import statement on line 3 makes the constants and methods of the *Font* class available for use by that statement.

2.10 FORMATTING NUMERIC OUTPUT: A FIRST PASS

In this chapter, we have discussed how to perform numeric output, but we have not discussed how to format numeric output to improve its readability, such as adding a comma every three digits to the left of the decimal point, or adjusting the precision of the fractional part of a number output to the right of the decimal point. The `format` method in the `DecimalFormat` class can be used to accomplish both of these commonly used types of output formatting. We will conclude this chapter with an introduction to the techniques used to format numeric output; we will present more details on these techniques in Chapter 5.

The application presented in Figure 2.14 uses the `DecimalFormat` class's `format` method to format the output of a real number (line 12) and an integer (line 13). The method returns a string containing the formatted numeric value and is sent one argument. The argument is the numeric variable to be formatted: `speedOfLight` and `population` on lines 12 and 13 respectively.

This nonstatic method is invoked (on lines 12 and 13) using the `DecimalFormat` object `df` declared on line 10. The formatting to be performed is associated with the decimal format object and is specified as a string literal coded inside the parentheses at the end of line 10. The string literal `#,###.##` coded on this line indicates that commas will appear every three digits to the left of

```
1    import java.text.DecimalFormat;
2
3    public class BasicNumericFormatting
4    {
5      public static void main(String[] args)
6      {
7        double speedOfLight = 299792458.7153;
8        int population = 1097603176;
9
10       DecimalFormat df = new DecimalFormat("#,###.##");
11
12       System.out.println(df.format(speedOfLight));
13       System.out.println(df.format(population));
14     }
15   }
```

Figure 2.14
The application **BasicNumericFormatting**.

the decimal point, and *real* numbers (nonintegers) will be output with two digits of precision. The level of precision used in the formatting can be changed by adding or removing pound signs to the right of the decimal point on line 10.

The output produced by the program is given in Figure 2.15. As this output shows, real numbers are always rounded up (299792458.7153 was output as 299792458.72), and integer output does not contain a decimal point.

```
299,792,458.72
1,097,603,176
```

Figure 2.15
The output produced by the **BasicNumericFormatting** application.

2.11 CHAPTER SUMMARY

This chapter introduced the basic components of a Java program and the Java template for developing a program that performs input, mathematical calculations, and output. Variables are declared to store data during the program's execution. Primitive variables store one data value, and reference variables store a memory address where the object that contains the data is located. The type of the data (for example, character or integer), must also be declared. Good coding style dictates that variable names be meaningful as well as syntactically correct. Meaningful variable names indicate what the data represents. They begin with a letter and cannot contain spaces.

The print and println methods are used to output a string to the console window to which the object System.out is attached. Escape sequences permit characters with special meaning to be used in output statements. The concatenation operator joins data values and strings into a single output string.

String objects, which are reference variables store the memory address that refers to, or references, the actual string. Strings can be created and initialized using either a one-line or two-line grammar. The default value for an uninitialized string is null. Strings have to be converted into numeric values to perform mathematical operations, and there is a set of classes in the API, called wrapper classes, which contain static methods to perform this conversion.

Java, like most programming languages, provides the ability to perform basic arithmetic calculations and provides additional features, including the API Math class, to perform more complex calculations. Arithmetic calculations are performed in Java using arithmetic expressions. Arithmetic expressions consist of a series of operands separated by operators. The parts of an arithmetic expression inside the parentheses are evaluated first using the rules of precedence to determine the order of the operations. If the operators are of equal precedence, they are evaluated from left to right. Higher precedence operators are evaluated first. The division of two integers always results in a truncated integer value, and the mod operator is used to determine the remainder of integer division.

Values are assigned to variables using the assignment operator. Generally, the type of the value being assigned to a variable should match the type of the variable. Type casting and promotion are provided and are used with mixed-mode expressions to ensure that the variable types are compatible and there is no loss of precision.

Dialog boxes are a graphical way to communicate with the user of a Java program and offer an alternative to console-based input and output. The method `drawString` in the API `Graphics` class can be used to perform text output to a graphics window, and the setFont method can be used to change the default font, style and size. The counting algorithm is used to keep track of elapsed seconds in a game program. Chapter 3 will extend the concepts of objects, classes, and methods and their application to creating game programs.

Finally, the `DecimalFormat` class is introduced to provide ways to format numeric output to improve its readability.

Knowledge Exercises

1. True or False:
   a) The type of the data stored in a variable can change as the program executes.
   b) Variables must be declared in a program before they are used.
   c) Variables must be initialized when they are declared.
   d) It is grammatically incorrect to begin a variable name with an upper-case letter.
   e) Spaces can be used in variable names for better readability.

2. Which statement in a Java application program is executed first?

3. What are variables? Name two types of variables and the information each one stores.

4. Which of the following is not a primitive data type?
   a) boolean   b) char   c) String   d) int

5. Give the default initial values for variables declared to be of the following types:
   a) boolean   b) char   c) double   d) int

6. Write a well-composed declaration statement to declare variables that can store:
   a) Maggie's age initialized to 32
   b) The first initial of Ryan's name initialized to the letter 'R'
   c) The cost of a taco
   d) The number 21,234,096,464
   e) The fact that it is snowing

7. Is a numeric literal, coded in a program, represented as a float or a double? Explain.

8. Determine if each of the following variables is well composed and valid. For those that are not, explain why not.
   a) 2ndplace   b) middleInitial   c) winningTeam
   d) fgp3   e) test1 grade   f) myScore
   g) SalePrice

9. Give the code to output two lines to the system console. The first line will contain your name, and the second line will contain the town in which you live, using:
   a) Two statements   b) One statement

10. Write a well-composed variable declaration statement to declare a string String object initialized to Skyler's address, which is 21 First Avenue, using the:

    a) One-line object-declaration grammar   b) Two-line object-declaration grammar

11. Draw a picture of the memory allocated by the statements:

    a) `int distance = 675;`   b) `String myName = new String("Jane");`

12. Give one statement to:

    a) Output the annotated contents of the memory cell `priceOfCorn`

    b) Output the sentence: Martin said: "I had a dream."

    c) Change the contents of the variable `myBalance` to 234.54.

13. Evaluate each of these expressions:

    a) 17 - 5 * 2 + 12   b) 31 - 7 * 2 + 14

    c) (48 + 12) / 12 + 18 * 2   d) 21 - 9 + 18 + 4 * 3.7

14. Give the code to:

    a) Declare the variable `quizAverage` and store the average of the variables `quiz1`, `quiz2`, `quiz3`, and `quiz4` in it

    b) Calculate the sine of 45 degrees and store the value in the variable `sineOf45`

    c) Calculate and output the square root of 45.67

    d) Calculate and output 34.7 to the 5th power

15. Write the variable declaration to declare the variable `average` and the assignment statement to store the average of three speed limits: 55, 57, and 60 miles per hour.

16. Give an assignment statement to store the integer part of the value stored in the double variable `bankBalance` in the variable `dollars`.

17. True or False:

    a) You must include an import statement in a program to perform I/O using dialog boxes.

    b) A message dialog box can be used to obtain input from the program user.

    c) A string is always returned from an input dialog box.

    d) When the user clicks "OK" without making an input into an input dialog box, null is returned.

    e) Dialog boxes will size themselves to accommodate the string argument sent to them.

18. Write the code to output two lines to a message dialog box. The first line will contain your first and last name, and the second line will contain your date of birth in the format "My birthday is: dd\mm\yyyy" (yes, those are backslashes).

19. Give the code to allow the program user to enter a checking account balance using an input dialog box. Include a well-composed user prompt.

20. Think of a game. Write the code to output the name of the game and its creator, the task (objective) of the game, and how the game pieces are controlled to a message dialog box of reasonable size.

21. Give the code to declare a double variable named `deposit` and to parse the input contained in the string `sDeposit` into it.

22. Write the code to declare an integer variable named `speedLimit` and to parse the input contained in the string `sSpeedLimit` into it.

Programming Exercises

1. Write a Java application that outputs your name on one line followed by the town in which you live to the system console.

2. Write a program to calculate the average of five quiz grades: 100, 97, 67, 85, and 79. Output the quiz grades and the average to the system console. The output should be well annotated with the quiz grades on one line and the output on another.

3. Write a program to accept an angle (input in degrees) and a real number. Then, output the angle and its sine, cosine, and tangent. Follow that output with the output of the input real number, its cube, and the square root of the number. The outputs should occupy several lines and be sent to both the system console and to a message dialog box. The input prompts should be well composed, and the outputs should be well annotated.

4. Repeat Programming Exercise 3, but output the information to the system console and to the middle of the game board. Use 20-point italic Arial font for the game-board output.

5. Write a program to ask the user to enter the product of a pair of real numbers (of your choosing), with the input rounded to one digit of precision. After the product is entered, output the user's input and the correct product, rounded to one digit of precision. The outputs should occupy several lines, and be sent to the system console and to a message dialog box. The input prompts should be well composed, and the outputs should be well annotated.

6. Write a program to ask the user to enter the product of a pair of real numbers of your choosing. After the product is entered, output the correct answer and the number of seconds it took the user to enter the product to the center of the game board and to the system console. Use 20-point italic Arial font for the game-board output. The output should be on two lines and well annotated.

7. Repeat Programming Exercise 6, but output the numbers with commas every three digits on the left side of the decimal point, and use one digit of precision.

Endnotes

[1] The URL of the Edition 7 API documentation is: *http://docs.oracle.com/javase/7/docs/api/* It is named: Java Platform, Standard Edition 7 API Specification.

[2] http://www.randomnumbers.info/content/Random.htm

CHAPTER 3

METHODS, CLASSES, AND OBJECTS: A FIRST LOOK

3.1   *Methods We Write* *76*

3.2   *Information Passing* *79*

3.3   *The API* **Graphics** *Class* *89*

3.4   *Object Oriented Programming* *93*

3.5   *Defining Classes and Creating Objects* *94*

3.6   *Adding Methods to Classes* *102*

3.7   *Overloading Constructors* *121*

3.8   *Passing Objects To and From Worker Methods* *125*

3.9   *Chapter Summary* *128*

In this chapter

This chapter extends the concepts of methods, classes, and objects discussed in the previous chapter to enable us to design and implement our own classes and the methods that they contain. These concepts facilitate the development of our programs by allowing us to divide a large program into several smaller classes, separately develop these classes, and then integrate them into the larger program. Once written, these classes can also be used in other programs, just as the API classes are. Several design tools will be introduced in the chapter to methodize the specification of a class and the object it defines. The understanding of material presented in this chapter is the foundation of the advanced OOP topics discussed in Chapters 7 and 8.

After successfully completing this chapter, you should:

- Be able to write void and nonvoid methods
- Understand how to share primitive information and objects between methods
- Understand the concept of value parameters
- Be able to read a Unified Modeling Language (UML) diagram and use it to specify a class
- Understand how to design and specify graphical and nongraphical objects
- Be able to identify, write, and use a set of methods that most classes contain
- Understand the concept and use of public and private data members and methods
- Be able to design, construct, modify, and access an object using its class's methods
- Use methods of the Graphics class to draw lines, rectangles, ovals, and circles
- Have acquired the foundational skills required for a study of Chapters 7 and 8

3.1 METHODS WE WRITE

In Chapter 2, we became familiar with several methods available in the Java Application Programming Interface. For example, the methods `println` and `print` perform output to the system console, `pow` and `sqrt` perform calculations, and `drawString` and `setFont` perform text output to the program window. Being resident in the API, these methods are available to all Java programmers, and their use expedites the program development process because only one programmer, the API programmer, had to discover their algorithms and then write, test, and debug their code. The rest of us simply use the methods by importing them into our program and writing a one-line invocation statement. Because most of the cost of software development is the salaries paid to the programmers, the use of prewritten methods also makes software more affordable.

In this section, we will learn how to write our own methods. Not only will this allow us to reuse the code that we write in other programs, but it also facilitates the development of our programs by dividing a large program into several smaller subprograms called methods. By dividing a large program into subprograms, these methods can be developed by several programmers working in parallel, which greatly reduces the calendar time required to produce a program.

> **The Motivation for Writing Methods**
>
> *Extends our problem solving capabilities: Humans are good at solving small problems but not large problems*
>
> **NOTE** *Reduces development time: Methods can be developed in parallel by several members of a programming team*
>
> *Reduces cost: Methods can be written in such a way that they can be used in any program using a one-line invocation statement*

3.1.1 Syntax of a Method

In Java, all the methods we write must be part of a class. They must be coded within the class's code block, the open and close braces that begin and end a class statement. The class statement can be the one that contains the program entry point, the method `main`, or some other class that we will learn how to create later in this chapter. When methods are coded inside the class that contains the method `main`, good coding style dictates that they be coded after it.

The minimum code required to create a method is:

```
returnType methodName( )
{
    //the code of the method is placed here
}
```

The first line of the method is called the method's *signature.* The signature is followed by a set of open and close braces that define the bounds of the method's *code block.* The statements to be executed when the method is invoked are coded inside this code block.

The method's signature, the first line of the method's code, must include the type of the information returned from the method, followed by the method's name, followed by an open and close set of parentheses. If the method does not return a value to the invoker, for example, simply output a string value, the keyword `void` is used as the return type. In this case, the method is said to be a `void` method.

A method that simply outputs the name of the student newspaper to the system console every time it is invoked would be an example of a `void` method.

```
void outputNewspaperName()
{
    System.out.println("The Student Voice");
}
```

The syntax and coding style used for naming methods are the same as those used to name variables:

- they cannot contain spaces
- they should begin with a lower-case letter
- new words should begin with an upper-case letter

Normally, they are only comprised of letters. Digits, the dollar sign, and the underscore are not normally used in their names. For example, a method that adds two integers together and returns the result could be named `addTwoInts` rather than `add _ 2 _ Ints`.

Figure 3.1 presents the application `AVoidMethod` that contains the implementation and two different invocation forms of the void method `outputNewspaperName`. The output it produces is shown in Figure 3.2.

```
1    public class AVoidMethod
2    {
3        public static void main(String[] args)
4        {
5            AVoidMethod.outputNewspaperName(); //1st method invocation
6            System.out.println("Page 1\n");
7            outputNewspaperName();              //2nd method invocation
8            System.out.println("Page 2\n");
9        }
10
11       static void outputNewspaperName()    //method signature
12       {
13           System.out.println("The Student Voice");
14       }
15   }
```

Figure 3.1
The console application **AVoidMethod**.

```
The Student Voice
Page 1

The Student Voice
Page 2
```

Figure 3.2
The output produced by the console application **AVoidMethod**.

The program consists of two methods: the method `main` (lines 3–9) and the method `output-NewspaperName` (lines 11–14). Both of these methods are coded within the program class's code block that begins on line 2 and ends on line 15.

NOTE   *A method cannot be coded inside of another method's code block.*

The signature of the method `outputNewspaperName`, coded on line 11, begins with the keyword **static**. Not all method signatures begin with this key word. As we have learned, methods fall into two categories: those that operate on objects (static methods) and those that do not (nonstatic methods). An example of a method that operates on an object is the method `println`. It operates on, or sends its output string to, the console object whose name is `System.out`. Methods that do not operate on an object must include the key word **static** in their signature. The method `outputNewspaperName` does not operate on an object, so its signature begins with the key word static. In Section 3.5, we will discuss methods that we write that do operate on objects, and we will gain more insight into what it means to say a method operates on an object.

NOTE   *Methods that do not operate on an object must include the key word **static** in their signature.*

The method `outputNewspaperName` is invoked in lines 5 and 7 of the application's main method. Line 7 just mentions the name of the method followed by open and close parentheses. This invocation syntax is valid because the static method is coded within the same class, `AVoid-Method`, as the invocation statement (line 7). The more generalized syntax for invoking a static method is used on line 5. Here, the invocation statement begins with the name of the class in which the method is coded followed by a dot:

```
AVoidMethodApp.outputNewspaperName();
```

We used this syntax to invoke the static methods `pow` and `sqrt` that are coded in the Math class.

```
double ans = Math.pow(3.0, 2.0);
double root = Math.srt(9.0);
```

Because these two methods are not coded in the same class in which they are normally invoked, the name of the class must be included in the invocation statement. The only exception to this is the use of a static import statement. When either syntax is valid, the shorter syntax makes our programs more readable and is therefore preferred.

The execution sequence of the application begins on line 5 of the main method. This invocation statement causes the code in the code block of the `outputNewspaperName` method to execute (lines 12–14), which produces the first line of output (Figure 3.2). Then line 6 of the main method executes, producing the second line of output. Line 7 causes the `outputNewspaperName` method to execute a second time, which produces the third line of output. Finally, line 8 executes, which produces the last output line.

NOTE   *After a method executes, the next statement to execute is the statement immediately after the statement that invoked it.*

3.2 INFORMATION PASSING

For a method to function properly, information must often be passed to it when it is invoked, and some methods must return one piece of information to the invoking statement. Consider the Math class's nonvoid static method `pow`. When it is invoked, a number (n) and a power (p) are passed to it, and the method returns the result of its calculation: n^p. The left side of Figure 3.3 depicts this sharing of information between the invoker (top left) of the method `pow` and the method (bottom left). The right side of the figure generalizes this concept of shared information between the invoker, often called the client, and the method that performs some "work" for the client, often referred to as the worker method. For example `pow`'s work is to compute a given number (n) raised to a given power (p).

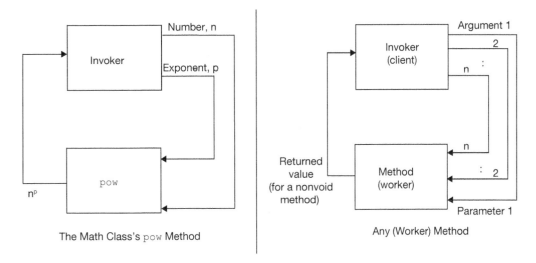

The Math Class's `pow` Method

Any (Worker) Method

Figure 3.3
The sharing of information between a method and its invoker.

As depicted in the right side of Figure 3.3, an unlimited number of pieces of information can be sent from the invoking client to a worker method, however, only one piece of information can be sent back to the client from the worker method. We say that the client sends the method an *argument list* containing the shared information, and the worker method receives the shared information in its *parameter list* (either or both of which could be empty).

NOTE   *No more than one piece of information can be returned from a method.*

3.2.1 Parameters and Arguments

If a method is to receive information passed to it from the client, then its signature must contain a parameter list. The parameter list is coded inside the open and close parenthesis of the method's signature. The parameters in the list are separated by commas, and each parameter consists of a variable name preceded by its type. For example, the signature of a method whose work is to output a person's age and weight would have an `int` and a `double` parameter in its parameter list.

```
static void outputAgeAndWeight(int age, double weight)
{
    System.out.println(age: "  + age + " weight: " + weight);
}
```

Each parameter receives *one* piece of information sent to it by the client code's invocation statement, and the *type* of the parameter must match the type of the information sent to it. The client's statement used to invoke the method `outputAgeAndWeight` would contain two arguments in its argument list, within parentheses.

```
outputAgeAndWeight(myAge, myWeight);
```

This statement passes the contents of the variables `myAge` and `myWeight` to the method.

Arguments, information that is to be shared with the worker method, can be variables (e.g., `myAge, myWeight`) that have been previously declared in the client code, or string or primitive literals.

> **NOTE** *The order, number, and type of the arguments in a method invocation statement must match the order, number, and type of the parameters in the method's signature.*

Each time a method is invoked, the variables in the method's parameter list are allocated and paired up with the arguments in the invocation's argument list (the first parameter paired with the first argument, the second parameter paired with the second argument, etc.), and the value stored in each of the arguments is copied into the paired parameters. For the invocation statement

```
outputAgeAndWeight(myAge, myWeight);
```

the value in the argument `myAge` is copied into the parameter `age` of the method `outputAgeAndWeight`, and the value contained in the argument `myWeight` is copied into the parameter `weight`. This type of information passing is called *passing by value*, and the parameters are called *value parameters* because the values contained in the arguments are copied into the parameters. Once the parameters have been allocated and this transfer of information is complete, the code in the worker method's code block begins execution.

Consider the sequence of code that contains a main method and the method `outputAgeAndWeight`:

```
public static void main(String[] args)
{   int myAge = 23;
    double myWeight = 185.4;

    outputAgeAndWeight(myAge, myWeight);
}

static void outputAgeAndWeight(int age, double weight)
{
    System.out.println("age: "  + age + " weight: " + weight);
}
```

Figure 3.4 depicts a sequence of seven events that occur when this code executes and illustrates the process of passing information using value parameters. The left side of figure shows the main method's (client) code and its execution sequence (events 1, 2, 3), which includes the RAM memory allocated to its two arguments (event 2 is depicted in the bottom left portion of the figure).

The right side of the figure shows the code of the method and its execution sequence (events 4, 5, 6, and 7), which includes the RAM memory allocated to its two parameters (event 5 is depicted in the bottom right portion of the figure). The passing of the values stored in the client's arguments into the paired worker parameters is depicted as event 6 in the bottom center of the figure. After the information is passed, the code block of the method executes (event 7).

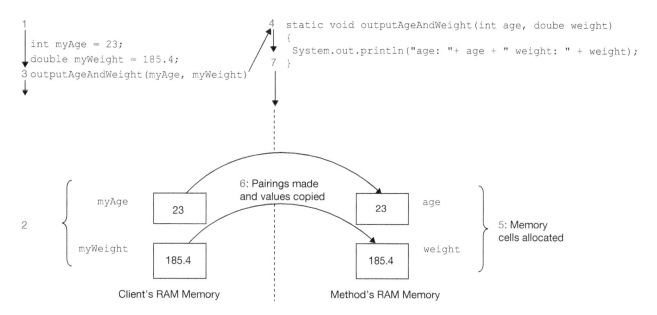

Figure 3.4
The transfer of information to a method via value parameters.

The dotted line in the figure is a line that the code in the client and worker methods cannot cross. The client code on the left of the figure cannot access the contents of the member cells `age` and `weight`, and the worker method code cannot access the memory cells `myAge` and `myWeight`. Inserting the statement

```
myAge = myAge + 1;
```

into the code of the method `outputAgeAndWeight` would result in a translation error because `myAge` is only known to the client code.

When the method completes its execution, the variables named in its parameter list are de-allocated, and their storage is returned to the memory manager. The result is that the values stored in these memory cells are lost, in that they are no longer available to the program. An understanding of this is fundamental to the notion of value parameters. It is also important to realize that the four memory cells created during events 2 and 5 are separate and distinct. To emphasize this, the names of the parameters (`age` and `weight`), coded in the worker method's signature, were intentionally chosen to be different than the names of the arguments passed to method (myAge and myWeight). Even if the argument and parameter names were the same (e.g., both coded as age and weight), event 5 would still create two distinct memory cells on the right side of Figure 3.4 named age and weight. A coding of the symbols age and weight in the worker method would refer the contents of these to memory cells, which would be de-allocated when the method ends its execution.

> **NOTE** *Every time a method is invoked, the variables in its parameter list are allocated, and they are de-allocated when the method ends its execution.*

3.2.2 Scope and Side Effects of Value Parameters

The only way to pass information between arguments and parameters (i.e., between client code and worker method code) in Java is via value parameters, so it is important that we understand the limitations of the value parameter memory model presented in Figure 3.4 and its implications. As depicted in the figure, the client code has two variables it can access, myAge and myWeight, and the method has two variables it can access, age and weight. The client code cannot access the variables age and weight, and the worker method cannot access the variables myAge and myWeight.

In programming language jargon, we say that the worker method's variables age and weight are defined within the **scope** of its code, and the variables myAge and myWeight are out of its scope. A Java statement can only access variables that are within its scope.

> **Definition**
>
> The **scope** of a variable is the portion of a program in which it is defined and can therefore be accessed.

It is syntactically correct to make the argument names in a method invocation the same as the parameter names coded in the method's signature. For example, the names of the variables declared in the main method and the worker method's parameter list could both be named myAge and myWeight.

```
public static void main(String[] args)
{   int myAge = 23;
    double MyWeight = 185.4;

    outputAgeAndWeight(myAge, myWeight);
}

static void outputAgeAndWeight(int myAge, double myWeight)
{
    System.out.println("age: "  + myAge + " weight: " + myWeight);
}
```

As previously mentioned, this coding of the method would still create two memory cells assigned to the method's parameters on the lower right side of Figure 3.4, but their names would now be myAge and myWeight. Now, the statement

```
myAge = myAge + 1;
```

written into the worker method's code would not result in a translation error because there is now a variable named myAge that is within its scope. The method's code would access the contents of its memory cell myAge, and the contents of that variable would be changed to 24. When the method ends and execution returns to the client code, the contents of the client code's memory cell myAge would be unchanged. It would still contain the value 23.

Normally, this is a good thing because it prevents an unwanted *side effect* of the method's code changing the client's data. Preventing this side effect assures that the values stored in the client code variables before the method was invoked will be the same values stored in those variables after the method completes it execution. In some cases, however, this is not what we want.

Consider the case of a method, named swap, that the client invokes to swap the contents of two of its variables, a and b, via the statements

```
int a = 10;
int b = 20;
swap(a, b);
System.out.println("a is: " + a + " and b: is " + b);
```

If the method is successful, the output produced after swap completes its execution should be a is 20 and b is 10.

The method swap would have two integer parameters to receive the values to be swapped, and its code would implement the swapping algorithm. The code of the method, preceded by a main method that invokes it, is given below:

```
public static void main(String[] args)
{
    int a = 10;
    int b = 20;

    swap(a, b);
    System.out.println("a is:" + a + " and b: " + b);
}

static void swap(int a, int b)
{
    int temp = a;
    a = b;
    b = temp;
}
```

Unfortunately, because Java uses value parameters, this coding of the method does not swap the client's variables, and the output produced by the last statement in the main method is a is 10 and b is 20.

Consistent with the memory model of value parameters, the client and the method each have their own memory cells named a and b. The method swaps the values contained in its two memory cells a and b, which has no side effects on the contents of the memory cells a and b allocated in the client code. These two cells remain unchanged (they still contain 10 and 20, respectively), which makes it appear that the swap algorithm was improperly coded in the worker method.

It turns out that it is impossible to write a method that swaps the contents of two client variables using primitive-type parameters because, by design, value parameters prevent a method from changing the values in the client's argument list. Some programming languages (e.g., C and C++) solve this problem by allowing another type of parameter called a reference parameter. Java does not support this type of parameter because it can lead to some undesirable side effects

3.2.3 Returned Values

A worker method can return one, and only one value to the method that invokes it. A method that returns a value is called a value returning or nonvoid method, and the key word `void` is not used in its signature. It is replaced with the type of the information the method returns. For example, the method `showInputDialog` in the API class `JOptionPane` is a nonvoid method that returns a reference to a `String`, so its signature contains the type `String` rather than the keyword `void`.

Methods can return the contents of reference variables, as the method `showInputDialog` does, or they can return the contents of primitive variables. In both cases, the returned value should be thought of as replacing the invocation of the method in the statement that invoked the method after the method executes. If the value is to be used later in the program, the invocation should be coded as the right part of an assignment statement that assigns the returned value to a variable.

For example, the two statements below prompt the user to enter a person's age and return the characters that are entered, but only the second one retains the location of the `String` object that is returned.

```
JOptionPane.showInputDialog("enter a person's age");
String sAge = JOptionPane.showInputDialog("enter a person's age");
```

A nonvoid method must contain a `return` statement or the method will not translate. The statement begins with the keyword **return**, which is followed by the value that is to be returned. The value to be returned can be a literal, a variable, the value of an arithmetic expression, or a value returned from a method invocation. The following code segment contains a nonvoid method `multiply` preceded by the code of the main method that invokes it. The method `multiply` calculates and returns the product of two numbers passed to it.

```
public static void main(String[] args)
{
    double a = 10.0;
    double b = 20.0;

    double product = multiply(a, b);
    System.out.println(a + " x " + b + " = " product);
}
```

```
static double multiply(double a, double b)
{
    double c;
    c = a * b;
    return c;
}
```

Because, as previously mentioned, an arithmetic expression can be coded in a `return` statement, the method could have been coded more succinctly as:

```
static double multiply(double a, double b)
{
    return a * b;
}
```

There can be more than one return statement in a nonvoid method, but we will not have a use for that feature of the language until we gain an understanding of the material presented in the next chapter.

3.2.4 Class Level Variables

Class level variables are another way of sharing information among methods. However, the manner in which the information is shared and the syntax used to code class level variables are both very different than when arguments, parameters and `return` statements are used to share information.

To begin with, unlike using arguments and parameters to pass information to a worker method, in order for methods to share information using class variables, the methods must be coded in the same class. The information sharing is accomplished by coding the variable outside of the code blocks of the methods in the class. Good coding style dictates that they be coded at the top of the class before the code of any of the methods. When this done, the variable is within the scope of all of the methods in the class. The methods actually share the same variable, which permits any method in the class to fetch and overwrite the variable's contents. Unlike arguments and parameters, class variables provide a two-way path for methods to share information. One method can write a value into the variable, and another method can read the value from it.

Although we did not explain class variables in this much detail in Chapter 2, the program presented in Figure 2.12 used a class variable named `count` (line 8) to share the game's time between the method `timer` that was incrementing it (line 23), and the method `draw` that was outputting it to the game board (line18). As shown on line 8 when a class variable is used in the program's class, its declaration must begin with the keyword `static`:

```
static int count = 0;
```

Aside from that, its declaration syntax is the same as that used to declare a variable inside of a method's code block.

A variable can be declared inside a method's code block that has the same name of a class-variable. When this is done, a memory cell is created with the same name as the class variable and is called a *local variable*. All uses of the variable's name inside the method's code block refer to the local variable, and the local variable can only be accessed by the method's code. To access the class variable from inside the method, the name of the variable would be preceded by the name of the class followed by a dot (just as when we invoke static methods).

Wherever possible, it is good programming practice not to use the names of class variables for naming variables declared inside of methods. For one thing, it reduces the program's readability because, if we fail to realize that the local variable is declared, we would erroneously believe that the class variable is being used inside the method. In addition, if we neglect to declare the local variable when coding the method, the translator will assume we want to use the class variable, and it will not remind us that we neglected to declare the local variable.

 It is good programming practice not to use the names of class variables for naming local variables declared inside of methods.

Figure 3.5 presents a program that contains four worker methods and demonstrates information sharing via value parameters, return statements, and class variables, the use of local variables, and the features of methods that make them reusable. The inputs to the program and the outputs the program produces are shown Figure 3.6.

Lines 30–36 contain the code of the method inputInteger. Its signature (line 30) indicates that it is a nonvoid method that returns an integer and has a String parameter named prompt. The method passes the string sent to it to an input dialog box (line 33) to be displayed as a prompt to the program user. The returned user input is parsed into the integer variable a (line 34), and then the parsed value is returned to the invoker (line 35). The inclusion of a string parameter in its signature allows the invoker to specify the prompt sent to the input dialog box. In addition, the method parses the input integer, freeing the invoker from that responsibility. Both of these features make this a highly reusable method. It is invoked five times within the program (on lines 11, 17, 18, 23, and 24), and each time it is sent a different prompt.

Two class variables, a and b, are declared on lines 4 and 5 with a initialized to 10. The value in the class variable a is included in the string passed to the invocation of inputInteger on line 11, which is displayed as the prompt in the input dialog box (Figure 3.6a) produced by line 33. The method inputInteger declares its own local variable a on line 32, so the assignment of the parsed value of the user input into the variable a (line 34) changes the contents of the local variable, leaving the class variable unchanged. This is verified by the first output (Figure 3.6b) produced by the program (lines 14–15), which indicates that a 10-year-old child will be 13 in 3 more years.

The method dif is invoked on line 13 to calculate the first output: the years to reach the desired age. It is passed the desired age, input on lines 11-12, as the first argument on line 13. Because the method main does not declare a local variable named a, the second argument on line 13, a, is the class variable. The method then calculates the difference between the two values passed to its two parameters (line 40), the desired age and the value stored in the class variable. Because the desired age was input as 13, and the output indicates that it will be reached in 3 more years, the class variable passed to the method's second parameter must have contained the value 10 at the time `dif` was invoked. The previous assignment into the local variable `a` on line 34 had no effect on it.

It should be noted that even if the parameter `a` was reassigned inside the method `dif`, the class variable would still retain the value 10 because Java uses value parameters. All references in the method `dif` to the variable `a` refer to the parameter, which can be thought of as a local variable.

Two swap methods, `swapParameters` and `swapClassLevels`, are coded on lines 43–55. The first of these methods is invoked on line 19. It contains two parameters, `a` and `b` (line 43), to receive the values to be swapped, which are input on lines 17 and 18 (Figures 3.6 c and d). Although the names of the parameters are the same as the names of the class-level variables, they are not the same memory cells as the class variables. When the values stored in the parameters are swapped (lines 45–47), the output produced by lines 20–21 of the main method confirms a feature of value parameters: changes to parameters have no effect on the arguments sent to the method. The numbers output by the main method are output in the same order in which they were input: 1111 followed by 2222 (Figure 3.6 e).

Because the main method does not declare local variables named `a` and `b`, lines 23 and 24 store the values returned from `inputInteger` in the program's class variables (Figures 3.6 f and g). The second swap method, `swapClassLevels`, is invoked on line 25. It has an empty parameter list (line 50) and only one local variable, `temp`. Therefore, the variables `a` and `b` used in this method default to the class-level variables. Because these are shared with the main method, the swapping of the values in these variables performed on lines 52–55 does have an effect on the output produced by the main method (lines 26–27). As a result, the numbers input on lines 23 and 24 (8888 and 9999) are output in reverse order (9999 followed by 8888) by lines 26 and 27 (Figure 3.6 h).

```java
1    import javax.swing.JOptionPane;
2
3    public class MethodsAndParms
4    {  static int a = 10; // Two classlevel variables
5       static int b;
6
7       public static void main(String[] args)
8       {
9          int desiredAge, first, second, difference; // local Variables
10
11         desiredAge = inputInteger("You are " + a + " years old" +
12                                   "\nHow old do you wish you were?");
13         difference = dif(desiredAge, a);
14         JOptionPane.showMessageDialog(null, + "Only " + difference +
15                                       " Years to go");
16
17         first = inputInteger("Enter the first number to swap");
18         second = inputInteger("Enter the second number to swap");
19         swapParameters(first, second);
20         JOptionPane.showMessageDialog(null, "Swapped using parameters: " +
21                                       first + " " + second);
```

```
22
23        a = inputInteger("Enter the first number to swap");
24        b = inputInteger("Enter the second number to swap");
25        swapClassLevels();
26        JOptionPane.showMessageDialog(null, "Swapped using class " +
27                                    "levels: " + a + " " + b);
28     }
29
30     static int inputInteger(String prompt)
31     {
32        int a; // a local variable
33        String sInput = JOptionPane.showInputDialog(prompt);
34        a = Integer.parseInt(sInput);
35        return a;
36     }
37
38     static int dif(int desiredAge, int a)
39     {
40        return desiredAge - a;
41     }
42
43     static void swapParameters(int a, int b)
44     {
45        int temp = a;
46        a = b;
47        b = temp;
48     }
49
50     static void swapClassLevels()
51     {
52      int temp = a;
53      a = b;
54      b = temp;
55      }
56 }
```

Figure 3.5
The application **MethodsAndParameters**.

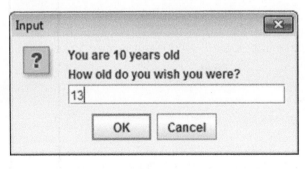

(a)

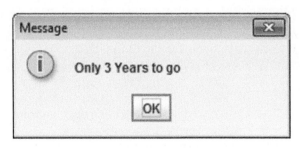

(b)

Figure 3.6
Inputs and resulting outputs produced by the application **MethodsAndParameters.**

3.3 THE API GRAPHICS CLASS

Having gained a deeper understanding of methods and the techniques for sharing information between methods and the program code that invokes them, we will reinforce those concepts in this section by examining several worker methods in the API Graphics class. As discussed in Chapter 2, this class contains methods for drawing text on Graphics objects. It also contains methods used to change the drawing color and for drawing lines, rectangles, ovals, and circles on Graphics objects.

3.3.1 Changing the Drawing Color

All drawing performed on a Graphics object is performed in the current color. The default current color is black. The setColor method in the Graphics class can be used to change the current drawing color. One argument, used to specify the new value of the current drawing color, is passed to the method. Table 3.1 gives the names of the thirteen predefined color variables in the class Color. Because these variables are static variables, they are referred to by their name preceded by Color followed by a dot. For example, to set the color of all subsequent drawings on the Graphics object g to red, we would code:

```
g.setColor(Color.RED);
```

As previously discussed, the Graphics object attached to our game board is passed into the draw method's parameter g when the game environment invokes the draw method. Therefore, if this statement were coded in the draw call back method, the current drawing color of the game board would be changed to red.

Table 3.1
Thirteen of the Predefined Colors in the Color Class

Color	Variable Name
black	BLACK
blue	BLUE
cyan	CYAN
dark gray	DARK_GRAY
gray	GRAY
green	GREEN
light gray	LIGHT_GRAY
magenta	MAGENTA
orange	ORANGE
pink	PINK
red	RED
white	WHITE
yellow	YELLOW

3.3.2 Drawing Lines, Rectangles, Ovals, and Circles

Figure 3.7 presents five of the methods in the Graphics class. These methods are nonstatic void methods. As their names imply, the first method is used to a draw line, and the remaining four methods are used to draw rectangles and ovals. To specify the location of the item to be drawn, all of the methods are passed (x, y) coordinates whose units are pixels.

The line drawing method, drawLine, is passed two sets of (x, y) coordinates, which are the endpoints of the line to be drawn. For example, to draw a line from (30, 50) to (60, 80) on the Graphics object g, we would code:

```
g.drawLine(30, 50, 60, 80);
```

The rectangle drawing methods drawRect and fillRect are used to draw the outline of a rectangle and to draw a filled (solid) rectangle, respectively. Their first two arguments specify the coordinates of the upper left corner of the rectangle, and the third and forth coordinates specify the width and height of the rectangle in pixels. For example, to draw the outline of a rectangle whose upper left corner is at (100, 200) and is 50 pixels wide and 75 pixel high on the Graphics object g, we would code:

```
g.drawRect(100, 200, 50, 75);
```

To draw this rectangle as a solid rectangle, filled with the current drawing color, we code:

```
g.fillRect(100, 200, 50, 75);
```

The method drawOval is used to draw the outline of an oval, and the method fillOval is used to draw a solid oval filled with the current color. These ovals are drawn within a specified rectangle (which is not drawn). The method's four parameters are identical to those of the rectangle methods previously discussed and are used to specify the rectangle's (x, y) location and its width and height. For example, to draw the outline of an oval 50 pixels wide and 70 pixels high inscribed inside a rectangle whose upper left corner is at (100, 200), we would code:

```
g.drawOval(100, 200, 50, 75);
```

To draw this oval as a solid oval filled with the current drawing color, we code:

```
g.fillOval(100, 200, 50, 75);
```

`drawLine(int x1, int y1, int x2, int y2)`   Draws a line, using the current color, between the points (x1, y1) and (x2, y2)
`drawRect(int x, int y, int width, int height)`   Draws the outline of a rectangle whose upper left corner is at (x, y) and whose width and height are width and height, using the current color
`drawOval(int x, int y, int width, int height)`   Draws the outline of an oval bounded by the rectangle whose upper left corner is at (x, y) and whose width and height are width and height, using the current color
`fillRect(int x, int y, int width, int height)`   Draws a rectangle whose upper left corner is at (x, y) and whose width and height are width and height, filled with the current color
`fillOval(int x, int y, int width, int height)`   Draws an oval bounded by the rectangle whose upper left corner is at (x, y) and whose width and height are width and height, filled using the current color

Figure 3.7
Primitive-shape drawing methods in the **Graphics** class.

The oval drawing methods can be used to draw circles by making the third and fourth arguments, the height and width of the rectangle that encloses the oval, the same number of pixels. For example, to draw a solid circle 50 pixels in diameter inscribed inside a rectangle whose upper left corner is at (100, 200) we would code:

```
g.fillOval(100, 200, 50, 50);
```

When the statements presented in this section are coded in the game environment's `draw` call back method, the lines and shapes they draw appear on the game board because, as mentioned at the end of Section 3.3.1, the `Graphics` object passed into the `draw` call back method's parameter `g` is attached to our game board.

Figure 3.8 presents the application `LinesAndShapes` that draws two lines in the default color (black), two dark-gray rectangles, a red oval, and a blue circle on the game-board object. The graphical output of the program is shown in Figure 3.9. Lines 16–26 coded inside the draw method perform the drawing. Consistent with the variable names given in Table 3.1, the argument sent to the `setColor` method on line 19 has an underscore separating the words DARK and GRAY.

```
1    import edu.sjcny.gpv1.*;
2    import java.awt.*;
3
4    public class LinesAndShapes extends DrawableAdapter
5    {
6      static LinesAndShapes ga = new LinesAndShapes( );
7      static GameBoard gb = new GameBoard(ga, "Lines and Shapes");
8
9      public static void main(String[] args)
10     {
11       showGameBoard(gb);
12     }
13
14     public void draw(Graphics g) // the drawing call back method
15     {
16       g.drawLine(100, 75, 260, 75);      //Lines
17       g.drawLine(300, 50, 400, 100);
18
19       g.setColor(Color.DARK_GRAY);
20       g.drawRect(100, 170, 100, 60);    //Rectangles
21       g.fillRect(280, 170, 150, 40);
22
23       g.setColor(Color.RED);
24       g.drawOval(55, 300, 180, 80);     //Ovals
25       g.setColor(Color.BLUE);
26       g.fillOval(280, 300, 100, 100);
27
28     }
29   }
```

Figure 3.8

The application **LinesAndShapes**.

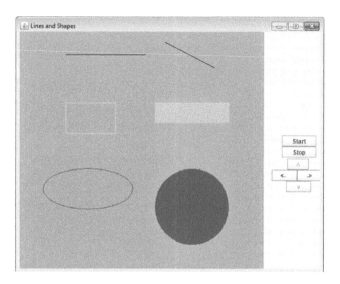

Figure 3.9
The output produced by the application **LinesAndShapes**.

3.4 OBJECT ORIENTED PROGRAMMING

Early programming languages were designed in the procedural paradigm. In this paradigm, a program is decomposed into smaller parts called subprograms, and the language provides a mechanism for combining the subprograms into the larger program. During the design process, the programmer focuses on the definition of the subprograms and how the program's data will be stored. In this paradigm, the subprograms and the program's data are separated and coded into two distinct entities.

Object oriented programming is a more recent programming paradigm. The paradigm is an attempt to facilitate the development of programs that deal with objects, such as starships, or people, or Web pages. In this paradigm, the program is decomposed into the various classes to which the objects belong. During the design process, the programmer focuses on determining the objects the program will deal with, the attributes of each object (e.g., a starship's name), and the operations that can be performed on each object (e.g., changing a starship's location). In this paradigm, the operations (subprograms) and attributes (data) are collected and coded into one entity called a class.

Both paradigms are in use today. Some programming solutions are better designed and more easily implemented using the procedural paradigm, and others are more easily designed and implemented using the object paradigm. C is a procedural language, C++ is a language that can be used in both the procedural and object paradigm, and Java is an object oriented language. If the program deals with objects, then the object paradigm should be strongly considered.

3.4.1 What Are Classes and Objects?

A **class** is a blueprint of how to construct an item, and an **object** is a particular item or instance of a class. For example, we all belong to the class human. That class contains a genetic blueprint of how to construct a human object, which we call a person. As per the human blueprint, all people have common attributes. For example, all people have colored-eyes, colored-hair, and eventually grow to an adult height. But clearly, all people (except identical twins) are also different. For example, people grow to different heights, have different-colored eyes, and different hair colors, what makes objects different is that each object contains its own value of the attributes contained in the blueprint.

> **Definition**
>
> A **class** is a blueprint of how to construct an item, and an **object** is a particular item or instance of a class.

The value of Mary's three attributes could be 63 inches for height, blue for eye color, and red for hair color. The value of her sister Kate's attributes could be 68 inches for height, brown for eye color, and black for hair color. No wonder these two objects look different. Now suppose Kate, who always admired her sister's red hair and blue eyes, dyed her hair to a red color and inserted a set of blue contact lenses into her eyes. These hair coloring and lens insertion operations would change the values of two of Kate's attributes, and she would then look like a taller version of Mary.

In object oriented languages, a class is the mechanism for defining the blueprint of an entity. As such, it contains the attributes that each object in the class will have (e.g., height, hair color, and eye color). To store the different values of these attributes for each object constructed from the blueprint, the attributes are represented within the class as variables. In addition, because the values of the attributes of an object can change, the class contains methods (e.g., `setEyeColor` and `setHairColor`) that can operate on the variables to change, or set, the values they store to new values.

3.5 DEFINING CLASSES AND CREATING OBJECTS

During the design process of an object oriented program, the programmer focuses on determining the objects the program will deal with, the attributes of each object, and the operations that can be performed on them. The blueprint for each type of object will be coded into a programming construct called a class that will represent the attributes as variables and the operations as methods. In the remainder of Section 3.5, we will discuss a graphical tool used to specify a class and the Java syntax used to code that specification into a Java program.

> **NOTE** *The programming construct* **class** *is comprised of variable definitions and method definitions.*

3.5.1 Specifying a class: Unified Modeling Language Diagrams

A unified modeling language (UML) diagram is a graphical representation of a class. The diagram consists of three rectangles stacked on top of each other. From top to bottom, as shown in Figure 3.10, these rectangles are used to specify the class name, the variables that will be part

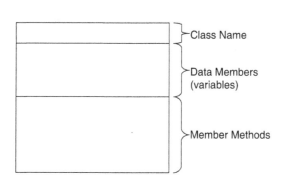

Figure 3.10
The template of a UML diagram.

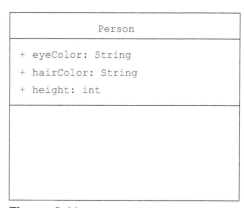

Figure 3.11
The specification of the class Person, Version 1.

of the class, and the class's methods. The variables are called data members (of the class), and the methods are called member methods because they are both part of (members of) the class being specified.

As an example, consider a program that is going deal with people objects where each person has three attributes: eye color, hair color, and height. The UML diagram used to specify the class, whose name was chosen to be `Person`, is shown in Figure 3.11. The name of the class appears at the top of the diagram, and the class's three data members are tabulated in the second box of the diagram.

To succinctly convey information about a class's data members and methods, UML diagrams employ a standardized notation, some of which is included in Figure 3.11. For example, the type of each data member is specified by following its variable name with a colon and the type of the variable. As shown in the figure, the class `Person` has two String data members and one integer data member.

The three data members of the class `Person` are preceded with a plus (+) sign. The plus sign is used to denote the *access* property of a data member of a class. When the UML specification of a class is coded into a Java class construct, the + sign is coded as the keyword `public`. Another alternative is to precede the names of the data members with a minus (–) sign, which is coded as the keyword `private`. We will learn more about the implications of the use of access modifiers in the next section.

3.5.2 The Class Code Template

Like the data members of a class, a class itself can be public or private, although most classes are public. We will discuss private classes in Chapter 7. The code template for a public Java class is given below:

```
public class ClassName
{
    //data members are coded here
    //member methods are coded here
}
```

The name of the class, given at the top of the UML diagram, is substituted for `ClassName` on the first line of the template. The declaration of the class's data members and the code of its member methods are coded inside of a pair of braces that make up the class's code block. The variables that represent a class's data members are coded before the code of the class's member methods. While this is not a Java syntax rule, it is considered good coding practice. The code of the class specified by the UML diagram presented in Figure 3.11 is given in Figure 3.12 with the data members set to initial values.

```java
public class Person
{
    //data members
    public String eyeColor = "blue";
    public String hairColor = "red";
    public int height = 65;

    //member methods

}
```

Figure 3.12
The code of the class Person specified in Figure 3.11.

Normally, the initial values are chosen to be the most common value of the data members. In this case, the assumption is that most people have blue eyes, red hair, and are 65 inches tall.

3.5.3 Creating Objects

In Section 2.5, we examined a two-line syntax for declaring objects in the class `String`. For example:

```java
String firstName;
firstName = new String("John");
```

The first line creates the reference variable `firstName` that can store the address of a `String` object, which is initialized to the default value **null**. The second line creates a new `String` object, stores the string "John" inside of it, and then overwrites the **null** value stored in the variable `firstName` with the address of the object. Alternately, the two lines of code can be consolidated into one line:

```java
String firstName = new String("John");
```

When talking about the object created with either the two- or one-line syntax, in the interest of brevity we say that "we created a string object named `firstName`," or we might be asked to "output the object `firstName`." However, experienced programmers know that it is more accurate to say, "we created a string object referenced by the variable `firstName`," or "output the object referenced by `firstName`." With that understanding, we will use the brief version in the remainder of this text.

By changing the name of the class coded in the one- or two-line syntax and usually the code inside the parentheses, both versions of the syntax can be used to declare an object in any class. The code fragment below uses the one-line grammar to create two `Person` objects, one named `mary` and the other named `kate`:

```
Person mary = new Person();
Person kate = new Person();
```

The memory allocated by these two statements is shown in Figure 3.13. As defined in the `Person` class (Figure 3.12), each object contains the same three variables set to initial values. The variables `hairColor` and `eyeColor` store the address of string objects that contain the initial values. At this point, Mary and Kate are identical twins and will remain so until we add methods to the class that can change the values of the data members.

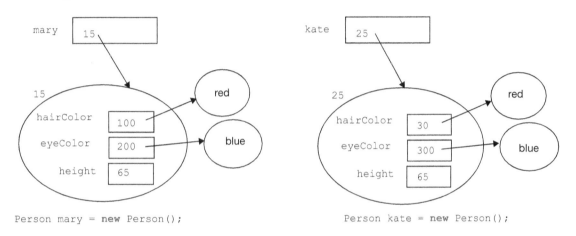

Figure 3.13
Two Person objects and the statements that constructed them.

Constructor methods

Let us assume that the two lines of code that created the objects `mary` and `kate`

```
Person mary = new Person();
Person kate = new Person();
```

were coded in the main method of a program that dealt with people, or more precisely, `Person` objects. These two lines of code should be thought of as the main method's request to the class to create two `Person` objects. If I call a carpenter and request that he create, or construct, a shed for me, I become his client. The two terms, *construct* and *client*, used in this analogy are used in the programming jargon of classes and objects. We would say that the class `Person` has constructed two objects for the client code main. Any section of code that declares an object in a class is considered to be client code (of that class), and the class is said to have constructed the objects for the client code.

Every class has at least one member method that constructs new objects. These non-void methods are called *constructors*, and they execute every time the object declaration syntax is used to declare an object. During the execution of a constructor method, the storage is allocated for the class's data members, the initial values are stored in the data members, the collection of data members is assigned a memory location (considered to be the location of the object), and that location is returned to the client code. The assignment operator included in the object-declaration grammar then stores the returned location of the object in the object's reference variable (e.g., `mary`).

The name of a constructor method is always the name of its class, so the code to the right of the keyword **new** in the declaration of `mary`'s object

```
Person mary = new Person();
```

is actually an invocation to the constructor method named `Person` that has no parameters and returns the address of a newly created `Person` object.

The class `Person` shown in Figure 3.12 does not contain a constructor method, which in this case would be a method named `Person`. When a class does not contain a constructor, a Java-provided constructor method is used to construct objects. This constructor, referred to as the default constructor, has no parameters, and it performs the functions previously mentioned:

1. Allocates the storage for the data members of the class
2. Stores the initial values in the data members
3. Assigns the collection of data members a memory location
4. Returns the location to the client code

Because the class `Person` does not contain any methods, the two `Person` objects `mary` and `kate` declared as

```
Person mary = new Person();
Person kate = new Person();
```

would be created by the default constructor, which would perform the four functions listed above. Each object's data members would be set to the initial values specified in the data-member portion of their class (Figure 3.12) during function 2. In Section 3.6.2, we will learn how to add constructor methods that we write to a class. These methods can contain parameters and code to extend the four functions performed by the default constructor.

3.5.4 Displaying an Object

Objects can be displayed to the system console and to a graphical game board in one of two ways. We can simply mention the name of the object or invoke the `toString` method on the object inside a method invocation used to display strings, or we can add a method to the object's class that, when invoked, outputs the object. The following statements use the first approach to display the `Person` object `mary` to the system console object, `System.out` and then to a `GameBoard` object named `g` at location (210, 100).

```
System.out.println(mary );
g.drawString(mary.toString(), 210, 100);
```

This approach is usually not too interesting because what is displayed is the location of the object that is stored in the reference variable `mary` preceded by an ampersand (@) and the name of the object's class. Referring to Figure 3.13, Mary's object is located at address 15, so the output to the system console and the game board would be Person@15. The second alternative, adding a method to the object's class that when invoked outputs the object, produces a more interesting and useful output. This technique will be discussed in Section 3.6.

Figure 3.14 presents an application that creates two Person objects, whose class is defined in Figure 3.12, and outputs their locations to the system console and the game board. The output is shown in Figure 3.15, except that the program does not produce the more interesting output of the actual object Mary shown in the middle of the game board. As previously mentioned, the techniques for producing that output will be discussed Section 3.6, and the code to produce the output will be left as an exercise for the student.

Lines 7, 10, and 11 create two Person objects using the two-line syntax. The reference variables mary and kate are declared as class variables on line 7, so they can be accessed from the main method and the draw call back method. Lines 13–14 and lines 21–22 output the object's locations to the system console and the game board, respectively. These locations can be thought of as the locations assigned to the two objects by Java's memory manager when lines 10–11 execute.

```
1   import edu.sjcny.gpv1.*;
2   import java.awt.*;
3   public class ClassAndObjectBasics extends DrawableAdapter
4   {
5      static ClassAndObjectBasics ge = new ClassAndObjectBasics();
6      static GameBoard gb = new GameBoard(ge, "Class & Object Basics");
7      static Person mary, kate;
8
9      public static void main(String[] args)
10     {  mary = new Person();
11        kate = new Person();
12
13        System.out.println(mary);
14        System.out.println(kate);
15
16        showGameBoard(gb);
17     }
18
19     public void draw(Graphics g)
20     {
21        g.drawString(mary.toString(), 210, 100);
22        g.drawString(kate.toString(), 210, 120);
23     }
24  }
```

Figure 3.14
The application **ClassAndObjectBasics**.

System console output:
Person@3a6727
Person@4a65e0

Game board output:

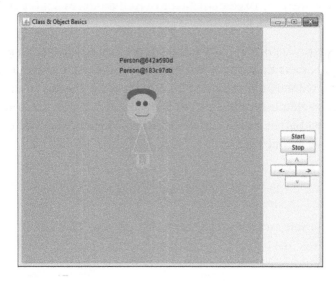

Figure 3.15
The object locations output by the application **ClassAndObjectBasics**.

3.5.5 Designing a Graphical Object

During the specification and design of a program we identify the types of objects that the program will deal with and the operations to be performed on them. Then during the program development process, a class is developed for each of the object types, and the operations performed on the objects become the methods of the class. A common operation performed on objects is to display them, and in the previous section we were able to display a Person object's location without adding a method to the Person class. To produce the more interesting display of an object, such as the drawing of the object mary with her red hair and blue eyes shown in the middle of Figure 3.15, we add a method to the object's class that uses the shape and line drawing methods of the Graphics class to produce the output.

In Section 3.6, we will learn how to add this method, whose name usually begins with the prefix show, and other methods that perform common operations on objects to an object's class. In preparation for the coding of this method, the programmer has to design each type of graphical object using the basic drawing shapes available in the Graphics class. In this section, we will become familiar with techniques used to design these objects so that the drawing can be easily coded into a show method, and the object can be easily manipulated by other class methods that perhaps relocate the object, erase the object, or animate the object.

Drawing an Object

To begin, we draw a picture of the object using the graphical shapes available in the API Graphics class discussed in Section 3.3. The object should be inscribed in a rectangle, and if ovals are used, they should be inscribed in their own rectangle. Figure 3.16 shows a sketch of a snowman-type object comprised of two rectangles and two circles. The rectangles that inscribe the ovals and the entire object are shown in red.

The dimensions, in pixels, of each of the basic shapes that make up the game piece should be given in the drawing. For example, the snowman's hat is specified on the upper right side of the figure to be 10 pixels wide and 15 pixels high. Ovals that are circles, such as a snowman's head and body, can be specified with one dimension (e.g., the diameter of the snowman's head is 20 pixels). After the dimensions of all of the shapes that make up the object have been noted on the drawing, the overall width and height of the inscribing rectangle is added to the drawing. This is shown in Figure 3.16 on the bottom and left side of the inscribing rectangle. The width is simply the width of the snowman's body, 40, and the height is the sum of the heights of the shapes that make up the snowman, 77 (15 + 2 + 20 + 40).

The color of each shape that makes up the object should also be given, as shown in the lower right portion of the figure. The word default used in the object's color specification implies that snowmen objects could be constructed with hats that are not black. Finally, a point that will be used to locate the object on the game board is noted on the drawing. As shown in the upper left side of the figure, this point is typically the upper left corner of the inscribing rectangle.

The next step in this design process is to determine the locations of each of the shapes' upper-left corner relative to the (x, y) location of the game piece, which for our snowman is the upper left corner of the inscribing rectangle. These locations, along with the width and

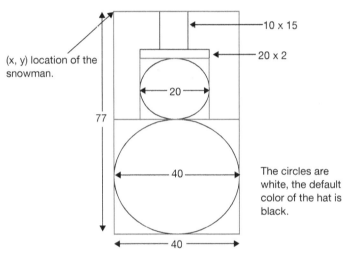

Figure 3.16
The design of a snowman game piece.

height of each of the shapes, are entered into in a table that will be used in the show method to draw each of the shapes. The table is a digital representation of the object, and the process of determining the data is referred to as digitizing the object.

The digital representation of our snowman object is given in Table 3.2. As previously mentioned, each location in the table is relative to the (x, y) location of the upper corner of the rectangle that inscribes the snowman object. Therefore, each location given in the table begins with an x or y followed by the x or y distance to the corner of the shape. When reading the locations in the table, it should be remembered that the positive x direction is to the right, and the positive y direction is down.

To determine these distances, we either consider the dimensions of each of the shapes given in Figure 3.16, or we draw the object on a piece of graph paper whose origin is the upper left corner of the object's inscribing rectangle. Then, the x and y distances to the upper-left corner of each shape

Table 3.2
Digital Representation of the Snowman Object Shown in Figure 3.16

Component	Shape	Shape's X or Line's X_1 Coordinate	Shape's Y or Line's Y_1 Coordinate	Width or Line's X_2 Coordinate	Height or Line's Y_2 Coordinate
Hat	Rectangle	$x + (20 - 5)$	y	10	15
Hat Brim	Rectangle	$x + (20 - 10)$	$y + (15)$	20	2
Head	Circle	$x + (20 - 10)$	$y + (15 + 2)$	20	20
Body	Circle	x	$y + (15 + 2 + 20)$	40	40

are simply the x and y coordinates of the shape's inscribing rectangle's upper left corner. The following two examples illustrate the technique of determining the x and y coordinates of each shape by considering the dimensions given in Figure 3.16.

1. To determine the x location of the upper left corner of the snowman's hat, which is x + (20-5) as indicated in the first row and third column of the table, half the width of the snowman's inscribing rectangle (20) is added to x because the center of the hat is at the center of the inscribing rectangle. Half the width of the hat (5) is subtracted from x because the left side of the hat is half the width of the hat closer to the left side of the snowman's inscribing rectangle than is the center of the hat.

2. To determine the y location of the upper left corner of snowman's head, which is y + (15+2) as indicated in the third row and fourth column of the table, the height of the hat (15) and the height of the hat brim (2) are added to y.

It should be noted that when lines are used in the object's drawing, each line is entered on a separate row of the table and, as indicated in the column headings of Table 3.2, the coordinates of the endpoints of the lines are entered into the rightmost four columns of the table. During the design phase of the program, a table is produced for each type of object in the program.

3.6 ADDING METHODS TO CLASSES

Many of the methods added to a class perform operations on the objects in the class. Some of these operations are so commonly performed, such as a method to display an object or a method to change the value of a data member, that they are included in most classes. To improve program readability, the names of these methods usually begin with a designated prefix. For example, the names of methods that display objects usually begin with the prefix `show`, and a method that begins with the prefix `set` usually changes the value of one of an object's data members.

In this section, we will study the techniques for adding methods to classes and how to use them to perform operations on objects. These methods will be added to a class named `SnowmanV1` that defines the object depicted in Figure 3.16 and digitized in Table 3.2. Its UML diagram will be progressively developed, by adding methods to it, as we move through the next few sections of this chapter.

Our starting point will be the UML diagram shown in Figure 3.17, which is implemented in Figure 3.18. The class has three data members, two integers, and a reference variable used to specify the location of a SnowmanV1 object and its hat color. As shown in the UML diagram, the data member hatColor will refer to a color constant in the class Color. The code of the class SnowmanV1 is presented in Figure 3.18. The three data members are coded on lines 4–6. The default location of the snowman is (5, 30), which is the upper left corner of the game board. The hat color has been initialized to the color constant BLACK.

Figure 3.17
The UML diagram of the class **SnowmanV1**

```
1    public class SnowmanV1
2    {
3        //data members
4        public int x = 5;
5        public int y = 30;
6        public Color hatColor = Color.BLACK;
7    }
```

Figure 3.18
The Class **SnowmanV1**

The use of a graphical snowman in this chapter will make the concept of operating on an object less abstract, and therefore more easily understood. For example, rather than the class' show method simply displaying an object's (x, y) location, its show method will display the object in a more tangible way: by drawing it on the game board at its (x, y) location. Rather than simply outputting the increased value of an object's x location, we will see the object move to the right.

3.6.1 The show Method

A method that begins with the prefix show is used to display an object and is a nonstatic method. Because the drawing methods of the Graphics class cannot be used to draw on the system console, we have to define what it means to show an object on the system console. The commonly accepted meaning is that the output would consist of the annotated values of the object's data members. This version of a show method, named showXYToSC (SC for system console) would invoke the println method and pass it a string that concatenates the annotation and the class's x and y data members. For example:

```
public void showXYToSC()
{
    System.out.println("x is: " + x +
                       "\ny is: " + y);
}
```

After this code is added to the class then snowman `sm1` could be output to the system console using the statement:

```
sm1.showXYToSC();
```

which would produce the output:

x is: 5

y is: 30

The statement `sm1.showXYToSC();` can be read in three different ways:

1. The object `sm1` is invoking the `showXYToSC` method.
2. The method `showXYToSC` is invoked on the object `sm1`.
3. The `showXYToSC` method is operating on the object `sm1`.

All three of these are synonymous; that is, they mean the same thing. In general, to cause a method to operate on an object, we precede the name of the method with the name of the object followed by a dot.

An important point to remember is that if we just focused on the code of the `showXYToSC` method and asked the question, when it mentions the data members x and y, which object's data members is it talking about, the answer is the data members of the object that invoked it. The true meaning of the statement "a method operates on an object" is that all occurrences of the names of the data members coded inside the method refer to the data members of the object that invoked it.

Figure 3.19 presents the expanded UML diagram that reflects the addition of two show methods, `showXYToSC` and `show`. The method `show` will use the digitized version of a snowman, presented in Table 3.2, to display a `SnowmanV2` object on the game board. Because the `shape` drawing methods in the `Graphics` class will need access to the game board object, the `show` method will have one parameter: a reference to a `Graphics` object. The characters g: `Graphics` that appear inside the parentheses of this method in the UML diagram is UML notation to indicate that this method has one parameter named g that is a reference to a `Graphics` object.

The code of this expanded class is given in Figure 3.20. A client application that declares a `SnowmanV2` object and outputs the object's address to the system console and the object to both the system console and the game board is shown in Figure 3.21. The application's output is shown in Figure 3.22.

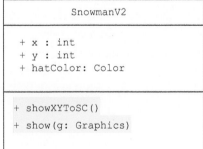

Figure 3.19
The UML diagram of the class
`SnowmanV2`.

The client code (Figure 3.21) invokes the default constructor on line 7 to declare a `SnowmanV2` object named `sm1`. The declaration uses the one-line object declaration syntax and is at the class level, so the object can be accessed by the `main` method and the `draw` call back method. Line 11 outputs the object's location to the system console, and line 12 invokes the `showXYToSC` method of the `Snowman`'s class to display snowman `sm1` to the system console. This method is coded on lines 12–16 of the `Snowman` class (Figure 3.20).

Line 19 of the application invokes the SnowmanV2 class's show method to display snowman sm1 on the game board. This invocation is coded in the draw call back method for two reasons. First, the show method must be passed a Graphics object on which to perform its drawing, and the draw method is the only call back method that is passed a Graphics object when it is invoked. It passes the Graphics object to the show method as an argument on line 19. Secondly, when the game board needs to be redrawn, the game environment invokes draw, which will then invokes show to redraw the snowman.

Lines 18–26 of Figure 3.20 are the code of the show method. The method's signature (line 18) includes the parameter g specified in the class's UML diagram (Figure 3.19). It uses this parameter to invoke methods in the Graphics class used to change the current drawing color (setColor lines 20 and 23) and to draw the rectangles and circles specified in Table 3.2. All of the shape locations sent to the Graphics class methods as arguments on lines 21–25 are those contained in the table. They contain the variables x and y because they are relative to the upper left corner of the rectangle that inscribes the snowman. Because the method does not declare local variables named x and y, the class-level data members x and y are used in these arguments. As a result, the snowman is drawn as shown in Figure 3.21 with the upper left corner of its inscribing rectangle at (5, 30).

```
1    import java.awt.Color;;
2    import java.awt.Graphics;; //needed for drawing shapes
3
4    public class SnowmanV2
5    {
6      //data members
7      public int x = 5;
8      public int y = 30;
9      public Color hatColor = Color.BLACK;
10
11     //member methods
12     public void showXYToSC()
13     {
14       System.out.println("x is: " + x +
15                          "\ny is: " + y);
16     }
17
18     public void show(Graphics g) //g is passed to the method
19     {
20       g.setColor(hatColor);
21       g.fillRect(x + 15, y, 10, 15);   //hat
22       g.fillRect(x + 10, y + 15, 20, 2); //brim
23       g.setColor(Color.WHITE);
24       g.fillOval(x + 10, y + 17, 20, 20); //head
25       g.fillOval(x, y + 37, 40, 40);    //body
26     }
27   }
```

Figure 3.20
The class **SnowmanV2**.

```
1    import edu.sjcny.gpv1.*;
2    import java.awt.Graphics;
3    public class ShowMethods extends DrawableAdapter
4    {
5      static ShowMethods ga = new ShowMethods( );
6      static GameBoard gb = new GameBoard(ga, "Show Methods");
7      static SnowmanV2 sm1 = new SnowmanV2();
8
9      public static void main(String[] args)
10     {
11       System.out.println(sm1);
12       sm1.showXYToSC();
13
14       showGameBoard(gb);
15     }
16
17     public void draw(Graphics g)  //the drawing call back method
18     {
19       sm1.show(g);
20
21     }
22   }
```

Figure 3.21
The application **ShowMethods**.

System Console Output
SnowmanV2@3a6727

x is: 5

y is: 30

Graphical Output

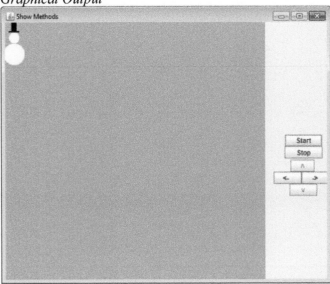

Figure 3.22
The console and graphical output produced by the application **ShowMethods**.

3.6.2 Constructors and the Keyword `this`

In Section 3.5.3, we learned that constructors are methods that construct objects, and the names of these methods must be the same as the class of the objects they construct. If a constructor method is not included in the specification and code of a class, a Java provided default constructor creates the object by performing the following four functions:

1. Allocate the storage for the data members of the class
2. Set the initial values into the data members
3. Assign the collection of data members a memory location
4. Return the location to the client code

Because the class `SnowmanV2` does not contain a constructor method, the default constructor is used to create all instances of this class (objects declared in this class). As a result, function 2 would locate them all at (5, 30), and they would all have black hats. When displayed, they would be displayed on top of each other giving the appearance that only one of them was displayed.

To allow the client code to specify the values of the data members of a newly constructed object, we add a constructor method to its class. Its code template is the same as the template used to code any other method, except its name must be the same as the class's name, and its signature cannot contain a return type. Its signature can contain a parameter list, and it can contain Java statements in its code block. When a constructor method is included in the code of a class, the default constructor is no longer available to construct objects in the class.

Figure 3.23 presents the UML diagram of the class `SnowmanV3` that contains a two-parameter constructor, which is a constructor with a parameter list that contains two parameters. When the client code uses this constructor method to create an object, just before the fourth function normally performed by the default constructor is performed, the constructor method executes. Storage is allocated for the constructor's parameters, the values of the client's arguments are copied into them, and then the code of the constructor executes.

As with any method, the values copied into the parameters of the constructor could be used anywhere in the constructor's code block by coding the names of the parameters. It is often the case that these parameters are used by the client code to specify the initial values of the data members. When this is the case, the constructor's code block simply assigns the parameters to the data members:

```
public SnowmanV3(int xLoc, int yLoc)
{   x = xLoc;
    y = yLoc;
}
```

SnowmanV3
+ x : int + y : int + hatColor: Color
+ SnowmanV3(xLoc: int, yLoc: int) + showXYToSC() + show(g: Graphics)

Figure 3.23
The UML diagram of the class **SnowmanV3**.

After this two-parameter constructor's code is included in the code of the class `SnowmanV3`, the client could use the following code to declare two snowmen located at the upper right and lower left corners of the game board:

```
SnowmanV3 sm1 = new SnowmanV3(5, 30);
SnowmanV3 sm1 = new SnowmanV3(460, 423);
```

The Keyword `this`

A method in a class can contain a parameter whose name is the same as the name of one of the class's data members. When this occurs, we say that the parameters *shadow* the data members. For example, the signature of the SnowmanV3 class's two-parameter constructor could have been coded as:

```
public SnowmanV3(int x, int y)
```

When the parameter names shadow data member names, the use of the name within the constructor refers to the parameter, not to the data member. As previously stated, parameters should be considered to be local variables. An assignment into the variable x within the constructor's code body changes the value stored in the parameter, not the value stored in the class-level data member x. We can refer to the data member within the code of constructor (or any other member method whose parameter list employs shadowing), by preceding the data member's name with the key word `this` followed by a dot, e.g., `this.x`. This syntax could be thought of as the variable x that is a data member of *this* class. Using this syntax, the SnownanV3 class's two-parameter constructor could be coded as:

```
public SnowmanV3(int x, int y)
{   this.x - x;
    this.y = y;
}
```

This coding of the two-parameter constructor, which uses shadowing, is actually preferred when the parameter list is being used to reset the initial values of the data members. When shadowing is used, the name and type of the parameters and the class's data members in the UML diagram (Figure 3.24) are the same, which is a cue to anyone looking at the UML diagram that the constructor will reset the initial values of the data members.

Figure 3.25 is the implementation of the SnowmanV3 class specified in Figure 3.24. A client application that declares and displays two instances of the class is shown in Figure 3.26, and the output to the game board produced by the application is shown in Figure 3.27.

The two-parameter constructor is coded on lines 12–16 of Figure 3.25. It is good programming style to code the constructor as the first method after the data member declarations. Because the names of the constructor's parameters are the same as the class's data members, the keyword `this` is used on lines 14 and 15 to access the class's data members and assign the initial values passed into the parameters to them.

The client code (Figure 3.26) invokes the constructor twice, once on line 9 and again on line 10, to create two snowmen named sm1 and sm2. The arguments sent to the constructor specify the initial (x, y) locations of the snowmen, which the constructor stores in the two data members of the objects. Lines 19 and 20 of the client code invoke the show method. During the first execution of the

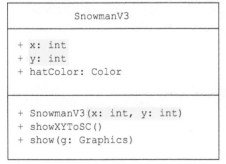

Figure 3.24
The modified UML diagram of the class
SnowmanV3.

method, the variables x and y on lines 27–31 of Figure 3.25 refer to the x and y data members of snowman sm1. Because these variables contain the coordinates (5, 30), this snowman is drawn in the upper left corner of the game board. Similarly, during the second invocation of the show method of the SnowmanV3 class, the variables x and y on lines 26–31 refer to the x and y data members of snowman sm2, and it is drawn at the lower right corner of the game board (460, 423).

3.6.3 Private Access and the set/get Methods

In the interest of simplicity, the data members and the member methods of the classes we have discussed all had public assess as indicated by the plus (+) sign that precedes them in their UML diagrams. Another type of access available in Java is private access, which is denoted in a UML diagram by a minus (-) sign. In this section, we will examine the difference between public and

```java
1   import java.awt.Color;
2   import java.awt.Graphics; //needed for drawing shapes
3
4   public class SnowmanV3
5   {
6     //data members
7     public int x = 5;
8     public int y = 30;
9     public Color hatColor = Color.BLACK;
10
11    // member methods
12    public SnowmanV3(int x, int y)
13    {
14      this.x = x;
15      this.y = y;
16    }
17
18    public void showXYToSC()
19    {
20      System.out.println("x is: " + x +
21                         "\ny is: " + y);
22    }
23
24    public void show(Graphics g) // g is passed to the method
25    {
26      g.setColor(hatColor);
27      g.fillRect(x + 15, y, 10, 15); //hat
28      g.fillRect(x + 10, y + 15, 20, 2); //brim
29      g.setColor(Color.WHITE);
30      g.fillOval(x + 10, y + 17, 20, 20); //head
31      g.fillOval(x, y + 37, 40, 40); //body
32    }
33  }
```

Figure 3.25
The class **SnowmanV3**.

```
1      import edu.sjcny.gpv1.*;
2      import java.awt.Graphics;
3
4      public class ConstructorAndThis extends DrawableAdapter
5      {
6        static ConstructorAndThis ga = new ConstructorAndThis();
7        static GameBoard gb = new GameBoard(ga,"Constructors and " +
8                                            "Key Word:this");
9        static SnowmanV3 sm1 = new SnowmanV3( 5, 30);
10       static SnowmanV3 sm2 = new SnowmanV3(460, 423);
11
12     public static void main(String[] args)
13     {
14       showGameBoard(gb);
15     }
16
17     public void draw(Graphics g) //the drawing call back method
18     {
19       sm1.show(g);
20       sm2.show(g);
21     }
22     }
```

Figure 3.26
The application **ConstructorAndThis**.

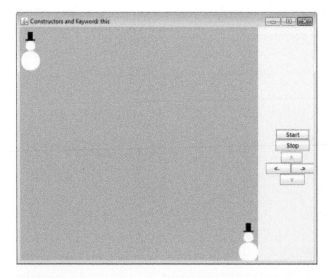

Figure 3.27
The output from the application **ConstructorAndThis**.

private access and learn which access modifier is normally used for the data members and member methods of a class. This will lead us to a discussion of methods that begin with the prefixes set and get that are commonly coded in most classes.

Public and Private Access

In the case of a member method, *access* is the act of invoking the method. In the case of a data member, access is the act of fetching or assigning the contents of the data member. Designating *private* access to the data members or methods of a class places no restrictions on the code of the methods contained in the class. Any line of code in a method of a class can invoke any private or public method in the class and can fetch and assign the value stored in any of its data members.

Private access places restrictions on client code. Client code cannot invoke methods of a class that are assigned private access, nor can it access the data members of a class that are assigned private access. If an application declared an object named `mary`, and the object's class contained a method named `show`, then the client code statement

```
mary.show();
```

would result in a translation error if the method was assigned private access.

> **NOTE** *Public access allows client code to access a class's data member or method, but private access does not.*

The syntax we have used in client code to access (invoke) a public method can also be used in client code to access an object's public data. The syntax is the member (method or data) name proceeded by the object name followed by a dot. This syntax was used on line 12 of the application shown in Figure 3.21

```
sm1.showXYToSC()
```

to invoke the public method `showXYToSC` coded on lines 12–16 of Figure 3.20. This method outputs two data members, `x` and `y`, to the system console. Because the access modifier used in the declaration of these two data members is public, their contents could have been fetched and then output by the client code by replacing line 12 of the client code (Figure 3.21) with the statement:

```
System.out.println("x is: " + sm1.x + "\ny is: " + sm1.y);
```

In addition, the client code could set the x location of snowman `sm1` to 10 by coding:

```
sm1.x = 10;
```

Normally, methods in a class are assigned public access. Exceptions to this will be given in subsequent chapters. Assigning them public access allows the client code to invoke them.

Good programming practice dictates that all data members in a class be assigned private access because allowing the client public access to an object's data members can lead to some insidious and difficult to find programming errors.

That being said, it is often the case that client code has a need to obtain (get) the value stored in an object's private data member, or set the value to a new value. Because any method in a class can access both private and public data members that are part of its class, public methods that begin with the prefixes `get` and `set` are added to the class. The client then invokes these methods to fetch and change the values stored in an object's private data members.

Normally, methods in a class are assigned public access, and data members are assigned private access. Client code invokes the set *and* get *methods of the class to access an object's private data.*

set Methods

A set method is a void method used to change, or set, the value stored in an object's private data member to a new value. The new value is passed into it as an argument. Because most classes have more than one data member, set is not a method name, but a prefix used in naming methods. Normally, we code a set method for every private data member in the class. The method names begin with the set prefix, which is followed by the name of the data member they operate on. For example, setX would be the name of the method the client code would invoke to change the contents of an object's private data member named x.

The signature of a set method contains one parameter and its code block contains one line of code. The method's parameter receives the new value of the data member, and the line of code simply assigns the new value to the data member. Because the value passed into the method is to be the new value of the data member, the parameter's type always matches the type of the data member. Below is the code of the setX method that sets the value of a private integer data member named x to the value of the argument passed to it.

```java
public void setX(int x)
{
    this.x = x;
}
```

Because the method is public, the client code could invoke it to change the data member x of the object sm1 to 100:

```java
sm1.setX(100);
```

String Immutability

The String class does not contain set methods to change the value of the characters stored in a String object. This is because Java strings are *immutable*. Once a value has been stored in a String object, the value cannot be changed. Although the following code fragment appears to change the value "Robert" stored in the string object created on the first line to "Bob", in fact it does not. Rather, it creates a new string object, stores "Bob" in it, and assigns the address of the newly created object to the variable name.

```java
String name = "Robert";
name = "Bob";
```

Although this gives the appearance that the value stored in the object has changed, in reality, the new string value "Bob" is stored in a different object. The process is illustrated in Figure 3.28.

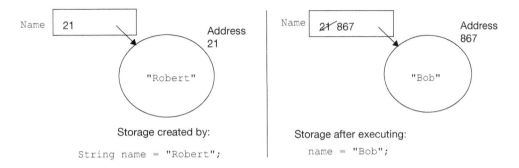

Figure 3.28
The immutability of **String** objects.

get Methods

A get method is a nonvoid method used to fetch, or get, the value stored in an object's private data member. The value is returned via a return statement. Like set, get is a prefix used in naming methods that fetch and return private data, and normally, a get method is coded for every private data member in a class.

Good programming practice dictates that the names of these methods begin with the prefix get, which is followed by the name of the data member on which they operate. For example, getX would be the name of the method the client code would invoke to fetch the contents of an object's private data member named x.

The signature of a get method contains a return type, and its parameter list is empty. The return type is always the same as the type of the data member it fetches. Its code block contains one line of code that simply returns the value of the data member. Below is the code of the getX method that returns the integer value of an object's private data member named x:

```
public int getX()
{
    return x;
}
```
Assuming a client application had declared an object named sm1, the following client code increases the object's private data member x by one:

```
int currentX = sm1.getX();
sm1.setX(currentX + 1);
```

Figure 3.29 shows the code of the class SnowmanV4. It is the same code as the class SnowmanV3 shown in Figure 3.25, except its three data members have been assigned private access (lines 6–8) and the console output method has been removed. In addition, set and get methods for its private data members x and y have been added to the class. The code of these four methods, getX, setX, getY, and setY begin on lines 27, 32, 37, and 42, respectively.

```
1    import java.awt.*;
2
3    public class SnowmanV4
4    {
5      //data members
6      private int x = 7;
7      private int y = 30;
8      private Color hatColor = Color.BLACK;
9
10     // member methods
11     public SnowmanV4(int x, int y)
12     {
13       this.x = x;
14       this.y = y;
15     }
16
17     public void show(Graphics g) // g, is passed to the method
18     {
19       g.setColor(hatColor);
20       g.fillRect(x + 15, y, 10, 15); //hat
21       g.fillRect(x + 10, y + 15, 20, 2); //brim
22       g.setColor(Color.WHITE);
23       g.fillOval(x + 10, y + 17, 20, 20); //head
24       g.fillOval(x, y + 37, 40, 40); //body
25     }
26
27     public int getX()
28     {
29       return x;
30     }
31
32     public void setX(int newX)
33     {
34       x = newX;
35     }
36
37     public int getY()
38     {
39       return y;
40     }
41
42     public void setY(int newY)
43     {
44       y = newY;
45     }
46   }
```

Figure 3.29
The class **SnowmanV4**.

The application class `SetGetButtonClick` shown in Figure 3.30 illustrates the use of `set` and `get` methods to access private data members.

```
1    import edu.sjcny.gpv1.*;
2    import javax.swing.*;
3    import java.awt.Graphics;
4
5    public class SetGetButtonClick extends DrawableAdapter
6    {
7      static SetGetButtonClick ga = new SetGetButtonClick ( );
8      static GameBoard gb = new GameBoard(ga,"Get Set and Button Click");
9      static SnowmanV4 sm1 = new SnowmanV4(5,30); //top-left corner
10     static SnowmanV4 sm2 = new SnowmanV4(460,423); //bottom-right corner
11
12     public static void main(String[] args)
13     {
14       String s = JOptionPane.showInputDialog("sm2's new x location?");
15       int newX = Integer.parseInt(s);
16       sm2.setX(newX);
17       showGameBoard(gb);
18     }
19
20     public void draw(Graphics g) //the drawing call back method
21     {
22       sm1.show(g);
23       sm2.show(g);
24     }
25
26     public void rightButton() //moves sm1 one pixel right per click
27     {
28       int currentX = sm1.getX( );
29       sm1.setX(currentX + 1);
30     }
31   }
```

Figure 3.30
The application **SetGetButtonClick**.

The program is identical to the `ConstructorAndThis` application shown in Figure 3.26, except that lines 14–16 and 26–30 have been added. Lines 16 and 29 illustrate the use of the `setX` method to change the x value of Snowman `sm2` and thus reposition it horizontally. Lines 26–30 illustrate the use of the `getX` method and the `rightButton` call back method to move snowman `sm1` to the right one pixel every time the right button is clicked.

When the program begins, two snowmen, `sm1` and `sm2`, declared on lines 9 and 10, are displayed on the game board by lines 22 and 23 of the `draw` call back method (Figure 3.30) at the upper-left and lower-right corners of the game board. Then, line 14 displays an input dialog box asking the user to enter the new value of snowman `sm2`'s x coordinate. Line 16 invokes the `setX` method to operate on snowman sm2, passing it the new x coordinate parsed on line 15. The method stores the new value in sm2's x data member (line 34 of Figure 3.29). The result is that when the game board is redrawn after the dialog box closes, the snowman is drawn at its new x position. Figure 3.31 shows snowman sm2 in its new location, at the middle of the game board, after the user enters 250 in the input dialog box.

Lines 26–30 is an implementation of the game environment's rightButton call back method. As its name implies, this method is invoked every time the button on the game window with the right arrow head (→) is clicked. It uses the getX method on line 28 to fetch the current x coordinate of sm1. Then it invokes the setX method to set the x data member of snowman sm1 to one more than its current value. Because the rightButton call back method executes every time the right button is clicked, and the draw method is invoked when it completes its execution, sm1 moves one pixel to the right very time the button is clicked. The upper portion of Figure 3.31 shows sm1's new location after 60 clicks of the game board's right (→) button.

3.6.4 The toString and input Methods

The methods we have developed in Section 3.6 perform work for a client application. They construct objects, display objects, and access the values of an object's private data members. The methods toString and input are two other methods that perform work for the client applications. These methods expand the client's ability to access private data members, and both of the methods normally permit access to all of an object's data members in one invocation.

The toString Method

The toString method is a nonvoid method that returns a string containing all the annotated values of an object's data members to the client application. The method's parameter list is empty. Its code progressively concatenates identifying annotation with the value of each of an object's data members, and the resulting string is the method's returned value. For example, the SnowmanV4 class shown in Figure 3.29 contains three data members: x, y, and hatColor. A typical coding of this class's toString method would be:

```
1    public String toString()
2    {
3        String s;
4        s = "x is: " + x +
5            "\ny is: " + y +
6            "\nhatColor is: " + hatColor;
7        return s;
8    }
```

Because a class can have an unlimited number of data members, it is good coding practice to code the concatenation of each data member's annotation and variable name on a separate line, as coded on lines 4, 5, and 6. Because the client code often sends the returned string to an output device, the inclusion of a new-line escape sequence in all but the first data member's annotation improves the readability of the output.

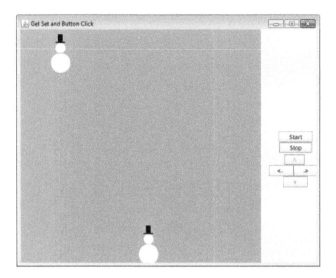

Figure 3.31
The output of the application **SetGetButtonClick** after the snowmen are relocated.

The variable hatColor, coded at the end of line 6, is declared as a reference variable in the SnowmanV4 class. When a reference variable is coded where a string is expected (as is expected here because the variable is preceded by the concatenation operator), the translator considers it to be an implicit invocation of another toString method. In Section 3.5.4, the location stored in the reference variable mary was output with an explicit invocation of a Java-provided default toString method. Because the class Color contains its own toString method, that method is implicitly invoked on line 6, and the string it returns is then concatenated into the string s. Rather than returning contents of the variable hatColor (an address), Color's toString method places a description of the color stored in the Color object hatColor into the returned string.

The input Method

The input method is a void method that allows the program user to enter new values for all of the data members of an object. The method's parameter list is empty. Its code prompts the user to enter new values for each of an object's data members, parses numeric inputs, and assigns the new values to the object's data members. For example, the SnowmanV4 class shown in Figure 3.29 contains three data members: x, y, and hatColor. A typical coding of this class's input method would be:

```
1    public void input()
2    {
3        String s;
4        int red, green, blue;
5
6        s - JOptionPane.showInputDialog("enter the value of x");
7        x = Integer.parseInt(s);
8        s = JOptionPane.showInputDialog("enter the value of y");
9        y = Integer.parseInt(s);
```

```
10        s = JOptionPane.showInputDialog("enter hat's red intensity");
11        red = Integer.parseInt(s);
12        s = JOptionPane.showInputDialog("enter hat's green intensity");
13        green = Integer.parseInt(s);
14        s = JOptionPane.showInputDialog("enter hat's blue intensity");
15        blue = Integer.parseInt(s);
16        hatColor = new Color(red, green, blue);
17    }
```

Because the variables x,y, and `hatColor` are not declared within the method, assignments into them (on lines 7, 9, and 16) change the values stored in the `SnowmanV4` object's data members.

Line 16 creates a new color object using the `Color` class's three-parameter constructor and stores its address in the data member `hatColor`. The arguments sent to the constructor are the shade intensities of the colors red, green, and blue that combine to produce the desired new color. The range of a color's intensity is 0 (lowest intensity) to 255 (highest intensity). High intensities produce bright colors. The program user would have to have knowledge of how to mix shade intensities of these three colors to produce a desired color. These intensities are input and parsed on lines 10–15. In the simplest case, if the desired color were to be either red, green, or blue, the intensity of the other two colors would be input as zero. White is an equal mix of the three colors, and black is the absence (zero intensity) of the three colors.

Figure 3.32 presents the class `SnowmanV5` that includes the code of the `toString` (lines 29–36) and `input` methods (lines 38–54) discussed in this section, and Figure 3.33 presents the application `ToStringAndInput` that demonstrates the use of these methods. The console and graphical outputs produced by the program are presented in Figure 3.34.

Lines 8 and 9 of the application (Figure 3.33) declares two snowmen, `sm1` and `sm2`, located at (7, 30) and (460, 420), respectively. The `SnowmanV5` class's `toString` method is invoked inside of the `println` method's argument list on lines 13 and 14 to obtain annotated versions of the current values of each snowman's data members. The returned string is concatenated with the names of the snowman and output to the system console (top of Figure 3.34).

The output contains a description of each the snowman's current hat color: *java.awt. Color[r=0,g=0,b=0]*. This is the string returned from the `SnowmanV5` class's `toString` method's implicit invocation of the `Color` class' `toString` method (line 34 of Figure 3.32). The *r=0, g=0, b=0* portion of the output indicates that the red (r), green (g), and blue (b) intensities of the color are all zero: the default hat color black.

Line 15 of the application displays the game board, with the two snowmen drawn on it at their initial locations wearing their black hats (Figure 3.34a). The `SnowmanV5` class's `input` method is invoked on lines 20 and 21 of the application (Figure 3.33), which allows the user to input new values of the two snowmen's data members. Finally, line 18 redisplays the game board, and the two snowmen are drawn at their new locations with their new colored hats as shown on in Figure 3.34b. This output reflects user inputs of:

(200, 200) for `sm1`'s location and (0, 255, 0) for its (red, green, blue) color intensities;
(250, 200) for `sm2`'s location and (0, 0, 255) for its (red, green, blue) color intensities.

```
1    import java.awt.*;
2    import javax.swing.*; // needed for dialog box input
3
4    public class SnowmanV5
5    {
6      //data members
7      private int x = 7;
8      private int y = 30;
9      private Color hatColor = Color.BLACK;
10
11     //member methods
12     public SnowmanV5(int x, int y)
13     {
14       this.x = x;
15       this.y = y;
16     }
17
18     public void show(Graphics g) //g is passed to the method
19     {
20       g.setColor(hatColor);
21       g.fillRect(x + 15, y, 10, 15); //hat
22       g.fillRect(x + 10, y + 15, 20, 2); //brim
23       g.setColor(Color.WHITE);
24       g.fillOval(x + 10, y + 17, 20, 20); //head
25       g.fillOval(x, y + 37, 40, 40); //body
26
27     }
28
29     public String toString()
30     {
31       String s;
32       s = "x is: " + x +
33           "\ny is: " + y +
34           "\nhatColor is: " + hatColor;
35       return s;
36     }
37
38     public void input()
39     {
40       String s;
41       int red, green, blue;
42
43       s = JOptionPane.showInputDialog("enter the value of x");
44       x = Integer.parseInt(s);
45       s = JOptionPane.showInputDialog("enter the value of y");
46       y = Integer.parseInt(s);
47       s = JOptionPane.showInputDialog("enter hat's red intensity");
48       red = Integer.parseInt(s);
49       s =JOptionPane.showInputDialog("enter hat's green intensity");
```

```
50        green = Integer.parseInt(s);
51        s = JOptionPane.showInputDialog("enter hat's blue intensity");
52        blue = Integer.parseInt(s);
53        hatColor = new Color(red, green, blue);
54      }
55  }
```

Figure 3.32
The class `SnowmanV5`.

```
1    import edu.sjcny.gpv1.*;
2    import java.awt.*;
3
4    public class ToStringAndInput extends DrawableAdapter
5    {
6      static ToStringAndInput ge = new ToStringAndInput();
7      static GameBoard gb = new GameBoard(ge,"toString And input
                                                Methods");
8      static SnowmanV5 sm1 = new SnowmanV5(7, 30);
9      static SnowmanV5 sm2 = new SnowmanV5(460, 420);
10
11     public static void main(String[] args)
12     {
13       System.out.println("sm1's\n" + sm1.toString());
14       System.out.println("sm2's\n" + sm2.toString());
15       showGameBoard(gb);
16       sm1.input();
17       sm2.input();
18       showGameBoard(gb);
19     }
20
21     public void draw(Graphics g)
22     {
23       sm1.show(g);
24       sm2.show(g);
25     }
26  }
```

Figure 3.33
The application `ToStringAndInput`.

Console Output:

sm1's
x is: 7
y is: 30
hatColor is: java.awt.Color[r=0,g=0,b=0]
sm2's
x is: 460
y is: 420
hatColor is: java.awt.Color[r=0,g=0,b=0]

Game Board Output:

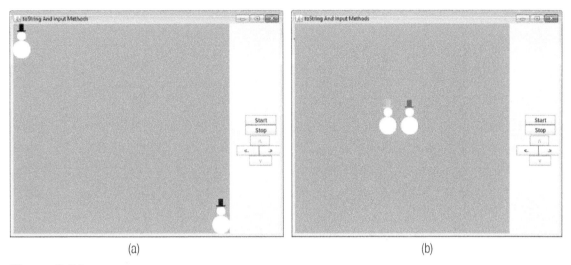

(a)   (b)

Figure 3.34
The console and game board output from the application `ToStringAndInput`.

3.7 OVERLOADING CONSTRUCTORS

Overloading constructors is an object oriented programming term used to describe a class that contains more than one constructor method. The code of each constructor is different, which is the motivation for coding more than one constructor. There is no limit on the number of constructors a class can contain. The name of a constructor method must be the name of the class, so all of the constructor methods in a class have the same name. For example, if the class's name is SnowmanV4, then the name of all of the constructors would be SnowmanV4.

Any of a class's constructors can be used by a client application to allocate an object in the constructor's class. Because the names of the methods are the same, the only way the Java translator knows which constructor is being used is to examine the type and number of arguments in the client's invocation statement.

Consider the code of the class SnowmanV6 presented in Figure 3.35. It contains three constructors, which begin on lines 12, 15, and 20. The signature (line 12) of the first of these constructors contains no parameters and is therefore referred to as the no-parameter constructor. To use the no-parameter constructor, the client's declaration statement would not contain any arguments:

```
SnowmanV6 s1 = new SnowmanV6();
```

Because the constructor's code block is empty, the snowman's x, y, and hatColor data members would retain their default values set on lines 7–9, and when the snowman was drawn it would appear at (7, 30) with a black hat.

To use the two-parameter constructor on line 15, the client's declaration statement would have to contain two integer arguments:

```
SnowmanV6 s1 = new SnowmanV6(250, 250);
```

This constructor allows the client to specify the initial location of the newly created snowman. Lines 17–18 would execute and set the value copied into the method's parameters (250) into the object's x and y data members. When the snowman was drawn, it would appear at (250, 250) wearing a black hat.

To use the three-parameter constructor on line 20, the client's declaration statement would have to contain two integer arguments and a reference to a `Color` object:

```
SnowmanV6 s1 = new SnowmanV6(350, 250, Color.BLUE);
```

This constructor allows the client not only to specify the initial location of the snowman, but also its hat color. Lines 22–24 would execute and set the values 350 and 250 into the object's x and y data members, and it would set the object's data member `hatColor` to blue. In this case, when the snowman was drawn, it would appear at (350, 250), and because line 28 of Figure 3.35 uses the object's `hatColor` data member to set the current color before drawing the hat, it would be wearing a blue hat.

An attempt to create a snowman with an argument list that does not match one of the parameter lists on lines 12, 15, or 20 would result in a translation error. For example, the client statement

```
SnowmanV6 s1 = new SnowmanV6(350.34, 200, Color.BLUE);
```

would result in a translation error indicating that the translator cannot find a constructor whose parameters are a double, followed by an integer, followed by a `Color` object.

_____
NOTE *Each constructor in a class must have a unique parameter list, and the type and number of the arguments in the client's object declaration statement must match one of these lists.*

It should be noted that once a constructor is coded in a class, the Java-provided default constructor discussed in Section 3.5.3 can no longer be used to create an instance of the class. As a result, to default to the values in data member's declaration statements, a no-parameter constructor (e.g., lines 12–14 of Figure 3.35) must be added to the class.

Figure 3.36 presents the application `OverloadingConstructors` that uses the three constructors shown in Figure 3.35 to construct three snowmen on lines 8, 9, and 10: one at the default location (7, 30), one at the center of the game board (250, 250), and one to its right at (350, 250) with a blue hat. Before each snowman's hat is drawn, line 28 of the snowman's class's show method (Figure 3.35) sets the current drawing color to the snowman's hat color. As a result, when the three snowmen are drawn on the game board (lines 19–21 of Figure 3.36) at their initial locations, one is wearing a blue hat (Figure 3.37).

```java
1    import java.awt.Color;
2    import java.awt.Graphics; // needed for drawing shapes
3
4    public class SnowmanV6
5    {
6      //data members
7      private int x = 7;
8      private int y = 30;
9      private Color hatColor = Color.BLACK;
10
11     // member methods
12     public SnowmanV6( )
13     {
14     }
15     public SnowmanV6(int x, int y)
16     {
17       this.x = x;
18       this.y = y;
19     }
20     public SnowmanV6(int x, int y, Color hatColor)
21     {
22       this.x = x;
23       this.y = y;
24       this.hatColor = hatColor;
25     }
26     public void show(Graphics g)    // g is passed to the method
27     {
28       g.setColor(hatColor);
29       g.fillRect(x + 15, y, 10, 15);        // hat
30       g.fillRect(x + 10, y + 15, 20, 2);  // brim
31       g.setColor(Color.WHITE);
32       g.fillOval(x + 10, y + 17, 20, 20); // head
33       g.fillOval(x, y + 37, 40, 40);        // body
34     }
35     public int getX()
36     {
37       return x;
38     }
39     public void setX(int newX)
40     {
41       x = newX;
42     }
43     public int getY()
44     {
45       return y;
46     }
47
48     public void setY(int newY)
49     {
```

```
50        y = newY;
51     }
52  }
```

Figure 3.35
The class **SnowmanV6**.

```
1    import edu.sjcny.gpv1.*;
2    import java.awt.*;
3
4    public class OverloadingConstructors extends DrawableAdapter
5    {
6       static OverloadingConstructors ga= new OverloadingConstructors();
7       static GameBoard gb = new GameBoard(ga, "Overloading
                                                Constructors");
8       static SnowmanV6 sm1 = new SnowmanV6( 7, 30);
9       static SnowmanV6 sm2 = new SnowmanV6 (250, 250);
10      static SnowmanV6 sm3 = new SnowmanV6(350, 250, Color.BLUE);
11
12      public static void main(String[] args)
13      {
14         showGameBoard(gb);
15      }
16
17      public void draw(Graphics g) //the drawing call back method
18      {
19         sm1.show(g);
20         sm2.show(g);
21         sm3.show(g);
22      }
23   }
```

Figure 3.36
The application **OverloadingConstructors**.

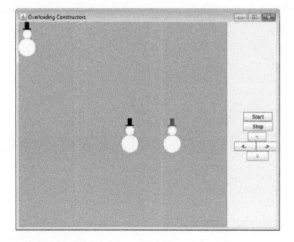

Figure 3.37
The output from the application **OverloadingConstructors**.

3.8 PASSING OBJECTS TO AND FROM WORKER METHODS

The techniques and syntax used to pass primitive information (i.e., values stored in primitive variables) between client and worker methods were discussed in Section 3.2. The same techniques and syntax presented in that section can be used to pass objects between client and worker methods. In the case of objects, the information passed is actually the addresses of the objects stored in the reference variables that refer to the objects. An unlimited number of object addresses can be passed to a worker method via its parameter list, and the address of one object can be returned from a worker method via its `return` statement.

Passing Objects to Worker Methods

The first row of Table 3.3 gives the syntax used to invoke the `Game` class's *static* method `add-1ToX` passing it the address of the `SnowmanV6` object `sm1`. The right-most column gives the syntax of the method's signature. For comparative purposes, the second row of the table gives the syntax used to pass the integer `age` to static method `add1toAge` and the syntax of the method's signature. As shown in the table, the syntax used to pass objects to worker methods is the syntax used to pass primitive values to worker methods. The primitive type coded in the method's parameter list is replaced with the type of the reference variable (i.e., the object's class name), as shown in the rightmost column of the table.

The following code segment is a `static` worker method named `moveRight` that increases the `x` data member of the `SnowmanV6` object passed to it by one pixel:

```
public static void moveRight(SnowmanV6 aSnowman)
{
 int currentX = aSnowman.getX( );
 aSnowman.setX(currentX + 1);
}
```

Table 3.3
Syntax Used To Pass Objects and Primitives to Worker Methods

Information Passed	Client Method's Invocation Statement	Worker Method's Signature Coded in the Class Game
An Object's address	Game.add1ToX(sm1)	static void add1ToX(SnowmanV6 sm)
An Integer value	Game.add1ToAge(age1)	static void add1ToAge(int age)

Figure 3.38 is modified version of the program presented in Figure 3.30 that moves a snowman one pixel to the right every time the game board's right arrow button is clicked. The method `moveRight` has been added to the program (lines 32–37), and it is used to move two snowmen to the right every time the right arrow button is clicked. This method is invoked on lines 28 and 29 to move the two `SnowmanV6` objects, `sm1` and `sm2`, to the right one pixel. The objects are created on lines 9 and 10 using the class's three-parameter constructor. The first invocation of `moveRight` (line 28) passes the location of `sm1` to the method, and the second invocation (line 29) passes `sm2`'s location to the method. Because the static method `moveRight` is coded in the same class as the invocation statements on lines 28 and 29, the name of the class need not be included in the invocations.

```
1    import edu.sjcny.gpv1.*;
2    import javax.swing.*;
3    import java.awt.*;
4
5    public class ObjectsAsParameters extends DrawableAdapter
6    {
7      static ObjectsAsParameters ga = new ObjectsAsParameters();
8      static GameBoard gb = new GameBoard(ga, "Objects As Parameters");
9      static SnowmanV6 sm1 = new SnowmanV6(5, 40, Color.RED);
10     static SnowmanV6 sm2 = new SnowmanV6(460, 423, Color.BLUE);
11
12     public static void main(String[] args)
13     {
14       String s = JOptionPane.showInputDialog("sm2's new x location?");
15       int newX = Integer.parseInt(s);
16       sm2.setX(newX);
17       showGameBoard(gb);
18     }
19
20     public static void draw(Graphics g) // the drawing call back method
21     {
22       sm1.show(g);
23       sm2.show(g);
24     }
25
26     public void rightButton() //moves sm1 & sm2 one pixel right per
                                              click
27     {
28       moveRight(sm1);
29       moveRight(sm2);
30     }
31
32     public void moveRight(SnowmanV6 aSnowman)
33     {
34       int currentX = aSnowman.getX( );
35       currentX++;
36       aSnowman.setX(currentX);
37     }
38  }
```

Figure 3.38
The application `ObjectsAsParameters`.

Figure 3.39 illustrates the passing of the location from the reference variable sm1 into the method's moveRight parameter aSnowman, and the change in the x data member of the object after the method executes. The client code's RAM memory is shown on the left side of the figure, and the worker method's RAM memory is shown on the right side of the figure. Each time the method is invoked, the value stored in the invocation's argument is copied into the parameter

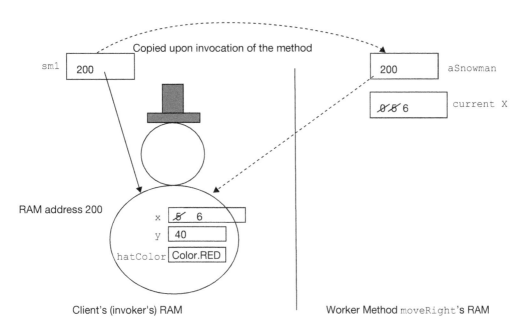

Figure 3.39
The passing of the object sm1 to the worker method `moveRight`.

`aSnowman`. The dashed arrow at the top of the figure illustrates this process for the first invocation of the method (line 28) when the location of snowman `sm1` is passed to the parameter `aSnowman`.

After the snowman's location, 200, is copied into the worker method's parameter `aSnowman`, the use of this variable on lines 34 and 36 of Figure 3.38 refers to the client's snowman object `sm1`. Line 34 fetches `sm1`'s x data member, and line 36 changes the value stored in this data member. While the method is in execution, the snowman object is shared between the client code and the worker method it invoked. Although we normally say we are "passing an object to a method," we really should say we are "passing the address of the object to a method."

> **NOTE** *Technically speaking, objects are not passed to and from methods. Rather, the addresses of the objects are passed between the methods.*

Because the `sm1`'s address is shared, when the worker method ends the initial value of its x data member (5) stored inside the object has been overwritten with the value 6 to be consistent with Figure 3.39. This is not a contradiction of the idea that value parameters prevent worker methods from changing the client's information passed to it as parameters because the information passed to the method `moveRight` is the contents of the variable `sm1`, not the object's data member x. This is a subtle but important point to understand. While it is true that the worker method can change the contents of the data members of the object `sm1` because `aSnowman` stores the object's address, it cannot change the address stored in the variable `sm1` (which was passed to it).

Returning an Object from a Worker Method

An object's address can be returned from a method using the same syntax used to return a primitive value from a method. The keyword **void** in the method's signature is replaced with the type of the information being returned. To return the location of an object from a method, the name of the returned object's class replaces the keyword `void`. As is the case when primitive values are returned from a method, if the returned address is to be used by the client code that invoked the method, the client code must assign the returned address to a variable.

The static method shown in Figure 3.40 creates a snowman object located half way between the two snowmen whose addresses are passed into its parameters, and returns the address of the newly created snowman. Assuming the method is added to the class `SnowmanV6`, the following code fragment invokes the method and stores the returned address of the newly created snowman in the reference variable `aSnowman`:

```
SnowmanV6 aSnowman;
aSnowman = SnowmanV6.halfWayBetween(snowman1, snowman2);
```

The signature of the method on line 1 of Figure 3.40 states that the address of a `SnowmanV6` object will be returned from the method. A `SnowmanV6` object is created on line 4, and its address is returned on line 9.

```
1    public static SnowmanV6 halfWayBetween(SnowmanV6 sm1,SnowmanV6 sm2)
2    {
3      int x, y;
4      SnowmanV6 aSnowman = new SnowmanV6();
5      x = (sm1.getX() + sm2.getX()) / 2);
6      y = (sm1.getX() + sm2.getX()) / 2);
7      aSnowman.setX(x);
8      aSnowman.setY(y);
9      return aSnowman;
10   }
```

Figure 3.40
A method that returns an object.

3.9 CHAPTER SUMMARY

This chapter began our study of the concepts used to design and implement classes, which will be expanded in Chapters 7 and 8. We learned that a class is similar to a blueprint enabling us to define and construct an item, and that an object is a particular item or instance of the class. In the same manner that we use the classes and methods available in the Java API to facilitate the design and development of a program, we can also use and reuse the classes we create.

Methods are subprograms, which are key components of classes. They perform the work of the class by creating, displaying, and manipulating the class's objects. Several versions of a class's constructor methods are normally available in a class to create an object and initialize various subsets of its data members. The names of methods that perform tasks common to most classes have been standardized, and they are included in most classes. The methods named `toString` and `show` are used to display an object on the console or on the game board, and the `input` method and methods that whose names begin with the prefixes `set` and `get` are used to change the values of an object's data members.

The first line of a method is called the method's signature. Java uses value parameters to pass information to a method and a return statement to transfer one value from a method. The list of information passed to a method is called an argument list, which is a sequence of variables and literal values separated by commas. This information is copied into the list of variables declared in the method's signature, which is called a parameter list. Before the method begins execution, the value stored in the ith argument of the invocation statement is copied into the ith parameter of the method. An argument's type must match the type of its corresponding parameter. Value parameters prevent a method from changing the value stored in thevariables coded in the argument list.

Several methods in a class can have the same name if their parameter lists are different. When this feature is used in the coding of a class's methods, we say that the methods with the same name are overloaded. Constructor methods are often overloaded because their names must be the same as the class's name. Normally, methods have public access to permit methods defined outside of the class to invoke them, and data members have private access to prevent methods defined outside of the class from inadvertently changing their values.

A class's data members are declared as class level variables. Class level variables are variables declared outside of the code block of a method and inside the code block of the class. It is good programming practice to declare these class-level variables at the beginning of the class's code block before the implementation of the class's methods.

All class variables declared in a class, whether they are declared public or private, can be directly accessed within the class's methods by simply coding the name of the variable. The only exceptions to this are if the method declares a parameter, or variable, within its code block with the same name. When this is the case, the class variable is accessed within the method by preceding its name with the `key word` this followed by a period. The context in which direct access syntax can be used to access a variable is called the scope of the variable.

A UML diagram is a graphical depiction of a class developed during the design of the class. This tool not only facilitates the design of the class, but it also documents the data members and methods that make up the class. It is used as the starting point for the implementation of the class. Other class design tools discussed in this chapter are the techniques used to depict and digitize a graphical object, which serve as the basis for the implementation of their `show` methods.

The methods in the API `Graphics` class can be used to implement a graphical object's `show` method. This class provides methods for drawing lines and basic shapes on a previously declared `Graphics` object. The units of the (x, y) location of the lines, shapes, and the size of the shapes passed to these methods is pixels or picture elements. These methods provide the foundation for the rest of the graphical topics in this text.

Knowledge Exercises

1. Indicate whether the following statements are true or false:
   a) Methods must be coded inside the code block (i.e., the open and close brackets) of a class.
   b) The first line of a method is called its title.
   c) The first line of a method always ends with a semicolon.
   d) All methods must contain a code block.
   e) The method `pow` in the `Math` class is an example of a void method.
   f) We can invoke methods we did not write.

2. Indicate whether the following statements are true or false.
   a) It is good programming practice to begin a method name with an uppercase letter.
   b) It is good programming practice to make the names of methods representative of the work they perform.
   c) A method's name should not contain capital letters.

3. Fill in the blank:
   a) The signature of a method that does not operate on an object must contain the key word.
   b) The signature of a method that does not return a value must contain the key word _____.
   c) When we invoke a static method, we begin the invocation statement with the name of _____ followed by a dot.
   d) When we invoke a nonstatic method, we begin the invocation statement with the name of _____ followed by a dot.

4. Give the invocation statement to invoke the class `Boat`'s `moveBoat` method whose signature is: `public static void moveBoat()`.

5. Indicate whether the following statements are true or false:
   a) Client code is code that invokes a method.
   b) A method can invoke the same method more than once.
   c) Parameters are used to pass information to a method, and the information is passed into the method's arguments.
   d) One or more pieces of information can be passed to a method.
   e) One or more pieces of information can be returned from a method.
   f) The type of a parameter must match the type of the information it receives.
   g) Parameters and arguments share the same variable.
   h) Java passes information to methods using the concept of reference parameters.
   i) When a method changes the value of an integer passed to it, the original value is no longer available to the client code.

6. Give the signature of a public method named `add` that adds two integers sent to it and returns the result.

7. After an invoked method completes its execution, which statement executes next?

8. Indicate whether the following statements are true or false:
   a) A class-level variable must be coded inside a method in the class.
   b) Class-level variables are used to share information among all of the methods defined in the class.
   c) A method cannot declare a variable with the same name as a class-level variable.
   d) When a method changes the value stored in a class-level variable, the original value is no longer available to the other method in the class.
   e) More than one class-level variable can be coded in a class.

9. Give the declaration of a class-level variable named checkAmount that is coded in the program's class.

10. Fill in the blank:
    a) The method _____ in the Graphics class is used to change the current drawing color.
    b) The constant_____in the Color class stores the color red.
    c) The import statement _____ is used to access the methods defined in the Graphics class.
    d) The import statement _____ is used to access the color constants defined in the Color class.

11. Give the name of the method in the Graphics class used to:
    a) Draw the outline of a rectangle
    b) Draw a filled rectangle
    c) Draw the outline of an ellipse
    d) Draw the outline of a circle
    e) Draw a filled circle
    f) Draw a line

12. Give the Java statement (or statements) to draw the following shapes and lines on the Graphics object g:
    a) A line from (200, 30) to (100, 75) drawn in the current color
    b) The outline of a 100-pixel wide by 50-pixel high rectangle located at (20, 200) drawn using the current color
    c) A blue filled circle whose diameter is 30 pixels located at (250, 300)
    d) A blue filled ellipse 100-pixel wide by 50-pixel high located at (300, 100)

13. Fill in the blank:
    a) Using the words object and class in: House is to _____ as blueprint to _____.
    b) Classes are comprised of member _____ and _____.
    c) The name of the graphic used to specify a class is a _____ diagram.

d) Data members of a class are usually designated to have _____ access.

e) Member methods of a class are usually designated to have _____ access.

14. Give the Java code to declare an object named `joe` in the class `Person` using the class's no-parameter constructor, and:

   a) the one-line declaration syntax.

   b) the two-line declaration syntax.

15. Referring to Exercise 14:

   a) What is actually stored in the variable `joe`?

   b) Is `joe` a primitive-type variable? If not, what is the its type?

   c) Draw a picture (similar to Figure 3.13) of the memory allocated by Exercise 14a, assuming the class `Person` has two integer data members named `age` and `idNumber`.

16. Give the Java code to declare a class whose object will be coffee cups. Each coffee cup will have a size (ounces) and a price. The class will not contain any methods.

17. Referring to Exercise 16:

   a) Give the code of the two-parameter constructor of the class defined in Exercise 16.

   b) Give the client code used to declare a $3.85 coffee cup whose size is 8 ounces.

   c) Give the code to output the coffee cup declared in part B to the system console using an implicit invocation of the `toString` method.

   d) Repeat part C of this question using an explicit invocation of the `toString` method.

   e) What is output to the console by the invocation in part C and B?

   f) Give the code to produce the same output generated by part D to the graphic object `g`.

18. Give the code of a method named `toString` that, when added to the class defined in Exercise 16, returns the values of its two data members fully annotated.

19. Give the code of a method named `show` that, when added to the class defined in Exercise 16, outputs the values of its two data members to the center of a 500 wide by 500 high `Graphics` object named `g`.

20. Using a sketch similar to Figure 3.16, show the design of a recreational vehicle (RV) that has two side windows, tires a large entrance door.

21. Give a table similar to Table 3.2 that contains the digitized version of the RV design specified in Exercise 20.

22. When must the keyword `this` be used in a method to access one of the data members of its class?

23. A class contains one integer data member named `total` whose access is private.

   a) Use the key word `this` in a statement coded inside one of the class's method that doubles the value stored in the data member `total`.

   b) Give a statement coded inside one of the class's method that doubles the value stored in the data member `total` without using the key word `this`.

   c) Give the code of a `set` method that client code could use to change the value of the data member `total`.

d) Give the code of a `get` method that client code could use to fetch the value of the data member `total`.

e) Assuming the appropriate `set` and `get` methods exist, give the client code to double the value of the total of the object named `myAccount` that uses the `set` and `get` methods.

f) Assuming the data member `total` was declared to have public access, give the client code to double the value of the total of the object named `myAccount` without using `set` and `get` methods.

g) Give the code of the class's `toString` method.

h) Give the code of the class's `input` method.

i) Which access modifier keyword, `public` or `private`, results in more restricted access?

24. Indicate whether the following statements are true or false:

a) A class need not contain an explicitly coded constructor.

b) A class can contain several constructors.

c) A class can contain several constructors with different names.

d) A class can contain several constructors with the same signature.

e) When a constructor invocation is proceed by the keyword `new`, an object is created, and its address is returned.

f) The Java provided default constructor has no parameters.

25. A client application has declared three objects named `ship1`, `ship2`, and `ship3` that are instances of the existing class `Starship`. Each starship contains a data member that stores the color used to draw the starship.

a) Give the signature of a static method in the `Starship` class named `largest` that is passed two `Starship` objects and returns the address of one of them.

b) Give the client code statement used to invoke the static method described in part A of this exercise and place the returned address in `ship1`.

c) If the method changed the value of the color data member of one of the starships passed to it, would it be drawn in the new or old color after the method completes its execution?

d) Give the signature of a nonstatic method in the `Starship` class named `sameModel` that compares two `Starship` objects and returns a Boolean value.

e) Give the client code statement used to invoke the nonstatic method described in part D of this exercise and store the returned Boolean value in the variable `isSame`.

26. Using a sketch similar to Figure 3.16, show the design of the user-controlled game piece that is part of the game you specified in Preprogramming Exercise 1 of Chapter 1.

27. Give a table similar to Table 3.2 that contains the digitized version of the game piece design specified in Exercise 26.

Programming Exercises

1. Write a nongraphical application that contains a static method with an empty parameter list that outputs your name and your age on one line to the system console. The main method of the application should invoke it three times. The output it produces should be annotated as shown

below (assuming your name is Tommy and you are 18 years old):

The author of this program is Tommy who is 18 years old.

2. Write a graphical application that contains a static method that is invoked by the draw call back method. It should have one parameter to receive the Graphics object g passed to it. When invoked, the method should output your name and your age to the center of the game board as shown below (assuming your name is Tommy and you are 18 years old):

The author of this program is Tommy who is 18 years old.

3. Write a nongraphical application that contains a static method to compute and return the square root of the product of three real numbers passed to it. The main method of the application should invoke it and then output the three numbers and the returned value clearly annotated.

4. Write a graphical application that contains a static method to compute and return the square root of the product of three real numbers passed to it. The draw method should invoke it and then output the three numbers and the returned value clearly annotated.

5. Write a nongraphical application that contains a static method to compute and return the square root of the product of three real numbers that are declared and initialized as class-level variables. The main method of the application should invoke it and then output the three numbers and the returned value clearly annotated.

6. Write a graphical application whose draw method displays an old television on a table with an antenna on it.

7. The statistics kept for each player on a ladies softball team include each player's name, number of homeruns, and batting average as a real number.

   a) Give the UML diagram for a class named TeamMember whose objects can store the three private pieces of data for a player. The class should include a three-parameter constructor, a toString method, a method to input the statistics for a player, and a showSC method to output a player's statistics to the system console.

   b) Progressively implement and test the TeamMember class by adding one method and verifying it before adding the next method. A good order to add the methods is the toString method, followed by the constructor, the show method, and finally the input method. (The client code can create a TeamMember object using the Java supplied default constructor to test the toString method.)

   c) After all of the methods are verified, comment out the test code in the client application and add two TeamMember instances to the program whose statistics are passed to the three-parameter constructor. Output these players to the system console and then output them again after the user inputs new names, homerun counts, and batting averages for each player.

8. Write a graphical application that contains a class named RV whose objects are the recreational vehicle designed and digitized as described in Knowledge Exercises 20 and 21. The class's private data members should be the vehicle's body color and (x, y) location.

   a) Give the UML diagram for the class. It should include a three-parameter constructor, a toString method, a method to input the values of all of an object's data members, and a show method to draw the RV at its current (x, y) location.

b) Progressively implement and test the RV class by adding a method and verifying it before adding the next method. A good order to add the methods to the class is the three-parameter constructor, followed by the `toString` method, the `show` method, and finally the `input` method. The client code should create an RV object using the three-parameter constructor to test all of the methods as they are progressively added to the class.

c) After all of the methods are verified, comment out the test code in the client application and add two RV instances to the program whose location and color are passed to the three-parameter constructor. Output these vehicles to the system console and the game board and then output them again after the user inputs a new color and a new (x, y) location for each vehicle.

9. After implementing and testing the class described in Programming Exercise 7, progressively add a `set` and a `get` method to the class for each of the class's data members. After the `set` and a `get` methods have been verified, create two instances of the class using the three-parameter constructor and display them to the system console. Then, ask the user how many home runs and batting average points should be added to each player's statistics. Use the `set` and a `get` methods to change the statistics and then output the two players to the system console.

10. After implementing and testing the class described in Programming Exercise 8, progressively add a `set` and a `get` method to the class for each of the class's data members. After the `set` and a `get` methods have been verified, create an instance of the class using the three-parameter constructor and display it on the system console and the game board. Every time one of the game board's directional buttons is clicked, the RV's location should be changed by two pixels in the appropriate direction.

11. Using the skills developed in this chapter, begin to implement the game you specified in Preprogramming Exercise 1 of Chapter 1. Begin by completing Knowledge Exercises 26 and 27 to design and digitize the user-controlled game piece. Then, implement the class of the digitized game object, beginning with a UML diagram of the game piece that includes a constructor with the appropriate number of parameters, a `show` method to draw the object on the game board at its current (x, y) location, a `toString` method, and a `set` and a `get` method for each of the class's data members. After progressively implementing and testing all of the class's methods, write a graphical application that displays the game piece on the game board and then moves the game piece by two pixels in the appropriate direction every time one of the game board's directional buttons is clicked.

Endnotes and References

[1] Lanzinger, Franz. *Classic Game Design: From Pong to Pac-Man with Unity.* Dulles, Virginia: Mercury Learning and Information, 2014.

[2] Schell, Jesse. *The Art of Game Design.* Burlington, MA: Morgan Kaufmann Publishers, 2010.

BOOLEAN EXPRESSIONS, MAKING DECISIONS, AND DISK INPUT AND OUTPUT

4.1   *Alternatives to Sequential Execution* *138*

4.2   *Boolean Expressions* *138*

4.3   *The* **if** *Statement* *144*

4.4   *The* **if-else** *Statement* *150*

4.5   *Nested* **if** *Statements.* *158*

4.6   *The* **switch** *Statement* *160*

4.7   *Console Input and the* **Scanner** *Class.* *169*

4.8   *Disk Input and Output: A First Look* *172*

4.9   *Exceptions: A First Pass* *179*

4.10 *Chapter Summary* *185*

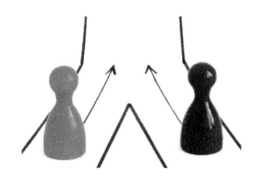

In this chapter

To control the sequence of operations, Java provides three decision-making statements, and in this chapter, we will learn how to write the Boolean condition on which these decisions are based. By default, Java statements execute in the order in which they are coded, although at some point in most algorithms, a decision has to be made as to which of its steps should be executed next. When depicted in a flow chart, this part of the algorithm begins with a diamond shape. To implement these algorithms, programming languages include decision statements that use Boolean expressions as conditions to determine whether to execute or skip statements. Java also provides two statements that always skip a predetermined set of statements, one of which will be discussed in this chapter.

In addition, this chapter extends the input and output techniques of the previous chapters to include input from the system console as well as disk I/O, and it introduces a technique used to alter the sequential execution path of a program when an unexpected error occurs.

After successfully completing this chapter, you should:

- Be familiar with the logical and relational operators and their order of precedence
- Be able to write and evaluate simple and complex Boolean expressions
- Understand how to compare strings and determine their alphabetic order
- Be able to write `if`, `if-else`, and `switch` statements to implement the decision-making part of an algorithm

- Understand the use of the `break` statement
- Be able to perform console input using the `Scanner` class and its methods
- Be able to create, open, read, and write sequential text files to and from a disk
- Begin to understand how to use `try` and `catch` blocks to handle an error exception
- Use decision-making statements to control a timer, a graphical object's visibility and motion, and detect collisions between two objects

4.1 ALTERNATIVES TO SEQUENTIAL EXECUTION

When a Java application begins, the first statement to execute is the first executable statement in the method main. The order in which the remainder of the instructions execute is referred to as the *execution path* of the program, or the *flow* of the program. The default execution path of a Java statement block is sequential. It can be thought of as the statements executing in line number order. After the first statement in the block executes, the remaining statements execute in the order in which they are written unless one of the statements specifically alters the execution path.

Many algorithms cannot be formulated in a way that all of its steps are executed sequentially. Therefore, programming languages provide statements to change the default sequential execution path. Programmers use these statements, or constructs, to alter the sequential flow of the program, so they are referred to as *control-of-flow* or *control* statements. We have already used one of these constructs: the invocation of a method. Assuming a method was invoked on line 10 of a program, the next statement to execute would not be line 11, but rather, the first executable statement in the method's code block. Line 11 would execute after the method completed its execution.

Aside from method invocation statements, programming languages provide additional control-of-flow statements to alter the default execution path. Some of these statements are used to skip a group of statements, and others are used to repeat a group of statements. Most often, these control-of-flow statements include a logical expression, called a Boolean expression, to decide when to skip statements or to decide how many times to repeat statements. In this chapter, we will discuss the Java statements used to skip a group of statements. The Java statements that are used to repeat a group of statements will be discussed in Chapter 5.

4.2 BOOLEAN EXPRESSIONS

Boolean (logical) expressions are named after George Boole, an English mathematician who conceived of a symbolic algebra for logic. Like mathematical algebraic expressions, Boolean expressions consist of operators and operands. Unlike mathematical expressions, Boolean expressions evaluate to one of two values: `true` or `false`. Boolean expressions used in control-of-flow statements can either be a *simple* Boolean expression, or a combination of two or more simple Boolean expressions called compound Boolean expressions.

4.2.1 Simple Boolean Expressions

A simple Boolean expression evaluates to either `true` or `false`. In Java, these expressions consist of a relational or an equality operator surrounded by two operands. Java's four relational operators are given at the top of the Table 4.1, and its two equality operators are at the bottom of the table. The first column in the table gives the name (which implies the meaning) of each operator, and the second column gives the Java symbols (keystrokes) that represent them. The symbols for the last four operators in the table are typed as two keystrokes without spaces. The third column of the table gives examples of simple Boolean expressions involving each of the six operators, all of which evaluate to `true`.

Table 4.1
Java's Relational and Equality Operators

Operator	Java Symbol	Examples that Evaluate to true
Less than	<	5 < 7
Greater than	>	6.31 > 3.14
Less than or equal to	<=	5 <= 5
Greater than or equal to	>=	'c' >= 'a'
Equal to	==	6 == 3 * 2
Not equal to	!=	23 != 54

A common mistake made when coding simple Boolean expressions is to code the equal to operator as a single equal (=) keystroke, which is interpreted by the translator as the assignment operator. Think of this operator as "is equal" to (= =).

When one of the four relational operators is used, the two operands can be anything that can be converted to (interpreted as) a numeric. This includes numeric literals, numeric variables, and arithmetic expressions, as well as character literals and character variables. When a character literal or character variable is used, the character (e.g., `'A'`) is interpreted as an integer (e.g., 65), and the numeric value is used to evaluate the relational expression. The following code fragments are syntactically correct, and the third one evaluates to `true` because `'A'` and `'C'` are interpreted as 65 and 67 (see Appendix C), then the expression is evaluated.

```
int age = 13;
5 < 2 * 21
100 >= age
'A' < 'C'
25 <= 2 * (age + 1)
```

The interpretation of characters in simple Boolean expressions as numeric imposes an ordering on them called *lexicographical* or dictionary order, which is the order in which they appear in the Extended ASCII table (Appendix C).

When the types of the operands used with one of the four relational operators do not match (e.g., one is a float and one is a double, or one is an integer and the other is a character), one of the operands is promoted before the expression is evaluated. For example, the following simple Boolean expressions are syntactically correct and evaluate to `true`:

```
4.521 < 10        // 10 is promoted to the double 10.0
Math.PI >= -2     // -2 is promoted to double -2.0
2 < 'A'           // 'A' is promoted to 65
```

When one of the two equality operators is used in a simple Boolean expression, the choices for the operands are expanded. Not only can the two operands be anything that can be converted to a numeric, but they can also be two Boolean operands (literals or variables) or two reference variables (including the value `null`). For example:

```
4.535 != 21
65 == 'A'
true != false
myName != yourName
name == null
```

Like the arithmetic operators, the operators in Table 4.1 have an order of precedence associated with them. The four relational operators have equal precedence, and the two equality operators have equal precedence. The precedence value of the relational operators is higher than the precedence value of the equality operators. The expression

```
true == 'C' >= 'A'
```

is syntactically correct and evaluates to `true` because first `'C' >= 'A'` evaluates to `true`, and then `true == true` evaluates to `true`. As shown in Appendix E, the arithmetic operators have higher precedence than the relational and equality operators.

NOTE   *Arithmetic expressions in simple Boolean expressions are evaluated first. In more complex expressions, the relational operators are evaluated next, followed by the equality operators, and then the logical operators. The assignment operator is evaluated last.*

4.2.2 Compound Boolean Expressions

Like simple Boolean expressions, compound Boolean expressions also evaluate to either `true` or `false`. When used in a control-of-flow statement, compound Boolean expressions use the Java conditional binary logical operators AND and OR to combine the truth values of two or more operands. Alternately, compound Boolean expressions can use the unary logic operator NOT to reverse the truth value of a single operand, just as the negation operator reverses the sign of an operand in a mathematical expression. The operands in compound Boolean expressions must evaluate to Boolean values (`true` or `false`). Most often, these operands are simple Boolean expressions but could be a Boolean literal or a non-void method invocation that returns a Boolean value.

Table 4.2 gives the three Java logical operators normally used in control-of-flow statements and the symbols used to represent them. The three operators are shown in decreasing precedence order: the NOT operator has the highest precedence, followed by the AND operator, and the OR operator has the lowest precedence. As shown in Appendix E, the arithmetic operators and the relational and equality operators have higher precedence than the logic operators. The Java symbols for the AND (&&) and OR (||) operators given in the second column of the table are each two keystrokes. The keystrokes (||) used in the symbol for the OR operator is located above the Enter key on the keyboard.

Table 4.2
Java's Logical Operators

Logical Operator	Java Symbol	Examples that Evaluate to true
Not	!	! ('p' > 'x')
And	&&	8 < 10 && 6 == 2 * 3
Or	||	7 < 4 || 8 >= 5

All of the compound logical expressions shown in the rightmost column of Table 4.2 evaluate to `true`. To evaluate the truth value of a complex Boolean expression, we must know the meaning of the conditional logic operators. As previously stated, the meaning of the unary NOT(!) operator is simply to reverse the truth value of its operand. For example, because 'p' comes before 'x' in the extended ASCII table, ('p' > 'x') evaluates to `false` and !('p' > 'x') evaluates to `true`. Similarly, !(6 > 10) evaluates to `true`.

The meaning of the two binary logical operators, AND and OR, is usually conveyed in truth tables such as the one shown in Table 4.3. The four possible combinations of the truth values of their two Boolean operands, A and B, are given in the two columns on the left side of the table. The corresponding values of the AND and OR operators for each of the four possible values of their operands is given in the two columns on the right side of the table. Summarizing the resulting values, A && B evaluates to `true` only when A and B are both `true`, and A || B evaluates to `false` only when A and B are both `false`. The compound Boolean expression in the third row of Table 4.2 evaluates to `true` because one of the operands, 8 >= 5, is `true`.

Table 4.3
Meaning of Java's Binary Logical Operators

Operand Truth Values		Meaning of Operators	
A	B	A && B	A || B
true	true	true	true
true	false	false	true
false	true	false	true
false	false	false	false

Figure 4.1 presents an application that evaluates simple Boolean expressions whose operands are literals, primitive and reference variables, and a compound Boolean expression. The output produced by the program is given at the bottom of the figure.

When a compound expression is evaluated, it follows the order of precedence from left to right. Parentheses can also be used to make the ordering clear or to enforce a certain ordering in the evaluation. For example, the expression on line 23 might be written as

```
((i1 == 5 || c1 < 'A') && (d1 != 21.8 ))
```

to specify the order of evaluation. Evaluating the sub-expressions in a different order might give a different result.

```
1    public class BooleanExpressions
2    {
3       public static void main(String[] args)
4       {
5       int i1 = 5;
6       double d1 = 3.53;    double d2 = 54.88;
7       char c1 = 'A';    char c2 ='C';
8       boolean b1 = true;    boolean b2 = false;
9       String s1 = new String("Bob");
10      String s2 = new String("Bob");
11
12      System.out.println(i1 < 5);
13      System.out.println(d1 > d2);
14
15      System.out.println(i1 >= d1); // integer i1 promoted
16      System.out.println(d1 <= 3); // integer 3 is promoted
17
18      System.out.println(c1 < c2); // lexicographical order used
19      System.out.println(10 > c2); // c2 promoted to numeric 67
20
21      System.out.println(b1 == b2) ;
22
23      System.out.println( i1 == 5 || c1 < 'A' && d1 != 21.8 );
24
25      System.out.println(s1 == s2); // compares contents of s1 and s2
26      }
27   }

Output
false
false
true
false
true
false
false
true
false
```

Figure 4.1
The application **BooleanExpressions** and the output it produces.

Lines 5–8 declare and initialize integer, double, character, and Boolean variables. These variables are used in simple Boolean expressions that are evaluated and output on lines (12–21). The types of the operands in the expressions on lines 15, 16, and 19 do not match, so promotion is used before these expressions are evaluated. The contents of the character variables on line 18 are interpreted as numerics before the Boolean expression is evaluated. Because 65 ('A') is less than 67 ('C'), the fifth output is true.

Line 23 contains an example of a compound Boolean expression containing two conditional logical operators OR and AND. Although the order of the operations in this expression is not important, the AND operation, having higher precedence, is evaluated first. This reduces the expression to

```
i1 == 5 || false
```

which evaluates to `true` (the next to the last output in Figure 4.1).

The operands in the Boolean expression output on line 25 are the two string variables declared on lines 9 and 10. Both strings are initialized to "Bob" by the `String` class's one-parameter constructor, yet the comparison for equality on line 25 produces an output of `false` (the last output). This is because the equality operators always compare the contents of the reference variables rather than the contents of the objects they refer to. Because the objects `s1` and `s2` are stored in different locations, the contents of `s1` and `s2` are not equal, and the Boolean expression on line 25 evaluates to `false`. Most often, to compare the contents of two objects, we have to add a method to the object's class that performs the comparison and then returns a Boolean value.

4.2.3 Comparing String Objects

In Chapter 7, we will discuss techniques for comparing the contents of any two objects. Strings are used so often in programs that the `String` class provides several methods for comparing them. One of these is the `equals` method. It is a non-static method that returns a Boolean value. The returned value is `true` when the contents of the string object sent to it is the same as the contents of the string object that invoked it. The comparison of the two strings is case sensitive. The following code fragment demonstrates the use of the method. The first three invocations to the method return `true`, and the last two return `false`.

```
String name1 = new String("Bob");
String name2 = new String("Bob");
String name3 = "BOB";
String name4 = "Mary";
System.out.println(name1.equals(name2));
System.out.println(name1.equals("Bob"));
System.out.println(name1.equals("Bob") || name1.equals("Mary"));
System.out.println(name1.equals(name3)); // false, case mismatch
System.out.println(name1.equals(name4)); // false, different names
```

The third invocation demonstrates that a method that returns a Boolean value can be used as an operand in a compound Boolean expression.

The `String` class contains three other non-static methods for comparing strings. Their names are: `equalsIgnoreCase`, `compareTo`, and the `compareToIgnoreCase`. Like the `equals` method, the `equalsIgnoreCase` method returns a Boolean value, which is `true` when the contents of the string object sent to it is the same as the contents of the string object that invoked it. Unlike the `equals` method, case sensitivity is ignored when making the comparison.

The `String` class's `compareTo` and `compareToIgnoreCase` methods determine the relative lexicographical order of two `String` objects. These non-static methods return an integer whose value reflects the lexicographical order of the string that invoked it relative to the string sent to it as an argument. The `compareTo` method considers case sensitivity, and the `compareToIgnore-Case` ignores case sensitivity. The code fragment below compares the lexicographical order two strings `s1` and `s2`:

```
int order1 = s1.compareTo(s2);
int order2 = s2.compareToIgnoreCase(s2);
```

The values returned to the variables `order1` and `order2` would be:

- negative when `s1` comes before `s2` in lexicographical order
- positive when `s1` comes after `s2` in lexicographical order
- zero when `s1` and `s2` are equal in lexicographical order

Although the `compareTo` and the `CompareToIgnoreCase` methods can be used to determine when two strings are equal, it is good coding practice to use the `equals` and `equalsIgnoreCase` methods when testing two strings for eq uality because it makes our code more readable.

4.3 THE `if` STATEMENT

The `if` statement is one of two Java control-of-flow statements that can be used to alter the default sequential execution of a program based on the truth value of a Boolean expression. The other statement is the `if-else` statement, which will be discussed in Section 4.4.

The syntax of the `if` statement begins with the keyword if, followed by a Boolean expression inside parentheses, followed by a statement or group of statements to be skipped or executed. When there is a group of statements, they must be coded as a statement block; that is, they must be enclosed in braces. The group of statements will be executed when the Boolean condition is `true`, and skipped when the Boolean expression is `false`. Thus, the syntax of the statement is:

One Statement Syntax	Multiple Statement Syntax

`if`(a Boolean expression)
a Statement to be skipped
or executed
	`if`(a Boolean expression)
	{ Statement*1* to be skipped or executed
	             :
	  Statement*n* to be skipped or executed
	}

Even when there is just one statement, it is better coding practice to enclose the one statement in braces, which makes the statement more readable and less prone to errors. For example, if during the development of the program we were to decide to add a second statement and neglected to add the open and close braces around the two statements, the second statement would not be considered part of the `if` statement. It would always execute. The two coding examples given below are not equivalent:

```
if(a false Boolean expression)          if(a false Boolean expression)
    statement1                          {   statement1
    statement2                              statement2
                                        }
```

The code on the left always executes `statement2`, even though the indentation seems to imply that its execution is dependent on the truth value of the Boolean expression. A good habit to acquire when writing an `if` statement is to write this code fragment first:

```
if( )
{

}
```

and then fill in the Boolean condition and the statements to be skipped when the condition is `false`. Most often, we see the `if` statement coded as:

```
if(a Boolean expression)
{
    //One or more statements possibly to be skipped
}
```

The meaning, or *semantics*, and the execution path of the `if` statement is illustrated in Figure 4.2

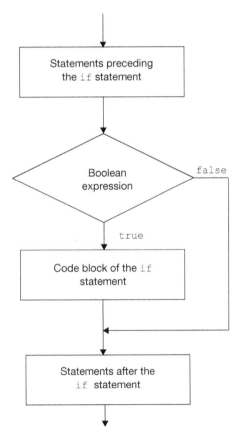

Figure 4.2
The meaning and execution path of the **if** statement.

We conclude this section with a discussion of a use of the `if` statement, making game objects disappear, and then present a game programming application that demonstrates several uses of the `if` statement.

Using the `if` Statement

In many games, the game's objects disappear based on events that occur as the game progresses. When Pac-Man collides with a food pellet, the pellet disappears, or when Frogger is hit by a car, she disappears. Often, after the event occurs the object not only becomes invisible, but it is eliminated from the game. Graphic objects can be made to disappear by either drawing them in the color of the program's window (or in our case the game board), or by not drawing them at all.

To convey the visibility status of a game piece object, e.g., a food pellet, a Boolean data member is added to the object's class. When an event occurs that changes the status (for example, when food pellet `p1` is eaten by Pac-Man), the truth value of the data member is reversed by the code that detected the event. The `draw` call back method can use the truth value of this data member in an `if` statement's Boolean condition to decide whether or not to draw the object. If a Boolean data member named `eaten`, initialized to `false`, was added to the class of Pac-Man's pellets, and the data member was set to `true` when the pellet was eaten, then adding the following code fragment to the `draw` call back method would make pellet `p1` disappear after the pellet was is eaten.

```
if( p1.getEaten( ) == false )
{
  p1.show(g);
}
```

If the variable `count` was being used to keep track of the game's time, and pellet `p1` was only to appear after the game had been played for 20 seconds, then a compound Boolean expression would be used in the above code fragment.

```
if( p1.getEaten( ) == false && count >= 20)
{
  p1.show(g);
}
```

In this case the pellet, `p1`, would appear 20 seconds into the game, and it would disappear when an event changes that pellet's data member `eaten` to `true`.

In Section 2.9.1 (Figure 2.12), the counting algorithm was used to keep track of a game's time. Figure 4.3 presents the code discussed in that section with three `if` statements added to it: two to the `draw` call back method (lines 17–31) and one to the `timer1` method (lines 33–40). In addition, a `BoxedSnowman` object `s1`, whose class is given Figure 4.4, has been added to the application (line 10). The graphical output produced by the program is given in Figure 4.5.

When the application shown in Figure 4.3 is launched, the number of elapsed seconds is displayed on the game board starting from zero (top left side of Figure 4.5). To begin the game the start button is clicked, which causes the elapsed time to be updated every second. Five seconds into the game, the snowman `s1` appears at the center of the game board (top right side of Figure 4.5). After ten seconds, the game ends. The elapsed time remains at ten seconds, a message appears on the game board indicating that the game is over, and the snowman disappears from the game board (bottom portion of Figure 4.5).

Line 20 of the application displays the number of elapsed seconds, which is stored in the class variable count. This variable is incremented on line 35 of the timer1 call back method, which (by default) executes once a second. Ten seconds into the game, the Boolean condition of the if statement that begins on line 36 becomes true, and line 38 invokes the game environment's stop-Timer method to stop timer 1 from ticking. As described in Appendix B, this method is passed one argument, which specifies the timer number (1, 2, or 3) that is to be stopped. It is a nonstatic method, invoked on the program's GameBoard object gb, which was declared on line 8.

The Boolean data member visible has been declared on line 9 of the BoxedSnowman class (Figure 4.4) to store the visibility status of a snowman, and the class contains a set and get method (lines 51–59) to allow client code to access this private data member. To make the snowman appear after five seconds has elapsed, snowman s1's visibility status is fetched by a call to the getVisible method on line 21 of the application, and the returned value is used in the compound Boolean expression to decide when to show the snowman on the game board. The snowman will be shown when its visible data member is true *and* the game's time is five seconds or greater. Since visible is initialized to on line 9 of the BoxedSnowman class to true, the snowman is displayed on the game board five seconds into the game.

To make the snowman disappear after ten seconds, the if statement inside the timer1 call back method (lines 33–41) sets snowman s1's visible property to false (line 36) when count equals ten. This causes the first term in the Boolean expression on line 21 to become false, and line 23, which displays the snowman on the game board, does not execute.

The if statement that begins on line 26 displays the game ending messages when the game time reaches ten seconds.

```
1    import edu.sjcny.gpv1.*;
2    import java.awt.Graphics;
3    import java.awt.Font;
4
5    public class IfStatement extends DrawableAdapter
6    {
7      static IfStatement ga = new IfStatement();
8      static GameBoard gb = new GameBoard(ga, "The if Statement");
9      static int count = 0;
10     static BoxedSnowman s1 = new BoxedSnowman(250, 215, Color.BLACK);
11
12     public static void main(String[] args)
13     {
14       showGameBoard(gb);
15     }
16
17     public void draw(Graphics g) // the draw call back method
18     {
19         g.setFont(new Font("Arial", Font.BOLD, 18));
```

```
20        g.drawString("Your game time is: " + count, 10, 50);
21        if(s1.getVisible() == true && count >= 5)
22        {
23            s1.show(g);
24        }
25
26        if(count == 10)
27        {
28            g.drawString("Game Over", 10, 70);
29            g.drawString("Have a Good Day", 10, 90);
30        }
31    }
32
33    public void timer1()
34    {
35        count = count + 1;
36        if(count == 10)
37        {
38            gb.stopTimer(1);
39            s1.setVisible(false);
40        }
41    }
42  }
```

Figure 4.3
The application **IfStatement**.

```
1     import java.awtGraphics;
2     import java.awt.Color;
3
4     public class BoxedSnowman
5     {
6       private int x = 8;
7       private int y = 30;
8       private Color hatColor = Color.BLACK;
9       private boolean visible = true;
10
11      public BoxedSnowman(int intialX, int intialY, Color hatColor)
12      { x = intialX;
13        y = intialY;
14        this.hatColor = hatColor;
15      }
16
17      public void show(Graphics g) //g is the game board object
18      {
19        g.setColor(hatColor);
20        g.fillRect(x + 15, y, 10, 15); //hat
21        g.fillRect(x + 10, y + 15, 20, 2); //brim
```

```
22        g.setColor(Color.WHITE);
23        g.fillOval(x + 10, y + 17, 20, 20); // head
24        g.fillOval(x, y + 37, 40, 40); //body
25        g.setColor(Color.RED);
26        g.fillOval(x + 19, y + 53, 4, 4); //button
27        g.setColor(Color.BLACK);
28        g.drawRect(x, y, 40, 77); //inscribing rectangle
29      }
30
31      public int getX()
32      {
33        return x;
34      }
35
36      public void setX(int newX)
37      {
38        x = newX;
39      }
40
41      public int getY()
42      {
43        return y;
44      }
45
46      public void setY(int newY)
47      {
48        y = newY;
49      }
50
51      public boolean getVisible()
52      {
53        return visible;
54      }
55
56      public void setVisible(boolean newVisible)
57      {
58        visible = newVisible;
59      }
60    }
```

Figure 4.4
The **BoxedSnowman** class.

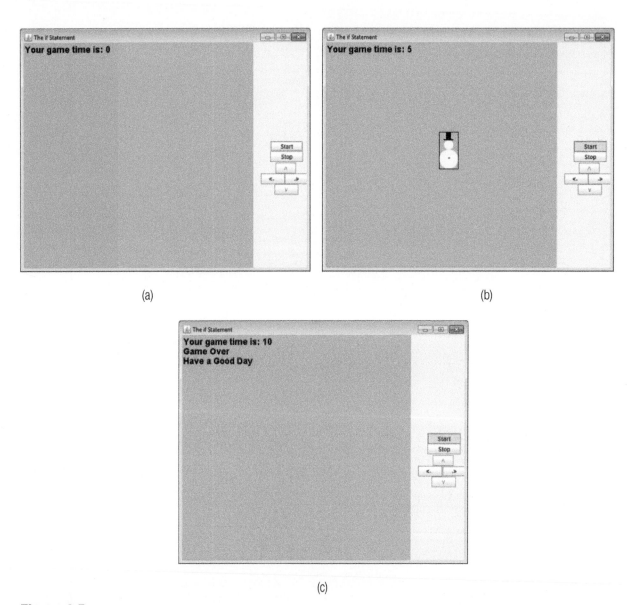

Figure 4.5
The output produced by the application **IfStatement**.

4.4 THE if-else STATEMENT

Like the if statement, the if-else statement is a Java control-of-flow statement that can be used to alter the default sequential execution path of a program by skipping statements based on the truth value of a Boolean expression. This statement can be thought of as having two clauses: an if clause and an else clause. Each clause has a statement block associated with it. One, and only one, of these blocks will execute. When the Boolean condition is true, the statement block associated with the if clause executes. When it is false, the statement block associated with the else clause executes. The syntax of the if-else statement is:

```
if(a Boolean expression)
{
    // One or more if clause statements
}
else
{
    // One or more else clause statements
}
```

and its meaning and execution path is given in Figure 4.6

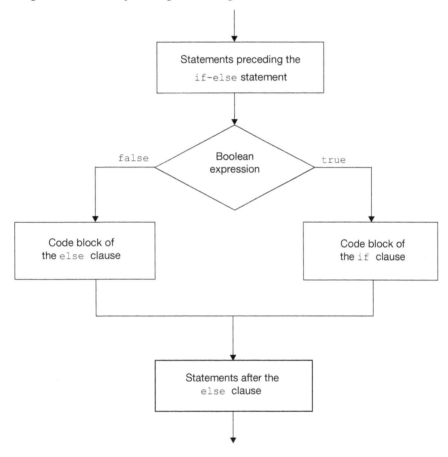

Figure 4.6
The meaning and execution path of the **if-else** statement.

Because the statements in the code block that follow the else clause are executed when the if statement's Boolean expression is false, the else clause does not contain its own Boolean expression. The following code fragment determines what weight jacket to wear based on the temperature stored in the memory cell temperature:

```
if(temperature <= 45)
{
    System.out.println("It is a frigid " + temperature + " degrees,");
```

```
        System.out.println("Wear your heavy jacket.");
    }
    else
    {
      System.out.println("It is rather mild " + temperature + " degrees,");
      System.out.println("Wear your light weight jacket");
    }
```

The `if-else` statement is used to choose one of two statement blocks to execute: the first when the `if` statement's Boolean condition is `true` and the second when it is `false`. By coding just one statement into the `else` clause's statement block that is another `if-else` statement, we can choose between one of three mutually exclusive alternatives, as illustrated in the following coding template:

```
    if(Boolean expression 1)
{
   // One or more if clause statements in code block 1
}
    else if(Boolean expression 2)
{
   // One or more if clause statements in code block 2
}
    else
{
   // One or more else clause statements in code block 3
}
```

As indicated by the second comment in the template, the second set of open and close parentheses defines the code block of the second `if` statement. Because the second `if` statement is the only statement in the first `else` clause's code block, not coding it inside a set of brackets improves readability. Figure 4.7 illustrates the meaning and execution path of the code template.

This coding process can be progressively repeated when there are more than three mutually exclusive alternatives. The following code template illustrates the use of this concept to choose one of four mutually exclusive Code blocks to execute:

```
if(Boolean expression 1)
{
   // One or more if clause statements in code block 1
}
else if(Boolean expression 2)
{
   // One or more if clause statements in code block 2
}
else if(Boolean expression 3)
{
   // One or more if clause statements in code block 3
}
else
```

```
{
   // One or more else clause statements in code block 4
}
```

To improve the readability, it is good programming practice to indent as shown above and to keep the first line of the `if` statements on the same line as the `else` clauses that proceeded them.

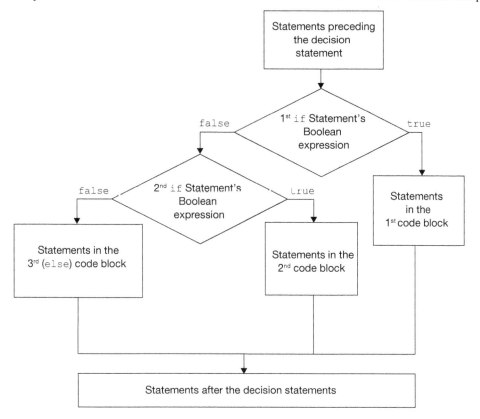

Figure 4.7
The meaning and execution path of an **if-else** statement whose **else** clause statement is an **if-else** statement.

As an example, the following code fragment determines which one of four colors, red, green, blue, or white, was contained in the `String` object `carColor`.

```
if(carColor.equals("Red"))
{
   System.out.println("the car color is Red");
}
else if(carColor.equals("Green"))
{
   System.out.println("the car color is Green");
}
else if( carColor.equals("Blue") )
{
   System.out.println("the car color is Blue");
```

```
    }
    else
    {
        System.out.println("the car color is White");
    }
```

These decision statements are executed in the sequence shown in Figure 4.8. The Boolean expressions are evaluated in the order in which they are coded. Only one of the statement blocks will execute, which will be the statement block associated with the first `true` Boolean condition. When none of the Boolean conditions are `true`, the statement block associated with the last `else` clause executes. The last `else` clause and its associated statement block are optional. When it is included, one and only one statement block in the construct always executes.

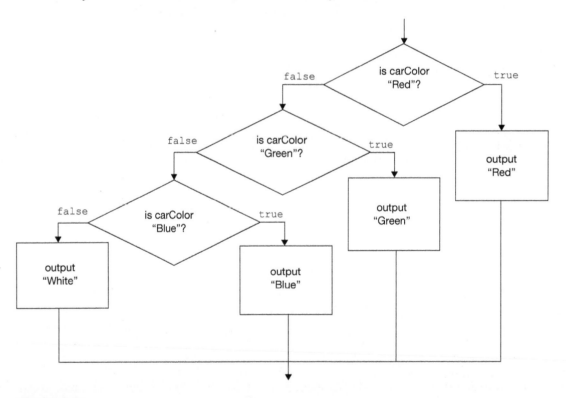

Figure 4.8
Determining the color contain in the **String** object **carColor**.

We conclude this section with a discussion of a common use of the `if-else` statement (detecting collisions between game pieces) and then present a game-programming application that utilizes this common game event.

Detecting Collisions: Use of the `if` and `else-if` Statements

Most games involve some sort of interaction between the game-piece objects. For example, the ball in a Pong game rebounds off a paddle, the frog in a Frogger game is hit by a truck, or a meteorite collides with a space craft. All of these interactions are referred to as collisions, and usually the score or the length of the game is influenced by these collisions. The Boolean conditions in an `if-else` construct are used to detect the occurrence of collisions, and the code blocks inside the construct are used to take the appropriate action (e.g., change the score or end the game) when a collision occurs.

There are several algorithms used to detect collisions, all of which involve the use of decisions statements. In one of the simplest algorithms, we imagine a rectangle enclosing each game piece. That is, the entire game piece is inscribed inside a rectangle, as shown in Figure 4.9, and the location of the upper-left corner of the rectangle is the game piece's (x, y) location. Then, we consider two objects to be in a collided state when their rectangles touch or overlap.

For example, consider the two snowmen `s1` and `s2` depicted in Figure 4.9a that are 40 pixels wide and 77 pixels high. If snowman `s2` were moving to the left, a collision with snowman `s1` would occur when the left side of `s2`'s rectangle was at the same x location as the right side of `s1`'s rectangle. This situation is depicted in Figure 4.9b. The following Boolean expression, which is true when this event occurs, can be used to detect this collision state.

```
s2.getX( ) == s1.getX + 40; // The snowmen are 40 pixels wide
```

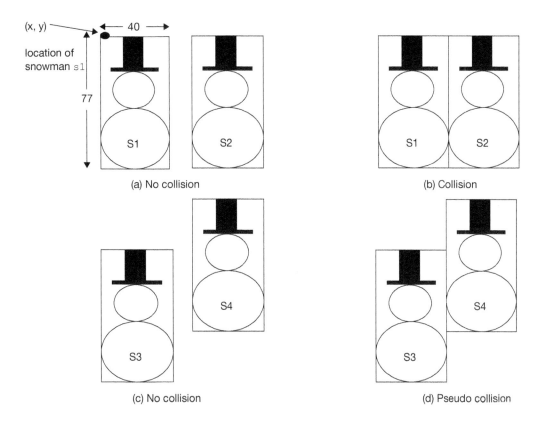

(a) No collision   (b) Collision

(c) No collision   (d) Pseudo collision

Figure 4.9
Noncollided and collided game pieces.

Although this collision detection scheme is simple, it is not always accurate. When the rectangles of the two snowmen depicted in Figure 4.9b are at the same x location, the bodies of the two snowmen are touching each other. This is not the case for the two snowmen, s3 and s4, shown in Figure 4.9c. If snowman s4 were moving to the left when the left side of its rectangle is at the same x location as the right side of s3's rectangle, as shown in Figure 4.9d, the two snowmen would not be in a collided state. There would still be a small amount of separation between the left side of s4's body and the right side of s3's head.

Fortunately, in most cases, the game's player would not notice the separation and would visually confirm this pseudo-collision as an actual collision. If we are willing to accept this limitation of our collision-detection scheme, we can extend this simple scheme to detect a collision between the two snowmen as they approach each other from any direction.

Figure 4.10 depicts snowman s2 in the following four positions relative to snowman s1:

- Position 1: s2 is to the right of s1
- Position 2: s2 is to the left of s1
- Position 3: s2 is below s1
- Position 4: s2 is above s2

When snowman s2 is in any of these positions relative to snowman s1, then the two snowmen cannot be in a collided state. In fact, s2 could be in two of these positions simultaneously, e.g., to the right and above of snowman s1, which would also be a non-collided state.

Each of the four positions depicted in Figure 4.10 can be easily detected with a simple Boolean expression. Assuming the snowman is inscribed inside a rectangle that is w pixels wide and h pixels high, the right column of Table 4.4 gives the Boolean conditions that evaluate to `true` when the snowmen are in each of the four positions.

Table 4.4
Boolean Expressions to Detect the Four Non-collided Positions in Figure 4.8

Position of Snowman s2 Relative to s1	Boolean Expression to Detect the Position
1. s2 is to the right of s1	`s2.getX( ) > s1.getX( ) + w`
2. s2 is to the left of s1	`s2.getX( ) + w < s1.getX( )`
3. s2 is below s1	`s2.getY( ) > s1.getY( ) + h`
4. s2 is above s1	`s2.getY( ) + h < s1.getY( )`

These four Boolean expressions can be used in `if-else` statements to determine when the two snowmen have not collided; otherwise they have collided.

```
if(s2.getX() > s1.getX() + w) // s2 right of s1
{
  System.out.println("no collision");
}
else if(s2.getX() + w < s1.getX()) // s2 left of s1
{
  System.out.println("no collision");
```

```
}
else if(s2.getY() > s1.getY() + h) // s2 below s1
{
   System.out.println("no collision");
}
else if(s2.getY( ) + h < s1.getY( )) // s2 above s1
{
   System.out.println("no collision");
}
else // collision
{
    System.out.println("collision");
}
```

Alternately, the Boolean conditions could be combined to form a compound Boolean condition that would evaluate to `true` for a non-collision.

```
(s2.getX( ) > s1.getX() + w || s2.getX() + w < s1.getX() ||
  s2.getY( ) > s1.getY() + h || s2.getY() + h < s1.getY())
```

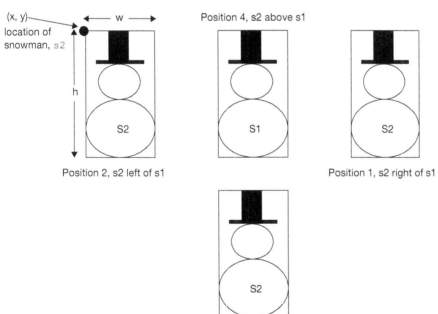

Figure 4.10
The non-collided positions of snowman **s2** relative to snowman **s1**.

Using this compound Boolean expression, the series of if-else statements to detect a colli-sion would become

```java
if(s2.getX( ) > s1.getX() + w || s2.getX() + w < s1.getX() ||
    s2.getY( ) > s1.getY() + h || s2.getY() + h < s1.getY())
{
  System.out.println("no collision");
}
    else //collision
{
  System.out.println("collision");
}
```

The truth value of the Boolean condition could also be reversed, using Java's not (!) logical operator, and the if clause of the if-else statement would detect a collision between the two snowmen.

```java
if( !(s2.getX( ) > s1.getX() + w || s2.getX() + w < s1.getX() ||
    s2.getY( ) > s1.getY() + h || s2.getY() + h < s1.getY()) )
{
  System.out.println("collision");
}
else // no collision
{
  System.out.println("no collision");
}
```

The following code fragment uses an expanded version this if-else statement's Boolean ex-pression to detect when a collision occurs and snowman s2 is in a visible state. When this occurs, the game's score (the variable score) is increased by 1, and snowman s1's visible property is set to false.

```java
if( !(s2.getX( ) > s1.getX() + w || s2.getX() + w < s1.getX()||
       s2.getY( ) > s1.getY() + h || s2.getY() + h < s1.getY()) &&
       s1.getVisible == true) // collision and s1 is visible
{
    score = score + 1;
    s1.setVisible(false);
}
```

An additional term has been added at the end of the Boolean expression. Because it is preceded by the && (AND) operator, the expanded expression is only true when the two snowmen collide *and* snowman s1 is visible. This prevents the score from increasing when a game object (i.e., s2) collides with an invisible game object that is no longer part of the game (i.e., s1).

4.5 NESTED if STATEMENTS

Just as the else clause of an if-else statement can contain an if statement, the statement block of an if statement can also contain other if statements. This method of coding is referred to as nested `if` statements, because the second `if` statement can be thought of as an egg inside the nest formed by the first `if` statement's code block.

The following code fragment contains a Boolean variable `raining` and an integer variable `temperature`, and uses a nested `if` statement to determine if a sweater and a raincoat should be carried on a cold day when it is raining.

```
if(raining == true)
{
  System.out.println("Take your umbrella, ");
  if(temperature <= 50) // begins a nested if-else statement
  {
     System.out.println("take a sweater, ");"
     System.out.println("and your raincoat.");
  }
}
```

An `if-else` statement can also be nested inside an `if` statement as demonstrated in the below code fragment:

```
if(raining == true)
{
  System.out.println("Take your umbrella, ");
  if(temperature <= 50) // begins a nested if statement
  {
     System.out.println("take a sweater, ");"
     System.out.println("and your raincoat.");
  }
  else // temperature is > 50 degrees
  {
     System.out.println("and your raincoat");
  }
}
```

The `else` clause in an `if` statement is always paired with the `if` statement whose code block ends just before the `else` clause. The indentation used in the code fragment above is considered good programming practice because it implies this pairing: the `else` clause is part of the `if` statement that checks the temperature. This code fragment is equivalent to the code fragment below, which is considered to be poor programming style because its indentation erroneously implies that the `else` clause is part of the `if` statement that determines if it is raining.

```
if(raining == true)
{
  System.out.println("Take your umbrella, ");
  if(temperature < 50) // begins a nested if statement
  {
     System.out.println("and carry your raincoat too");
  } // end of the inner if statement
else
```

```
    {
        System.out.println("but not your raincoat");
    }
  { // end of the outer if statement
```

The following code segment is another example of the use of a nested `if` statement. It is an alternate way of determining when snowmen `s1` and `s2` have collided *and* `s1` is visible.

```
if( !(s2.getX( ) > s1.getX() + w || s2.getX() + w < s1.getX()||
      s2.getY( ) > s1.getY() + h || s2.getY() + h < s1.getY()))//collision
{
    if(s1.getVisible == true) // and s1 is visible
    {
      score = score + 1;
      s1.setVisible(false);
    }
}
```

4.6 THE switch STATEMENT

The `switch` statement is another control-of-flow statement available in Java. It is not as versatile as the `if` and `if-else` statements in that the decisions these statements make cannot be based on an explicitly written simple or compound Boolean expression. The syntax of the `switch` statement limits the operator used in its decision making to equality. In addition, the equality must be between:

- two `String` objects
- two `byte`, `short`, `char`, or `int` primitive-data types (or classes that "wrap" these data types), or
- two instances of a previously defined enumerated type (which will be discussed in Chapter 7)

All uses of the `switch` statement can be coded using an `if-else` statement, but not vice-versa. That being said, there are times when the use of the `switch` statement makes our programs more readable and therefore easier to understand, modify, and maintain. It can only be used when the decision as to which statements to execute and which statements to skip is based on a choice selected from a group, or menu, of *finite* choices. When this is the case, the use of the `switch` statement is considered to be good programming practice.

The syntax of the `switch` statement is depicted in Figure 4.11. The indentation used in the figure also reflects good programming practice.

```
switch (choiceExpression)
{
  case choiceValue1:
  {
      // statement block for choiceValue1
      break;
  }
  case choiceValue2:
  {
      // statement block for choiceValue2
      break;
  }

      :
      :
  case choiceValueN:
  {
      // statement block for choiceValueN
      break;
  }
  default:
  {
      // default statements
  }
}
```

Figure 4.11
The syntax of the **switch** statement.

As shown in the figure, the first line of the statement begins with the keyword switch, and the remaining lines of the statement consist of case clauses and a default clause enclosed in a set of brackets. When typing the statement, it is best to begin by typing the following required syntax and then filling in the remainder of the statement's first line and the case and default clauses that are appropriate to the particular use of the statement.

```
switch( )
{

}
```

Referring to Figure 4.11, the three most common (and difficult to discover) syntax errors made when coding a switch statement are:

1. neglecting to code the open and close parentheses after the keyword switch
2. coding a semicolon after the close parenthesis on the first line of the statement
3. neglecting to code the colon (not semicolon) after the choiceValue1, or choiceValue2... or after the keyword default

The entity enclosed in the parentheses after the keyword switch is referred to as the *choice expression*. The choice expression must be a variable whose type is one of the allowable types previously mentioned (e.g., a `String` object, an integer variable, etc.) or it can be an expression that evaluates to one of these types.

| ```java
switch(choice)
{
   case choiceValue1:
   {
     // statements for choiceValue1
     break;
   }

   case choiceValue2:
   {
     // statements for choiceValue2
     break;
   }
        :
        :
   case choiceValueN:
   {
     // statements for choiceValueN
     break;
   }
   default
   {
     // default statements
   }
}
``` | ```java
if (choice == choiceValue1)
{
   {
       // statements for choiceValue1
   }
}
else if(choice == choiceValue2)
{
   {
       // statements for choiceValue2
   }
        :
        :
else if(choice == choiceValueN)
   {
       // statements for choiceValueN
   }
else
   {
       // default statements
   }
}
``` |
| (a) | (b) |

Figure 4.12
Semantically equivalent **switch** and **if-else** statements.

When a `switch` statement begins execution, the value of the choice expression is determined and then the statement block of the *first* case clause whose choice value is equal to that value is executed. If the choice expression is not equal to one of the choice values, the default clause's statement block executes. Figure 4.12 illustrates the meaning and execution path of a `switch` statement (Figure 4.12a) by comparing it with an equivalent `if-else` statement (Figure 4.12b).

As an example, the following code fragment determines which one of four colors, red, green, blue, or white, is contained in the `String` object `carColor`:

```java
switch (carColor)
{
  case "red":
  {
     System.out.println("the car color is red");
     break;
  }
  case "green":
```

```
    {
       System.out.println("the car color is green");
       break;
    }
    case "blue":
    {
       System.out.println("the car color is blue");
       break;
    }
    default:
    {
       System.out.println("the car color is white");
    }
}
```

The following code fragment illustrates the use of an arithmetic expression as the choice expression in a switch statement:

```
int i;
String s = JOptionPane.showInputDialog("enter an integer");
i = Integer.parseInt(i);

switch (i * 2)
{
  case 10:
  {
     System.out.println("two times the number is 10");
     break;
  }
  case 20:
  {
     System.out.println("two times the number is 20");
     break;
  }
  default:
  {
     System.out.println("two times the number is not 10 or 20");
  }
}
```

There is no limit to the number of case clauses that can be used in a switch statement. The default clause is optional and, if used, must be coded as the last clause in the statement. The brackets surrounding the statements in the case and default clauses are not necessary and are only used to improve readability.

Several cases can be assigned to the same statement block using the syntax

```
case 2: case 5: case 7:
{
  // statement block for all three cases
   break;
}
```

The previous statement block would execute when the choice expression evaluates to 2, 5, or 7.

The `break` statement at the end of the code block of each `case` is also optional. However, unlike the optional bracket pairs, its presence has a major impact on the execution path of the construct. A `break` statement is a control-of-flow statement that does not use a logical expression to decide when to execute or skip statements. Rather, when a `break` statement is executed inside a `switch` statement, it always ends the execution of the `switch` statement in which it is coded. Basically, it means: break out of this statement. It can also be used inside `if` or `if-else` statements to end their execution.

When a `break` statement inside a control-of-flow statement is executed, the next statement to execute is the one that immediately follows the control-of-flow statement. When executed inside a `switch` statement, the statement blocks in all of the subsequent `case` clauses and the statement block in the `default` clause are skipped, and the next statement to execute is the one that follows the close brace at the end of the `switch` statement. (That is, the close brace that is paired with the open brace after the keyword `switch`.)

When the `break` statement is not coded at the end of a `case` clause, after the statements in that clause execute, the statements in all subsequent case clauses execute until a `break` statement is encountered. If a `break` statement is not encountered, the `default` clause also executes. Because most times the choices coded into the `switch` construct are mutually exclusive, a `break` statement is usually coded as the last statement in each `case` clause.

Figure 4.13 shows a game application that uses the `switch` and `break` statements to change the position of a snowman on a game board, uses the `if` and `if-else` statements to determine the game's score, make a second snowman disappear and then reappear at a new location, and to determine when the game is over.

When the application is launched, two snowmen, one wearing a black hat and the other wearing a green hat, appear on the game board below the game's score and remaining time (Figure 4.14a). The game begins when the player clicks the Start button on the game board. The objective of the game is to make the two snowmen collide as many times as possible before time runs out, using the keyboard cursor control keys to move the black-hat snowman. Each time they collide, a point is awarded and the green-hat snowman disappears. It reappears at a new location after the black-hat snowman has been moved to a location such that the two snowmen are no longer in a collision state.

The game's snowmen, s1 and s2, are instances of the `BoxedSnowman` class (Figure 4.4). They are created on lines 9 and 10 of the application shown in Figure 4.13 using a three parameter constructor to specify the snowmen's position and hat color: s1 green, s2 black. Line 29 of the `draw` call back method outputs the remaining time, and line 60 outputs the player's score just before the draw method ends.

Lines 54–58 invokes the `BoxedSnowman` class's `show` method to draw the snowmen on the game board at their current (x, y) locations. The `if` statement that begins on line 55 checks the visibility status of snowman s1 to decide if it should be drawn (line 57). The initial value of a `BoxedSnowman`'s visible property is `true` (Figure 4.4, line 9), so when the game is launched, it appears on the game board.

```
1     import edu.sjcny.gpv1.*;
2     import java.awt.*;
3     //Use of decision statements
4
5     public class DecisionsControlOfFlow extends DrawableAdapter
6     {
7        static DecisionsControlOfFlow ge = new DecisionsControlOfFlow();
8        static GameBoard gb = new GameBoard(ge, "Control Of Flow");
9        static BoxedSnowman s1 = new BoxedSnowman(300, 200, Color.GREEN);
10       static BoxedSnowman s2 = new BoxedSnowman(30, 100, Color.BLACK);
11       static int score = 0;
12       static int count = 10;
13
14       public static void main(String[] args)
15       {
16          showGameBoard(gb);
17       }
18
19       public void draw(Graphics g) //call back method
20       {
21          int w = 40;
22          int h = 77;
23          int s1X, s1Y, s2X, s2Y, temp;
24
25          s1X = s1.getX(); s1Y = s1.getY();
26          s2X = s2.getX(); s2Y = s2.getY();
27          g.setColor(Color.BLACK);
28          g.setFont(new Font("Arial", Font.BOLD, 18));
29          g.drawString("Time remaining: " + count, 260, 50);
30
31          if(count == 0) //game over
32          {
33             g.setColor(Color.BLACK);
34             g.drawString("Game Over", 205, 70);
35             g.drawString("Have a Good Day", 175, 90);
36          }
37          else if( !(s2X > s1X + w || s2X + w < s1X || s2Y > s1Y + h ||
38               s2Y + h < s1Y) && s1.getVisible() == true) // collision
39          {
40             score = score + 1;
41             s1.setVisible(false);
42          }
43          else if( s2X > s1X + w || s2X + w < s1X || s2Y > s1Y + h ||
44               s2Y + h < s1Y) // no collision
45          {
46             if(s1.getVisible() == false) // not visible
47             {  temp = s1.getX();
48                s1.setX(s1.getY());
49                s1.setY(temp);
```

```
50                    s1.setVisible(true);
51              }
52          }
53
54          s2.show(g);
55          if(s1.getVisible() == true)
56          {
57              s1.show(g);
58          }
59          g.setColor(Color.BLACK);
60          g.drawString("Score: " + score, 150, 50);
61      }
62
63      public void keyStruck(char key) // call back method
64      {
65          int newX, newY;
66
67          switch (key)
68          {
69              case 'L':
70              {
71                  newX = s2.getX() - 2;
72                  s2.setX(newX);
73                  break;
74              }
75              case 'R':
76              {
77                  newX = s2.getX() + 2;
78                  s2.setX(newX);
79                  break;
80              }
81              case 'U':
82              {
83                  newY = s2.getY() - 2;
84                  s2.setY(newY);
85                  break;
86              }
87              case 'D':
88              {
89                  newY = s2.getY() + 2;
90                  s2.setY(newY);
91              }
92          } // end of switch statement
93      }
94      public void timer1() // call back method
95      {
96          count = count - 1;
97          if(count == 0)
```

```
98              {
99                  gb.stopTimer(1);
100             }
101         }
102 }
```

Figure 4.13
The **DecisionsControlOfFlow** application: A decision statement case study.

The use of a switch statement is illustrated on lines 67–92. In this case, the switch statement is used to determine which of the four cursor-control keyboard keys was struck to move the snowman s2 two pixels from its current location. The statement is coded inside the game environment's call back method keyStruck (line 63), which is invoked by the game environment every time a keyboard key is struck. The method has one parameter named key whose type is char, and the game environment passes a character, the key that was struck, into it. After keyStruck completes its execution, the game environment invokes the draw call back method.

The parameter key on line 63 is used as the switch statement's choice expression on line 67. When the keyboard left, right, up, or down cursor-control keys are struck, they generate the characters 'L', 'R', 'U', or 'D', respectively. These characters are used as the switch statement's cases on lines 69, 75, 81, and 87 to decide in which direction to move snowman s2.

When a key on the keyboard is held down, it transmits characters 20 times a second just as if the key was being pressed and released 20 times a second. For this reason, to control the motion of game pieces, key strokes are preferred over button clicks.

Figure 4.14b shows the game board three seconds after the Start button was clicked and the right and down cursor keys were used to move snowman s2 adjacent to snowman s1. One more right cursor keystroke will cause a collision.

Line 31 begins an if-else statement that contains a nested if-else statement (line 37) and two nested if statements (lines 43 and 46). The keyword else that appears on lines 37 and 43 are part of the if-else statements that begin on lines 31 and 37, respectively. Line 31 decides if the game is over, and when it is, it announces it to the game's player.

The if-else statement that begins on line 37 decides if the two snowmen have collided when snowman s2 is visible. Its Boolean expression, as discussed at the end of Section 4.4, is true when it is not the case that snowman s2 is to the right, to the left, or below or above snowman s1, and s1 is visible. When this is the case, the if clause's code block increases the player's score by one point using the counting algorithm (line 40) and sets the visible property of snowman s1 to false (line 41). Setting s1's visible property to false causes it to disappear from the game board (Figure 4.14c) because the Boolean condition in the if statement that draws s1 (line 55) is now false. The setting of s1's visible property to false also prevents the awarding of points until s1 is again visible which occurs when the two snowmen are no longer in a collision state. The determination that the two snowmen are no longer in a collision state is performed by the if statement on line 43. Its Boolean condition is the same as the condition on lines 37 and 38, except that the NOT (!) operator and the test for visible have been removed. This Boolean condition is `true` when the snowmen are not in a collision state. Then the nested `if` statement that begins on line 46 executes and decides if snowman `s1` is invisible. When it is invisible, the nested `if` statement's code block executes relocating snowman `s1` by swapping its x and y coordinates. This code block also sets `s1`'s `visible` property to `true` (line 50), which causes the `if` statement that begins on line 55 to draw snowman `s1` on the game board at its new location (Figure 4.14d).

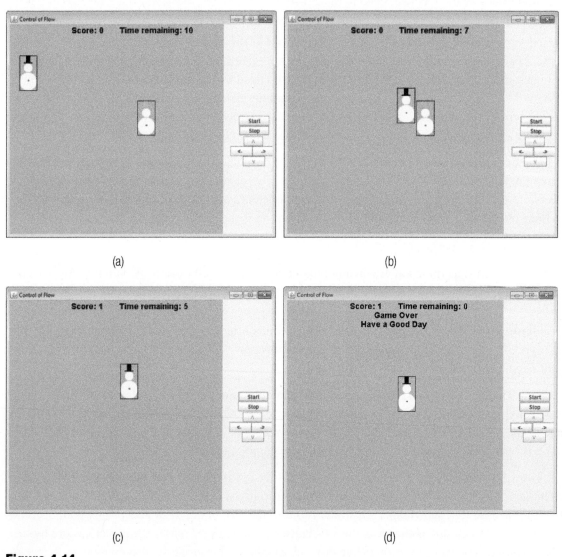

(a)

(b)

(c)

(d)

Figure 4.14
The output of the **DecisionsControlOfFlow** application.

4.7 CONSOLE INPUT AND THE Scanner CLASS

We have already learned how to perform input and output using message dialog boxes and how to send output to the system console using the `println` method. The system console can also be used to perform keyboard input using methods in the `Scanner` class. These nonstatic methods can also be used to perform input from a disk file, which will be discussed in the next section.

Just as there is a predefined output object attached to the system console, `System.out`, there is a predefined input object attached to the console, `System.in`. However, before we use the input methods in the `Scanner` class we have to declare a `Scanner` object and pass the console object to the `Scanner` class's one-parameter constructor. The following code fragment declares the `Scanner` object `consoleIn`:

```
Scanner consoleIn = new Scanner(System.in);
```

The `Scanner` object, `consoleIn`, can then be used to invoke non-void methods in the `Scanner` class, which accept input from the system console. As the user types the input, the keystrokes are output to the console. The names of the three most frequently used methods in this class all begin with the word next. Their full names and the type of data they return are given in Table 4.5. To use the methods, include the following import statement in your program:

```
import java.util.Scanner;
```

Table 4.5
Commonly Used Input Methods in the **Scanner** Class

Method Name	Returned Type
nextInt	int
nextDouble	double
nextLine	String

As their names imply, `nextInt` and `nextDouble` are both used to accept numeric input. When the input is an integer, `nextInt` is used, and `nextDouble` is used when the input is a real number. Both methods parse the input characters into a numeric value, and so there is no need to use the parsing methods in the wrapper classes `Integer` and `Double`. The method `nextLine` is used to accept `String` input.

When these methods are invoked, the program's execution is suspended until the user completes the keyboard input by striking the Enter key. Then, the methods return the input value. Until that point, the user can edit the input using the Backspace and Delete keys. It is good programming practice to precede the method invocations with a well-composed prompt output to the system console. The following code fragment accepts a person's name, age, and weight entered into the system console:

```
Scanner consoleIn = new Scanner(System.in);
String name;
int age;
double weight;
```

```
System.out.print("Enter your name: ");
name = consoleIn.nextLine();

System.out.print("\nEnter your age: ");
age = consoleIn.nextInt();

System.out.print("\nEnter your weight: ");
weight = consoleIn.nextDouble();
```

Several numeric inputs can be entered on one line as long as they are separated (delimited) by at least one space. Spaces that precede a numeric input are ignored. The following code segment accepts a person's age and weight input on one line to the system console.

```
int age;
double weight;
Scanner consoleIn = new Scanner(System.in);

System.out.print ("Enter your age and weight on one line " +
    "separated by at least one space: ");
age = consoleIn.nextInt();
weight = consoleIn.nextDouble();
```

 Several numeric inputs, separated by at least one space, can be input on the same line.

Spaces that precede a string input are not ignored. They are considered, and become, part of the input string. Spaces typed after a numeric input will become part of a string input subsequently read from the same line. For this reason, strings should not be input on the same line as numeric inputs.

 Numeric and string inputs should not be input on the same line.

When a numeric input and a string are read from two separate input lines, and the numeric input precedes the string, two invocations of nextLine are required to capture the string. This is because numeric inputs leave the character generated by the Enter key "behind," and the nextLine method considers this a valid input string (the empty string ""). The following statements accept a person's age, followed by the person's name and address. The first string input is properly preceded by an additional invocation of the nextLine method.

```
Scanner consoleIn = new Scanner(System.in);
int age;
String name;
String address;

System.out.print("\nEnter your age: ");
age = consoleIn.nextInt();
```

```
consoleIn.nextLine(); // clears the enter keystroke left behind
System.out.print("Enter your name: ");
name = consoleIn.nextLine();

System.out.print("Enter your address: ");
address = consoleIn.nextLine();
```

To fully understand Scanner class input, we must recognize that the characters the user types are transferred to a memory resident storage area called an input *buffer*. When a Scanner method is invoked and the buffer is empty, the method pauses until an Enter key is struck. If the buffer is not empty, the method accepts an input from the buffer, and then the input is deleted from the buffer. The nextLine method also deletes the Enter keystroke from the buffer; however, Scanner methods that return numeric values do not remove this character from the buffer.

When reading numeric inputs, this is not a problem because the numeric input methods not only skip leading spaces in the buffer, they also skip the Enter keystroke. This whitespace is ignored until the buffer is empty or they find an input to process. However, the newline method does not skip the Enter keystroke. As a result, when an invocation to nextLine follows a numeric input it encounters a nonempty buffer containing an Enter keystroke. The nextLine method reads and removes the Enter keystroke from the buffer and returns the empty string ("").

___
NOTE

When reading a string from the console after a numeric input, two invocations of the newLine method are required to read the string. The first invocation flushes the new line (empty string) from the buffer.

Figure 4.15 presents an application that demonstrates the use of the Scanner class's methods to accept input from the system console. The console inputs and corresponding outputs are given at the bottom of the figure.

Line 1 imports the Scanner class's methods into the application, and line 6 uses the Scanner class's one-parameter constructor to create the object consoleIn passing it the predefined console input object System.in. Lines 11–16 accept a string, integer, and a double from the system console, each input on a separate line. These values are output on lines 17–18.

Lines 20-25 change the order of the inputs beginning with two numeric inputs on the same console line (lines 20–22). Then, a string is input (lines 23–25). Line 24 clears the Enter keystroke left in the buffer after the second numeric is read (line 22). Lines 26–27 outputs the second set of inputs. Referring to the bottom of Figure 4.15, the user entered several spaces between the input age, 5, and the input weight, 35. These spaces were ignored by the nextDouble method invoked on line 22. The weight output (35.4) on the last line of the figure confirms this.

```
1    import java.util.Scanner;
2    public class ScannerConsoleInput
3    {
4       public static void main(String[] args)
5       {
```

```
6       Scanner consoleIn = new Scanner(System.in);
7       String name;
8       int age;
9       double weight;
10
11      System.out.print("Enter your name: ");
12      name = consoleIn.nextLine();
13      System.out.print("Enter your age: ");
14      age = consoleIn.nextInt();
15      System.out.print("Enter your weight: ");
16      weight = consoleIn.nextDouble();
17      System.out.println("Age: " + age + " Weight: " + weight +
18                          " Name: " + name);
19
20      System.out.print("\nEnter your age and weight on one line: ");
21      age = consoleIn.nextInt();
22      weight = consoleIn.nextDouble();
23      System.out.print("Enter your name: ");
24      consoleIn.nextLine(); // clears the enter keystroke from buffer
25      name = consoleIn.nextLine();
26      System.out.println("Age: " + age + " Weight: " + weight +
27                          " Name: " + name);
28   }
29   }
```

Console inputs and outputs:
Enter your name: Breanne
Enter your age: 18
Enter your weight: 125.7
Age: 18 Weight: 125.7 Name: Breanne

Enter your age and weight on one line: 5   35.4
Enter your name: Nora
Age: 5 Weight: 35.4 Name: Nora

Figure 4.15
The application **ScannerConsoleInput** followed by sample inputs and the corresponding outputs.

4.8 DISK INPUT AND OUTPUT: A FIRST LOOK

Unlike RAM memory, disk storage is nonvolatile, which means it retains the information stored on it when the computer system is powered down. As a result, it is used to archive data and program instructions. There are two types of disk files: text files and binary files. Information stored in binary files normally occupies less storage on the disk, and the information transfer is faster. That being said, text files are in wide use because all of the information in the file is stored as ASCII characters, which means it can be opened, read, modified, and restored using any text editor.

In this section, we will limit our discussion of disk file I/O to text files and the techniques for accessing the file's data items in the order in which they appear in the file. This type of access is called sequential access. The alternate form of access, called random *access*, allows the data items to be accessed in any order. We will extend our discussion of disk I/O in subsequent chapters.

4.8.1 Sequential Text File Input

Information stored in a text file can be sequentially read into a program using the Scanner class's methods presented in Table 4.5. In fact, all of the concepts discussed in Section 4.7 used to read or input data from the system console apply to sequential text file input. The one exception is the creation of the Scanner object.

To accept input from the system console, the object was created by passing the predefined object System.in to the Scanner class's one-parameter constructor. To accept input from a sequential text file, a File object is passed to the Scanner class's one-parameter constructor. This File object is created using the File class's one-parameter constructor that accepts a string argument containing the file's path and name. Case sensitivity in this string is ignored. The import statement import java.io.*; is used to access the File class.

The code fragment presented in Figure 4.16 reads an integer from the beginning of the file named data.txt resident on the root of the C drive.

```
1    File fileObject = new File("c:/data.txt");
2    Scanner fileIn = new Scanner(fileObject);
3    int score;
4
5    score = fileIn.nextInt();
```

Figure 4.16
Code fragment to read an integer from the disk file **data.txt** resident on the root of the C drive.

The string argument sent to the File class's constructor (on line 1 of Figure 4.16) contains a forward slash, which is preferred over the backslash for two reasons. First, all operating systems accept a forward slash in a path definition. Second, to use a backslash the escape sequence for a backslash (\\) would have to be used inside the string argument. Most Windows-friendly programmers often forget to code the escape sequence and code the string argument as "c:\data.txt". This would result in a translation error: illegal escape character, because \d is not a valid escape sequence.

A more insidious error occurs when a single backslash is erroneously coded, and the character that comes after it is a valid escape character. For example, if the file name was newData.txt, and it was located on the root of the C drive, the following line of code would not result in a translation error on a Windows system because \n is a valid escape sequence.

```
File fileObject = new File("c:\newData.txt");
```

However, it would result in a runtime error indicating that the file does not exist because the \n would be replaced at compile time with a new line or line feed (LF) character, and the name of the file passed to the constructor would be the LF character followed by ewData.txt.

 Always use forward slashes (/) when specifying a file path.

Even when the forward slash is used to specify the path to the file, the file must exist or a runtime error indicating that the file does not exist will occur. If the path is not specified (i.e., just the file name and its extension is coded), the file is assumed to be inside the project folder created by the IDE or a subfolder of that folder. The exact location may be IDE-specific.

Except for lines 1 and 2 of Figure 4.16, the code used to read data from a text file is the same as the code used to read data from the system console, except that no prompts are output. We simply imagine that instead of the user typing the data into the system console in response to input prompts, the same data (character for character, line for line) was typed into a text editor and then saved to the disk file.

For example, if a person's age, weight, and name were typed into the C-drive resident text file data.txt whose contents are shown in Figure 4.17, then the code fragment presented in Figure 4.18 would read these values from the disk file. With the exception of lines 1 and 2, Figure 4.18 contains the same code used to read an age, weight, and name from the system console (lines 7–9 and 20–25 of Figure 4.15) with the two user prompts (lines 20 and 23) removed and the name of the Scanner object changed.

```
5      35.4
Nora
```

Figure 4.17
The data contained in the disk file **data.txt** resident on the root of the C drive.

```
1    File fileObject = new File("c:/data.txt");
2    Scanner fileIn = new Scanner(fileObject);
3    String name;
4    int age;
5    double weight;
6
7    age = fileIn.nextInt();
8    weight = fileIn.nextDouble();
9    fileIn.nextLine();
10   name = fileIn.nextLine();
```

Figure 4.18
The code fragment to read the data contained in the file shown in Figure 4.17.

To process a sequential file, Java maintains a read position pointer that is initially positioned at the first character in the file. Each time a data item is read from the file, this pointer is moved to the next item in the file. After the last item in the file has been read, the pointer is positioned at a special character called an end of file (EOF), which is automatically placed at the end of all disk files. In Chapter 5, we will discuss the importance of the addition of the EOF character to the file and how to detect when we have reached it.

There are some additional issues to consider when reading data from a text file that do not arise when performing console input. These include the need to know:

- the name and the path to the file to declare the `File` object (line 1 of Figure 4.18)
- the order of the information in the file, so the statements on lines 7, 8, 9, and 10 of Figure 4.18 are coded in the proper sequence
- the type of each piece of information in the file, so the proper `Scanner` class method can be invoked to read each piece of information

This information is described in a file specification given to the programmer by the software engineer who designed the file.

4.8.2 Determining the Existence of a File

Another issue to consider when reading data from a text file that does not arise when performing console input is how to prevent a runtime error if the data file does not exist. The `File` class contains a non-void method named `exists` that can be used to detect the existence of a file, and the `System` class contains a static method named `exit` that can be used to end a program.

The `exists` method in the `File` class returns `true` when the file exists, and the `exit` method in the `System` class has one integer parameter, which is usually passed a zero. The following code segment demonstrates the use of these two methods to bring a program to a more informative user-friendly ending when it tries to use a disk file that does not exist:

```
File fileObject = new File("c:/data.txt");



if(!fileObject.exists()) // file does not exist
{
  System.out.println("the file does not exist, the program is terminating")
  System.exit(0);
}
```

 It is good programming practice to check for a disk file's existence to avoid a runtime error that is normally difficult for the user to understand.

4.8.3 Sequential Text File Output

Information can be sequentially output (written) to a text file using the `print` and `println` methods that are used to write information to the system console. In addition, the Java syntax used to format console output data, such as the spacing of the output information, moving to a new line, and specifying the precision of numeric outputs, is the same syntax used to format disk-file output. The one exception to this is the output annotation.

Output annotation is normally not included in the string sent to the methods and `print` and `println` when writing to a disk file because most disk files are read by programs, not people. When the file's data will not be processed or read by a program (perhaps the file's contents will be examined after it is printed), output annotation is included. Alternately, the reader could refer to the file's specification to identify unannotated file information.

To write to the system console, the `print` and `println` methods operate on a predefined object `System.out` attached to the system console. To write to a sequential text file, these methods operate on a programmer-defined object in the `PrintWriter` class. This object is created using two lines of code that are analogous to the two lines used to create the `Scanner` object used to perform disk input.

The `PrintWriter` object is created using the class's two-parameter constructor, which is passed to an object in the `FileWriter` class. The file's path and name is passed to the `FileWriter` object when it is created. Case sensitivity in this string is ignored. The import statement `import java.io.*;` is used to access the `PrintWriter` and the `FileWriter` classes.

The code fragment presented in Figure 4.19 creates a sequential text file named `data.txt` on the root of the C drive and then outputs the contents of the variable `score` followed by a new-line character to the beginning of the file.

```
1    FileWriter fileWriterObject = new FileWriter("c:/data.txt");
2    PrintWriter fileOut = new PrintWriter(fileWriterObject, false);
3    int score = 20;
4
5    fileOut.println(score);
```

Figure 4.19
Code fragment to write an integer to the beginning of the disk file **data.txt** resident on the root of the C drive.

Lines 1 and 2 of Figure 4.19 create the disk file and the object `fileOut` that is used to invoke the `println` method on line 5. A generic term used to describe the functionality of these two lines is that they create and open the file. If the file had already existed, it would have been deleted and then recreated. All the information previously written to a deleted file is lost.

Data written to a text file using the `print` and `println` methods should be thought of as being placed in the file exactly as the data would have appeared on the system console (line for line, character for character) had the methods operated on `System.out`. The only exception is that a new-line character does not appear on the system console. Rather, it causes the cursor to move to the beginning of the next line. The characters of the first data item are followed in the file by the characters of the second item, which are followed by the third, etc.

Figure 4.20 presents an application that writes a person's age, weight, and name to a sequential text file named `data.txt` and then reads the data from the file and outputs the information to the system console. The system console output produced by the program is shown at the end of the figure, and the characters written to the disk file are shown in Figure 4.21.

Lines 1 and 2 of Figure 4.20 make the `Scanner`, `File`, `FileWriter`, and `PrintWriter` classes available to the program. Their constructors are used on lines 8–12 to create objects `fileIn` and `fileOut`, which are used on lines 18–19 and lines 23–26, respectively, to write to and read from the file.

```
1     import java.util.Scanner;
2     import java.io.*;
3
4     public class DiskIO
5     {
6       public static void main(String[] args) throws IOException
7       {
8         File fileObject = new File("data.txt"); // input
9         Scanner fileIn = new Scanner(fileObject);
10        FileWriter fileWriterObject = new FileWriter("data.txt"); // output
11        PrintWriter fileOut = new PrintWriter(fileWriterObject, false);
12
13        String name = "Nora Smith";
14        int age = 5;
15        double weight = 35.4;
16
17        // write three data items to the disk file
18        fileOut.println(age + " " + weight);
19        fileOut.println(name);
20        fileOut.close();
21
22        //read the data from the disk file
23        age = fileIn.nextInt();
24        weight = fileIn.nextDouble();
25        fileIn.nextLine(); // clears New Line after a numeric from the buffer
26        name = fileIn.nextLine();
27        fileIn.close();
28
29        System.out.println("Age: " + age + " Weight: " + weight +
30                           " Name: " + name);
31      }
32    }
```

System console output
Age: 5 Weight: 35.4 Name: Nora Smith

Figure 4.20
The application **DiskIO** and the console output it produces.

> 5 35.4**n**^{l}Nora Smithn^l**e**^{of}
> **n**^{l} represents a new-line character
> **e**^{of} represents an end of file (EOF) character

Figure 4.21
The characters output to the file data.txt by the application **DiskIO**.

A `throws` clause has been added to the end of the signature of the main method (line 6). This tells the translator that the programmer is aware that some serious runtime problems (e.g., an attempt was made to read past the EOF character) could develop during the execution of the program. However, the programmer has chosen not to include code to deal with those problems. Without the throws clause, this program will not translate. We will discuss the code to deal with these problems in the next section of this chapter.

The string containing the name of the file on lines 8 and 10 does not contain a path. Therefore, the file is created inside the project folder created by the IDE. This is not always desirable but is often used in game programs because the file contains information about the game, such as the highest score achieved to date.

Line 18 writes two numbers to the file separated by a space as shown in Figure 4.21. The space is a very important part of the output. Without it, Nora's age (5) and her weight (35.4) would be adjacent to each other and would therefore be considered one number (534.4) by anyone reading the file including line 23 of the program. The result would be one of the serious runtime errors the programmer chose to ignore because a double, 534.4, cannot be parsed into the integer variable age.

Lines 20 and 27 invoke the `close` method in the `FileWriter` and `Scanner` classes. These statements release the system resources required to perform disk I/O. If they are not included in a program that performs disk input and/or output, the Java Runtime Environment releases the resources when the program ends. It is not only good programming practice to code them immediately after the last disk I/O statements, but in this program it is essential that line 20 be part of the program.

Here's why: During the execution of a program that writes to a disk file, the data is actually written to a RAM resident buffer. The characters stored in the buffer are written to the disk file when the buffer is full or the `FileWriter`'s `close` method is executed. This method flushes a partially full buffer to the disk file during the program's execution. Because the number of characters written by this program does not fill the buffer, eliminating line 20 from the program presents line 23 with an empty disk file from which to read. This situation causes the program to terminate in a runtime error.

When the `FileWriter` class's `close` method executes an end of file (EOF) character is added to the end of the file.

NOTE

Always invoke the `FileWriter` *class's* `close` *method after the last file output statement.*
Always invoke the `Scanner`*'s class's* `close` *method after the last file input statement.*

4.8.4 Appending Data to an Existing Text File

Data can be appended (added to the end) of a disk file by changing the second argument sent to the `PrintWriter`'s two-parameter constructor from `false` to `true`. For example, line 11 of Figure 4.20 to would be changed to:

```
PrintWriter fileOut = new PrintWriter(fileWriterObject, true);
```

When the program is run, if the file does exist it would not be deleted. (If it does not exist, it would be created.) Each execution of the program would add data to the end of the file followed by an EOF character. Figure 4.22 shows the contents of the file after three executions of the program, assuming the file did not exist before the program's first execution and the value `true` was passed to the `PrintWriter` constructor.

---

5 35.4**n**^{l}Nora Smith**n**^{l}5 35.4**n**^{l}Nora Smith**n**^{l}5 35.4**n**^{l}Nora Smith**n**^{l}**e**^{of}

n^l represents a new-line character

e^{of} represents an EOF character

Figure 4.22
The output by 3 executions of **DiskIO** with the file open for append.

4.8.5 Deleting, Modifying, and Adding File Data Items

Java, like most programming languages, does not contain a method to delete or modify a file data item or add a data item anywhere in the file except at its end. These operations can be accomplished by including the disk I/O methods discussed in this chapter in algorithms that perform these tasks. For example, the delete algorithm would be:

1. Read all of the file's information into RAM memory
2. Close the file
3. Delete the file
4. Recreate the file
5. Write all of the information except the item to be deleted back into to the file
6. Close the file

Because the coding of these algorithms requires knowledge of the material covered in Chapters 5 and 6, we will return to this topic in Chapter 6.

4.9 EXCEPTIONS: A FIRST PASS

An exception is a Java feature that a method can use to communicate to its invoker that an unexpected event has occurred during the method's execution when the method does not contain code to deal with it. When the event is one that Java deems serious, a `throws` clause must be added to the signature of the method in which the invocation is coded, or instructions to deal with the event must be added to the code block that contains the invocation statement.

The former approach was taken in the program that appears in Figure 4.20 on line 6. The `Scanner` and `FileWriter` class constructors invoked on lines 9 and 10 are methods that can encounter serious unexpected events during their execution. Therefore, a `throws` clause was added to the signature of the main method (line 6) because the main method contains these two invocations. In this section, we will cover a brief introduction to the alternative to the `throws` clause: adding instructions to deal with the event in the code block that contains the invocation statements. Chapter 10, "Exceptions, A Second Pass" contains a more in-depth discussion of exceptions.

As the word "throws" implies, a baseball analogy was used in the selection of the Java keywords associated with exceptions, and the analogy is helpful in gaining an understanding of exceptions. Imagine that when the serious event occurs during a method's execution the method says, "I take *exception* to that event, and I am not going to continue executing. My last action will be to let my invoker know of this problem by *throwing* an exception object back to it."

If the invoker wants to deal with the problem, its code block *catches* the exception object and deals with the problem. Otherwise it *throws* the exception object on to the Java Runtime Environment. The term `throws` is a Java keyword we have already used (line 6 of Figure 4.20) when we did not want to deal with an unexpected problem. Two other keywords, `try` and `catch`, are used when we want to deal with the problem.

Each of these keywords begins a code block, and the `try` code block is always coded immediately before the `catch` code block. The following code fragment is a template for a `try` statement that will catch a thrown `IOException` object. As shown in the template, the type of exception object caught is coded in a parameter list after the keyword `catch`.

```
try
{
  // the code containing the method invocations and other statements
}
catch(IOException e)
{
  // the statements to deal with the unexpected events
}
```

The statements that invoked the methods that could throw the exception object must be coded inside the `try` block. Other statements can be included in the `try` block. Effectively, you are trying these invocation statements to see if the methods they invoke throw an exception object.

When an exception object is thrown by a method invoked inside the `try` block, the remainder of the statements in the `try` block does not execute, and execution passes to the first statement in the `catch` block. If an exception is not thrown, the statements in the `try` block complete their execution, and the `catch` block statements are not executed. In either case, the statements following the `catch` code block executes after the `try` block or the `catch` block completes execution.

The use of the template is illustrated in the following code fragment. It attempts to read the value stored in a disk file into the variable `score` and catches the `IOException` object thrown by the `Scanner` class's constructor when this constructor encounters a problem.

```
int score;
try
{
  File fileObject = new File("data.txt"); // input
  Scanner fileIn = new Scanner(fileObject);

  score = fileIn.nextInt();
  fileIn.close();
}
catch(IOException e)
{
  System.out.print ("The score could not be read from the disk file,");
  System.out.println(" but the game will continue.");
}
//rest of the game's statements
```

If the reading of the score was essential to the continuation of the program, the second statement in the `catch` block would be replaced with the following two statements to terminate the program's execution:

```
System.out.println(" the program is terminating.");
System.exit(0);
```

The program in Figure 4.23 illustrates the use of disk input and output in a game program and the use of exceptions to deal with unexpected disk I/O problems. It is the same program presented in Figure 4.13, modified to keep track of the highest game score ever achieved. When the game is over, this score is read from a disk file. If a new high score was not achieved, the game player is informed and encouraged to keep practicing. Otherwise, the new high score is written to the disk file and the game player is congratulated.

```
1    import edu.sjcny.gpv1.*;
2    import java.awt.*;
3    import java.util.Scanner;
4    import java.io.*;
5    //illstrates basic exceptions
6
7    public class ExceptionBasics extends DrawableAdapter
8    {
9      static ExceptionBasics ge = new ExceptionBasics ();
10     static GameBoard gb = new GameBoard(ge, "Exception Basics");
11     static BoxedSnowman s1 = new BoxedSnowman(300, 200, Color.GREEN);
12     static BoxedSnowman s2 = new BoxedSnowman(30, 100, Color.BLACK);
13     static int score = 0;
14     static int count = 10;
15
16     public static void main(String[] args)
17     {
18       showGameBoard(gb);
19     }
```

```
20
21    public void draw(Graphics g) // a call back method
22    {
23      int w = 40;
24      int h = 77;
25      int s1X, s1Y, s2X, s2Y, temp;
26
27      s1X = s1.getX(); s1Y = s1.getY();
28      s2X = s2.getX(); s2Y = s2.getY();
29      g.setColor(Color.BLACK);
30      g.setFont(new Font("Arial", Font.BOLD, 18));
31      g.drawString("Time remaining: " + count, 260, 50);
32
33      if(count == 0) // the game is over
34      {
35        g.setColor(Color.BLACK);
36        g.drawString("Game Over", 205, 70);
37        g.drawString("Have a Good Day", 175, 90);
38
39        try
40        {
41          int highScore;
42          File fileObj = new File("HiScore.txt");
43          Scanner fileIn = new Scanner(fileObj);
44          highScore = fileIn.nextInt();
45          fileIn.close();
46
47          if(score >= highScore) // a new high score
48          {
49            g.drawString("Great, Your Score is the Highest Ever.," +
50                         "It Will Be Saved", 10, 110);
51            FileWriter fileWriterObj = new FileWriter("HiScore.txt");
52            PrintWriter fileOut = new PrintWriter(fileWriterObj, false);
53
54            fileOut.println(score);
55            fileOut.close();
56          }
57          else // not a new high score
58          {
59            g.drawString("Best Score is: " + highScore +
60                         ", Keep Practicing", 110, 110);
61          }
62        }
63        catch(IOException e)
64        {
65          g.drawString("Problems With High Score File", 120, 110);
66        }
67      }
```

```
68        else if( !(s2X > s1X + w || s2X + w < s1X || s2Y > s1Y + h ||
69                    s2Y + h < s1Y) && s1.getVisible() == true)
70        {
71          score = score + 1;
72          s1.setVisible(false);
73        }
74        else if( s2X > s1X + w || s2X + w < s1X || s2Y > s1Y + h ||
75                 s2Y + h < s1Y) // no collision
76        {
77          if(s1.getVisible() == false) // not visible
78          {  temp = s1.getX();
79             s1.setX(s1.getY());
80             s1.setY(temp);
81             s1.setVisible(true);
82          }
83        }
84
85        s2.show(g);
86        if(s1.getVisible() == true)
87        {
88          s1.show(g);
89        }
90          g.setColor(Color.BLACK);
91          g.drawString("Score: " + score, 150, 50);
92      }
93
94      public void keyStruck(char key) // a call back method
95      {
96        int newX, newY;
97
98        switch (key)
99        {
100         case 'L':
101         {
102           newX = s2.getX() - 2;
103           s2.setX(newX);
104           break;
105         }
106         case 'R':
107         {
108           newX = s2.getX() + 2;
109           s2.setX(newX);
110           break;
111         }
112         case 'U':
113         {
114           newY = s2.getY() - 2;
115           s2.setY(newY);
116           break;
```

```
117            }
118         case 'D':
119         {
120            newY = s2.getY() + 2;
121            s2.setY(newY);
122         }
123      }
124   }
125   public void timer1() // a call back method
126   {
127      count = count - 1;
128      if(count == 0)
129      {
130         gb.stopTimer(1);
131      }
132   }
133 }
```

Figure 4.23
The **ExceptionBasics** Application: A decision and exceptions case study.

When the application is launched, two snowmen, one wearing a black hat and the other wearing a green hat, appear on the game board below the game's score and remaining time (Figure 4.24a). The game begins when the player clicks the Start button on the game board. The objective of the game is to make the two snowmen collide as many times as possible before time runs out using the keyboard cursor-control keys to move the black-hat snowman. Each time they collide, a point is awarded, and the green-hat snowman disappears. It reappears at a new location after the black-hat snowman has been moved to a location such that the two snowmen are no longer in a collision state.

The changes to the program are the additions of the lines 3–4 that make the Scanner, File, FileWriter, and PrintWriter classes needed to perform disk I/O available to the program, the elimination of the throws clause in the main method's signature and the addition of lines 40–67 that perform the disk I/O. Figure 4.24 presents several outputs produced by the program under various game conditions.

The signature of the main method (line 16) does not contain a throws clause because the disk I/O is performed inside the code block of a try statement (line 39). Line 44 reads the highest score ever achieved from the disk file HiScore.txt using the Scanner object inFile created by lines 42–43. Then, the file is closed (line 45). Normally, the programmer would use a text editor to create the file and store a score of zero in it as part of the program's development. Because the file's path is not specified on line 42, the file must be stored inside the project folder created by the IDE.

When a new high score is achieved, as determined by line 47, line 49–50 informs the game player of this achievement (Figure 4.24b). The new high score is written to the disk file (line 54) using the PrintWriter object fileOut created on lines 51–52, and the file is closed (line 55). Because the second argument sent to the PrintWriter constructor on line 52 is false, the file containing the old high score is deleted and recreated before the new high score is written to it. (The new high score is not appended to the file.)

When a new high score is not achieved, lines 59–60 of the `if-else` statement that begins in line 47 produces the output shown in Figure 4.24c. If a problem occurs during the disk I/O performed inside of the `try` block, execution of the `try` block is terminated, and the `catch` block (lines 63–66) executes producing the error message at the end of the text output shown in Figure 4.24d.

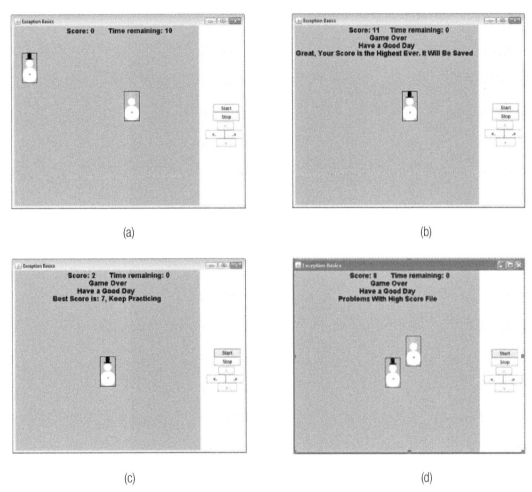

(a)   (b)

(c)   (d)

Figure 4.24
Outputs produced by the application **ExceptionBasics**.

4.10 CHAPTER SUMMARY

Ordinarily, a Java program executes its statements sequentially. The `if`, `if-else`, and `switch` statements are used to alter this sequential path of execution by selecting which statement, or group of statements, to execute next. When the resulting decision of an `if` or `if-else` construct effect more than one statement, these statements must be coded inside a code block.

Both the `if` and `if-else` statements evaluate Boolean expressions to determine whether to execute or skip the statements included in their code blocks. Boolean expressions use the logical and relational operators (all of which have a precedence order associated with them) and evaluate to `true` or `false`. These statements may be nested, which allows them to test for several conditions, or several conditions can be tested by one statement using compound Boolean conditions. The `if` statement is used to decide to skip or execute one group of statements, and the `if-else` statement is used to decide which of two mutually exclusive groups of statements to execute.

Although all uses of the `switch` statement can be coded using an equivalent set of nested `if-else` statements, the use of the `switch` statement makes our programs more readable when the decision to be made is based on one or more discrete values. The values can be references to a strings or primitive values whose type is `byte`, `short`, `char` or `int`, or the values of an enumerated type.

Most often, a `break` statement is used to prevent the cases coded below the one that is equivalent to the current value of the switch variable from executing. A `default` clause can be included at the end of the statement that will execute when the value of the switch variable does not match any of the statement's cases. Decision statements have many applications to game programming, such as controlling the value of a timer, increasing a score when an event occurs, testing to see when there is a collision between objects, and determining which keystroke has been entered and responding to it.

The `String` class provides methods for comparing `String` objects because they cannot be compared using the relational operators. The equality operator compares the contents of variables, but `String` reference variables contain the address of the strings they refer to, not the strings themselves. Therefore, to compare strings, the `String` class provides methods such as `equals` and `compareTo`, which make case sensitive comparisons, and `equalsIgnoreCase` and `compareToIgnoreCase`, which ignore case sensitivity.

Disk I/O is useful for storing game data, such as the highest score achieved, and any other type of data that must be retained after a program ends. When data is stored in RAM buffers, it is volatile and is not preserved from one game to the next. In contrast, when data is stored in a text file, it can be read and compared each time the game is played. The constructors in the `File` and `Scanner` classes, and the constructors in the `FileWriter` and `PrintWriter` classes, can be used to "attach" `Scanner` and `PrintWriter` I/O objects to a file. Text output can then be sent to the file using the methods in the `PrintWriter` class, and information can be read from the file using the `Scanner` class's methods. Methods in the scanner class can also be used to accept input from the system console. The `File` class method, `exists`, can determine if a file exists before attempting to use it, and it is always good programming style to close a file after using it.

Disk I/O often causes errors such as when code attempts to access a file that does not exist or whose pathname is incorrect. This causes an exception error to be generated, which disrupts the normal flow of a program. Java provides two exception-related constructs, called `try` and `catch` blocks. When an exception occurs within the code of a `try` block, the program's execution path is transferred into the code of the `catch` block, which is designed to process (handle) and recover from runtime exceptions. A `System` class method, `exit`, can be used inside a `catch` block to terminate a program gracefully.

Knowledge Exercises

1. The variables i, j, k and m have been declared as: **int** i = 10; **int** j = 20; **int** k = 30; **int** m = 40. Evaluate the following as true or false:

   a) i <= j

   b) k == 30

   c) i != j && j >= k

   d) i != j || j >= k

   e) (i <= k && k >= m) || (j * 2 == m && k > j)

   f) m <= k || i + j + k >= m

2. What is the normal default execution sequence (path) of all Java programs?

3. What are the two types of statements available in Java to alter the default execution path?

4. Write the Java code to output the contents of the variable myBalance when it stores the value 10.0 to the system console.

5. Modify the Java code in Question 4 by adding a statement to output *my balance is not 10.0* when the memory cell myBalance does not store 10.0.

6. Write an if or if-else statement to perform each of these tasks:

   a) Add 5 to a grade if the grade is greater than 75

   b) Produce the output *buy tickets* if the cost is less than $150.00, otherwise output *too expensive*.

   c) Output the value stored in the variable GPA to the system console if the String object name contains the string Anna

   d) For the strings referenced by s1 and s2, if s1 comes before s2 in alphabetical order, output *in alphabetical order* otherwise output the message *not in order*.

7. True or false:

   a) An if statement must contain one Boolean expression.

   b) An if-else statement must contain two Boolean expressions.

   c) An if statement must contain a statement block.

   d) The code block of an if statement executes when its Boolean condition is true.

   e) The code block of an if statement can contain another if statement.

   f) The code block of an else clause cannot contain another if statement.

   g) An if or if-else statement may be nested within another if statement's code block.

   h) Java contains an if-else-if statement.

8. The string s1 just received input from an input dialog box. Give the statement to output *OK* to the system console when the user enters *Stop Sign* (case sensitive).

9. True or false:

   a) A switch statement must contain a default clause.

   b) A switch statement can have multiple cases.

c) The choice values of a `switch` statement can be strings.

d) A `switch` statement must contain at least one `break` statement.

e) A `switch` statement is normally used to determine a choice between several alternatives.

f) Every `switch` statement can be written as equivalent `if-else` statements.

g) A sequence of `if-else` statements can always be written as an equivalent `switch` statement.

10. Write the `switch` statement to output the menu selection stored in the string variable `item`, assuming the choices are *Hamburger*, *Taco*, or *BLT* (use system-console output).

11. Write the equivalent `if-else` statements to output the menu selections given in Question 10.

12. What API class must be imported into your program to accept input from the system console?

13. Give all of the statements, excluding import statements, to:
   a) accept the year of a person's birth input from the system console (include a prompt)
   b) accept a person's name input from the system console (include a prompt)

14. What is the advantage of saving information in disk files versus saving the information in main memory?

15. True or false:
   a) Text files can be viewed using the program Notepad.
   b) Text files cannot be printed on a printer.
   c) By convention, text files end with the extension .txt
   d) It is best to use two forward slashes to specify the path name where the file is located.

16. Write all of the import statement(s) necessary to perform disk I/O.

17. Give all of the statements, excluding import statements, to:
   a) read the year of a person's birth from the disk file `Dates.txt` stored on the root of the E drive
   b) read a person's age and name from the disk file `Names.txt` stored on the root of the E drive
   c) read the year of a person's birth from the disk file `bDays.txt` stored on the root of the E drive

18. Give all the statements necessary to append the contents of the variables `myBalance` and `yourBalance` to the disk file `Balances.txt` stored on the root of the C drive.

19. Give all the statements necessary to output the contents of the variables `myBalance` and `yourBalance` to the disk file `Balances.txt` stored on the root of the C drive. If the file already exists, delete it before performing the output.

20. Give all the statements necessary to determine if the file `Data.txt` exists on the root of the C drive, and output *The File Exists* to the system console if it does.

21. Write the statement needed to close the file attached to the scanner object `inputFile`.

22. Briefly discuss how the `try` and `catch` block can be used to handle exceptions detected by methods invoked within a program.

Programming Exercises

1. Write a program to ask a user to input two strings from the system console. If the strings are identical output *Stings* Identical to the system console. Otherwise output them in alphabetical order.

2. Write a program for a travel agency, which presents the user with the following menu as a console input prompt:

   Where do you want to vacation?

   Enter: 1 for Disney World, 2 for Las Vegas, 3 for Paris or 4 for Alaska

   After accepting the customer's numeric response from the system console, use either an `if-else` or a `switch` statement to output two destination-appropriate messages to the text file `vacation.txt` (for example, if the user chose 4 for Alaska, you might want to output the messages *Bring a warm jacket and enjoy Alaska* and *Say "Hello" to Frosty for me*). Feel free to add bells and whistles such as adding a welcome message or adding additional destinations.

3. Write a program to ask a user to enter a student name, major, and GPA from the system console. If the GPA is greater than 3.5, set a Boolean variable, `honors`, to `true`, otherwise set it to `false`. Create a text file called `StudentInfo.txt` and output the name, major, GPA, and the student's honors status to four separate lines of the file.

4. Extend the program described in Programming Exercise 4 to ask the user the name of the file in which to store the data. After writing the data to a text file with that name, add the phrase *End of Student Record* as the last line of the file. Then, read five lines store in the file and output them on five separate lines to a message box with the appropriate annotation. Before reading the data, ask the user the name of the file from which to read. Use a `try` and a `catch` block to output the message *problems opening or reading the file* when an `IOException` is thrown.

5. Write a graphical game application that contains a class named `RV` whose objects are the recreational vehicle designed and digitized as described in Knowledge Exercises 20 and 21 of Chapter 3. When the application is launched, the RVs appear on the screen. The game player is given 10 seconds to move any part of the RV beyond the top, bottom, right side, and left side of the game board using the keyboard cursor control keys. The game begins when the game player clicks the Start button and ends when the time expires or some part of the RV has moved beyond all four boundaries of the game board. During the game, a countdown of the time remaining should be displayed at the top of the game board, and the countdown should stop at the end of the game.

6. Write a graphical game application that contains a class named `RV` whose objects are the recreational vehicles designed and digitized as described in Knowledge Exercises 20 and 21 of Chapter 3. The application should also contain a class named `Mouse` whose objects are designed and digitized in a similar manner. When the application is launched, one RV

and one mouse appear on the screen at different random locations. The user is given 10 seconds to move the mouse to the RV using the keyboard's cursor control keys. The game begins when the game player clicks the Start button and ends when the time expires or the mouse has collided with the RV. During the game, a countdown of the time remaining should be displayed at the top of the game board, and the countdown should stop at the end of the game. The game begins when the game player clicks the Start button and ends when the time expires or some part of the mouse has collided with the RV.

7. Write the game application described in Programming Exercise 7 modified to include three RVs at different locations. In this version of the game, the game player has to make the mouse collide into all three RVs and the RVs disappear when the mouse collides with them. The player's score will be the time remaining after all the RVs have disappeared. A record of the lowest score ever achieved will be kept in the disk file LowScore.txt.

8. Using the skills developed in this chapter, continue the implementation of the parts of your game (specified in Preprogramming Exercise 1 of Chapter 1) that require cursor-key motion control, disk I/O, collision detection, and stopping a time countdown. To test the collision detection, you will have to add a class to your application that implements your second type of game piece.

CHAPTER 5

REPEATING STATEMENTS: LOOPS

5.1   *A Second Alternative to Sequential Execution. 192*
5.2   *The* for *Statement. 193*
5.3   *Formatting Numeric Output: A Second Pass. 202*
5.4   *Nesting* for *Loops 208*
5.5   *The* while *Statement 212*
5.6   *The* do-while *Statement 219*
5.7   *The* break *and* continue *Statements 221*
5.8   *Which Loop Statement to Use 222*
5.9   *The* Random *Class 224*
5.10 *The Enhanced* for *Statement. 228*
5.11 *Chapter Summary 229*

In this chapter

In this chapter, we will learn the techniques used to repeat the execution of a designated group of statements an unlimited number of times, which gives us the ability to perform a significant amount of processing with just a few repeated statements. Not only does this reduce the time and effort required to produce a program, but it also allows us to utilize algorithms whose implementation require the use of these repetition, or loop, statements. We will discuss the syntax and execution path of Java's three repetition statements, consider which one is best suited for particular applications, and learn how to nest these statements. Our knowledge of these statements will be expanded in Chapter 6, which covers the concept of arrays, because loops are used to unlock the power of arrays.

We will learn why repetition statements are an integral part of repetition statements, consider which one is best suited for particular applications, and learn of two fundamental algorithms, summing and averaging, and how to generate a repeatable sequence of pseudorandom numbers using loops and the methods in the class `Random`. In addition, we will extend our knowledge of numeric formatting introduced in Chapter 2 and learn to produce output consistent with any of the world's currency systems.

After successfully completing this chapter you should:

- Understand the syntax and execution path of Java's `for`, `while`, and `do-while` statements
- Know which statement to use for a particular application
- Understand why a `for` loop is an automatic counting loop
- Understand the role of sentinels and their use in `while` and `do-while` loops

- Be able to explain the totaling and counting algorithms and the role loops play in their implementation
- Know how to generate a set of random numbers using the `Random` class methods
- Be able to use the `NumberFormat` class's methods to format currency output in a local specific format
- Be able to use the `DecimalFormat` class's methods to format numeric output with leading/trailing zeros and comma separators and display a numeric value as a percentage or using scientific notation

5.1 A SECOND ALTERNATIVE TO SEQUENTIAL EXECUTION

Often, the proper execution path of a program's statements requires that a sequence of instructions be executed several times. For example, a program accepts three input deposits and adds them to a bank balance after each input. In this case, the input statement and the arithmetic statement to add the input deposit to the bank balance would be repeated three times.

One alternative would be to code one input and one arithmetic statement, copy and paste them into the program two more times, and then execute the three groups of statements sequentially. Another alternative would be to enclose one input and one arithmetic statement in a repetition statement's code block, which is repeated three times. Although both approaches would produce the same result, the second alternative is most often preferred, especially when the statements are to be repeated a large number of times. Not only does this approach save coding time, but it also improves the readability of our programs by significantly reducing the length of the program, and, more importantly, making it obvious to the reader that the statements are being repeated.

A repetition statement is most often referred to as a *loop* statement. The term loop comes from an aircraft "loop" maneuver often performed at air shows during which the aircraft repeatedly travels in a vertical circle. Figure 5.1 illustrates the maneuver and programming analogy.

Like many programming languages, Java provides three repetition or loop statements: the `for`, the `while`, and the `do-while` statements. While there is the possibility for significant overlap in

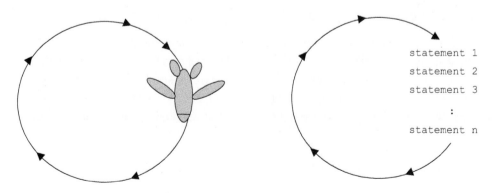

Figure 5.1
Airplane and programming loops.

the use of these three statements in our programs, good coding practice and ease of use greatly narrow the choice of which statement to use in a particular context. One of the objectives of this chapter is to specify clear criteria for when each of these three statements is best used in our programs. We will begin our study of repetition statements with the for statement.

5.2 THE for STATEMENT

The for statement is often called an automatic counting loop. It is most often used when we know how many times to repeat the loop's statements. In some cases, this is known at the time the program is written; for example, a program that always processes three deposits. In other cases, the number of times the loop is to execute is specified, or determined, during the program's execution. For example, before entering deposits the program users are asked to enter the number of deposits they will be making into their bank account during this execution of the program. The criterion common to both of these alternatives is that *before* the loop executes the number of repetitions is known. When this is the case, the for loop is the best repetition statement to use.

5.2.1 Syntax of the for Statement

The left side of Figure 5.2 shows an example of a for statement containing a group of statements that will execute its statement block three times. The meaning of the statement and its execution path are illustrated on the right side of Figure 5.2. The integer variable i is called the loop or

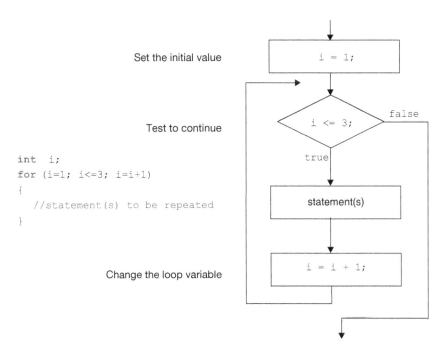

```
int  i;
for (i=1; i<=3; i=i+1)
{
    //statement(s) to be repeated
}
```

Set the initial value

Test to continue

Change the loop variable

Figure 5.2
A **for** loop that executes three times and its execution path.

loop control variable. The statement(s) enclosed inside the braces are called the loop's code block, or the *body of the loop*. They are said to be inside the loop. These are the statements to be repeated.

When a loop is correctly written, the loop variable is initialized, tested, and changed. In a `for` loop, all three of these actions are coded within the `for` statement's parentheses. Referring to the left side of Figure 5.2, the statement i=1; sets the initial value, i<=3; tests to see if i has reached its terminating value or if the loop should continue, and i=i+1; changes or increments the value of the loop's control variable.

Referring to the items enclosed inside the parentheses after the keyword `for`, the code:

- i=1; is called the initialization expression
- i<=3; is called the condition to continue expression or continuation condition
- i=i+1; is called the increment

The initialization expression is an assignment statement. As shown on the top-right side of Figure 5.2, this assignment statement always executes once to initialize the loop variable just before the loop begins. The condition to continue expression is a Boolean expression involving the loop variable, which executes at least once. The loop body is repeatedly executed while this Boolean expression is `true`. If the Boolean condition is `false` when the loop begins, the statements in the loop body are not executed. The increment is an assignment statement. The statement is used to change the loop variable after the statements in the loop body are executed. When the increment is one, the equivalent coding i++; is commonly used.

The loop shown in Figure 5.2 executes its statement body three times. When the `for` statement begins, the loop variable i is initialized to 1. The condition to continue (i <= 3) evaluates to `true` (1 <= 3), and the statements in the loop body execute for the first time. The loop variable is then incremented to 2, the condition is tested and is still `true` (2 <= 3), and the statements execute a second time. The loop variable is then incremented to 3, the condition is still `true` (3 <= 3), and the statements execute a third time. Finally, the loop variable becomes 4, the condition (4 <= 3) is `false`, and the loop ends. After the loop ends, the statement immediately following its close brace executes.

The following code fragment contains a `for` statement that executes its loop body 500 times:

```
int i;
for(i=1; i<=500; i=i+1)
   {
     //statement(s) to be repeated
   }
```

The most common errors made when coding the `for` statement are:

- placing a semicolon after the close parenthesis
- neglecting to code the semicolon after the initial condition or after the condition to continue, both of which result in a translation error
- neglecting to code the open and close braces around the statements when more than one statement is to be repeated

- modifying the loop variable within the body of the loop which alters the automatic counting

When a semicolon is coded after the close parenthesis, the statement is syntactically correct, however, none of the statements that would have normally formed the loop body are considered to be part of (inside) the loop. They default to sequential execution and each statement executes once. When braces are not coded, the statement is also syntactically correct, however, the first statement after the `for` statement is the only statement considered to be part of the loop. Regardless of the indentation used, it is the only statement repeated.

The generalized syntax of the `for` statement and its execution path are shown at the top and bottom of Figure 5.3, respectively.

```
for(initialization expression; condition to continue; increment)
{
    //statement(s) to be repeated
}
```

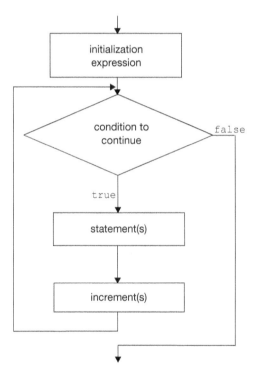

Figure 5.3
The generalized syntax of the **for** statement and its execution path.

In addition to the loop variable, the initialization expression, test to continue, and the increment can all contain other variables that can be used to adjust the flow of the statement at runtime. For example, the following code fragment outputs the values in the five times table from 10 to 50 on one line:

```
int i;
int beginValue = 10;
```

```
int endValue = 50;
int tableValue = 5;

for(i=beginValue; i<=endValue, i=i+tableValue)
{
System.out.print(i + " ");
}
```

Figure 5.4 presents a console application named ForLoopCounting that utilizes this feature of the statement to count from a user input starting value to a specified ending value, by a specified increment. The bottom part of the figure gives the user prompts and inputs and the corresponding outputs generated by the program.

The input starting and ending values, and the increment to count by, are parsed into the variables start, end, and increment on lines 10, 12, and 14 of Figure 5.4. These variables are used in the initialization expression, condition to continue, and increment of the for statement that begins on line 18. As indicated by the input and output at the bottom of Figure 5.5, the program user inputs 3 as a starting value, 27 as an ending value, and an increment of 5. After the value 23 is output, the loop variable i becomes 28 (= 23 + 5). Because 28 is not less than or equal to the ending value 27, the loop ends and 28 is not output.

```
1     import javax.swing.*;
2
3     public class ForLoopCounting
4     {
5       public static void main(String[] args)
6       { int start, end, increment;
7         String input;
8
9         input = JOptionPane.showInputDialog("Enter the starting value:");
10        start = Integer.parseInt(input);
11        input = JOptionPane.showInputDialog("Enter the ending value: ");
12        end = Integer.parseInt(input);
13        input = JOptionPane.showInputDialog("Count by?: ");
14        increment = Integer.parseInt(input);
15
16        System.out.println("Counting from " + start + " to " + end +
17                           " by " + increment + "s:");
18        for(int i=start; i<=end; i=i+increment)
19        {
20           System.out.println(i);
21        }
22      }
23    }
```

Input prompts and user inputs:
Enter the starting value: 3
Enter the ending value: 27
Count by?: 5

```
Outputs:
Counting from 3 to 23 by 5s:
3
8
13
18
23
```

Figure 5.4
The application **ForLoopCounting** and typical inputs and outputs.

Line 18 presents a feature of the `for` statement we have not previously discussed. It declares the loop variable `i` as part of the initialization expression by proceeding its assignment statement with the keyword `int`. When this is done, the scope of the loop variable is limited to the `for` statement and its statement body. The loop variable cannot be used by statements that follow the loop or by statements that precede the loop. After the loop ends, the Java memory manager reclaims the storage assigned to the loop variable, and the variable's lifetime is said to be over. If another variable named `i` had been declared in the program before or after the loop statement, all references to the variable `i` inside the `for` statement (lines 18-21) would refer to the loop variable, not the variable declared outside the loop. This feature ensures that the loop will count correctly.

A `for` loop can also be used to count down to an ending value. In this case, the loop variable is initialized to the starting countdown value, and it is decremented each pass through the loop. The statement's Boolean condition checks to see if the ending value is reached. The following code fragment counts down from ten to zero:

```java
for(int i= 10; i>= 0; i--)
{
  System.out.println(i);
}
```

In general, the initialization expression and the increment can contain more than one assignment statement. When this is the case, they are separated with commas as shown in code fragment below. The loop's execution path is shown in Figure 5.5.

```java
int i, j, k;
for(i=1, j=10, k=4; i<= 3; i=i+1, j=j+3, k=k-1)
{
  //statement(s) to be repeated
}
```

5.2.2 A for Loop Application

Figure 5.6 shows a graphical application that draws the first row of a checkerboard on a light-gray-colored game board as shown in Figure 5.7. The program uses a `for` loop to draw the eight checkerboard squares and then uses another `for` loop to draw a red checker on the row's black squares.

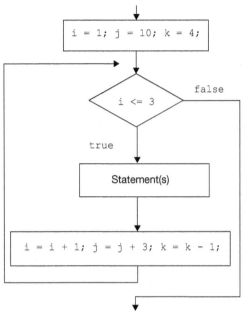

Figure 5.5
Execution path of a **for** loop containing multiple initialization-expression and increment-assignment statements.

Inside the draw method, line 26 of Figure 5.6 uses the game environment's setBackground method to change the game board's background color to light gray. Then line 29 begins a for loop that executes eight times. During each iteration of the loop, a black or red checkerboard box is drawn (line 36) using the current drawing color. The first statement in the loop body (line 31) sets the current color to firstColor (black), then line 32 uses the modulus operator to determine if the loop variable, col, is even (col % 2 == 0). If it is, the current color is changed to secondColor (red), which causes the even checkerboard boxes (2, 4, 6, and 8) to be drawn in red. The counting algorithm, whose increment is the width of the checkerboard boxes, is used on line 37 to calculate the x location of the next checkerboard box to be drawn.

Line 42 begins a second for loop that draws a red checker (line 45) on the black checkerboard boxes. Before the loop begins, the current drawing color is set to red (line 41). Because the for statement's increment adds 2 to the loop variable col, this variable stores the column numbers 1 (firstChecker-Col), then 3, 5, and 7. These are the column numbers of the black boxes, which are used on line 44 to calculate the x location of each column's checker. In this calculation, one is subtracted from the column number col before it is multiplied by the box width because column 1's checker should be drawn at an x value of 20.

```
1    import java.awt.*;
2    import edu.sjcny.gpv1.*;
3
4    public class CheckerBoardRow extends DrawableAdapter
5    {
6        static CheckerBoardRow ge = new CheckerBoardRow();
7        static GameBoard gb = new GameBoard(ge, "Checker Board Row");
8
9        public static void main(String[] args)
10       {
11           showGameBoard(gb);
12       }
13
14       public void draw(Graphics g)
15       {
16           int boxX = 12;
17           int boxY = 50;
18           int boxWidth = 60;
19           int boxHeight = 53;
20           int checkerX = 20;
```

```
21        int checkerY = 55;
22        int firstCheckerCol = 1;
23        Color firstColor = Color.BLACK;
24        Color secondColor = Color.RED;
25
26        gb.setBackground(Color.LIGHT_GRAY);
27
28        //Draw the Checker board boxes
29        for(int col = 1; col <= 8; col++)
30        {
31          g. setColor(firstColor); //black
32          if(col % 2 == 0)
33          {
34            g. setColor(secondColor); //red
35          } //end if
36          g.fillRect(boxX, boxY, boxWidth, boxHeight);
37          boxX = boxX + boxWidth;
38        } //end for loop
39
40        //Draw the Red checkers
41        g.setColor(Color.RED);
42        for(int col = firstCheckerCol; col <=8; col= col + 2)
43        {
44          checkerX = 20 + (col - 1) * boxWidth;
45          g.fillOval(checkerX, checkerY, 40, 40);
46        }
47      }
48  }
```

Figure 5.6
The application **CheckerBoardRow**.

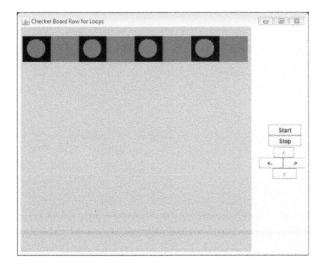

Figure 5.7
The output from the application **CheckerBoardRow**.

5.2.3 The Totaling and Averaging Algorithms

The totaling or summation algorithm, like the counting algorithm, is a fundamental algorithm of computer science. Both of these algorithms are used in most programs. As the totaling algorithm's name implies, it is used to calculate a total, or sum, of a group of values. For example, it could be used to calculate the total of a group of deposits input to a program, and once the total is known, the average deposit can be easily determined by dividing the total by the number of deposits.

The totaling algorithm is very similar to the counting algorithm, except that the counting algorithm adds (or subtracts) a *constant* increment to the current value of the counter every time it is executed, and the totaling algorithm adds the *next item* to be totaled to the current value of the total every time it is executed:

counting algorithm: `count = count ± constantIncrement;`
totaling algorithm: `total = total + newItem;`

If we were adding a group of deposits, the variable `newItem` would contain the next deposit. As was the case with the counting algorithm, the name of the variable on the left side of the assignment operator can be any valid variable name. Similarly, the same variable name must be used on the right side of the assignment operator, and the name should be representative of what it stores. For example, when calculating a new bank balance:

```
balance = balance + deposit;
```

The chosen variable is generically referred to as the totaling or summation variable. Before the algorithm is used, the variable is set to an initial value, which is the current (beginning) value of the sum. For example, it could be the bank balance before the new deposits are made. Often, this value is zero. As is the case with the counting algorithm, once the initial value is set, the summation algorithm is repeatedly executed.

The following code fragments add up the integers from one to four:

```
int sum = 0;                          int sum = 0;
sum = sum + 1;                        for(int i = 1; i <= 4; i = i + 1)
sum = sum + 2;              OR        {
sum = sum + 3;                            sum = sum + i;
sum = sum + 4;                        }
```

The contents of the memory cell `sum` would progress from 0, to 1, to 3, to 6, and finally to 10. In most cases, as shown on the right, a loop is used to repeat the summation algorithm.

Figure 5.8 presents a Java console application named `TotalingLoop` that demonstrates the use of the totaling algorithm and the calculation of an average. A set of sample inputs and the program's corresponding outputs is given at the bottom of the figure. The monetary outputs produced by lines 15–16 and lines 30–34 are formatted as U.S. currency using an object in the `NumberFormat` class declared on line 13. This class and its methods used to produce this currency formatting will be discussed in the next section.

The program accepts a given number of input deposits and uses the totaling algorithm (line 25) to calculate their total. The number of deposits to be processed is input on line 17, then the parsed value is used in the Boolean condition of the for statement that begins on line 21 to process that number of deposits.

Before the loop begins, the totaling variable, total, is initialized to zero (line 20). During each iteration of the loop that begins on line 21, a new deposit is input and parsed. Then, the total algorithm is used on line 25 to add the new deposit to the total of the previously input deposits. After all the deposits are processed, the new balance (line 27) and the average deposit (line 28) are calculated. Lines 15–16 output the beginning balance, and lines 30–34 output the total of the deposits, the average deposit, and the new balance to the system console.

```
1    import javax.swing.JOptionPane;
2    import java.text.NumberFormat;
3    import java.util.Locale;
4
5    public class TotalingLoop
6    {
7      public static void main(String[] args)
8      {
9        double balance = 1000.24;
10       int numOfDeposits;
11       double deposit, total, newBalance, averageDeposit;
12       String input;
13       NumberFormat us = NumberFormat.getCurrencyInstance(Locale.US);
14
15       System.out.println("Your beginning balance is: " +
16                          us.format(balance));
17       input = JOptionPane.showInputDialog("How Many Deposits?");
18       numOfDeposits = Integer.parseInt(input);
19
20       total = 0.0;
21       for(int i = 1; i <= numOfDeposits;  i++)
22       {
23         input = JOptionPane.showInputDialog("Enter a deposit");
24         deposit = Double.parseDouble(input);
25         total = total + deposit;
26       }
27       balance = balance + total;
28       averageDeposit = total / numOfDeposits;
29
30       System.out.println("The total of the " + numOfDeposits +
31                          " deposits is " + us.format(total));
32       System.out.println("The average deposit was: " +
33                          us.format(averageDeposit));
34       System.out.println("Your new balance is: " + us.format(balance));
35     }
36   }
```

```
Inputs
3
20.10
30.20
40.30

Outputs
Your beginning balance is: $1,000.24
The total of the 3 deposits is $90.60
The average deposit was: $30.20
Your new balance is: $1,090.84
```

Figure 5.8
The application **TotalingLoops** and typical inputs and outputs.

5.3 FORMATTING NUMERIC OUTPUT: A SECOND PASS

The use of the `DecimalFormat` class to improve the readability of numeric outputs was briefly discussed in Chapter 2 (Section 2.10). In this section, we will expand that discussion and also discuss the use of the `NumberFormat` and `Locale` classes that were used to format the currency outputs produced by the program shown in Figure 5.8. We will begin with an introduction to the techniques used to format numeric output as currency.

> **NOTE** *All numeric formatting rounds up the fractional part of a numeric value, and all of the digits in the integer portion of the numeric value are always included in the formatted version of the number.*

5.3.1 Currency Formatting

The monetary outputs produced by the program shown in Figure 5.8 are formatted as United States currency. There is a leading dollar sign and a decimal point separating the dollar amount from the cents, which are displayed as two rounded digits to the right of the decimal point. In addition, a comma is used as a thousands separator in the dollar amount. Had the output been negative, it would have been enclosed in parentheses. All of this formatting conforms to the way U.S. currency is displayed within the world of finance and makes the units of the output recognizable as dollars and cents.

Two methods in the `NumberFormat` class, `getCurrencyInstance` and `format`, and constants defined in the class `Locale` can be used to format numeric values as currency. The constants in the class `Locale` are used to specify which of the world's currencies to use in the formatting.

The `NumberFormat` class's method `getCurrencyInstance` is used on line 12 of Figure 5.8 to create a currency formatting object named `us`. The method accepts one argument, which is normally one of the predefined static constants in the `Locale` class. As the name of the class implies, this argument specifies the locale of the format that will be associated with the formatting object. Line 13 uses the constant Locale.US, to specify that the currency formatting associated with the object us will be United States currency: dollars and cents.

The object us is then used on lines 15-16 and lines 30-33 to invoke the NumberFormat class's format method. This method converts the numeric value passed to it to a string using the formatting associated with the object that invoked it. As a result, the four numeric outputs produced by the program are formatted as U.S. currency.

By changing the argument passed to the method getCurrencyInstance on line 13, the numeric output produced by the program could be made to conform to other currency formats used in the financial world. For example, the following code fragment produces the two outputs, which are formatted as pounds (the United Kingdom's currency) and euros (the European Union currency), respectively. The output of the code fragment is given below the code.

```
double price - 1234567.889;
NumberFormat uk = NumberFormat.getCurrencyInstance(Locale.UK);
NumberFormat france = NumberFormat.getCurrencyInstance(Locale.FRANCE);

    System.out.println(uk.format(price));
    System.out.println(france.format(price));
```

Output:

```
£1,234,567.89
1 234 567,89 €
```

NOTE *The formatting performed does not take into account monetary exchange rates.*

The Default Locale

The getCurrencyInstance method invoked on line 13 of Figure 5.8 is overloaded. There are two version of it: a one-parameter version that was invoked on line 13 and a no-parameter version. The no-parameter version of the method can be used to format numeric currency in the default locale of the computer's operating system. Assuming the default locale of the operating system was Italy, the following code fragment would produce two identical lines of output formatted as euros (Italy's currency).

```
double price = 1435.2;
NumberFormat italy = NumberFormat.getCurrencyInstance(Locale.ITALY);
NumberFormat osDefault = NumberFormat.getCurrencyInstance();

System.out.println(italy.format(price));
System.out.println(osDefault.format(price));
```

5.3.2 The DecimalFormat Class: A Second Look

The methods in the DecimalFormat class, which were briefly discussed in Section 2.10 of Chapter 2, can also be used to format numeric output. Normally, these methods are used when the numeric value is not currency.

Like the NumberFormat class, the DecimalFormat class contains a nonstatic method named format that returns a string containing the formatted version of the numeric value sent to it as an argument. This method is invoked with a DecimalFormat object that can be declared using the class's one-parameter constructor. The constructor is passed a string argument, called the *formatting string*, which contains the formatting information. In Section 2.10, we used the formatting string argument "#,###.##" to produce an output that contained a comma every three digits to the left of the decimal point and to format real numbers (nonintegers) with a maximum of two digits of precision.

Other characters can be used in the formatting string to produce other forms of numeric output formatting. The pound signs (#) to left and right of the decimal point can be replaced with zeros, which are used to format the numeric value with leading and trailing zeros. In addition, a percent sign (%) can be added to the end of the formatting string. The percent sign is used to format the numeric value as a percentage. For example, the value 0.237 would be formatted as 23.7%, assuming one digit of precision was specified in the formatting string. Numeric values can also be formatted in scientific notation.

Regardless of the characters used in the formatting string, the fractional part of a numeric value is always rounded up and all of the digits in the integer portion of the numeric value or a leading zero are always included in the formatted value unless scientific notation is being used.

Leading and Trailing Zeros

Inserting zeros into the formatting string adjacent to the decimal point will add leading or trailing zeros to the formatted value. For example, when the numeric value being formatted does not have an integer part (e.g., .254), inserting a zero to the left of the decimal point in the formatting string will format the value as 0.254. Adding a zero the right of the decimal point will format the value 167 as 167.0. If the number does have a fractional or integer part, then the digit adjacent to the decimal point in the numeric value always appears in the formatted value.

The code fragment below formats numeric values with one leading zero and two trailing zeros and produces the output shown below the code. The third output value is rounded to the specified two digits of precision.

```java
double n1 = .2;
double n2 = 167.0;
double n3 = 1.4672
DecimalFormat ltz = new DecimalFormat("#,##0.00");
System.out.print(ltz.format(n1) + " " + ltz.format(n2) + " " +
                 ltz.format(n3));
```

Output:
```
0.20 167.00 1.47
```

Percentages

A formatting string that ends with a percent sign is used to format a numeric value as a percentage. The value will be multiplied by 100, and a percent sign will be added to the right side of the string from the `format` method. For example, the value 0.254 would be formatted as 25.4%. The code fragment below formats numeric values as percentages with one leading zero and one trailing zero. The output it produces is shown below the code.

```
double n1 = 0.002;
double n2 = 0.16 DecimalFormat pct = new DecimalFormat("#,##0.0%");
System.out.println(pct.format(n1) + " " + pct.format(n2));
```

Output:

```
0.2% 16.0%
```

Scientific Notation

Scientific notation is a formatting of a numeric value into a mantissa followed by an exponent. Usually, the mantissa and the exponent are separated by the letter E. The mantissa contains the digits of the numeric value with its decimal point shifted left or right. To determine the numeric value, the mantissa is multiplied by 10 raised to the value of the exponent. For example, `23.971E2` represents the numeric value `2,397.1`.

A formatting string that ends with the character E followed by the number of leading zeros to be displayed in the exponent is used to format a numeric value in scientific notation. At least one zero must be included after the letter E in the formatting string. The formatted value will contain the mantissa and the exponent separated by the letter E. The mantissa is formatted using the portion of the formatting string to the left of the letter E, which should contain only zeroes and a decimal point.

The code fragment below formats numeric values in scientific notation with the mantissa shown with one digit to the left of the decimal. The output it produces is shown below the code.

```
double n1 = 0.00000215;
double n2 = 16123067533.1
DecimalFormat sn = new DecimalFormat("0.0000E0");
System.out.println( sn.format(n1) + " " + sn.format(n2));
```

Output:

```
2.1500E-6 1.6123E10
```

NOTE   *All digits of the exponent will always be included in the scientific formatted version of a numeric value.*

Table 5.1 summarizes the characters used in the `DecimalFormat` class's format string and the formatting they produce. All digits in the integer portion of numeric value will always be included in the formatted version of the numeric unless scientific notation is being used. All digits of the exponent are always displayed when using scientific notation.

Table 5.1

The **`DecimalFormat`** Class's Formatting Characters and Their Meaning

Character	Formatting Produced	Formatting String Example
.	Output a decimal point in this position	
#	Output a digit in this position if it exists	`"#.#"`
0	Output a digit in this position if it exists, else a zero	`"0.00"` One leading zero, two digits of precision
,	Output a comma separator in this position, as necessary	`"#,##0.00"` Comma separator every three digits (with one leading zero and two digits of precision)
%	Output a numeric value as a percentage (Multiply the numeric by 100 and add a percent sign to its right)	`"0.000%"` Convert numeric to a percentage followed by a percent sign (with one leading zero, three digits of precision)
E	Output the numeric value in scientific notation	`"0.0000E0"` Mantissa formatted with 5 digits x.xxxxEx All digits of the exponent are displayed

Figure 5.9 illustrates the use of the methods in the `DecimalFormat` class to format numeric outputs. The program produces four groupings of outputs, which are shown in Figure 5.10. Each grouping outputs the same three numbers: n1, n2, and n3 (lines 15–33) using different formatting strings, which are defined on lines 7–10.

The first three output groupings use comma separators every three digits. The second and third groupings also use leading and trailing zeros, with the outputs in the third grouping displayed as percentages. The fourth output grouping uses scientific notation.

The first numeric output in the first grouping (0.006) has been truncated because its formatting string (line 7) only contains three digits of precision. It contains a leading zero because all numeric values contain a leading zero unless scientific notation is being used. The last two outputs in the first grouping do not contain trailing zeros because the pound sign (#) was used on line 7 to specify their precision.

The outputs in the second grouping contain trailing zeros because a zero was used in their formatting string to specify their precision (line 8). Finally, the exponent (11) in the second numeric output of the last grouping contains two digits even though its formatting string specifies one digit of precision. All the digits of an exponent are always displayed, regardless of the number of zeros used to specify the leading zeros of the exponent.

```
1 import java.text.DecimalFormat;
2
3 public class DecimalFormatClass
4 {
5    public static void main(String[] args)
6    {
7       DecimalFormat cs = new DecimalFormat("#,###.###"); //commas
8       DecimalFormat ltz = new DecimalFormat("#,##0.000"); //zeros
9       DecimalFormat pct = new DecimalFormat("#,##0.00%"); //percentages
10      DecimalFormat sn = new DecimalFormat("0.0000E0"); //scientific
11      double n1 = 0.0062;
12      double n2 = 161234563468.5;
13      double n3 = 1.530;
14
15      System.out.println("Comma-separators");
16      System.out.println(cs.format(n1));
17      System.out.println(cs.format(n2));
18      System.out.println(cs.format(n3));
19
20      System.out.println("\nLeading & Trailing Zeros, & Commas");
21      System.out.println(ltz.format(n1));
22      System.out.println(ltz.format(n2));
23      System.out.println(ltz.format(n3));
24
25      System.out.println("\nPercentages");
26      System.out.println(pct.format(n1));
27      System.out.println(pct.format(n2));
28      System.out.println(pct.format(n3));
29
30      System.out.println("\nScientific Notation");
31      System.out.println(sn.format(n1));
32      System.out.println(sn.format(n2));
33      System.out.println(sn.format(n3));
34    }
35 }
```

Figure 5.9
The application **DecimalFormatClass**.

Comma separators
0.006
161,234,563,468.5
1.53

Leading & Trailing Zeros &Commas
0.006
161,234,563,468.500
1.530

Percentages
0.62%
16,123,456,346,850.00%
153.00%

Scientific Notation
6.2000E-3
1.6123E11
1.5300E0

Figure 5.10
The output produced by the application **DecimalFormatClass**.

5.4 NESTING for LOOPS

As we have learned, loops can be used to repeat a statement or a group of statements contained inside a statement block. When the statement block contains a loop, we say that the loop that is inside the statement block is *nested* inside the other loop. The loop in the statement block is called the *inner* loop because it is inside the other loop, which is referred to as the *outer* loop. The loop in the statement block can be thought of as an egg inside the nest formed by the outer loop. Consider the following code fragment that computes the average of a runner's ten qualifying race times:

```
total = 0;
for(int i = 1; i<=10;  i++)
{
  input = JOptionPane.showInputDialog("Enter a race time");
  aRaceTime = Double.parseDouble(input);
  total = total + aRaceTime;
}
System.out.println(" Your average time is " + total / 10);
```

This code could be used to process 100 runners by nesting it inside an outer loop that executes 100 times.

```
for(int j = 1; j<=100; j++) //each runner (the outer loop)
{
```

```
    total = 0;
    for(int i = 1; i<=10;  i++) //each race (the inner loop)
    {
      input = JOptionPane.showInputDialog("Enter a race time");
      aRaceTime = Double.parseDouble(input);
      total = total + aRaceTime;
    }
    System.out.println(" Your average time is + total / 10);
  }
```

As is the case with nested decision statements, there is no limit on how many loops can be nested inside of other loops. The following code fragment processes the 10 qualifying times for 100 racers in 5 states using two levels of nesting.

```
for(int k = 1; k<=5; k++) //each state
{
  for(int j = 1; j<=100; j++) //each runner
  {
    total = 0;
    for(int i = 1; i<=10;  i++) //each race
    {
      input = JOptionPane.showInputDialog("Enter a race time");
      aRaceTime = Double.parseDouble(input);
      total = total + aRaceTime;
    }
    System.out.println("Your average time is + total /10);
  }
}
```

The indentation used in the above code fragment is considered good programming practice because it makes the use of nested loops, and the nesting levels, obvious to anyone reading the code. It can be quickly determined that the three statements in the innermost loop will execute 5,000 times (= 5 * 100 * 10). When using nested loops, it is also good programming practice to progressively develop the code from the inside of the nest outward. The innermost loop (e.g., one that processes 10 races) is coded first, tested, and corrected. Then, this loop is enclosed in a loop (e.g., one that processes 100 runners), and this nested structure is again tested. The process continues until the outermost loop (e.g., one that processes 5 states) is complete.

Figure 5.11 contains a graphics application that illustrates the use of nested `for` loops to draw the checkerboard shown in Figure 5.12, and a second set of nested `for` loops to draw three rows of red checkers on the board. A significant portion of the code is the same as the code shown in Figure 5.6 that drew *one* row of a checkerboard containing red checkers.

Lines 31 to 49 contain the first set of nested `for` loops used to draw the eight rows of the checkerboard. The inner loop, that begins on Lines 33 and ends on Line 42, is same code used on Lines 29 to 38 of Figure 5.6 to draw one row of a checkerboard. This loop is now nested inside an outer loop that begins on line 31, which executes eight times. With each pass through the outer loop, the inner loop draws another row of the board. To prevent the rows from being drawn on top of each other, line 43 increases the y location of the next row of boxes to be draw in the inner loop by the

```
1     import edu.sjcny.gpv1.*;
2     import java.awt.Color;
3     import java.awt.Graphics;
4
5     public class CheckerBoard extends DrawableAdapter
6     {
7        static CheckerBoard ge = new CheckerBoard();
8        static GameBoard gb = new GameBoard(ge, "Nested For loops");
9
10       public static void main(String[] args)
11       {
12          showGameBoard(gb);
13       }
14
15       public void draw(Graphics g)
16       {
17          int xBox = 12;
18          int yBox = 50;
19          int boxWidth = 60;
20          int boxHeight = 53;
21          int firstCheckerCol = 1;
22          int checkerX = 20;
23          int checkerY = 55;
24          Color firstColor = Color.BLACK;
25          Color secondColor = Color.RED;
26          Color temp;
27
28          gb.setBackground(Color.LIGHT_GRAY);
29
30          //Draw the checker board boxes
31          for(int row = 1; row <= 8; row++) //each row
32          {
33             for(int col = 1; col <=8; col++) //each column
34             {
35                g. setColor(firstColor);
36                if(col % 2 == 0)
37                {
38                   g. setColor(secondColor);
39                }
40                g.fillRect(xBox, yBox, boxWidth, boxHeight);
41                xBox = xBox + boxWidth;
42             }
43             yBox = yBox + boxHeight;
44             xBox = 12;
45
46             temp = firstColor; //swap the box colors
47             firstColor = secondColor;
48             secondColor = temp;
49          }
```

```
50
51      //Draw the red checkers
52      for(int row = 1; row <= 3; row++) //first three rows
53      {
54        if(row % 2 == 0) //an even numbered row
55        {
56          checkerX = checkerX + boxWidth;
57          firstCheckerCol = 2;
58        }
59        g.setColor(Color.RED);
60        for(int col = firstCheckerCol; col <=8; col= col + 2)
61        { //red checker locations
62          checkerX = 20 + (col -1) * boxWidth;
63          g.fillOval( checkerX, checkerY, 40, 40);
64        }
65        checkerY = checkerY + boxHeight;
66        checkerX - 20;
67        firstCheckerCol = 1;
68      }
69   }
70 }
```

Figure 5.11
The graphical application **CheckerBoard**.

height of the boxes, and line 44 resets the x location of the each row's first box to 12. Before the outer loop ends, lines 46–48 swap the colors of the odd and even column boxes. This will make the colors of the boxes to be drawn in each column of the next row different from the color of the boxes in the row above them.

The inner loop that begins on lines 60 and ends on line 64 is the same code used on lines 42–46 of Figure 5.6 to draw one row of red checkers. This loop is now nested inside an outer loop that begins on line 31, which executes three times. With each pass through the outer loop, the inner loop draws the next row of checkers. After a row is drawn, the y location of the next row of checkers is calculated and assigned to the variable checkerY on line 65. The value stored in this variable is increased by the height of the boxes then used during the next iteration of the inner loop (line 63) to draw a row of checkers.

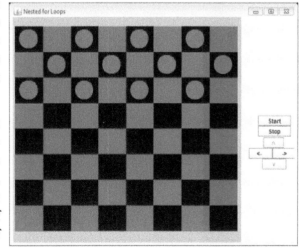

Figure 5.12
The output produced by the application **CheckerBoard**.

Line 66 reinitializes the x location of the first checker in a row to 20. The if statement on line 54 decides when the row number is even. Because only the odd-numbered rows (rows 1 and 3) should have a checker in the first column of the board (at x = 20), checkerX is increased by the width of a checkerboard box (line 56) when the row number is even. Then, line 57 sets the variable firstCheckerCol, used on line 60 as the column number of a row's first checker, to 2 (line 57)

5.5 THE while STATEMENT

Many applications require that a sequence of statements be repeated until a Boolean condition becomes `false`, rather than repeating until the statements have been executed a given or known number of times. For example, a program might continue to ask for a password until the correct password is entered. When this is the case, the `while` or the `do-while` statements are normally used to code the loop that repeats the statements. If the statements should be executed at least once, the `do-while` statement is used. Otherwise, the `while` statement is used. In this section, the `while` statement will be discussed, and the `do-while` statement will be discussed in Section 5.6.

5.5.1 Syntax of the while Statement

The generalized syntax of the `while` statement and its execution path are shown on the left and right sides of Figure 5.13, respectively:

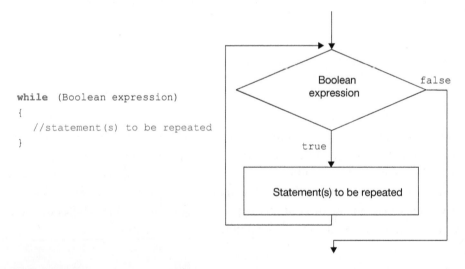

```
while (Boolean expression)
{
    //statement(s) to be repeated
}
```

Figure 5.13
The syntax and execution path of the **while** statement.

The statement begins with the keyword `while` followed by a Boolean expression enclosed in parentheses, which is followed by a code block containing the statements to be repeated. While it is the case that a single statement to be repeated need not be coded inside a statement block, as discussed in Section 5.2.1, it is good programming practice to do so.

As shown on the right side of Figure 5.13, the statements in the block will be repeated as long as the Boolean condition is `true`. If, when the statement begins execution, the Boolean condition is `false`, the statement block will not be executed.

The following code fragment outputs the square root of 1.2, 2.3, 3.4, and 4.5:

```
double n = 1.2;
while(n != 5.6)
{
```

```
System.out.println(Math.sqrt(n));
n = n + 1.1;
}
```

The most common errors made when coding the `while` statement are:

- placing a semicolon after the close parenthesis
- neglecting to code the open and close brace around the statements when more than one statement is to be repeated

When a semicolon is coded after the close parentheses, the statement is syntactically correct, however, none of the statements that would have normally formed the loop body are considered to be part of (inside) the loop. They default to sequential execution, and each statement executes once. When braces are not coded, the statement is also syntactically correct, however, the first statement after the `while` statement is the only statement considered to be part of the loop. Regardless of the indentation used, it is the only statement repeated. When coding a `while` loop, it is good programming practice to code the following fragment and then add the Boolean condition and the statements to be repeated:

```
while()
{

}
```

A common logic error made when coding the `while` statement is that the statements inside the statement block, during some repetition of the loop, do not change the Boolean expression to `false`. The statement, or statements, intended to do that were either incorrectly coded or were not included in the loop's statement block. In either case, once the loop begins, it never ends, and the loop is said to be an *infinite* loop. The following code fragment is an infinite loop because the statement that increments n is not part of the loop's statement block. On each iteration through the loop, n's value remains 1.2, and the Boolean condition never becomes `false`.

```
double n = 1.2;
while(n != 5.6)
{
   System.out.println(Math.sqrt(n));
}
n = n + 1.1;
```

Infinite loops can also occur when the loop's Boolean expression is improperly coded, as is the case in the following code fragment. The variable n assumes the values 1.2, 2.3, 3.4, 4.5, 5.6 ..., but never the value 5.5.

```
double n = 1.2;
while(n != 5.5) //n never becomes 5.5
{
   System.out.println(Math.sqrt(n));
   n = n + 1.1;
}
```

5.5.2 Sentinel Loops

Many applications require that a sequence of instructions be repeated until a signal to stop is detected. The signal is referred to as a sentinel value, and a loop that ends when it detects a sentinel value is called a *sentinel* loop.

Sentinel loops are commonly used to process a set of input data, and the sentinel value is chosen to be a specific value of the input data. The value selected must be a value that would never occur in that data set (for example, a student grade of -1). As another example, you might want to continue to process bank deposits until a negative deposit is entered, or when data is being read from a disk file to continue to process data until an End of File (EOF) marker is encountered. Although `for` loops that contain `break` statements could be used to code sentinel loops, they are more easily coded using the `while` and `do-while` statements.

Often, the use of sentinel loops in our programs makes them easier to use. Imagine you are a data-entry person using the program shown in Figure 5.8 to process a group of input deposits. When the program is launched, you are asked for the number of deposits. If the first item on the list of deposits you were given to enter was the number of deposits, the automatic counting performed by the `for` loop used in the program would be perfect for the application.

However, if the number of deposits was not included in the list of deposits, then before you used the application, you would have to count the number of deposits. Not only would this be time consuming when the list of deposits was long, but if you miscounted the number of deposits, the program would either terminate before all the deposits were entered (because your count was too low) or ask you to enter a deposit that did not exist (because your count was too high). Generally speaking, when the number of data items to be processed is not easily determined, sentinel loops make our programs much easier to use.

The following code fragment is a template for a sentinel loop that uses a `while` statement to process a set of inputs. Each input is read into a variable called the sentinel variable.

```
//obtain the first input into the sentinel variable
while( //the input is not the sentinel value )
{
    //statement(s) to perform the loop's processing
    //obtain the next input into the sentinel variable
}
```

The template begins with a statement to accept the first input and the same statement, which accepts all subsequent inputs, is also coded as the last statement in the `while` statement's code block. The other statements in the statement block perform the processing of each input. This placement of the input statements in a sentinel loop prevents the processing of the sentinel value, even if it is the first input (i.e., the data set is empty).

The three most common errors made when coding a sentinel loop are:

- neglecting to code the statement to accept the first sentinel variable input before the `while` statement

- neglecting to code the statements to accept all subsequent inputs of the sentinel variable at the end of the loop's code block
- coding the statements to accept all subsequent inputs of the sentinel variable inside the loop's code block before the processing statements

The first error results in the loop processing the default value of the sentinel variable, or if the default value is the sentinel value, the loop does not execute at all. The second error results in an infinite loop because once the loop is entered, the sentinel variable is not changed. When the third error is made, the first input is not processed.

The application SentinelWhileLoop presented in Figure 5.14 demonstrates the use of the code template. It is a sentinel loop version of the program shown in Figure 5.8 that totals and averages a set of input deposits. Typical inputs and outputs are shown at the bottom of Figure 5.14. As previously discussed, this version would be preferred if the number of deposits was not the first data item.

Following the format of the while loop sentinel template, line 18 accepts the initial value of the sentinel variable input. The Boolean expression (on line 19) of the while statement uses this variable to decide if the statement's code block should be executed. If anything other than the sentinel value (-1) has been input, an execution of the loop's statement block is performed.

Because an average is to be calculated and the user is no longer required to enter the number of deposits, the counting algorithm is used on line 23 to count the number of deposits processed. The counting variable, numOfDeposits, is initialized to zero on line 15. Consistent with the while sentinel loop template, the last line of the loop's code block (line 24) accepts the next input value and stores it in the sentinel variable input.

```
1    import javax.swing.JOptionPane;
2    import java.text.NumberFormat;
3
4    public class SentinelWhileLoop
5    {
6      public static void main(String[] args)
7      {
8        double balance = 1000.24;
9        int numOfDeposits;
10       double deposit, total, newBalance, averageDeposit;
11       String input;
12       NumberFormat us = NumberFormat.getCurrencyInstance();
13
14       System.out.println("Your beginning balance was:
                           "+ us.format(balance));
15       numOfDeposits = 0;
16       total = 0.0;
17
18       input = JOptionPane.showInputDialog("Enter a deposit, -1 to end");
19       while( !input.equals("-1") ) //input is not "-1"
```

```
20       {
21          deposit = Double.parseDouble(input);
22          total = total + deposit;
23          numOfDeposits++;
24          input = JOptionPane.showInputDialog("Enter a deposit, -1 to end");
25       }
26
27       balance = balance + total;
28       averageDeposit = total / numOfDeposits;
29
30       System.out.println("The total of the " + numOfDeposits +
31                          " deposits is "+ us.format(total));
32       System.out.println("The average deposit was: " +
33                          us.format(averageDeposit));
34       System.out.println("Your new balance is: " + us.format(balance));
35    }
36  }
```

Inputs
20.10
30.20
40.30
-1

Outputs
Your beginning balance was: $1,000.24
The total of the 3 deposits is $90.60
The average deposit was: $30.20
Your new balance is: $1,090.84

Figure 5.14
The console application **SentinelWhileLoop** and the output it produces.

Another commonly used form of a while sentinel loop parses the input after each input is accepted. This adaptation of the while loop sentinel template in the program shown in Figure 5.14 would be coded as:

```
input = JOptionPane.showInputDialog("Enter a deposit, -1 to end");
deposit = Double.parseDouble(input);
while (!deposit == -1.0)
{
   //statement(s) to perform the loop's processing, less the parsing
   input = JOptionPane.showInputDialog("Enter a deposit, -1 to end");
   deposit = Double.parseDouble(input);
}
```

5.5.3 Detecting an End Of File

Often, large data sets are stored in disk files, and the programs that process them read the data from the disk file until a sentinel value is detected. Because the sentinel value is chosen to be a value outside the range of the data set's values, most sentinel values vary from one application to another. In the case of a disk-based data file, there is one sentinel value that works for all data sets: the End of File (EOF) marker that is placed at the end of each file.

In Section 4.8.1 of Chapter 4, we used the methods in the `Scanner` class to read data from a disk text file. The `Scanner` class also contains a method named `hasNext` that can be used to detect the EOF marker in a file. The method has no parameters and returns `false` when the EOF marker is encountered. The following code fragment uses a sentinel loop to read all the integer data values from the disk text file `data.txt` stored on the root of the C drive and outputs the values to the system console. The value returned from the method `hasNext` is stored in the sentinel-variable `notEOF`.

```java
int dataItem;
File fileObject = new File("c:/data.txt");
Scanner fileIn = new Scanner(fileObject);
boolean notEOF; //the sentinel variable

notEOF = fileIn.hasNext(); //fetch the 1st sentinel variable value
while(notEOF) //more data to process
{
  dataItem = fileIn.nextInt();
  System.out.println(dataItem);
  notEOF = fileIn.hasNext(); //fetch next sentinel value
}
fileIn.close();
```

The following code fragment is a more succinct and more commonly used version of an EOF sentinel loop:

```java
int dataItem;
File fileObject = new File("c:/data.txt");
Scanner fileIn = new Scanner(fileObject);

while(fileIn.hasNext()) //more data to process
{
    dataItem = fileIn.nextInt();
    System.out.println(dataItem);
}
fileIn.close();
```

Figure 5.15 presents a modified version of the program shown in Figure 5.14 that processed a group of deposits entered from the keyboard. The new version of the program reads the deposits from a disk file using the file's EOF marker as a sentinel value. A set of file inputs and the corresponding program outputs are given at the bottom of Figure 5.15.

The instructions in Figure 5.14 that accept input from the keyboard have been removed from the program. Lines 1 and 2 of Figure 5.15 have been added to access the `Scanner` and `File` classes. In the interest of brevity, exceptions that could be generated during the disk file input performed by the program are not processed by the modified program. Rather, a `throws` clause has been added to the end of line 7.

Line 21 begins a sentinel `while` loop that ends when an EOF marker is detected. Inside the loop, line 23 reads and parses the next deposit using the `Scanner` object created by lines 13 and 14. Line 35 closes the disk file after the console output is performed.

```
1    import java.util.Scanner;
2    import java.io.*;
3    import java.text.NumberFormat;
4
5    public class EndOfFile
6    {
7      public static void main(String[] args) throws IOException
8      {
9        double balance = 1000.24;
10       int numOfDeposits;
11       double deposit, total, newBalance, averageDeposit;
12       NumberFormat us = NumberFormat.getCurrencyInstance();
13       File fileObject = new File("c:/data.txt");
14       Scanner fileIn = new Scanner(fileObject);
15
16       numOfDeposits = 0;
17       total = 0.0;
18
19       System.out.println("Your beginning balance is: " +
20                          us.format(balance));
21       while(fileIn.hasNext())  //more data to process
22       {
23         deposit = fileIn.nextDouble();
24         total = total + deposit;
25         numOfDeposits++;
26       }
27       balance = balance + total;
28       averageDeposit = total / numOfDeposits;
29
30       System.out.println("The total of the " + numOfDeposits +
31                          " deposits is " + us.format(total));
32       System.out.println("The average deposit was: " +
33                          us.format(averageDeposit));
34       System.out.println("Your new balance is: " + us.format(balance));
35       fileIn.close();
36     }
37   }
```

Disk File Inputs
20.10
30.20
40.30

Outputs
Your beginning balance was: $1,000.24
The total of the 3 deposits is $90.60
The average deposit was: $30.20
Your new balance is: $1,090.84

Figure 5.15
The application **EndOfFile**, a set of file inputs, and corresponding outputs.

An alternate approach to using the Scanner class's hasNext method to detect the end of a file is to write the number of data items into the file as the file's first value. If the data file processed by the program shown in Figure 5.15 had been written this way, lines 21-26 would be coded as shown below:

```
21      numOfDeposits = fileIn.nextInt();  //read the number of data items
22       for(int i = 1; i <= numOfDeposits; i++) //each data item
23       {
24         deposit = fileIn.nextDouble();
25         total = total + deposit;
26       }
```

Most often, the use of the hasNext method to detect the end of the file is the better approach because if new data were added to end of the file, updating the number of data items at the beginning of the file would require reading, deleting, and rewriting the entire file. This is a time-consuming process.

5.6 THE do-while STATEMENT

As previously discussed, when a loop in an application is to execute a known number of times, the for statement is best suited for the application. When the number of times to execute the loop is not known, either the while or the do-while statements are preferred. Of these two statements, the do-while statement is the better alternative when the loop's statements should be executed *at least once*. For example, the code to check a password is normally coded inside a do-while loop because the password has to be entered at least once.

5.6.1 Syntax of the do-while Statement

The generalized syntax of the do-while statement and its execution path are shown on the left and right sides of Figure 5.16, respectively.

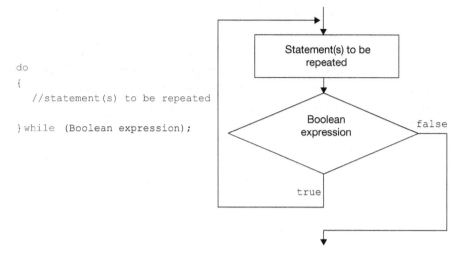

```
do
{
    //statement(s) to be repeated

}while (Boolean expression);
```

Figure 5.16
The generalized syntax of the do-while statement.

The statement begins with the keyword do followed by the loop's statement block. The keyword while and the statement's Boolean expression enclosed in parentheses are coded after the statement block's close brace. It is good programing style to code the keyword while and the Boolean expression on the same line as the close brace because it improves the readability of the statement. The do-while statement ends with a semicolon coded after the close parentheses that terminates the Boolean expression.

As shown on the right side of Figure 5.16, the loop's statement(s) will be executed at least once because they are executed before the Boolean condition is tested. After they execute, the Boolean expression is tested, and the statements are repeated until the Boolean condition becomes false. The do-while loop is called a *post-test* loop because the test to terminate the loop is performed after the loop's statement block has executed at least once.

The most common syntactical errors made when coding the do-while statement are:

• placing a semicolon after the keyword do
• neglecting to include a semicolon after the Boolean expression
• neglecting to code the open and close braces around the statements when more than one statement is to be repeated

All of these coding errors are syntax errors and are detected and reported by the Java translator. When coding a do-while loop, it is good programming practice to code the following code fragment and then add the statements to be repeated and the Boolean condition, even if only one statement is to be repeated.

```
do
{

}while( );
```

The most common logic error made when coding this statement is that the statements inside the statement block, during some repetition of the loop, do *not* change the Boolean expression to `false`. In this case, once the loop begins, it never ends and is said to be an infinite loop. For example, the following code sequence is an infinite loop because the loop's statement does not change the string variable `password`, which is used in the Boolean condition. The user-entered password is mistakenly stored in the string object `pw` leaving the string `password` unchanged each time through the loop.

```
String password = "";
String pw;
do
{
    pw = JOptionPane.showInputDialog("Enter The Password");
}while(!password.equals("Mercury"));
```

The following code fragment is the correct coding of a `do-while` statement that verifies the entry of the correct password, *Mercury*.

```
String password = "";
do
{
    password = JOptionPane.showInputDialog("Enter The Password");
}while(!password.equals("Mercury"));
```

Infinite loops can also occur when the loop's Boolean expression is improperly coded. In the code fragment below, the logical operator NOT(`!`) has been left out of the Boolean expression, and any password other than the correct password, *Mercury*, is accepted.

```
String password = "";
do
{
    password = JOptionPane.showInputDialog("Enter The Password");
}while(password.equals("Mercury"));
```

5.7 THE break AND continue STATEMENTS

The `break` and `continue` statements are used inside a `for`, `while`, or `do-while` loop's code block to alter the loop's execution path. Just as a `break` statement terminates the execution of a `switch` statement, a `break` statement may also be used to terminate a loop. Execution continues with the statement that follows the loop.

NOTE — *When a* `break` *statement is executed inside a loop, the execution of the loop terminates.*

When a `continue` statement is executed in a loop, the *current* iteration of the loop is terminated, and statements that come after it in the loop's body are not executed during that iteration of the loop. Execution continues with the testing of the loop statement's Boolean condition. When a `continue` statement is executed inside a `for` loop, the loop variable is incremented before the Boolean condition is tested.

NOTE   *When a* `continue` *statement is executed inside a loop, the current iteration of the loop terminates.*

To illustrate the use of these two statements, the code fragment below gives a game player three chances to enter the password "*Mars*" to access a game. The `break` statement is used to exit the loop after the message *Look up your password* is output. The `continue` statement is used to skip the message box output and the `break` statement until three incorrect passwords are entered.

```java
int count = 1;
String password = "";
do
{
   if(count <= 3)
   {
     password = JOptionPane.showInputDialog("Enter your password");
     count++;
     continue;
   }
   JOptionPane.showMessageDialog(null, "Look up your password");
   break;
}while(!password.equals("Mars"));
```

5.8 WHICH LOOP STATEMENT TO USE

When the number of times to repeat the loop's statements is known, the `for` statement should be used to code the loop. The number of times to repeat the loop could be known at the time the program is written (e.g., the program will always process 100 race times), or it is determined during the program's execution before the loop statement is executed. For example, before entering a group of deposits, the program users are asked to enter the number of deposits they will be making into their bank account. In both of these cases the `for` loop is the preferred loop statement.

When the number of times to execute the loop is not known, either a `while` or a `do-while` loop is preferred to a `for` loop. The `while` statement is the better alternative when there are times (cases) when the loop body should not execute even once. The `do-while` statement is the better alternative when the loop's statements should always be executed at least once. Table 5.2 summarizes the criteria for selecting the best loop statement for a particular application.

Table 5.2
Criteria for Selecting the Best Loop Statement

Is the Number of Times the Loop Will Execute Known?	Loop Statement
Yes	for
No, and there are cases when the loop body should *not* execute even once	while
No, and the loop body should always execute *at least once*	do-while

The boundaries between the use of the three loop statements become somewhat blurred with the use of the counting algorithm inside a `while` loop and the use of a `break` statement inside a `for` loop. For example, to average 100 items, most programmers would use a `for` loop. However, a `while` loop that contains the counting algorithm can also be used, as illustrated in the following code fragment:

```
int count = 1;
double total = 0;
double average;
String sItem;
while (count <= 100)
{
    sitem = JOptionPane.showInputDialog("Enter an item");
    total = total + Double.parseDouble(sItem);
    count++;
}
average = total / 100;
System.out.println("The average of the 100 items is: " + average);
```

The `for` loop is preferred for this application because when a `while` loop is used and we neglect to increment the counter (`count++;`) in the loop's body, the loop becomes an infinite loop. If we use a `for` loop and neglect to increment the counter in the first line of the `for` statement, the translator would alert us to the oversight.

Consider a program that totals input items until a -1 is entered or 100 items have been entered. Most programmers would use a `while` loop for this application. However, it can be coded using a `for` loop that contains a `break` statement.

```
double total = 0;
String sItem;

for(int i = 1; i <= 100; i++)
{
    sItem = JOptionPane.showInputDialog("enter an item");
    if(sItem.equals("-1"))
    {
        break;
    }
    total = total + Double.parseDouble(sItem);
}
System.out.println("The total of the items is: " + total);
```

When this `for` loop is used it would appear that the loop will always execute 100 times. However, the loop terminates before 100 iterations when the `break` statement executes. From a code readability point of view, the following `while` loop is the preferred loop statement for this application because the first line of the `while` loop clearly states the two conditions that will end the input loop.

```
int count = 1;
double total = 0;
String sItem;
```

```
sItem = JOptionPane.showInputDialog("enter an item, or -1");
while (!sItem.equals("-1") && count <= 100) //tests both conditions
{
    total = total + Double.parseDouble(sItem);
    count = count++;
    sItem = JOptionPane.showInputDialog("enter an item, or -1");
}
System.out.println("The total of the items is: " + total);
```

5.9 THE Random CLASS

Pseudorandom numbers, their use in computer programs, and the ability to generate them with the Math class's random method were discussed in Section 2.6.4 of Chapter 2. The methods in the class Random can also be used to generate pseudorandom numbers. In fact, these methods do the work of the Math class's random method in that the method random invokes the Random class's methods to generate the numbers it returns.

Table 5.3 lists the Random class's constructors and some of its methods used to generate pseudorandom numbers. Each time these methods are invoked, they return the next number in a sequence of random numbers. An object in the class Random is used to invoke them, which is created using one of the class's constructors.

```
Random randomObject1 = new Random();
Random randomObject2 = new Random(123456);
```

Table 5.3
Random Class Methods

Method	Description	Coding Example
Random()	Creates a Random object based on the seed value time of day	Random ro = new Random();
Random(long seed)	Creates a Random object based on the seed argument sent to it	Random ro = new Random(675);
nextDouble()	Returns the next pseudo-random real number in the range: 0.0<=randomNumber<1.0	double rn = ro.nextDouble();
nextInt()	Returns the next pseudorandom integer in the range of the int primitive type	int rn = ro.nextInt();
nextInt(int max)	Returns the next pseudo-random integer in the range zero to one less than max	int rn = ro.nextInt(20);

When the one-parameter constructor is used to create the object, the sequence of numbers the methods generate is based on the integer argument sent to the constructor, which is called a *seed* value. When the no-parameter constructor is used to create the object, the sequence of numbers the methods generate is based on the time of day because the seed value defaults to the real-time clock's value expressed in milliseconds. Sequences of numbers generated with objects created using the same seed value will be identical.

The one-parameter constructor is used when it is desirable to generate the same sequence of pseudorandom numbers every time the program is run. Conversely, the no-parameter constructor is used when it is desirable to generate a sequence of pseudorandom numbers that rarely repeats because the program would have to be run at exactly the same time of day to generate the same sequence of numbers.

Like the `Math` class's `random` method, the method `nextDouble` generates and returns a pseudorandom real number (a `double`) in the range: 0.0 <= randomNumber < 1.0. The method can be used to generate a real number in the range: min ≤ randomNumber < max using the following assignment statement (and sample object declaration):

```
Random randomObject2 = new Random(98765);
randomNumber = min + randomObject2.nextDouble() * (max - min);
```

The following code sequence outputs a sequence of ten pseudorandom real numbers in the range 20.0 ≤ randomNumber < 50.0. It would be very unusual for this code to generate the same sequence of numbers during two executions of the program because the sequence's seed value is the time of day in milliseconds. (The `Random` object is created with the no-parameter constructor.) Alternately, the one-parameter constructor could be used to generate a repeatable sequence of numbers.

```
double randomNumber;
double min = 20.0;
double max = 50.0;
Random randomObject2 = new Random(); // time of day seed value

for(int i = 1; i<=10; i++)
{
   randomNumber = min + randomObject2.nextDouble() * (max - min);
   System.out.println(randomNumber);
}
```

As shown in the Table 5.3, there are two versions of the `nextInt` method, which is used to generate and return a random integer (of type `int`). The no-parameter version returns a pseudorandom number over the full range of an `int` type variable (see Table 2.1).

The one-parameter version of the `nextInt` method is used to generate a sequence of integers, each of which are within a specified range. The numbers returned from the method are in the range zero to one less than the argument sent to it. The following code sequence generates a pseudorandom number between zero and nine, inclusive:

```
Random randomObject2 = new Random();
randomNumber = randomObject2.nextInt(10)
```

The use of this method can be generalized. The following code sequence outputs ten random integers in the range three to six, *inclusive*. The initial values of the variables max and min specify the lowest and highest numbers generated in the sequence. Every time this code is run, the same sequence of numbers is generated (5, 5, 5, 4, 3, 5, 5, 3, 6, 4) because the one-parameter constructor was used to create the Random object.

```
int randomNumber;
int min = 3;
int max = 6;
Random randomObject1 = new Random(98765); //repeatable random set

for(int i = 1; i<=10; i++)
{
   randomNumber = min + randomObject1.nextInt(max - min + 1);
   System.out.println(randomNumber); //in the range min to max inclusive
}
```

Figure 5.17 shows a number-guessing game program in which the player is asked to guess a number between 32 and 38, inclusive. The inputs and outputs for a correct answer on the second guess are shown in Figure 5.18.

Line 1 imports the Random class into the program. Line 8 declares an instance of this class, randomObject, which is used to invoke the nextInt method on line 15. The use of the no-parameter constructor on line 8 ensures that each time the program is run, there is the possibility that a different pseudorandom number will be generated by line 15. The maximum and minimum values of the pseudorandom numbers used on line 15 are specified on lines 9 and 10.

```
1    import java.util.Random;
2    import javax.swing.*;
3
4    public class RandomClass
5    {
6      public static void main(String[] args)
7      {
8        Random randomObject = new Random(); //time of day seed value
9        int min = 32;
10       int max = 38;
11       int secretNumber;
12       String sGuess;
13       int count = 1;
14
15       secretNumber = min + randomObject.nextInt(max - min + 1);
16       JOptionPane.showMessageDialog(null, "Secret Number Guessing Game" +
17                                     "\nguess a number between " +
18                                     max + " and " + min);
19       do
20       {
```

```
21          sGuess = JOptionPane.showInputDialog("Enter guess" + count +
22                                    "\nOr click Cancel to quit");
23          count++;
24          if(sGuess == null) //Cancel was clicked
25          {
26            break;
27          }
28       }while(secretNumber != Integer.parseInt(sGuess));
29
30       if(sGuess == null) //Cancel was clicked
31       {
32          JOptionPane.showMessageDialog(null, "Secret Number was " +
33                                    secretNumber);
34       }
35       else
36       {
37          JOptionPane.showMessageDialog(null, "Great, you guessed it.");
38       }
39    }
40 }
```

Figure 5.17
The application `RandomClass`.

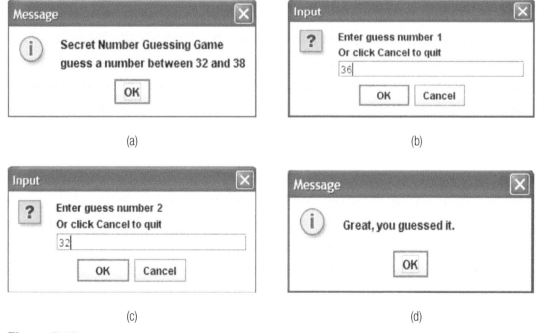

(a)

(b)

(c)

(d)

Figure 5.18
The inputs and corresponding outputs produced by the application `RandomClass`.

5.10 THE ENHANCED for STATEMENT

The enhanced `for` statement is an alternate syntax of a `for` loop that is used to fetch *all* of the elements of an array sequentially. During the execution of the loop, the elements of the array cannot be modified, so its use is limited. It can be used to output or total the elements of an array.

The syntax of the statement is given below, in which `anElement` is a variable whose type, `aType`, is always the type of the elements of the array `arrayName`:

```
for( aType anElement: arrayName )
{
   //statement(s) that use the variable anElement
}
```

For example, if the array is an array of references to `String` objects, the statement would be coded as shown below:

```
for( String anElement: arrayName )
{
   //statement(s) that use the variable anElement
}
```

A colon is always coded after the variable `anElement`. If there is only one statement to be executed within the loop, the open and close braces need not be coded, but it is good programming practice to include them.

The number of times the loop executes is always equivalent to the length of the array, in the above case `arrayName.length`. During the execution of the loop, the variable `anElement` assumes the value of each element of the array in ascending order, beginning with the first element (during the first iteration of the loop) and ending with the last element (during the last iteration of the loop). The two loops shown below are equivalent, and both produce the system console output `Nora Ryan Logan`.

```
String anArray = {"Nora", "Ryan", "Logan"};

for(String anElement: arrayName )
{
   System.out.print (anElement + " ");
}

System.out.println( );

for(int i = 0; i < 3; i++)
{
   System.out.print (arrayName[i] + " ")
}
```

Within the loop's body, the variable used in the enhanced `for` statement (e.g., `anElement`), can be used anywhere it is syntactically correct to use a variable of its type. An advantage of the enhanced `for` loop is that it cannot produce an `ArrayIndexOutOfBounds` error because it does not use a loop variable to access the elements of the array. The disadvantage is that the elements of the array cannot be changed inside the loop. We will see a more practical use of the enhanced for statement in Chapter 13, "Generics."

5.11 CHAPTER SUMMARY

Many applications require that the statements in a statement block be repeated, and in this chapter we discussed three ways to perform this repetition: a `for` loop, a `while` loop, and a `do-while` loop. The `for` loop is an automatic counting loop used when the number of times to repeat the statements is known. The `do-while` and `while` loops end when their Boolean condition becomes `false` and they are usually used to detect a sentinel value of the data they are processing. The `do-while` loop is used whenever the loop's block should be executed at least once, and the `while` loop is a more general-purpose loop that can be used in most applications.

The loop control variable of a `for` loop is used to control the number of iterations of the loop. The statement's initialization expression sets its initial value. At the end of each loop iteration, the increment expression executes, which normally changes the value of the loop variable. The `for` and `while` loops are called pretest loops: they test their Boolean condition to continue at the beginning of the loop; the `do-while` loop is a posttest loop, testing its condition to continue at the end of an iteration.

The totaling or summation algorithm is a loop-based algorithm because it sums a set of items by repeatedly adding the value of a new item to an existing subtotal and making the result the new subtotal. Its template is: `total = total + newItem`. Each time through the loop, the value of the variable `newItem` assumes the next value to be totaled, which is often input by the user or from a disk file. The variable total is initialized to zero before the totaling loop begins. The counting algorithm can use used inside a loop's statement block to count the number of times the loop executes and can then be divided into the total the loop calculates to determine the average of the totaled values.

Often, a sentinel value is used to terminate a loop when the number of input values to be processed is unknown. Two Java statements, `break` and `continue`, also enable us to control the number of times all or some of the statements within the body of the loop will be executed. When a `break` is executed within a loop, the loop terminates. The `continue` statement can be used to end the current iteration of the loop and is useful when conditions dictate that the remaining statements in the loop's block should be skipped during the current iteration. When a loop is used to obtain and process an unknown number of inputs from a file, Java's End of File (EOF) character or the `Scanner` class's `hasnext` method can be used as a sentinel to terminate the loop.

Nested loops are used to repeat loop-based algorithms. Examples include averaging 10 grades and repeating this for 20 students or processing a set of race times for 100 runners. Nested loops are particularly useful in creating two-dimensional graphics that are composed of many instances of the same repetitive shape, such as the eight rows of eight squares of a checkerboard.

The `Random` class's `nextInt` and `nextDouble` methods can be used to generate a random integer or real number and, when used inside of a loop, to generate a set of random numbers. The `nextInt` method is easier to use than the `Math` class's `random` method because it returns an integer in the positive range of the `int` type or within a specified range. This makes it ideal for generating random game board pixel locations. In addition, when the methods are invoked using a `Random` object created with the class's one-parameter constructor, they generate a repeatable sequence of pseudorandom numbers. This is particularly useful in applications that require the same starting point every time they are launched and is always used when the random numbers are generated within a graphics call back method.

The methods in the `DecimalFormat` class can be used to insert leading/training zeros and comma separators into numeric output, specify the output's precision, and convert the output to a percentage or display it using scientific notation. The methods in the `NumberFormat` and `Locale` classes are used to produce local dependent currency formatting for use in financial and international applications.

Our knowledge of these statements will be expanded in Chapter 6, which covers the concept of arrays because loops are used to unlock the power of arrays. Also, in the next chapter, we will see how loops can be used with arrays to enable us to input, output, and process large data sets.

Knowledge Exercises

1. True or false:
   a) The body of a `while` loop will always execute at least once.
   b) The `for` loop is an automatic counting loop and should be used where the number of repetitions is known.
   c) A sentinel is a data value that can be used to terminate a loop.
   d) The `do-while` loop will continue until the Boolean expression in the `while` statement becomes `true`.
   e) A `while` loop is a posttest loop.
   f) Checking for the EOF condition can be used to control a loop.
   g) A nested loop is a loop within a loop.
   h) Every `while` loop can be written as a `for` loop without using a break statement.
   i) Every `for` loop can be written as a `while` loop.
   j) The `break` statement ends the current iteration of a loop.
   k) A `for` loop ends when Boolean condition becomes `true`.
   l) The `continue` statement can be coded inside any loop.
   m) Placing a semicolon after the parenthesis in a `while` loop can cause an infinite loop.
   n) The statement block of a do-`while` loop may not be executed.
   o) A `for` loop may be designed to count down by decrementing the control variable.
   p) Loops may be used to validate user input or to give the user another chance to enter a value, such as a password, that was typed incorrectly.

2. Write a loop that outputs the integers from 20 to 100 to the system console and the appropriate term, odd or even, next to each output value.

3. Write a loop that outputs the sum of the even integers from 1 to n, where n is a value input by the user, to a message box.

4. Consider the following code fragment:
```
int i = 10;
int  sum = 0;
while (i <= 100)
{
   sum = sum + i;
   i++;
}
System.out.println("The sum of the integers from 10 to 100 is: " +
                    sum);
```
a) How many times does this loop execute?

b) Write an equivalent for loop.

c) Write an equivalent do-while loop.

5. Consider the following code fragment:
```
int i = 1;
while (i != 20)
{
   i = i + 2;
}
System.out.println("The value of i is " + i);
```
a) Will this loop terminate? If not, why not?

b) What numbers does it output?

6. Consider the following code fragment:
```
int num = 4;
for (int i = 2; i <= 7; i++)
{ System.out.println( "Number is " + num);
  num = num + i;
}
```
a) What is the value of num after the loop has executed twice?

b) How many times will the body of the loop be executed?

c) What value will be output on the fourth time through the loop?

d) What is the value of num when the loop ends?

e) What causes this loop to terminate?

7. Consider the following code fragment:
```
int x = 11;
while (x > 0)
{   x = x - 3;
    System.out.println(x);
}
```

     a) Give its output

     b) Write an equivalent `for` loop

8. Write the code fragment for an input validation loop that asks a user to enter an integer in the range of zero to five, displays an error if the input is out of range, and gives the user an *unlimited* number of chances to enter it correctly.

9. Write the code fragment for an input validation loop that asks a user to enter an integer in the range of zero to five, displays an error if the input is out of range, and gives the user at most three chances to enter it correctly.

10. Explain the difference in the execution paths of a `while` loop and a `do-while` loop.

11. Give a code fragment to produce the following output to the system console every time it is executed:

     a) A different set of 20 random integers in the range 0 to 500

     b) The same set of 20 random integers in the range 0 to 500

     c) The same set of 20 random integers in the range 7 to 500

     d) The same set of 20 random integers in the range `min` to `max`

12. Give the declarations and output statements required to display the value stored in the double variable `balance`, formatted as specified below. Also give the resulting formatted output.

     a) US currency

     b) One leading and one trailing zero, with comma separators every three digits to the left of the decimal point

     c) Scientific notation with four digits of precision

     d) Two trailing zeros, comma separators every three digits to the left of the decimal point, and a leading zero only when the balance contains a value that only has a fractional part

     e) Spanish currency

Programming Exercises

1. Write a program that uses a `for` loop to calculate and output the product of the integers from n to 1 (n factorial) to a message box. For example, when n = 4, the output would be 24 = 4 * 3 * 2 * 1. The value of n will be input by the user via an input dialog box, and the output should be properly annotated.

2. You have just been hired by the TravelStars agency, and your first assignment is to produce a histogram to graphically represent the ratings that travelers have given to various hotels. Your program will begin by asking the user to enter the number of hotels to be including in the histogram. Then, ask a user to input each hotel's name, the hotel's star rating, an integer between 1 and 10 stars inclusive. The histogram should be output to the system console and formatted as shown below.

Hotel Name	Rating
Hotel 1	**********
Hotel 2	******

Hotel 3	********
Hotel 4	**
Hotel 5	****

3. Write a program that uses nested loops to output one or more of these patterns (or create some of your own):

```
a)  * * * * * * * * * *        b)  *                c)          *
    * * * * * * * * * *            * * *                      *   *
    * * * * * * * * * *            * * * * *                *   *   *
    * * * * * * * * * *            * * * * * * *          *   *   *   *
    * * * * * * * * * *            * * * * * * * * *    *   *   *   *   *
```

4. Write a program that asks the program users for the country in which they were born and their salary for the each of the last 12 months. Output each month's salary, as well as the total pay for that year in the format of their local currency, to the system console, properly annotated.

5. Write a program that outputs 25 random integers to the system console that are within a range (minimum value and maximum value) specified by the user.

6. Write a program to simulate the toss of two dice. Every time the user clicks the OK button on a message generate two random outputs between 1–6, as well as the sum of the two dice. If the total is 7 or 11, output *You win*, otherwise output *Better luck next time*.

7. Write a graphical application that displays 650 of the 2,500 stars that can be seen in the night time sky. The stars will be drawn on the game board as filled ovals whose diameter is a random number between one and three pixels. There will be 400 white, 200 yellow, and 50 red stars, positioned at random (x, y) locations on a black-colored game board. You can change the color of the game board by invoking the `Component` class's `setBackground` method in the `main` method and passing it the color black.

8. Write the application described in Programming Exercise 7 using three nested loops to draw the stars.

9. Write a graphical application to simulate a journey to the sun by Captain Burk. Before the game board is displayed, the captain will be required to enter the noncase sensitive password "SS" (short for Starship). Then, he will be asked to enter the tonnage of each item in his cargo. When a -1 is entered, output the total weight of the cargo to a message box and display the game board described in Programming Exercise 7 or 8 with a 50-pixel-diameter sun positioned at the center of the game board. The sun will be a yellow instance of a `HeavenlyBodies` class you will add to the application that contains:
   - The four data members of a heavenly body: its (x, y) location coordinates, its diameter, and its color
   - A four-parameter constructor
   - A `show` method, and `set` and `get` methods for all the data members

Use an input dialog box for all input.

10. Write the graphical application described in Programming Exercise 9 expanded to include these features:
    - Before the game board is displayed, the captain will be asked how many (of a maximum of three) planets to add to the night sky and then asked to enter the location and diameter of each planet. The color of the three planets will be red, green, and brown, respectively, and they will be instances of `HeavenlyBodies` displayed on the game board.

    - When the Start button is clicked, the diameter of the sun should increase by 2 pixels every 20 milliseconds to simulate the Captain Burk's journey to the sun.

    - When the Start button is clicked a white comet (a `HeavenlyBodies` object) will travel from the upper-left to the lower-right corner of the gameboard with its diameter increasing from 3 to 50 pixels.

11. Using the skills developed in this chapter, continue the implementation of the parts of your game requiring knowledge of loops. Be sure to add this feature:
    - Do not permit the game to be played until the case-sensitive password "gp" (game player) is entered. After three unsuccessful password entries, output the statement *passwords are case sensitive* and terminate the program by invoking the `System` class's `exit` method.

CHAPTER 6

ARRAYS

6.1 *The Origin of Arrays* *236*
6.2 *The Concept of Arrays* *236*
6.3 *Declaring Arrays* *238*
6.4 *Arrays and Loops* *241*
6.5 *Arrays of Objects* *243*
6.6 *Passing Arrays Between Methods* *250*
6.7 *Parallel Arrays* *258*
6.8 *Common Array Algorithms.* *265*
6.9 *Application Programmer Interface Array Support* .*278*
6.11 *Deleting, Modifying, and Adding Disk File Items* . *286*
6.12 *Chapter Summary.* *290*

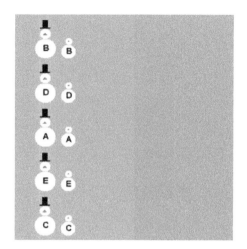

In this chapter

In this chapter, we will introduce the concept of an array and the powerful features of the construct that make it a part of most programs. These features include the ability to store and retrieve large data sets, and, when combined with the concept of a loop, these data sets can be processed with only a few instructions. Array processing algorithms such as sorting, searching, and copying will be discussed and implemented, as will algorithms introduced in Chapter 4 for inserting and deleting items stored in a disk text file. We will also explore the API methods that implement many of the classical array processing algorithms.

One-dimensional arrays, which can be used to store a list of items, will be discussed as well as multi-dimensional arrays, and we will use two-dimensional arrays to organize data in tables as rows and columns.

After successfully completing this chapter you should:

- Understand the advantages and importance of using arrays
- Be familiar with the Java memory model used to store arrays
- Be able to construct and use arrays of primitives and objects
- Understand and be able to implement the algorithms used to search an array, sort it, and find the minimum and maximum values stored in it
- Be familiar with and be able to use the array-processing methods in the API
- Understand the concept of parallel arrays and use them to process data sets
- Know how to use arrays to insert, delete, or update data items stored in a disk file
- Be able to apply array techniques to game programs

6.1 ■ THE ORIGIN OF ARRAYS

The machines we call computers received their name because the first operational versions of these machines were primarily used by mathematicians to perform rapid computations on large data sets. They were machines whose task was to compute; they were computers. However, long before computers were operational, mathematicians were using subscripted variables, such as x_2 or x_4, to represent the data used in their formulas and calculations, so it was natural for them to want to use these subscripted variables in the formulas evaluated by these early computing machines.

To facilitate the writing of these subscripted variables into a program, the designers of FORTRAN (which stands for *For*mula *Tran*slation), the first high level programming language used by mathematicians, included a construct that modeled subscripted variables. The construct was named *array*. Thus, the computer concept of an array has its roots in the mathematical model of subscripted variables.

6.2 ■ THE CONCEPT OF ARRAYS

Consider a program that processes five people's ages stored in the integer memory cells `age0`, `age1`, `age2`, `age3`, and `age4`. The declaration of these variables would be rather straightforward:

```
int age0, age1, age2, age3, age4;
```

But suppose that instead of processing five people's ages, the program processed five million people's ages. Although the declaration syntax for the five million memory cells would still be straight forward, it would be quite lengthy and very time consuming to write. In fact, a good typist would take more than a month to type just the variable declarations for this program, assuming the typist typed continuously for eight hours each day without stopping to eat. (This, by the way, is a violation of the federal labor laws.) Using the construct array, the same typist could type the declaration of the five million memory cells in seconds.

That's all an **array** is: a technique used to declare memory cells, which is rooted in the mathematical concept of subscripted variables.

Definition

An **array** is a programming concept used to declare groups of related memory cells in which each member of the group has the same data type, the same first name, the array's name, and a unique last name called an **index**.

The memory cells are related in the same way that our integer memory cells `age0` through `age4` were related: each one stores a person's age, or perhaps a person's weight, or perhaps an address of a snowman game piece. In Java the unique last names, the indexes (or indices), are always sequential integers beginning with zero (i.e., 0, 1, 2, 3, 4, …). In addition, Java syntax requires that the unique last name is enclosed in open and close brackets, for example, [2].

Figure 6.1 shows ten memory cells used to store people's ages. The five memory cells on the left were declared to be five separate integer variables with the statement

```
int age0, age1, age2, age3, age4;
```

The five memory cells on the right were declared to be part of a five-member or element array named `age`.

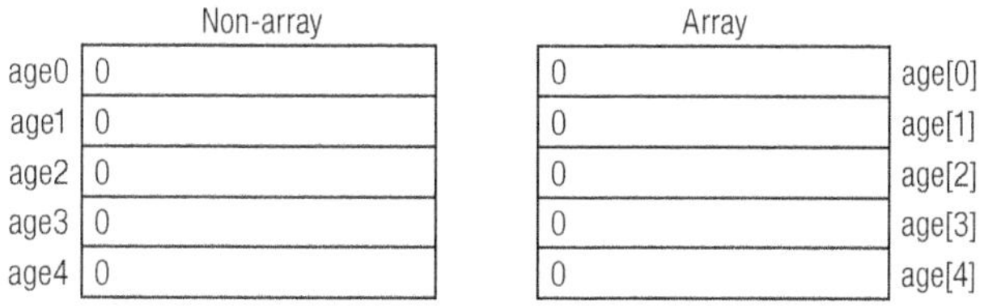

Figure 6.1
Storage allocated to five integer variables and to a five-element array named age.

As shown in Figure 6.1, the amount of storage allocated to the integer variables on the left side of the figure is the same as the amount of storage allocated to array elements shown on the right side of the figure: five distinct integer memory cells. From a memory-allocation viewpoint, the only difference in the way memory is allocated to the memory cells that make up the elements of an array is that the array elements are always allocated as contiguous memory; that is, if each memory cell occupied four bytes of storage, and `age[0]` was stored in bytes 100–103, the memory allocated to the subsequent four elements of the array would begin at byte addresses 104, 108, 112, and 116. (In contrast, the five integer variables might be stored in different locations scattered around memory.)

Array elements can be used in our programs anywhere it is syntactically correct to code the name of a memory cell: in input and output statements, in arithmetic and logic expressions, on the left side of an assignment operator, and as arguments and parameters. To use them, we simply code their complete names. For example, the statements on the left and right sides of Figure 6.2 are equivalent, although they are syntactically different because the statements on the right side of the figure use the array construct.

Without arrays	With arrays
``age3=new Scanner(System.in).nextInt();
age3 = age3 + 1;
System.out.println("Your age is" +
                age3);
if(age3 >= 18)
{
   System.out.println("You can " +
                "Drive now");
}

double avgAge = averageTwo(age0,
                age1);``` | ```age[3]=new Scanner(System.in).nextInt();
age[3] = age[3] + 1;
System.out.println("Your age is" +
                age[3]);
if(age[3] >= 18)
{
   System.out.println("You can " +
                "Drive now");
}

double avgAge = averageTwo(age[0],
                age[1]);``` |

Figure 6.2
Equivalent statements with and without the use of arrays.

Although the syntax involved in using arrays is a bit more cumbersome because of the coding of the open and close brackets, as previously mentioned, they do give us the ability to rapidly declare large numbers of variables. In addition, as we will see later in this chapter, when arrays are used inside of loops they also give us the ability to process large data sets with just a few lines of code. For these two reasons, most programs use arrays.

6.3 DECLARING ARRAYS

In Java, all arrays are stored inside of an object. Although we most often state that we are "declaring an array," it is more accurate to state that we are "declaring an object that contains an array." In fact, as we shall see, the object contains not only the array but an also an integer data member named `length`.

The syntax used to declare an array object is similar to the syntax used to declare non-array objects in that a reference variable is declared that will refer to the array object, and the keyword `new` is used to construct the object. Where they differ is that the array-object declaration syntax also includes a set of brackets to indicate that the reference variable will refer to an array object, and the number of elements the array will contain (called the size of the array) is enclosed in another set of brackets. The generalized syntax is:

```
aType[] arrayName = new aType[arraySize];
```
where:

`aType` is the type of the elements of the array

`arrayName` is the name of a reference variable that will store the address of the array object, also considered to be the name of the array

`arraySize` is the number of elements in the array

To declare an array object that could store five integer ages we would write:

```
int[] ages = new int[5];
```

This statement allocates the memory shown in Figure 6.3. Not only is the storage for the array's elements allocated inside the object, but an integer named `length` is allocated and initialized to the size of the array. The index of the first element of an array is always zero, and the indexes of the remaining elements of an array are assigned sequential integer values in ascending order. This implies that the index of the last element of an array is always one less than the size of the array. In a five-element array, `ages[5]` does not exist, which is somewhat counterintuitive, and attempting to access it results in a runtime error.

NOTE   *The indices of an array containing n elements are 0 through n-1, and the size of the array is n.*

Conceptually, the array object declaration would be drawn as shown on the right side of Figure 6.1, which is the way we most often visualize an array. Figure 6.3 gives a more accurate depiction of the storage allocated to the array object created by the declaration given in the figure's caption and the reference variable, `ages`, that refers to the array object.

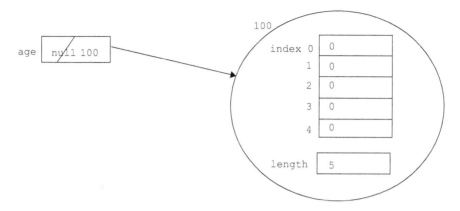

Figure 6.3
The array object created by the statement `int[] ages = new int[5];`.

When an array object is created, the elements of the array are initialized to their default values (e.g., zero for an array of integers), and the array object is assigned an address (address 100 in Figure 6.3). The data member `length` is initialized to the size of the array. For example in Figure 6.3, `length` stores the value 5 inside the array object `ages`.

The data member `length` is a public data member, so rather than using a `get` method to access it, it can be accessed by coding the name of the array object followed by `length`, preceded by a dot. The following code fragment outputs a 5, the size of the array `ages`:

```
int[] ages = new int[5];
System.out.println(ages.length);
```

The data member `length` is a final variable and cannot be assigned a value. The following code fragment results in a translation error:

```
int[] ages = new int[5];
ages.length = 23; //syntax error: can't re-assign a final constant
```

6.3.1 Dynamic Allocation of Arrays

An array object, like any other object, can be allocated dynamically during the execution of the program. As we have learned, to do this we most often use the two-line object declaration syntax. The first line is used to declare the reference variable that will refer to the object, and good programming practice dictates that this line is coded at the top of the method or class in which the array will be used. The second line of the syntax is used to allocate the object and set the reference variable pointing to it. This line is normally coded further down in a method.

The splitting of the array object declaration syntax permits the size of the array to be determined by the processing the program performs. For example, the size of the array could be read from the first line of a disk file that also contains the data that will be stored in the array, or the size of the array could be input by the user. For example:

```
int[] ages;
String sSize = JOPtionPane.showInputDialiog("How many ages" +
                                            "will be entered?");
```

```
int size = Integer.parseInt(sSize);
ages = new int[size];
```

Many applications, in which the number of data items to be processed is determined at run time, would be very difficult to code without the use of arrays. For example, consider an application that outputs a set of input data in reverse order. This requires declaring a variable for every data item because they must all be saved until the last data item is input and then output. Because the number of inputs is not known until runtime, without the use of arrays, we would have to guess the maximum number of inputs, allocate that number of variables, and keep our fingers crossed that we did not guess too low.

The fact that the `length` data member of an array object cannot be changed is consistent with the fact that, in Java, the size of an array cannot be changed. As is the case with all objects, the reference variable that refers to the object can be assigned to another object. In the case of an array, we can make use of this fact to effectively resize the array at runtime by assigning the reference variable to the address of a smaller, or a larger, array object.

For example, an array initially sized to five elements could be made to refer to a new array object whose size is based on a user input.

```
int[] data = new int[5];
        :
        :
String sSize = JOPtionPane.showInputDialiog("How many ages" +
                                        "will be entered?");
int size = Integer.parseInt(sSize);
data = new int[size];
```

Assuming the user entered a "3" in response to the above prompt, Figure 6.4 shows the changes in the contents of the reference variable `data` and the array object that `data` refers to, resulting from the execution of the above code. It should be noted that if the original five-element array contained five people's ages, these ages would be lost after the dynamic allocation.

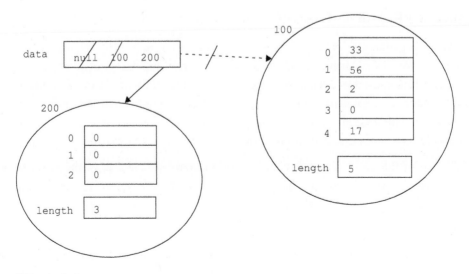

Figure 6.4
The effect of the statement data = new int[3];.

As shown in Figure 6.4, the five-element array object's address is overwritten with the address of the new three-element array object, causing the storage allocated to the five-element array to be reclaimed by the Java runtime memory manager. In Java, the storage allocated to objects that are not referred to by a reference variable is reclaimed for use by other programs. In Section 6.9, we will discuss techniques for transferring the values into a resized array when it is created.

6.4 ARRAYS AND LOOPS

Using arrays inside loops gives us the ability to process large data sets with just a few lines of code. This is because the index used to specify which element of the array is being processed can not only be a numeric literal (e.g., `a = age[2];`), but it can also be an integer variable. The only restriction on the integer variable is that the value stored in it must be a valid element number of the array. The following code segment outputs the third element of the array `price` twice. When the last statement executes, the current contents of the variable `index` is fetched, substituted for the variable `index`, and the output is performed.

```
double[] price = new double[100];
int index = 2;

System.out.println(price[2]);
System.out.println(price[index]);
```

This array feature is commonly used with the loop variable of a `for` statement as the array index. Using this approach, the code to decrease the price of each of the 10,000 items a department store sells by 10% in preparation for its annual Labor Day sale can be coded in just two lines of code:

```
for(int i = 0; i < 10000; i++)
{
    salePrice[i] = price[i] * 0.9;
}
```

The first time through the loop the variable `i` stores the value 0, and `salePrice[0]` is computed. The second time through the loop `i` stores the value 1, and `salePrice[1]` is computed. This process continues until finally `salePrice[9999]` is computed.

Two common mistakes are made when processing arrays inside of loops, both of which are syntactically correct:

- the loop variable is initialized to 1 instead of to 0
- the Boolean condition is incorrectly coded using the <= operator instead of <

The first mistake stems from the fact that most of us begin with 1 when we count: 1, 2, 3, etc., so our natural tendency is to initialize the loop variable to 1 instead of 0. When this mistake is made, the first element of the array (element zero) is not processed.

Coding the Boolean condition incorrectly is the most common mistake. When all the elements of the array are to be processed, our code is much more understandable if we use the size of the array, `price.length`, in the Boolean condition. However, when we do this, we must use the less than (<) operator in the condition (e.g., `i < price.length`). Unfortunately, most novice programmers, intent on processing the last element of the array, use the <= operator, and the last iteration of the loop generates an index that is one greater that of the last element of the array (e.g., 5 for a five-element array). The result is a runtime error indicating that the program generated an `Array-IndexOutOfBoundsException`. This error occurs whenever a program uses an array index that is not in the range 0 to one less than the array's size.

Figure 6.5 presents the application `ArraysAndLoops` that uses many of the array concepts discussed thus far in this chapter to compute, and output, the sale price of a group of input items. It accepts the prices of a set of items to be placed on sale, then computes and outputs the sale price of the items. A sample set of inputs and the corresponding outputs produced by the program are given at the bottom of the figure.

```
1    import javax.swing.*;
2    import java.text.NumberFormat;
3
4    public class ArraysAndLoops
5    {
6      public static void main(String[] args)
7      {
8        double[] price, salePrice;
9        String s;
10       int size;
11       NumberFormat fm = NumberFormat.getCurrencyInstance();
12       s = JOptionPane.showInputDialog("How many sale items?");
13       size = Integer.parseInt(s);
14       price = new double[size];
15       salePrice = new double[size];
16
17       for(int i = 0; i < size; i++)
18       {
19         s = JOptionPane.showInputDialog("Enter item " + (i + 1) +
20                                     " 's price");
21         price[i] = Double.parseDouble(s);
22       }
23
24       for(int i = 0; i < price.length; i++)
25       {
26         salePrice[i] = price[i] * 0.9;
27         System.out.println("The sale price of item " + (i + 1)  +
28                            " is " + fm.format(salePrice[i]));
29       }
30     }
31   }
```

Inputs:
5
10.00
20.00
30.00
40.00
50.00
Outputs:
The sale price of item 1 is $9.00
The sale price of item 2 is $18.00
The sale price of item 3 is $27.00
The sale price of item 4 is $36.00
The sale price of item 5 is $45.00

Figure 6.5
The application **ArraysAndLoops** and a set of inputs and corresponding outputs.

After the user enters the number of items to be placed on sale (line 12), two array objects are dynamically allocated on lines 14 and 15, and their addresses are assigned to the reference variables `price` and `salePrice`. These variables were declared on line 8.

The program uses two `for` loops that begin on lines 17 and 24. The first loop accepts the input of the non-sale prices, and the second loop computes and outputs the sale prices. The loop variable, `i`, of the `for` loop that begins on line 17 is used to change the element of the array `price` (line 21) that stores the parsed input. The second `for` loop, which begins on line 24, uses its loop variable to index its way through the array `price` and the array `salePrice` (line 26) as it computes the new values of the `salePrice` array.

The first loop uses the variable `size`, which was used to size both arrays on lines 14 and 15, in its Boolean condition. The second loop uses the `length` data member of the array object `price` in its Boolean condition. Either approach can be used. However, the latter approach is preferred because it more clearly indicates that the entire array is being processed within the loop, and eliminates the chance that an incorrect variable (other than size) would be coded in the Boolean condition. The second approach is also preferred when the array is passed into a method that will process the array's contents for reasons that we will discuss in Section 6.6. Both `for` statements correctly use the less than operator (<) in their Boolean conditions.

6.5 ARRAYS OF OBJECTS

Technically speaking, there is no way to declare an array of objects. The elements of an array cannot be objects; they can only be primitive or reference variables. However, when the array elements are reference variables, each element of the array can contain the address of an object. When this is the case, we often say that we have "an array of objects" because it is easier to say than "an array of reference variables that refer to objects" (which is what we actually have).

Leaving aside the technical jargon, when we set each element of an array of reference variables to point to an object, we can rapidly process all of the objects by indexing through the array of reference variables. In addition, just as it was easy to declare a large number of variables using arrays, we can easily declare a large number of objects using arrays of reference variables.

The first step in applying the power of arrays to programs that process objects is to declare (an array object that contains) an array of reference variables. The second step is to declare the objects and set their addresses into the elements of the array. The syntax used to declare the array of reference variables is the same syntax used to declare an array of primitive variables. The following declaration creates an array of reference variables that could refer to five Snowman objects:

```
Snowman[] sm = new Snowman[5];
```

The storage allocated by this declaration is shown in Figure 6.6. Because the array contains reference variables, they are initialized to the default value of a newly created reference variable: null. Otherwise, the figure is identical to Figure 6.3, which shows the storage allocated when an array of five integers is declared.

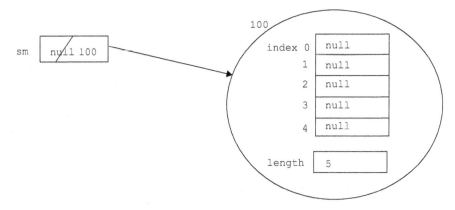

Figure 6.6
The storage created by the declaration **Snowman[] sm =new Snowman[5];**.

As shown in Figure 6.6, the declaration of the array object does not allocate any Snowman objects. To do this, we have to invoke a constructor in the Snowman class and set the returned address of the newly constructed Snowman into an element of the array. Assuming the class has a two-parameter constructor, one way to do this is to write five declaration statements:

```
sm[0] = new Snowman(50, 100);
sm[1] = new Snowman(100, 100);
sm[2] = new Snowman(150, 100);
sm[3] = new Snowman(200, 100);
sm[4] = new Snowman(250, 100);
```

Assuming the constructor's parameters are the (x, y) location of a Snowman object, our five newly created snowmen will be standing shoulder to shoulder (at x = 50, 100, 150, 200, and 250) when they are drawn on the game board. An equivalent but more efficient way to construct the five snowmen would be to place the invocation of the constructor inside a loop. The use of a loop is the preferred coding technique, which we would quickly realize if we had to declare a group of 5,000 snowmen.

```
for(int i = 0; i < 5; i++)
{
    sm[i] = new Snowman(50 +  i * 50, 100);
}
```

Because the loop variable is used as the index into the array sm, sm[0] receives the address of the first Snowman created inside the loop. During each additional pass through the loop, the next sequential element of the array receives the address of a newly created Snowman. In addition, the loop variable is used to change the x coordinate of the snowmen, using the expression (50 + i * 50), each time through the loop. The storage created after the loop completes its execution is shown in Figure 6.7.

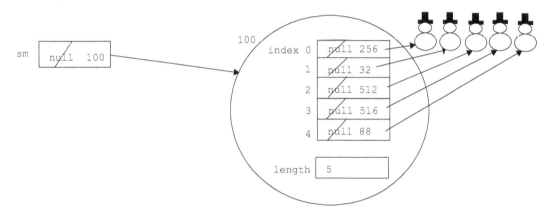

Figure 6.7
An array of five reference variables pointing to five **Snowman** objects.

6.5.1 Processing an Array's Objects

In Section 6.4, we learned that large primitive data sets could be processed with just a few lines of code using the concepts of arrays and loops. To accomplish this, the data set was stored in an array of primitive variables, and the processing instructions were coded inside a loop. The loop variable was used as the index into the array, which caused the processing instruction(s) to operate on a different element of the array during each pass through the loop.

Similarly, we can process large sets of objects with just a few lines of code by storing the objects' addresses inside an array of reference variables and then perform the processing on each object inside a loop. The only difference is that instead of performing the processing on the array elements themselves, the array elements are used to invoke the class's processing methods on the objects they reference.

For example, the code to add one to each of five people's ages stored in an array of integers named ages is very similar to the code that moves each of five snowmen stored in an array of objects named sm one pixel to the right. The following code fragment illustrates the similarities:

```
int x;
for(int i = 0; i < 5; i++)
{
   ages[i] = ages[i] + 1; //increment the ages

   x = sm[i].getX(); //move the snowmen
   sm[i].setX(x + 1);
}
```

Each time through this loop, the loop variable is used to change the element of the two arrays involved in loop's processing instructions. In the case of the integer array, the value stored in one of the elements of the array, `ages`, is incremented by one; that is, the contents of the array `ages` is changed. However, the loop processing does not change the contents of the array `sm`. Rather, it uses the contents of the array `sm` to specify which `Snowman` object will be changed (operated on) by the `getX` and `setX` methods during each pass through the loop. In this case, the `x` data member of each `Snowman` object is increased by one.

That is not to say that the contents of an array of reference variables cannot be changed inside a loop. As we have already seen, this is done when objects are constructed and the default `null` values stored in the elements of the array are overwritten with the location of the newly constructed (`Snowman`) objects. Conversely, all five snowmen could be eliminated from a game by overwriting their addresses stored in the array with the value `null`:

```
for(int i = 0; i < 5; i++)
{
   sm[i] = null;
}
```

This would cause the Java memory manager to recycle the storage allocated to the five `Snowmen` objects and make it available to other programs running on the system.

The game application in Figure 6.8 uses the concepts discussed in this section to conduct a parade of eight snowmen whose class is shown in Figure 6.9. The output produced by the program when it is launched and the output produced several seconds after the start button is clicked are shown on the left and right sides of Figure 6.10, respectively.

An array of reference variables named `parade` that will be used to store the addresses of eight `Snowman` objects, is created on line 7 of Figure 6.8. When the game is launched, the snowmen are displayed along a left-to-right downward-sloping diagonal (as shown in Figure 6.10a), until the Start button is clicked. Then they parade around the game board reflecting off its boundaries, eventually coming to the positions shown in Figure 6.10b.

The creation, display, animation, and reflection of the snowmen are performed inside four loops. Within each iteration of these loops, a different snowman is processed because the loop variable is used as an index into the `parade` array. The first of these loops (lines 11–14 of Figure 6.8) is used to create the snowmen and place the addresses of these eight objects in the reference variable array `parade`. On line 13, the loop variable, `i`, is used inside the argument list sent to the `SnowmanV7` class's two-parameter constructor to calculate each snowman's initial (x, y) location along a downward-sloping diagonal. During each iteration of the loop that begins on line 21, a different snowman is displayed on the game board at its current (x, y) location.

The remaining two loops, which begin on lines 31 and 41, move the snowmen around the game board and bounce (reflect*)* them off the vertical and horizontal boundaries of the game board. The loops are coded inside the `timer3` call back method (lines 27–56), whose interval is set to 20 milliseconds on line 15. As a result, every 20 milliseconds (1/50th of a second), the game environment invokes this method, and the loops are executed. After the `timer3` method completes its execution, the game environment invokes the application's `draw` method (line 19), which displays the snowmen at their new (x, y) position.

The `for` loop coded on lines 31–39 of the application performs the animation of the snowmen. By using the loop variable, `i`, as an index into the parade array, each snowman's x and y position is fetched (lines 33 and 36), incremented by their corresponding speed data members (lines 34 and 37), and set to their new values (lines 35 and 38). Being coded inside the `timer3` method, this code changes each snowman's (x, y) position every 20 milliseconds. The rapid repositioning and redrawing of the snowmen (every 1/50th of a second) gives the appearance of continuous motion.

The `for` loop coded on lines 41–55 of Figure 6.8 performs the reflection of the snowmen off the boundaries of the game board. The two data members, `xSpeed` and `ySpeed` were added to the class `SnowmanV7` (Figure 6.9, lines 7 and 8) along with their corresponding `set` and `get` methods (lines 41, 45, 49, and 53) to perform this reflection. The loop variable, `i`, is used inside two `if` statements (that begin on lines 43 and 49 of Figure 6.8) to index into the `parade` array. Their Boolean conditions determine when a snowman's current (x, y) position is at or beyond the vertical (line 43) and horizontal (line 49) boundaries of the game board.

When this is the case, the snowman's speed is fetched (lines 45 and 51), its sign is reversed (lines 46 and 50), and the new value is set into the snowman's speed data member (lines 47 and 53). Then, during the next execution of the `timer3` method, when each snowman's speed is used to reposition it on the game board, those that reached a game board edge appear to bounce off the edge because the sign of their speed has been reversed.

```
1    import java.awt.Graphics;
2    import edu.sjcny.gpv1.*;
3
4    public class SnowmanParade   extends DrawableAdapter
5    { static SnowmanParade ge = new SnowmanParade();
6      static GameBoard gb = new GameBoard(ge, "Snowman Parade");
7      static SnowmanV7[] parade = new SnowmanV7[8];
8
9      public static void main(String[] args)
10     {
```

```
11        for(int i=0; i < parade.length; i++) //create each snowman
12        {
13           parade[i] = new SnowmanV7(10 + i * 50 , 100 + i * 30);
14        }
15      gb.setTimerInterval(3, 20);
16      showGameBoard(gb);
17    }
18
19    public void draw(Graphics g) //draw each snowman
20    {
21      for(int i = 0; i < parade.length; i++)
22      {
23         parade[i].show(g);
24      }
25    }
26
27    public void timer3()
28    {
29      int x, speed, y;
30
31      for(int i = 0; i  <parade.length; i++) //move each snowman
32      {
33        x = parade[i].getX();
34        x = x + parade[i].getXSpeed();
35        parade[i].setX(x);
36        y = parade[i].getY();
37        y = y + parade[i].getYSpeed();
38        parade[i].setY(y);
39      }
40
41      for(int i = 0; i < parade.length; i++) //reflect each snowman
42      {
43        if(parade[i].getX() >= 460 || parade[i].getX() <= 6)//x
44        {
45           speed = parade[i].getXSpeed();
46           speed = -speed;
47           parade[i].setXSpeed(speed);
48        }
49        if(parade[i].getY() >= 420 || parade[i].getY() <= 30)//
50        {
51           speed = parade[i].getYSpeed();
52           speed = -speed;
53           parade[i].setYSpeed(speed);
54        }
55      }
56    }
57  }
```

Figure 6.8
The application **SnowmanParade**.

```
1    import java.awt.*;
2
3    public class SnowmanV7
4    {
5      int x;
6      int y;
7      int xSpeed = 2;
8      int ySpeed = 2;
9
10     public SnowmanV7(int x, int y)
11     { this.x = x;
12       this.y = y;
13     }
14
15     public void show(Graphics g) // g is the game board object
16     { g.setColor(Color.BLACK);
17       g.fillRect(x + 15, y, 10, 15); // hat
18       g.fillRect(x + 10, y + 15, 20, 2); // brim
19       g.setColor(Color.WHITE);
20       g.fillOval(x + 10, y + 17, 20, 20); // head
21       g.fillOval(x, y + 37, 40, 40); // body
22       g.setColor(Color.RED);
23     }
24
25     public int getX()
26     { return x;
27     }
28
29     public void setX(int newX)
30     { x = newX;
31     }
32
33     public int getY()
34     { return y;
35     }
36
37     public void setY(int newY)
38     { y = newY;
39     }
40
41     public int getXSpeed()
42     { return xSpeed;
43     }
44
45     public void setXSpeed(int newXSpeed)
```

```
46      { xSpeed = newXSpeed;
47      }
48
49      public int getYSpeed()
50      { return ySpeed;
51      }
52
53      public void setYSpeed(int newYSpeed)
54      { ySpeed = newYSpeed;
55      }
56  }
```

Figure 6.9
The class **SnowmanV7**.

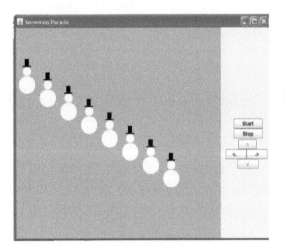

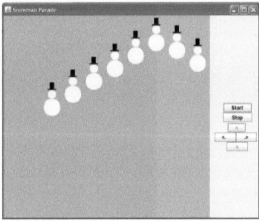

(a) Initial output   (b) Output several seconds after Start is clicked

Figure 6.10
The output of the application **SnowmanParade**.

6.6 PASSING ARRAYS BETWEEN METHODS

As discussed in Section 3.8, reference variables can be part of a worker method's parameter list. This gives us the ability to pass the location of objects declared in a method into a worker method it invokes. Knowing the object's location enables the worker method to perform some processing on the object by referring to it using the parameter name that received the object's location. In addition, when the returned type of a non-void worker method is the name of a class, the worker method can return the location of *one* object in that class to the method that invoked it.

Because arrays are stored in objects, the ability to pass reference variables to and from worker methods also gives us the ability to pass arrays to and from worker methods. To do this, we simply pass the array object's reference variable to and from the worker method. While there are no conceptual differences to consider when passing array and non-array objects to and from worker methods, there are some minor syntactical differences in the signature of the worker method.

In the remainder of this section, we will discuss these differences and present examples of passing arrays to and from worker methods. We will begin with a discussion of passing arrays to a worker method and conclude with a discussion of returning an array from a worker method.

6.6.1 Passing Arrays of Primitives to a Worker Method

Consider the array age, shown on the left side of Figure 6.11, which stores the ages of five people that have the same birthday. The following code fragment defines and initializes this array and passes it to the static worker method birthday coded in the class Party.

```
int[] age = new int[5];
for(int i=0; i < age.length; i++)
{
   age [i] = 21 + i;
}
Party.birthday(age); //method invocation statement
```

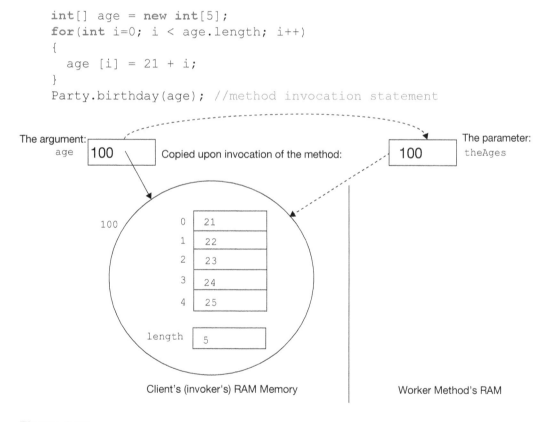

Figure 6.11
Passing an array of primitives to a method.

Looking at the method invocation statement, there is no way to tell if the argument age sent to the method birthday is a primitive variable or an array. This is because the syntax of an invocation statement used to pass an array reference to a worker method is the same syntax used to pass a primitive variable to a worker method, which is also the same syntax used to pass any reference variable to a worker method. From an invocation statement's viewpoint, there is nothing new to learn about passing arrays to worker methods.

As previously discussed, it is the syntax of the signature of the worker method that is different. When a parameter listed in a method's signature is an array, a pair of braces [] is coded in between the parameter's name and its type. The following is the code of the static worker method `birthday` that is passed an integer array. The work of the method is to add one to each element of the array.

```
static void birthday(int[] theAges)
{
  for(int i=0; i < theAges.length; i++)
  {
    theAges[i] = theAges[i] + 1;
  }
}
```

NOTE *When a parameter in a worker method's signature is an array, code a pair of braces [] in between the parameter's name and its type. For example:*
```
static void birthday(int[] theAges)
```

As indicated by the dashed arrows at the top of Figure 6.11, when the method is invoked and passed the argument `ages`, Java's use of value parameters copies the value stored in the argument (100) into the method's parameter `theAges`. Then the method's code is able to access the elements of the array object because its parameter, `theAges`, now stores the array's address. Effectively, while the method is executing, the array object is *shared* between the client code and the worker method it invokes. Although we normally say we are "passing an array to a method," we really should say we are "passing the *address* of an array object to a method."

NOTE *When passing an array to a worker method, the address of the array is passed to the method, and the array object is shared between the client and worker methods.*

Because the array's address is shared, if the worker method changes the contents of the array, the client code no longer has access to the original contents of the array. This is not a contradiction of the idea that value parameters prevent worker methods from changing the client's information passed to it because the information passed to the worker method is the array's *address*, not the array's *elements*. This is a subtle but important point to understand. Referring to Figure 6.11, while it is true that the worker method can change the contents of the elements of the array because `theAges` stores the object's address, it cannot change the address of the array stored in the variable `age` (which was the information passed to it).

If the worker method contained the statement below, it would lose access to the client's array object, but the client code would not. The address of the client's array object would still be stored in the variable `age`.

```
theAges = new int[20];
```

6.6.2 Passing Arrays of Objects to a Worker Method

As mentioned in Section 6.5, technically speaking, Java does not support arrays of objects. However, an array's elements can be reference variables that each store the address of an object. When this is the case, we often say that the array is "an array of objects" because it is simpler than saying the array is "an array of reference variables that point to objects." When passing an array of objects to a method, the invocation statement and the method's signature use the same syntax used to pass an array of primitive variables to a method. As discussed in the previous section, the only indication that arrays are being passed is the inclusion of a pair of braces [] in between the parameter's name and its type in the signature of the worker method.

The left side of Figure 6.12 shows the array, `parade`, containing five reference variables that store the addresses of five `SnowmanV7` objects whose class is shown in Figure 6.9. To pass this array to a worker method, we take advantage of Java's value parameter implementation and pass the address of the array to the method using the same syntax we used to pass the address of an array of primitives to a method.

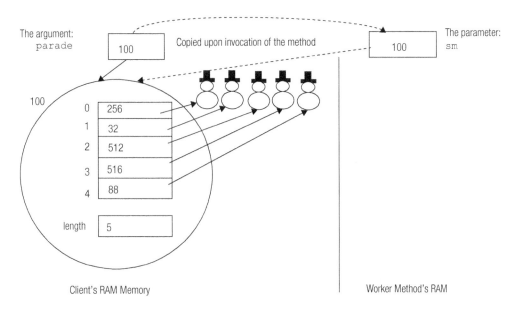

Figure 6.12
Passing the location of an array of objects to a method.

For example, suppose we wanted to use the static worker methods `move` and `bounce` coded in the class `PassingArrays` to reposition the `SnowmanV7` objects on the game board and reflect them off the edges of the board. Assuming these methods each had one parameter used to pass the array of snowmen named `parade` to the methods, the client code statements to invoke the worker methods would be:

```
PassingArrays.move(parade);
PassingArrays.bounce(parade);
```

If the parameter name in the worker methods was `sm`, the signature of the methods would be:

```
static void move(SnowmanV7[] sm);
static void bounce(SnowmanV7[] sm);
```

The dashed arrows at the top of Figure 6.12 illustrate the passing of the array's location into the method's parameter, sm, which permits the methods to reference the array of snowmen during their execution. The result is that while the methods are executing, the client code and the worker methods share the array of reference variables *and* the objects they refer to. If the worker methods' code writes new values into the data members of the snowmen objects, then these new values would be available to the client code after the worker methods completed their execution.

The application PassingArrays, shown in Figure 6.13, illustrates the sharing of the information contained in integer and object arrays with invoked methods and the methods' ability to change the contents of the array's elements and the objects they reference. Figure 6.14 shows the console output produced by the program, and Figure 6.15 shows the graphical output it produces (which is the same as that produced by the application SnowmanParade). The class SnowmanV7 referred to in Figure 6.13 is the same class (shown in Figure 6.9) used in the SnowmanParade application.

To verify the concept that the client and worker methods share primitive arrays, we have also included the array object ages and the method birthday within the PassingArrays application. Referring to Figure 6.13, the application's main method declares an array of five integers named ages on line 11. These variables are initialized to the values 21 through 25 inside the for loop that begins on line 13. On line 17, this array is passed to the method birthday (lines 45–51), and the address of the array is stored in the method's parameter theAges (line 45). The code of the method increases each element of the array by 1 inside its for loop (line 49). When the method ends, the for loop in the method main (lines 18–20) outputs the contents of the array, producing the console output shown in Figure 6.14. The fact that all of the ages output by the method main have been increased by 1 verifies that the methods main and birthday shared the same array of integers.

The code of the graphical portion of the applications PassingArrays is the same as the code of the application SnowmanParade (Figure 6.8) except that the code that moves and reflects the snowmen (coded on lines 29–55 of Figure 6.8) have been placed inside the static methods move and bounce (lines 53–87 of Figure 6.13). In addition, invocations of these methods have been placed inside the game environment's timer3 method, lines 41 and 42. Thus, the graphical output of the two programs is the same. When the game is launched, the snowmen are displayed along the left-to-right downward-sloping diagonal, as shown Figure 6.15a. When the Start button is clicked, they parade around the game board bouncing off its edges. Figure 6.15b shows the program's graphical output several seconds after the Start button is clicked.

The timer3 method now consists of two statements: the invocations of the move and reflect methods (lines 41 and 42 of Figure 6.13). The address of the array parade (declared on line 7) is passed into the parameter sm of these methods, whose signatures are given on lines 53 and 68. Inside their for loops, the methods change the (x, y) location (lines 61 and 64) and speed data members (lines 78 and 84) of the snowmen referenced by sm's elements. Because the array is shared between these methods and the timer3 method, the new locations and speed of the snowmen have been placed into the `Snowman` array reference by `parade`. This fact is verified during the next invocation of the game environments `draw` method when the snowmen are drawn at their new locations and reflected off the edges of the game board.

```
1    import edu.sjcny.gpv1.*;
2    import java.awt.*;
3
4    public class PassingArrays   extends DrawableAdapter
5    { static PassingArrays ge = new PassingArrays();
6      static GameBoard gb = new GameBoard(ge, "Snowman Parade");
7      static SnowmanV7[] parade = new SnowmanV7[8];
8
9      public static void main(String[] args)
10     {
11       int[] ages = new int[5];
12
13       for(int i = 0; i < 5; i++)
14       {
15         ages[i] = 21 + i;
16       }
17       birthday(ages);
18       for(int i = 0; i < 5; i++)
19       { System.out.print(ages[i] + " ");
20       }
21
22       for(int i = 0; i < 8; i++)
23       {
24         parade[i] = new SnowmanV7(10 + i * 50, 100 + i * 30);
25       }
26
27       gb.setTimerInterval(3, 20);
28       showGameBoard(gb);
29     }
30
31     public void draw(Graphics g)
32     {
33       for(int i = 0; i < 8; i++)
34       {
35         parade[i].show(g); // show the parade at its current location
36       }
37     }
38
39     public void timer3()
40     {
41       move(parade);
42       bounce(parade);
43     }
44
45     static  void birthday(int[] theAges)
```

```
46      {
47        for(int i = 0; i < theAges.length; i++)
48        {
49         theAges[i] = theAges[i] + 1;
50        }
51      }
52
53      static void move(SnowmanV7[] sm)
54      {
55        int x, y;
56
57        for(int i = 0; i < 8;  i++)
58        {
59          x = sm[i].getX();
60          x = x + sm[i].getXSpeed();
61          sm[i].setX(x);
62          y = sm[i].getY();
63          y = y + sm[i].getYSpeed();
64          sm[i].setY(y);
65        }
66      }
67
68      static void bounce(SnowmanV7[] sm)
69      {
70        int speed;
71
72        for(int i - 0; i < 8; i++)
73        {
74          if(sm[i].getX() >= 460 || sm[i].getX() <= 6)
75          {
76            speed = sm[i].getXSpeed();
77            speed = -speed;
78            sm[i].setXSpeed(speed);
79          }
80          if(sm[i].getY() >= 420 || sm[i].getY() <= 30)
81          {
82            speed = sm[i].getYSpeed();
83            speed = -speed;
84            sm[i].setYSpeed(speed);
85        }
86        }
87      }
88  }
```

Figure 6.13
The application **PassingArrays**.

```
22 23 24 25 26
```

Figure 6.14
The console output produced by the application **PassingArrays**.

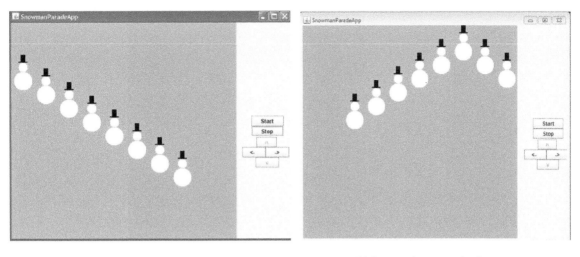

(a) Initial output   (b) Output after several reflections

Figure 6.15
The graphical output of the application **PassingArrays**.

6.6.3 Returning an Array from a Worker Method

As discussed in Section 3.8, an object's address can be returned from a method via a `return` statement. Because arrays are stored in objects, this also gives us the ability to return the address of an array from a worker method. The only syntactical difference to consider when returning the address of an array object is in the signature of the worker method. When a method returns an array, a pair of braces `[]` is coded in between the method's name and its returned type. As is the case when any value or address is returned from a method, if the returned address is to be used by the client code that invoked the method, the client code must assign the returned address to a variable.

The following is the code of the static worker method `birthdayV2` that is passed an integer array and returns a copy of the array with all of its elements increased by one. The contents of the array `theAges` passed into the method are unchanged.

```
static int[] birthdayV2(int[] theAges)
{
  int[] newAges = new int[length.theAges]; //declares the returned array
  for(int i = 0; i < theAges.length; i++)
  {
     newAges[i] = theAges[i] + 1;
  }
     return newAges; //returns the address of the new array
}
```

The syntax of the signature of a method that returns an array of objects is the same as the syntax used in the above method's signature, except the primitive type is replaced with the name of the object's class (e.g., `SnowmanV7[]` would replace `int[]`). In Chapter 7, we discuss and present a very important example of returning an array of objects from a method.

NOTE

When a method returns an array, a pair of braces [] *is coded in between the method's name and its returned type in the method's signature. For example:*

```
static int[] birthday(int[] theAges)
```

The return statement only contains the name of the array without the braces. For example:

```
return newAges;
```

6.7 PARALLEL ARRAYS

Suppose you were writing a program to maintain a database of student information for a school that had 1,000 students. Specifically, three pieces of information would be stored for each student: the student's identification number, age, and grade point average (GPA). If you were an object oriented programmer, you would begin by creating a class, probably named Student, which contained three data members, one for each piece of information. In addition, the class would contain a constructor to construct student objects and an input method to input information into a student object. Your application could then create the database as shown below:

```
Student[] studentInfo = new Student[1000]; //1,000 Student object array

for(int i = 0; i < 1000, i++)
{
    studentInfo[i] = new Student(); //create a new Student object
    student[i].input; //input a student's information
}
```

Now suppose that your program was going to be maintained by Anna, a programmer who was not trained in object oriented programming. She is not familiar with the concept of classes, the construction of objects, data members, and the idea that a class's non-static methods (e.g., the input method) can operate on an object's data members.

Anna's programming training was in the alternate programming paradigm, the *procedural* paradigm, in which objects do not play a central role in the language's constructs. She is not "object friendly". Because both the procedural and object oriented paradigms include the concept of arrays, you have decided to eliminate the use of the Student class from your program and simply use three arrays. One array will store all the student identification numbers, another will store all the student ages, and the third array will store all the student grade point averages (GPAs). Your application would then create the database as shown below:

```
1  int[] id = new int[1000];
2  int[] age = new int[1000];
3  double[] gpa = new double[1000];
4  String sInput;
```

```
5
6  for(int i = 0; i < 1000, i++)
7  {
8    sInput = JOptionPane.showInputDialog("Enter a student's ID number);
9    id[i] = Integer.parseInt(sInput);
10   sInput = JOptionPane.showInputDialog("Enter THAT student's age);
11   age[i] = Integer.parseInt(sInput);
12   sInput = JOptionPane.showInputDialog("Enter THAT student's GPA);
13   gpa[i] = Double.parseDouble(sInput);
14 }
```

The code that is used to input the student information is an example of the use of parallel arrays. This is easily recognized when we examine the input prompts on lines 8, 10, and 12. On line 8, the user is instructed to *input a student's ID number*, implying that any of the 1,000 student IDs could be entered. Perhaps ID number 15647. However, on lines 10 and 12, the user is instructed to enter *THAT student's age* and *THAT student's GPA*. This implies that the next two entries must be the age and GPA of the student whose ID number was just entered.

Because the loop variable is used as the index into the three arrays, a student's information is stored in the *same* element of all three arrays. This is the concept of parallel arrays. Each piece of data that is associated with a particular student is stored in the same element of each of the three arrays that comprise the data set. We would not be using the concept of parallel arrays if a particular student's ID number was stored in element 3 of the id array, and that student's age and GPA were stored in element 24 of the age array and element 6 of the GPA array, respectively.

The name *parallel arrays* comes from the idea that if we were to draw the three arrays side by side and then draw parallel horizontal lines below and above each element of the array, as depicted in Figure 6.16, all of a student's information would be contained between two of the lines. For example, the age of the student whose ID is 76892 would be 19, and the student's GPA would be 4.0. All of Al's information, including his GPA of 1.7, would have been entered during the first iteration of the input loop. (Please study more, Al.)

	id		age		gpa	
0	15647		18		1.7	Al's info
1	3452		21		2.55	Flo's info.
2	76892		19		4.0	Bob's info.
3	34376		22		3.85	Jo's info.
4	77834		19		3.3	Ed's info.
:	:		:		:	:
999	45823		20		2.3	Jen's info.

Figure 6.16
Three parallel arrays.

It is important to remember that parallel arrays are a concept or a model, not a programming language construct. The concept is used when the programmer stores all the data for a particular entity in the same elements of two or more arrays.

Parallel arrays are used less frequently in programs coded in object oriented programming languages like Java because all of the data for a particular entity can be stored inside an object as its data members, rather than in the elements of several arrays. However, if we wanted to group several different objects together, e.g., a snowman and its child, then a set of parallel arrays of objects is a perfect way to do this.

For example, suppose that five snowmen had one snow child each. Then, if the arrays `parent` and `child` were used to store the addresses of the snowmen and the snow children, respectively, by considering the two arrays to be parallel, we could quickly locate a child's parent or locate a parent's child. The address of a parent and the address of its child would be stored in the same two elements of the arrays: `parent[2]`'s child's address would be stored in `child[2]`.

Figure 6.17 shows the graphical application `ParallelArrays` that uses three parallel arrays to associate a parent snowman with its snow child and their family name. The parent snowman's class, `ParentSnowman`, is shown in Figure 6.18, and the snow child's class, `SnowChild`, is shown in Figure 6.19.

When the program is launched, the graphical output shown in Figure 6.20a is produced. The parent snowmen are lined up vertically on the left of the game board, and the snow children are located at random locations to their right. Every child and parent has their family name (last name) displayed on their bellies. When a key is struck, the children are repositioned next to their parents as shown Figure 6.20b. Parallel arrays are used to make the association between a parent, its child, and the family name.

Three array objects are created on lines 14–16, with the first of these (the array `names`) initialized to the names of the five families (B, D, A, E, and C). Then the other two array objects are filled with references to `ParentSnowman` and `SnowChild` objects inside the `for` loop that begins on line 20. The constructors used to create the objects on lines 24 and 25 accept three arguments. The first two are the x and y location of the object, which for the children are random numbers generated on lines 22 and 23. The third parameter is the family name that will appear on the object's belly. The constructors store this name in the parent and child classes' data member `name` on line 17 of Figures 6.18 and 6.19, respectively.

The loop that begins on line 20 of Figure 6.17 establishes the arrays as parallel arrays. With each pass through the loop, the loop variable `i` is used on lines 24 and 25 as an index into the array `names` to select the family name of a parent (line 24) and its child (line 25). This name is passed to the `ParentSnowman` and `SnowChild` constructors, and the returned addresses are stored in the element `i` of the `parent` and `child` arrays. Because the same index number is used in all three arrays, a parent, its child, and their family name are all stored in the same element number of their respective arrays.

The parallel construction of the arrays makes it easy to reposition the children next to their parents, which is done in the `for` loop that begins on line 42 of the `keyStruck` call back method. Lines 44 and 45 fetch the (x, y) location of the ith child's parent, and these values are used on lines 46 and 47 to reposition the ith child to the right of its parent. Fifty pixels are added to the parent's x coordinate to move the child to the right of its parent, and 35 pixels are added to the y coordinate of the parent to account for the difference in height of the parent and child objects.

Parallel arrays are also used in the API `Graphics` class's method `fillPolygon`. This method is used on lines 31 and 28 of Figures 6.18 and 6.19, respectively, to draw the triangular noses of the parent snowmen and their children. The method has three parameters, two of which are arrays of integers:

```
public void fillPolygon(int[] xPoints, int[] yPoints , int nPoints)
```

The parameters are used to specify the x coordinates of the vertices of a polygon (`xPoints`), the y coordinates of the vertices of a polygon (`yPoints`), and the number of vertices (`nPoints`). Within the method, the two arrays are used as parallel arrays. The coordinate of the ith vertex of the polygon is assumed to be (`xPoints[i]`, `yPoints[i]`). That is, the x and y coordinates of a vertex are assumed to be at the same element number in the `xPoints` and `yPoints` arrays. Knowing this, the two arrays `xPoly` and `yPoly` passed to the method on line 31 of Figure 6.18 have been set up as parallel arrays on lines 20 and 21. Because the desired coordinates of the three vertices of a parent's nose are (x + 20, y + 25), (x + 15, y + 30), and (x + 25, y + 30), these x and y parings are coded in the same elements of both arrays. A similar set of parings defines a child's nose on lines 21 and 22 of Figure 6.19, which are used to draw the child's nose on line 28 of that figure.

```
1    import edu.sjcny.gpv1.*;
2    import java.awt.*;
3    import java.util.Random;
4
5    public class ParallelArrays extends DrawableAdapter
6    {
7      static ParallelArrays ge = new ParallelArrays();
8      static GameBoard gb = new GameBoard(ge, "Parallel Object ArraysApp");
9      static ParentSnowman[] parent;
10     static SnowChild[] child;
11
12     public static void main(String[] args)
13     {
14       String[] names = { "B", "D", "A", "E", "C"};
15       parent = new ParentSnowman[5];
16       child = new SnowChild[5];
17       Random rn = new Random(500);
18       int x, y;
19
20       for(int i = 0;  i < 5;  i++)
21       {
22         x = 100 + rn.nextInt(500 - 100 - 30);
23         y = 30 + rn.nextInt(500 - 30 - 30);
24         parent[i] = new ParentSnowman(50, 50 + 90*i, names[i]);
25         child[i]  = new SnowChild(x, y, names[i]);
26       }
```

```
27          showGameBoard(gb);
28      }
29
30      public void draw(Graphics g)
31      {
32        for(int i = 0; i<5; i++)
33        {
34          parent[i].show(g);
35          child[i].show(g);
36        }
37      }
38
39      public void keyStruck(char key)
40      {
41        int x, y;
42        for(int i = 0; i< 5; i++)
43        {
44          x = parent[i].getX();
45          y = parent[i].getY();
46          child[i].setX(x + 50);
47          child[i].setY(y + 35);
48        }
49      }
50  }
```

Figure 6.17
The application **ParallelArrays**.

```
1    import java.awt.*;
2
3    public class ParentSnowman
4    {
5      private int x = 8;
6      private int y = 30;
7      private boolean visible = true;
8      private String name;
9
10     public ParentSnowman()
11     {
12     }
13
14     public ParentSnowman(int intialX, int intialY, String name)
15     { x = intialX;
16       y = intialY;
17       this.name = name;
18     }
19
20     public void show(Graphics g) //g is the game board object
21     { int[] xPoly = {x + 20, x + 15, x + 25};
```

```
22        int[] yPoly = {y + 25,  y + 30,  y + 30};
23
24        g.setColor(Color.BLACK);
25        g.fillRect(x + 15, y, 10, 15); //hat
26        g.fillRect(x + 10, y + 15, 20, 2); //brim
27        g.setColor(Color.WHITE);
28        g.fillOval(x + 10, y + 17, 20, 20); //head
29        g.fillOval(x, y + 37, 40, 40); //body
30        g.setColor(Color.RED);
31        g.fillPolygon(xPoly, yPoly, 3); //nose
32        g.setColor(Color.BLACK);
33        g.setFont(new Font("Arial", Font.BOLD, 16));
34        g.drawString(name, x + 16, y + 62); //name
35     }
36
37     public int getX()
38     { return x;
39     }
40
41     public void setX(int newX)
42     { x = newX;
43     }
44
45     public int getY()
46     { return y;
47     }
48
49     public void setY(int newY)
50     { y = newY;
51     }
52
53     public boolean getVisible()
54     { return visible;
55     }
56
57     public void setVisible (boolean newVisible)
58     { visible  = newVisible;
59     }
60
61     public String getName()
62     { return name;
63     }
64  }
```

Figure 6.18
The class **ParentSnowman**.

```java
1    import java.awt.*;
2
3    public class SnowChild
4    {
5      private int x = 8;
6      private int y = 30;
7      private boolean visible = true;
8      private String name;
9
10     public SnowChild()
11     {
12     }
13
14     public SnowChild(int intialX, int intialY, String name)
15     { x = intialX;
16       y = intialY;
17       this.name = name;
18       }
19
20     public void show(Graphics g) //g is the game board object
21     { int[] xPoly = {x + 15, x + 12, x + 18};
22       int[] yPoly = {y + 5, y + 8, y + 8};
23
24       g.setColor(Color.WHITE);
25       g.fillOval(x + 8, y, 14, 14); //head
26       g.fillOval(x, y + 14, 28, 28); //body
27       g.setColor(Color.RED);
28       g.fillPolygon(xPoly, yPoly, 3); //nose
29       g.setColor(Color.BLACK);
30       g.setFont(new Font("Arial", Font.BOLD, 16));
31       g.drawString(name, x + 10, y + 33);   //name
32     }
33
34     public int getX()
35     { return x;
36     }
37
38     public void setX(int newX)
39     { x = newX;
40     }
41
42     public int getY()
43     { return y;
44     }
45
46     public void setY(int newY)
47     { y = newY;
48     }
49
```

```
50      public boolean getVisible()
51      { return visible;
52      }
53
54      public void setVisible (boolean newVisible)
55      { visible  = newVisible;
56      }
57
58      public void setName(String newName)
59      { name = newName;
60      }
61
62      public String getName()
63      { return name;
64      }
65    }
```

Figure 6.19
The class **SnowChild**.

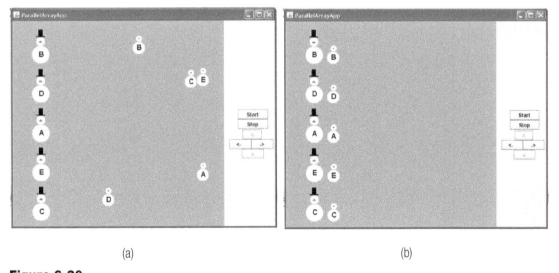

(a)   (b)

Figure 6.20
The graphical output of the application **ParallelArrays**.

6.8 COMMON ARRAY ALGORITHMS

As we have seen, arrays can be used to easily declare and process large data sets. Often, the processing performed on these data sets involves searching for a particular piece of data (e.g., the snowman family whose name is C), finding the name of the snowman family that is first or last in alphabetical order, or displaying the snowman families in sorted order based on their names. Searching, finding minimums and maximums, and sorting are all array-processing algorithms that are very commonly used in programs. We will begin our study of these algorithms with the array searching algorithm.

6.8.1 Searching

As its name implies, this algorithm is used to search an array to determine the element number of the array that contains a given value. For example, it could be used to search an array containing a group of people's ages to find the element number whose value is 32. If a parallel array contained the names of the people, then the element number could be used as an index into the name array to output the name of a person who is 32 years old. In an object oriented context, it could be used to search an array of parent snowmen to find the element number of the snowman whose `name` data member contains the string "C" and then use this element number to display its family name on the game board.

The algorithm to search for, or locate, a particular value contained in an array is shown in Figure 6.21. The implementation on the left side of the figure searches the *integer* array `ages` for the value 32, and the code on the right searches the *object* array `parent` for an object whose `age` data member is 32. These *target* values are specified on line 1. Lines 2–12 constitute the searching algorithm. Except for the names of the arrays and the Boolean conditions on line 6, the algorithms are identical. Line 6 of the array of objects version of the algorithm (the right side of the figure) assumes that the class of the objects contains a `getAge` method to fetch an object's `age` data member.

| ```
1 int target = 32;
2 int elementNumber = -1;
3 boolean found = false;
4 for(int i = 0; i < ages.length; i++)
5 {
6   if(ages[i] == target)
7   {
8     found = true;
9     elementNumber = i;
10    break;
11  }
12}
``` | ```
1 int target = 32;
2 int elementNumber = -1;
3 boolean found = false;
4 for(int i = 0; i< parent.length; i++)
5 {
6   if(parent[i].getAge() == target))
7   {
8     found = true;
9     elementNumber = i;
10    break;
11  }
12}
``` |
| **Searching an Array of Primitives** | **Searching an Array of Objects** |

Figure 6.21
The array searching algorithm.

The initializing value on line 1 of Figure 6.21 is the target value to be found. Line 2 initializes the Boolean variable `found` to `false`. This variable will be set to `true` if the target being searched for is found. The loop that begins on line 4 indexes its way through the array. Inside that loop, the `if` statement on line 6 determines if element `i` of the array contains the target value. If it does, `found` is set to `true` (line 8), `elementNumber` is set on line 9 to the element number that contains the target value, and the code breaks out of the loop (line 10). Subsequent code would have to examine the variable `found` before using the index stored in the variable `elementNumber` because, if the target value is not found, the value stored in the variable `elementNumber` would be out of bounds (i.e., equal to its initial value, -1).

The algorithm on the right side of Figure 6.21 can be used to locate a value stored in any primitive-type data member contained in the array's objects, as long as the class of the objects contains a get method to fetch the data member (which would be invoked on line 6). If the data member is not a primitive-type variable, but rather a reference variable, then the class of the object it references also must contain an equals method to be used in the Boolean condition on line 6. Typically, this method returns true when the object that invoked it is equal to the argument sent to it (the variable target). The String class contains an implementation of this method.

Assuming the data member's name was lastName that referenced a string, and we were searching for the name Jones, lines 1 and 6 of the algorithm would become:

```
Line 1: String target = "Jones";
Line 6: if(parent[i].getLastName().equals(target))
```

It should be noted that if several elements of the array contained the target value, the variable elementNumber would be set to the index of the lowest of these elements. If the highest element number of the array that contains the minimum value is desired, then the break statement on line 10 of Figure 2.21 would be eliminated from the algorithm. In addition, when the algorithms are implemented as a method that returns the element number of the target value, the method returns the variable elementNumber. The signature of the method would be:

```
public static int findValue(ArrayType[] arrayOfvalues, TargetType target)
```

where ArrayType and TargetType are the types of the array and the value being searched for, respectively. The method below searches the array of SnowChild objects passed to its first parameter and returns the index of the first child whose name is the string passed to its second parameter. Otherwise, it returns a -1.

```
public static int findValue(SnowChild[] anArray, String target)
{
  int elementNumber = -1;

  for(int i = 0; i < anArray.length; i++)
  {
    if(anArray[i].getName().equals(target))
    {
      elementNumber = i;
      break;
    }
  }
  return elementNumber;
}
```

6.8.2 Minimums and Maximums

The algorithms to locate the minimum or maximum value contained in an array are very similar to the searching algorithm discussed in the previous section. They also use a for loop to search the entire array, but when the loop terminates, the variable elementNumber contains the element number of the minimum or maximum value in the array. When the array is an array of objects, this value is the minimum or maximum value stored in a particular data member of the objects.

The code shown on the left side of Figure 6.22 is an implementation of the algorithm to locate the *minimum* value contained in an array of primitive values (in this case, an array of people's ages). The code on the right searches the object array `parent` for the minimum value stored in one of the object's data members (in this case, the integer data member `age`). Except for lines 1, 6, and the different array names the algorithms are identical.

Lines 1 and 6 of the array of objects version of the algorithm (right side of the figure) assume that the class of the objects contains a `getAge` method to fetch the object's data member (`age`).

Both algorithms begin with the assumption that the minimum value is stored in, or is referenced by, the first element of the array. Therefore, line 1 sets the variable `min` to that value, and line 2 stores its index (zero) in the variable `elementNumber`. The `for` loop that begins on line 4 compares the value stored in the variable `min` to all of the other members of the array. If it finds a value smaller than the value stored in `min` (line 6), it saves that value in `min` (line 8) and its element number in the variable `elementNumber` (line 9). When the loop ends, `elementNumber` contains the index of the minimum value in the array.

``
1 int min = ages[0];
2 int elementNumber = 0;
3
4 for(int i = 1; i < ages.length; i++)
5 {
6   if(ages[i] < min)
7   {
8   min = ages[i];
9   elementNumber = i
10   }
11 }
``
	``
	1 int min = parent[0].getAge();
	2 int elementNumber = 0;
	3
	4 for(int i = 1; i< parent.length; i++)
	5 {
	6 if(parent[i].gctAgc() < min)
	7 {
	8 min = parent[i].getAge();
	9 elementNumber = i
	10 }
	11 }
	``

Minimum Primitive Array Value Algorithm	**Minimum Object Array Value Algorithm**

Figure 6.22
The minimum value algorithm.

Using an approach similar to the search algorithm, the algorithm on the right side of Figure 6.22 can be used to locate the minimum value of any primitive type data member contained in the array's objects, as long as the objects' class contains a `get` method to fetch the data member (invoked on lines 1, 6, and 8). If the data member is not a primitive type variable, but rather a reference variable, then the class of the object it references also must contain a `compareTo` method to be used in the Boolean condition on line 6. Typically, this method returns a negative number when the object that invoked it is less than the argument sent to it (the variable `min`). The `String` class contains an implementation of this method.

Assuming the data member referenced a `String` object, and the data member's name was `lastName`, lines 1 and 6 of the algorithm would become:

```
Line 1: String min = parent[0].getLastName();
Line 6: if(parent[i].getLastName().compareTo(min) <  0)
```

Finally, when the array is an array of `String` objects, lines 1 and 6 of the algorithm would become:

```
Line 1: String min = parent[0];
Line 6: if(parent[i].compareTo(min) <  0)
```

It should be noted that if several elements of the array contained the minimum value, the variable `elementNumber` would be set to the index of the lowest value of these elements. If the highest index of the array that contains the minimum value is desired, then the less than operator (<) used in the Boolean expression on line 6 would be changed to the less than or equal to operator (<=). When the algorithms are coded as a method that returns the element number of the minimum value, the method returns the variable `elementNumber`. The signature of the method would be:

```
public int findMin(ArrayType[] arrayOfvalues)
```

where `ArrayType` is the types of the array elements (e.g., `double`, `String`, `SnowChild`, etc.). The following method searches the array of `SnowChild` objects passed to it and returns the index of the snow child that contains the minimum value of the primitive data member `x`.

```
public int findMin(SnowChild[] arrayOfvalues)
{
  int min = arrayOfValues[0].getX();
  int elementNumber = 0;

  for(int i = 1; i  <  arrayOfValues.length; i++)
  {
    if(arrayOfValues[i].getAge() < min)
  {
    min = arrayOfValues[i].getAge();
    elementNumber = i;
  }
  return elementNumber;
}
```

Locating Maximums

The algorithm to locate the maximum value contained in an array is the same as that used to locate the minimum value, except that the less than operator (<) used on line 6 of Figure 6.22 is replaced with the greater than operator (>), and good coding style dictates that the variable `min` be renamed `max`.

6.8.3 Sorting

There are many algorithms for sorting the elements of an `n` element array. One of the simplest is the Selection Sort algorithm. It begins by locating the minimum value contained in elements 1 to n-1, and if it is smaller than element zero (j = 0), it is swapped into element zero. Then it locates the next smallest value, and if it is smaller than element one (j = 1), swaps it into element one. This process is repeated for j = 2, 3, ... n-2. When the algorithm ends, the array is sorted in ascending order.

For example, suppose we wanted to sort an array of five integers, 12, 9, 3, 4, and 11, shown in the left column of Table 6.1 in ascending order. First, we locate the smallest value among 9, 3, 4, and 11 which is 3. Because it is less than 12 (the value in element j = 0), it is swapped with 12, which produces the ordering shown in the second column of the table. Then the smallest value among 12, 4, and 11 is located, which is 4. Because it is less than **9** (the value in element j = 1), it is swapped with 9, producing the ordering shown in the third column of the table. The remaining two steps for j = 2 and j = 3 and the final sorted array are shown in the three right-most columns. When the array is an array of objects, the algorithm sorts the objects based on the value of one of the class's data members.

Table 6.1
The Progression of the Selection Sort Algorithm

	j = 0	j = 1	j = 2	j = 3	
index 0	12	3	3	3	3
1	9	9	4	4	4
2	3	12	12	9	9
3	4	4	9	12	11
4	11	11	11	11	12
	Original Array	After 12 and 3 were swapped	After 9 and 4 were swapped	After 12 and 9 were swapped	After 12 and 11 were swapped

The code shown on the left side of Figure 6.23 is an implementation of the Selection Sort algorithm for sorting an array of primitive values (in this case an array of people's ages). It uses nested loops: the inner loop searches for a minimum value, and the outer loop places it into its correct position in the array. The right side of the figure is an implementation of the algorithm used to sort an array of ParentClass objects based on the value of one of their primitive type data members (in this case, the integer data member age). Except for the names of the arrays, the type of the variable declared on line 2, and the use of the getAge method on lines 6, 10, and 12 on the right side of the figure, the implementations are identical.

The code that begins on line 6 and ends on line 15 is essentially the algorithm to locate the minimum value of an array's elements, which was discussed in Section 6.8.2 and implemented in Figure 6.22. The differences are that line 6 initializes the minimum value, min, to the jth element of the array rather than the first element, and line 7 initializes the minimum element number, iMin, to j rather than zero. In addition, the loop that begins on line 8 initializes its loop variable to j + 1 rather than one. The variable j is the loop variable of an outer loop that begins on line 4 and ends on line 23. Because it is initialized to zero on line 4 the first time lines 6–15 execute, this code is in fact identical to the minimum value algorithm.

After the search for the minimum value ends (line 15), if j is not the index of the minimum value of the remaining unsorted portion of the array (as determined by the if statement on line 17), then lines 19–21 place the minimum value in element j by swapping element j with element iMin. The first time through the outer loop, element zero stores the minimum value contained in the array. After the second iteration of the outer loop, the next lowest element is stored in element 1. When the algorithm ends, the array is sorted in ascending order. To sort the elements of an array in *descending* order, the less than (<) operator in the Boolean condition on line 10 is changed to the greater than (>) operator.

It should be noted that when sorting an array of objects (right side of Figure 6,23), lines 19–21 swaps the references to the objects contained in the array parents. For example, on the first iteration of the outer loop, the location of the object whose age data member is the minimum value is placed in the first element of the array parents. The alternative is to swap the contents of the data members of the objects, which is more time consuming. In either case, if the sorted objects were output from the first element of the array to the last, they would appear in sorted order based on the contents of the age data member.

Sorting an Array of Primitives	The selection sort algorithm.

<pre>1   int iMin, min;
2   int temp;
3
4   for (int j = 0; j < ages.length; j++)
5   {
6   min = ages[j];
7   iMin = j;
8   for (int i = j+1; i < ages.length; i++)
9   {
10   if (ages[i] < min)
11   {
12   min = ages[i];
13   iMin = i;
14   }
15   }
16
17   if (iMin != j)
18   {
19   temp = ages[j];
20   ages[j] = ages[iMin];
21   ages[iMin] = temp;
22   }
23   }</pre>
	<pre>1 int iMin, min;
	2 ParentClass temp;
	3
	4 for (int j = 0; j < parent.length; j++)
	5 {
	6 min = parent[j].getAge();
	7 iMin = j;
	8 for (int i = j+1; i < parent.length; i++)
	9 {
	10 if (parent[i].getAge() < min)
	11 {
	12 min = parent[i].getAge();
	13 iMin = i;
	14 }
	15 }
	16
	17 if (iMin != j)
	18 {
	19 temp = parent[j];
	20 parent[j] = parent[iMin];
	21 parent[iMin] = temp;
	22 }
	23 }</pre>

Figure 6.23
The minimum value algorithm.

The algorithm on the right side of Figure 6.23 can be used to sort an array of objects based on any primitive type data member contained in the array's objects, as long as the class of the objects contains a `get` method to fetch the data member (which would be invoked on lines 6, 10, and 12).

If the data member is *not* a primitive type variable, but rather a reference variable, then the class of the object it references also must contain a `compareTo` method to be used in the Boolean condition on line 10. Typically, this method returns a negative number when the object that invoked it is less than the argument sent to it (the variable `min`). The `String` class contains an implementation of this method. Assuming the data member referenced a `String` object and the data member's name was `lastName`, line 10 of the algorithm would become:

Line 10: `if(parent[i].getLastName().compareTo(min) <  0)`

When the array is an array of `String` objects, line 10 of the algorithm would become:

Line 10: `if(parent[i].compareTo(min) <  0)`

An Array Algorithm Case Study

Figure 6.24 presents the graphical application `ArrayAlgorithms` that illustrates the use of the array processing algorithms discussed in this chapter to process parallel arrays of snow families. When the application begins, the user is asked to enter the names of five snow families (e.g., "I", "B", "N", "E", and "G"). Then the five families, each consisting of a `ParentSnowman` and a `SnowChild` object, whose classes are shown in Figures 6.18 and 6.19, respectively, are displayed (Figure 6.25a).

After the program is launched, when the user types the name of a snow family (e.g., "I"), the family is searched for and alternately disappears (Figure 6.25b) and reappears (Figure 6.25a). When the up-arrow cursor key is struck, the family whose name is the minimum in sorted order (e.g., "B"), alternately disappears (Figure 6.25c) and reappears (Figure 6.25a). Finally, when the "S" key is struck, the visible snow families are displayed in sorted order by family name (Figure 6.25d).

```
1    import edu.sjcny.gpv1.*;
2    import java.awt.*;
3    import javax.swing.*;
4
5    public class ArrayAlgorithms extends DrawableAdapter
6    {
7      static ArrayAlgorithms ge = new ArrayAlgorithms();
8      static GameBoard gb = new GameBoard(ge, "ArrayAlgorithmsApp");
9      static ParentSnowman[] parent;
10     static SnowChild[] child;
11
12     public static void main(String[] args)
13     {
14       String name;
```

```
15        parent = new ParentSnowman[5];
16        child = new SnowChild[5];
17
18        for(int i = 0;  i < 5;  i++)
19        {
20          name = JOptionPane.showInputDialog("enter a family name");
21          name = name.toUpperCase();
22          child[i] = new SnowChild(50 + 60, 80 + 90 * i, name);
23          parent[i] = new ParentSnowman(50, 50 + 90 * i, name);
24        }
25        showGameBoard(gb);
26      }
27
28      public void draw(Graphics g)
29      {
30        for(int i = 0;  i<5;  i++)
31        {
32          if(parent[i].getVisible() == true)
33          { parent[i].show(g);
34            child[i].show(g);
35          }
36        }
37      }
38
39      public void keyStruck(char key)
40      {
41        int index;
42
43        String sKey = Character.toString(key);
44        index = findValue(parent, sKey);
45        if(index != -1) //name is valid, reverse family's visibility
46        {
47          if(parent[index].getVisible() == true)
48          {
49            parent[index].setVisible(false);
50          }
51          else
52          {
53            parent[index].setVisible(true);
54          }
55        }
56
57        if (key == 'U') //up arrow struck, reverse visibility of min name
58        {
59          index = findMin(parent); //index of first family in alphabetic order
60          if(parent[index].getVisible() == true)
61          {
62            parent[index].setVisible(false);
```

```java
63          }
64        else
65        {
66          parent[index].setVisible(true);
67        }
68      }
69    if(key == 'S') //sort the families
70    {
71      selectionSort(parent);
72    }
73  }
74
75  public static int findValue(ParentSnowman[] parent, String targetValue)
76  {
77    int elementNumber = -1;
78    for(int i = 0; i< parent.length; i++)
79    {
80      if(parent[i].getName().equalsIgnoreCase(targetValue))
81      {
82        elementNumber = i;
83        break;
84      }
85    }
86    return elementNumber;
87  }
88
89  public static int findMin(ParentSnowman[] parent)
90  {
91    String min = parent[0].getName();
92    int elementNumber = 0;
93    for(int i = 1; i <  parent.length; i++)
94    {
95      if(parent[i].getName().compareToIgnoreCase(min) < 0)
96      {
97        min = parent[i].getName();
98        elementNumber = i;
99      }
100   }
101   return elementNumber;
102 }
103
104 public static void selectionSort(ParentSnowman[] parent)
105 {
106   int iMin, tempInt;
107   ParentSnowman tempParent;
108   SnowChild tempChild;
109   String min;
110
```

```
111     for (int j = 0; j < parent.length; j++)
112     {
113       min = parent[j].getName();
114       iMin = j;
115       for (int i = j+1; i < parent.length; i++)
116       {
117         if (parent[i].getName().compareToIgnoreCase(min) <  0)
118         {
119           min = parent[i].getName();
120           iMin = i;
121         }
122       }
123       if(iMin != j) //swap element j with minimum element
124       {
125         tempParent = parent[j]; //swap array references
126         parent[j] = parent[iMin];
127         parent[iMin] = tempParent;
128         tempChild = child[j];
129         child[j] = child[iMin];
130         child[iMin] = tempChild;
131
132         tempInt = parent[j].getY(); //swap Y positions
133         parent[j].setY(parent[iMin].getY());
134         parent[iMin].setY(tempInt);
135         child[j].setY(parent[j].getY() + 30);
136         child[iMin].setY(parent[iMin].getY() + 30);
137       }
138     }
139   }
140 }
```

Figure 6.24
The application **ArrayAlgorithms**.

The loop that begins on line 18 of the main method accepts the five family names (line 20) and allocates the five child and parent objects (lines 22 and 23). With each pass though the loop, a child and a parent object is created, assigned positions next to each other on the game board, and given their family name. Then, the loop variable is used to write the addresses of these two newly created family members into the same (ith) element of the child and parent arrays, making these two arrays parallel.

The loop that begins on line 30 of the draw method displays the five snow families on the game board, if they are visible as determined by the if statement's Boolean condition on line 32. When the Boolean condition is true, the ith parent and the ith child are drawn. Because the arrays were set up to be parallel, a parent and its child are drawn (lines 31–34).

Use of the Search Algorithm

The code, to make a family alternately disappear and reappear when their one-character family name is typed, is on lines 43–55 of the keyStruck method. This method is invoked by the game environment whenever a key is typed, and the typed character is passed into the method's parameter, key (line 43). To locate a ParentSnowman object with that family name, line 44 invokes the findValue method (lines 75–87) passing it the parent array (parent) and the string version of the family name (sKey). The method findValue is an implementation of the object version of the search algorithm discussed at the end of Section 6.8.1. If an object is found with that family name (the returned array index is not -1 on line 45), then the index is used on lines 47–54 to reverse the visibility of the parent object. Assuming an "I" was struck twice, the game board would change from the board displayed in Figure 6.25a to that shown in Figure 6.25b and then back again.

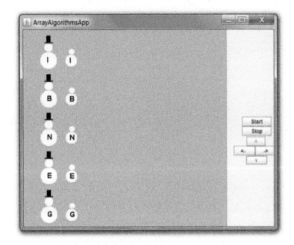

(a) After the program is launched

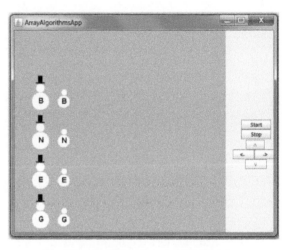

(b) After the "I" key is struck the first time

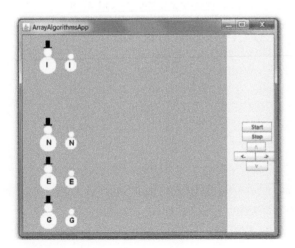

(c) Second strike of "I" key followed by a strike of the up cursor key

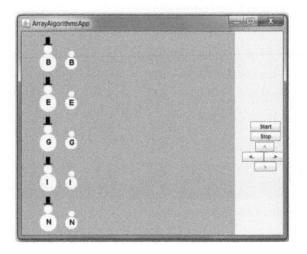

(d) After the "S" key is struck

Figure 6.25
The graphical output of the application **ArrayAlgorithms**.

Because in this application the search is for a particular value of a String object (the case-insensitive family name), this implementation of the search algorithm uses the String class's equalsIgnoreCase method on line 80 to compare the name passed to it (contained in the parameter targetValue) to the name returned by the ParentSnowman class's getName method.

Use of the Minimum Value Algorithm

The code to make a family whose name is first in alphabetical order alternately disappear and reappear when the up-arrow curser key is struck is coded on lines 57–68 of the keyStruck method. To locate a ParentSnowman object whose family name is first in alphabetic order, line 59 invokes the findMin method (lines 89–102), passing it the parent array. The method findMin is an implementation of the algorithm discussed in Section 6.8.2 that searches an array for a minimum value. In this coding of the algorithm, the method returns the array element number (line 101) that references the object whose name data member is first in alphabetic order (line 95). The returned element number is used on lines 60–67 to reverse the visibility of the parent object. Because the draw method (lines 28–37) only draws the snowman parent and its child when the parent's visible data member is true (line 32), both the parent and child disappear and reappear when the up-arrow key is typed.

In this application, the search is for a minimum value of a String object (the case-insensitive family name), findMin uses the String class's compareToIgnoreCase method on line 95 to determine if the name returned by the ParentSnowman class's getName method is less than the string referenced by min.

Use of the Selection Sort Algorithm

The code to sort the parent and child arrays in ascending order based on family names when the S key is struck is coded on lines 69–72 of the keyStruck method. To sort the parent and child arrays, line 71 invokes the selectionSort method (lines 104–139) passing it the parent array. The method selectionSort is an implementation of the sorting algorithm discussed in Section 6.8.3. In this coding of the algorithm, the method not only swaps the elements of the array passed to it (lines 125–127) but also the elements of its parallel array child (lines 128–130). (Because the address of the child array is declared as a class-level variable, the selectionSort method has access to it.) In addition, the method swaps the y data members of the parent objects (lines 132–134) and then positions the children next to their parents (lines 135–137), so the families will appear in sorted order from the top to the bottom of the game board.

Because in this application, the sorting is based on a String object (the case-insensitive family name), the method selectionSort uses the String class's compareToIgnoreCase method on line 117 to determine if the name returned by the ParentSnowman class's getName method is less than the string referenced by min.

6.9 APPLICATION PROGRAMMING INTERFACE ARRAY SUPPORT

The System and Arrays classes in the Java Application Programming Interface contain methods for processing arrays, and the API class ArrayList provides a means of storing data in an "array-like" object that can expand beyond its original size. The ArrayList class is one of the API's generic collection classes, which will be discussed in Chapter 12 after the topic of generics is introduced. We begin our discussion with the System class's arraycopy method.

6.9.1 The arraycopy Method

As its name implies, the arraycopy method in the System class is used to copy the contents of one array (called the *source* array) into another array (called the *destination* array). The method is a static method and is therefore invoked by first coding the name of its class, System, rather than the name of an object. Its signature contains five parameters, and a typical invocation would be:

```
System.arraycopy(sourceArray, sourceIndex, destinationArray,
                 destinationIndex, numElements);
```

where:

```
sourceArray is the name of the array that is being copied (an array
            object reference variable)
sourceIndex is the index of the first element copied from sourceArray
            (an int)
destinationArray is the name of the array being copied to (an array
                 object reference variable)
destinationIndex is the index of the first element copied into
                 destinationArray (an int)
numElements is the number of sequential elements to be copied (an int)
```

Both the source array and destination arrays must exist (have been previously declared) before the method is invoked. Figure 6.26 shows the result of executing the invocation:

```
System.arraycopy(age, 0, sum, 1, 2);
```

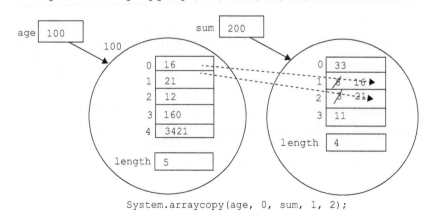

```
System.arraycopy(age, 0, sum, 1, 2);
```

Figure 6.26
The use of the System class's **arraycopy** method.

If the `sourceIndex`, `destinationIndex`, and `numElements` values passed to the method are such that the copying causes element numbers to be generated that do not exist, a runtime error (ArrayIndexOutOfBoundsException) will occur.

6.9.2 The Arrays Class

The API `Arrays` class contains two methods that can be used to copy one array into another and contains several other useful methods for processing arrays of primitives and strings. These include a method to facilitate the output of all of the elements of an array by converting them to a single string, a sorting method, a search method, a method to determine if the corresponding elements of two arrays are equal, and a method that sets the elements of an array to a specified value. The searching and sorting method algorithms execute faster than the algorithms discussed in Sections 6.8.1 and 6.8.3. Some of the methods in the class `Arrays` are summarized in Table 6.2.

Table 6.2
Methods in the API Arrays Class

Function	Method Name	Typical Invocation
Copies all or a portion of an array beginning with the *first* element	copyOf	`int[] a = Arrays.copyOf(sourceArray, 10);` Returns an array containing the first *ten* elements of the array `sourceArray`
Copies an array beginning with *any* element	copyRangeOf	`int[] a = Arrays.copyOfRange(sourceArray, 2, 10);` Returns an array containing the *third* (index 2) through the *ninth* elements of array `sourceArray`
Converts an array's contents to a string	toString	`String arrayContents = Arrays.toString(anArray);` Returns a string enclosed in braces containing the contents of the array's elements, each separated by a comma and a space
Sorts the elements of an array in ascending order	sort	`Arrays.sort(anArray);` Sorts all of the elements of the array `anArray` `Arrays.sort(anArray, 1, 5);` Sorts the values at index 1 through index 4 of the array `anArray`
Searches for (locates) a target value in a *sorted* array	binarySearch	`int[] i = Arrays.binarySearch(anArrray, targetValue)` Returns the index of an occurrence of `targetValue` in the sorted array anArray or returns a negative value if an occurrence is not found
Sets the elements of an array to a given value	fill	`Arrays.fill(intArray, 4);` Sets all of the elements of the array `intArray` to the value 4 `Arrays.fill(stringArray, 1, 4, "FillValue");` Sets the second (index 1) to the fourth (index 3) elements of the array `stringArray` to "FillValue"

All of these methods are static methods, and the program presented in Figure 6.27 illustrates their use. The output generated by this program appears in Figure 6.28.

Lines 15 and 16 of Figure 6.27 output all of the elements of the string and integer arrays `stringArray` and `intArray` created on lines 6 and 8. The parameter sent to the `println` method on lines 15 and 16 is the string returned from the `Arrays` class's `toString` method. The returned string is a concatenation of all of the elements of the array sent to the method separated by a comma and a space (lines 2 and 3 of Figure 6.28). It begins with an open bracket [and ends with a close bracket].

Lines 21 and 23 of Figure 6.27 use the `Arrays` class's static `copyOf` method to create a copy of the arrays `stringArray` and `intArray` and assign the newly created array addresses to the variables `copyStringArray` and `copyIntArray`, respectively. The second parameter sent to this method specifies the number of elements to be copied, and the copy always begins at element 0. If the number of elements to be copied exceeds the size of the source array (as it does on line 21), the elements are filled in with default values consistent with their type (`null` for string references) as shown on line 6 of Figure 6.28.

The `Arrays` class's `equals` method is used on lines 29 and 31 of Figure 6.27 to compare two integer arrays for equality. The method returns `true` if all of the corresponding elements of the two arrays passed to it are equal, as they are on line 29; otherwise, it returns `false` (line 31). The returned Boolean values are output and shown on lines 10 and 11 of Figure 6.28.

Line 36 of Figure 6.27 uses the one-parameter version of the `Arrays` class's static method `sort` to sort all of the elements of the array `stringArray`, and line 38 uses the three-parameter version of the method to sort the values at indices 1 through 4 of the array `intArray`. The third argument sent the three-parameter version of the method is always one larger than the index of the highest element to be sorted. This can be verified by comparing the output of the unsorted values (line 7 of Figure 6.28) to the output of the sorted values (line 15 of Figure 6.28). The sort is always performed inside the arrays passed to the method.

After the array `stringArray` is sorted (line 36), the `Arrays` class's method `binarySearch` can be used to determine the index of a given value in the array. Line 44 invokes this method to search the array for the index of the element containing the string "Fred." This string's position in sorted order is index 2 (line 14 of Figure 6.28), so the method returns the value 2 (line 18 of Figure 6.28). If there were several occurrences of the item being searched for in the array, it is uncertain as to which occurrence's index would be returned. Line 45 searches for the name "Doris," which is not contained in the array. When the item searched for is not in the array, a negative index is returned, in this case the value -3 (line 19 of Figure 6.28). When the search value is not found, the absolute value of the returned index is one greater than the index where the item would be if it were in its sorted position in the array. Line 14 of Figure 6.28 shows the sorted version of the array.

The `Arrays` class's methods `copyOf` and `copyOfRange` can be used to copy all or part of the elements of an array. As previously stated, the `copyOf` method always begins its copy at index 0 of the array, and the second argument passed to it indicates the number of elements to copy. The method is used on line 50 of Figure 6.27 to copy the first four elements of the array intArray into a newly created array whose address is assigned to the variable copyIntArray. The contents of the returned array is shown on line 22 of Figure 6.28, which can be compared to the contents of the array intArray shown on line 15 of the figure.

When the copyOfRange method is used, the copying can begin and end anywhere in the source array. As shown on line 52 of Figure 6.27, the source array is specified as the first argument sent to the method, the starting index is the second argument, and the third argument is always one more that the last index to be copied. Therefore, line 52 specifies that the elements at index 2–9 should be copied into a newly created array. If the value of the last argument specifies an index that is beyond the bounds of the source array (as it is on line 52), default values (e.g., zero for numeric types, null for char and String types) are entered into the out-of-bounds elements of the returned array. Thus, the last four elements in the integer array returned from the invocation on line 52 contain zeros (line 22 of Figure 6.28).

Lines 58 and 60 of Figure 6.27 use the Arrays class's fill method to set sequential elements of the arrays intArray and stringArray (specified as the first argument sent to this method) to a value specified by the last argument sent to the method. The two-parameter version of this method (invoked on line 58) fills all of the elements of the array sent to it. The four-parameter version of this method, invoked on line 60, fills a specified sequential range of elements of the array sent to it. The index at which to start the fill is the second argument sent to the four-parameter version of the method, and the third argument is always one more than the last index to be filled. The contents of the filled arrays are shown on lines 25 and 26 of Figure 6.28.

```
1    import java.util.Arrays;
2    public class ArraysClass
3    {
4      public static void main(String[] args)
5      {
6        String[] stringArray = {"Tom","Mary","Bob","Alice","Joe","Fred"};
7        String[] copyStringArray;
8        int[] intArray = { 3, 5, 2, 8, 6, 4};
9        int[] copyIntArray;
10       int[] filledIntArray;
11
12       //outputting the elements of an arrays
13       System.out.println("Outputing arrays using the " +
14                          "Arrays.toString method");
15       System.out.println(Arrays.toString(stringArray));
16       System.out.println(Arrays.toString(intArray));
17
18       //copying the elements of an array;
```

```
19      System.out.println("\nCopying arrays using the " +
20                         "Arrays.copyOf method");
21      copyStringArray = Arrays.copyOf(stringArray, 10);
22      System.out.println(Arrays.toString(copyStringArray));
23      copyIntArray = Arrays.copyOf(intArray, intArray.length);
24      System.out.println(Arrays.toString(copyIntArray));
25
26      //determining if all the elements of two arrays are equal
27      System.out.println("\nTesting two arrays for equality " +
28                         "using the Arrays.equals method");
29      System.out.println(Arrays.equals(intArray, copyIntArray));
30      copyIntArray[0] = 1;
31      System.out.println(Arrays.equals(intArray, copyIntArray));
32
33      //sorting arrays
34      System.out.println("\nSorting all or part of an array: " +
35                         "the Arrays.sort method");
36      Arrays.sort(stringArray);
37      System.out.println(Arrays.toString(stringArray));
38      Arrays.sort(intArray, 1, 5);
39      System.out.println(Arrays.toString(intArray));
40
41      //searching for an element of a sorted array
42      System.out.println("\nSearching for a value: the " +
43                         "Arrays.binarySearch method");
44      System.out.println(Arrays.binarySearch(stringArray, "Fred"));
45      System.out.println(Arrays.binarySearch(stringArray, "Doris"));
46
47      //copying a part of an array
48      System.out.println("\nPartial copies: the " +
49                         "Arrays.copy and copyRange methods");
50      copyIntArray = Arrays.copyOf(intArray, 4);
51      System.out.println(Arrays.toString(copyIntArray));
52      copyIntArray = Arrays.copyOfRange(intArray, 2, 10);
53      System.out.println(Arrays.toString(copyIntArray));
54
55      //setting all elements of a array to one value
56      System.out.println("\nFilling all or part of an array: " +
57                         "the Arrays.fill method");
58      Arrays.fill(intArray, 4);
59      System.out.println(Arrays.toString(intArray));
60      Arrays.fill(stringArray, 1, 4, "FillValue");
61      System.out.println(Arrays.toString(stringArray));
62   }
63 }
```

Figure 6.27
The application **ArraysClass**.

```
1    Outputting arrays using the Arrays.toString method
2    [Tom, Mary, Bob, Alice, Joe, Fred]
3    [3, 5, 2, 8, 6, 4]
4
5    Copying arrays using the Arrays.copyOf method
6    [Tom, Mary, Bob, Alice, Joe, Fred, null, null, null, null]
7    [3, 5, 2, 8, 6, 4]
8
9    Testing two arrays for equality: the Arrays.equals method
10   true
11   false
12
13   Sorting all or part of an array: the Arrays.sort method
14   [Alice, Bob, Fred, Joe, Mary, Tom]
15   [3, 2, 5, 6, 8, 4]
16
17   Searching for a value: the Arrays.binarySearch method
18   2
19   -3
20   Partial copies: the Arrays.copy and copyRange methods
21   [3, 2, 5, 6]
22   [5, 6, 8, 4, 0, 0, 0, 0]
23
24   Filling all or part of an array: the Arrays.fill method
25   [4, 4, 4, 4, 4, 4]
26   [Alice, FillValue, FillValue, FillValue, Mary, Tom]
27
```

Figure 6.28
The output produced by the application **ArraysClass**.

6.10 Multi-dimensional Arrays

Java, like most programming languages, supports multidimensional arrays. Like one-dimensional arrays, each memory cell in a multidimensional array shares the same "first name," the name of the array, and all of the array's element must be the same type. To close out this analogy, unlike one-dimensional arrays, each element of multi-dimensional arrays have *two or more* unique last names.

The simplest multi-dimensional array is a two-dimensional array, which conceptually is a group of memory cells arranged in rows and columns (left side of Figure 6.29). In Java, there is no limit to the number of dimensions an array can have. Three-dimensional arrays can be visualized as multiple two-dimensional arrays each in a different plane (right side of Figure 6.30). In effect, we have added a depth dimension to the two-dimensional array. Because we live in a three-dimensional world, multi-dimensional arrays with more than three dimensions are not often used in programs, although there are times when they are useful.

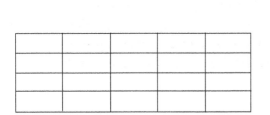

A Two-Dimensional Array

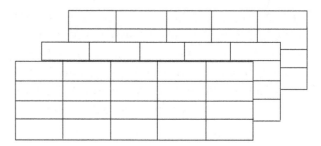

A Three-Dimensional Array

Figure 6.29
Visualization of a two- and three-dimensional array.

6.10.1 Two-Dimensional Arrays

A two-dimensional array is similar to a two-dimensional table with rows and columns. Two-dimensional arrays are typically used to store a group of data items for several entities. For example, a group of 5 examination grades for each of 4 students, or the 10 qualifying times for each of the 100 cyclists in the Tour de France. (A three-dimensional array with five planes could store the last five years' Tour de France qualifying time results, one year per plane.)

The names of the memory cells (elements) that make up a two-dimensional array begin with the name of the array followed by the element's row and column number. Figure 6.30 shows the names of all of the twenty elements of a four-row by five-column two-dimensional array named `grades`.

The name of an array element can be used anywhere the name of a non-array variable can be used, e.g., in arithmetic expressions, in output and input statements, in argument lists, and on the right side of the assignment operator. When they are used, the element's row number is always written *before* its column number. Thus, we would code `grades[2][4]` to access the contents of the third row and fifth column of the `grades` array shown in Figure 6.30.

NOTE   *The indices of both the row and column numbers start from zero.*

	column 0	column 1	column 2	column 3	column 4
row 0	grades[0][0]	grades[0][1]	grades[0][2]	grades[0][3]	grades[0][4]
row 1	grades[1][0]	grades[1][1]	grades[1][2]	grades[1][3]	grades[1][4]
row 2	grades[2][0]	grades[2][1]	grades[2][2]	grades[2][3]	grades[2][4]
row 3	grades[3][0]	grades[3][1]	grades[3][2]	grades[3][3]	grades[3][4]

Figure 6.30
The element names of a four-by-five two-dimensional array named grades.

The syntax used to declare a two-dimensional array is a simple extension of the one-dimensional array declaration syntax discussed in Section 6.3. The only difference is that an additional set of empty brackets is added before the name of the array, and the number of columns is specified after the number of rows. (In a similar way, a third set of empty brackets and the number of planes is added to declare a three-dimensional array.) The Java statement to declare the two-dimensional *integer* array `grades`, shown in Figure 6.30, would be:

```
int[][] grades = new int[4][5]; //four rows and five columns
```

The equivalent two-line syntax is:

```
int[][] grades;
grades = new int[4][5];
```

The numeric literals in the second line of the two-line grammar can be replaced with integer variables to specify or change the size of the array at run time.

As is the case with all array declarations, these declarations create a reference variable named `grades` that refers to an array object containing the array's elements. To facilitate the processing of all of the elements of a two-dimensional array, the array object also contains one additional `public` data member *per row* that stores the number of elements (columns) in each row of the array. For the array `grades`, depicted in Figure 6.30, each of these variables would store the integer value 5, and their names would be:

`grades[0].length`, `grades[1].length`, `grades[2].length`, and `grades[3].length`

The array object would still contain the `public` data member `grades.length` that stores the number of rows contained in the array (the integer value 4).

Initializing Two-Dimensional Arrays

The elements of a two-dimensional array can be initialized when the array is declared. As with one-dimensional arrays, when this is done the number of rows and columns in the array is not specifically stated but is implied from the number of initial values, and an initial value must be specified for each element of the array. The initialization syntax is most easily understood if we consider a two-dimensional array to be a one-dimensional array with each of its elements being a row of the two-dimensional array. In addition, it is most easily read if we write each row's initial values on a separate line. The array declaration below uses this coding style to declare the two-dimensional array `ages` depicted in Figure 6.31, initializing all of its values to those shown in the figure.

```
int[][] ages = { {10, 11, 12, 13, 14},
                 {20, 21, 22, 23, 24},
                 {30, 31, 32, 33, 34},
                 {40, 41, 42, 43, 44} };
```

NOTE   *If one element of an array is to be initialized, all of the elements must be initialized.*

	column 0	column 1	column 2	column 3	column 4
row 0	10	11	12	13	14
row 1	20	21	22	23	24
row 2	30	31	32	33	34
row 4	40	41	42	43	44

Figure 6.31
The elements of the array grades after its initialization.

The number of initial values specified in each row of a two-dimensional array need not be the same. The following declaration produces the array ages, shown in Figure 6.32, which has a different number of elements in each of its three rows:

```
int[][] ages  = { {10, 11, 12},
                  {20, 21, 22, 23, 24},
                  {30, 31} };
```

Inside the array object ages, the public variables named ages[0].length, ages[1].length, and ages[2].length would store the integer values 3, 5, and 2, respectively. These variables are used in the code fragment below to output all of the elements of the array ages shown in Figure 6.32 and are often used by methods that are passed two-dimensional arrays to determine the number of columns in each row of the array.

```
for(int row = 0; row < ages.length; row++) //each row
{
    for(int col = 0, col < ages[row].length; col++) //each column in a row
    {
        System.out.print(ages[row][col] + " ");
    }
    System.out.println();
}
```

	column 0	column 1	column 2	column 3	column 4
row 0	10	11	12		
row 1	20	21	22	23	24
row 2	30	31			

Figure 6.32
The elements of the array ages after its initialization.

6.11 DELETING, MODIFYING, AND ADDING DISK FILE ITEMS

In Section 4.8.5, it was mentioned that Java, like most programming languages, does not contain a method to delete or modify a file data item or to add a data item anywhere in the file except at its end. These operations can be performed by algorithms that *combine* the disk I/O methods discussed in Chapter 4 with the use of arrays and loops. An array is used because *all* of the data must be read into RAM memory to delete or modify a data item or to add an item to an arbitrary position in a data file. Because disk data files normally contain large data sets, this can easily be accomplished by reading each item into an element of the array and placing the read statement inside a loop.

In the remainder of this chapter, we will discuss these algorithms and their processing of a file of primitive data items that are all of the same type. The use of algorithms to process a file that contains the data members of several objects, with the data members possibly being different types, will be discussed in Chapter 7.

Deleting an Item From a Disk File

The algorithm to delete a data item from a file would be:

1. Open the file, read the number of items contained in the file, and allocate an array of that size
2. Inside a `for` loop, read all of the file's data items into the array
3. Close the file
4. Delete and recreate the file and write the new number of items to the file
5. Inside a `for` loop, write the elements of the array, *except* the item to be deleted, to the file
6. Close the file

When the algorithm ends, there would be one less item in the file, the deleted item, and the remaining data would be in their original order.

The item to be deleted can be specified by its position in the file, e.g., "delete item number 25," or by specifying the data value to be deleted, e.g., "delete the deposit 34.56." When the position in the file is specified, Step 5's loop variable is used to decide if the next element of the array should be written to the file. Assuming Step 1 of the algorithm stored the number of items read from the file in the variable `count`, and Step 2 reads the data into the array `data`, the following code fragment illustrates Step 5's process when deleting item 25 from the file:

```
//delete item 25
for(int i = 0; i < count; i++)
{
  if(i != 25 - 1)
  {
    //write the item, data[i], to the file
  }
}
```

When the value of the data item to be deleted is specified, the decision to write the next element of the array back into the file is based on the contents of the array element. Assuming Step 1 of the algorithm stored the number of items read from the file in the variable `count` and then read the data into the array data, the following code fragment illustrates Step 5's process when deleting all of the occurrences of 35.56 from the file:

```
//delete 35.56 from the file
for(int i = 0; i < count; i++)
{
  if(data[i] != 35.56)
  {
    //write the item, data[i], to the file
  }
}
```

The application DeleteFileItem shown in Figure 6.33 deletes a game score input by the program's user from the disk text file scores.txt. It uses the six-step algorithm discussed in this section and the file input and output methods discussed in Chapter 4. The number of items in the file is read from the file on line 16 and then used to size the array on line 17. It is also used on line 31 to write the new number of file items into the file after it is deleted and recreated by lines 29 and 30. The value to be deleted from the file is parsed into the variable deletedItem on line 35 and then used in the Boolean condition on line 38 to prevent the deleted item from being rewritten to the file.

```
1    import java.util.Scanner;
2    import java.io.*;
3    import javax.swing.*;
4
5    public class DeleteFileItem
6    {
7      public static void main(String[] args) throws IOException
8      {
9        double[] data;
10       double deletedItem;
11       int count = 0;
12
13       //Step 1: Open the file, read the number of items, allocate the array
14       File fileObject = new File("score.txt");
15       Scanner fileIn = new Scanner(fileObject);
16       count = fileIn.nextInt();
17       data = new double[count];
18
19       //Step 2: Read all of the file's data items into the array
20       for(int i = 0; i < count; i++)
21       {
22         data[i] = fileIn.nextDouble();
23       }
24
25       //Step 3: Close the file
26       fileIn.close();
27
```

```
28        //Step 4: Delete and recreate the file
29        FileWriter fileWriterObject = new FileWriter("data.txt");
30        PrintWriter fileOut = new PrintWriter(fileWriterObject, false);
31        fileOut.println(count - 1);
32
33        //Step 5: write the elements of the array without the deleted item
34        String s = JOptionPane.showInputDialog("enter score to delete");
35        deletedItem = Double.parseDouble(s);
36        for(int i = 0; i < count; i++)
37        {
38          if(data[i] != deletedItem)
39          {
40            fileOut.println(data[i]);
41          }
42        }
43
44        //Step 6: Close the file
45        fileOut.close();
46    }
47 }
```

Figure 6.33
The application **DeleteFileItem**.

Detecting an End of a File

If the number of items in the file was not stored in the file, then line 16 of Figure 6.33 would be replaced with the following code fragment that counts the number of items in the file before the array is declared and then closes and reopens the file. In addition, line 31 would be removed from the program.

```
while(fileIn.hasNext()) //count the data items
{
  count++;
  fileIn.nextDouble();
}
fileIn.close();
fileObject = new File("data.txt");
fileIn = new Scanner(fileObject);
```

Modifying an Item Stored in a Disk File

The algorithm to modify an item in a disk file would be the same as the deletion algorithm except that an else clause would be added to Step 5's if statement (line 38 of Figure 6.33). Assuming the new value of the data item was stored in the variable newValue, the else clause would be coded as:

```
else
{
  //write the new value to the file
}
```

Because the number of data items in the file would remain the same, Step 4 (line 31 of Figure 6.33) would write the original number of data items back into the file.

Inserting a New Item into a File

To insert a new item into a file, its position in the file and its value must be known. The algorithm, shown below, is the same as the deletion algorithm except for Step 5, and the number of items in the file written to the file in Step 4 would be increased by one:

1. Open the file, read the number of items contained in the file, and allocate an array of that size
2. Inside a `for` loop, read all of the file's data items into the array
3. Close the file
4. Delete and recreate the file and write the new number of items to the file
5. Inside a `for` loop, write the elements of the array, *and the new item* to the file
6. Close the file

Assuming the following: the new item's position in the file is stored in the variable `itemNumber`; the new value is stored in the variable `newValue`; and position numbers in the file begin at zero, then the Step 5 `for` loop becomes:

```
//add newValue to the file at position itemNumber
for(int i = 0; i < count; i++)
{
  if(i == itemNumber)
  {
    //write the newValue to the file
  }
  //write the item, data[i], to the file
}
```

In addition to modifying text files and data files, these file operations will also enable us to record players' scores and update the high scores of a game.

6.12 CHAPTER SUMMARY

The concept of an array presented in this chapter provides us with a powerful tool for storing, retrieving, and processing data, especially large data sets. Unlike primitive variables, which contain only a single value, an array contains multiple data elements that are all of the same type. When an array is created, its data items are all initialized to their default values. The index of an array always begins at zero and extends to n-1, where n is the number of elements in the array (the *size* of the array). To distinguish one element from another, we use an index after the array name, as in an element's name, `grade[4]`, which is the name of the fifth element of the array.

In Java, all arrays are stored inside an object. This object is declared using a syntax similar to that used to declare non-array objects. A set of brackets is added to the declaration after the object's type, and a second set of brackets containing the size of the array is written after the keyword `new`.

Every array has a public data member named `length`, which stores the size of a one-dimensional array or the number rows in a two-dimensional array. Two-dimensional arrays also contain an array of public data members named `length` whose elements store the number of elements in each row of the array.

Loops are often used to efficiently input, output, and process the data in an array using the loop variable as an index into the array. Array elements can be used in any Java statement where a variable can be used; they can receive input and be output, used in mathematical expressions, assigned values, passed as an argument into a method, and returned from a method. In addition, like any object, the location of an array object can be passed to a method and returned from it. The concept of parallel arrays is implemented using either multiple one-dimensional arrays or using multidimensional arrays. In either case, we can use this concept to organize related information such as student ID numbers and GPAs and quickly and efficiently access it.

Sorting and searching for particular values, including minimum and maximum values, are very common programming operations, and their algorithms are very similar. The Selection Sort algorithm can be used to sort an array in ascending or descending order. It uses nested loops to locate the smallest (or largest) value in the array and to store it in the first element. Then, it searches for the next smallest value and stores it in the second element, and repeats this process until the entire list is sorted.

An array's elements can be either primitive or reference variables. An array of objects can be simulated by creating an array in which each element is a reference variable. For example, we can create an array of snowmen, or more correctly, an array of reference variables that refer to `Snowman` objects. The position or speed of all these `Snowmen` objects can easily be changed within a loop to create a parade of `Snowmen` objects that appear to be marching around the game board screen.

The `System` class method `arraycopy` is used to copy a sequential set of elements from one array into another array. Other API methods include `toString`, `sort`, and `fill`, which converts all of an array's elements to a single string, efficiently sorts the elements into ascending order, or sets an array's elements to a given value, respectively.

Finally, arrays are used in the implementation of algorithms that insert new items into a text file and that delete or update existing items. These algorithms use the disk I/O methods discussed in Chapter 4 to read an existing data set from a disk file into an array. Then, the file is deleted and recreated, and the data set is written back to the file with new items inserted into it, or existing items deleted or updated.

Knowledge Exercises

1. True or false:
   (a) An array is a technique for naming groups of memory cells.
   (b) All the elements of an array need *not* be of the same data type.
   (c) The size of an array can be dynamically allocated.

(d) Once an array is created, its size cannot be changed.

(e) The largest index of an array is its length - 1.

(f) An array cannot be passed into a method.

(g) Arrays can only be one or two dimensional.

(h) Arrays can be initialized when they are created.

(i) An efficient way to perform an operation on an entire array is to process it in a loop.

(j) In Java, the first index or subscript always begins with 1.

2. Give two features of an array that makes it more powerful than a set of non-array variables.

3. Mention at least two differences between an array element and a non-array variable.

4. Explain the difference between an array and an array object.

5. Assume that the array `gameScores` has been created using the following declaration:

   `int[] gameScores = new int[100];`

   Answer the following questions with respect to this array:

   True or false:

   (a) The size of this array is 100.

   (b) The first element in this array is `gameScores[1]`

   (c) The last element in this array is `gameScores[100]`

   (d) This is a valid assignment to this array: `gameScores[5] = 93.2;`

   (e) When invoked, `gameScores.length` would return the value 99.

   (f) Give the Java statement to store the value 12 the second element of the array.

   (g) Give the statement to output the last element of the array to the system console.

   (h) Give the Java statements to output all of the elements of the array to the system console.

   (i) Give the Java statements to output the average of all of the elements of the array.

   (j) Draw a picture of the memory allocated by the declaration.

6. Find at least two errors in the following code and explain what should be done to fix them:

```
//prices start at $0 (not available) and increase from $5, to $10, $15....
    int size = 25;
    double[] ticketPrice = new double [size];
    for (int i = 1; i <= 25; i++)
    {
      ticketPrice[i] = i * 5;
    }
    System.out.println ("The price of a tier " + " " i " + " ticket is:  " +
                       ticketPrice[i]);
```

7. Assume that you have been given these declarations below, answer the questions that follow them.

```
    final int MAX = 45;
    int[] x = new int[MAX];
    double[] y = {22.54, 3.6, 54.76, 10.8, 5.62};
    double z;
```

(a) How many elements does the array x contain?

(b) What is the subscript or index of the last element of array x?

(c) What is the largest valid subscript of array y?

(d) Write the statements to multiply the very first element of the array by 7.

(e) Write the statements that increase the last element of array y by 20.5.

(f) Write a statement that assigns the sum of the first 3 elements of array y to z.

8. Give a statement to allocate an array that can store:

(a) Three thousand characters using the one-line declaration syntax

(b) Two hundred strings using the two-line declaration syntax

(c) Five thousand Snowmen objects using the one-line declaration syntax

(d) Five quiz scores for 100 students

9. Give the statement(s) to:

(a) Declare three parallel arrays that can store the names, weights, and target weights for 50 people in a weight loss clinic

(b) Output all of the information stored in the arrays declared in part a to the system console, one person per line

(c) Output Joe Smith's weight and target weight to the system console

(d) Output all of the names to the system console in alphabetical order

10. Write a method that is passed two arrays of doubles, each of the same size, and returns an array whose ith element is the sum up to the ith elements of the two arrays passed to it.

Programming Exercises

1. Refer to the program in Figure 6.24. Modify the code in the keyStruck method to include the instructions to move the third parent snowman and its child 20 pixels to the right each time the "M" key is struck.

2. As part of a research project, you have collected the following data and have initialized and stored it in an initialized array using the declaration:

```
int[ ] ages = {21, 32, 45, 23, 19, 41, 27, 20 , 21, 43,
               39, 24, 25, 22, 44};
```

Write a program to do each of the following tasks (with all output going to the system console):

(a) Search for a value input by the user and report if it is found or not

(b) Search for and output the minimum and maximum ages in the data set

(c) Calculate and output the average age

(d) Copy the ages to a new array called sortedAges, sort this array in ascending order, and then output both arrays

3. Write a program to accept a given number of names, input by the program user, and write the names in sorted order to a disk file named Students.txt. Then, ask the user which name should be eliminated from the file and eliminate that name from the file. Finally, read all of the names from the modified file and output them in reverse alphabetical order.

4. Write a graphical application that includes a class that defines a solid disk object whose diameter, color, and location are specified when an object is constructed. When the program is launched, the user should be asked how many disks to display on the game board, then asked the size, color, and location of each disk. The disks should then be displayed on the game board at their specified locations.

5. Modify the program described in Programming Exercise 4 so only disks whose diameters are 50 pixels or smaller are displayed when the down-arrow key is struck and only those disks that are larger than 50 pixels are displayed when the up-arrow key is struck.

6. Write a graphical application that includes a class that defines a flower with a red center whose petal color and location is specified when a `Flower` object is constructed. When launched, the program should display a garden of 100 flowers at random locations on the lower portion of the game board. The (x, y) locations of the flowers will be randomly generated and be in the range ($7 \leq x \leq 500 - w$) and ($300 \leq y \leq 500 - h$), where w and h are the width and height of the flower.

7. Modify the program described in Programming Exercise 6 so every time the down-arrow game board button is clicked, 20 of the remaining flowers disappear from the garden.

8. Write a graphical application that includes a class that defines a light-gray colored raindrop whose height is 4 pixels and whose width is 6 pixels. When the application is launched, 300 raindrops should appear on the game board at random locations. The (x, y) locations of the raindrops will be in the range ($7 \leq x \leq 496$) and ($30 \leq y \leq 494$).

9. Modify the program described in Programming Exercise 8 so when the Start button on the game board is clicked, the raindrops move downward two pixels every 40 milliseconds, giving the appearance that it is raining. When a raindrop reaches the bottom of the game board (the y coordinate of its location is greater than 500), reset its y coordinate to 30.

10. Add the garden described in Programming Exercise 6 to Programming Exercise 8.

11. Add the garden described in Programming Exercise 6 to Programming Exercise 9.

12. Using the skills developed in this chapter, continue the implementation of the parts of your game that require multiple instances of one of your game pieces. To facilitate the processing of these objects, they should be part of an array of objects.

Enrichment

Investigate at least two other sorting algorithms and discuss their advantages and disadvantages over the Selection Sort algorithm.

Investigate why the `binarySearch` method in the API `Arrays` class is faster than the search method presented in this chapter.

References

Knuth, Donald, *The Art of Computer Programming, Volume 3: Sorting and Searching,* 2nd ed. New York: Addison-Wesley, 1998.

Levitin, Analy. *Introduction to the Design and Analysis of Algorithms*, 3rd ed. New York: Addison-Wesley Longman, 2011.

McAllister, William. *Data Structures and Algorithms*. Sudbury, MA: Jones and Bartlett Publishers, 2009.

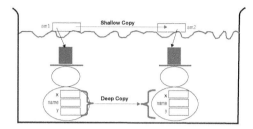

METHODS, CLASSES, AND OBJECTS: A SECOND LOOK

7.1   Static Data Members 298
7.2   Methods Invoking Methods Within their Class. 301
7.3   Comparing Objects. 303
7.4   Copying and Cloning Objects. 306
7.5   The **String** Class: A Second Look. 318
7.6   The Wrapper Classes: A Second Look 322
7.7   Aggregation 328
7.8   Inner Classes 337
7.9   Processing Large Numbers. 340
7.10 Enumerated Types. 343
7.11 Chapter Summary. 347

■ ■ ■ ■ ■

In this chapter

In this chapter, we will extend our knowledge of the features that can be incorporated into the classes we write, our knowledge of the String and the wrapper classes, and explore two other often-used classes defined in the Java Application Programming Interface (API). We will learn the techniques and motivation for writing classes whose objects share a data member and whose methods invoke each other, as well as the techniques and motivation for defining classes whose data members are objects. In addition, we will discuss what it means to compare, copy, and clone objects and how to write methods that perform these operations. An understanding of the topics in this chapter will enable us to more efficiently write complex programs, increase the reusability of the classes we write, and process numeric values that are beyond the size and precision of the primitive numeric types.

After successfully completing this chapter, you should:

- Understand static data members and their ability to share storage among all instances of a class within an application
- Become more familiar with the distinction between public and private methods
- Understand the fundamental differences between deep and shallow comparisons and copies
- Be able to compare two instances of a class
- Be able to use the deep copy technique to copy data members and clone objects

- Know how to create strings from primitive values, convert strings to characters, tokenize a string, and utilize other common string-processing methods
- Be able to create and use a wrapper class object and its autoboxing feature
- Understand how to aggregate an object into a class and the advantages of doing so
- Comprehend the relationship between, and implementation of, inner and outer classes
- Be able to use the `BigInteger` and `BigDecimal` classes for processing large numbers of arbitrary precision

7.1 STATIC DATA MEMBERS

Consider a worker class named `Student` that contains two data members named `idNumber` and `gpa` and a two-parameter constructor. The following code fragment would produce the `Student` objects `ryan` and `mary` depicted in Figure 7.1, assuming the first and second arguments passed to the constructor are used to initialize data members `idNumber` and `gpa`, respectively. As discussed in Chapter 3, each instance contains storage for its two data members.

```
Student ryan = new Student(1567, 3.26);
Student mary = new Student(2373, 2.87);
```

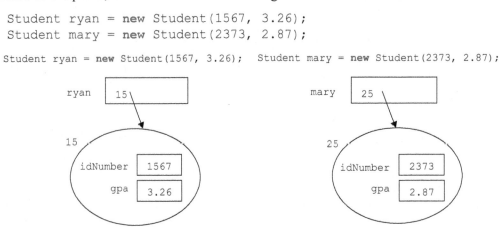

Figure 7.1
Two **Student** objects and the data members allocated to them.

Like methods, data members of a worker class can be declared to be static data members by including the keyword `static` in the data member's declaration statement. For example:

```
private static int studentCount = 0;
```

When a data member of a class is declared to be static, each instance of the class declared within an application does not contain storage for the data member. Rather, *one* storage cell is *shared* among all objects declared within an application. For example, if an additional static data member named `studentCount` were added to the class `Student`, the memory allocated to the two `Student` instances `ryan` and `mary` shown in Figure 7.1 would be expanded by one shared integer variable shown at the bottom of Figure 7.2.

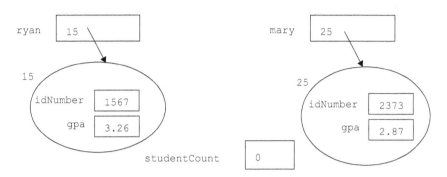

Figure 7.2
Two **Student** objects and the shared static data member **studentCount**.

A very common use of static data members is to keep track of the number of instances of a class (objects) that have been declared within an application. To accomplish this, a line of code to increment the static data member is included in each of the class's constructors. Below is an implementation of the Student class's two-parameter constructor that uses the class's static data member studentCount to keep track of the number of objects declared in the class:

```
public Student(int idNumber, double gpa)
{
   studentCount++; //counts the number of Student objects declared
   this.idNumber = idNumber;
   this.gpa = gpa;
}
```

Figure 7.3 shows the changes to the data member studentCount after two Student objects have been constructed with this version of the constructor. Normally, static data members in a class are declared with *private* access, and a get method is coded in the class to fetch the value of the data member. When the data member is being used to count the instances of a class, a set method is not coded to generally limit the data member's write access to the class's methods (and specifically, to the class's constructors).

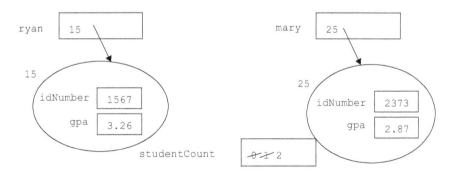

Figure 7.3
The changes to the static data member **studentCount** after two objects are created.

It is good coding style to declare the get method to be a static method. This forces the invoker (as shown below) to code the name of the class in the invocation statement rather than the name of an object, which implies to its reader that the value being fetched does not belong to a particular object. For example:

```
int numberOfStudents = Student.getStudentCount();
```

Figure 7.4 uses the concepts discussed in this section to keep track of the number of instances of the class Student that are declared within in a program. Line 2 declares the static data member studentCount and initializes it to zero. This variable is incremented within the class's two-parameter constructor on line 8 every time the constructor is invoked to create an object. The class's toString method (lines 13–18) does not return the value of the static variable because normally the string it returns includes only the values of a particular object's data members. The number of Student instances declared in a program can be fetched by invoking the class's getStudent-Count method (lines 20–23). As previously discussed, this is a static method, and the class does not contain a setStudentCount method to restrict applications' write access to the static variable.

```
1    public class Student
2    { private static int studentCount = 0;
3      private int idNumber;
4      private double gpa;
5
6      public Student(int idNumber, double gpa)
7      {
8        studentCount++; //counts the number of Student objects declared
9        this.idNumber = idNumber;
10       this.gpa = gpa;
11     }
12
13     public String toString()
14     {
15       String s = "id is " + idNumber +
16                  "\ngpa is "  + gpa;
17       return s;
18     }
19
20     public static int getStudentCount()
21     {
22       return studentCount;
23     }
24   }
```

Figure 7.4
The worker class **Student**.

7.2 METHODS INVOKING METHODS WITHIN THEIR CLASS

A method in a worker class can invoke another method in its class. This is a common coding technique and, if used properly, can reduce the time required to develop a class and make our programs easier to read and understand.

Suppose that the UML diagram that specified the class Student shown in Figure 7.4 also required a method named show to be part of the class that outputs the annotated values of the data members of an object to the system console. One way to code the method would be:

```
public void show()
{
   String s = "id is " + idNumber +
              "\ngpa is "  + gpa;
   System.out.println(s);
}
```

However, a better way to code this method would be to take advantage of the fact that the UML diagram also specified that a toString method would be part of the class, and a method in a class can invoke other methods in its class. Knowing this, the show method would be coded after the toString method was completed and verified (taken for a test drive), so it could be invoked to perform some work for the show method. This approach reduces the code of the show method to one executable statement, as shown below:

```
public void show()
{
   System.out.println(toString()); //toString does all the work
}
```

Figure 7.5 is an expanded version of the class Student shown in Figure 7.4 with this coding of the show method added to it (lines 25–28).

Normally, when a nonstatic worker method is invoked within client code, its name is preceded by the name of an object followed by a dot. It would be impossible to use this syntax to invoke the toString method on line 27 of Figure 7.5 because objects (instances of worker classes) are declared in client code. Because line 27 is syntactically correct, the question of which object's data members will be output to the console by the invocation of toString on line 27 arises. The answer is: the object the client code used to invoke the show method. When a nonstatic method of a class is invoked by another method in the class, the method operates on the same object upon which the method invoking it is operating.

For example, the toString method invoked on line 27 of Figure 7.5 would return a string containing Ryan's student information when the following client-code fragment was executed:

```
StudentV2 ryan = new StudentV2(1567, 3.26);
ryan.show();
```

When a method in a class invokes another method in its class, the invocation state-ment is not preceded by the name of an object followed by a dot, and both methods operate on the same object.

```
1    public class StudentV2
2    { private static int studentCount = 0;
3      private int idNumber;
4      private double gpa;
5
6      public StudentV2(int idNumber, double gpa)
7      {
8        studentCount++; //counts the number of Student objects declared
9        this.idNumber = idNumber;
10       this.gpa = gpa;
11     }
12
13     public String toString()
14     {
15       String s = "id is " + idNumber +
16                  "\ngpa is "  + gpa;
17       return s;
18     }
19
20     public static int getStudentCount()
21     {
22       return studentCount;
23     }
24
25     public void show()
26     {
27       System.out.println(toString());
28     }
29   }
```

Figure 7.5
The class **StudentV2**.

Private Class Methods

Another example of a worker class method invoking a method in its class evolves from the design process discussed in Section 1.7. When a UML diagram of a class specifies that a compli-cated method is to be included in the class, it is good programming practice to divide it into several simpler methods that are added to the complicated method's class. This is consistent with the divide and conquer problem-solving technique. Once each of the simpler methods have been coded and tested, often in parallel by several different programmers, the complicated method is written as a series of invocations of the simpler methods that are part of its class.

Because the only reason the simple methods were written was to perform the work of a more complex method in their class, the simpler methods are normally declared to be *private* methods. Private methods can only be invoked by the code of other methods within their class, and their signature begins with the keyword `private` rather than with the keyword `public`. When this is done, we say that the method has private access, and an attempt to invoke a private method from within a method that is not a member of its class results in a translation error. Often, methods are declared private to prevent methods that are not part of their class from invoking them. We will discuss this further in Section 7.4.

7.3 COMPARING OBJECTS

In Section 6.8, we discussed algorithms for searching, finding minimums and maximums, and sorting an array of objects. Fundamental to all of these algorithms is the ability to compare two objects. Generally speaking, the phrase "compare two objects" is ambiguous. It could mean that we want to compare the contents of a particular data member of two objects or the contents of two or more data members of two objects, or it could mean that we want to compare the contents of the reference variables that refer to the objects. Therefore, before we write a method that compares two objects for a particular application, we have to define what it means to "compare two objects" in the context of that application.

The simplest case is when the objects being compared are strings, but even then we would have to decide whether to simply compare the length of the strings or compare the strings for equality or lexicographical order and decide if these comparisons should be case sensitive. Once we define what it means to compare two string objects for a particular application, then in most cases, either the `String` class's length method or its `equals` or `compareTo` method (or its case-insensitive versions of these methods) can be used to compare the strings. The use of these methods to compare string objects was discussed in Section 4.2.3, and the use of these methods to compare data members of objects that are strings was discussed in Section 6.8.

When the objects being compared are not strings, we normally add a method to the object's class to perform the comparison after defining what it means to compare two objects. It is good coding style to name these methods `equals` or `compareTo`, or to at least use these words in a longer method title.

A fish tank analogy is useful in gaining an understanding of how to write and use these methods as well as the methods that will be discussed in the next section of this chapter. Figure 7.6 depicts two snowman objects: `sm1` and `sm2` in a fish tank. In this analogy, reference variables float at the top of the tank because they are light (They only contain one address). Objects are depicted at the deeper levels of the tank because they contain multiple data members, which make them heavy. Our snowmen contain three data members: each snowman's (x, y) location and a reference variable name.

A *shallow* comparison is performed at the surface of the tank. It compares the contents of the two reference variables that float on the surface of the tank (e.g., `sm1` and `sm2` in Figure 7.6). A *deep* comparison is performed at the bottom of the tank. A deep comparison compares the contents of two objects. The methods that perform shallow and deep comparisons are fundamentally different and will be discussed separately.

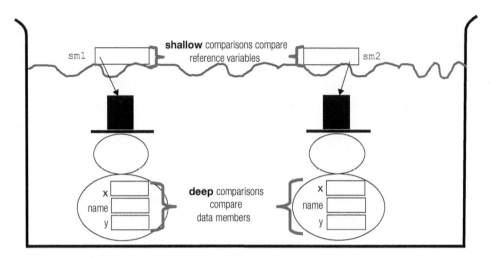

Figure 7.6
A fish tank analogy of shallow and deep comparisons.

7.3.1 Shallow Comparisons

In Chapter 4, we used the relational operators to compare two primitive values. For example, to determine if the values stored in the integer variables `age1` and `age2` are equal, we used the equality operator (==):

```
if(age1 == age2)
```

This comparison is a *shallow comparison* because primitive variables contain one value, so they would float on the top of a fish tank. Because reference variables also float, the same syntax used to perform a shallow comparison of two primitive values can be used to perform a shallow comparison of two objects. In effect, a shallow comparison of two objects determines if two reference variables refer to the same object.

Normally, a method named `equals`, such as the method `equals` in the `String` class, performs a *deep* comparison of two objects. It compares information contained inside the objects. For this reason, when coding a shallow `equals` method in the class of the objects being compared it is good coding practice to name the method `shallowEquals`. This name clearly indicates that the method is making a shallow comparison. The following method, which would be coded inside the class `ParentSnowman` (Figure 6.18), performs a shallow comparison of the `ParentSnowman` object that invoked it and the object passed to its parameter. It uses the equality relational operator to perform the comparison.

```
public boolean shallowEquals(ParentSnowman ps) //a shallow comparison
{
    if(this == ps) //this contains the address of the invoking object
```

Chapter 7· Methods, Classes, and Objects: A Second Look ■ 305

```
      {
        return true; //the invoking object and ps refer to the same object
      }
      else
      {
        return false; //ps does not reference the invoking object
      }
    }
```

An exception to this comparison-method naming convention is the method `equals` in the API class `Object`. It performs a shallow comparison of two objects. The following code fragment illustrates the use of this shallow comparison method. It outputs the Boolean value `true` and then `false` because the variables `ps1` and `ps2` contain the same address and `ps1` and `ps3` do not.

```
ParentSnowman ps1 = new ParentSnowman();
ParentSnowman ps2 = ps1; //ps2 is initialized to the address in ps1
ParentSnowman ps3 = new ParentSnowman();
boolean sameAddresses;

sameAddresses = ps1.equals(ps2); //shallow comparison, returns true
System.out.println(sameAddresses);
sameAddresses = ps1.equals(ps3); //shallow comparison, returns false
System.out.println(sameAddresses);
```

7.3.2 Deep Comparisons

Deep comparisons compare the contents of two objects' data members. As previously mentioned, before we write a method that performs a deep comparison for a particular application, we have to determine which of the objects' data members to compare for that application. For example, if we decide that two snowmen are equal if they are at the same game board position, then the x and y data member of the two objects would be compared. Once this decision is made, the class's `get` methods are used to fetch the data members, and they are compared using the relational operators if they are primitive variables. If they are reference variables that refer to other objects, they are compared using the deep comparison method in the objects' class.

The method shown in Figure 7.7, which would be coded in the class `ParentSnowman`, performs a deep comparison of two `ParentSnowman` objects: the object that invokes it and the object passed to its parameter. As depicted in Figure 7.6, each `ParentSnowman` object contains its (x, y) location and a reference to its family name (a string). The method returns `true` when the two objects are at the same game board (x, y) location *and* the objects' family name, referenced by string data member `name`, are the same.

```
1  public boolean equals(ParentSnowman ps) //a deep comparison
2  {
3    if(x == ps.getX() && y == ps.getY() &&
4        name.equals(ps.getName()))
5    {
```

```
6        return true; //same location and family name
7    }
8    else
9    {
10       return false; //different location and/or family name
11   }
12 }
```

Figure 7.7
A deep comparison method named **equals** that would be part of the **ParentSnowman** class.

It should be noted that the invocation of the equals method on line 4 of Figure 7.7 is an invocation of the String class's equals method. This method is invoked because name is a string variable and the argument that follows its name on line 4, ps.getName(), returns a reference to a String object.

There are four common errors made when coding the third term of the Boolean condition on lines 3 and 4 of Figure 7.7:

```
1. name == ps.getName()
2. this.getName() == ps.getName()
3. name.equals(ps)
4. this.equals(ps)
```

When either of the first two errors is made, a shallow comparison of the name data members is performed, and the Boolean condition evaluates to false even when the strings are the same. The two addresses, not the strings, are being compared. When the third error is made, a string is being compared to a ParentSnowman object, and the Object class's equals method is invoked, which also makes a shallow comparison.

When the fourth error is made, the program ends in a runtime *StackOverflow* error. Two ParentSnowman objects are being compared causing line 4 to repeatedly invoke the same method of which it is a part. This is a concept called recursion. It is not considered a syntax error because when recursion is properly used, it can facilitate the coding of many algorithms. We will learn more about the proper use of this coding technique in Chapter 9.

Deep comparisons are also performed to compare the relative order of two objects. A method that compares two objects to determine their relative order is normally named compareTo, and it returns an integer. The string class contains a method named compareTo that determines the lexicographical order of two String objects. Aside from changing the name of the method presented in Figure 7.7 and the returned type and value, compareTo methods would use the less than (<) or the greater than (>) operator to compare primitive data members and use previously coded compareTo methods to compare data members that are objects.

7.4 COPYING AND CLONING OBJECTS

The deep and shallow fish tank analogy also helps us to understand the techniques used to copy and clone objects. We can make both shallow and deep copies of objects, and clones of objects can easily be created from deep copies of objects. Figure 7.8 illustrates the difference between a shallow and a deep copy. Shallow copies copy the contents of one object's reference variable into another object's reference variable. Deep copies copy all of the values of one object's data members into the data members of another object. We will begin with a discussion of shallow copies.

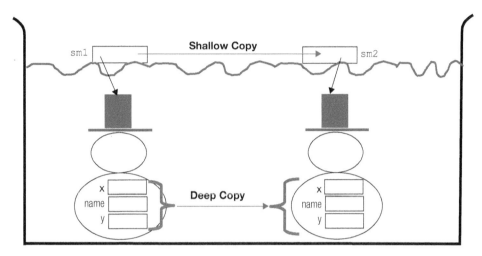

Figure 7.8
A fish tank analogy of shallow and deep copies.

7.4.1 Shallow Copies

In Chapter 2, we used the assignment operator to copy the contents of one primitive variable into another. For example, the following line of code copies the value stored in the integer variable age1 into the variable age2:

```
age2 = age1;
```

This statement actually performs a shallow copy between two primitive variables because primitive variables contain only one value, so they would float on the top of a fish tank. Because reference variables also float (contain one value, an address) and the assignment operator can be used to assign reference variables, the same syntax is used to make a shallow copy of an object. The following line of code makes a shallow copy of object sm1 into object sm2:

```
sm2 = sm1; //a shallow copy of object sm1 into object sm2
```

Although we say we are making a shallow copy of an object, we are actually copying the contents of one object's reference variable into the other object's reference variable, as shown at the top of Figure 7.8. It is important that we understand the consequences of this.

Referring to Figure 7.8, after the shallow copy of object sm1 into sm2 is complete, the address of the snowman object on the right side of the fish tank that was stored in the reference variable sm2 has been overwritten with the address of the snowman object on the left side of the fish tank. Now both reference variables, sm1 and sm2, refer to the *same* object. As a result, the snowman on the left now has two names. In addition, the snowman on the right side of Figure 7.8 is no longer part of the program (unless another variable in the program also stored its address) because the address of the object is no longer known to the program. When an object's address is not stored in a program reference variable, the Java memory manager reclaims its storage.

NOTE *A shallow copy gives one object two names, and it may eliminate an object from the program.*

The following code fragment makes a shallow copy of object ps1 into ps2, and as a result outputs the data members of the object declared on line 1 twice:

```
1   ParentSnowman ps1 = new ParentSnowman(250, 250, "A");
2   ParentSnowman ps2 = new ParentSnowman(10, 20, "X");
3
4   ps2 = ps1; // makes a shallow copy of object sm1 into object ps2
5   System.out.println(ps1.show());
6   System.out.println(ps2.show());
```

7.4.2 Deep Copies and Clones

As shown in the bottom of Figure 7.8, when we make a deep copy of an object, the values of its data members are copied into the data members of another object. Unlike performing a shallow copy, when a deep copy is complete both objects *still exist*, and the values stored in their data members are identical. The method arraycopy discussed in Section 6.9.1 can be used to deep copy one array object into another.

Generally speaking, a method has to be added to a class to be able to make deep copies of instances of the class. A deep copy method uses the class's set methods to copy the data members of the object that invoked it into the data members of the object sent to its parameter.

The method shown in Figure 7.9 is a deep copy method, which would be coded in the class ParentSnowman. As depicted in Figure 7.8, each ParentSnowman object contains its (x, y) location and the object's family name, referenced by the string data member name:

```
1   public void deepCopy(ParentSnowman ps) //a deep copy into ps method
2   {
3       ps.setX(x);
4       ps.setY(y);
5       ps.setName(name);
6   }
```

Figure 7.9
A **deepCopy** method that would be part of the **ParentSnowman** class.

In some cases, it is desirable to deep copy a subset of one object's data members into another object. When this is the case, it is good programming practice to name the method copy, rather than deepCopy, to alert the reader of the method's signature to the fact that not all of an object's data members are being copied.

Cloning Objects

When an object is cloned, a new instance of the object's class is *created*, and the values of all of an existing object's data members are copied into the corresponding data members of the new object. If one object existed before the clone was created, *two* objects exist after it is created. To create a clone of an object, a method (usually named `clone`) is coded in the object's class. The method is a nonvoid method that returns the address of the newly created clone object.

Figures 7.10 and 7.11 show two alternate codings of a clone method, which would be coded in the class `ParentSnowman`. Both methods return the address of a newly created clone of the object that invoked them. The version shown in Figure 7.10 invokes the class's `deepCopy` method on line 4 to copy the values of the data members of the object that invoked the method into the clone object created on line 3. This version of the method assumes that the class contains a deep copy method and a no-parameter constructor. The new object is identical to (an exact copy of) an existing object.

```
1   public ParentSnowman clone() //a deep copy
2   {
3      ParentSnowman theClone = new ParentSnowman();
4      this.deepCopy(theClone);
5      return theClone;
6   }
```

Figure 7.10
A clone method using a **deepCopy** method that would be part of the class **ParentSnowman**.

The alternate coding of the clone method presented in Figure 7.11 uses the class's three-parameter constructor on line 3 to copy the values of the data members into the clone when it is constructed. If each object only contains three data members, then the newly created object is identical to (an exact copy of) an existing object. Generally speaking, to produce an exact copy of an object with n data members, this version of the clone method would have to invoke an n-parameter constructor on line 3 of Figure 7.11.

```
1   public ParentSnowman clone() //a deep copy
2   {
3      ParentSnowman theClone = new ParentSnowman(x, y, name);
4      return theClone;
5   }
```

Figure 7.11
An alternate clone method that would be part of the class **ParentSnowman**.

If it is appropriate to a particular application for the clone method to copy only a subset of an object's data members into the newly created object, then line 4 of Figure 7.10 would be changed to an invocation of the class's `copy` method, and the clone method would be renamed `partialClone` to indicate that invocations of this method do not make an identical copy of the object that invoked it.

Figure 7.12 is the code of a class named ParentSnowmanV2 that is an expanded version of the ParentSnowman class shown in Figure 6.18. The expanded version adds the following methods to the class:

- a copy method (lines 29–35) that copies four of an object's data members into another object
- a partial-clone method (lines 36–41) that invokes the copy method
- a shallow comparison method (lines 42–52)
- a deep comparison method (lines 53–63) that compares the hatColor data members of two objects
- a method that detects collisions (lines 64–75) between two snowmen

In addition, three static data members (lines 5–7) and a get method (lines 93–96) to fetch one of these data members have also been added to the class.

As discussed in Section 7.1, the three static data members declared on lines 5, 6, and 7 of Figure 7.12 are shared by all instances of this class. The first of these, snowmanCount initialized to zero, will be used to count the number of snowmen constructed. It is incremented inside the no-parameter constructor (line 18) and the four-parameter constructor (line 27) every time these constructors execute. The client can fetch the value of the variable snowmanCount using the get method coded on lines 93–96.

The other two static variables, w and h, store the width (40) and height (77) of a snowman, as depicted in Figure 4.9. Because the class's show method draws all snowmen with the same width and height, it is appropriate that these two variables be shared by all instances of the class. The variables are used in the Boolean condition coded within the collidedWith method (lines 64–75) that detects a collision between the snowman that invoked it and the snowman passed to its parameter ps. The values of the variables x and y used on lines 66 and 67, and within other methods of the class, are the values of the x and y data members of the snowman that invoked the method. Alternately, we could code these data members as this.x or this.y.

The class's copy method (lines 29–35) copies four of a snowman's seven nonstatic data members (lines 31–34). When the method completes its execution, the snowman passed to its parameter will have the same name, hat color, and location as the snowman that invoked the method. To prevent methods that are not part of the ParentSnowmanV2 class from erroneously invoking this method to make a deep copy of *all* of an object's data members, it is declared as a private method on line 29.

The copy method is invoked on line 39 by the class's partialClone method, which means that clones will have only the same name, hat color, and location as the snowman from which they were cloned. Their xSpeed, ySpeed, and visible data members will retain their default values (set on lines 12–14). As previously discussed in Section 7.2, the fact that the copy method is a private method does not prevent the class's clone method from invoking it.

The deep comparison performed on line 55 of the equals method determines if two snowmen have the same hat color by invoking the API Color class's equals method. If they do, the method returns the value true.

```
1    import java.awt.*;
2
3    public class ParentSnowmanV2
4    {
5      private static int snowmanCount = 0;
6      private static int w = 40;
7      private static int h = 77;
8      private int x = 8;
9      private int y = 30;
10     private String name;
11     private Color hatColor= Color.BLACK;
12     private int xSpeed = 2;
13     private int ySpeed = 2;
14     private boolean visible = true;
15
16     public ParentSnowmanV2()
17     {
18       snowmanCount++;
19     }
20     public ParentSnowmanV2(int intialX, int intialY, String name,
21                            Color hatColor)
22     {
23       x = intialX;
24       y = intialY;
25       this.name = name;
26       this.hatColor = hatColor;
27       snowmanCount++;
28     }
29     private void copy(ParentSnowmanV2 ps) //copies 4 data members
30     {
31       ps.setX(x);
32       ps.setY(y);
33       ps.setName(name);
34       ps.setHatColor(hatColor);
35     }
36     public ParentSnowmanV2 partialClone()
37     {
38       ParentSnowmanV2 theClone = new ParentSnowmanV2();
39       this.copy(theClone);
40       return theClone;
41     }
42     public boolean shallowEquals(ParentSnowmanV2 ps)
43     {
44       if(this == ps)
45       {
46         return true;
47       }
48       else
49       {
```

```
50            return false;
51          }
52        }
53        public boolean equals(ParentSnowmanV2 ps)
54        {
55          if(hatColor.equals(ps.getHatColor())) //same hat color
56          {
57            return true;
58          }
59          else
60          {
61            return false;
62          }
63        }
64        public boolean collidedWith(ParentSnowmanV2 ps)
65        {
66          if( !(x > ps.getX( ) + w || x + w < ps.getX( ) ||
67                y > ps.getY( ) + h || y + h < ps.getY( )))
68          {
69           return true;
70          }
71          else
72          {
73           return false;
74          }
75        }
76        public void show(Graphics g) // g is the game board object
77        {
78          int[] xPoly = {x + 20, x + 15, x + 25};
79          int[] yPoly = {y + 25, y + 30, y + 30};
80
81          g.setColor(hatColor);
82          g.fillRect(x + 15, y, 10, 15);  // hat
83          g.fillRect(x + 10, y + 15, 20, 2);  // brim
84          g.setColor(Color.WHITE);
85          g.fillOval(x + 10, y + 17, 20, 20); // head
86          g.fillOval(x, y + 37, 40, 40);  // body
87          g.setColor(Color.RED);
88          g.fillPolygon(xPoly, yPoly, 3); // nose
89          g.setColor(Color.BLACK);
90          g.setFont(new Font("Arial", Font.BOLD, 16));
91          g.drawString(name, x + 16, y + 62); // name
92        }
93        public static int getSnowmanCount()
94        {
95          return snowmanCount;
96        }
97        public int getXSpeed()
98        {
```

```
99       return xSpeed;
100    }
101    public void setXSpeed(int newXSpeed)
102    {
103      xSpeed = newXSpeed;
104    }
105    public int getYSpeed()
106    {
107      return ySpeed;
108    }
109    public void setYSpeed(int newYSpeed)
110    {
111      ySpeed = newYSpeed;
112    }
113    public void setHatColor(Color newHatColor)
114    {
115      hatColor = newHatColor;
116    }
117    public Color getHatColor()
118    {
119      return hatColor;
120    }
121    public int getX()
122    {
123      return x;
124    }
125    public void setX(int newX)
126    {
127      x = newX;
128    }
129    public int getY()
130    {
131      return y;
132    }
133    public void setY(int newY)
134    {
135      y = newY;
136    }
137    public String getName()
138    {
139      return name;
140    }
141    public void setName(String newName)
142    {
143      name = newName;
144    }
145    public boolean getVisible()
146    {
```

```
147        return visible;
148    }
149 }
```

Figure 7.12
The class `ParentSnowmanV2`.

The application shown in Figure 7.13 uses most of the concepts discussed up to this point in this chapter. When the game board's Start button is clicked, a snowman guard, whose family name is "G" patrols his game board garden looking for three green-hat snowmen who have wandered into the garden (Figure 7.14a). When he finds (collides with) one, he positions the green-hat snowman behind himself and continues his search (Figure 7.14b). Each time he reaches the border of his garden, he clones himself and posts the clone at the garden's edge (Figure 7.14c) to guard the garden from wandering snowmen. After the guard has found the three green-hat snowmen and posted six clones at the garden's boundaries, the animation ends (Figure 7.14d).

```
1     import edu.sjcny.gpv1.*;
2     import java.awt.*;
3
4     public class DeepAndShallow extends DrawableAdapter
5     { static DeepAndShallow ge = new DeepAndShallow ();
6       static GameBoard gb = new GameBoard(ge, "Deep and Shallow");
7       static ParentSnowmanV2[] ps;
8       static boolean gameOver = false;
9
10      public static void main(String[] args)
11      { ps = new ParentSnowmanV2[10];
12        ps[0] = new ParentSnowmanV2(100, 200, "G", Color.BLUE);
13        ps[1] = new ParentSnowmanV2(300, 275, "1", Color.GREEN);
14        ps[2] = new ParentSnowmanV2(300, 400, "2", Color.GREEN);
15        ps[3] = new ParentSnowmanV2(100, 100, "3", Color.GREEN);
16
17        gb.setTimerInterval(3, 20);
18        showGameBoard(gb);
19      }
20
21      public void draw(Graphics g)
22      {
23        for(int i = 1; i < ps.length; i++)
25        {
26          if(ps[i] != null) //the snowman exists
27          {
28            ps[i].show(g);
29          }
30        }
31        ps[0].show(g); //the patrolling guard
32      }
33
34      public void timer3()
```

```
35    { int x, speed, y;
36      if(ParentSnowmanV2.getSnowmanCount()== 10)
37      {
38        gb.stopTimer(3);
39        gameOver = true;
40      }
41      //move the guard
42      x = ps[0].getX();
43      x = x + ps[0].getXSpeed();
44      ps[0].setX(x);
45      y = ps[0].getY();
46      y = y + ps[0].getYSpeed();
47      ps[0].setY(y);
48
49      //is ps[0] at a border?
50      if(ps[0].getX() >= 460 || ps[0].getX() <= 6)
51      {
52        speed = ps[0].getXSpeed();
53        speed = -speed;
54        ps[0].setXSpeed(speed);
55        ps[ParentSnowmanV2.getSnowmanCount()] = ps[0].partialClone();
56      }
57      if(ps[0].getY() >= 423 || ps[0].getY() <= 30)
58      {
59        speed = ps[0].getYSpeed();
60        speed = -speed;
61        ps[0].setYSpeed(speed);
62        ps[ParentSnowmanV2.getSnowmanCount()] = ps[0].partialClone();
63      }
64
65      // has ps[0] found a green-hat wandering snowman?
66      for(int i = 1; i <= ps.length; i++)
67      {
68        if(ps[i] != null && ps[0].collidedWith(ps[i]) &&
69          !ps[0].equals(ps[i]))
70        {
71          ps[i].setX(ps[0].getX()); //position wanderer behind ps[0]
72          ps[i].setY(ps[0].getY());
73        }
74      }
75    }
76
77    public void leftButton()
78    {
79      if(gameOver == true)
80      { for(int i=0; i<=3; i++) //move the three intruders left
81        {
82          ps[i].setX(ps[i].getX() - (i * 3));
```

```
83              }
84            ps[0].setX(ps[0].getX() - 1); // move the guard
85          }
86        }
87    }
```

Figure 7.13
The application **DeepAndShallow**.

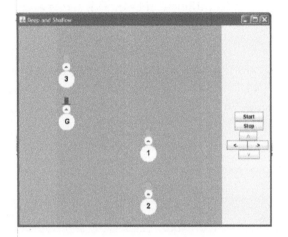

(a) Game board when the program is launched

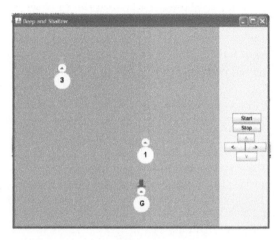

(b) Game board after green-hat snowman 2 is found and placed behind the guard

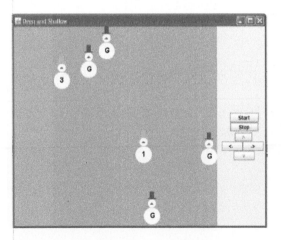

(c) Game board after three clones are posted and green-hat snowman 3 is about to be found

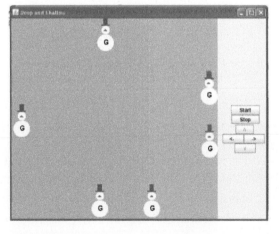

(d) Game board after six clones have been posted and all the wonderers have been found

Figure 7.14
Graphical output produced by the application **DeepAndShallow**.

This animation uses an array of ten ParentSnowmanV2 snowmen objects, whose class is shown in Figure 7.12; the array, ps, is declared on line 11 of Figure 7.13. The patrolling snowman guard and the three green-hat snowmen, declared on lines 12–15, are referenced by indices 0 and 1–3, respectively. The remaining six elements of the array will be used to reference the clone snowmen.

The patrolling of the guard and the game termination are dependent on timer3. Line 17 of the main method sets timer3's increment to 20 milliseconds, which means that the timer3 call back method (lines 34–75) executes every 20 milliseconds. Its code determines if the patrol is over (lines 36–40), moves the patrolling guard (lines 42–56), posts clone guards (lines 50–63) and gathers up the intruders (lines 66–74). Line 36 determines if ten snowmen have been constructed, which would mean that all six guards have been posted. If so, the patrol is ended by line 38, which stops timer3. While the timer is ticking, lines 42–47 use the Snowman class's set and get methods to fetch, change, and overwrite the current values of the patrolling guard's (x, y) location every 20 milliseconds. This keeps the snowman on patrol.

Lines 50 and 57 determine if the guard has reached a vertical (line 50) or horizontal (line 57) edge of the garden. If it has, lines 52–54 and lines 59–61 reflect the guard off the edge by changing the sign of the x and/or y speed data member. Then, lines 55 and 62 invoke the partialClone method to create the clone snowman and store its returned address in the next available element of the array ps. The index of this element is the static value returned from the getSnowmanCount method, which is invoked on the left side of these lines. Because the partialClone method in the ParentSnowmanV2 class (Figure 7.12) copies the current (x, y) position of the patrolling snowman into the clone, the clone is positioned at an edge of the garden.

Just before the timer3 method ends, the for loop that begins on line 66 indexes through the last nine elements of the array. For each of these elements, the if statement's Boolean condition on lines 68 and 69 determines if:

- the element of the array references a snowman (is not null)
- the referenced snowman has collided with the patrolling guard (ps[0]) as determined by the collidedWith method
- the referenced snowman is an intruder as determined by the equals method (Its hat color is not equal to the guard's hat color.)

When this is the case, the (x, y) position of the green-hat wandering snowman is set to the (x, y) position of the patrolling guard (lines 71–72). On the next tick of timer3, the patrolling guard is only moved two pixels, so the guard and the snowman remain in a collided state, and the wandering snowman's position is reset by lines 71–72 to the patrolling guard's new position. The resulting effect is that the wandering snowman goes on patrol with the guard. It cannot be seen on patrol because line 31 of the draw method draws the patrolling guard, ps[0], last (i.e., on top of the green-hat snowmen that have joined the patrol).

After the game ends, a series of left button clicks will separate the patrolling guard from the green-hat guards that have joined the patrol as shown in the center portion of Figure 7.15. This is accomplished by decrementing the x coordinates of each green-hat patrolling snowman (line 82) and the guard (line 84) by a different amount on each button click. Until the game ends, the left button is inactive because the body of the if statement on line 79 that separates the snowmen is only executed when the Boolean variable gameOver is set to true on line 39 of the timer3 call back method.

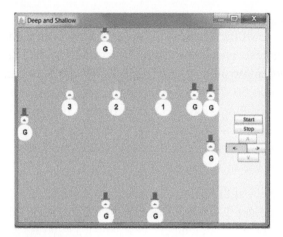

Figure 7.15
Graphical output produced by the application **DeepAndShallow**
after the animation ends and several left button clicks have been performed.

7.5 THE STRING CLASS: A SECOND LOOK

In Section 2.5, we discussed the creation of String objects, and in Section 4.2.3, we discussed the String class's methods equals and compareTo, which are used to compare two strings. In addition to these methods, the class contains a rich collection of methods used to create strings, to convert strings to characters, and to process string data.

7.5.1 Creating Strings from Primitive Values

Aside from the one-parameter constructor discussed in Chapter 2 that is passed a string literal or a string object such as

```
String name1 = new String("Robert");
String name2 = new String(name1);
```

the String class also contains several overloaded constructors. Each of these creates a new string object and returns its address. Two of the most frequently used constructors have a character array passed to them. The following code fragment uses the one-parameter version of these two methods to create the string name1 initialized to *Joanne Jones* and the three-parameter version to create the string name2 initialized to *anne Jo*. (The second argument sent to the three-parameter version of the constructor would be *zero* to include the first character of the array in the string object.)

```
char[] c = {'J', 'o', 'a', 'n', 'n', 'e', ' ', 'J', 'o', 'n', 'e', 's'};
String name1 = new String(c); //all characters used
String name2 = new String(c, 2, 7); //7 characters used, starts @ index 2
```

The static method valueOf in the String class also can be used to create and return the address of a string object initialized to the argument passed to it. Overloaded versions of this method use a `char`, `int`, `long`, `float`, or `double` parameter. Integer type `byte` and `short` arguments can be passed to the `int` parameter version of this method. In addition, there is a version of the method that accepts a character array passed to it. The following code fragment demonstrates the use of this overloaded method, to output the string: *x102030405.556.66yz*.

```
char c = 'x';
byte b = 10;
short s = 20;
int i = 30;
long l = 40;
float f = 5.55f;
double d = 6.66;
char[] cArray = {'y', 'z'}

String s2 = String.valueOf(c) + String.valueOf(b) + String.valueOf(s) +
            String.valueOf(i) + String.valueOf(f) + String.valueOf(l) +
            String.valueOf(d) + String.valueOf(cArray);

System.out.println(s2);
```

7.5.2 Converting Strings to Characters

The `String` class method `charAt` can be used to convert a particular character contained in the string object that invoked it to type `char`, and it returns the character. The following code fragment stores the character `'S'` in the variable `c`.

```
String aString = "Joe Smith";
char c = aString.charAt(4);   //character numbers begin at zero
```

The method `toCharArray` converts a string object that invokes it to an array of characters and returns the address of the array. After the following code fragment executes, the character arrays `c1` and `c2` contain the same character sequence:

```
char[] c1 = {'J', 'o', 'a', 'n', 'n', 'e', ' ', 'R', 'a', 'y'};
char[] c2;
String aString = "Joanne Ray";
c2 = aString.toCharArray();
```

7.5.3 Processing Strings

The `String` class contains several methods to process string data. Two of these methods, `compareTo` and `equals` (and their related methods `compareToIgnoreCase` and `equalsIgnoreCase`) were discussed in Section 4.2.3. Table 7.1 describes other `String` class methods often used to process strings.

All of these methods are nonstatic methods. They can be used to determine the existence or location of a given substring in a string, fetch a substring from a specified position in the string, produce an uppercase or lowercase version of a string, replace the first or all occurrences of a substring with a given string, and tokenize a string determine if a string begins or ends with a specified string.

Table 7.1

String Processing Methods in the String Class

Function	Method and Parameter Type	Example and Description

Locate a given substring in a string	`indexOf`
	
	Parameter(s): String *or*
	
	String, `int`
		`int i = s1.indexOf(target);`
		Returns the index of the *first* occurrence of substring `target` in the string `s1`
		`int i = s1.indexof(target, start);`
		Returns the index of the first occurrence of substring `target` that begins at or after the index `start` in the string `s1`

Fetch a substring from a string	`substring`
	
	Parameter(s):
	`int` *or*
	`int, int`
		`String s2 = s1.substring(start);`
		Returns the substring of `s1` from index `start` to the end of `s1`
		`String s2 = subString(start, end);`
		Returns the substring of `s1` from index `start` to
		index end −1

Convert a string to upper or lower case characters	`toUpperCase`
	
	`toLowerCase`
		`String s2 = s1.toUpperCase();`
		Creates a clone of string `s1` consisting of all uppercase characters
		`String s2 = s1.toLowerCase()`
		Creates a clone of string `s1` consisting of all lowercase characters

Replace a given substring in a string with a given substring	`replaceFirst`
	Parameter(s): String, String
	`replaceAll`
	Parameter(s): String, String
		`String s2 = s1.replaceFirst(target, new);`
		Returns a string with the first occurrence of the substring `target` in `s1` replaced with the string `new`
		`String s2 = s1.replaceAll(target, new);`
		Returns a string with all occurrences of the substring `target` in `s1` replaced with the string `new`

Determine if a string begins or ends with a given string	`startsWith`
	Parameter: String
	`endsWith`
	Parameter: String
		`boolean b = s1.startsWith(s2);`
		Returns *true* if the string `s1` begins with the string `s2`
		`boolean b = s1.endsWith(s2);`
		Returns *true* if the string `s1` ends with the string `s2`

Tokenize a string	`split`
	
	Parameter(s): String *or*
	
	String, `int`
		`String[] s1 = s1.split(" +");`
		Returns a string array whose elements are the substrings of `s1` that are separated by one or more spaces
		`String[] s1 = s1.split(" +" , n);`
		Returns a string array whose elements are the substrings of `s1` that are separated by one or more spaces; there will be `n` or fewer elements in the returned array

The application `StringProcessing` presented in Figure 7.16 uses some of the methods described in Table 7.1 to process a sentence input by the user. If the word *Hello* appears at the beginning of the sentence it is eliminated, and if the word *Tom* is in the sentence it is changed to *XXX*. A typical input and corresponding output are given in the left and right sides of Figure 7.17, respectively.

Line 16 uses the `String` class method `split` to create a new `String` array and place each word of the sentence input on line 11 into its elements. Then, it stores the address of the array returned from `split` in the variable `sArray` that is declared on line 8. The string consisting of a space followed by a plus sign passed to `split` on line 16 instructs the method to consider one or more spaces as tokens, in this case, word delimiters in the sentence. Line 19 clones the string input on line 11 and stores its address in the variable s2.

Lines 20–23 remove the word Hello from the beginning the cloned string s2. The `indexOf` method is used in the `if` statement's Boolean condition on line 20 to determine if the substring "Hello" begins at the index zero of the string s2. If it does, the `substring` method is used on line 22 to return the substring of s2 that begins at index 6 (after the word *Hello* and the space that follows it). The address of this new string object is stored in (shallow copied into) s2. Line 20 could have been coded as shown below:

```
if(s2.startsWith("Hello"))
```

The `replaceAll` method is invoked on line 24. It effectively creates a clone of the string object s2 and replaces all occurrences of the word *Tom* with the string literal "XXX." The returned address of the modified clone is then assigned to (shallow copied into) the variable s2.

```
1    import javax.swing.*;
2
3    public class StringProcessing
4    {
5      public static void main(String[] args)
6      {
7        String s1, s2;
8        String[] sArray;
9        int nWords;
10
11       s1 = JOptionPane.showInputDialog("Enter a sentence, Please\n" +
12                                        "Don't begin it with Hello,\n" +
13                                        "don't include the word Tom.\n" +
14                                        "Hello will be removed, and \n" +
15                                        "Tom replaced with XXX.");
16       sArray = s1.split(" +"); //stores each word in separate elements
17       nWords = sArray.length; //the number of words
18
19       s2 = new String(s1);
20       if(s2.indexOf("Hello") == 0)
21       {
```

```
22          s2 = s2.substring(6);
23      }
24      s2 = s2.replaceAll("Tom", "XXX");
25
26      JOptionPane.showMessageDialog(null, "There are " + nWords +
27                             " words in your sentence:\n" +
28                             s1 + "\nThe revised sentence is:\n" +
29                             s2);
30   }
31 }
```

Figure 7.16
The application **StringProcessing**.

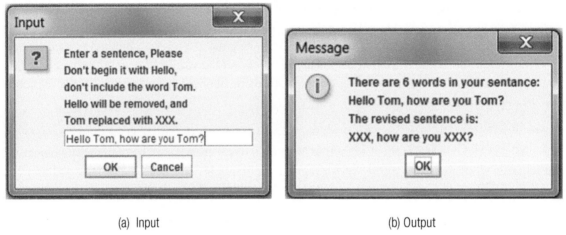

(a) Input   (b) Output

Figure 7.17
Input to the application **StringProcessing** and the corresponding output.

7.6 THE WRAPPER CLASSES: A SECOND LOOK

As discussed in Section 2.7.3, the six numeric wrapper classes (e.g., Integer, Double, etc.) contain methods that parse a string into integer or real values that can then be stored in primitive variables. In addition to these methods, all of the wrapper classes contain constructors to create a wrapper class object and also contain a collection of useful constants. A seventh wrapper class, the class Character, contains methods to perform common operations on characters. In this section, we will discuss these additional features of the wrapper classes and a related topic called autoboxing.

7.6.1 Wrapper Class Objects

A wrapper class's one-parameter constructor can be used to create a wrapper object. Wrapper class objects contain a single private primitive data member whose type is consistent with the class's name. For example, an object in the class Double contains a double primitive data member, and an instance of an Integer contains an int data member. The argument passed to the one-parameter constructor is stored in the object's data member. Envisioning the primitive value being wrapped in the object is the basis of the phrase *wrapper classes*.

The wrapper classes contain methods that return the value stored in an object's data member. These methods perform the function of `get` methods, but their names begin with the primitive type they return followed by the word *Value*. For example, the `Integer` class contains a method named `intValue` that returns the value of the class's integer data member, and the `Character` class contains the method `charValue` that returns the value of the class's character data member.

The `Integer` class also contains the methods `byteValue`, `shortValue`, `longValue`, `floatValue`, and `doubleValue` that cast the returned value of the data member into the other numeric primitive types. The other numeric wrapper classes contain five similarly named methods used to cast the data member they return into different numeric types. The following code segment wraps the value 20 in an `Integer` object and outputs the value as an integer and a double (e.g., 20 followed by 20.0):

```
Integer n = new Integer(20);
System.out.println(n.intValue() + " " +
                   n.doubleValue()); //outputs: 20 20.0
```

Each of the wrapper classes contains an `equals` and a `compareTo` method to perform a deep comparison of the data wrapped in the object that invoked them and the object sent to their parameter. The `equals` method returns the Boolean value `true` when the two objects are equal, otherwise it returns `false`. The equality operator (==) can be used to perform a shallow comparison to determine if two wrapper class reference variables refer to the same object.

The `compareTo` method returns an integer, which is negative, zero, or positive when the invoking object is less than, equal to, or greater than the object sent to its parameter, respectively. This version of the method coded in the numeric wrapper classes always returns -1, 0, or 1. The integer returned from the `Character` class's version of the method also gives an indication of the lexicographic separation of the characters contained in the objects being compared.

The following code fragment outputs the value -25. The value is negative because the character 'a' appears before 'z' in the Unicode table, and its absolute value is 25 because 'a' is 25 characters before 'z'.

```
Character c1 = new Character('a');
Character c2 = new Character('z');
System.out.println(c1.compareTo(c2));  //outputs: -25
```

The wrapper classes do not contain set methods to change the value of the data member wrapped in the object. This is because wrapper class objects, like `String` objects, are *immutable*. Once a value has been stored in a wrapper class's data member or inside a `String` object, the value cannot be changed. As is the case with `String` objects, the assignment operator can be used to reassign the address stored in the object's reference variable to a newly created object that contains the assigned (different) value. Although this gives the appearance that the value stored in the object has changed, in reality, the new value has been stored in a different object.

The assignment operator can also be used to shallow copy (the address of) two wrapper class objects. The following code fragment outputs the value 12.5 twice. Although it initially creates two instances of a `Double`, d1 and d2, after the third line executes, these variables reference the same object. The object containing the value *54.6* is reclaimed by the Java memory manager. The coding of the variables d1 and d2 in the argument sent to the `println` method are two implicit invocations of the `Double` class's `toString` method.

```
Double d1 = new Double(12.5);
Double d2 = new Double(54.6);
d2 = d1; //d1 and d2 reference the same object which contains 12.5;
System.out.println(d1 + " " +  d2); //outputs: 12.5 12.5
```

7.6.2 Autoboxing and Unboxing

The autoboxing feature of wrapper classes makes it easier to use wrapper class objects in our programs. This feature automatically "wraps" primitive values into wrapper objects. For example, wrapper class objects can be declared using the abbreviated syntax used to declare `String` objects, as discussed in Section 2.5. The following line of code wraps, or boxes, the integer 20 in an `Integer` object and writes its address in the variable n1:

```
Integer n1 = 20; //autoboxing of the value 20 in an object declaration
```

When this statement executes, the autoboxing feature creates an `Integer` wrapper object, stores (boxes) 20 in its data member, and returns the object's address. The statement is equivalent to the following statement:

```
Integer n1 = new Integer(20);
```

Autoboxing can also be used to effectively reassign or set the primitive value stored in a wrapper class object. The following code fragment outputs the value 3.6. The right side of line 2 uses autoboxing to create a new `Integer` wrapper object, stores 3.6 in its data member, and returns its address. The returned address is then stored in the variable n1. The wrapper object containing the value 2.5 is reclaimed by the Java memory manager.

```
1    Double n1 = 2.5;
2    n1 = 3.6; //Autoboxing of the value 3.6 in an assignment statement
3    System.out.println(n1);
```

It should be noted that if the value to be boxed in a wrapper class object (e.g., n2) is already stored in another wrapper class object (e.g., n1) of the same type, then a new object is not created. Rather, n2 is set to refer to n1's object. The only exception to this is if the long form of the object-declaration grammar is used to declare and initialize the new object. This caveat also applies to `String` objects. The code fragment shown in Figure 7.19 demonstrates these concepts, as well as the use of the equality operator and the wrapper class's `equals` method. The output it produces is shown at the bottom of the figure.

Lines 2, 7, and 11 do not create a new object but simply assign n2 the object's address that is stored in n1. Line 16 creates a new object even though the object n1 created on line 15 stores the same value because the long form of the object-declaration syntax (which includes the keyword **new**) is used to create it.

```
1    Integer n1 = 20;
2    Integer n2 = 20; //a new object is not created, n2 is assigned n1
3    if(n1 == n2) System.out.println("n1 and n2 refer to the same object");
4    if(n1.equals(n2)) System.out.println("n1 & n2 contain the same value");
5
6    n1 = 30;
7    n2 = 30; //a new object is not created, n2 is assigned n1
8    if(n1 == n2) System.out.println("n1 & n2 refer to the same object");
9    if(n1.equals(n2)) System.out.println("n1 & n2 contain the same value");
10
11   n2 = n1; //a new object is not created, n2 is assigned n1
12   if(n1 == n2) System.out.println("n1 & n2 refer to the same object");;
13   if(n1.equals(n2)) System.out.println("n1 & n2 contain the same value");
14
15   n1 = 40;
16   n2 = new Integer(40); //a new object is created
17   if(n1 == n2) System.out.println("n1 & n2 refer to the same object");
18   if(n1.equals(n2)) System.out.println("n1 & n2 contain the same value");
```

Output produced:

n1 & n2 refer to the same object
n1 & n2 contain the same value
n1 & n2 refer to the same object
n1 & n2 contain the same value
n1 & n2 refer to the same object
n1 & n2 contain the same value
n1 & n2 contain the same value

Figure 7.18
Examples of when autoboxing creates new objects.

The *unboxing* feature of wrapper classes allows us to use the name of a numeric wrapper class object in arithmetic expressions. The following code fragment outputs the values *7* and *16*. The value stored in the object n2 is unboxed from it on lines 2, 3, and 4. The unboxing fetches the value 7 from the object on lines 2 and 3, and the value 8 on line 4.

```
1    Integer n2 = 7;
2    int n3 = n2; //auto Unboxing of n2
3    n2++; //auto Unboxing of n2, incrementing, and Autoboxing the new value
4    n2 = n2 * 2; //auto Unboxing, multiplying, and Autoboxing the new value
5    System.out.println(n3 + " " + n2);
```

The location of wrapper class objects can be passed to and returned from a method using the same syntax used to pass any object's location to or from a method. The most common use of wrapper class objects is to pass a primitive value to a generic method that is expecting an object or to store a group of primitive values in a Java collection object. Generic methods and collections, and the role wrapper objects play in their use, will be discussed in Chapter 12.

7.6.3 Wrapper Class Constants

The six numeric wrapper classes all contain static data members named MAX _ VALUE, MIN _ VALUE, and SIZE. The values of a class's MAX _ VALUE and MIN _ VALUE constants are the maximum and minimum values that can be stored in the primitive numeric data member of an instance of that class. The value of the constant SIZE is the number of bits that make up the primitive data member's storage cell.

The following code fragment produces the output *127 - 128 8*, which are the maximum and minimum values that can be wrapped in a Byte object, and the size of the object's data member (8 bits). These are the same values presented on the first row of Table 2.1, which specified the range and size of the primitive numeric types.

```
System.out.println(Byte.MAX_VALUE, + " " + Byte.MIN_VALUE, +
                   " " + Byte.SIZE);
```

7.6.4 The Character Wrapper Class

The wrapper class Character contains all of the methods, constants, and the autoboxing features of the numeric wrapper classes discussed previously in Section 7.6. Its value method, named charValue, returns the character stored inside the Character instance that invokes it. Naturally, the Character class's constants such as MAX _ VALUE, MIN _ VALUE, and SIZE store values relevant to primitive char values, and the class's methods operate on Character objects and are passed char parameters.

In addition to the analogous numeric wrapper class methods, the Character class contains two static methods named toUpperCase and toLowerCase that change the case of a character primitive passed to their char type parameter. The Character class also contains seven other static methods described in Table 7.2 that return a Boolean value. These methods can be used to determine if the character passed to it is a digit or a letter, an uppercase or lowercase letter, or is Java whitespace. The methods are very useful in programs that process text information.

Figure 7.19 contains a program ParseSentence that demonstrates the use of four of the methods shown in Table 7.2 to determine the number of upper and lowercase letters, digits, and whitespace in an input sentence. A typical input sentence and the corresponding output the program produces is shown in Figures 7.20a and 7.20b, respectively.

The code inside the for loop that begins on line 14 of Figure 7.19 counts the number of occurrences of the four different types of characters contained in the sentence input on line 13. The String class's length method is invoked on line 14 to determine the number of characters in the sentence.

Each time through the loop, the loop variable is passed to the String class's charAt method to fetch the ith character from the sentence. Lines 17, 21, 25, and 29 use four of the character-testing methods presented in Table 7.2 to determine if the character returned from the charAt method is an upper- or lowercase letter, digit, or whitespace.

Table 7.2

The Character-Testing Methods in the Class Character

Method Name and Parameter List	Returns true if the Character Passed to its Parameter is:	Code Example
isDigit(char c)	a digit in the range 0 to 9	Character.isDigit('4'); returns true
isLetter(char c)	an upper or lower case letter of the alphabet	Character.isDigit('C'); returns true
isLetterOrDigit(char c)	an upper- or lowercase letter or digit (0-9)	Character.isLetterOrDigit('C'); returns true Character.isLetterOrDigit('6'); returns true
isLowerCase(char c)	a lowercase letter of the alphabet	Character.isDigit('c'); returns true
isSpaceChar(char c)	a space character	Character.isSpaceChar(' '); returns true
isUpperCase(char c)	an uppercase letter of the alphabet	Character.isUpperCase('B'); returns true
isWhiteSpace(char c)	Java defined white space (e.g., space, tab, or a new line character)	Character.isWhiteSpace(' '); returns true

```
1     import javax.swing.*;
2
3     public class ParseSentence
4     {
5       public static void main(String[] args)
6       {
7         int upperCase = 0;
8         int lowerCase = 0;
9         int numeric = 0;
10        int whitespace = 0;
11        char c;
12
13        String sentence = JOptionPane.showInputDialog("Enter a sentence");
14        for(int i = 0; i < sentence.length(); i++)
15        {
16          c = sentence.charAt(i);
17          if(Character.isUpperCase(c))
```

```
18          {
19             upperCase++;
20          }
21          else if(Character.isLowerCase(c))
22          {
23             lowerCase++;
24          }
25          else if(Character.isDigit(c))
26          {
27             numeric++;
28          }
29          else if(Character.isWhitespace(c))
30          {
31             whitespace++;
32          }
33       }
34       JOptionPane.showMessageDialog(null, "The sentence contains:\n" +
35                                     upperCase + " Upper case letters,\n" +
36                                     owerCase + " Lower case letters,\n" +
37                                     numeric + " Digits and\n" +
38                                     whitespace + " Whitespace characters");
39    }
40 }
```

Figure 7.19
The application **ParseSentence**.

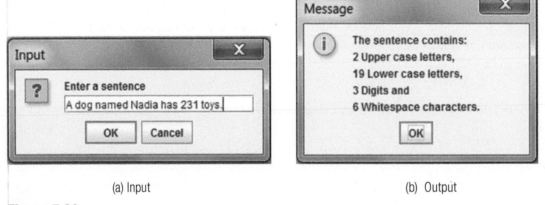

        (a) Input   (b) Output

Figure 7.20
An input to the application **ParseSentence** and the resulting output.

7.7 AGGREGATION

Just as a group of primitive variables can be collected into an object by declaring them as data members in the object's class, instances of other types of objects can also be collected, or aggregated, into an object. We have already utilized this concept many times in this textbook. For example, lines 10 and 11 of Figure 7.12 indicate that a String and a Color object will be part of a `ParentSnowmanV2` object. As a result, the `ParentSnowmanV2` class would be considered an **aggregated** *class*.

Definition

An **aggregated** class is a class that includes in its data members instances of other classes.

Aggregating an object into a class is a simple task. As shown in Figure 7.21, which contains lines 10–11 and lines 20–28 of Figure 7.12, we simply declare a data member that can reference the object (lines 10 and 11) and assign the reference variable the address of an object (lines 11, 25, and 26).

```
10      private String name;
11      private Color hatColor= Color.BLACK;
 :
20      public ParentSnowmanV2(int intialX, int intialY, String name,
21                             Color hatColor)
22      {
23        x = intialX;
24        y = intialY;
25        this.name = name;
26        this.hatColor = hatColor;
27        snowmanCount++;
28      }
```

Figure 7.21
A code fragment from an aggregated class.

The difficult part of the aggregation shown in Figure 7.21 falls on the authors of the `String` and `Color` classes. They had to anticipate the operations that would be performed on aggregated strings or `Color` objects and provide methods to perform these operations. In the case of the `String` class, this includes operations such as comparing two strings, outputting a string to the console, and all of the other operations that were discussed in Section 7. 5. These methods are invoked by the code of the aggregated class to operate on the objects.

Properly anticipating the operations that will be performed on an aggregated object is a key component of the concept of aggregation. In addition, where possible, the signatures of these methods are standardized, as is the case for the `equals` method in the `String` and `Color` classes. Providing commonly used methods whose signatures are standardized facilitates the use of aggregation in our programs.

Instances of a class that we write can also be aggregated into other classes using the same syntax discussed above. (In this case, the burden of identifying the operations that will be performed on the aggregated objects and writing the classes falls on us.) This use of aggregation gives us the ability to extend the design concept of divide and conquer, used to divide complicated methods into smaller methods, to classes we write. The component objects of a large class (e.g., a `ParentSnowman` class) can be identified (e.g., a `Hat` object and a `Nose` object), and then the component classes can be written. Once written, instances of these classes can be aggregated into the larger class. In addition, instances of component classes can be aggregated into the classes of other programs just as instances of API classes are used in most Java programs.

The concept of aggregation gives us the ability to:

- use instances of existing objects in classes we write
- extend the design concept of divide and conquer to classes we write
- define a complicated object as an aggregation of component objects defined in other classes
- easily operate on aggregated component objects as separate entities

Figure 7.22 shows the UML representation of a class named SnowmanV8 that aggregates a Hat and String object into it. The symbol for aggregation in a UML diagram is the diamond shown below the SnowmanV8 class. The lines that connect it to the Hat and String classes indicate that the SnowmanV8 class aggregates at least one Hat and one String object into it. The last two data members of the SnowmanV8 class specify that one of each of these objects is aggregated into the class.

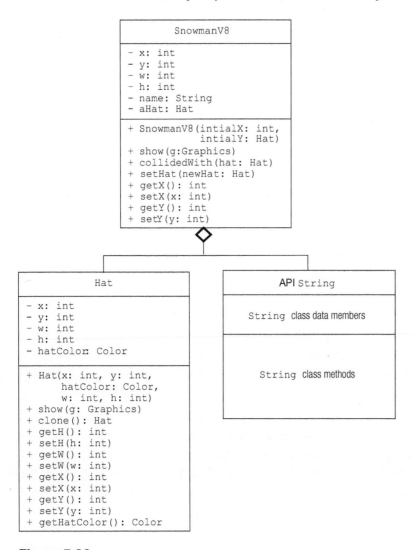

Figure 7.22
UML diagram of the **SnowmanV8** and the **Hat** classes.

During the design of the Hat class, it was anticipated that classes that aggregate hats will want to include hats of different colors and sizes. The last three parameters of the class's constructor were included in its parameter list to allow for this, as were its last three data members. The Hat class's show method will use these data members to draw a properly sized and colored hat. In addition, it has been anticipated that classes that aggregate Hat objects will want to clone them, so the class includes a clone method. Finally, it was assumed that once created, a hat's color would not be changed, so a setHatColor data member was not included in the Hat class.

Figure 7.23 shows the code of the class Hat that is specified in Figure 7.22. Lines 22 and 23 of the show method scale the hat top and its brim using the hat's specified width (w) and height (h). This unburdens the authors of all classes that aggregate hats from knowing how to scale a Hat object. That task is left to the hat specialist, which illustrates another advantage of aggregation. In addition, they do not have to include the Hat class's data members and method in their class, making the aggregated easier to code and understand. The clone method, lines 25–29, invokes the class's constructor in line 27 to create a clone of the Hat object that invokes it and returns the address of the newly created clone on line 28.

```
1    import java.awt.*;
2
3    public class Hat
4    {
5      private int x;
6      private int y;
7      private int w = 20;
8      private int h = 17;
9      private Color hatColor;
10
11     public Hat(int x, int y, Color hatColor, int w, int h)
12     {
13       this.x = x;
14       this.y = y;
15       this.hatColor = hatColor;
16       this.w = w;
17       this.h = h;
18     }
19     public void show(Graphics g)
20     {
21       g.setColor(hatColor);
22       g.fillRect(x + w/4, y, w/2, (int)(h*0.9));   // hat top
23       g.fillRect(x, y + (int)(h*0.9), w, (int)(h*0.2));   // brim
24     }
25     public Hat clone()
26     {
27       Hat theClone = new Hat(x, y, hatColor, w, h);
28       return theClone;
29     }
30     public int getW()
```

```
31      {
32          return w;
33      }
34      public int getH()
35      {
36          return h;
37      }
38      public int getX()
39      {
40          return x;
41      }
42      public void setX(int newX)
43      {
44          x = newX;
45      }
46      public int getY()
47      {
48          return y;
49      }
50      public void setY(int newY)
51      {
52          y = newY;
53      }
54      public Color getHatColor()
55      {
56          return hatColor;
57      }
58  }
```

Figure 7.23
The class `Hat`.

Figure 7.24 shows the code of the class `SnowmanV8` that is specified in Figure 7.22. This class begins the aggregation of a `String` and a `Hat` object with the declaration of its last two data members on lines 9 and 10. Line 16 of the constructor completes the aggregation of the `String` object by creating a string and setting its address into the data member `name`.

The aggregation of the `Hat` object is completed on line 52 of the `setHat` method that assigns the address of a `Hat` object passed to its parameter on line 50 to the data member `aHat` declared on line 10. This means that until the `setHat` method is invoked, a `SnowmanV8` object should be drawn without a hat on his head. This is easily accomplished by including an `if` statement (line 22) in the class's `show` method that only invokes the `Hat` class's `show` method (line 26) when the data member `aHat` does contain its default value, `null`. This demonstrates another advantage of aggregation: aggregated objects can easily be treated as separate entities in a program. The snowman can be drawn with or without a hat.

Before the hat is drawn, it must be positioned on the snowman's head. This is accomplished by lines 24 and 25, which use the `Hat` class's `setX` and `setY` methods to set the (x, y) position of the hat above the snowman's head. The argument sent to these methods uses the `Hat` class's `setW` and `setH` methods to fetch the height and width of the hat, which are used to center the hat on the snowman's head.

Lines 38–49 of Figure 7.24 contain the code of the `SnowmanV8` class's `collidedWith` method specified in Figure 7.22. It detects a collision between the snowman that invokes it and the `Hat` object passed to its parameter. It uses the `Hat` class's `get` methods in the Boolean expression on lines 40 and 41 to decide if a collision has occurred.

```
1    import java.awt.*;
2
3    public class SnowmanV8
4    {
5      private static int w = 40;
6      private static int h = 77;
7      private int x;
8      private int y;
9      private String name; //data members for aggregated objects
10     private Hat aHat;
11
12     public SnowmanV8(int intialX, int intialY)
13     {
14       x = intialX;
15       y = intialY;
16       name = "sm"; //aggregates a String object into this class
17     }
18     public void show(Graphics g)
19     { int[] xPoly = {x + 20, x + 15, x + 25};
20       int[] yPoly = {y + 8, y + 13, y + 13};
21
22       if(aHat != null) //snowman has a hat
23       {
24         aHat.setX(x + w/2 - aHat.getW()/2); //locate the hat on head
25         aHat.setY(y - aHat.getH());
26         aHat.show(g); //draw the hat
27       }
28       g.setColor(Color.WHITE);
29       g.fillOval(x + 10, y, 20, 20); // head
30       g.fillOval(x, y + 20, 40, 40); // body
31       g.setColor(Color.RED);
32       g.fillPolygon(xPoly, yPoly, 3); // nose
33       g.setColor(Color.BLACK);
34       g.setFont(new Font("Arial", Font.BOLD, 16));
35       g.drawString(name, x + 10, y + 45); // name
36     }
37
38     public boolean collidedWith(Hat hat)
39     {
40       if( !(x > hat.getX( ) + hat.getW() || x + w < hat.getX( ) ||
```

```
41                    y > hat.getY( ) + hat.getH() || y + h < hat.getY( )))
42          {
43            return true;
44          }
45          else
46          {
47            return false;
48          }
49        }
50        public void setHat(Hat newHat)
51        {
52          aHat = newHat; //aggregates a Hat object into this class
53        }
54        public int getX()
55        {
56          return x;
57        }
58        public void setX(int newX)
59        {
60          x = newX;
61        }
62        public int getY()
63        {
64          return y;
65        }
66        public void setY(int newY)
67        {
68          y = newY;
69        }
70      }
```

Figure 7.24
The class SnowmanV8.

Figure 7.25 presents the application Aggregation. When launched, it displays a hatless snowman and a hat rack containing six different hats, as shown in Figure 7.26a. The keyboard cursor-control keys are used to move the snowman to the hat he wishes to wear, perhaps the blue hat as shown in the upper right side of the figure (7.26b). The chosen hat is cloned and positioned on his head (Figure 7.26c), and follows him around the game board as shown on the lower right side of the figure (7.26d).

The application's draw method (lines 23–32) draws the hat rack on lines 25 and 26, and then its for loop invokes the hat class's show method to draw the six hats created on lines 12 to 17. The parameters sent to the Hat class's five-parameter constructor specify different locations, colors, and sizes for each hat.

Line 31 of the draw method invokes the SnowmanV8 class's show method to draw the snowman that was created on line 8 on the game board. When the application is launched, the snowman's data member, aHat, declared on line 10 of the Figure 7.24, still contains its null default value. This causes the snowman to be drawn without a hat, as shown in Figure 7.26a, because the Boolean condition on line 22 of Figure 7.24 is `false`.

Every time a cursor key is struck, the code of the switch statement (Figure 7.25, lines 37–62) inside the `keyStruck` call back method moves the snowman two pixels left, right, up, or down. Then, the `if` statement (lines 66–69) uses the loop variable of the `for` loop to check each hat in the array `hats` to determine if the snowman has chosen (collided with) any of the hats on the hat rack.

When a hat is chosen it is cloned, and the clone is aggregated into the snowman object by invoking the hat class's `setHat` method and passing it the address of the cloned hat (line 68). The aggregation is accomplished by line 52 of Figure 7.24, which assigns the cloned hat's address (passed to the `setHat` method) the snowman's data member `aHat`. Because the data member is no longer `null`, lines 24–25 of Figure 7.24 position the aggregated hat centered and on top of the snowman's head at its current position, and line 26 draws the hat at that position.

```
1    import edu.sjcny.gpv1.*;
2    import java.awt.*;
3
4    public class Aggregation extends DrawableAdapter
5    { static Aggregation ge = new Aggregation();
6      static GameBoard gb = new GameBoard(ge, "Aggregation");
7      static Hat[] hats = new Hat[6];
8      static SnowmanV8 sm;
9
10     public static void main(String[] args)
11     {
12       hats[0] = new Hat(40, 100, Color.RED, 20, 17);
13       hats[1] = new Hat(120, 100, Color.ORANGE, 25, 21);
14       hats[2] = new Hat(200, 100, Color.YELLOW, 20, 17);
15       hats[3] = new Hat(280, 100, Color.GREEN, 40, 34);
16       hats[4] = new Hat(360, 100, Color.BLUE, 30, 25);
17       hats[5] = new Hat(440, 100, Color.MAGENTA, 35, 29);
18       sm = new SnowmanV8(250, 250);
19
20       showGameBoard(gb);
21     }
22
23     public void draw(Graphics g)
24     {
25       g.setColor(Color.BLACK); //the hat rack
26       g.fillRect(20, 95, 460, 5);
27       for(int i=0; i<hats.length; i++)
28       {
29         hats[i].show(g);
30       }
31       sm.show(g);
32     }
```

```
33      public void keyStruck(char key) //call back method
34      {
35        int newX, newY;
36
37        switch (key) //to move the snowman
38        {
39          case 'L':
40          {
41            newX = sm.getX() - 2;
42            sm.setX(newX);
43            break;
44          }
45          case 'R':
46          {
47            newX = sm.getX() + 2;
48            sm.setX(newX);
49            break;
50          }
51          case 'U':
52          {
53            newY = sm.getY() - 2;
54            sm.setY(newY);
55            break;
56          }
57          case 'D':
58          {
59            newY = sm.getY() + 2;
60            sm.setY(newY);
61          }
62        }
63        //acquiring a new Hat
64        for(int i = 0; i<hats.length; i++)
65        {
66          if(sm.collidedWith(hats[i])) //a hat is chosen
67          {
68            sm.setHat(hats[i].clone()); //clone the hat and add it to sm
69          }
70        }
71      }
72 }
```

Figure 7.25
The application **Aggregation**.

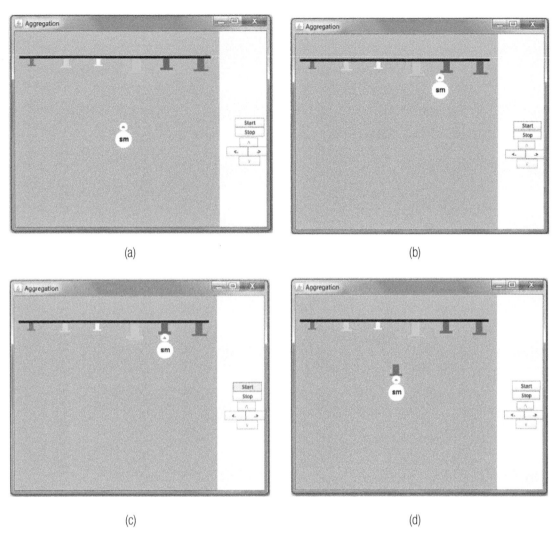

Figure 7.26
Output generated by the application **Aggregation**.

7.8 ■ INNER CLASSES

An *inner class* is a class defined inside another class. Just as classes can contain data members and methods, they can contain other classes. The class that contains the inner class is called the *outer* class. Normally, a class is defined as an inner class only if the outer class will aggregate instances of the inner class. Consider the Hat class (Figure 7.23) discussed in the previous section. Because both the class SnowmanV8 and the application Aggregation declared Hat objects, the Hat class was not coded inside the SnowmanV8 class. Inner classes are most often used in Java programs that use a Graphical User Interface (GUI), also called a point-and-click interface. In this section, we will become familiar with the syntax of inner classes and the ability of the inner and outer classes to access each other's data members and methods.

Figure 7.27 presents the class PhoneBook that contains an inner class PhoneNumbers, which begins on line 28 and ends on line 48. Instances of the inner class contain a person's office, cell, and home phone numbers. These three strings are declared as aggregated data members of the inner class on lines 30–32, and the class's constructor assigns them input values (lines 36–40) when a PhoneNumbers object is created. The class's show method (lines 43–47) outputs the three phone numbers to the system console.

```java
1    import javax.swing.*;
2
3    public class PhoneBook
4    {
5      private String[] name;
6      private PhoneNumbers[] numbers;
7
8      public PhoneBook() //a phone book has three listings
9      {
10       name = new String[3];
11       numbers = new PhoneNumbers[3];
12
13       for(int i = 0; i < name.length; i++)
14       {
15         name[i] = JOptionPane.showInputDialog("enter your name");
16         numbers[i] = new PhoneNumbers(i);
17       }
18     }
19     public void showAll()
20     {
21       for(int i = 0; i < name.length; i++)
22       {
23         System.out.println("\nName: " + name[i]);
24         numbers[i].show();
25       }
26     }
27
28     private class PhoneNumbers //an inner class
29     {
30       private String home;
31       private String cell;
32       private String office;
33
34       public PhoneNumbers(int i)
35       {
36         home = JOptionPane.showInputDialog("enter " + name[i] +
37                                     "'s HOME number");
38         cell = JOptionPane.showInputDialog("enter " + name[i] +
39                                     "'s CELL number");
40         office = JOptionPane.showInputDialog("enter " + name[i] +
41                                     "'s OFFICE number");
```

```
42        }
43        public void show()
44        {
45           System.out.println("PhoneNumbers: home:" + home +
46                              " cell:" + cell +  " office:" + office);
47        }
48     } //end of the inner class Phonenumbers
49  }
```

Figure 7.27
The class **PhoneBook** and its inner class **PhoneNumbers**.

The outer class PhoneBook declares two parallel arrays each containing three elements on lines 10 and 11 and assigns their addresses to the variables name and numbers, declared on lines 5 and 6. After creating the arrays, the for loop (lines 13–17) in the outer class's constructor completes the aggregation of the String and PhoneNumbers objects into the outer class by creating new instances of these classes and assigning their addresses to the elements of the parallel arrays name and numbers (lines 15 and 16).

> **NOTE**   *The code of an outer class can invoke a constructor in an inner class.*

Each time the inner class's constructor is invoked on line 16, it not only creates a new object, but it also accepts input into the data members of the newly created object on lines 36–41. The argument passed to this one-parameter constructor on line 16 is the loop variable declared on line 13. Lines 36, 38, and 40 of the constructor use this value to index into the outer class's name array, which causes the person's name that was just input on line 10 to become part of the prompts output by lines 36–41.

> **NOTE**   *The code of an inner class can access the data members of its outer class.*

The outer class's showAll method (lines 19–26) outputs all of the names and numbers in the two parallel arrays to the system console. Inside its for loop, line 23 outputs a person's name, and then line 24 invokes the inner class's show method to output that person's phone numbers.

> **NOTE**   *The code of an outer class can invoke the methods in an inner class.*

In general:

- the code of an inner and outer class can access each other's members (both data members and methods)
- an inner class is not visible outside of the outer class

The application InnerClass, shown in Figure 7.28, declares a PhoneBook object to store the names and phone numbers of a person's three best friends. Then, it invokes the class's showAll method to output the names and numbers input by the program user. Figure 7.29 shows two typical first inputs and a typical console output produced by the program.

```
1    public class InnerClass
2    {
3      public static void main(String[] args)
4      {
5        PhoneBook bestFriends = new PhoneBook();
6        bestFriends.showAll();
7      }
8    }
```

Figure 7.28
The application **InnerClass**.

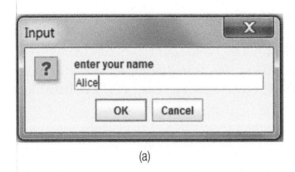
(a)

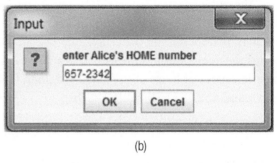
(b)

Console Output:
Name: Alice
PhoneNumbers: home:657-2342 cell:574-8976 office:345-6589

Name: Tom
PhoneNumbers: home:367-4367 cell:754-3564 office:386-1212

Name: Annie
PhoneNumbers: home:456-4698 cell:765-8294 office:839-5623

Figure 7.29
Two typical inputs to the application **InnerClass** and a typical set of outputs.

7.9 PROCESSING LARGE NUMBERS

Occasionally, there is a need to process an integer that is larger or smaller than the maximum or minimum values that can be stored in the primitive type `long`. For example, the encryption used on the Internet involves processing prime numbers that contain 309 digits, which far exceeds the 19-digit maximum value that can be stored in the primitive type `long`. Similarly, we might need to process a real number that is larger or smaller than the maximum or minimum values of the primitive type `double` or require more than the 15 digits of precision the type `double` provides.

The Java API contains two classes that can be used to process numbers that are too large or too small to be stored in primitive types or that require more than 15 digits of precision; they are the `BigInteger` and `BigDecimal` classes. As their names imply, they can be used to process numbers beyond the range of the primitive integer and real types, and the `BigDecimal` can also provide a specified number of digits of precision. Objects in these classes, like `String` and wrapper class objects, are immutable.

Processing of objects in these classes is performed by using the methods that are part of these classes. For example, addition is performed by the method `add`, which adds the object that invoked it to the object passed to its parameter and returns a reference to an object that contains their sum. There are methods to perform all of the operations normally performed on primitive numeric types, including modulo arithmetic, methods that are analogous to the `Math` class's methods, and methods to perform other common operations on numbers such as finding the greatest common denominator, generating a prime number, and determining if a number is prime.

The `BigInteger` Class

Consider a program to generate a specified term of the Fibonacci sequence. The first two terms of this sequence, f1 and f2, are both defined as 1. Any other term in the series is defined as the sum of the two previous terms: fn = fn-2 + fn-1. From term 93 (f93) on, the values of the terms exceed the size of the primitive type `long`.

The application `FibonacciTerm`, shown in Figure 7.30, demonstrates the use of some of the constants and methods in the class `BigInteger`. The program calculates and outputs a specified term (greater than 2) of the sequence and identifies those terms that are larger than the maximum value of the primitive type `long`. A set of program inputs and corresponding outputs are shown in Figure 7.31.

Line 1 of Figure 7.31 imports the class `BigInteger` into the program, and lines 10–12 create three instances of the class. The first two are assigned the address of the class's static object that stores the value 1. There are two other static objects defined in the class, `TEN` and `ZERO`, which store the values 10 and 0, respectively. Line 12 uses the class's `valueOf` method that returns the address of a `BigInteger` object set to the value passed to its parameter. In this case, the maximum value of the primitive type `long` is passed to the method, which is a static constant in the wrapper class `Long`.

The `for` loop that begins on line 16 computes the terms of the sequence from 3 to the number input on line 14. Each time through the loop, the `add` method is used on line 19 to calculate the next term of the sequence and the address of the object containing the value returned from the method is assigned to the variable `fn`. Line 20 sets `fnMinus1` to the previous value of `fn`.

When the loop ends, line 22 uses the class's `toString` method to convert the calculated value stored in the object `fn` to a string before it is output. The conversion could have been coded as an implicit invocation of the `toString` method:

```
System.out.println("f" + n + " - " + fn);
```

Finally, the `BigInteger` class's `compareTo` method is used in the Boolean condition on line 23 to determine if the calculated term of the sequence is larger than the maximum value of a `long` type primitive. The integer value the method returns is interpreted in the same way as the integer value retuned from the `String` class's `compareTo` method.

```
1    import java.math.BigInteger;
2    import javax.swing.*;
3
4    public class FibonacciTerm
5    {
6      public static void main(String[] args)
7      {
8        int n;
9        BigInteger temp;
10       BigInteger fnMinus1 = BigInteger.ONE;
11       BigInteger fn = BigInteger.ONE;
12       BigInteger longMaxValue = BigInteger.valueOf(Long.MAX_VALUE);
13
14       String s = JOptionPane.showInputDialog("enter the term number");
15       n = Integer.parseInt(s);
16       for(int i = 3; i <= n; i++)
17       {
18         temp = fn;
19         fn = fnMinus1.add(fn);
20         fnMinus1 = temp;
21       }
22       System.out.println("f" + n + " = " + fn.toString());
23       if(fn.compareTo(longMaxValue) > 0)
24       {
25         System.out.println("Which EXCEEDS the maximum value of " +
26                            "type long");
27       }
28       else
29       {
30         System.out.println("Which does NOT exceed the maximum value of " +
31                            "type long");
32       }
33     }
34   }
```

Figure 7.30
The application **FibonacciTerm**.

Inputs to Three Executions of the Program:

92

93

300

Corresponding Outputs:

f92 = 7540113804746346429

Which does NOT exceed the maximum value of type long

f93 = 12200160415121876738
Which EXCEEDS the maximum value of type `long`

f300 = 222232244629420445529739893461909967206666939096499764990979600
Which EXCEEDS the maximum value of type `long`

Figure 7.31
Sample inputs to the application **FibonacciTerm** and the corresponding outputs they produce.

The `BigDecimal` Class

As previously mentioned, the `BigDecimal` class can be used to represent real values to a specified precision. The code fragment shown in Figure 7.32 computes and rounds up the number 176 divided by 7 to a precision of 19, 18, 17, and 16 digits. The resulting `BigDecimal` object, returned from the three-parameter version of the class's `divide` method, is output at the bottom of the figure using an implicit invocation of the `BigInteger` class's `toString` method. The `divide` method divides the object that invoked it by the first argument sent to it.

The second argument sent to the `divide` method specifies the precision of the computed value. The third argument specifies the rounding mode used to determine the rightmost digit of precision. This can either be an integer or a constant defined in the class `RoundingMode`. The class's constant HALF_UP, used in Figure 7.32, is used to perform the conventional upward rounding.

```
    BigDecimal one76 = BigDecimal.valueOf(176);
    BigDecimal seven = BigDecimal.valueOf(7);

    System.out.println(one76.divide(seven, 19, RoundingMode.HALF_UP));
    System.out.println(one76.divide(seven, 18, RoundingMode.HALF_UP));
    System.out.println(one76.divide(seven, 17, RoundingMode.HALF_UP));
    System.out.println(one76.divide(seven, 16, RoundingMode.HALF_UP));
```

Output:

25.1428571428571428571
25.142857142857142857
25.14285714285714286
25.1428571428571429

Figure 7.32
Use of the **BigDecimal** class's divide method.

7.10 ENUMERATED TYPES

Enumeration is the process of defining a new type and specifying, or enumerating, a finite set of values that instances of the type can assume. The use of enumeration can make our programs more readable. Java supports enumerated types. The following enumeration statement defines the enumerated type `Team` and specifies that there are three values in its set of values: `Yankees`, `Braves`, and `Giants`.

```
// Declaration of an enumerated type
   enum Team {Yankees, Braves, Giants}
```

An enumeration statement is coded at the class level; it cannot be coded inside (local to) a method. The values that appear in the statement can be any valid identifier, which implies that they cannot be strings or primitive literals. The following declarations are invalid:

```
// Invalid enumeration statements: values not identifier names
enum Team {"Yankees", "Braves", "Giants"} //can't contain quotes
enum ID {NY Yankees, Atlanta Braves, SF Giants} //spaces not allowed
```

An enumeration statement can also be written in a separate Java file whose name is the same as the statement's enumerated type name; e.g., `Team`.

At an abstract level, the identifiers can be thought of as static constants in a class whose name is the enumerated type name (e.g., `Team`) and whose values are the identifier names. In this abstract view, the enumerated values are analogous to the static `double` constant `PI` in the `Math` class whose value is the double 3.141592653589793. The following code fragment outputs *3.141592653589793 Yankees* to the system console:

```
// Accessing the values of enumerated types
enum Team {Yankees, Braves, Giants}

System.out.println(Math.PI + " " + Team.Yankees);
```

Continuing the analogy, just as the numeric constant `Math.PI` can be assigned to a variable of its type (i.e., `double`), an enumerated constant can be assigned to a variable of its type (e.g. `Team`). The following code fragment also outputs *3.141592653589793 Yankees* to the system console:

```
// Assigning an enumerated type value
enum Team {Yankees, Braves, Giants}

Team myTeam = Team.Yankees;
double valueOfPi = Math.PI;
System.out.println(valueOfPi + " " + myTeam);
```

For the most part, considering the identifiers in an enumeration statement to be analogous to static constants is consistent with the Java syntax of enumerations. An exception to this is when an enumerated type variable is used in a switch statement after the keyword `switch`. In this context, the enumerated type name is not used to qualify the identifier coded as the choice value after the keyword `case`. In the code fragment shown in Figure 7.33, when an enumerated value such as Yankees is used within the switch statement, the type name `Team` is not used to qualify the identifier, as shown on line 6. When the identifier is used in other statements (e.g., line 7 of Figure 7.33), the type qualifier is used.

```
    // Using enumerated types in switch statements
1   enum Team {Yankees, Braves, Giants}
2
3   Team myTeam = Team.Yankees;
4   switch (myTeam)
5   {
6     case Yankees: // no type name qualifier used here
7       System.out.println(myTeam + " " + Team.Yankees);
8   }
```

Figure 7.33
Syntax of enumerated types in a **switch** statement.

The API interface Enum defines a set of methods that implement operations commonly performed on enumerated types. When discussing them, it useful to move away from the abstract view of an enumeration's identifiers being static constants to a more concrete view of them. While it is true that the enumerated type is a class, it is a special kind of class. In addition, the identifiers are not static constants in the class, but rather each identifier is a static reference variable that refers to an instance of the class.

As such, like static constants, we access the contents of these reference variables by the name of the identifier proceed by the name of the class followed by a dot (just as we have been doing). Figure 7.34 shows the three objects created by the enumeration shown below, the variables that reference them, and the contents of the variable myTeam after the assignment statement is executed:

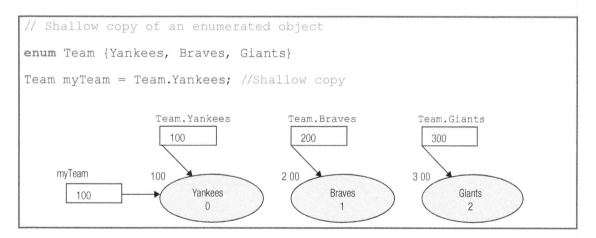

Figure 7.34
Three objects of the enumeration **Team**.

As shown in Figure 7.34, each object has an ordinal value associated with it, which always begins with zero. The values are assigned sequentially to the identifiers in the order (left to right) in which they appear in the enumeration statement. The Enum class's method ordinal returns the ordinal value assigned to the object that invoked it. The code fragment below outputs 1 to the system console.

```
// Invocations of the Team class' ordinal method
enum Team {Yankees, Braves, Giants}

Team myTeam = Team.Braves
System.out.println(myTeam.ordinal());
```

The `ordinal` method can also be used with an enumerated type object in the same way any other method is used with an instance of its class. For example, the statement

```
System.out.println ( "The ordinal value of " + Team.Giants +
                    " is " + Team.Giants.ordinal() );
```

results in the console output *The ordinal value of Giants is 2.*

NOTE   *The ordinal values of an enumerated type always begin with zero.*

The methods in the class `Enum`, four of which are shown in Table 7.3, operate on an enumerated type's objects. The class's `toString` method returns the name of the object's identifier converted to a string. The code fragment below outputs *Yankees Yankees* using an explicit and implicit invocation of the method:

```
// Invocations of the Enum class's toString method
enum Team {Yankees, Braves, Giants}

Team myTeam = Team.Yankees
System.out.println(Team.Yankees.toString() + " " + myTeam.Yankees);
```

The `Enum` class's `compareTo` method is an implementation of the method defined in the interface `Comparable`. The comparison it makes is based on the ordinal values associated with the object that invoked the method and the argument passed to it. The following code fragment outputs -2 because the identifier `Yankees`' ordinal value (0) is two less than the identifier `Giants`' value (2).

Table 7.3
Commonly Used Methods in the Class Enum

Method Name and Parameter List	Returned Type	Description
compareTo(EnumType enum2)	int	diff = enum1.compareTo(enum2) Returns the difference between the ordinal values of enum1 and enum2, positive for emum1 > enum2
equals(EnumType enum2)	boolean	equal = enum1.equals(enum2) Returns true when the ordinal values of enum1 and enum2 are equal, otherwise false
ordinal()	int	value = enum1.ordinal() Returns the ordinal values of enum1
toString()	String	value = enum1.toString() Returns the value of enum1

```
// Invocations of the Team class' compareTo method
enum Team {Yankees, Braves, Giants}

Team myTeam = Team.Yankees
System.out.println(myTeam.compareTo(Team.Giants));
```

The `Enum` class's method `equals` returns `true` when the object that invoked it has the same ordinal value as the object passed to its parameter.

7.11 CHAPTER SUMMARY

Java classes consist of data members and methods that operate on the data, and an object is an instance of a class. When a data member is declared to be static, all instances of the class share the variable. Often, a static variable is incremented inside a class's constructor to keep track of the number of objects that have been created.

It is good programming practice to write a complicated method as several simpler methods that it can invoke. Usually, the simpler methods are given private access to prevent methods that are not part of the class from invoking them. Methods can invoke private methods that are part of their class by simply coding the method's name and an argument list.

The object addresses stored in two reference variables can be compared using the relational operators, and they can be copied using the assignment operator. These are referred to as a shallow comparison and a shallow copy, respectively. After a shallow copy, two reference variables refer to the same object. To compare or copy objects, we first need to define which of their data members will be compared or which will be copied. Comparing and copying the data members of two objects is referred to as deep comparisons and deep copies. In both cases, a method has to be written to perform these operations.

Deep comparison methods return a Boolean value, and it is good programming practice for the methods to be named `compareTo`, as defined in the API interface `Comparable`, or named `equals` when the comparison is performed to determine equality. The `String` class contains deep comparison methods with these names. Deep copy methods either copy all of the data members from one object to another or copy all of the data members into a newly created object called a clone and return the address of the clone object. The names of deep copy methods ordinarily contain the word "copy," such as the `arraycopy` method in the `System` class, and clone methods are usually named `clone`.

In addition to deep comparison methods, the `String` class contains methods to perform common operations on `String` objects. These include locating and fetching substrings (the methods `indexOf` and `substring`), changing the case of a string (`toUpperCase` and `toLowerCase`), replacing a part of a string with another string (`replaceFirst` and `replaceAll`), and determining if a string begins or ends with a particular string (`startsWith` and `endsWith`). In addition, its `split` method can be used to place substrings of a string separated by a designated delimiter, usually white space, into the elements of the array it creates and returns. The substrings are called tokens, and the process is called tokenizing the string.

Autoboxing is the automatic construction of a wrapper class object without having to explicitly invoke the class' constructor, and auto-unboxing is the process of fetching the primitive value stored in a wrapper class object without having to invoke a `get` method. This feature can be used to pass a primitive value to a wrapper-class parameter or to assign a retuned wrapper class object to a primitive variable. The `Character` wrapper class contains a variety of methods used to process characters such as determining if a character is a letter or a digit, if it is lower or upper case, or if it is white space. The numeric wrapper classes contain static constants whose values are the maximum and minimum numeric values that they can wrap. The methods in the classes `BigInteger` and `BigDecimal` give us the ability to process numbers whose absolute value is too large to be stored in primitive types or that require more than 15 digits of precision. Objects in these classes, like `String` and wrapper class objects, are immutable.

Aggregation is the process of declaring a data member of a class to be a reference to an object. This permits us to define a complex object as an aggregate of simpler component objects, extending the concepts of reusable code and divide and conquer to the design of classes. A class, called an inner class, can also be defined within another class called an outer class. The inner class can access the data members defined in the outer class and vice versa. The outer class can create instances of the inner class and invoke its methods. Enumeration is the process of defining a type and specifying, or enumerating, the values that instances of the type can assume. The use of enumeration can make our programs more readable.

Knowledge Exercises

1. True or false:
   a) Static data members allow one storage cell to be shared among all instances of their class.
   b) A method cannot invoke another method in its class.
   c) Methods that are declared `private` can be invoked by other methods within their own class.
   d) A deep comparison determines if two reference variables refer to the same object.
   e) To make a clone of an object, we make a shallow copy of it.
   f) The variables `s1` and `s2` refer to two different objects. After I make a shallow copy of `s2` into `s1`, I have two identical objects.
   g) Autoboxing constructs a wrapper class object without explicitly invoking the class's constructor.
   h) An outer class can invoke the methods of its inner class.

2. Consider the class `Student` shown in Figure 7.4.
   a) Why is its data member `studentCount` declared to be static?
   b) Why is the class's `get` method declared to be a static method?
   c) Write the statement to output the variable `studentCount` to the system console.
   d) Why does the class not contain a public method named `setStudentCount`?

3. Explain the difference between a deep and a shallow comparison.

4. Explain the difference between a deep and a shallow copy.

5. Explain the difference between a deep copy and a clone.

6. How does the method `equals` in the API `Object` class differ from the `equals` method in the `String` class?

7. Write a code fragment to output *Two Objects* to the system console if the variable `s1` and `s2` refer to two different objects.

8. Write a method that could be added to the class `Student`, shown in Figure 7.5, which would clone the `Student` object that invoked it.

9. What is output by these statements, assuming the following declarations have been made:

```
String s1 = "Computers rock"; String s2 = "Hello world";
```
a) `System.out.println(s2.indexOf("world"));`
b) `System.out.println(s1.substring(10));`
c) `System.out.println(s2.replaceFirst("world", "everyone"));`
d) `System.out.println(s2.starts("world"));`
e) `String[] s = s2.split();`
   `System.out.println(s[1]);`
f) `if(s1.equalsIgnoreCase("Computers Rock")`
   `{`
   `System.out.print("True - these are the same.");`
   `}`
   else
   `{`
   `System.out.print("False - they are not the same.");`
   `}`

10. Give the code to:
   (a) create an instance of the wrapper class `Integer` that contains the value 20 without explicitly invoking the class's constructor
   (b) set the integer variable `age` to the value stored in the `Integer` instance `number`
   (c) output the maximum and minimum values that can be stored in a primitive variable declared to be type `long` to the system console
   (d) output `true` to the system console if the character contained in the variable `aCharacter` is white space or a digit

11. Define aggregation in the context of a Java class.

12. Give three advantages of using aggregation in the classes we design.

13. How would you represent an integer in your program that was larger than the maximum value of the primitive type `long`?

14. How would you input an integer to your program that was larger than the maximum value of the primitive type `long`?

15. How would you double the integer discussed in Exercise 13?

16. Give the code to define two `BigInteger` objects initialized to 1,234,567,890,123,456 and 9,876,543,210,654,321, multiply the numbers, and output the result.

17. Assume an enumerated type `CarColor` has been declared as:

    `enum CarColor` {RED, WHITE, SILVER, BLACK, BLUE}
    a) What is the ordinal value of SILVER?
    b) Write a statement to create a variable, `favoriteColor`, of type `CarColor` and set it to BLUE.
    c) Write a statement to output the `favoriteColor` and its ordinal value to the system console.

Programming Exercises

1. Add a deep comparison method and a clone method to the class shown in Figure 7.4. The deep comparison method should return 0 when two instances of the class are equal (i.e., both objects' id numbers and GPA are equal). Then write an application that declares an instance of the class named `s1` and two other instances named `s2` and `s3`. The object `s2` should have the same id as `s1`, and `s2` should have the same GPA as `s1`. Output the three objects to the system console followed by *s1 equals s2* or *s1 equals s3*, as determined by two invocations of the deep comparison method. Then clone `s1`, store the returned address in `s2`, and repeat all of the output.

2. Write a program that accepts an arithmetic expression that does not contain parentheses and verifies that is correctly written. It is correctly written if each of the operators in the expression is between two operands preceded and followed by a space: for example 2 * 3 + 5. Output a correct expression to the system console. Otherwise, output the expression up to the point were the first error was detected, then a caret (Shift 6 key stroke), and then the remainder of the math expression. The second line of output, in both cases, should be the number of tokens (operators and operands) that were in the original expression. (Use the `split` method in the `String` class.)

3. Modify the class `PhoneBook` shown in Figure 7.27 so each of the three listings in a `PhoneBook` instance will also have an address consisting of a street, city, state, and zip code. To accomplish this, add another inner class named `Address` to the class `Phonebook`. The new information should be input in a similar way to that of the phone numbers. To verify your modifications to the class, write an application that declares an instance of a `PhoneBook`, accepts user inputs, then outputs the entire phonebook.

4. Write a program that calculates and outputs the sum of the integers from 1 to 10,000,000,000. Hint: the sum is (10,000,000,000 * 10,000,000,001)/2, which is not equal to 3,883,139,820,726,120,960.

5. Write a program to multiply two real numbers of any size input via a dialog box and output their product with seven digits of precision, rounded up.

Enrichment

1. Investigate and learn who was the first to discover that the sum of the integers from 1 to n is (n * (n +1)) /2 and the circumstances under which he discovered it.

2. Explore the Fibonacci sequence to discover its presence in art, architecture, music, and nature and investigate the relationship of the Fibonacci sequence to the Golden ratio.

3. Research the Fibonacci searching algorithm.

INHERITANCE

8.1 *The Concept of Inheritance* *354*

8.2 *The UML Diagrams and Language of Inheritance* . . . *355*

8.3 *Implementing Inheritance* *357*

8.4 *Using Inheritance in the Design Process* *372*

8.5 *Polymorphism.* *385*

8.6 *Interfaces.* *398*

8.7 *Serializing Objects* *406*

8.8 *Chapter Summary* *411*

In this chapter

In this chapter, we expand our knowledge of object oriented programming into the advanced topics of inheritance, polymorphism, interfaces and adapter classes, and the serialization of objects. These OOP concepts can significantly reduce the time and effort required to design and develop a software product.

We will learn that Java supports two forms of inheritance, chain inheritance and multiple child inheritance. Both of these allow us to rapidly create a class from a similar existing class and to easily expand and/or modify the new class to adapt it to the requirements of a particular project. When used as a design tool, inheritance not only reduces the cost of a software product under development, but it also reduces the cost of future products by increasing the reusability of the classes we write. Using inheritance, application-dependent parts of a method can be written in a way that they can invoke methods that implement the yet-to-be-determined requirements of future products.

Polymorphism is another fundamental characteristic of OOP, which allows things to exist in many ("poly") different forms ("morph"), such as when one array references many different types of objects or when one invocation morphs itself into an invocation of a method appropriate to a particular launch of a program. Polymorphism also allows us to pass different types of objects to one type of parameter.

Interfaces allow us to define the signature and functionality of related methods without having to implement them, and adaptor classes facilitate the use of interfaces. Using object serialization, we can easily save a collection of objects to a disk file and reuse the objects in a future launch of the same or different program.

After successfully completing this chapter you should:

- Understand the advantages, terminology, syntax, and importance of using inheritance
- Know how to implement a child class that inherits data members and methods from an existing parent class using the `extends` clause
- Be able to invoke and modify an inherited method and expand inherited methods and data members
- Be able to distinguish between overriding and overloading methods
- Know how to use inheritance as part of the design process
- Understand the processes that Java uses to locate a method at translation and run time
- Be able to comprehend and use polymorphism and polymorphic arrays
- Understand abstract classes, interfaces, and adapter classes and how to implement and use them
- Write and read a group of objects to and from a disk file

8.1 THE CONCEPT OF INHERITANCE

Definition

Inheritance is an OPP programming concept in which new classes that contain all of the data members and methods of an existing class can be efficiently created and then expanded and/ or modified. The concept of inheritance implies that two classes have a relationship with each other in which one class, called a *child* class, inherits attributes from the other class, called the *parent* class.

The concept of **inheritance** is fundamental to object oriented programming. If properly used, it can greatly reduce the time and effort required to develop a software product. For example, suppose that one of the classes specified during the design of a new program is similar to an existing class in that the existing class contains many of the data members and methods listed in the new class's UML diagram. The best way to develop the new class would be to simply add the existing class to the program and modify and/or add to it. One approach to this would be to copy the source code of the existing class, paste the code into a new class, and then modify the copied code. A better approach would be to use the concept of inheritance.

Although we may have been importing the existing class into our programs for many years, we may not have its source code. For example, the Java API does not contain the source code of any of the classes included in it. Rather, it contains the classes' translated byte codes. This fact would eliminate the copy and paste alternative but not the inheritance alternative. To use the concept of inheritance, we only need the byte codes of the existing class. In addition, software engineering studies reveal that copying, pasting, and modifying code that we did not write can be more time consuming than a completely independent development of a new class. Inheritance allows us to modify an existing class that was added to a new program in a way that does not introduce the errors that are associated with the copy-paste-modify alternative.

Even if there are no existing classes that contain many of the data members and methods of the classes specified for a new program, the time and cost to develop the program can still be reduced using the concept of inheritance during the design process. Finally, the use of inheritance in the design of our programs also makes them easier to read and intuitively easier to understand because the classes we write better model the real world. Because we know that children inherit attributes from their parents, it is intuitive that a game's new `ChildSuperHero` class would inherit attributes from an existing game's `ParentSuperHero` class. The attributes inherited by the `ChildSuperHero` class would be the data members and the methods of the `ParentSuperHero` class, which could then be efficiently expanded or modified to model the child super hero.

In summary:

- Inheritance reduces the cost and time to develop a software product
- Inheritance is the best way to incorporate and then morph an existing class into a new class
- We do not need the source code of the existing class, only its byte code translation, to utilize the concepts of inheritance
- Inheritance is used in the OOP program-design process even when there are no existing classes to be morphed and incorporated into the program

8.2 THE UML DIAGRAMS AND LANGUAGE OF INHERITANCE

Inheritance introduces a new feature into UML diagrams and has a set of terms associated with it. An early understanding of this feature and the jargon of inheritance is fundamental to the remainder of the material in this chapter.

Inheritance UML Diagrams

Figure 8.1 shows the UML diagram of the classes `RowBoat` and `SailBoat`. The `RowBoat` class's UML diagram contains five data members and twelve methods, and the UML diagram of the `SailBoat` contains no data members and one constructor method. Instances of the class `SailBoat` will actually contain more data members and methods than those listed in the class's UML diagram because the upward-pointing arrow in the center of the figure indicates that the `SailBoat` class *inherits from* the `RowBoat` class. As noted next to the arrow in the figure, the Java keyword used to establish this relationship is `extends`.

The Parent-Child Relationship

The concept of inheritance implies that two classes have a relationship with each other in which one class, called a *child* class, inherits attributes from the other class, called the *parent* class. The attributes inherited are all of the data members and all of the methods of the parent class *except* for the parent class's constructors. As indicated on the left side of Figure 8.1, there are two other pairs of terms that are used in the literature to refer to the parent and child class. The parent class is sometimes called the *super class*, and then the child class is called the *subclass*. Alternately, the term *base class* can be substituted for parent class, in which case the child class is referred to as a

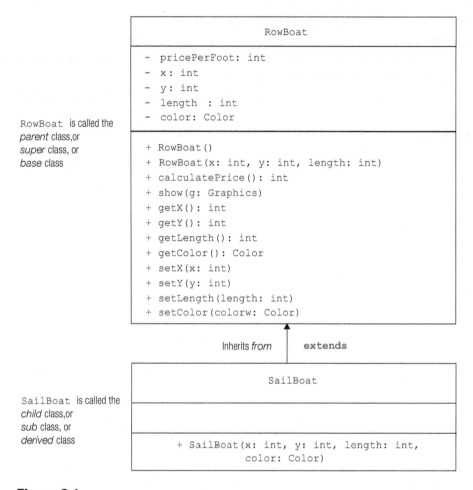

RowBoat is called the
parent class,or
super class, or
base class

SailBoat is called the
child class,or
sub class, or
derived class

Figure 8.1
The class **RowBoat** and the class **SailBoat**.

derived class. These three pairs of terms: *parent* class-*child* class, *super* class-*sub* class, and *base* class-*derived* class should not be unpaired and intermixed.

Because a child class inherits all of the data members and methods of the parent class and contains all of the data members and methods specified in its own UML diagram, a child class's data members and methods add to, or *extend*, a parent class. As specified in Figure 8.1, all instances of the classes SailBoat and RowBoat will have five data members, but the SailBoat class extends the complement of methods that can operate on a SailBoat object from 12 to 13.

> **NOTE** *Inheritance does not work in reverse. Parents do not inherit the data members and methods added to the child class.*

Establishing the Parent-Child Relationship

When a child class is implemented, the parent-child relationship is established by the inclusion of an extends *clause* on the right side of the class's heading. This clause begins with the keyword extends followed by the name of the parent class. For example:

```
public class SailBoat extends RowBoat
```

> **NOTE**
> *To establish an inheritance relationship, an* `extends` *clause is included at the end of the class statement of the child class:*
> ```
> public class ChildClassName extends ParentClassName
> ```

Forms of Inheritance

A class can only extend or inherit from *one* class. In *chain inheritance* a child class can be the parent of another class. This is supported in Java, as is the ability for several child classes to inherit from the same parent class. These two forms of inheritance are illustrated in the upper-left and upper-right portions of Figure 8.2, respectively.

Multiple inheritance, the concept that a child class can inherit attributes from *more than one* parent, is not supported in Java. Multiple inheritance is depicted in the lower-right portion of Figure 8.2.

We say that class B on the top left side of Figure 8.2 *directly* inherits from class A, as do classes B, C, and D at the top right side of the figure. A class that directly inherits from another class extends it by including an `extends` clause in its heading. We say that classes C and D on the top left side of Figure 8.2 *indirectly* inherit from class A because they either inherit from a class that directly inherits from class A (in C's case) or directly inherit from a class that indirectly inherit from class A (in D's case).

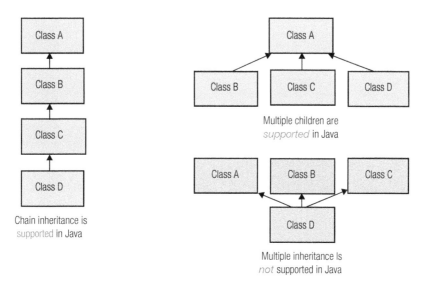

Figure 8.2
Various forms of inheritance.

8.3 IMPLEMENTING INHERITANCE

In addition to the keyword `extends`, which is used to indicate that a child class inherits from a parent class, there are other keywords and concepts that are associated with inheritance. Most of these are used in the implementation of a child class, but an understanding of some of these keywords, such as `final` and `abstract`, and the concepts associated with them, apply to the implementation of a parent class. In the remainder of this section, we will discuss the keywords and concepts of inheritance that apply to the implementation of a child class; we will discuss the relevant parent class issues in Section 8.4.

Figure 8.3 presents the code of the class RowBoat specified in the top portion of Figure 8.1. The class does not utilize any of the concepts of inheritance presented in this chapter. Nevertheless, it can become a parent class if another class extends it. This class will be the parent of child classes used in parts of this chapter to demonstrate the basic of concepts inheritance and the use of the keywords associated with these concepts.

```java
1    import java.awt.*;
2    public class RowBoat
3    {
4      private static int PRICE_PER_FOOT = 10;
5      private int x, y, length;
6      private Color color = Color.GREEN;
7
8      public RowBoat()
9      {
10
11     }
12     public RowBoat(int x, int y, int length)
13     {
14       this.x = x;
15       this.y = y;
16       this.length = length;
17     }
18     public int calculatePrice()
19     {
20       return length * PRICE_PER_FOOT;
21     }
22     public void show(Graphics g)
23     {
24       int[] xBoat = {x , x + length, x + 6 * length/7,  x + length/14};
25       int[] yBoat = {y,   y, y + length / 7, y + length / 7};
26       int price = calculatePrice();
27       g.setColor(color); //draw the Boat
28       g.fillPolygon(xBoat, yBoat, xBoat.length);
29       g.setColor(Color.BLACK); //draw the boat's price in black
30       g.setFont(new Font("Arial", Font.BOLD, 16));
31       g.drawString("$" + String.valueOf(price), x + 10, y + 16);
32     }
33     public int getX()
34     {
35       return x;
```

```
36      }
37      public int getY()
38      {
39        return y;
40      }
41      public int getLength()
42      {
43        return length;
44      }
45      public Color getColor()
46      {
47        return color;
48      }
49      public void setX(int x)
50      {
51        this.x = x;
52      }
53      public void setY(int y)
54      {
55        this.y = y;
56      }
57      public void setLength(int length)
58      {
59        this.length = length;
60      }
61        public void setColor(Color color)
62      {
63        this.color = color;
64      }
65    }
```

Figure 8.3
The class **RowBoat**.

The RowBoat class's three-parameter constructor (lines 12–17 of Figure 8.3) can be used to create and position a rowboat on the game board at the (x, y) location passed to its first two parameters. The value passed to the constructor's third parameter is the size (length) of the rowboat. The x, y, and length data members of a rowboat created with the class's default constructor (lines 8–11) would retain the default value of the type int: 0. Because the constructor does not include a parameter to specify the color of the boat, it would default to green (line 6).

The show method (lines 22–32) draws a rowboat on the game board at its current (x, y) location and then draws the price of the boat on it (lines 29–31). The price is returned from the invocation of the class's calculatePrice method on line 26. Line 20 of this method multiplies the length of the boat by the static variable PRICE _ PER _ FOOT to determine the price of the boat.

The application ShowTwoRowBoats shown in Figure 8.4 creates two rowboats of lengths 200 and 150 feet (lines 7-8) and displays them on the game board (lines 16-17) as shown in Figure 8.5.

```
1    import edu.sjcny.gpv1.*;
2    import java.awt.*;
3
4    public class ShowTwoRowBoats extends DrawableAdapter
5    { static ShowTwoRowBoats ge = new ShowTwoRowBoats();
6      static GameBoard gb = new GameBoard(ge, "Show Two Row Boats");
7      static RowBoat rb1 = new RowBoat(30, 150, 200);
8      static RowBoat rb2 = new RowBoat(30, 250, 150);
9
10     public static void main(String[] args)
11     {
12        showGameBoard(gb);
13     }
14     public void draw(Graphics g)
15     {
16        rb1.show(g);
17        rb2.show(g);
18     }
19   }
```

Figure 8.4
The application **ShowTwoRowBoats**.

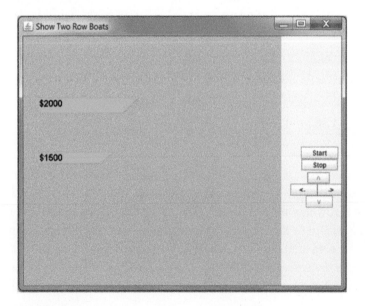

Figure 8.5
The output produced by the application **ShowTwoRowBoats**.

8.3.1 Constructors and Inherited Method Invocations

The class SailBoat is specified in the bottom portion of Figure 8.1. Sailboats use rowboats for their hull and are delivered without a mast and sail. As delivered, they actually are rowboats, except for the fact that the purchaser can specify the color of the boat. Because they are so similar to rowboats, we can utilize the concept of inheritance to rapidly develop their class.

To begin with, they will inherit all of a rowboat's attributes as indicated by the arrow that connects them to the class RowBoat in Figure 8.1. This will save the time and cost associated with declaring a sailboat's five data members, writing and verifying the associated set and get methods, and writing and verifying the methods to draw them and to calculate their price.

To implement the expanding capability into the SailBoat class, the ability to specify the color of the boat when it is purchased, a four-parameter constructor is included in the SailBoat class. When a sailboat is constructed, the color of the new boat will be passed to the constructor's fourth parameter.

Figure 8.6 presents the code for the class SailBoat. Because we are using inheritance by including the extends clause at the end of its heading (line 3), the class consists of only ten lines of code. A sailboat's location, price per foot, length, and color can be stored in its inherited data members. In addition, the values stored in the data members can be fetched and set, the sailboat's price can be calculated, and the boat can be drawn on the game board using the methods inherited from the RowBoat class.

Invoking A Parent Class Constructor

Parent class constructors are *not* inherited, but they can be invoked within the code of a child class's constructor. The SailBoat class's constructor (lines 5–9 of Figure 8.6) invokes the parent class's constructor on line 7 and passes it the (x, y) location of the sailboat and its length. The invocation begins with the keyword **super**, rather than the name of the parent (also known as super) class, followed by an argument list. This is the syntax a child class uses to invoke a parent class constructor. Lines 14–16 of Figure 8.3 then execute and place the values passed to it into the SailBoat object's inherited data members x, y, and length.

NOTE   *When a child class constructor invokes a parent class constructor, the invocation statement must be coded as the first line of the child class constructor.*

Every time a child class constructor is executed, a parent constructor must be executed before the remainder of the child class's constructor is executed. If an explicit invocation, such as the one on line 7 of Figure 8.6, is not included as the first line of a child class constructor, the parent's no-parameter constructor is automatically executed. In this case, the parent class must:

1. contain the code of a no-parameter constructor, or
2. contain no constructors at all, in which case the Java default constructor will be executed

If one of these two conditions is not met, and the first line of the child class is not an explicit invocation of a parent constructor, the child class will not translate.

Invoking a Parent Class Method

A child class method can invoke any parent method whose access is designated public or whose access is designated protected. We will discuss protected access, its use, and its implications later in this chapter.

Because the RowBoat class does not contain a four-parameter constructor, line 8 of Figure 8.6 invokes the method setColor to store the color of the new sailboat that was passed to the constructor on line 3. If the SailBoat class contained a setColor method, it would have executed. Because it does not, we move up the inheritance chain to the parent class. The parent class does contain a public setColor method (lines 61–64 of Figure 8.3), and the invocation on line 8 causes it to execute.

```
1    import java.awt.*;
2
3    public class SailBoat extends RowBoat
4    {
5      public SailBoat(int x, int y, int length, Color color)
6      {
7        super(x, y, length); //invoke parent constructor
8        setColor(color);  //access parent's protected data method
9      }
10   }
```

Figure 8.6
The class **SailBoat**.

An alternate and equivalent coding for line 8 of Figure 8.6 would be:

```
this.setColor(color);
```

Because all of the RowBoat class's set methods are public, line 7 of Figure 8.6 could have been coded as the following three lines. The one-line alternative shown in the figure is preferred.

```
setX(x); //or this.setX(x);
setY(y); //or this.setY(y);
setLength(length); //or this.setLength(length);
```

NOTE *The syntax used to invoke a parent method from within a child method is the same syntax (that was discussed in Chapter 7) used to invoke another method in its class.*

The application InheritanceBasics presented in Figure 8.7 creates two rowboats and a cyan-colored sailboat and then displays them on the left and right sides of the game board, respectively. The program's output is shown in Figure 8.8

The show method is invoked on line 20 of Figure 8.7 to display the sailboat whose location, size, and color is specified on line 9. Because a SailBoat object (sb1) invoked the method, the search for the method begins in the SailBoat class just as it does for classes that do not extend other classes. If the SailBoat class contained a show method with a graphics parameter, it would have been executed. Because it does not, we move up the inheritance chain to the parent class RowBoat. It contains a public show method with a graphics parameter (line 22 of Figure 8.3), and the invocation on line 20 causes it to execute. The inherited show method draws the sailboat object sb1.

Line 26 of the inherited show method invokes the method calculatePrice. The search for this method also begins in the SailBoat class because the show method that issued the invocation is operating on an instance of this class, sb1. Because the SailBoat class does not contain a calculatePrice method, the search continues up the inheritance chain, and RowBoat class's version of the method executes.

```
1    import edu.sjcny.gpv1.*;
2    import java.awt.*;
3
4    public class InheritanceBasics extends DrawableAdapter
5    { static InheritanceBasics ge = new InheritanceBasics();
6      static GameBoard gb = new GameBoard(ge, "Inheritance Basics");
7      static RowBoat rb1 = new RowBoat(30, 150, 200);
8      static RowBoat rb2 = new RowBoat(30, 250, 150);
9      static SailBoat sb1 = new SailBoat(260, 150, 200, Color.CYAN);
10
11     public static void main(String[] args)
12     {
13       showGameBoard(gb);
14     }
15
16     public void draw(Graphics g)
17     {
18       rb1.show(g);
19       rb2.show(g);
20       sb1.show(g);
21     }
22   }
```

Figure 8.7
The application **InheritanceBasics**.

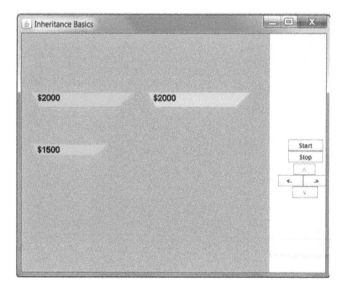

Figure 8.8
The output produced by the application **InheritanceBasics**.

8.3.2 Overriding Methods

Consistent with the concept of inheritance, the SailBoat class's four-parameter constructor added to the attributes inherited from its parent class. As previously mentioned, child classes can also modify the inherited attributes. The mechanism for modifying an inherited method is called *overriding* a method, which allows a child class to contain a method whose signature is exactly the *same* (same returned type, name, and parameter list) as the parent's method it is modifying.

Suppose that a second version of a sailboat, named SailBoatV2, was being offered for sale. This type of sailboat is not only delivered in a specified color, but it also has a mast installed on it. In order to properly display the new type of sailboat (with a mast), the RowBoat's show method would be overridden. The modified version of the method, coded in the new SailboatV2 class, would incorporate the drawing of the mast into its version of the method.

Because the UML diagram of the RowBoat shown in Figure 8.1 contains many more data members and methods than the UML diagram of the SailBoat class, we may be tempted to make the new class a child of the RowBoat class. If we do this, in addition to overriding the inherited show method, we would also have to rewrite the code of the SailBoat class's four-parameter constructor when the new class is coded. A better approach would be to take advantage of the fact that Java supports chain inheritance, which is depicted on the left side of Figure 8.2, and make the new class a child of the SailBoat class. The new class would then inherit all of the attributes (data members and methods) of both the RowBoat and the SailBoat classes, which gives it the ability to invoke the SailBoat class's four-parameter constructor. This approach to the design of the new class is depicted in Figure 8.9.

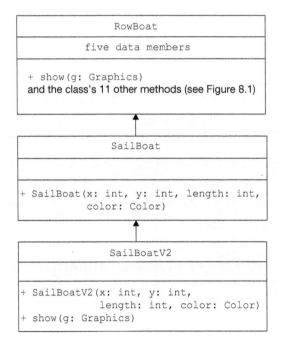

Figure 8.9
The inheritance chain of the class **SailBoatV2**.

The implementation of the class `SailBoatV2` is shown in Figure 8.10. As specified in Figure 8.9, it extends the class `SailBoat` (line 3). Its four-parameter constructor (lines 5–8) simply invokes its parent's four-parameter constructor on line 7, passing it the (x, y) location, length, and color of the new sailboat that was passed to it. It also overwrites the `show` method it inherits from the `RowBoat` class (lines 11–17).

```
1    import java.awt.*;
2
3    public class SailBoatV2 extends SailBoat //overriding a parent method
4    {
5      public SailBoatV2(int x, int y, int length, Color color)
6      {
7        super(x, y, length, color); //invoke the parent's constructor
8      }
9
10     @Override //translator verified an inherited method has this signature
11     public void show(Graphics g) // overwrites the parent's method
12     {
13       super.show(g); //invoke the parent's method to draw the boat
14       g.setColor(Color.BLACK); //draw the mast
15       g.fillRect(getX() + getLength()/2, getY() - getLength()/2,
16                  3, getLength()/2);
17     }
18   }
```

Figure 8.10
The class **SailBoatV2**.

Invoking a Parent's Version of an Overwritten Method

The overridden version of the `show` method coded in the `SailBoatV2` class begins by invoking its inherited `show` method (line 13 of Figure 8.10) to draw the hull of the sailboat. As when invoking an inherited constructor, the keyword `super` is used in the invocation. When invoking a nonconstructor inherited method, the keyword **super** is followed by a dot.

The `SailBoatV2` class's inheritance chain is used to locate the invoked method. The syntax `super.` that proceeds the name and argument list of the invocation on line 13 tells the translator that we do not want the search to begin for the invoked method in the `SailBoatV2` class but rather to begin the search in its parent class. Otherwise, the `SailBoatV2` class's `show` method would invoke itself.

Because the `RowBoat` does contain a `show` method whose parameter is a `Graphics` object (line 22 of Figure 8.3), this method executes and draws the hull of the boat. Then, lines 14–16 of Figure 8.10 incorporate the modification to this method by drawing the sailboat's mast. If the search up the inheritance chain did not locate a `show` method whose parameter was a `Graphics` object, the translation of the `SailBoatV2` class would have ended in a translation error.

The @Override directive

The `@Override` directive that appears on line 10 of Figure 8.10 instructs the translator to search up the `SailBoatV2` class's inheritance chain for a method with the same signature that is coded on the line that follows it. If it cannot find a method with that signature, the translation ends in an error.

It is good programming practice to include this translation directive before the signature of a method that is meant to override an inherited method. Suppose the method name or parameter list typed on line 11 was syntactically correct but did not match the parameter list of the method it was overriding. For example, suppose the signature with the method's name was misspelled as shown below:

```
11  public void shown(Graphics g) //does NOT override inherited show method
```

Without the directive on line 10, the class would translate, but the inherited `show` method would not have been overridden. The client invocation on line 20 of Figure 8.11 would then cause the inherited method to execute, and the sailboat would be drawn without a mast.

Figure 8.11 presents the application `OverridingMethods`, which is the same application presented in Figure 8.7, except the sailboat it creates on line 9 is now a `SailBoatV2` object. As a result, the `SailBoatV2` class's overridden `show` method is invoked on line 20, and the sailboat is drawn with a mast. The output it produces is shown in Figure 8.12

```
1    import edu.sjcny.gpv1.*;
2    import java.awt.*;
3
4    public class OverridingMethods extends DrawableAdapter
5    { static OverridingMehtods ge = new OverridingMethods();
6      static GameBoard gb = new GameBoard(ge, "OVERRIDING METHODS");
7      static RowBoat rb1 = new RowBoat(30, 150, 200);
8      static RowBoat rb2 = new RowBoat(30, 250, 150);
9      static SailBoatV2 sb1 = new SailBoatV2(260, 150, 200, Color.CYAN);
10
11     public static void main(String[] args)
12     {
13       showGameBoard(gb);
14     }
15
16     public void draw(Graphics g)
17     {
18       rb1.show(g);
19       rb2.show(g);
20       sb1.show(g);
21     }
22   }
```

Figure 8.11
The application **OverRidingMethods**.

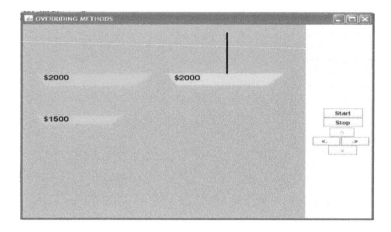

Figure 8.12
The output produced by the application **OverRidingMethods**.

Final Methods

A method can be declared to be a `final` method by coding the keyword `final` in its signature immediately after the method's access modifier. When a method is declared to be final, it cannot be overridden by a child class. An attempt to do so results in a translation error. For example, if the signature of the `show` method on line 22 of the `RowBoat` class (Figure 8.3) was coded as shown below, the `SailBoatV2` class shown in Figure 8.10 could not override it.

```
22      public final void show(Graphics g)
```

Methods that enforce security on systems are usually declared to be final to prevent them from being overridden.

Overriding versus Overloading Methods

The concepts of overriding and overloading methods are often confused because both concepts can be used to code a new method that has the same name as an existing method. In addition, the two topics are often considered to be more restrictive than they actually are. Before concluding our discussion of overriding methods, we will discuss the differences between, and commonalities shared by, these concepts.

One difference between the concepts of overriding and overloading methods also allows us to identify which concept is being used. When two methods in an inheritance chain have the same name and the same parameter list, the concept of *overriding* methods is being used. When two methods in an inheritance chain, or within the same class, have the same name and different parameter lists (i.e., either the number and/or type of the parameters are different), the concept of *overloading* methods is being used.

A second difference is that the concept of overriding a method cannot be used to modify the functionality of a method coded in its class because two methods with the same name and parameter list cannot be coded in the same class. The code of an overridden method and the code of the method that overrides it must appear in two different classes in an inheritance chain. The concept of overloading a method is less restrictive. The code of an overloaded method and that of the method it overloads can appear in the same class or in different classes within an inheritance chain.

The concepts of overriding and overloading methods have many things in common:

- both concepts are used to modify or expand the functionality of an existing method
- both concepts can be used to produce a new method that has the same name as an existing method
- both static and nonstatic methods can be overridden and overloaded
- a child class can overload and override any of its inherited methods
- the translator always uses the same technique to locate and identify a method that is being invoked regardless of the whether the method has been overridden or overloaded

This section will conclude with a summary of the search path the translator uses to locate an invoked overridden or overloaded method, and a summary of the syntax used to invoke inherited methods.

Summary of the Method Search Path

When an overloaded or overridden method is invoked, the translator uses the same search process to locate the method that it uses to locate all invoked methods. The class of the object's reference variable, or the class of an invoked static method, is searched for a method whose name and parameter list matches the name and argument list in the invocation statement. If a match is *not* found in that class, the search continues up the class's inheritance chain.

Summary of the Inherited Method Invocation Syntax

As we have learned, a child class method can invoke a method inherited from its parent. If the method is not overridden in the child class, the method is invoked by coding the name of the method followed by an argument list. When the method is a static method, this syntax is preceded by the name of the parent class followed by a dot. If the parent method is overridden and is not a static method, the invocation is preceded by the keyword `super` followed by a dot.

8.3.3 Extending Inherited Data Members

A child class's ability to extend the attributes it inherits is not limited to overriding and overloading inherited methods or including new methods in its class. It can also extend the data members it inherits by declaring additional data members inside its class definition. Figure 8.13 presents the inheritance chain of a class named `SailBoatV3`, which is a sailboat delivered with a mast and a sail. To facilitate the implementation of the new class, it extends the `SailboatV2` class because, in all other aspects, this new type of sailboat is a `SailBoatV2` object.

As shown in its UML diagram, the `SailBoatV3` class will override its inherited `calculatePrice` method. The new version of this method will use the class's new data members `sailArea` and `pricePerSquareFoot` to calculate and include the cost of the sail in the boat's price. The boat's `sailArea` will be specified using the last parameter of the class's five-parameter constructor. In addition, the inherited `show` method will be overwritten. This version of the method will be used to draw the sail on the boat's mast.

NOTE   *The name of a data member added to a child class can be the same as the name of an inherited data member, but it is good programming practice to avoid duplicating inherited data member names.*

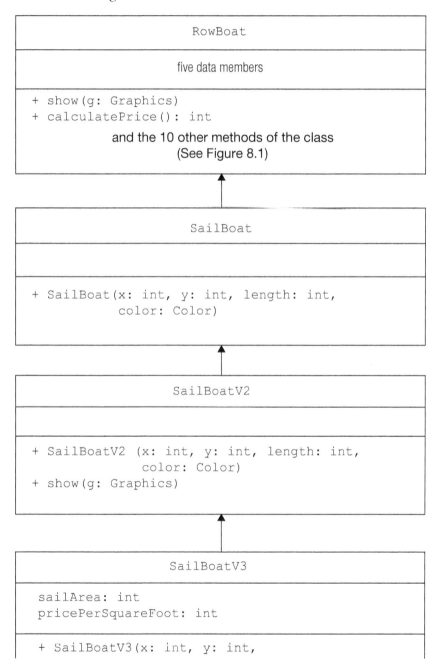

Figure 8.13
The inheritance chain of the class **SailBoatV3**.

Figure 8.14 shows the implementation of the SailBoatV3 class that extends the class Sail-BoatV2 (line 3). Its two additional data members, pricePerSquareFoot and sailArea, are declared on lines 5 and 6. Line 12 of the class's constructor stores the sail area passed to its last parameter in the data member sailArea. Line 19 of the expanded calculatePrice method multiplies these data members to determine the sail's price and then adds this product to the price returned from line 18's invocation of RowBoat's version of the method.

Lines 25–31 implement additional functionality of the overridden show method by defining the (x, y) coordinates of the triangular sail's vertices and then drawing the sail. Line 32 invokes the class's inherited show method to draw the boat's hull and mast.

Figure 8.15 presents the application ExtendingDataMembers, which is the same application presented in Figure 8.11, except it creates a yellow instance (sb2) of the class SailBoatV3 on line 10. As a result, the SailBoatV3 class's version of the show method is invoked on line 22, and the

```java
1     import java.awt.*;
2
3     public class SailBoatV3 extends SailBoatV2
4     {
5       private static int pricePerSquareFoot = 2;
6       private int sailArea; // additional data members
7
8       public SailBoatV3(int x, int y, int length,
9                         Color color, int sailArea)
10      {
11        super(x, y, length, color);
12        this.sailArea = sailArea;
13      }
14
15      @Override
16      public int calculatePrice() //invokes the method it overrides
17      {
18        int hullPrice = super.calculatePrice(); //invokes RowBoat's method
19        return hullPrice + sailArea * pricePerSquareFoot;
20      }
21
22      @Override
23      public void show(Graphics g)
24      {
25        int[] xSail = {getX() + getLength()/2, getX(),
26                       getX() + getLength()/2,};
27        int[] ySail = {getY() - getLength()/2, getY() - getLength()/8,
28                       getY() - getLength()/8};
29
30        g.setColor(Color.WHITE); //draw the sail
31        g.fillPolygon(xSail, ySail, xSail.length);
32        super.show(g);
33      }
34    }
```

Figure 8.14
The class **SailBoatV3**.

yellow sailboat is drawn with a sail as shown in the bottom right portion of Figure 8.12. Although the lengths of the two sailboats declared in the application (lines 9–10) are both 200, the cost of the second boat (sb2) is higher because of the $600 additional cost of the boat's 300-square-foot sail (at $2 per square foot as per line 5 of Figure 8.14).

```
1    import edu.sjcny.gpv1.*;
2    import java.awt.*;
3
4    public class ExtendingDataMembers extends DrawableAdapter
5    { static ExtendingDataMembers ge = new ExtendingDataMembers ();
6      static GameBoard gb = new GameBoard(ge, "EXTENDING DATA MEMBERS");
7      static RowBoat rb1 = new RowBoat(30, 150, 200);
8      static RowBoat rb2 = new RowBoat(30, 250, 150);
9      static SailBoatV2 sb1 = new SailBoatV2(260, 150, 200, Color.CYAN);
10     static SailBoatV3 sb2 = new SailBoatV3(260, 300, 200, Color.YELLOW, 300);
11
12     public static void main(String[] args)
13     {
14       showGameBoard(gb);
15     }
16
17     public void draw(Graphics g)
18     {
19       rb1.show(g);
20       rb2.show(g);
21       sb1.show(g);
22       sb2.show(g);
23     }
24   }
```

Figure 8.15
The application **ExtendingDataMembers**.

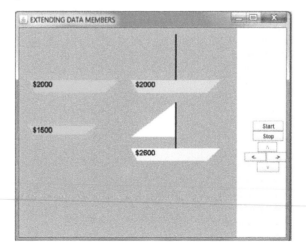

Figure 8.16
The output produced by the application **ExtendingDataMembers**.

Parent Class Methods Invoking Child Class Methods

As previously discussed at the end of Section 8.3.1, when the RowBoat class's show method invokes the method calculatePrice (line 26 of Figure 8.3), the search for the method begins in the class of the object that invoked the show method. When line 22 of Figure 8.15 executes, the search for the calculatePrice method begins in sb2's class, SailBoatV3. Because this class overrides the inherited version of the calculatePrice method, sb2's price is calculated by its version of the method coded on lines 16–20 of Figure 8.14. This is precisely what should happen because otherwise the cost of the sail would not be included in the price of the sailboat sb2. The Java process used to locate invoked methods, which is summarized at the end of Section 8.3.2, causes the RowBoat class's show method to invoke the SailBoatV3 class's calculatePrice method to determine the price of a SailBoatV3 sailboat instance.

8.4 USING INHERITANCE IN THE DESIGN PROCESS

The time and effort required to create a new class can be greatly reduced if we can extend the attributes of an existing class using the basic techniques of inheritance discussed in the previous section. These techniques include inheriting methods and data members into the new class, overriding and overloading these methods to change and extend their functionality, and adding new methods and data members to the new class. But even if there are no existing classes that provide some of the functionality of the classes specified for a new program, the time and cost to develop the program can still be reduced using the concept of inheritance during the design process.

Suppose your Uncle Ed asked you to develop a Java program to "keep track of the inventory" of a boat store he was about to open that will carry rowboats, sailboats, and powerboats. After several follow-up conversations with him, you have determined that "keeping track of the inventory" means knowing the location of each boat on his storage lot, knowing each boat's price and size, and other details that are particular to the type of the boat such as the number of oars, the sail area, and the horsepower of a powerboat. Translating all of this into an OPP design, you concluded there will be three worker classes in the program and produced the UML diagrams shown in Figure 8.17.

Before proceeding to the coding phase of Uncle Ed's (or any other) program, we should apply the basic concepts of inheritance previously discussed in this chapter and the other more advanced inheritance concepts, such as *abstract classes*, to the design process.

8.4.1 Abstract Classes

After the UML diagrams that describe the objects that will be part of the program are prepared, their data members and methods should be compared to determine their commonalities. An examination of the data members of the classes specified in Figure 8.17 reveals that the first five data members in all three classes are the same. In addition, the signatures of all of their methods, except for their constructors, are the same. If we were to give these UML diagrams to three programmers to implement, each programmer would have to code the same five data members into their class and write the same six set and get methods to change and fetch the values of the data members. In addition, the code of their `calculatePrice`, `show`, and `toString` methods would share some similar code.

RowBoatV2
- pricePerFoot: int - x: int - y: int - length : int - color: Color - oars : int

+ RowBoatV2 (x: int , y: int,
           length: int, c: Color,
           oars: int)
+ calculatePrice(): int
+ show(g: Graphics)
+ toString(): String
+ getX(): int
+ getY(): int
+ getLength(): int
+ getColor(): Color
+ setX(x: int)
+ setY(y: int)

SailBoatV4
- pricePerFoot: int - x: int - y: int - length : int - color: Color - sailArea: int

+ SailBoatV2 (x: int , y: int,
           length: int, c: Color,
           sailArea : int)
+ calculatePrice(): int
+ show(g: Graphics)
+ toString(): String
+ getX(): int
+ getY(): int
+ getLength(): int
+ getColor(): Color
+ setX(x: int)
+ setY(y: int)

PowerBoat
- pricePerFoot: int - x: int - y: int - length : int - color: Color - horsePower: int

+ PowerBoat (x: int , y: int,
           length: int, c: Color,
           horsepower: int)
+ calculatePrice(): int
+ show(g: Graphics)
+ toString(): String
+ getX(): int
+ getY(): int
+ getLength(): int
+ getColor(): Color
+ setX(x: int)
+ setY(y: int)

Figure 8.17
The class design of a boat store's inventory application.

To avoid this duplication among the three classes, a forth class named `Boat` is added to the design as shown at the top of Figure 8.18. This class will be an *abstract class*. A class is designated to be abstract by including the keyword `abstract` in its heading. For example:

```
public abstract class Boat //an abstract class
```

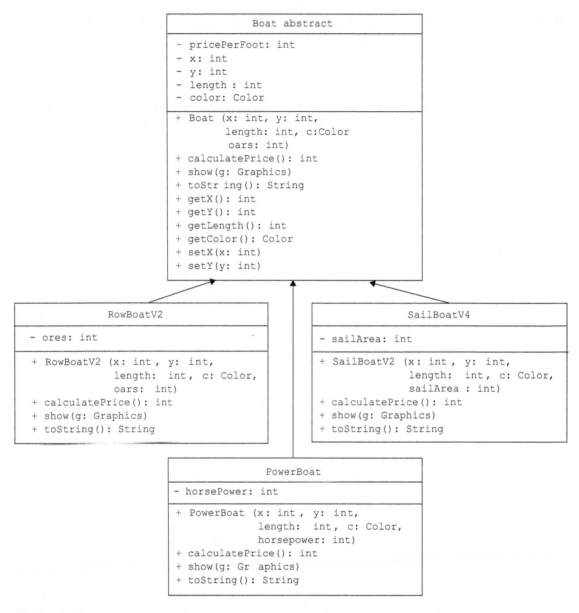

Figure 8.18
The use of inheritance in the design of a boat store's inventory application.

An abstract class is used to collect data members and methods that are common to several classes into one class. It is not meant to be the class of one of the types of objects that will make up a program. For example, you cannot purchase an instance of a `Boat` object from Uncle Ed. He only sells rowboats, sailboats, and powerboats. Consistent with this use of abstract classes, an attempt to declare an object in an abstract class results in a translation error.

As shown in the bottom portion of Figure 8.17, after the abstract `Boat` class is added to the design of Uncle Ed's program, the duplicated five data members and the `set` and `get` methods are eliminated from the original three classes and moved into the UML diagram of the `Boat` class.

Then, as indicated by the arrows in the figure, the original three classes become subclasses of the `Boat` class. By simply including the keyword `extends` in the heading of the classes they code, the authors of the original three classes no longer have to code five of their class's six data members or the six `set` and `get` methods. But the reduction in effort does not end here.

Each of the original classes also contained methods to draw the boat it defines and calculate its price as well as a `toString` method. The signatures of these methods are the same in all three classes, and your conversations with Uncle Ed revealed that they share some common functionality. He has told you that the base price of each type of boat is calculated in the same way because they share a common hull. In reflecting on what he said, you realize that this introduces some common functionality into the `show` methods because each boat's hull will look the same. It also introduces some common functionality into the `calculatePrice` method because each boat's hull will be priced in the same way. Because each of the `toString` methods will return the annotated values of the classes' first five data members, these methods also share some common functionality.

Methods in the child classes that have the same signature and share some common functionality also become part of the parent class's UML diagram, as shown in the UML diagram of the `Boat` class, which now includes a `calculatePrice`, a `show`, and a `toString` method. Unlike the `set` and `get` methods that were eliminated from the child classes, some trace of these relocated methods are retained in the UML diagrams of the child classes to provide the functionality that is not common to each child class.

For example, the functionality of calculating the additional cost of a powerboat's motor would have to be retained in the `PowerBoatV2` class, and the cost of a rowboat's oars would be calculated in the `RowBoat` class. In the design presented in Figure 8.18, the child classes provide additional functionality by overriding the `Boat` class's `calculatePrice`, `show`, and `toString` methods. The code of these methods would invoke `Boat`'s version of the method to calculate and return the price of the boat's hull, draw the boat's hull, and to build and return a string containing the annotated versions of `Boat`'s five data members.

Comparing the UML diagrams in Figures 8.17 and 8.18, we can see that the use of inheritance in the design presented in Figure 8.18 has significantly reduced the effort required to produce Uncle Ed's program. The number of data members to be coded by the programmers has been reduced from 18 to 8, and the number of methods has been reduced from 30 to 22. In addition, the constructor in the `Boat` class will implement the commonality within the constructors in the other three classes, which will reduce the effort required to produce the constructors in the other three classes.

Figures 8.19–8.22 present the implementation of the design depicted in Figure 8.18. The `Boat` class is declared abstract on line 4 of Figure 8.19. Consistent with our design philosophy, it includes all of the data members common to the other three classes, and its methods provide the functionality shared by the other three classes. Those classes extend the `Boat` class (line 3 of Figures 8.20–8.22). They each include a data member particular to their type of boat (e.g., line 5 of Figure 8.20), and their methods invoke `Boat`'s methods (e.g., lines 9, 15, 21, and 31 of Figure 8.20) before adding the functionality particular to their type of boat. For example, line 16 of Figure 8.20 computes the cost of the oars, lines 22-26 draw the oars, and line 31 adds the number of oars to `toStrings` returned strings. The `implements` clause in the heading of the class `Boat` (line 4 of Figure 8.19) will be discussed in Section 8.7.

The application DesignTechniques shown in Figure 8.23 uses the new design to add a row-boat with four oars (line 8), a sailboat with a 200-square-foot sail (line 9), and a powerboat with a 400-horsepower motor (line 10) to Uncle Ed's inventory. The boats are then displayed on his lot (Figure 8.24).

```java
1    import java.awt.*;
2    import java.io.Serializable;
3
4    public abstract class Boat implements Serializable //contains attributes
5    {                                                  //common to all boats
6      private static int PRICE_PER_FOOT = 10;
7      private int x, y, length; //data members common to all types of boats
8      private Color color;
9
10     public Boat(int x, int y, int length, Color color)
11     {
12       this.x = x;
13       this.y = y;
14       this.length = length;
15       this.color = color;
16     }
17     public int calculatePrice() //will be overridden
18     {
19       return length * PRICE_PER_FOOT;
20     }
21     public void show(Graphics g) //will be overridden
22     {
23       int[] xBoat = {getX() , getX() + length, getX() + 6*length/7,
24                     getX() + length/14};
25       int[] yBoat = {getY(), getY(), getY() + length/7,
26                     getY() + length/7};
27       int price = calculatePrice();
28       g.setColor(color);
29       g.fillPolygon(xBoat, yBoat, xBoat.length);
30       g.setColor(Color.BLACK);
31       g.setFont(new Font("Arial", Font.BOLD, 16));
32       g.drawString("$" + String.valueOf(price), x + 10, y + 16);
33     }
34     public String toString() //will be overridden
35     {
36       return "Location: (" + x + ", " + y +"), length: " + length +
37                     ",Color: " + color;
38     }
39     public int getX() //get & set methods common to all types of boats
40     {
41       return x;
```

```
42      }
43      public int getY()
44      {
45        return y;
46      }
47      public int getLength()
48      {
49        return length;
50      }
51      public Color getColor()
52      {
53        return color;
54      }
55      public void setX(int x)
56      {
57        this.x = x;
58      }
59      public void setY(int y)
60      {
61        this.y = y;
62      }
63    }
```

Figure 8.19
The abstract class **Boat**.

```
1     import java.awt.*;
2
3     public class RowBoatV2 extends Boat
4     {
5       private int oars; //extended (additional) data member
6
7       public RowBoatV2(int x, int y, int length, Color c, int oars)
8       {
9         super(x, y, length, c);
10        this.oars = oars;
11      }
12      @Override
13      public int calculatePrice() //overrides parent method
14      {
15        int hullPrice = super.calculatePrice();
16        return hullPrice + oars * 10;
17      }
18      @Override
19      public void show(Graphics g) //overrides parent method
20      {
21        super.show(g);
```

```
22        g.setColor(Color.BLACK);
23        for(int i = 1; i <= oars; i++) //each ore
24        {
25          g.fillRect(getX() + i*10, getY() - 20, 2, 20); //handle
26          g.fillOval(getX() + i*10-2, getY() - 30, 6, 10); //paddle
27        }
28     }
29   public String toString() //overrides parent method
30   {
31      return super.toString() + ", Oars: " + oars;
32   }
33  }
```

Figure 8.20
The child class **RowBoatV2**.

```
1    import java.awt.*;
2
3    public class SailBoatV4 extends Boat
4    {
5      private int sailArea; //extended (additional) data member
6
7      public SailBoatV4(int x, int y, int length,
8                        Color color, int sailArea)
9      {
10       super(x, y, length, color);
11       this.sailArea = sailArea;
12     }
13     @Override
14     public int calculatePrice() //overrides parent method
15     {
16       int hullPrice = super.calculatePrice();
17       return hullPrice + sailArea * 2;
18     }
19     @Override
20     public void show(Graphics g) //overrides parent method
21     {
22       int[] xSail = {getX() + getLength()/2, getX(),
23                      getX() + getLength()/2};
24       int[] ySail = {getY() - getLength()/2, getY() - getLength()/8,
25                      getY() - getLength()/8};
26
27       super.show(g);
28       g.setColor(Color.BLACK); //draw the mast
29       g.fillRect(getX() + getLength()/2, getY() - getLength()/2, 3,
30                  getLength()/2);
31       g.setColor(Color.WHITE); //draw the sail
32       g.fillPolygon(xSail, ySail, xSail.length);
33     }
```

```
34     public String toString() //overrides parent method
35     {
36       return super.toString() + ", Sail Area: " + sailArea;
37     }
38  }
```

Figure 8.21
The child class **SailBoatV4**.

```
1    import java.awt.*;
2
3    public class PowerBoat extends Boat
4    {
5      private int horsePower; //extended (additional) data member
6
7      public PowerBoat(int x, int y, int length,
8                      Color color, int horsePower)
9      {
10       super(x, y, length, color);
11       this.horsePower = horsePower;
12     }
13     @Override
14     public int calculatePrice() //overrides parent method
15     {
16       int hullPrice = super.calculatePrice();
17       return hullPrice + horsePower * 3;
18     }
19     @Override
20     public void show(Graphics g) //overrides parent method
21     {
22       int[] xSail = {getX() + getLength()/2, getX(),
23                      getX() + getLength()/2,};
24       int[] ySail = {getY() - getLength()/2, getY() - getLength()/8,
25                      getY() - getLength()/8};
26
27       super.show(g);
28       g.setColor(Color.BLACK); //draw the shaft
29       g.fillOval(getX() - 13, getY() + getLength()/7 , 30, 4);
30       g.setColor(Color.GRAY); //draw the propeller
31       g.fillOval(getX() - 20, getY() + getLength()/7, 20, 6);
32       g.fillOval(getX() - 13, getY() + getLength()/7 - 7, 6, 20);
33     }
34     public String toString() //overrides parent method
35     {
36       return super.toString() + ", Horsepower: " + horsePower;
37     }
38  }
```

Figure 8.22
The child class **PowerBoat**.

```
1    import edu.sjcny.gpv1.*;
2    import java.awt.*;
3
4    public class DesignTechniques extends DrawableAdapter
5    {
6      static DesignTechniques ge = new DesignTechniques();
7      static GameBoard gb = new GameBoard(ge, "Design Techniques");
8      static RowBoatV2 rb1 = new RowBoatV2(50, 200, 120, Color.YELLOW, 4);
9      static SailBoatV4 sb1 = new SailBoatV4(220, 200, 200, Color.GREEN, 200);
10     static PowerBoat pb1 = new PowerBoat(50, 300, 200, Color.MAGENTA, 400);
11
12     public static void main(String[] args)
13     {
14       showGameBoard(gb);
15     }
16
17     public void draw(Graphics g)
18     {
19       rb1.show(g);
20       sb1.show(g);
21       pb1.show(g);
22     }
23   }
```

Figure 8.23
The application **DesignTechniques**.

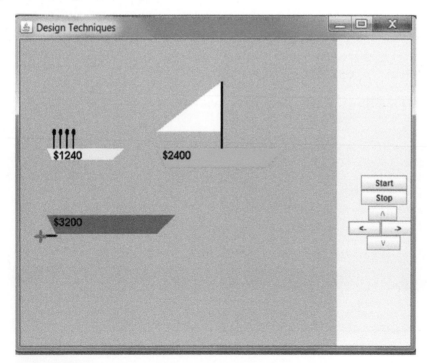

Figure 8.24
The output produced by the application **DesignTechniques**.

8.4.2 Designing Parent Methods to Invoke Child Methods

In addition to creating an abstract class to collect the common attributes shared by the various objects that will be part of a program, there are other inheritance concepts that should be considered when designing and coding the methods in an abstract or nonabstract parent class. One of them is the ability of a parent method to invoke a child class's method.

As discussed at the end of Section 8.3.3, the code of a method in a super class that is operating on an instance of a direct or indirect subclass can invoke a method coded in the subclass. The syntax used is the familiar syntax of coding the method's name followed by the appropriate argument list. For example, if a nonstatic method named extras is added to the child class RowBoatV2, shown in Figure 8.20, then it could be invoked inside any of the methods of its parent class Boat, shown in Figure 8.19, by coding: extras();

This presents an alternate approach to adding functionality to an inherited method during the design phase. Instead of child classes overriding an inherited method, they simply include a method that implements their version of the added functionality, and the code of the parent's inherited method includes an invocation of this method. The signature of the method added to the child classes must be the same in all of the child classes that intend to add functionality to the inherited method.

If this design approach was taken to calculate the price of a rowboat, sailboat, and powerboat, the Boat class's calculatePrice method, lines 17–20 of Figure 8.19, would be changed to the version of the method at the top Figure 8.25. This version of the method invokes the method extras to calculate an additional cost to be added to the price of the hull for oars, a sail, or a motor. The empty version of the method extras shown at the bottom of the figure has to be added to the Boat class or it will not compile. The child classes' calculatePrice methods in Figures 8.20, 8.21, and 8.22 would be replaced with the code of the extras method shown in the upper, middle, and lower portions of Figure 8.26, respectively.

```
public int calculatePrice()
{
  return length * PRICE_PER_FOOT + extras();
}

public int extras()
{

}
```

Figure 8.25
A parent method that invokes the child's method **extras** and the empty implementation of the **extras** method coded in the parent class.

```
public int extras() //RowBoatV2's version of the method extras
{
   return oars * 10;
}

public int extras() //SailBoatV4's version of the method extras
{
   return sailArea * 2;
}

public int extras() //PowerBoat's version of the method extras
{
   return horsePower * 3;
}
```

Figure 8.26
Three child class implementations of the method **extras**

8.4.3 Abstract Parent Methods

An alternative to including the empty version of the method `extras` shown at the bottom of Figure 8.25 is to code it as an abstract method in the parent class, in this case, the class `Boat` (Figure 8.19). Abstract methods include the keyword **abstract** in their signature before their returned type. In addition, their signature ends with a semicolon. As shown below, they do not contain an open and close brace or any code.

```
public abstract int extra();
```

When this approach is used, the parent class must be declared abstract because the parent class no longer contains an implementation of a method it invokes. In addition, the translator will verify that each nonabstract class that inherits directly or indirectly from the abstract class implements a method whose signature matches the signature of the abstract method. If it does not, the child class will not translate. In effect, the inclusion of an abstract method in a parent class is a promissory note, enforced by the translator, that child classes will implement (override) the abstract method.

The use of abstract methods in a super class is considered to be good programming practice when:

- The super class will not be instantiated. Its sole purpose is to collect the common data members and functionality shared by its direct and indirect subclasses.
- Most of its direct and indirect subclasses will add functionally to the super class method that invokes the abstract method.

In the event that a subclass does not need to add functionality to the super class method that invokes an abstract method, the subclass would implement the abstract method with an empty code block.

8.4.4 Final Classes

A class can be declared to be a `final` class by coding the keyword `final` in its heading immediately after the class's access modifier. When a class is declared `final`, it cannot be extended. An attempt to do so results in a translation error. For example, if the heading of the `PowerBoat` class (line 3 of Figure 8.22) was coded as shown below, then it could not be a parent class.

```
3    public final class PowerBoat extends Boat
```

Classes that contain methods that enforce security on systems are usually declared to be `final` to prevent their methods from being overridden.

A class cannot be declared `abstract` and `final` because it would be rendered useless. If it were abstract, instances of the class could not be created; if it were also final, it could not be extended. In short, nothing could be done with it.

8.4.5 Protected Data Members

When a method or a data member in a class is designated to have private access, the method can only be invoked and the data member can only be directly accessed by the methods defined inside the class. A private method cannot be invoked by methods defined outside of its class. A private data member can be indirectly accessed by a method defined in another class by invoking its `set` and `get` methods. When a method or a data member is designated to have public access the method can be invoked, and the data member can be directly accessed, by methods defined outside of its class.

A class's methods and data members can also be declared to have protected access by beginning their declaration with the keyword `protected`.

```
protected int count;
```

The access modifier `protected` is less restrictive than `private` access and more restrictive than `public` access. Restrictions imposed by protected access are package dependent.

When a method or a data member is designated to have `protected` access, the method can be invoked, and the data member can be directly accessed, by methods defined inside its class *and* its direct and indirect subclasses. As illustrated in the bottom and top left portions of Figure 8.27, the access is permitted whether or not the parent's protected data members/methods and the child classes are defined in the same package.

Methods in nonchild classes can only access another class's protected methods, and directly access its protected data members, if the nonchild class is defined in the same package as the protected methods and data. This restriction is illustrated in the top right and bottom portions of Figure 8.27.

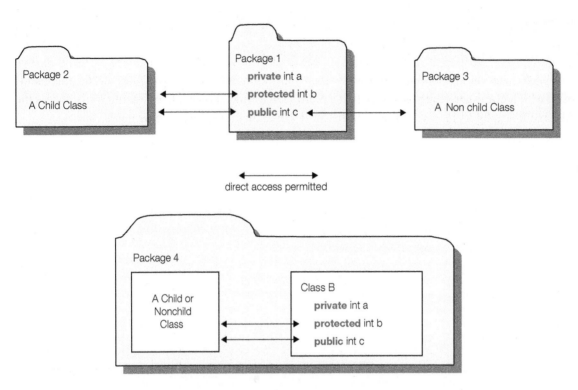

Figure 8.27
Restrictions imposed by `private, protected`, and `public access`.

> **NOTE** *Protected methods and data members are hidden from nonchild classes defined in separate packages.*

8.4.6 Making a Class Inheritance Ready: Best Practices

When designing a class, we should always consider the possibility that other classes may extend it. If for some reason we want to prevent the class from being extended, the class is declared `final`. If a nonfinal class contains a constructor, it should also contain a no-parameter constructor even if its code block is empty, otherwise the child class's constructors will always have to explicitly invoke a parent constructor. A parent class that was created to collect the methods and data members common to other classes should be declared abstract.

Each method in a nonfinal class should be examined to decide if its functionality could be compromised if it were overridden in a subclass. When that is the case, the method should be declared `final`. To permit restricted modifications to a `final` method, the method should invoke an abstract method whose signature is defined within the `final` method's class, then subclasses can add functionality to a `final` method by implementing the abstract method. This abstract method approach should also be used when the algorithm of a parent class method requires that child classes add functionality particular to them because the translator will verify that the child classes implement the abstract method. This approach should also be considered when it is anticipated that a child class is likely to override a parent method.

A parent data member that stores a constant should always be declared as `final` to prevent it from being changed. Generally speaking, it is good programming practice to declare all nonfinal data members in a parent class to be private rather than protected and, where appropriate, include `set` and `get` methods to permit access to them. This maintains the encapsulation of the data members, which eliminates the possibility that a method in a child class could unintentionally access the data members by using a variable with the same name that it neglected to declare.

8.5. POLYMORPHISM

Polymorphism is the idea that something can exist in several different forms. We have already discussed several uses of polymorphism in computer science. One use of polymorphism we discussed is overloading methods. A method can be overloaded or morphed into a new form, with the new form having a different parameter list. These different forms of the method can be coded inside the same class, such as constructors with several different parameter lists, or one form of a method's parameter list can be coded in a super class, and another form could be coded in its subclass.

Other uses of polymorphism occur within the concept of inheritance. Two of these uses were already discussed. The first is the inheritance concept of overriding methods. In this use of polymorphism, one form of a method exists in the super class, and another form of the method, with the exact same signature, exists in the subclass. The second involves the invocation of a method by a parent method. Due to the search path used to locate the invoked method at run time, this invocation could take on the form of an invocation of a parent class method or a child class method with the same signature.

Polymorphism is also used to indicate that a child can take on the form of a parent because a child is also a parent. This should not be surprising because we have already learned that a child class inherits everything from a parent: all of its data members and all of its methods (except for its constructors). This polymorphic inheritance concept opens up a set of programming practices that makes our programs easier to write and easier to understand. In the remainder of this section, we will discuss these programming practices and the syntax used to incorporate them into the programs we write.

8.5.1 Parent and Child References

Because a child object is also considered to be a parent object, a parent reference variable can store the address of, or point to, a child object. This is a form of polymorphism because it permits a parent reference variable to assume many different forms. It can be a reference to a parent object, or it can be a reference to an instance of any class that inherits directly or indirectly from it.

Line 4 of the following code fragment illustrates the use of this form of polymorphism. Line 1 declares the variable `aBoat` to be a `Boat` class reference variable. Because the class `PowerBoat` (Figure 8.22) extends the class `Boat` (Figure 8.19), the variable can be morphed into a reference to a `PowerBoat` object. This is accomplished using the assignment statement on line 4. After line 4 executes, the variable `aBoat` stores the address of a `PowerBoat` object, the same object referenced by `pb1`.

```
//A super class reference variable can reference a subclass object
1    Boat aBoat; //declares a reference variable in the super class Boat
2    PowerBoat pb1 = new PowerBoat(50, 300, 200, Color.MAGENTA, 400);
3
4    aBoat = pb1; //aBoat and pb1 now reference the same powerboat
```

Consistent with this form of polymorphism, a super class reference variable that refers to one type of subclass object can be reassigned to reference an instance of another one of its subclasses. After the following code sequence executes, the variables `aBoat` and `sb1` both reference the same `SailBoatV4` object, whose class (Figure 8.21) also extends `Boat`.

```
//A super class reference variable can reference any subclass object
1    Boat aBoat; //declares a reference variable in the super class Boat
2    PowerBoat pb1 = new PowerBoat(50, 300, 200, Color.MAGENTA, 400);
3    SailBoatV4 sb1 = new SailBoatV4(220, 200, 200, Color.GREEN, 200);
4
5    aBoat = pb1; //aBoat references a powerboat
6    aBoat = sb1; //aBoat now reference a sailboat
```

NOTE *A super class reference variable can refer to any instance of a class that directly, or indirectly, inherits from it.*

Using the syntax of coercion, the address of a child class object stored in a parent reference variable can be coerced into a child reference variable. After line 6 of the following code fragment executes, the child reference variable `pb2` stores the address of a powerboat. If `pb2` were declared to be a reference to a subclass of `Boat` other than the `PowerBoat` class, line 6 would result in a translation error.

```
//A subclass reference can be coerced into a child reference variable
1    Boat aBoat; //declares a reference variable in the super class Boat
2    PowerBoat pb1 = new PowerBoat(50, 300, 200, Color.MAGENTA, 400);
3    PowerBoat pb2;
4
5    aBoat = pb1; //aBoat now references the same PowerBoat child
6    pb2 = (PowerBoat) aBoat; //valid when aBoat references a PowerBoat
```

There is one restriction on the use of assignment statements that mixes child and parent reference variables. A child class reference variable cannot be assigned the address of a parent class object because a parent object is not a child object. An attempt to do so results in a translation error. A good way to remember this restriction comes from the old family adage: Parents can point to their children when they correct them, but it is rude for children to point to their parents.

The following code fragment uses the nonabstract parent class `RowBoat` defined in Figure 8.3 and the `SailBoat` class that extends it (Figure 8.6). Assigning the location of the parent class object declared on line 1 to the child class reference variable, `sb1`, on line 4 produces a translation error, as does line 5, which attempts to coerce the address of the parent `RowBoat` object into the child class reference variable.

```
   //A subclass reference variable can NOT reference a superclass object
1  RowBoat rb1 = new RowBoat(30, 150, 200);
2  SailBoat sb1;
3
4  sb1 = rb1; //syntax error: child reference assigned a parent object
5  sb1 = (SailBoat) rb1; //coercion does not remedy the problem
```

NOTE   *The addresses of parent objects cannot be assigned to child reference variables.*

8.5.2 Polymorphic Invocations

Definition
A **polymorphic invocation** is the act of invoking a method using a parent reference variable that refers to a child object.

When a method is invoked using a parent reference variable that refers to a child object, it is referred to as a **polymorphic invocation**. Consider the client code fragment shown in Figure 8.28 that uses the super class `Boat` (Figure 8.19) and its subclass `PowerBoat` (Figure 8.22). Although the variable `aBoat` declared on line 1 is of type `Boat`, it has been assigned the address of a child `PowerBoat` object. This is valid because parents can point to children. The `show` method is invoked on line 5 using this parent reference variable, which makes line 5 a polymorphic invocation of the `show` method.

```
1   static Boat aBoat = new PowerBoat(50, 300, 200, Color.MAGENTA, 400);
2
3   public void draw(Graphics g)
4   {
5      aBoat.show(g);
6   }
```

Figure 8.28
Polymorphic invocation of the method **show** by the object referenced by **aBoat**.

The translator always looks into the class of the reference variable that invoked a nonstatic method to verify the signature of the method, for both polymorphic and nonpolymorphic invocations. As a result, line 5 begins its search in the class `Boat` for a method named `show` whose parameter list is a `Graphics` object. Because the `Boat` class contains a method with that signature (line 21 of Figure 8.19), line 5 is valid syntax. The parent class `Boat` need not implement the method `show`; it can simply define the method's name and its signature as an abstract method.

If the class `Boat` did not contain a `show` method whose parameter list matched line 5's argument list, the translator's search would progress *up* through the classes in `Boat`'s inheritance chain. Because the class `Boat` does not explicitly extend a class, the search would end unsuccessfully in the class `Object`, and line 5 of Figure 8.28 would produce a translation error.

_____ **NOTE**	*The class of the parent reference variable used in a polymorphic method invocation must include, or have inherited, an implementation or an abstract version of the invoked method.*

At runtime, the Java Runtime Environment uses a different starting point in its search to locate the method named in a polymorphic invocation. Unlike the translator that begins its search in the class of the parent reference variable coded in the invocation statement, the runtime environment begins its search in the class of the object referenced by the variable. For example, the search for the show method invoked on line 5 of Figure 8.28 would begin in the PowerBoat class because the variable aBoat references the PowerBoat object assigned to it on line 1. In effect, the invocation is morphed at runtime into an invocation of the show method that correctly draws a powerboat.

The programming language concept use to implement this form of polymorphism is called *dynamic binding*. The invocation is attached, or bound to, the method to be executed during runtime. Line 5 of Figure 8.29 is not a polymorphic invocation because line 1 declares pb1 to be a PowerBoat reference variable and assigns it the location of a PowerBoat object. For non-polymorphic invocations, the method located by the translator's search to verify the existence of a method with the appropriate signature is the method executed at runtime.

```
1    static PowerBoat pb1 = new PowerBoat(50, 300, 200, Color.MAGENTA, 400);
2
3    public void draw(Graphics g)
4    {
5      pb1.show(g);
6    }
```

Figure 8.29
Nonpolymorphic invocation of the method **show** by the object referenced by **pb1**.

The application PolymorphicInvocations shown in Figure 8.30 is a modification of the application DesignTechniques presented in Figure 8.23. This version of the application uses polymorphic invocations inside its draw call back method to produce the output shown in Figure 8.31, which is the same output produced by the original version (Figure 8.24).

Line 11 of Figure 8.30 creates three Boat reference variables, which are then assigned (lines 15–17) the location of the three objects created on lines 8, 9, and 10. This is valid syntax because all three of these objects' classes (Figures 8.20–8.22) extend the class Boat (Figure 8.19).

Because the variables boat1, boat2, and boat3 now reference child objects, the invocations on lines 23–25 are polymorphic invocations. The appearance of a properly drawn rowboat, sailboat, and powerboat on the game board shown in Figure 8.31 confirms that the search path used by the Java runtime environment to locate the show method it executed began in the classes of the objects rather than the class of the three reference variables (i.e., Boat). If the search had begun in the Boat class, its show method would have drawn three hulls without oars, or a sail, or a propeller (lines 23-32 of Figure 8.19).

```
1     import edu.sjcny.gpv1.*;
2     import java.awt.*;
3
4     public class PolymorphicInvocations extends DrawableAdapter
5     {
6       static PolymorphicInvocations ge = new PolymorphicInvocations();
7       static GameBoard gb = new GameBoard(ge, "Design Techniques");
8       static RowBoatV2 rb1 = new RowBoatV2(50, 200, 120, Color.YELLOW, 4);
9       static SailBoatV4 sb1 = new SailBoatV4(220, 200, 200, Color.GREEN, 200);
10      static PowerBoat pb1 = new PowerBoat(50, 300, 200, Color.MAGENTA, 400);
11      static Boat boat1, boat2, boat3;
12
13      public static void main(String[] args)
14      {
15        boat1 = rb1;
16        boat2 = sb1;
17        boat3 = pb1;
18        showGameBoard(gb);
19      }
20
21      public void draw(Graphics g)
22      {
23        boat1.show(g);
24        boat2.show(g);
25        boat3.show(g);
26      }
27    }
```

Figure 8.30
The application **PolymorphicInvocations**.

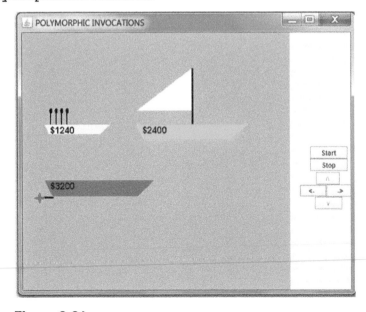

Figure 8.31
The output produced by the application **PolymorphicInvocations**.

8.5.3 Polymorphic Arrays

Definition

A **polymorphic array** is an array of parent reference variables that are used to store references to child objects.

Polymorphic arrays are declared using the syntax discussed in Section 6.5, which is used to declare any array of reference variables. For example, the array `inventory` declared below has the potential to become a polymorphic array because the class `Boat` defined in Figure 8.19 is the super class of the subclasses defined in Figures 8.20–8.22:

```
Boat[] inventory = new Boat[9];
```

If and when an element of the array `inventory` is assigned the address of a subclass object, it is then being used as a polymorphic array. Arrays of abstract class reference variables can only be used as polymorphic arrays because we cannot create an instance of an abstract class.

Each element of a polymorphic array could be assigned the address of the *same* type of subclass instance, in which case the array would be called a *homogeneous* polymorphic array. When at least two *different* subclass objects are referenced from within the array, the array is being used as a *nonhomogeneous* polymorphic array. Nonhomogeneous polymorphic arrays bring the power of arrays into the concept of inheritance and further reduce the number of lines of code required to produce an application.

The application `PolymorphicArrays` shown in Figure 8.32 is a modification of the application `PolymorphicInvocations` presented in Figure 8.30. It uses a polymorphic array to store a nine-boat inventory of Uncle Ed's boat store. The output it produces is shown in Figure 8.33.

Line 11 of Figure 8.32 creates a polymorphic array named `inventory` whose elements are reference variables in the abstract class `Boat` (Figure 8.19). Each time the loop that begins on line 15 executes, lines 17–21 create three new boats whose classes are shown in Figures 8.20–8.22. Then, lines 22–24 add them to Uncle Ed's inventory by storing them in the polymorphic array. The loop variable, i, is used on lines 17–20 to change the (x, y) location, number of oar, sail area, and size of the boats. It is also used on lines 22–24 to change the elements of the array that store the boats' addresses.

The `for` loop that begins on line 32 uses polymorphic invocations of the `show` method to draw each boat on the game board, which represents Uncle Ed's boat storage lot.

```
1    import edu.sjcny.gpv1.*;
2    import java.awt.*;
3
4    public class PolymorphicArrays extends DrawableAdapter
5    {
6      static PolymorphicArrays ge = new PolymorphicArrays();
7      static GameBoard gb = new GameBoard(ge, "POLYMORPHIC ARRAYS");
8      static RowBoatV2 rb;
9      static SailBoatV4 sb;
```

```
10    static PowerBoat pb;
11    static Boat[] inventory = new Boat[9];
12
13    public static void main(String[] args)
14    {
15      for(int i = 0; i < 3; i++)
16      {
17        rb = new RowBoatV2(10 + i * 130, 75, 120, Color.YELLOW, i * 2 + 2);
18        sb = new SailBoatV4(10 + i * 170, 250, 110 + i * 15, Color.GREEN,
19                            200 + i * 20);
20        pb = new PowerBoat(20 + i * 160, 350, 120 + i * 15, Color.MAGENTA,
21                            400);
22        inventory[i * 3] = rb;
23        inventory[i * 3 + 1] = sb;
24        inventory[i * 3 + 2] = pb;
25      }
26
27      showGameBoard(gb);
28    }
29
30    public void draw(Graphics g)
31    {
32      for(int i = 0; i < 9; i++)
33      {
34        inventory[i].show(g);
35      }
36    }
37  }
```

Figure 8.32
The application **PolymorphicArrays**.

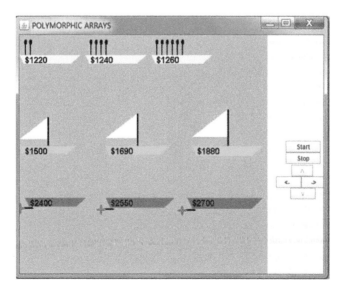

Figure 8.33
The output produced by the application **PolymorphicArrays**.

Advantages of Polymorphic Arrays

The addresses of the new boats created on lines 17–21 of Figure 8.32 could have been assigned directly into the array elements on these lines, in which case, lines 8–10 and 22–24 would be eliminated from the program. This approach would have reduced the program to 31 lines with much of the programs brevity coming from the use of a polymorphic array.

An alternative approach to this program would have been to declare three nonpolymorphic arrays, one for each type of boat, as shown below:

```
RowBoatV2[3]  rb = new RowBoatV2[3];
SailBoatV4[3]  sb = new SailBoatV4[3];
PowerBoat[3]  pb = new PowerBoat[3];
```

The addition of these three lines and the additions to the body of the output loop (line 34), which now requires an output of three arrays rather than one, would expanded the 31-line version of the program to a 36-line program. Reductions in coding effort are typically realized when polymorphic arrays are used.

In addition, if the details of the nine boats in Uncle Ed's inventory, including their type, were to be input by the program user instead of being hard coded (as on lines 17–21), the polymorphic approach would reduce the storage requirements of the program. Any mix of nine rowboats, sailboats, and powerboats could be saved in the nine-element polymorphic array, but the three-nonpolymorphic-array approach would require that all three arrays be expanded to nine elements to accommodate the case when all of the boats are of one type (e.g., all sailboats).

8.5.4 Polymorphism's Role in Parameter Passing

Because a super class can point to (i.e., store the address of) an instance of any of its subclasses, a parameter whose type is the super class can be passed an argument whose type is any of its subclasses. Taking this concept to its extreme, because all classes inherit directly or indirectly from the class Object, any object's address can be passed to a parameter whose type is Object. We will utilize this fact when we code generic classes in Chapter 13.

Suppose we wanted to code a method that determined if two of Uncle Ed's boats occupied the same (x, y) location. We would code the method in the super class Boat (Figure 8.19) to enable any instance of its subclasses (a rowboat, a sailboat, or a powerboat) to invoke it. The method would compare that object's x and y data members to those of the objects passed to its parameter. To ensure that any of these three types of boats could be passed to the method, the parameter's type would be the super class Boat. The code for the method is given below:

```
1    public boolean samePosition(Boat aBoat) //code in the superclass Boat
2    {
3      if(x == aBoat.x && y == aBoat.y)
4      {
5        return true;
6      }
7      else
```

```
8      {
9          return false;
10     }
11  }
```

If the method was to determine if any of Uncle Ed's boats occupied the same (x, y) location, the static method shown below could be coded in the super class Boat. The method signature contains one parameter, a reference variable that can store the address of an array of instances of the class Boat or instances of Boat's subclasses. When the method is invoked, it is passed the polymorphic array that contains Uncle Ed's boat inventory. It returns true if two or more boats are at the same (x, y) location.

```
1   public static boolean samePositionV2(Boat[] boats) //coded in the
2   {                                                  //superclass Boat
3     for(int i = 0; i< boats.length; i++)
4     {
5       for(int j = i + 1; j< boats.length; j++)
6       {
7         if(boats[i].x == boats[j].x && boats[i].y == boats[j].y)
8         {
9           return true;
10        }
11      }
12    }
13    return false;
14  }
```

8.5.5 The methods getClass and getName and the instanceof operator.

Suppose your Uncle Ed expanded the requirements of his inventory program to include output-ting the inventory of a specified type of boat. For example, print the details of all of the sailboats in the inventory. Then when a customer expressed an interest in a sailboat, Uncle Ed could give the customer a list of the sailboats currently in his inventory.

If the three nonpolymorphic arrays were used in the program, the type of the boat the customer was interested in could be used in the Boolean conditions of nested if-else statements to decide which of the three arrays to output. The following pseudocode fragment uses this approach to output the type of boat stored in the input string typeSpecified:

```
if(typeSpecfied.equalsIgnoreCase("rowboat")
{
    //a for loop to output the contents of the rowboat array
}
else if(typeSpecified.equalsIgnoreCase("sailboat")
{
    //a for loop to output the contents of the sailboat array
}
else
{
```

```
                //a for loop to output the contents of the powerboat array
        }
```

Although this implementation of the new requirement is rather straight forward, as discussed at the end of the previous section, this three-nonpolymorphic-array approach increases the program's size and its storage requirements. A more efficient single-polymorphic-array implementation of the new requirement could be used if there was some way of identifying the type each object referenced in the polymorphic array. The following pseudocode fragment could then be used to output only the type of boat stored in the input string `typeSpecified`:

```
for(int i=0; i < inventory.length; i++)//inventory is a polymorphic array
{
    if( //inventory[i] is of the typeSpedified )
    {
        System.out.println(inventory[i].toString());
    }
}
```

Fortunately, the API classes `Object` and `Class` provide the ability to identify the type, (i.e., the class) of any object.

The `getClass` Method in the Class Object

All classes inherit from the class `Object`. It is a super class of all classes contained in the API and the implied super class of every programmer defined class. The class `Object` is at the top of every class's inheritance chain. We have already taken advantage of this fact in Chapter 3 when we used the `toString` method inhcrited from the class `Object` to output the location of an object.

One of the other methods inherited from the class `Object` is its `getClass` method. This method has an empty parameter list and returns the location of an instance of a `Class` object.

The getName Method in the Class `Class`

When an object is constructed information about the object, such as its class name and the name of the class it extends, is recorded in an instance of a `Class` object that is created by the Java Virtual Machine and associated with the constructed object. The location of the associated `Class` object can be fetched by invoking `Object`'s `getClass` method on the constructed object, which can then be used to invoke any of the methods in the class `Class`.

One of these methods, `getName`, can be used to determine the name of any object's class. The method has an empty parameter list and returns a string containing the class's name. The following code fragment uses the five-parameter constructor of the class `PowerBoat` (Figure 8.22) to construct the object `pb` and uses the `getClass` and `getName` methods to output the name of `pb`'s class, `PowerBoat`:

```
1    PowerBoat pb = new PowerBoat(160, 350, 120, Color.MAGENTA, 400);
2    Class c = pb.getClass();
3    System.out.println(c.getName());
```

Often lines 2 and 3 are combined into one line:

```
System.out.println(pb.getClass.getName());
```

This abbreviated code version is used in the following code fragment to output only the Power-Boat objects stored in the polymorphic array inventory:

```
for(int i=0; i < inventory.length; i++)
{
  if(inventory[i].getClass().getName().equalsIgnoreCase("PowerBoat"))
    {
      System.out.println(inventory[i].toString());
    }
}
```

The application ObjectAndClass shown in Figure 8.34 is a modification of the application PolymorphicArrays presented in Figure 8.32. When launched, it asks the user what type of boat the customer is interested in and then uses the getClass and getName methods to identify that subset of Uncle Ed's inventory and outputs a description of these boats to the system console. The graphical and console output produced by the application is shown in Figure 8.35.

Line 8 of Figure 8.34 and the body of the loop that begins on line 15 create a polymorphic array named inventory whose elements are reference variables in the abstract class Boat defined in Figure 8.19. Each time the loop executes, lines 17–21 create three new boats whose classes are shown in Figures 8.20–8.22. The addresses of these objects are placed directly into the elements of the polymorphic array on lines 17, 19, and 21.

The Boolean condition of the *if* statement coded on line 29 uses the methods getClass and getName to determine if the class name of the object referenced by the ith element of the array inventory is the same as the string s input on line 25. If it is, the object is output to the console on line 31 using a polymorphic invocation of the toString method. The console output is shown in the bottom portion of Figure 8.35. Figure 8.35a shows the dialog box displayed by line 25 containing the user input *SAILBOATV4*, which resulted in the console output shown at the bottom of Figure 8.35. Figure 8.35b shows the graphical output produced by the polymorphic invocations of the show method (line 41 of Figure 8.34).

```
1    import edu.sjcny.gpv1.*;
2    import java.awt.*;
3    import javax.swing.*;
4
5    public class ObjectAndClass extends DrawableAdapter
6    { static ObjectAndClass ge = new ObjectAndClass();
7      static GameBoard gb = new GameBoard(ge, "getClass and getName Methods");
8      static Boat[] inventory = new Boat[9];
9
10     public static void main(String[] args)
11     {
12         String s;
13
```

```
14          // Use of a polymorphic array
15          for(int i = 0; i < 3; i++)
16          {
17            inventory[i*3] = new RowBoatV2(10 + i*130, 75, 120,
18                                    Color.YELLOW, i*2 + 2);
19            inventory[i*3 + 1] = new SailBoatV4(10 + i*170, 250 , 110+ i *15,
20                                    Color.GREEN, 200 + i*20);
21            inventory[i*3 + 2] = new PowerBoat(20 + i*160, 350 , 120+ i *15,
22                                    Color.MAGENTA, 400);
23          }
24
25          s = JOptionPane.showInputDialog("Interested in, a rowboatV2," +
26                                    "\na sailboatV4, or a powerboat?");
27          for(int i = 0; i < inventory.length; i++)
28          {
29              if(inventory[i].getClass().getName().equalsIgnoreCase(s))
30              {
31                System.out.println(inventory[i].toString());
32              }
33          }
34          showGameBoard(gb);
35    }
36
37    public void draw(Graphics g)
38    {
39      for(int i = 0; i < 9; i++)
40      {
41        inventory[i].show(g);
42      }
43    }
44  }
```

Figure 8.34
The application **ObjectAndClass**.

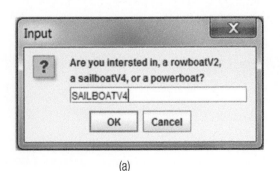

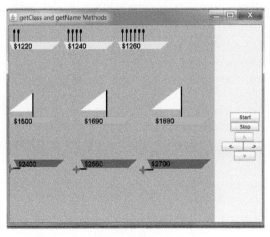

(a)   (b)

System Console Output:

Location: (10, 250), length: 110, Color: java.awt.Color[r=0,g=255,b=0], Sail Area: 200
Location: (180, 250), length: 125, Color: java.awt.Color[r=0,g=255,b=0], Sail Area: 220
Location: (350, 250), length: 140, Color: java.awt.Color[r=0,g=255,b=0], Sail Area: 240

Figure 8.35
The output produced by the application `ObjectAndClass`.

The instanceof Operator

Java provides a more succinct syntax than that used on line 29 of Figure 8.34 for determining the class of an object: its relational operator `instanceof`. This is a binary operator that can be used in a Boolean expression. Its first operand must be a reference variable, and its second operator must be a case-sensitive class name. The operator returns the value `true` when the class name is the class of the object referenced by the first operand. The Boolean condition on the last line of this code fragment evaluates to `true`.

```
Boat[] inventory = new Boat[2];
inventory[0] = new PowerBoat(50, 100, 200, Color.MAGENTA, 400);

if(inventory[0] instanceof PowerBoat)
```

Because a string variable cannot be used as one of the arguments, it cannot be used in the Boolean condition on line 29 of Figure 8.34 to determine if an element of the array `inventory` is an instance of the class whose name is stored in the string `s`.

The two most common uses of the `instanceof` operator are to:

1. Ensure that the casting of a polymorphic reference to an object does not result in a syntax error

2. Eliminate the need to include an implementation or an abstract version of a method in a parent class when the method is invoked polymorphically

The code fragment below demonstrates both of these uses. The `instanceof` operator is used on line 8 to prevent the translation error associated with an attempt to cast the `RowBoatV2` object declared in line 3 into a `PowerBoat` reference on line 10. In addition, because the casting permits a nonpolymorphic invocation of the `show` method on line 11, the translator looks into the `Power-Boat` class, rather than the `Boat` class, to verify the method's signature. The `Boat` class would not have to include a `show` method with the same signature as the `PowerBoat` class.

```
1   Boat[] inventory = new Boat[2]; //used as a polymorphic array
2   inventory[0] = new PowerBoat(50, 100, 200, Color.MAGENTA, 400);
3   inventory[1] = new RowBoatV2(50, 300, 75, Color.YELLOW, 2);
4   PowerBoat pb1;
5
6   for(int i = 0; i < inventory.length; i++)
7   {
8       if(inventory[i] instanceof PowerBoat) //show the powerboat(s)
```

```
9      {
10        pb1 = (PowerBoat) inventory[i];
11        pb1.show()
12     }
13  }
```

_____
NOTE

When using a preexisting super class to implement a polymorphic array, the use of the instanceof *operator and casting eliminates the syntax error associated with using the elements of the array to polymorphically invoke a child class method whose signature is not defined in the parent class. It also eliminates the need to include a version of the method in the super classes that we write.*

8.6 INTERFACES

An **interface** is very similar to an abstract super class that contains only abstract methods and/or static final constant definitions. They are most easily understood by comparing them to this type of super class. Like a class, the source code of an interface is saved in a file with a .java extension, and its translation is sorted in a file with a .class extension. In addition, it is good programming practice to begin the name of an interface with a capital letter.

Definition

An **interface** is a specification of the signatures of related methods that are implicitly abstract and/or a declaration of public constants that are implicitly static and final.

Figure 8.36 compares the syntax and keywords associated with an abstract super class and an interface. At the bottom of the figure, it also compares the syntax of heading of a class that *extends* an abstract super class and a class that *implements* an interface. As shown on the top right side of the figure, the heading of an interface substitutes the keyword interface for the two keywords abstract and class used in the definition of an abstract super class. In addition, the interface definition eliminates the keyword abstract used in the method signatures defined in an abstract class. Because the constant definitions included in an interface are implicitly static and final, these keywords are not used and the constants should be initialized. Interface methods and constant definitions are always implicitly public. They cannot be declared to be private or protected.

As shown in the bottom right side of Figure 8.36, a class that implements an interface uses the keyword implements in its heading rather than the keyword extends. Consistent with the use of these keywords, we say that a class implements an interface rather than extends it.

A syntactical difference not shown in Figure 8.36 is that while a class's heading can state that it extends one (and only one) super class, it can state that it implements more that one interface. When this is the case, the names of the interfaces in the class's implements clause are separated by commas. For example:

```
public class Class1 implements Interface1, Interface2, Interface3
```

Abstract Super Class	Interface
Definition of the super class `Parent`	Definition of the interface `AnInterface`

```
public abstract class Parent
{ public static final int a = 10;
  // other constants can
  // be included

  public abstract int extra();
  //other abstract methods
  //can be included
}
```

```
public interface AnInterface
{ public int a = 10;
  // other constants can
  // be included

  public int extra();
  //other signatures
  //can be included
}
```

Heading of a class that extends the super class Parent	**Heading of a class that implements the interface AnInterface**
`public class Child extends Parent`	`public class AClass implements  AnInterface`

Figure 8.36
A comparison of abstract super class and interface syntax.

When a class implements one or more interfaces and also extends a class, the `extends` clause is coded in its heading before the `implements` clause. For example:

```
public class Class2 extends Parent implements Interface1, Interface2
```

A class that includes an `implements` clause in its heading must implement all of the methods whose signatures are included in the interface. There are only two exceptions to this. The first exception is when the class is an abstract class, in which case it cannot implement any of the methods, and its subclasses must include implementations of all of the interface methods. The second exception is when the class inherits implementations of the methods. These inherited implementations are treated like any other inherited methods. For example, the same search techniques are used to locate them at translation and runtime, and subclasses can override the inherited implementations. In addition, the inherited version of the overridden method can be invoked by preceding the method name with the keyword `super` followed by a dot.

As is the case with abstract classes, we cannot declare an instance of an interface, but the type of a reference variable can be the name of an interface. A very important use of interface reference variables and interfaces in general is in the coding of generic classes, which will be discussed in Chapter 13.

In summary, an interface can be considered to be an abstract super class that contains only public abstract methods and public static final constant definitions, with the following idiosyncrasies:

- a class can implement several interfaces
- interfaces and abstract classes have syntactical differences (shown in Figure 8.36)
- interfaces cannot contain method implementations
- interfaces are used in the coding of generic classes

When to Define and Use an Interface

The similarities of an interface and an abstract class can be a source of confusion when trying to decide which construct to use for a particular programming application. An interface is preferred when we want to standardize the signatures and functionality of methods that implement a commonly performed task on objects that may not be related. By "may not be related," we mean that with the exception of the class `Object`, the classes that perform these common tasks may not share a common ancestor.

For example, the need to compare two objects was anticipated to be such a common task that an interface named `Comparable` is included in the Java API. It defines the signature of a method named `compareTo`, and the interface's documentation describes the functionality of the method. Many nonrelated classes included in the API, such as the `String` class and the `BigInteger` class, implement this interface, and they all implement the functionality described in the interface's documentation. They all compare two objects and return a zero, a negative or a positive value, that reflects the equality or ordering of the two objects being compared. This use of interfaces facilitates the use of any class's `compareTo` method if we know that the class has implemented the interface `Comparable`. In general:

- an *interface* is defined to standardize the signatures and functionality of methods that implement a commonly performed task on objects that may not share a common ancestor other than the class `Object`
- interfaces facilitate the use of methods by standardizing both their signature and their functionality, as described in their documentation

The code of the interface `Drawable` is shown in Figure 8.37. It defines the signatures of two methods commonly used in game applications. As is typically the case, the description of the interface, which is given in Table 8.1, contains the signatures of the methods and describes the functionality of the two methods. It is considered good programming practice that all implementations of an interface's methods conform to the functionality described in the interface's documentation.

```
1    import java.awt.*;
2
3    public interface Drawable
4    {
5      boolean canDraw(int drawableWidth, int drawableHeight);
6      void show(Graphics g);
7    }
```

Figure 8.37
The interface **Drawable**.

Table 8.1
The Documentation of the Interface Drawable

The Interface `Drawable`	
Methods	
Returned Type	**Signature and Functionality Description**
`boolean`	`canDraw(int width, int height)` Returns `true` if the object that invokes it can be drawn on a `Graphics` area whose lower right corner is at location (`width`, `height`)
`void`	`show(Graphics g)` Draws the game piece that invoked it on the graphic object `g` at its current (x, y) location

To close out our discussion of interfaces, consider the following scenario. The author of the game application `InterfaceUse`, shown in Figure 8.38, purchased a package containing the translated versions (bytecodes) of several game piece class implementations. The documentation of the package, which included a copy of Table 8.1, stated that all of the game-piece classes implemented the interface `Drawable` described in that table.

Six instances of two of these classes, `TopHat` and `SnowmanV9`, are declared on lines 11–16 of the application. Knowing that both of these classes implement the interface `Drawable`, the application programmer realized that the addresses of the six objects could be efficiently stored in a polymorphic array of type `Drawable` (which is declared on line 7 and assigned on lines 11–16 of Figure 8.38), and that the objects could then be efficiently drawn/not drawn using invocation of the two methods defined in the interface (lines 22–27 of Figure 8.38).

The output of the program is given in Figure 8.39, which reflects the fact that top hats can only be drawn if they are completely on the game board, and snowmen cannot be drawn if they are completely off the game board. The source code of the two game-piece classes and the class `GamePiece` that they extend (which in this hypothetical scenario, the application programmer never saw) are given in Figures 8.40, 8.41, and 8.42, respectively.

```
1    import edu.sjcny.gpv1.*;
2    import java.awt.*;
3
4    public class InterfaceUse extends DrawableAdapter
5    { static InterfaceUse ge = new InterfaceUse();
6      static GameBoard gb = new GameBoard(ge, "INTERFACES", 700, 700);
7      static Drawable[] items = new Drawable[6];
8
9      public static void main(String[] args)
10     {
```

```
11        items[0] = new TopHat(-10, 30, Color.BLUE, 51, 60); //part off
12        items[1] = new TopHat(350, 360, Color.BLACK, 51, 60);
13        items[2] = new TopHat(600, 640, Color.GREEN, 51, 60); //part off
14        items[3] = new SnowmanV9(-10, 120, Color.BLUE, 80, 152); //part off
15        items[4] = new SnowmanV9(200, 360, Color.BLACK, 80, 152);
16        items[5] = new SnowmanV9(400, 640, Color.GREEN, 80, 152); //part off
17        showGameBoard(gb);
18    }
19
20    public void draw(Graphics g)
21    {
22      for(int i = 0; i < items.length; i++)
23      {
24        if(items[i].canDraw(700, 700))
25        {
26          items[i].show(g);
27        }
28      }
29    }
30 }
```

Figure 8.38
The application **InterfaceUse**.

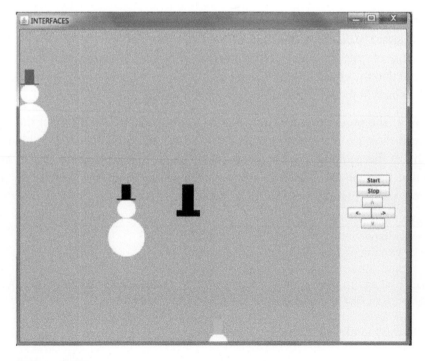

Figure 8.39
The output produced by the application **InterfaceUse**.

```
1     import java.awt.*;
2
3     public class TopHat extends GamePiece implements Drawable
4     {
5
6       public TopHat(int x, int y, Color hatColor, int w, int h)
7       {
8         this.x = x;
9         this.y = y;
10        this.hatColor = hatColor;
11        this.w = w;
12        this.h = h;
13      }
14      public void show(Graphics g)
15      {
16        g.setColor(hatColor);
17        g.fillRect(x + w/4, y, w/2, (int)(h*0.9));   // hat top
18        g.fillRect(x, y + (int)(h*0.9), w, (int)(h*0.2));   // brim
19      }
20      public boolean canDraw(int gbWidth, int gbHeight) //Completely on the
21      {                                                  //game board
22        if(x >= 6 && x + w <= gbWidth
23           &&
24           y >= 30 && y + (int)(h * 1.1) <= gbHeight)
25        {
26          return true;
27        }
28        else
29        {
30          return false;
31        }
32      }
33    }
```

Figure 8.40

The class **TopHat**.

```
1     import java.awt.*;
2     import javax.swing.*;
3
4     public class SnowmanV9 extends GamePiece implements Drawable
5     {
6       public SnowmanV9(int x, int y, Color hatColor, int w, int h)
7       {
8         this.x = x;
9         this.y = y;
10        this.hatColor = hatColor;
```

```
11        this.w = w;
12        this.h = h;
13     }
14     public void show(Graphics g)
15     {
16        g.setColor(Color.WHITE);
17        g.fillOval(x + 20, y + 30, 40, 40); //head
18        g.fillOval(x, y + 70, 80, 80); //body
19        g.setColor(hatColor);
20        g.fillRect(x + 30, y, 20, 30); //hat
21        g.fillRect(x + 20, y + 30, 40, 2); //brim
22     }
23     public boolean canDraw(int gbWidth, int gbHeight) //Not completely off
24     {                                                 //the game board
25        if(x + w >= 6 && x <= gbWidth
26           &&
27           y + h > 30 && y <= gbHeight)
28        {
29           return true;
30        }
31        else
32        {
33           return false;
34        }
35     }
36  }
```

Figure 8.41
The class **SnowmanV9**.

```
1     import java.awt.*;
2
3     public abstract class GamePiece
4     {
5        protected int x;
6        protected int y;
7        protected int w;
8        protected int h;
9        protected Color hatColor;
10
11    }
```

Figure 8.42
The abstract class **GamePiece**.

As shown in Figures 8.40 and 8.41, the TopHat and SnowmanV9 classes implement the interface Drawable and include an implementation of the functionality of the two Drawable methods particular to them. The implementer of the TopHat class decided that a top hat can only be drawn if it is completely on the game board, so the version of the method coded in Figure 8.40 returns true when this is the case. Snowmen will eventually be made to enter the game board from its edges, so they can be drawn if any part of them is on the game board. The code of the SnowmanV9's canDraw method coded in Figure 8.41 returns true when this is the case.

The output of the program shown in Figure 8.39 contains one top hat and three snowmen. This confirms the fact that the polymorphic invocations of the canDraw and show methods on lines 24 and 26 of Figure 8.38 are locating the correct subclass methods. As noted by the comments at the end of lines 11 and 13 of Figure 8.38, the blue and green top hats are partially off the game board, in which case their canDraw method returns false, and they are not drawn. All three snowmen are either partially or completely on the game board, in which case their canDraw method returns true, and they are all drawn.

The data members common to the classes TopHat and SnowmanV9 are collected in the abstract class GamePiece (Figure 8.42), which they extend. They are declared in this super class with protected access (lines 5–9 of Figure 8.42). As indicated in the top half of Figure 8.27, this gives the subclasses' methods the ability to access them directly without using set and get methods (e.g., lines 17 and 18 of Figure 8.40). In our hypothetical scenario, the application would be coded in a separate package, so it would not be able to access these data members.

8.6.1 Adapter Classes

When an interface contains a significant number of methods, it is good programming practice to provide an adapter class for the interface. The term adapter class is a generic term for a class that implements an interface with methods that contain empty code blocks. It is also good programming practice to assign the name of the adapter class the name of the interface class it implements, concatenated with the word "Adapter." For example, the name of the adapter class for the interface Drawable shown in Figure 8.37 would be DrawableAdapter. The code of this class is given in Figure 8.43.

```
public class DrawableAdapter implements Drawable
{
    boolean canDraw(int drawableWidth, int drawableHeight)
    {

    }
    void show(Graphics g);
    {

    }
}
```

Figure 8.43
The adapter class **DrawableAdapter**.

The adapter class is provided to permit a new class to implement only the methods defined in the interface that are relevant. When this is the case, the new class extends the adapter class and then overrides the empty methods with its implementation. For example, if the specification of the class `RocketShip` only required that it implement the `show` method in the `Drawable` interface, then, assuming the `DrawableAdapter` class shown in Figure 8.43 exists, the code of the `Rocket-Ship` class would be written as follows:

```
public class RocketShip extends DrawableAdapter
{
  // the data members of the class RocketShip

  @Override
  public show (Graphics g)
  {
    //the code to draw a RocketShip object
  }

  //the remainder of the methods of the class RocketShip
}
```

We will extend some of the adapter classes in the Java API when we study graphical user interfaces in Chapter 11. The game programming environment contains an interface named `Drawable` that defines the signatures of all of the `draw` call back methods described in Appendix A. The game environment also contains the adapter class `DrawableAdapter`, so a game program's class does not have to implement all of the call back methods if it extends `DrawAbleAdapter`, as does line 4 of Figure 8.37.

It should be noted that when a new class is a child class the use of an adapter class is not an alternative, because a class can only extend one class. The new class's heading would have to contain an `implements` clause, and all of the interface methods would have to be implemented. The interface methods not used by the class would simply contain an empty code block.

8.7 SERIALIZING OBJECTS

Definition

Object serialization is the act of disassembling objects before writing them to a disk file.

Object deserialization is the act of reassembling objects after they are read from a disk file.

In Section 4.8, we discussed techniques used to transfer information to and from a disk file. As part of these techniques, information is written to the disk using the methods in the `Print-Writer` class (e.g., `println` and `print`). These methods write a string to the file, which means that the information in the file is represented as ASCII characters. Any piece of information written to the file that is not a string must be converted to a string before it is written.

This means that when the contents of the variables `houseNumber` and `quantity` defined in the code fragment below are written to the disk, they produce the same output to the disk: the three characters *175*.

```
String houseNumber = "175"
int quantity = 175;
```

Because the type of the information written to the file (e.g., `String` and `int`)is not represented in the file, a written description of the information in the file must be provided with the file to properly read and process the data in the file. When a reference to an object is included in the parameter passed to the `PrintWriter`'s output methods, the object's `toString` method is implicitly invoked, and the returned string is written to the file. In this case, the file description should include not only the types of the data members written to the file, but also the order in which they were written and the objects' classes, so the object written to the file can be properly reconstructed by the program that reads the information from the file.

The `writeObject` method in the class `ObjectOutputStream` presents a better alternative for writing the data members of an object to a disk file. When this method is used to write an object to a file, all of the information required to reconstruct the object when it is read from the file (the data members' types, the order in which they were written, and the class of the objects) is written to the file by the method. This information can then be used by the `readObject` method contained in the `ObjectInputStream` class to reconstruct the object when the method is used to read the object from the file. The gleaning of all of this additional information from objects when they are written to a file is called **object serialization**, and the use of this information to efficiently recreate objects when they are read from a file is called **object deserialization**.

Object serialization allows us to write all of an object's data members to a disk file as a single entity by simply invoking the `ObjectOutputStream` class's `writeObject` method and passing the object to the method's parameter. Object deserialization allows us to read all of an object's data members from a disk file by simply invoking the `ObjectInputStream` class's `readObject` method. This method recreates a serialized object and returns the address of the recreated object. Because the class of each object is written to the file, the file can contain different types of objects. When these objects are related as subclasses of the same super class, the file can be written to and read from polymorphically.

The application `SerializingObjects` presented in Figure 8.44 demonstrates the serialized writing and reading of objects to/from a disk file. It is a modification of the application `PolymorphicArrays` shown in Figure 8.32. This version of the application outputs the nine-boat inventory of Uncle Ed's boat yard, stored in a polymorphic array, to a serialized disk file using the `writeObject` method and reads the objects back into the array using the `readObject` method. Sample outputs produced at various points in the program's execution are given in Figure 8.45.

Line 12 of Figure 8.44 creates a polymorphic array named `inventory` whose elements are reference variables in the abstract class `Boat` (Figure 8.19). Each time the loop that begins on line 16 executes, lines 18–22 create three new boats whose classes are shown in Figures 8.20–8.22. Then, lines 23–25 add them to Uncle Ed's inventory by storing them in the polymorphic array. When the program in Figure 8.44 is launched, line 37 of the `draw` method displays the boats on the game board because each element of the array `inventory` contains a non-null reference (line 35). The initial output of the program is shown in Figure 8.45a.

When the game board's right arrow button is clicked, line 59 of the button's call back method writes the serialized version of all of the boat objects to a disk file named "Inventory." The file is created and attached to the `ObjectOutputStream` object `outFile` on lines 52 and 53; this is the object used on line 59 to invoke the `writeObject` method.

After subsequent clicks of the game board's up arrow button, line 46 of the button's call back method deletes the boats from the polymorphic array by setting all of its elements to `null`. When the call back method ends, the game environment invokes the `draw` call back method. This method then displays an empty game board (Figure 8.45b) because line 35 prevents the `show` method from executing. If it had executed, the program would have been terminated by a `NullPointerException` because all of the elements of the array `inventory` are `null`.

To restore and redisplay Uncle Ed's inventory, line 77 of the left button call back method reads the serialized boat objects from the disk file "Inventory" and places their addresses into the polymorphic array. The file is opened and attached to the `ObjectInputStream` object `inFile` on lines 72 and 73; this is the object used on line 77 to invoke the `readObject` method. After the left button call back methods ends, the `draw` call back method executes and line 37 of the `draw` call back method displays the restored nine-boat inventory on the game board (left side of Figure 8.42) via polymorphic invocations to the boats' `show` methods. The redisplay of the inventory verifies that line 59 correctly wrote the serialized objects to the disk file, and line 77 correctly read them back into the polymorphic array.

The coercion used in Figure 8.44 on line 77 is necessary because the `readObject` method, invoked on that line, returns a reference whose type is `Object`. When writing and reading serialized objects, the exceptions coded on lines 64, 81, and 84 must be caught (as shown) or thrown (to be discussed in Chapter 10) inside the methods that perform the disk I/O. Alternately, a `throws` clause can be included in the methods' headings. If the methods override a method, the overridden method must contain the same `throws` clause, or the `throws` clause alternative cannot be used. Because the call back methods override the methods in the `DrawableAdapter` class, the `catch` clause alternative was used in this program.

```
1    import edu.sjcny.gpv1.*;
2    import java.awt.*;
3    import java.io.*;
4
5    public class SerializingObjects extends DrawableAdapter
6    {
7      static SerializingObjects ge = new SerializingObjects();
8      static GameBoard gb = new GameBoard(ge, "SERIALIZING OBJECTS");
9      static RowBoatV2 rb;
10     static SailBoatV4 sb;
11     static PowerBoat pb;
```

```
12      static Boat[] inventory = new Boat[9];
13
14      public static void main(String[] args)
15      {
16        for(int i = 0; i < 3; i++)
17        {
18          rb = new RowBoatV2(10 + i * 130, 75, 120, Color.YELLOW, i * 2 + 2);
19          sb = new SailBoatV4(10 + i * 170, 250, 110 + i * 15, Color.GREEN,
20                              200 + i * 20);
21          pb = new PowerBoat(20 + i * 160, 350, 120 + i * 15, Color.MAGENTA,
22                              400);
23          inventory[i * 3] = rb;
24          inventory[i * 3 + 1] = sb;
25          inventory[i * 3 + 2] = pb;
26        }
27
28        showGameBoard(gb);
29      }
30
31      public void draw(Graphics g)
32      {
33        for(int i = 0; i < 9; i++)
34        {
35          if(inventory[i] != null)
36          {
37            inventory[i].show(g);
38          }
39        }
40      }
41
42      public void upButton() //delete the RAM based inventory
43      {
44        for(int i = 0; i < 9; i++)
45          {
46              inventory[i] = null;
47          }
48      }
49      public void rightButton() //output inventory to the file
50      {
51        try
52        { FileOutputStream fos = new FileOutputStream("Inventory");
53          ObjectOutputStream outFile = new ObjectOutputStream(fos);
54
55          for(int i = 0; i < 9; i++)
56          {
57            if(inventory[i] != null)
58            {
59              outFile.writeObject(inventory[i]);
60            }
```

```
61          }
62          outFile.close();
63        }
64      catch(IOException e)
65        {
66        }
67      }
68
69    public void leftButton() //input inventory from the file
70      {
71        try
72        { FileInputStream fis = new FileInputStream("Inventory ");
73          ObjectInputStream inFile = new ObjectInputStream(fis);
74
75          for(int i = 0; i < 9; i++)
76          {
77              inventory[i] = (Boat) inFile.readObject();
78          }
79          inFile.close();
80        }
81      catch(IOException e)
82        {
83        }
84      catch(ClassNotFoundException e)
85        {
86        }
87      }
88  }
```

Figure 8.44
The application **SerializingObjects**.

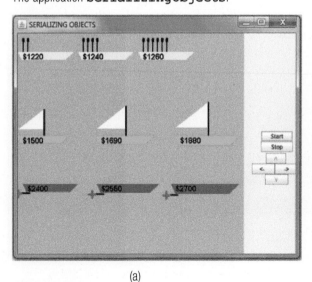
(a)

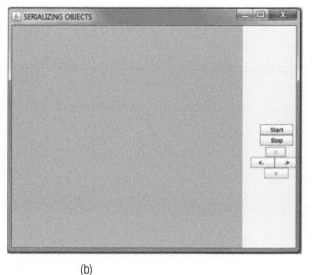
(b)

Figure 8.45
Outputs produced by the application **SerializingObjects**.

In order for an object to be serialized, its data members must be serializable. Primitive variables and strings are serializable, as are primitive arrays. The API documentation indicates that if a class implements the interface `Serializable`, then instances of the class are serializable; in addition, objects whose data members reference these serializable objects are serializable. The documentation of the API classes state which interfaces they implement. The API `Color` class, the `BigDecimal` and `BigInteger` classes, and many other API classes implement the interface `Serializable`.

The heading of the class whose objects are permitted to be serialized should indicate that it implements the interface `Serializable`, and all of its data members should be serializable. If any of the class's data members are not serializable, they should be declared `transient`.

The `Serializable` interface is imported from the API `java.io` package (line 3 of Figure 8.44), and it does not contain any method signatures to implement. Because all of the objects being serialized in the application `SerializingObjects` extend the class `Boat`, the `implements` clause was added to that class's heading (line 2 of Figure 8.19).

8.8 CHAPTER SUMMARY

Inheritance establishes a parent-child relationship between two classes in which all of the methods and data members of the parent class become part of the child class. Including the keyword `extends` in the class's heading of any Java class designates it as a child class, and the class name that follows it designates its parent class. A Java class can have one parent, and it can have multiple children unless the class is declared to be `final`. A child class also inherits the data members and methods of its parent's class's parent recursively. When a method is invoked on an object, the runtime environment begins its search for the method in the object's class and continues the search up the class's inheritance chain.

Functionality is added to an inherited class by coding additional data members and methods in the child class and by overriding an inherited method: that is, including a method in a child class that has the same signature as an inherited method. The translator will verify the signature of an overridden method if the child class includes the `@Override` directive before the signature of its version of the method. This is considered to be good programming practice. Inherited methods can be overloaded in the child class by changing the type or number of parameters in their parameter list.

To prevent a method from being overridden, the keyword `final` is used in its signature. When a class is declared to be `final`, it cannot be extended. Methods that enforce security on systems are usually declared to be `final` to prevent them from being overridden. An abstract class is used to collect data members and methods that are common to several classes into one parent class, which is considered to be good design practice. A class is designated to be abstract by including the keyword `abstract` in its heading before the keyword `class`. An abstract class cannot be instantiated.

Parent class constructors are not inherited, but they can be invoked as the first line of a child class constructor by coding the keyword `super` followed by an argument list. If the child does not explicitly invoke a parent constructor, the parent's default constructor is implicitly invoked. The child can also invoke inherited `public` or `protected` methods, including parent methods that were over-ridden, by beginning the invocation with the keyword **super** followed by a dot. This is often done in overridden methods to include the functionality of the parent method in the child's version of the method. Methods and data members whose access is designated `protected` are hidden from non-child classes contained in a separate package. Protected methods and data members of a class can be accessed by members in the same package as the class as well as by members in its subclass.

Polymorphism is a powerful feature of inheritance that is based on the fact that parent refer-ence variables can store the address of a child class object. This permits us to store references to any type of child object in one array of parent reference variables, and to execute each child's ver-sion of a method by invoking it on each element of the polymorphic array. It also permits a child class instance to be passed to, and processed by, a method whose parameter type is that of the parent class. The method can perform child class specific processing by using the `getClass` and `getName` methods and the `instanceof` operator to determine the name and class of the object passed to the method. Alternately, polymorphism also permits a parent method to invoke a child class method to perform child class specific processing. The parent class usually includes an ab-stract version of the method to impose a translator enforced requirement that its children provide an implementation of the method.

`Interfaces` are similar to `abstract classes` that only contain abstract methods and static final constants. Interfaces are used to share constants and to standardize the signatures and func-tionality of methods that perform common tasks on objects that may not share a common ancestor. When a class includes an `implements` clause in its heading, it must provide an implementation for every method defined in the interface. Alternately, it could extend a class (referred to as an `adapter class`) that provides empty implementations of the interface's methods and override one or more of the methods. A class can implement multiple interfaces, and interfaces play an impor-tant role in the implementation of generic methods and classes.

Objects can be transferred to and from disk files using the techniques called serializing and deserializing, respectively. Object serialization is the act of disassembling objects before writing them to a disk file, and object deserialization reassembles them after they are read from the disk file.

Knowledge Exercises

1. True or false:
   a) Parent class is to child class as base class is to super class.
   b) A parent class can inherit data members and methods from to a child class.
   c) A Java parent class can have multiple child classes that inherit its data members and methods.
   d) A parent class includes an `extends` clause in its heading to specify its child class.
   e) A child class inherits all the methods of its parent class including the parent's constructors.
   f) In Java, a child class may only extend (inherit from) one class.

g) Several child classes can inherit from the same parent.

h) Parent class constructors are not inherited, but they can be invoked from within the child class.

i) When two methods in an inheritance chain have the same name but different parameter lists, we say they are overridden.

j) An inherited method can be invoked by a method within a child class.

k) The keyword `final` is used to prevent a method from accidentally being overridden.

l) A class can implement more than one interface.

m) To extend a class, we must have the source code of the class.

n) By default, a parent's no-parameter construct is always invoked when a child class constructor begins execution.

2. Explain the difference between chain inheritance and multiple inheritance. Which one does Java support?

3. What are two advantages of using inheritance in the software design and implementation processes?

4. Give the statement used in a child class method to invoke an inherited two-parameter constructor.

5. Explain the restrictions imposed by these three types of access: public, private, and protected.

6. Give the statement used in a child class method to invoke an inherited method named `output` that has no parameters and is not overridden.

7. Give the statement used in a child class method to invoke an inherited method named `input` that has no parameters and is overridden.

8. Why should the `@Override` directive be used, and where is it coded?

9. How can we prevent a method from being overridden by a child class?

10. Give two reasons for overriding an inherited method.

11. Explain when you would overload a method instead of overriding it.

12. How can we prevent a class from being extended? Give an example of when we would want to impose this restriction.

13. Explain how an abstract class is used during the design process.

14. True or false:

   a) A parent reference variable can store the address of a child object.

   b) A child reference variable can store the address of a parent object.

   c) The address of a child object stored in a parent reference variable can be assigned to a child reference variable.

   d) When a method is invoked on a parent reference variable, the version of the method in the parent's class always executes.

   e) Child references variables can be passed to parent type parameters.

15. Give the declaration of a 200-element polymorphic array that can store instances of the child classes `Train` and `Airplane` that extend the class `Transporter`.

16. What are the differences between using `extends` and `implements` in a class's heading?

17. What can be included in an interface, and what is an advantage interfaces have over abstract classes?

18. What is an adapter class, and what is the advantage of extending an adapter class?

19. Explain what you would do to implement an adapter class for the interface `ManyMethods` that defines 20 method signatures.

Programming Exercises

1. Develop a UML diagram for a class named `Vehicle` that has three private data members: `price`, `color`, and `model`. Its methods will include a default and a three-parameter constructor, a `toString` method, `set` and `get` methods, and a method to input all of the values of its data members. Assume the class `Vehicle` extends the class `Transporter`.

2. Implement the class described in Exercise 1 and write an application that verifies your implementation. You can assume the `Transporter` class has no data members or methods.

3. Cars and trucks have a price, color, and model. Cars also have a radio type, and trucks have a maximum tonnage that they can haul. Develop the UML diagrams for a car and a truck class using the concepts of inheritance to reduce the time and effort required to develop the classes. All of the data members should be private, and each class should have a four-parameter constructor, a `toSting` method, `set` and `get` methods, and a method to input all of the values of its data members.

4. Implement the classes described in Exercise 3 and write an application that verifies your implementation. Then, change the application so it can be used to input a mix of 10 cars and trucks and output them to the system console.

5. Modify Exercise 4 to include the use of a polymorphic array.

6. Write an application that asks the user how many two-dimensional shapes (squares, rectangles, circles and ellipses) to draw on the game board, as well as the type, location, and color of each shape. Any of the circles or squares can be drawn filled or unfilled. After all inputs have been performed, the shapes will appear on the game board. The name of each shape will be displayed just above it, as will the formula to compute the shapes' area if the shape is a circle or a rectangle. When user strikes the S, R, C, or E key, all of the squares, rectangles, circles, or ellipses will alternately appear or disappear respectively. Your design should utilize the techniques of inheritance and polymorphism to minimize the effort required to produce the program.

7. Supermarkets carry three categories of items in their inventory: canned goods, flowers, and produce. Every item in the store has a name, a unit price, and a quantity in stock. In addition, produce items have an expiration date and a weight (because they are sold by the pound), and flower items have a color and a variety (i.e., house plant, garden plant, arrangement).

Develop UML diagrams for each of the three categories of items, canned goods, produce, and flowers, utilizing the techniques of inheritance and polymorphism to minimize the effort required to implement the classes, then implement the classes and verify their implementation. All of the data members should be private, and each class should have a constructor that can be passed the values of all of its data members, a `toString` method, `set` and `get` methods, a method to input all of the values of its data members, and a method to compute an item's price.

The price of an item is its base price plus a 15% profit margin. The base price of a canned-good item is just its unit price. The base price of a produce item is its unit price times its weight, and the base price a flower item is its unit price, except for arrangements which have a $5.00 preparation fee.

8. Design and implement a class called `SuperStore` that clients can use to declare a store that sells the canned goods, produce, and flowers described in Exercise 7. When an instance of this class is created, its constructor will be passed the number of items (canned goods plus produce plus flower items) that the store will carry, and the city location of the store (a string). The class will contain:

a) a method (named `Superstore(maxNumOfItems, city)`)

   to create an instance of a super store and specify its location and the maximum
   number of items the store will carry;

b) a method (named `addItem(anItem)`) to add a new canned good, produce, or flower item to the store's inventory (one method);

c) a method (named `OutputInventory()`) to output all the information for the entire inventory (all canned goods, produce, and flowers) to the system console preceded by the store's name and location,

d) a method (named `OutputGenericGroup(integerCategoryID)`) to output all the information for the entire inventory of either canned goods, produce, or flowers to the console, preceded by the store's location. Your design should include a polymorphic array to store the Superstore's inventory.

Note: Whenever an item is output, the output should include all of an item's input information, preceded by the item's generic category (e.g., *This item is a Canned Good*) and the item's calculated selling price.

9. Write an application that creates an instance of the superstore described in Exercise 8, allows the user to enter the initial inventory (items a–d below), and then repeatedly outputs the inventory (item e below).

a) What is the maximum number of items that will be in the new store's inventory?

b) What is the location of the store?

c) How many items will be in the initial inventory?

d) Repeatedly present a menu to allow the user to select the generic category of an item (an integer) and then request the information for that item until all items have been entered.

e) Repeatedly present the user with the following menu until a "3" is entered:

   Enter 1 to output all the information for all of the items in the inventory

   Enter 2 to output all the information for all of the items in a particular generic category

   Enter 3 to quit the program.

Enrichment

1. Why does Java not allow multiple inheritance? How is the diamond problem a consequence of multiple inheritance?

2. How can most of the features of multiple inheritance be simulated in Java?

RECURSION

9.1   *What is Recursion?* *418*

9.2   *Understanding a Recursive Method's Execution Path* . *421*

9.3   *Formulating and Implementing Recursive Algorithms*   *423*

9.4   *A Recursion Case Study: The Towers of Hanoi* *429*

9.5   *Problems with Recursion* *435*

9.6   *Chapter Summary* *444*

In this chapter

In this chapter we introduce recursion, a very powerful tool used in problem solving in which a problem's solution is expressed in terms of a simpler version of itself. The implementation of the recursive solution results in a method that invokes itself. We will examine the execution path of a recursive method, explore a methodology for discovering and implementing recursive algorithms, and practice this methodology on a set of progressively more difficult problems.

Although recursion can provide succinct and eloquent solutions to many problems, such as the Towers of Hanoi problem, the drawing of fractals, and the solution to many puzzles, the implementation of some recursive solutions can produce runtime problems. They can require large amounts of RAM memory and can result in unacceptably long execution times. We will identify the characteristics of recursion that cause these problems and learn a technique called dynamic programming used to solve one cause of unacceptably long execution times.

After successfully completing this chapter you should:

- Understand recursion and a recursive method's execution path
- Be able to design and implement a recursive solution to a problem by discovering its base case, a reduced solution, and a general solution
- Understand why recursive solutions require more time and storage than their iterative counterparts
- Know when to use a recursive solution and when an iterative solution would be more practical or efficient
- Understand how dynamic programming techniques can improve the efficiency of a recursive algorithm

9.1 WHAT IS RECURSION?

In general, recursion is defining something in simpler terms of itself, a property often referred to as self-similarity. In computer science, recursion is a technique used in the coding of methods and formulating algorithms. Usually, these methods or algorithms refer back to or are applied to themselves. When this technique is used to code a method, we say that the method is *recursive*. Before the execution of a recursive method ends, it either invokes itself or another method whose execution eventually leads to an invocation of the recursive method. Figure 9.1 illustrates both of these forms of recursion.

```java
public int aRecusiveMethod(int p)
{
   //code of the beginning
   //of the method

   int value = aRecusiveMethod(21)

   //remaining code of the method
}
```

A Method Reinvoked by Itself

```java
public void methodA()

 //beginning code
 //of the methodA

  methodB();

  //remaining code
  //of the method
}
```

```java
public void methodB()

 //beginning code
 //of the methodB

  methodC();

  //remaining code
  //of the method
}
```

```java
public void methodC()
{
 //beginning code
 //of the methodC

  methodA();

  //remaining code
  //of the method
}
```

A Method Eventually Reinvoked by
Another Method

A Reinvocation of `methodA`

Figure 9.1
The two forms of recursive methods.

In mathematics, recursion is often used to define functions and series that can also be defined without using recursion. For example, a non-recursive definition of ten factorial (10!) is:

$$10! = 10 * 9 * 8 * 7 * 6 * 5 * 4 * 3 * 2 * 1$$

This non-recursive definition of 10! can be generalized to a non-recursive definition of **n!** for any positive value of n.

Definition
The non-recursive definition of **n!** for values of $n \geq 0$
$n! \equiv n * (n - 1) * (n - 2) * (n - 3) * (n - 4) * .... * 3 * 2 * 1$ *and* $0! \equiv 1$

Alternately, the definition of 10! can be more succinctly stated recursively as

$$10! \equiv 10 * (10 - 1)! \ \ and \ \ 0! \equiv 1$$

This recursive definition can be generalized to a recursive definition of **n!** for any positive value of n.

Definition
The recursive definition of **n!**
$n! \equiv n * (n - 1)!$ *and* $0! \equiv 1$

The equivalence of the recursive and non-recursive definitions can be easily understood by examining the non-recursive definition of 10! and 9!

$$10! = 10 * \underbrace{9 * 8 * 7 * 6 * 5 * 4 * 3 * 2 * 1}_{(10 - 1)! = 9!}$$

$$9! = 9 * \underbrace{8 * 7 * 6 * 5 * 4 * 3 * 2 * 1}_{(9 - 1)!}$$

The last nine terms in the equation for 10! are contained in the right side of the equation for 9!, so 10! can certainly be expressed as 10 * 9!, which is the recursive definition of 10!. Having been shown this example, most of us would accept the fact that 9! can be used to calculate 10!, that is:

$$10! = 10 * 9!$$

This is the recursive way of calculating 10! which we now understand because we have realized that 9! = 9* 8 * 7 * 6 * 5 * 4 * 3 * 2 * 1. In effect, we have used the non-recursive definition of 9! to understand the recursive definition of 10!.

A recursive definition typically appears to define an entity in simpler terms of itself. The two uses of the factorial operator in the recursive definition of n! could be considered an example of this because the definition states that for positive values of n,

"n *factorial* is equal to n times n minus one *factorial*."

What makes this part of the recursive definition acceptable is that, although the word "factorial" is used in two phrases that make up the sentence ("n *factorial*" and "n minus 1 *factorial*"), the two phrases are different. In addition, the recursive definition of n! contains another crucial part: zero factorial is defined as one ($0! \equiv 1$).

The reason this second part of the definition is crucial to the validity of a recursive definition is that the recursive definition relies on being able to calculate $(n - 1)!$ in order to calculate n!. Knowing that the value of zero factorial is defined as one gives us the ability to calculate $(n - 1)!$. This fact may come as a surprise, but it becomes more obvious after a close examination of Figure 9.2, in which the recursive definition of n! is used in a progressive way to calculate (4)!. The right side of line 6 completes the calculation by substituting the value one (1), which is defined to be the value of zero factorial (0!)

The recursive definition of n factorial: $n! \equiv n * (n - 1)!$ *and* $0! \equiv 1$.

```
1    4! = 4 * (4 - 1)!
2       = 4 * 3!
3       = 4 * (3 * 2!)
4       = 4 * (3 * (2 * 1!))
5       = 4 * (3 * (2 * (1 * 0!)))
6       = 4 * (3 * (2 * (1 * 1)))
7       = 24
```

Figure 9.2
Calculating 4! using the recursive definition of n factorial.

The progression from lines 2 to 5 of Figure 9.2 is analogous to the progression of four phone calls shown at the top of Figure 9.3 initiated by you after your friend Evie asks you the value of four factorial. Remembering the recursive definition of n factorial, you know 4! is 4 * 3!. Because you don't know the value of 3!, you call your friend Logan and ask him the value of 3!. He realizes it is 3 * 2! and calls his friend Skyler to ask her the value of 2!, who calls Ryan to ask him the value of 1!. Finally, Ryan calls Breanne to ask her the value of 0!,

Figure 9.3
A progression of five phone calls to determine the value of four factorial.

This leads to the end of the sequence of four phone calls as depicted at the bottom-right of Figure 9.3. In response to Ryan's call, Breanne examines the definition of 0! and tells Ryan the value of 0! is *defined* as 1 and hangs up. Ryan multiplies 1 by the value of 0! that Breanne told him, 1, tells Skyler the value of 1! is 1, and hangs up his phone. This scenario continues with Skyler telling Logan the value of 2! is 2, and Logan telling you the value of 3! is 6. Finally, you multiply 4 by the value of 3! that Logan told you, 6, and you tell Evie the value of 4! is 24.

Recursion is not only used to more succinctly define formulas and series in mathematics, but it is also used to more succinctly define algorithms in computer science. It is for this reason that programming languages permit the two types of recursive invocations illustrated in Figure 9.1. If we were going to write a method that calculated n!, and the recursive definition of n! was used as the method's algorithm, then, when it was used to calculate 4!, the sequence of four phone calls illustrated in Figure 9.3 would be the method invoking itself four times. Evie asking you the value of 4! would be the initial invocation of the method.

Not all algorithms can be expressed recursively, but the effort expended in implementing those that can be is significantly less than implementing a non-recursive version of the algorithm. For this reason, an understanding of how recursive methods execute, how to formulate and implement a recursive algorithm, and some problems associated with the use of recursion is an essential tool to have in our programming toolbox.

9.2 UNDERSTANDING A RECURSIVE METHOD'S EXECUTION PATH

A recursive method is invoked, like any other method, by coding its name followed by an argument list used to pass values to the method's parameters. If the method returns a value, the value is either assigned to a variable for use in subsequent statements or used in the statement that contains the invocation of the method. Looking at the invocation statement, there is no way to determine if the method being invoked is recursive or not. Below is an invocation of a recursive method named `fact` that returns 4!, which could also be the invocation of a method with the same signature that is non-recursive:

```
long fourFactorial = fact(4);
```

The recursive version of this factorial method would differ from the non-recursive version within the implementation of the method. The recursive version implements the recursive definition of n factorial using the coding model shown at the top of Figure 9.1. Figure 9.4 shows the code of the method `fact` that calculates the value of n! recursively.

```
1   public long fact(int n)
2   {
3       long nMinus1Factorial, nFact;
4       if(n == 0) //return the definition of 0!
5       {
6           return 1;
7       }
8       else //calculate (n-1)! and then n!
9       {
10          nMinus1Factorial = fact(n-1); //fact invokes itself here
11          nFact = n * nMinus1Factorial;
12          return nFact;
13      }
14  }
```

Figure 9.4
A recursive method that calculates n!.

If the Boolean condition on line 4 of Figure 9.4 is `true`, line 6 returns 1, the value of 0! specified in the definition of n!. Otherwise, line 10 of the method invokes itself. Consistent with the first part of recursive definition of n!, it passes `fact` the value of n-1, and the method calculates and returns the value of (n-1)!. Then line 11 uses the returned value to calculate n factorial, which is returned on line 12.

Although the calculations performed by lines 10 and 11 are coded sequentially, they do not execute sequentially because line 10 of the initial invocation of the method initiates the first of the progression of four phone calls depicted at the top of Figure 9.3. When calculating 4!, the first of these phone calls (or, more accurately, recursive *invocations*) is passed the value 3 (i.e., 4 - 1).

The three subsequent recursive invocations of the method by line 10 pass the values 2, 1, and finally 0 to the method. The line-by-line execution sequence of the method to reach this point, beginning with the initial invocation of the method, is given below and is represented by the red arrows in Figure 9.5.

Lines 1, 2, 3, 4, 8, 9, 10 //which passes the *first* recursive invocation the value 3
Lines 1, 2, 3, 4, 8, 9, 10 //which passes the *second* recursive invocation the value 2
Lines 1, 2, 3, 4, 8, 9, 10 //which passes the *third* recursive invocation the value 1
Lines 1, 2, 3, 4, 8, 9, 10 //which passes the *fourth* recursive invocation the value 0

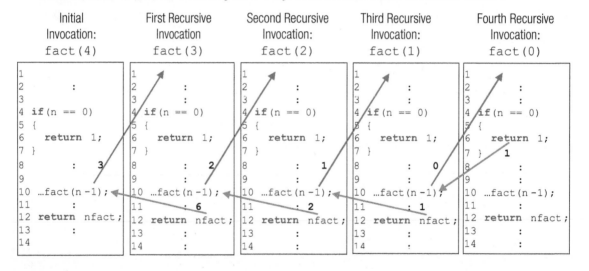

Figure 9.5
The execution sequence of the invocations of the method **fact** to calculate 4!

Because the fourth recursive invocation of the method is passed the value zero, its execution sequence is lines 1, 2, 3, 4, 5, and 6 because the Boolean condition on line 4 for this execution of the method evaluates to `true`. As a result, line 6 returns the value 1 (0!) to line 10 of the third recursive invocation (as indicated by the green arrow on the right side of Figure 9.5). Then lines 11 and 12 of the third, second, and first recursive invocations execute, returning the values 1, 2, and 6 (as indicated by the other three green arrows in Figure 9.5). Finally, lines 11 and 12 of the initial invocation of the method execute and return 24 = 4 * 6.

Two important observations to make from an examination of Figure 9.5 are that:

1. because of the recursive invocations spawned by line 10 of the initial invocation of the method, a considerable amount of time is required to complete the execution of this line of code

2. the recursive invocations of the method would have continued had it not been for the fact that the fourth recursive invocation was passed the value zero

Armed with an understanding of the execution path of recursive methods, we will discuss the techniques used to discover recursive algorithms and the nuances of implementing them.

9.3 FORMULATING AND IMPLEMENTING RECURSIVE ALGORITHMS

Most people do not possess an innate ability to think recursively. When shown the non-recursive and recursive definitions of n factorial, most of us would say that we are able to understand the non-recursive definition, but we are confused by its recursive counterpart. Therefore, it should come as no surprise that most of us have trouble recognizing that there is a recursive solution to a problem and have even more trouble trying to discover the algorithm even after we are told that one does exist.

Fortunately, we can learn to think recursively because the discovery of recursive algorithms can be methodized, and once discovered, many recursive algorithms are implemented in a very similar way. After gaining a basic understanding of the methodized process, lots of practice facilitates the learning curve.

9.3.1 The Base Case, Reduced Problem, and General Solution

The recursive-algorithm discovery process is broken into four discovery steps:

1. identify the *base case* or cases
2. identify the *reduced problem* or problems
3. identify the *general solution*
4. combine the base case, reduced problem, and general solution into a recursive algorithm

We have already used a base case, reduced problem, and general solution in the program presented in Figure 9.4 without identifying them by name. The base case, reduced problem, and general solution of the recursive algorithm for n factorial implemented in Figure 9.4 are identified in Table 9.1.

Prior to coding the method shown in Figure 9.4, we did not discover these three parts of the recursive algorithm for n!. They were discovered by the person that originally formulated the recursive definition of n!, who was probably born with the ability to think recursively. We simply discussed a method that implemented this definition of n! to gain insights into the execution path of a recursive method. This was a useful exercise because an understanding of the method's execution path, and an awareness of these three parts of the recursive definition of n!, do facilitate an understanding of the discovery process.

Table 9.1
The Base Case, Reduced Problem, and General Solution for n!

Base Case	Reduced Problem	General Solution
$0! \equiv 1$	$(n-1)!$	$n * (n-1)!$

Discovering the Base Case

The recursive-algorithm discovery process begins with the identification of the problem's base case. To discover the base case, we search for a particular instance of the problem whose solution is known. For example if we were trying to discover the recursive algorithm for n factorial, we would ask ourselves if there is a particular value of n: 0, or 1, or 2, or 3, or 4, etc., whose factorial value is known. Most people know that 0! is defined as 1, which is the base case for n factorial. The base case for another problem, x^n, is also a definition: x^0, which is also defined as 1. For some problems, the base case is not a definition but a trivial case of the problem that most of us know, such as $1 * 1 = 1$. Another example of a trivial base case is associated with the problem of outputting a string of n characters in reverse order. In this case, when n is one, we simply output the string.

When the problem involves an integer n, often (as we have seen) the base case is the solution to the problem when n = 0 or, for some problems, when n = 1. The determination of the base case is a crucial first step in the discovery process because it is used to discover the reduced problem, which is then used to discover the general solution. In addition, when we implement the algorithm, as shown on line 4 of Figure 9.4 and on the far right side of Figure 9.5, it is the base case that halts the progression of recursive invocations and is sometimes referred to as the *stopping condition*. Some problems, as we will see, contain multiple base cases.

Discovering the Reduced Problem

Identifying the reduced problem is often the most difficult part of the four-step discovery process. Usually, it can be identified by considering the following three criteria. The reduced problem:

1. is a problem similar to the original problem
2. is usually between the original problem and the base case and is usually closer to the original problem than it is to the base case
3. becomes the base case for all versions of the original problem when *progressively reduced*

For example, the reduced problem for n! is $(n-1)!$. Clearly, this is similar to the original problem in that it also involves n and uses the factorial operator. It is between the original problem and the base case (0!), and for most values of n (n > 2), it is closer to the original problem than it is to the base case. This would be an acceptable reduced problem if progressive reductions caused it to become the base case for all values of n.

By progressive reductions, we mean that we repeatedly apply the relationship between the candidate reduced problem and the original problem to the reduced problem to produce new versions of the problem. For n!, the relationship is that the number used in the reduced problem (n − 1) is one less than the number used in the original problem (n). Applying this relationship to the reduced problem (n − 1)!, the new version of the problem becomes ((n − 1) − 1)! = (n − 2)! on the first reduction. Subsequent new versions of the problem are ((n − 2) − 1)! = (n − 3)!, (n − 4)!, (n − 5)!, etc. Because this progressive reduction of (n − 1)! for any positive value of n will eventually become the base case, (n − 1)! is an acceptable reduced problem for n!.

An example of an unacceptable reduced problem for n! is (n − 2)!, although it satisfies most of our criteria. It is a problem similar to the original problem, it is between the base case (0!) and the original problem, and it is also closer to the original problem than it is to the base case. What makes it unacceptable is that progressive reductions, for *odd* values of n, do not result in the base case. For example, for n = 7 the reduced problem would be (7 − 2)! = 5!, and its progressive reductions would be:

$$(5 − 2)! = 3!, \quad (3 − 2)! = 1!, \quad (1 − 2)! = -1!.$$

The reductions skip over the base case, zero factorial. They never become the base case for odd values of n. Another unacceptable candidate reduced problem is (n + 1)!. For n = 7, the reduced problem would be (7 + 1)! = 8!, and its progressive reductions would be 8!, 9!, 10!, 11!, etc. The result would be an infinite series that never becomes the base case.

Some problems, as we will see, contain multiple reduced problems.

Discovering the General Solution

The general solution is the solution to the original problem. To discover the general solution, we think of a way to solve the original problem assuming that we have already found a valid reduced problem. That is, we think of a way of use the solution to the reduced problem in the solution of the original problem.

In the case of n!, this translates into the question of how (n − 1)! can be used to calculate n factorial. The answer is multiplying (n − 1)! by n, so the general solution for n! is n × (n − 1)!

The first three steps of the recursive-algorithm discovery process are summarized in Table 9.2.

9.3.2 Implementing Recursive Algorithms

Once we have discovered the base case, reduced problem, and general solution for a particular problem, they are combined into a recursive algorithm. Finding the correct combination usually involves some creativity, which comes naturally to some people while the rest of us have to develop this creative ability through practice.

For many problems, the base case, reduced problem, and general solution are combined in a similar way. For a subset of these problems, they are combined in an identical way, which is depicted in the flow chart shown in Figure 9.6. By working with this subset of problems, we will begin to develop the ability to think recursively. Continued practice with the super set of problems

Step	Process	Comments
2: Reduced Problem Discovery	Search for a version of the problem that: • is similar to the original problem • usually is between the original problem and the base case *and* closer to the original problem • when progressively reduced becomes the base case for *all versions* of the original problem	The reduced problem for n! is $(n-1)!$ $n! \leq (n-1)! \leq 0!$ The progressive reductions of $(n-1)!$ are: $(n-1)!, (n-2)!, (n-3)!$, etc., which becomes the base case, 0!, for all values of n.
3: General Solution Discovery	Think of a way to solve the original problem, assuming that we have already found a solution to the reduced problem.	The reduced problem is used in the general solution, e.g., $n! = n * (n-1)!$

will further develop our skills.

The algorithm shown in Figure 9.6 is most easily understood by comparing it to a particular implementation of it: the code of the method to recursively compute n! presented in Figure 9.4. The problem of calculating n! is one of the problems in the subset of problems whose three components (base case, reduced problem, and general solution) can be combined exactly as shown in Figure 9.6.

Figure 9.7 represents the code of this method with comments added to it to aid in an understanding of the manner in which the algorithm combines its three components. These comments refer to the blue-font numbers shown on the left side of each of the flow-chart symbols shown in Figure 9.6.

The `if` statement coded on line 4 of Figure 9.7 represents the question in symbol 2 of the flowchart, which is used to decide if the problem to be solved is the base case. The `return` statement (line 6) inside the `if` statement's code block represents flowchart symbols 3 and 4 that terminate the algorithm after returning the base case solution.

Symbol 5 of the flowchart is typically the most confusing part of the algorithm because it is the most confusing part of recursion. It calculates the solution to the reduced problem using this same algorithm. It is the recursive part of the algorithm. The right side of line 10 implements symbol 5 by re-invoking the method and passing it the reduced problem. As we have learned, this symbol of the flowchart can occupy a significant portion of the algorithm's execution time. Every time it is entered, it spawns another execution of the algorithm, beginning at symbol 1, to calculate the solution to a new (reduced) factorial problem.

After flowchart symbol 5 calculates the solution to the reduced problem, symbol 6 uses it to calculate the general solution to the original problem. Line 11 of Figure 9.7 implements flowchart symbol 6. After symbol 7 returns the problem's solution (line 12 of Figure 9.7), symbol 8 ends the algorithm.

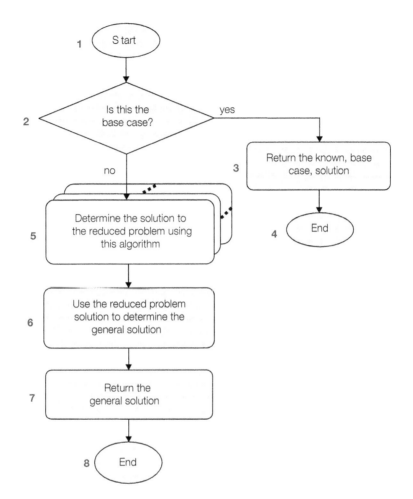

Figure 9.6
A template for some recursive algorithms.

```
1    public long fact(int n)
2    {
3      long nMinus1Factorial
4      if(n == 0) //Flow chart symbol 2
5      {
6        return 1; //Flow chart symbols 3 and 4
7      }
8      else
9      {
10       nMinus1Factorial = fact(n-1); //Flow chart symbol 5
11       nFact = n * nMinus1Factorial; //Flow chart symbol 6
12       return nFact; //Flow chart symbols 7 and 8
13     }
14   }
```

Figure 9.7
A recursive method that calculates n! commented to correlate to the algorithm presented in Figure 9.6.

9.3.3 Practice Problems

Now that we have acquired a basic understanding of recursion, the best way to extend our ability to think recursively is to apply our newly acquired skills to a set of problems that can be solved recursively. The problems presented in Table 9.3 are tabulated in an order intended to extend these skills in an incremental manner. As we move from the problems at the top of the table to those at the bottom of the table, their recursive solutions become increasingly dissimilar to the recursive solution of n!. For this reason, which is consistent with the adage that "practice makes perfect," it is best to work our way through all of the problems in the order in which they are tabulated. Table 9.4 (included in the Chapter Summary) presents the base case, reduced problem, and general solution for each of the problems presented in Table 9.3

Table 9.3
Several Problems That Have Recursive Solutions in Difficulty Order

Problem	Base Case	Reduced Problem	General Solution
Factorial of a positive integer, n!	$0! \equiv 1$	$(n-1)!$	$n * (n-1)!$
A number x raised to a positive integer, x^n			
Sum of the integers from 1 to n			
Product of two positive integers, $m \times n$			
Output an n character string, s, in reverse order			
Problems with Multiple Base Cases and Reduced Problems			
Generate the nth term of the Fibonacci Sequence, fn			
Find the greatest common divisor of two positive integers m and n, GCD(m, n), for m > n			
A Problem with Multiple Base Cases			
Search a sorted list of items for the item I			
A Problem that Uses the Reduced Problem Twice			
Towers of Hanoi: Move n rings from tower A to tower B using tower C			

As noted in the table, some problems have multiple base cases and reduced problems, and one problem uses its reduced problem twice in its general solution. As we have learned, the starting point is the determination of a problem's base case, then its reduced problem, and then its general solution. They should be entered into a copy of the last three columns of the table below the column entries for n!, and in most cases, they can be combined into a recursive solution using the algorithm depicted in Figure 9.6.

The correctness of the discovered base case, reduced problem, and general solutions should be verified by comparing them to the entries in Table 9.4 in the Chapter Summary. Implementing each problem's recursive solution before moving on to the next problem is highly recommended because it augments the learning process.

It is not unusual in the beginning, or at some other point in this learning process, not to be able to discover one or more of the three components of the recursive solution (i.e., its base case, reduced problem, or general solution). When this is the case, it is still useful to implement the recursive algorithm using the component(s) presented in Table 9.4. Consistent with this idea, many students begin by skipping the discovery process and simply implement a recursive method to calculate x^n using the components given in the second row of Table 9.4 and the flow chart presented in Figure 9.6.

A description of the last problem in Table 9.3, The Towers of Hanoi, is given in the beginning of the next section.

9.4 A RECURSION CASE STUDY: THE TOWERS OF HANOI

The recursive solution to the Towers of Hanoi problem is a good example of the simplicity and power of recursive algorithms. Its recursive solution can be implemented as seven lines of code. Applying the techniques we have learned to produce a recursive solution, this problem will serve as a good capstone to our discussion of how to formulate and implement recursive algorithms. Not only will this reinforce our knowledge of the discovery process, but the implementation of the problem's recursive algorithm will introduce an often-used nuance into the parameter list of a recursive method that is not used in the solutions of the other problems presented in Tables 9.3 and 9.4.

Statement of the Problem

The problem was conceived by the French mathematician Eduardo Lucas in 1883. It involves three towers and a set of n disks or rings, each with different diameters. The original legend claimed that the Brahmins of an ancient Indian temple were charged with moving 64 golden disks, and when the last one was in its final place, the world would come to an end.[1] As we will see, there is no need to worry about this because the disks had to be moved in a specified order, and if one disk were move per second it would take 585 billion years (2^{64} - 1 seconds) to relocate the disks.

The left side and right sides of Figure 9.8 illustrate the problem's starting and ending points for four rings (n = 4). The rings are initially stacked in decreasing order by size on one of the towers, which we will refer to as the starting tower. The left side of Figure 9.8 shows four rings stacked on a starting tower named A. The right side of the figure shows the four rings relocated to the tower named B, which we will refer to as the destination tower. We will refer to the third tower shown in the figure, whose name is C, as the extra tower.

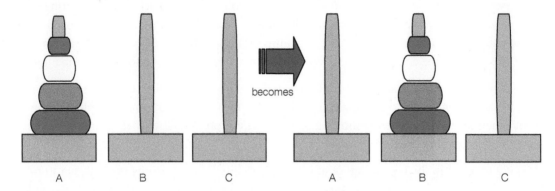

Figure 9.8
The Towers of Hanoi problem's starting and ending points using four rings.

The solution to the problem is a specification of the order in which to move the rings that will relocate all of them from a designated starting tower (tower A) to a designated destination tower (tower B) without violating the following two conditions:

1. Only one ring (a top ring) can be moved at a time, and it must be placed on a tower before another ring is moved.

2. A larger ring cannot be placed on top of a smaller ring.

These conditions imply that when the problem is solved, the rings will be stacked on the designated destination tower in decreasing size order, as shown on the right side of Figure 9.8. The problem solutions (i.e., the order in which the rings are moved to relocate them from tower A to tower B) for two, three, and four rings are given in Figure 9.9. Figure 9.10 depicts the three-ring solution.

Notice that there is a pattern to predicting the number of moves that will be needed for n rings. For two rings, there are three moves, for three rings, there are seven moves, and for four rings, there are fifteen moves. In general, the minimum number of moves for n rings will be $2^n - 1$. This is why moving the legendary 64 golden disks would require $2^{64} - 1$ moves and extraordinarily long time.

The Base Case

We have learned that the formulation of a recursive solution to a problem begins with a search for its base case: a known, defined, or trivial solution to the problem. We have also learned that when the problem involves n items, a good place to begin the search is when n = 0 or n = 1. This problem involves n rings, so we will begin by considering the case when there are zero rings. This is a legitimate base case for this problem because the trivial solution would be to do nothing. An alternate base case is when n = 1 because if we were asked to move one ring from tower A to tower B, we would simply state "move the top ring on tower A to tower B." Both of these are trivial solutions because most people would know them, and they do not require a consideration of the two conditions of the Towers of Hanoi problem. Either of these base cases can be used in the recursive solution to the problem. The n = 1 base case is the one that appears in Table 9.4.

Two-Ring Solution	Four-Ring Solution
1- move one ring from tower A to tower C	1- move one ring from tower A to tower C
2- move one ring from tower A to tower B	2- move one ring from tower A to tower B
3- move one ring from tower C to tower B	3- move one ring from tower C to tower B
	4- move one ring from tower A to tower C
Three-Ring Solution	5- move one ring from tower B to tower A
1- move one ring from tower A to tower B	6- move one ring from tower B to tower C
2- move one ring from tower A to tower C	7- move one ring from tower A to tower C
3- move one ring from tower B to tower C	8- move one ring from tower A to tower B
4- move one ring from tower A to tower B	9- move one ring from tower C to tower B
5- move one ring from tower C to tower A	10- move one ring from tower C to tower A
6- move one ring from tower C to tower B	11- move one ring from tower B to tower A
7- move one ring from tower A to tower B	12- move one ring from tower C to tower B
	13- move one ring from tower A to tower C
	14- move one ring from tower A to tower B
	15- move one ring from tower C to tower B

Figure 9.9
Three Towers of Hanoi problem solutions.

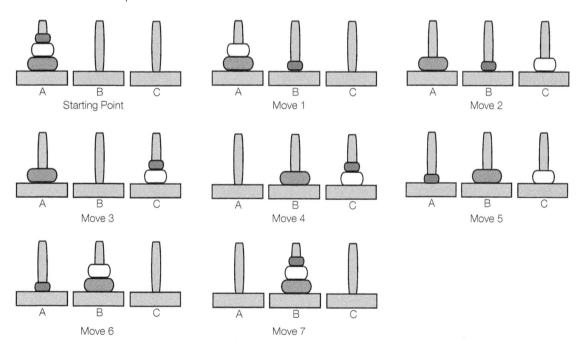

Figure 9.10
The solution to the three-ring Towers of Hanoi problem.

> **NOTE** *Towers of Hanoi base case:*
> *n = 1: Move 1 ring from one tower to another tower*

Reduced Problem

To discover the reduced problem, we can use a new tool often employed when the problem involves n items. We try to solve very simple versions of the problem, not quite as trivial as the base case, but close to it. Then, we examine the solutions looking for similarities and try to generalize the similarities into a reduced problem. For example, suppose we were able to produce the two- and three-ring solutions shown in Figure 9.9, which many non-recursive thinking people could probably do. If we are visual learners, it helps to sketch out each step of the solutions, as has been done in Figure 9.10 for the three-ring solution.

Examining Figure 9.10 and the two-ring solution in Figure 9.9, we notice that just before the half-way point of both solutions (move 4 of Figure 9.10 and move 2 of the two-ring solution), all of the rings except for one have been moved to tower C. Examining the moves made after the midpoint of both solutions (moves 5–7 in Figure 9.10 and move 3 of the two-ring solution in Figure 9.9), we realize that these also move all of the rings except for one.

Because the ability to move all but one ring from one tower to another tower is common to both the two- and three-ring solutions, perhaps this could be the reduced problem. When generalized, it becomes: move n-1 rings from one tower to another tower. This generalization does satisfy the three criteria for a reduced problem restated below and is the one that appears in Table 9.4:

1. It is similar to the original problem: move n rings from one tower to another tower.
2. It is closer to the original problem than either of the problem's base cases (n = 0 and n = 1), and it is between the original problem and these base cases.
3. When progressively reduced, it does eventually become one of the base cases: move one or move zero rings.

Another way of discovering this reduced solution would be to compare the illustration of the starting point in Figure 9.10 to the illustration of move 3 in that figure and to compare the illustrations of move 4 to move 7. From these comparisons, we would be likely to observe that the problem could be solved if we knew how to move n-1 rings, and then conclude that we need to make a call to a friend who knows how to move n-1 rings from one tower to another tower.

> **NOTE**
> *Towers of Hanoi reduced problem:*
> *Move n-1 rings from one tower to another tower.*

The General Solution

To discover the general solution, we ask ourselves how we can use the reduced problem to solve the original problem. In the case of the Towers of Hanoi, this question becomes: "how can we use the ability to move *n-1* rings to solve the problem of moving n rings from one tower to another tower?" The answer can often be found by examining the solutions developed to the very simple versions of the problem previously used to determine the reduced problem.

The three move sequences on both sides of move 4 in Figure 9.10, which shows the n = 3 solution, represent a movement of 3-1 rings from one tower to another. This means that if move 4 of Figure 9.10 was preceded and followed with a version of the reduced problem, it would be the general solution of the n = 3 ring problem:

1. use the reduced problem to move 2 rings from tower A to C (moves 1–3)
2. move 4 (move 1 ring from tower A to tower B)
3. use the reduced problem to move 2 rings from tower C to B (moves 5–7)

Once we have found a way to use the reduced problem to solve one of the simpler problems used in the discovery of the reduced problem (e.g., the 3 ring problem), its use is extrapolated to the n ring general solution. This is the general solution presented in Table 9.4.

NOTE
Towers of Hanoi general solution:
1. use the reduced problem to move n-1 rings from tower A to C
2. move 1 ring from tower A to tower B
3. use the reduced problem to move n-1 rings from tower C to B

Implementation

The base case, reduced problem, and general solution of this problem can be combined into a recursive algorithm using the flow chart shown in Figure 9.6. The application presented in Figure 9.11 implements this algorithm in a method named `hanoi` (lines 8–24). The signature of the method contains four parameters: the number of rings to be moved, followed by the name of the starting tower, the name of the destination tower, and the name of the third tower. It is invoked on line 5 to output the moves required to transfer four rings from tower A to tower B. The output produced by the program is shown in Figure 9.12.

As the names of the last three parameters in the signatures of the `hanoi` method on lines 8 and 9 indicate, the method uses the tower name passed to its parameter (`fromTower`) as the starting tower, and the tower names passed to the method's second and third parameters (`toTower and thirdTower`) are used as the destination tower and the extra tower, respectively. As a result, when the method is invoked recursively on line 20 of the general solution to move all but the bottom ring from the starting tower to the extra tower, the second argument used in the invocation is the parameter `thirdTower`, and the last argument is the parameter `toTower`. This effectively swaps roles of the extra tower and the destination tower during this invocation of the method, and n-1 rings are relocated to the extra tower.

Similarly, when the method is invoked on line 23 of the general solution to move the n-1 rings placed on the extra tower from the extra tower to the destination tower, the first argument used in the invocation is the method's parameter `thirdTower`, and the last argument is the method's parameter `fromTower`. This effectively swaps roles of the extra tower and the starting tower during this invocation of the method.

When the method `hanoi` is invoked, and line 12 detects the base case (the value passed to `nRings` is 1), the output produced by lines 14–15 includes the names of the towers passed to the method's first and second parameters `fromTower` and `toTower`. This ensures that when the invocations on lines 20 and 23 degenerate to the base case, the values of the first and second arguments passed to the method will be included in the base case's output (lines 14–15).

```
1    public class TowersOfHanoi
2    {
3      public static void main(String[] args)
4      {
5        hanoi(4, "A", "B", "C"); //output the solution for four rings
6      }
7
8      public static void hanoi(int nRings, String fromTower,
9                               String toTower, String thirdTower);
10     {
11
12       if(nRings == 1) //base case
13       {
14         System.out.println("move one ring from tower " + fromTower +
15                            " to tower " + toTower);
16         return;
17       }
18
19       //general solution
20       hanoi(nRings-1, fromTower, thirdTower, toTower); //reduced problem
21       System.out.println("move one ring from tower " + fromTower +
22                          " to tower " + toTower);
23       hanoi(nRings-1, thirdTower, toTower, fromTower); //reduced problem
24     }
25   }
```

Figure 9.11
The application **TowersOfHanoi**.

```
move one ring from tower A to tower C
move one ring from tower A to tower B
move one ring from tower C to tower B
move one ring from tower A to tower C
move one ring from tower B to tower A
move one ring from tower B to tower C
move one ring from tower A to tower C
move one ring from tower A to tower B
move one ring from tower C to tower B
move one ring from tower C to tower A
move one ring from tower B to tower A
move one ring from tower C to tower B
move one ring from tower A to tower C
move one ring from tower A to tower B
move one ring from tower C to tower B
```

Figure 9.12
The output produced by the application **TowersOfHanoi**.

9.5 PROBLEMS WITH RECURSION

Because only a small percentage of the population has an innate ability to think recursively, most of us need to be trained in how to discover and implement recursive algorithms. To a certain extent, the discovery and implementation process can be methodized, but a good deal of effort is necessary to become a good recursive programmer.

Another problem with recursion is that applications that use recursive algorithms tend to run more slowly. If two versions of the same application were developed, one that used a recursive algorithm and one that used a non-recursive algorithm, the non-recursive version would typically run faster. The difference in speed is due to the manner in which modern computer systems transfer execution to, and return from, an invoked method and the larger number of method invocations that recursive algorithms typically perform by repeatedly invoking themselves.

Every time a method is invoked, whether or not it is recursive, the runtime environment has to suspend the execution of the program to perform tasks associated with the invocation. Typically, these tasks include allocating the memory for the invoked method's parameters and local variables and transferring the value of the arguments into these parameters. Not only does this take time, but each method invocation requires additional RAM memory for the storage of the method's parameters and local variables.

Storage must also be allocated to save the contents of the CPU registers and the invoking method's return address to complete the invoking method's execution. Java stores this information in an area of storage called the *run-time stack*. After each invocation completes its execution, the invoking method cannot continue its execution until the information is retrieved from the run-time stack and stored in the CPU's registers.

As shown in Figure 9.5, the recursive method to calculate n! invokes itself four times to calculate 4!; to compute 40! requires 40 invocations, and n! requires n invocations. A non-recursive, or *iterative*, version of the method is given in Figure 9.13. It does not issue any method invocations during its execution regardless of the value of n. Its speed advantage over the recursive version increases with increasing values of n. In addition, it does not require storage allocated for the parameters, local variables, CPU register values and return addresses associated with the additional invocations of the recursive version of the method.

```
1    public static long factIterative(int n)
2    {
3      long nFact = 1;
4      for(int i = n; i >= 1; i--)
5      {
6        nFact = nFact * i;
7      }
8      return nFact;
9    }
```

Figure 9.13
An iterative method that calculates n!.

The number of invocations issued by some recursive algorithms can make the recursive solution incalculable from a time viewpoint. The implementation of the recursive definition of the **Fibonacci sequence** is one such example.

Definition

The recursive definition of the terms of the **Fibonacci sequence**:

$f_1 \equiv 1$ and $f_2 \equiv 1$;

for $n \geq 2$: $f_n = f_{n-1} + f_{n-2}$

Consistent with this definition, the first eight terms of the sequence are 1, 1, 2, 3, 5, 8, 13, and 21. This recursive definition has two base cases, $f_1 \equiv 1$ and $f_2 \equiv 1$, two reduced problems, f_{n-1} and f_{n-2}, and its general solution is $f_n = f_{n-1} + f_{n-2}$. While this may look innocent, when these base cases, reduced problems, and the general solution are combined as shown in Figure 9.6 and implemented into a recursive method, the number of recursive invocations made to calculate the 40th term in the sequence, f40, is 204,668,309. The reason there are this many invocations is illustrated in Figure 9.14, where the arrows in the figure should be interpreted as the method invoking itself to calculate a term of the series. Referring to the top of the figure, to calculate f40, the method is invoked to calculate f39 and f38. To calculate f39, the method is invoked to calculate f38 and f37. As shown in the remainder of the figure, during the recursive definition of f40, f39 is calculated once, but f38 is calculated twice, f37 three times, f36 five times, f35 eight times, etc.

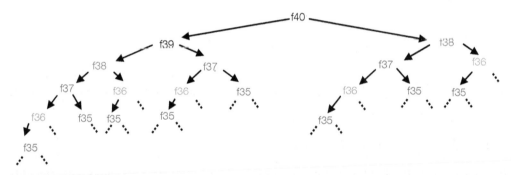

Figure 9.14
Some of the 204,668,309 invocations required to calculate the 40th term of the Fibonacci sequence.

Another problem with recursion is that during a recursive method's execution, if the recursive chain of invocations gets too long, the storage required for the return addresses and CPU register contents can exceed the capacity of the run-time stack. When this happens, the method's execution will produce a runtime `StackOverflowException` error, and unless the exception is caught, the application will be terminated. Below is a summary of the problems with recursion that were discussed in this section:

1. Most programmers need to be trained in how to discover and implement recursive algorithms.
2. The number of recursive invocations issued by a recursive method can make it significantly slower than its iterative counterpart.

3. Methods that implement recursive algorithms can require prohibitively large amounts of RAM storage.

4. Recursive methods are prone to terminating in a `StackOverflowException` error.

One solution to the last three problems will be discussed in Section 9.5.2.

9.5.1 When to Use Recursion

In light of the problems associated with recursion, and considering the fact that recursive algorithms have an iterative counterpart, the question of when we should use recursion in our programs arises. The short answer is when the recursive algorithm significantly reduces the algorithm-discovery and implementation time, and the additional storage requirements and execution time associated with a recursive method are acceptable.

This is not the case for most of the problems presented in Table 9.3. Certainly, the first five problems presented in the table would normally not be coded using recursion because their non-recursive (iterative) solution is easy to discover and simple to code. They were included in the table to facilitate the learning process. On the other end of the spectrum, recursion is usually used to find a greatest common divisor and in the solution to the Towers of Hanoi problem. The following three-line general solution of the Towers of Hanoi is much simpler than a non-recursive solution to the problem:

1. move n-1 rings from tower A to tower C
2. move one ring from tower A to tower B
3. move n-1 rings from tower C to tower B

Other common uses of recursion include the solution of puzzles, such as mazes, the Sudoku puzzle, the Eight Queens problem, the Knight's Tour, the searching and sorting of lists of data, and the drawing of fractals.

Fractals and the Sierpinsky Triangle

Fractals are mathematical or geometric objects that have the property of self-similarity, that is, each part of the object is a smaller or reduced copy of itself. Geometric fractals are implicitly recursive because they begin by drawing a shape and then extend the drawing by repeatedly redrawing the shape at smaller and smaller scales. Generally speaking, the repetitions are infinite, although the drawing process is normally terminated when the shapes become too small to see.

Given an equilateral triangle, the Sierpinsky fractal is produced by creating three equilateral triangles whose vertices are the three original vertices and the midpoints of the sides adjacent to these vertices. This process is then repeated recursively for the three resulting equilateral triangles. The first three steps in this process are shown in Figure 9.15.

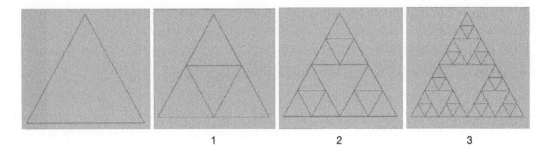

Figure 9.15
The first three steps in the creation of a Sierpinsky Triangle.

The fractal shown in Figures 9.16 is a Sierpinsky Triangle on which the process has been repeated seven times. It was created by the application RecursiveFractal shown in Figure 9.17. Line 20 of the application invokes the recursive method drawSierpinsky (lines 31–47) to draw the fractal. The invocation passes the method the number of times to repeat the Sierpinsky process (plus one for the drawing of the original triangle), the vertices of the original triangle (declared as Point objects on lines 8, 9, and 10), and the graphics object g because the method draws the triangles (lines 39–41). The vertex at the top of Figure 9.16 is p1, the lower left vertex is p2, and the lower right vertex is p3 (lines 8-10).

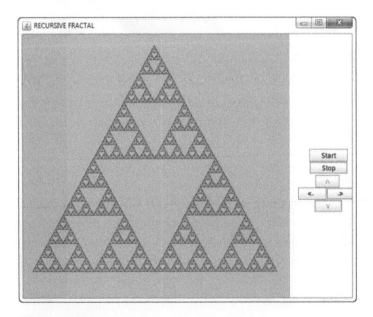

Figure 9.16
A six-iteration Sierpinsky fractal.

Line 34 tests for the base case, which is when the number of invocations of the method has been decremented to zero by line 42. The general solution is in lines 44–46, which recursively invokes the method to draw three triangles. The vertices of these triangles are one of the vertices passed to the method and the midpoints of the lines joining the other two vertices. Each of these three invocations spawns 363 additional invocations of the drawSierpinsky method for the fractal drawn by the application. The locations of the midpoints of the sides of the triangle passed as the third and fourth arguments on lines 44–46 are calculated by the midPoint method (lines 23–29). The two integer data members of the API Point class (x, y) are public data members, which eliminates the need to invoke set and get methods on lines 26 and 27.

The recursive execution sequence of the lines 44–46 draws all of the blue lines that make up the mostly blue large upper triangle shown in Figure 9.16, before the mostly blue large lower left triangle is drawn, which is drawn before the mostly blue large lower right triangle is drawn.

```
1    import edu.sjcny.gpv1.*;
2    import java.awt.*;
3
4    public class RecursiveFractal extends DrawableAdapter
5    {
6      static RecursiveFractal ge = new RecursiveFractal();
7      static GameBoard gb = new GameBoard(ge, "RECURSIVE FRACTAL");
8      static Point p1 = new Point(250, 70); //vertices of the 1st triangle
9      static Point p2 = new Point(25, 460);
10     static Point p3 = new Point(475, 460);
11
12     public static void main(String args[])
13     {
14       showGameBoard(gb);
15     }
16
17     public void draw(Graphics g)
18     {
19       g.setColor(Color.BLUE);
20       drawSierpinsky(8, p1, p2, p3, g);
21     }
22
23     public static Point midPoint(Point p1, Point p2)
24     {
25       Point midPoint = new Point();
26       midPoint.y = p1.y + (p2.y - p1.y)/2;
27       midPoint.x = p1.x + (p2.x - p1.x)/2;
28       return midPoint;
29     }
30
31     public static void drawSierpinsky(int iterations, Point p1, Point p2,
32                                       Point p3, Graphics g)
33     {
34       if(iterations == 0) //base case
35       {
36         return;
37       }
38       //general solution
39       g.drawLine(p1.x, p1.y, p2.x, p2.y); //draw a triangle
40       g.drawLine(p2.x, p2.y, p3.x, p3.y);
```

```
41        g.drawLine(p3.x, p3.y, p1.x, p1.y);
42        iterations--;
43     //reduced problems to draw top, left & right side triangles recursively
44        drawSierpinsky(iterations, p1, midPoint(p1,p2), midPoint(p1,p3), g);
45        drawSierpinsky(iterations, p2, midPoint(p2,p1), midPoint(p2,p3), g);
46        drawSierpinsky(iterations, p3, midPoint(p3,p1), midPoint(p3,p2), g);
47     }
48  }
```

Figure 9.17
The application **RecursiveFractal**.

9.5.2 Dynamic Programming

Dynamic programming is a technique that can sometimes be used to solve three of the problems associated with recursion: unacceptably long execution times, excessive memory requirements, and a StackOverflowException error. It does this by reducing the number of recursive invocations. The basis of this technique is the idea that once a value is computed recursively, it should not be computed again.

For example, Figure 9.18 shows the 25 invocations required to compute the seventh term of the Fibonacci series recursively. During this computation, once the first invocation to compute f3, shown on the lower left side of the figure, completes its execution, the other four invocations to compute f3 shown in the figure could be eliminated because the value of f3 is already known. Once computed, if that value was stored in a static class-level variable, the other four invocations of f3 could be replaced with a new base case that simply returned the value stored in the variable. A similar approach would eliminate four of the five invocations to compute f1, seven of the eight to compute f2, two of the three to compute f4, and one of the invocations to compute f5. The result would be that only seven invocations would be required to compute f7 recursively: one invocation to compute f7, and six more recursive invocations to compute f6, f5, f4, f3, f2, and f1 (see highlights in Figure 9.19).

Figure 9.19 illustrates this improved process of computing f7 = 13 using dynamic programming in the implementation of its recursive algorithm. The invocation of the method to compute f7 still spawns the recursive invocations shown on the far left side of Figure 9.18 to compute f6 though

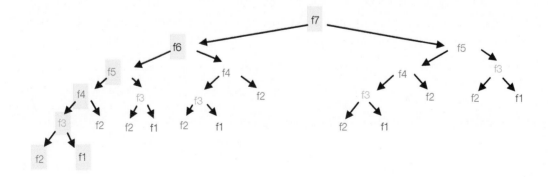

Figure 9.18
The 25 invocations required to compute the seventh term of the Fibonacci sequence recursively.

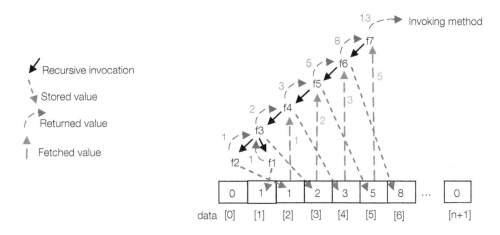

Figure 9.19
The seven invocations required to compute the seventh term of the Fibonacci sequence recursively using dynamic programming.

f1 (black arrows in Figure 9.19). Now, however, after these terms are computed and before they are returned (blue arrows in Figure 9.19), the computed values are stored in an array (red arrows) named `data` in Figure 9.19. In addition, before a recursive invocation is made to compute the value of fi, the ith element of the array is examined to see if it is nonzero. If it is, the value has already been computed, in which case the value is fetched from the array (green arrows in Figure 9.19), and the recursive invocation is not issued.

Referring to the left side of Figure 9.18, this eliminates the need to recalculate f2 when calculating f4, to recalculate f3 when calculating f5, to recalculate f4 when calculating f6, and to recalculate f5 when calculating f7. When dynamic programming is applied to the calculation of the 40th term of the Fibonacci series, the number of invocations of the recursive method is reduced from 204,668,309 invocations to 40 invocations.

The application `FibonacciDynamic` shown in Figure 9.20 contains two implementations of the recursive algorithm to calculate the nth term of the Fibonacci series. One of these implementations incorporates dynamic programming into the algorithm. After the user is asked to enter the number of the term to be calculated, the application invokes both methods and then outputs the calculated values and the number of invocations required to perform the calculations. A typical input and the resulting outputs produced by the application are shown in Figure 9.21.

The output statement that begins on line 18 invokes the non-dynamic implementation, `fib`, and produces the first two lines of output shown in Figure 9.21. It is passed the number of the term to be calculated, which was input and parsed on lines 13–16. The method `fib` (lines 28–42) counts the number of times it is invoked by incrementing the counter variable `invocations` on line 31. The variable is defined as a class-level variable on line 6, so all of the recursive invocations share it.

Line 33 of the method identifies the two defined base cases and returns the base case value, one, on line 35. Lines 38 and 39 invoke the method recursively to compute the two reduced problems, and their resulting sum is returned on line 40. A typical set of recursive invocations generated by this method when it is passed n = 40 and n = 7 are shown in Figures 9.14 and 9.18, respectively.

The output statement that begins on line 23 invokes the dynamic implementation, fibDynamic, and produces the last two lines of output shown in Figure 9.21. Before the dynamic version of the method is invoked on line 23, line 21 sets the invocation counter back to zero. Like its non-dynamic counterpart, fib, this method (lines 44–75) is passed the number of the term to be calculated (line 44), counts the number of times it is invoked (line 48), and identifies the two defined base cases on line 51. Unlike its dynamic counterpart, line 53 stores the value of these base cases (one) in the array data before returning the value. The array data is defined as a static class-level array on line 7, and its ith element is used to store the ith term of the sequence after it is calculated.

Lines 56–59 check for an additional base case, the value in the nth element of the array data is non-zero, in which case it returns the value. This prevents the recursive invocations to calculate fn-1 and fn-2 when the nth term of the sequence has already been calculated and stored in the array.

Line 62 checks the value data[n-1] to determine if the value of fn-1, the first reduced problem, has not been calculated. When that is the case, line 64 issues a recursive invocation to calculate it and stores the returned value in element n-1 of the array. Line 64 then sets the variable rp1 to the calculated value. Lines 67–71 perform the analogous operations for the second reduced problem, fn-2. The general solution, the value of fn, is calculated and returned on lines 72 and 73.

```java
1    import javax.swing.*;
2    import java.text.DecimalFormat;
3
4    public class FibonacciDynamic
5    {
6      static long invocations = 0;
7      static long[] data = new long[101];
8
9      public static void main(String[] args)
10     {
11       DecimalFormat f = new DecimalFormat("#,###");
12
13       String s = JOptionPane.showInputDialog("Enter the term number," +
14                                              " n, to be evaluated:" +
15                                              " 1<= n <=100");
16       int n = Integer.parseInt(s);
17
18       System.out.println("fn = " + f.format(fib(n)) +
19                          "\ncalculated making " + f.format(invocations) +
20                          " invocations");
21       invocations = 0;
22       System.out.println();
23       System.out.println("fn = " + f.format(fibDynamic(n)) +
24                          "\ncalculated making " + f.format(invocations) +
25                          " invocations");
26     }
27
28     public static long fib(int n)
29     {
```

```
30      long rp1, rp2;
31      invocations++;
32
33      if(n == 1 || n == 2) //defined base cases
34      {
35        return 1;
36      }
37      else //general solution
38      { rp1 = fib(n-1); //calculate first reduced problem
39        rp2 = fib(n-2); //calculate second reduced problem
40        return rp1 + rp2;
41      }
42    }
43
44    public static long fibDynamic(int n)
45    {
46      long rp1 = 0;
47      long rp2, gs;
48      invocations++;
49
50      //three base cases
51      if(n == 1 || n == 2) //defined base cases
52      {
53        data[n] = 1;
54        return 1;
55      }
56      else if(data[n] != 0) //dynamic programming base case
57      {
58        return data[n];
59      }
60      else //general solution
61      {
62        if(data[n-1] == 0) //calculate flrst reduced problem
63        {
64          data[n-1] = fibDynamic(n-1);
65        }
66        rp1 = data[n-1];
67        if(data[n-2] == 0) //calculate second reduced problem
68        {
69          data[n-2] = fibDynamic(n-2);
70        }
71        rp2 = data[n-2];
72        gs = rp1 + rp2;
73        return gs;
74      }
75    }
76  }
```

Figure 9.20
The application **FibonacciDynamic**.

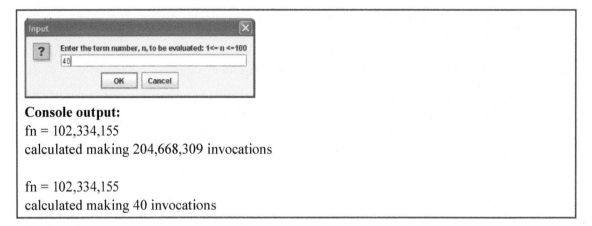

Figure 9.21
An input to the application **FibonacciDynamic** and the resulting outputs

9.6 CHAPTER SUMMARY

Recursion is a problem solving tool that can provide a more succinct, elegant solution to a problem than solutions based on other problem solving techniques. Recursive algorithms are implemented within a recursive method, which is a method that repeatedly invokes itself either directly or indirectly until a condition, called a base case, is reached and terminates the sequence of invocations. If the base case is not reached, the method terminates in a stack overflow runtime error because the RAM memory, dedicated to saving the information required to complete each invocation, has been exceeded. While most people don't naturally possess the innate ability to think recursively, they can learn how to do so via a divide-and-conquer methodology reinforced with lots of recursive problem solving practice.

The methodology consists of discovering a problem's base case, reduced problem, and general solution and combining these components into a recursive solution to the problem. The base case is a known, defined, or trivial solution to a similar but usually simpler problem. If the problem involves an integer, n, the base case is usually a version of the problem when n is zero or one. For example, the base case for x^n could be the definition, $x^0 \equiv 1$, or the trivial case $x^1 = x$.

The reduced problem is a simpler version of the problem that satisfies this condition: when the relationship between the problem and reduced problem is repeatedly applied to the reduced problem, it becomes the base case. For example, the relationship between x^n and the candidate reduced problem x^{n-1} is the reduction of the exponent by one. When this is repeatedly applied to the reduced problem x^{n-1}, it becomes x^{n-2}, which becomes x^{n-3}, which eventually becomes both base cases: first x^1 and then x^0. The discovery of the reduced problem is normally the most difficult part of the methodology.

The general solution is the recursive solution to the original problem under the assumption that the solution to the reduced problem is known. For example, if we know how to calculate x^{n-1}, then x^n can be calculated by multiplying x^{n-1} by x. Once a valid base case, reduced problem, and general solution have been discovered, the last step of the methodology is to combine them as shown in Figure 9.6. While the methodology cannot be used to formulate all recursive algorithms, by practicing with problems within its domain, we will develop the skills necessary to extrapolate the methodology to the recursive solution of problems beyond its domain.

It is important to understand not only how to use recursion, but when to use it or not use it as well. It should be used when the recursive algorithm significantly reduces the algorithm-discovery and implementation time and when the additional storage requirements and execution time are acceptable. Appropriate problems for recursive solutions are those whose structures are inherently recursive, such as trees, mazes, nested lists, and fractals.

Solutions for some of the common recursive problems are presented in Table 9.4.

Table 9.4
Base Cases, Reduced Problems, and General Solutions for Several Problems With Recursive Solutions

Problem	Base Case	Reduced Problem	General Solution
Factorial of a positive integer, n!	$0! \equiv 1$	$(n-1)!$	$n * (n-1)!$
A number x raised to a positive integer, x^n	$x^0 \equiv 1$	$x^{(n-1)}$	$x * x^{(n-1)}$
Sum of the integers from 1 to n	sum $\equiv 1$ for $n = 1$	Sum of the integers from 1 to $(n-1)$	$n +$ sum of the integers from 1 to $(n-1)$
Product of two positive integers, $m \times n$	$m * 1 = m$	$m * (n-1)$	$m + m * (n-1)$
Output an n character string s in reverse order	$n == 1$ output s	Output the last $n-1$ characters of string s in reverse order	Output the last $n-1$ characters of string s in reverse order. Then output the first character of s
Problems with Multiple Base Cases and Reduced Problems			
Generate the nth term of the Fibonacci Sequence, fn	$f_1 = 1$ and $f_2 = 1$	f_{n-1} and f_{n-2}	$f_{n-1} + f_{n-2}$
Find the greatest common divisor of two positive integers m and n, GCD(m, n), for $m > n$	if $m = n$, GCD = m	GCD(m − n, n) and GCD(m, n − m)	if(m > n) GCD(m − n, n) else GCD(m, n − m)

(Contd.)

Problem	Base Case	Reduced Problem	General Solution
A Problem with Multiple Base Cases			
Search a sorted list of items for the item I	If the list is empty, return not found If the middle item is I, return found	Search a designated sorted sub list for I	if I > middle item, sub list is the items after it, else sub list is items before it. Search the sub list for I
A Problem that Uses the Reduced Problem Twice			
Towers of Hanoi Move n rings from tower A to tower B using tower C	n = 1: Move 1 ring from one tower to another tower	Move n–1 rings from one tower to another tower	Move n–1 rings from A to C Move 1 ring from A to B Move n–1 rings from C to A

Knowledge Exercises

1. True or false:
   a) A method that invokes itself directly or indirectly is said to be recursive.
   b) By definition, zero factorial is equal to one.
   c) Finding the base case is the most difficult part of discovering a recursive algorithm.
   d) Every problem has a recursive solution.
   e) Implementations of recursive solutions can result in a `StackOverFlow` error.
   f) Recursion is useful in drawing fractals.
   g) Implementations of recursive solutions always execute quickly.

2. Which invocation of a recursive method takes the longest time to complete: the first invocation or the last?

3. Which of the flow-chart symbols in Figure 9.6 makes the algorithm it depicts recursive?

4. Calculate the value of 8! using both iterative and recursive techniques.

5. Calculate the value of the sixth term of the Fibonacci sequence using both iterative and recursive techniques.

6. How many terms of the Fibonacci sequence are calculated when the recursive technique (Figure 9.7) is used to calculate the sixth term of the sequence?

7. What is the name of the technique used to reduce the calculations performed in Exercise 6?

8. How many terms of the Fibonacci sequence are calculated when the technique of Exercise 7 is applied to Exercise 6?

9. Give the base case, reduced problem, and general solution used in the recursive solution of the calculation of the sum of the even integers from n up to m, where both n and m are even.

10. Explain why (n-2)! is not a valid reduced problem for n!.

11. Why is it important in the calculation of a factorial that zero factorial be defined as 1?

   $(0! \equiv 1)$

12. Use a recursive algorithm for the greatest common divisor to compute the greatest common divisor of 15 and 255.

13. What is the last step in the recursive solution-discovery methodology discussed in this chapter?

14. How many moves would be required in the Towers of Hanoi problem to move six rings? How many for ten rings? How many for n rings?

Programming Exercises

1. Write a recursive method that is passed two integers, x and y, and returns the value of x raised to the power y. Include the method in an application that verifies its functionality.

2. Write a recursive binary search method that is passed an array of integers and an integer value and returns the index of the array that contains the integer passed to it. If the integer is not found, the method returns -1. Include the method in an application that verifies its functionality.

3. Write a recursive method that calculates the sum of the elements of an integer array passed to it. Include the method in an application that verifies its functionality.

4. Write both a recursive and an iterative method to find and return the greatest common divisor of two integer arguments, x and y, passed to it. Include the methods in an application that verifies their functionality.

5. Write a recursive method that returns `true` when the string passed to it is a palindrome. A palindrome is a string that reads the same backwards and forwards. For example, "MADAMIMADAM," "TOOT," and "WOW." Include the method in an application that verifies its functionality.

6. Write a recursive method that outputs the string passed to it in reverse. Include the method in an application that verifies its functionality.

7. Write a graphical application that moves one of the Towers of Hanoi rings from one tower to another every time the up button of the game board is clicked. The program should begin by asking the user to input the number of rings to be relocated, and show the entire solution.

Enrichment

1. Binary trees are recursive structures. Find out how binary tree traversals are performed and explain the recursive algorithms for in-order, pre-order and post-order tree traversals. Why is recursion a suitable approach to tree traversals?

2. How can a recursive algorithm be used to count the nodes in a binary tree?

3. Fractals have the property of self-similarity, and they are often implemented recursively. Research the characteristics of some well-known fractals, such as the Koch snowflake, the Cantor Set, and the Mandelbrot and Julia sets. Explore their algorithms and implementations.

4. Investigate the Heap Sort and Quick Sort recursive algorithms to discover why they are so efficient. Explain briefly how the algorithms work.

5. The Eight Queens and the Knight's Tour problems both have recursive solutions. Investigate these problems and the recursive algorithms used to solve them.

6. Recursion is used in solving mazes. Research a recursive algorithm for traversing a maze and explain the base case, the reduced problem, and the general solution.

References

Barnsley, Michael. *Fractals Everywhere*. San Diego, CA: Academic Press, Inc., 1988.

Mandelbrot, Benoit. *The Fractal Geometry of Nature*. NewYok: W.H. Freeman and Co., 1977.

Peitgen, Heinz-Otto, et al. *Fractals for the Classroom, Strategic Activities*, Part One. New York: Springer-Verlag, 1991.

Peitgen, Heinz-Otto, et al. *Fractals for the Classroom, Complex Systems and Mandelbrot Set*, Vol. 2. New York: Springer-Verlag, 1992.

Roberts, Eric. *Thinking Recursively*. NewYork: John Wiley and Sons, 1986.

Roberts, Eric. *Thinking Recursively with Java,* 20th Anniversary Ed. NewYork: John Wiley and Sons, 2005.

Endnotes

[1] Epp, Suzanna, *Discrete Mathematics with Applications*, 3rd Ed., Brooks Cole, 2004. p, 461.

EXCEPTIONS: A SECOND LOOK

10.1 *An Overview* *450*

10.2 *Java's Exception Classes and Exception Objects* *451*

10.3 *Processing Thrown Exceptions* *453*

10.4 *The Throw Statement and Error Messages* *464*

10.5 *Defining Exception Classes* *472*

10.6 *Chapter Summary* *475*

In this chapter

In this chapter, we will discuss the features Java provides within its implementation of the concept of exceptions. This will expand our knowledge of the `try-catch` construct, the API exception classes, and the differences between checked and unchecked exceptions, which were discussed in the context of performing disk I/O. In addition, we will learn how to write methods that throw exceptions when they detect errors, as the methods in the API classes do, and how to create our own exception classes that make our programs more readable. We will also discuss ways of using exceptions to facilitate the implementation of methods that do not normally detect errors and the role of the `finally` clause in exception handling.

After successfully completing this chapter, you should:

- Be able to use the `try-catch` construct to process errors detected by methods you invoke and fully understand the execution path of the construct
- Know when to include a `finally` clause within a `try-catch` construct and its role in the construct's execution path
- Understand how to design and implement algorithms that detect errors and throw exception objects
- Be able to distinguish between the checked and unchecked exceptions as well as to know the differences between these two types of exceptions and their appropriate use
- Be able to define and use new exception classes to develop more readable code
- Know how to use the features of exceptions in non-error detecting methods to facilitate their development
- Understand the translator enforced coding order of multiple `catch` clauses coded within the `try-catch` construct

10.1 AN OVERVIEW

During the development of a program, a significant amount of time is spent testing the methods of the classes that make up the program because one very important programming goal is to produce an error free program. To improve the chances of attaining this goal, the development process begins by dividing a large program into smaller classes, and each class is divided into a collection of small methods because the solution to small problems tends to be less error prone. Then, each method is written and enters an iterative testing process aimed at exposing and eliminating the errors in the method's algorithm and its implementation. (Recall that the programming development process was explained in Chapter 1, and Figure 1.28 illustrates this process.)

Unfortunately, a successful completion of this process does not guarantee that a method will never produce a runtime error or an incorrect result because an unanticipated event could occur during its execution. For example, the user might input a zero divisor into a method that divides two inputs, or the user could direct the method to read data from a file that does not exist. To avoid these failure modes, during the design process we should identify the events that will result in a runtime error or an erroneous result and incorporate code into the method that recognizes them when they occur. For example, before a divisor is used, we should always make sure it is not zero, and we should check for the existence of a file before we attempt to read from the file.

Assuming that this error or failure mode recognition process is properly incorporated into the design of a method's algorithm, we are now faced with the task of deciding what actions to take when these anticipated events occur and incorporating these actions into the method's algorithm. When the method is part of a class that will be imported into someone else's program, this becomes an impossible task because the author of the method does not know what action the user of the class wants to take: terminate the program with an informative error message, give the user an opportunity to correct an erroneous input, or some other course of action.

To solve this dilemma, Java and other programming languages use the concept of exceptions. The name of this concept comes from the analogy of someone asking you to do something you cannot or should not do and you respond, "I take *exception* to your asking me to do that." A method that has determined it is being asked to divide by zero should take exception to that, and a method that has determined that it is being directed to read data from a disk file that does not exist should take exception to that.

The concept of exceptions is based on the idea that a method's algorithm should identify the occurrence of a problem and inform the invoker that it occurred. The burden of what is to be done after the problem occurs is passed on to the invoker. This allows for a recovery from the error that is appropriate to, and implemented by, each application that imports the method's class. For example, one application that received a divide-by-zero exception from a method it invoked could simply inform the program user that division by zero is not possible and terminate, while another application invoking the same method can give the user an opportunity to reenter the divisor.

Exception Terminology: A Baseball Analogy

As mentioned in Chapter 4, the terminology of exceptions comes from a communication analogy between two persons that involves a baseball. One person wraps a message around the ball and then throws the ball to the other person who catches it, unwraps the message, and reads it. Applying the analogy to the communication of error messages, when a method's algorithm detects a problem, it wraps an error message around an exception object and *throws* the object to the code block that invoked it. The code block can *catch* the thrown exception object, unwrap the error message, and process it.

To extend the analogy a bit further, if a person chooses not to catch a thrown ball, some other ordered collection of people can elect to catch it. The runtime environment maintains a history, or the order of a method's invocation sequence. For example, if the method main invoked method A, and method A invoked method B, and method B invoked method C, then C's invocation sequence would be main, A, B. Invocation sequences are stored in a structure called the runtime stack. If method C invoked method D during its execution, then C would be added to, or pushed onto, the runtime stack before D's execution began. The runtime stack would then contain the invocation sequence main, A, B, C.

To return to our analogy, if C chooses not to catch an exception that is thrown by the method it invoked during its execution, D, then each of the methods on the runtime stack are given a chance to catch it in the reverse order in which they were invoked (last in, first out). In our original example, B would be given the first chance to catch the thrown exception object, then A, and then main. We say that the exception object propagates up the runtime stack. If none of the methods on the runtime stack catch the exception, the Java Runtime Environment catches and processes it.

NOTE *All uncaught exception objects are caught by the Java Runtime Environment.*

After catching an exception, the Java Runtime Environment outputs an error to the System console that includes the unwrapped message and then terminates the program. This commonly occurs during the development process when a coding error results in a method being invoked that uses a reference variable that contains a null value or an array index is generated that is beyond the bounds of the array. The console outputs, produced by the Java Runtime Environment when these two errors occur, are familiar to most of us:

- exception in thread "main" java.lang.NullPointerException
- exception in thread "main" Java.lang.ArrayIndexOutOfBoundsException: -23

Using the techniques discussed in Chapter 4, which are expanded in this chapter, we can catch thrown exceptions and then either continue the program's execution after exceptions are caught or bring the program to a more informative "soft-landing" termination.

10.2 JAVA'S EXCEPTION CLASSES AND EXCEPTION OBJECTS

Figure 10.1 shows some of the API classes that are direct or indirect subclasses of the class Throwable. Instances of all of these classes are considered Java exception objects that can be thrown and caught by try-catch blocks. Error messages can be wrapped around these objects before they are thrown and unwrapped and processed when they are caught.

In Java, an exception object is an instance of the API class Throwable *or an instance of a class that is a direct or indirect subclass of it.*

Checked and Unchecked Exceptions Classes

As shown at the top of Figure 10.1, the classes Exception and Error are the two direct subclasses of Throwable. The class Error and all of its descendants are *unchecked* exception classes. Conversely, the class Throwable and the class Exception are *checked* exception classes. All direct and indirect subclasses of the class Exception are also checked exception classes except for the class RunTimeException and its descendants.

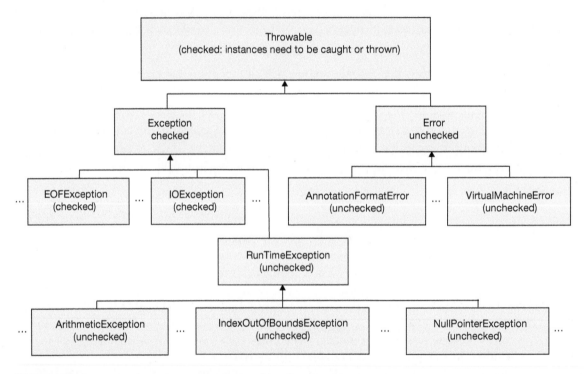

Figure 10.1
A subset of the exception classes included in the Java API and their inheritance chains.

When we invoke a method whose algorithm uses an instance of a *checked* exception to communicate to its invoker that an error has occurred, the invoking method must catch the object or include a throws clause in its heading to inform the translator that it is intentionally going to ignore the error detected by the method it invoked. The syntax of a throws clause is the keyword throws followed by one or more exception class names separated by commas. The exception object classes coded in the clause must be the type of the ignored checked exception or a direct or indirect super class of it.

As shown in Figure 10.1, the class IOException is a checked exception class. Instances of this class and its descendants are thrown by the methods discussed in Chapter 4 that perform disk I/O. That is why the two disk I/O programs shown in Figures 4.20 and 4.23 had to include a throws clause at the end of the main method's signature (line 6 of Figure 4.20) or perform the disk I/O from within a `try-catch` construct (lines 39–66 of Figure 4.23) that could catch the thrown checked exception object. If the disk I/O methods threw instances of *unchecked* exceptions, not including either a `throws` clause or the `try-catch` construct in the method that invoked them would be syntactically correct.

> **NOTE** *Thrown checked exceptions must be caught, or the signature of the invoking method must include a* `throws` *clause.*

Errors that cause instances of the class `Error` or its descendants to be thrown are considered abnormal conditions; they should normally not occur. They are not caused by programming errors, an I/O error, or something that can be dealt with within an application. When they do occur, they are best processed by the Java Runtime Environment, the catcher of all uncaught exceptions. Runtime errors that generate checked exceptions are considered to be situations that can be dealt with by a method within an application and are serious enough that the translator requires that they either are dealt with or that the method indicates that it is intentionally ignoring the error via a `throws` clause.

Errors that cause instances of the class `RunTimeError` or its descendants to be thrown are considered errors that will be eliminated during the testing phase of the application's development, and therefore, the translator does not require that the application process these errors or indicate that they are intentionally being ignored via a `throws` clause. In situations where the programmer feels that erroneous input or other non-programming error-related events could cause these unchecked exception objects to be thrown, a `try-catch` construct should be included in the portions of the application where these events could occur.

10.3 PROCESSING THROWN EXCEPTIONS

Exceptions are processed using a `try-catch` construct. The construct consists of a `try` clause that is immediately followed by a `catch` clause. The statements associated with each of these clauses are always enclosed in a set of brackets, even if there is only one statement associated with them. For this reason, they are commonly referred to as `try` and `catch` blocks.

The `try` block is used to detect thrown exceptions, and the `catch` block is used to process the errors that produced the exceptions. As illustrated in Figure 10.2, one `try` block can be followed by multiple `catch` blocks, and the `catch` blocks must immediately follow the `try` block. Coding statements in between any of the blocks is a syntax error. In the absence of a `finally` block, which will be discussed later in this chapter, at least one `catch` block must be included in the construct.

```
try
{
  //try to execute the statements in this statement block
}
catch(ExceptionClass1 thrownObject1)
{
  //statements to execute when an ExceptionClass1 object is thrown
}
```

```
catch(ExceptionClass2 thrownObject2)
{
    //statements to execute when an ExceptionClass2 object is thrown
}
          :
          :
catch(ExceptionClassN thrownObjectN)
{
    //statements to execute when an ExceptionClassN object is thrown
}
```

Figure 10.2
Syntax of the **try-catch** construct.

The first line of each catch block includes a single parameter that is a reference to an exception object. Its type must be Throwable or a descendent of that class. When multiple catch blocks are included in the construct, each block must contain a different parameter type.

The execution path of the try-catch construct is shown in Figure 10.3. The statements in the try block are executed until one of them causes an exception, at which point the execution of the

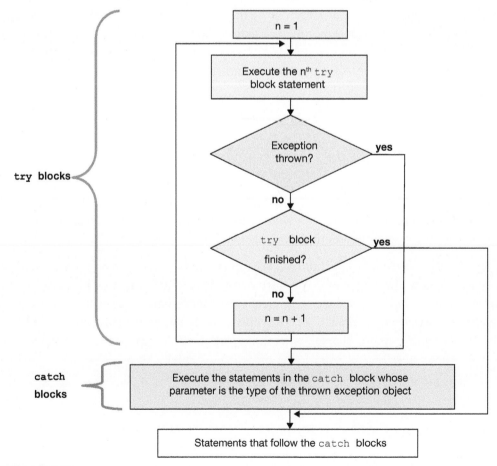

Figure 10.3
The execution path of the **try-catch** construct.

`try` block statement terminates, and the statements in the `catch` block whose parameter matches the type of the thrown exception object begins execution.

> **NOTE** *A thrown exception object can be caught by a* `catch` *block whose parameter type is a direct or indirect super class of the thrown exception type.*

After the statements in the `catch` block complete their execution, the statements that follow the `catch` blocks begin execution. If the type of the thrown exception object does not match any of the parameter types in the `catch` blocks, and it is an unchecked exception, the statements that follow the `catch` blocks are executed. If an uncaught exception is a checked exception, the method containing the `try-catch` construct terminates.

Figure 10.4 presents the application `ProcessingExceptions` that calculates the quotient and remainder of two input numbers and gives the user three opportunities to correct the erroneous input of a zero divisor. The `for` loop that begins on line 18 provides the three attempts to perform the division. Its statement block (line 19–42) includes the calculations, the error detection of a zero divisor, and the error processing.

Line 22 performs the division of the two numbers initially input and parsed on lines 12–16. Java's divide operator, used on line 22, throws an `ArithmeticException` object whenever the operation's divisor is zero. Because the statement is inside the `try` block that begins on line 20, whose `catch` block processes this type of exception (line 26), when the error occurs, the `if-else` statement that begins on line 28 executes. If three attempts to perform the division have not been made, the `if` statement's code block accepts another value of the divisor (Figure 10.5a), and the next iteration of the loop begins. After the third failed attempt to perform the division, the `else` clause's code block executes (lines 35–40) outputting an error message (Figure 10.5b), and line 39 terminates the program.

When the division performed on line 22 is successful, the `try` block completes its execution, and lines 43–45 output the result of the division (Figure 10.5c). The `break` statement at the end of the `try` block (line 24) should not be interpreted as breaking out of the `try-catch` construct; rather, its action is to terminate the `for` loop. The process of exiting a `try-catch` construct, illustrated in Figure 10.3, does not involve a `break` statement; this statement is used to terminate a switch or loop construct. If the `try-catch` construct were not coded inside the `for` loop that begins on line 18, the `break` statement on line 24 would have produced a translation error.

```
1    import javax.swing.*;
2
3    public class ProcessingExceptions
4    {
5      public static void main(String[] args)
6      {
7        String s;
8        int a, b;
9        int quotient = 0;
10       int remainder = 0;
```

```
11
12      s = JOptionPane.showInputDialog("This program calculates a / b " +
13                                    "\nEnter the value of a" );
14      a = Integer.parseInt(s);
15      s = JOptionPane.showInputDialog("Enter the value of b" );
16      b = Integer.parseInt(s);
17
18      for(int i=1; i<=3; i++) //three attempts to divide a and b
19      {
20        try
21        {
22          quotient = a / b; //throws an ArithmeticException
23          remainder = a % b;
24          break; //ends the for loop and Line 43 executes next
25        }
26        catch(ArithmeticException e)
27        {
28          if(i != 3) //three attempts to divide have not been made
29          {
30            s = JOptionPane.showInputDialog("A divisor cannot be zero." +
31                                        "\nPlease re-enter it");
32            b = Integer.parseInt(s);
33          }
34          else
35          {
36            JOptionPane.showMessageDialog(null, "Division by zero " +
37                                        "is undefined \n" +
38                                        "The program is ending");
39            System.exit(0); //terminate the program
40          }
41        } //end of the try-catch construct
42      }//end of for loop
43      JOptionPane.showMessageDialog(null, a + " / " + b + " = " +
44                                    quotient + ", with a " +
45                                    "remainder of " + remainder);
46    }
47  }
```

Figure 10.4
The application **ProcessingExceptions**.

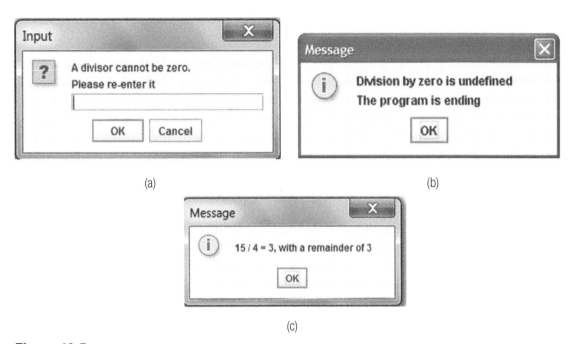

(a)

(b)

(c)

Figure 10.5
Outputs produced by the application **ProcessingExceptions**.

While it is true that the error checking performed with the `try-catch` construct used in the application shown in Figure 10.4 could be performed using an `if-else` statement, in most cases, the use of exceptions make our code more readable and simpler to code when more than one error can occur within in a code block.

The application `MultipleCatchBlocks` presented in Figure 10.6 is a modified version of the application presented in Figure 10.4. This version of the program uses a second `catch` block to verify that the two user inputs are integers, and, in the interest of brevity, ends after it processes this or the divide-by-zero error. Determining if the input string is an integer is a relatively simple thing to do because the `Integer` class's `parseInt` method throws a `NumberFormatException` object when the string passed to it contains any character other than a digit or a leading plus or minus sign. (The API online documentation of every method included in the API identifies the exceptions each method's throws.)

To take advantage of this fact, the parsing of the inputs has been moved into the program's `try` block (lines 17 and 19 in Figure 10.6), and the program's second `catch` block (lines 30–36) processes a `NumberFormatException` object. As shown in Figure 10.2, there is no limit to the number of `catch` blocks that can be associated with one `try` block.

Figure 10.7a shows an erroneous (non-integer) user input, which terminates the `try` block on line 17. Figure 10.7b shows the resulting error-message output by lines 32–34 before the program is terminated by line 35.

```
1    import javax.swing.*;
2
3    public class MultipleCatchBlocks
4    {
5      public static void main(String[] args)
6      {
7        String sa, sb;
8        int a = 0;
9        int b = 0;
10       int quotient = 0;
11       int remainder = 0;
12
13       try
14       {
15         sa = JOptionPane.showInputDialog("This program calculates " +
16                                     "a / b\nEnter the value of a");
17         a = Integer.parseInt(sa); //throws a NumberFormatException
18         sb = JOptionPane.showInputDialog("Enter the value of b" );
19         b = Integer.parseInt(sb); //throws a NumberFormatException
20         quotient = a / b;
21         remainder = a % b;
22       } //end of the try block
23       catch(ArithmeticException e) //process divide by zero
24       {
25         JOptionPane.showMessageDialog(null, "Division by zero " +
26                                     "is undefined. \n" +
27                                     "\nThe program is ending");
28         System.exit(0);
29       } //end of the first catch block
30       catch(NumberFormatException e) //process non-integer input
31       {
32         JOptionPane.showMessageDialog(null, "Enter only digits " +
33                                  "for the operands." +
34                                  "\nThe program is ending");
35         System.exit(0);
36       } //end of the second catch block
37       JOptionPane.showMessageDialog(null, a + " / " + b + " = " +
38                                  quotient + ", with a " +
39                                  "remainder of " + remainder);
40     }
41   }
```

Figure 10.6
The application **MultipleCatchBlocks**.

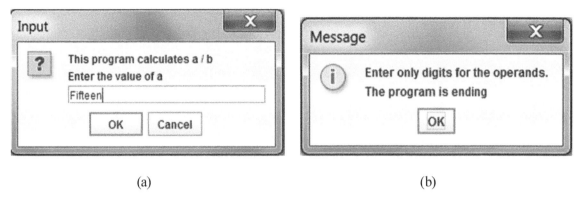

(a)   (b)

Figure 10.7
Outputs produced by the application `MultipleCatchBlocks`.

Unwrapping Error Messages

The `Throwable` class's `getMessage` method can be used to unwrap an error message. The method returns a string containing the message that was "wrapped around" the exception object that invoked it. The following code fragment outputs the message contained in the object caught by the `catch` statement:

```
catch (RuntimeException e)
{
    System.out.println(e.getMessage());
}
```

10.3.1 Non-error Checking Use of Exceptions

There are times when it is advantageous to use a `try-catch` construct not to detect and process errors but to efficiently identify and process data. Consider the case when an input string contains a mix of characters and numerics, and we want to process just the numerics. For example, add up the numbers in the string:

Please add up 3.4 plus 5 plus -2 OK?

After isolating the tokens (entities separated by white space) in the input string, we can avoid processing (totaling) the non-numeric tokens by using the `NumberFormatException` thrown by the `Double` class's `parseDouble` method to bypass the totaling algorithm. We are effectively using exceptions to identify the numeric tokens in the string. Normally, the `catch` block in this type of application is empty and is only included in the application to make it syntactically correct.

The application `ParsingNumerics`, shown in Figure 10.8, accepts an input string and outputs the sum of the numerics contained in the string. A typical input and output is shown in Figure 10.9.

Line 14 of the application uses the `String` class's `split` method to place the tokens of the string, input on line 12, into the elements of the `String` array `tokens`. The right side of the totaling algorithm on line 19 uses the loop variable of the `for` loop (that begins on line 15) to attempt to parse each token into a `double`. Because line 19 is inside a `try` block (lines 17–21), when the token is nonnumeric, the `parseDouble` method invoked on that line throws a `NumberFormatException` object, and line 19 does not complete its execution. The exception is caught by the `catch` statement (line 22), and the next iteration of the `for` loop begins.

When the parsed token is a numeric, line 19 completes its execution by adding the parsed token to the current total. Then, the token and a plus sign are concatenated into the string `numerics`. When the loop ends, line 27 replaces the rightmost plus sign in the string `numerics` with an equal sign. Then, the string and the total of the numeric values are output to a message box on line 28.

```java
1    import javax.swing.*;
2
3    public class ParsingNumerics
4    {
5      public static void main(String[] args)
6      {
7        String input;
8        String[] tokens;
9        double sum = 0;
10       String numerics = "";
11
12       input = JOptionPane.showInputDialog("Enter a String containing " +
13                                           "numerics");
14       tokens = input.split(" +");
15       for(int i = 0; i<tokens.length; i++)
16       {
17         try
18         {
19           sum = sum + Double.parseDouble(tokens[i]); //only numeric added
20           numerics = numerics + tokens[i] + " + "; //build output string
21         }
22         catch(NumberFormatException e) //non-numeric
23         {
24           //prevents termination of application when exception is thrown
25         }
26       } //replace the last plus sign with an equals and produce the output
27       numerics = numerics.substring(0, numerics.length() - 2) + "= ";
28       JOptionPane.showMessageDialog(null, numerics + sum);
29     }
30   }
```

Figure 10.8
The application **ParsingNumerics**.

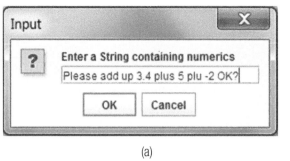
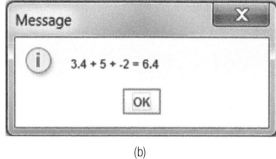

| (a) | (b) |

Figure 10.9
An input to the application **ParsingNumerics** and the resulting output.

10.3.2 The finally Clause

A `try-catch` construct can include a `finally` clause. When it does, as shown in Figure 10.10, the `finally` clause must immediately follow the last `catch` clause. Statements cannot be coded between the last `catch` clause and the `finally` clause. It is similar to the other two clauses in that it must contain a code block that could be empty or contain one or more statements.

```
try
{
   //try to execute the statements in this statement block
}
catch(ExceptionClass1 thrownObject1)
{
  //statements to execute when an ExceptionClass1 object is thrown
}
catch(ExceptionClass2 thrownObject2)
{
  //statements to execute when an ExceptionClass2 object is thrown
}
           :
           :
catch(ExceptionClassN thrownObjectN)
{
  //statements to execute when an ExceptionClassN object is thrown
}
finally
{
  //code executed after one of the above blocks completes execution
}
```

Figure 10.10
Syntax of the **try-catch-finally** construct.

The `finally` block's function is to implement the tasks associated with the construct that should be performed after the `try` block or one of the `catch` blocks completes its execution. The finally block *always* executes. Figure 10.11 shows the execution path of the try-catch-finally construct.

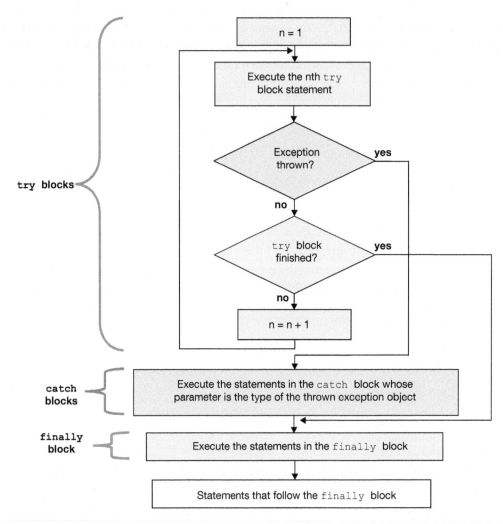

Figure 10.11
The execution path of the **try-catch-finally** construct.

The most common use of the finally clause is to close out the processing of the construct. Because the clause always executes, this processing includes the tasks that are common to, and would otherwise be implemented at, the end of the try block and all of the catch blocks. A proper understanding of the use of the finally block is that if it is not included in the construct, its code would have to be pasted into the end of the try block and into the end of all of the catch blocks. A good example of its use is to close all of the files that were opened during the execution of the other portions of the construct.

Java supports a try-finally construct. It is an error-detection and processing construct that does not contain a catch clause. The finally clause must immediately follow the try clause; statements cannot be coded in between them. After the try block completes its execution, the `finally` block executes, whether or not an exception is generated during the execution of the `try` block. When the `finally` block completes its execution, if an exception was not generated during the execution of the `try` block, the statements in the method that follow the `finally` block execute. If an exception was generated during the execution of the `try` block, the method of which it is a part terminates *after* the `finally` block completes execution. The statements that follow the `finally` block do not execute because the thrown exception was not caught. If the exception is a checked exception, the method's signature must contain a `throws` clause, or it will not translate.

The `try-finally` construct is used when the thrown exception is to be propagated up the runtime stack. The `finally` clause's code block can be empty, or it can contain the residual processing to be performed before the construct completes execution. For example, files being written to in the `try` block are closed or an output is performed. The exception thrown during the execution of the `try` block is not propagated up the runtime stack until the `finally` block completes its execution.

The application `TryFinally`, presented in Figure 10.12, contains a method named `append-DataItem` (lines 20–35), which is invoked on line 11, to write the string `data` to a disk file. The method uses a `try-finally` construct (lines 24–33) to make sure that the disk file to which it writes is closed when it ends execution. The signature of the method (lines 20 and 21) contains two string parameters; the first is the name of the file, and the second is the data item to be written to the file. The method does not contain a `catch` clause because it defers the decision as to what to do when a file output error occurs to its invoker. As a result, its signature contains a `throws` clause.

Line 28 writes to the file, and line 32 closes the file. Because the file is closed inside the `finally` block, it is executed whether or not an error occurs. Line 34 informs the user that the disk write was successful. It only executes if an exception is not thrown in the `try` block because the method does not include a `catch` clause. The console output shown at the bottom of Figure 10.12 was produced by line 34 after a successful disk write.

If the disk write is unsuccessful, the method ends after the `finally` block completes its execution. The thrown exception propagates up the runtime stack to the method `main`, where it is caught by line 13; then line 15 perform its output, and the program is terminated (line 16).

The declaration of the variable `fileOut`, which is assigned the address of a `PrintWriter` object on line 27, has to be coded outside of the `try` block (line 24). Otherwise, it would not be visible to and could not be used by line 32 to close the file.

```
1    import java.io.*;
2    import javax.swing.*;
3
4    public class TryFinally
5    {
6      public static void main(String[] args)
7      {
8        String data = JOptionPane.showInputDialog("Enter a data item");
9        try
10       {
```

```
11          appendDataItem("dataFile.txt", data);
12       }
13         catch(IOException e)
14          {
15            System.out.println("There were problems writing to the file");
16            System.exit(0);
17          }
18       }
19
20       public static void appendDataItem(String fileName,
21                                         String dataItem) throws IOException
22       {
23         PrintWriter fileOut = null;
24         try
25         {
26           FileWriter fileWriterObj = new FileWriter(fileName, true);
27           fileOut = new PrintWriter(fileWriterObj);
28           fileOut.println(dataItem);
29         }
30         finally
31         {
32           fileOut.close();
33         }
34         System.out.println("The data was written to the file");
35       }
36    }
```

Program output:
The data was written to the file

Figure 10.12
The application **TryFinally** and the output it produces.

10.4 THE THROW STATEMENT AND ERROR MESSAGES

When designing an algorithm for a method, we should always consider what could go wrong and include a strategy in the algorithm to detect the error. Even the design of a game piece's set method could include the ability to detect when the value passed to it is outside a valid range. For example, the setX method in a game piece's class could include an if statement to make sure the game piece's new x coordinate is within the boundaries of the game board: $minX \leq newX \leq maxX$, as shown below.

```
public void setX(int newX)
{
  if(newX < minx || newX > maxX)
  {
    // Take some action
  }
```

```
    else
    {
      x = newX;
    }
  }
```

To complete the algorithm, we must decide what action to take when the error is detected; that becomes the code of the `if` statement's code block. One strategy may be to set the x coordinate to a value that is within the bounds of the game board. However, this strategy may not be acceptable to all applications that use, or will use, this type of game piece. Even if one strategy can be found, such as asking the game player to re-enter the location of the game piece, one application may require a mouse click on the game board to identify the correct location and another may ask that the new location be entered via a dialog box.

When it is the case that one strategy may not suit the requirements for all applications that use instances of the game piece, the best strategy is for the method to throw an exception object whose message provides as much information as possible about the cause of the error. Then, each application can catch the object, examine the error message, and implement a recovery strategy that best suits the application.

The `throw` Statement

A method uses a `throw` statement to throw an exception. The statement begins with the keyword throw, which is followed by a reference to an exception object:

```
throw exceptionObject;
```

An exception object is an instance of an exception class, which is the API class `Throwable` or any of its direct or indirect subclasses. Referring to Figure 10.1, if we want the thrown exception to be an unchecked exception, the object thrown should be an instance of the class `RunTimeException` or one of its descendants. Checked exception objects are instances of the class `Exception` or one of its descendants other than `RunTimeException`.

NOTE *When a method throws a checked exception object, its signature must include a* `throws` *clause containing the name of the object's class or one of its ancestor classes.*

Once a decision has been made as to whether the exception will be checked or not, it is good programming practice to declare the exception object to be an instance of an exception class whose name best describes the error that was detected. This makes our programs more readable. For example, if a null reference was detected, the `NullPointerException` class would normally be chosen.

NOTE *A* `throws` *clause begins with the keyword* `throws` *followed by the name of one or more exception classes separated by commas.*

Creating Error Messages

An error message is created by passing a string containing the message to an exception class's one-parameter constructor when an exception object is created. The error is wrapped around, or contained in, the object when it is created. The setX method, shown in Figure 10.13, uses this approach on lines 5 and 9 to communicate which game board edge of a 500-pixel-wide board would have been breached by a 40-pixel-wide game piece. Exception object messages can be accessed using the Throwable class's getMessage method.

```
1    public void setX(int newX)
2    {
3      if(newX > 460) //beyond game board's right edge
4      {
5        throw new RuntimeException("Beyond the board's RIGHT edge");
6      }
7      if(newX < 6) //beyond game board's left edge
8      {
9        throw new RuntimeException("Beyond the board's LEFT edge");
10     }
11     x = newX;
12   }
```

Figure 10.13
A game piece's **setX** method that throws an exception containing a descriptive message.

The signature of the method shown in Figure 10.13 does not include a throws clause because a RuntimeException is an unchecked exception class. An alternative to the nameless objects created on lines 5 and 9 would be to use named exception objects, but the nameless-object approach used in the figure tends to be more readable.

```
// named exception object alternative to Line 5 of Figure 10.13
RuntimeException e =  new RuntimeException("Beyond the board's RIGHT");
throw e;
```

 NOTE *When a string is not passed to an API Exception class's constructor a default error message is used.*

Execution Path of the throw Statement

After a throw statement is executed within a method, the execution of the method ends, and the exception object propagates up the invocation sequence stored in the runtime stack. If the method is a non-void method, a value is not returned from the method.

On the client side, if the method was invoked inside a try block, the try block's execution ends, and the execution sequence of the catch and finally blocks begins. If the exception is not caught by the invoking method, it continues up the invocation sequence stored in the runtime stack until it is caught. If the Java Runtime Environment catches the exception object, the error message is displayed to the system console, and the application is terminated.

The class `BoxedSnowman2` is shown in Figure 10.14. Its `set` methods that begin on lines 37 and 53 throw a `RunTimeException` object when the value passed to them locates a portion of a snowman beyond the boundaries of the game board. The `if` statements on lines 39 and 43 of the `setX` method detect that an erroneous value of the snowman's `x` coordinate was passed into the method's parameter `newX`. When this is the case, lines 41 or 45 throw a nameless `RunTimeException` object containing appropriate error messages.

The throwing of the exception objects terminates the execution of the `setX` method, leaving the `x` data member unchanged. If an erroneous value is not detected, line 47 performs the normal function of a `setX` method: setting the value passed to the method into the object's `x` data member. Similar modifications have been made to the standard coding of the class's `setY` method (lines 53–64).

The class's three-parameter constructor (lines 9–19) has also been modified to only create snowmen that are completely on the game board. In the interest of brevity, this is accomplished by invoking the class's `setX` and `setY` methods (lines 12 and 13) to store the object's location in its x and y data members. If either of these method invocations, coded inside the `try` block that begins on line 11, produces a thrown exception (because the `intialX` or `intialY` value passed to the constructor is invalid), the constructor does not complete its execution, and it does not return the address of a newly created snowman. Because the constructor does *not* contain a `catch` clause, a thrown exception propagates its way up the invocation sequence stored in the runtime stack. The empty `finally` clause, lines 15-17, is included to make the use of the `try` clause syntactically correct.

```
1    import java.awt.*;
2
3    public class BoxedSnowman2
4    {
5      private int x = 8;
6      private int y = 30;
7      private Color hatColor = Color.BLACK;
8
9      public BoxedSnowman2(int intialX, int intialY, Color hatColor)
10     {
11       try
12       { setX(intialX); //x = intialX;
13         setY(intialY); //y = intialY;
14       }
15       finally
16       {
17       }
18       this.hatColor = hatColor;
19     }
20     public void show(Graphics g) //g is the game board object
21     {
22       g.setColor(hatColor);
```

```
23        g.fillRect(x + 15, y, 10, 15); //hat
24        g.fillRect(x + 10, y + 15, 20, 2); //brim
25        g.setColor(Color.WHITE);
26        g.fillOval(x + 10, y + 17, 20, 20); //head
27        g.fillOval(x, y + 37, 40, 40); //body
28        g.setColor(Color.RED);
29        g.fillOval(x + 19, y + 53, 4, 4); //button
30        g.setColor(Color.BLACK);
31        g.drawRect(x, y, 40, 77); //inscribing rectangle
32     }
33     public int getX()
34     {
35        return x;
36     }
37     public void setX(int newX)
38     {
39        if(newX > 460)
40        {
41           throw new RuntimeException("x is beyond the board's RIGHT");
42        }
43        if(newX < 6)
44        {
45           throw new RuntimeException("x is beyond the board's LEFT");
46        }
47        x = newX;
48     }
49     public int getY()
50     {
51        return y;
52     }
53     public void setY(int newY)
54     {
55        if(newY < 30)
56        {
57           throw new RuntimeException("y is beyond the board's TOP");
58        }
59        if(newY > 423)
60        {
61           throw new RuntimeException("y is beyond the board's BOTTOM");
62        }
63        y = newY;
64     }
65  }
```

Figure 10.14
The class **BoxedSnowman2**.

The application ThrowingExceptions, shown in Figure 10.15, displays a BoxedSnowman2 object on the game board at a user specified location, which can be moved around the game board using the keyboard cursor control keys. The application uses try-catch constructs on lines 24–32 and lines 50–82, to ensure that both the initial and subsequent game board locations of the snowman are within the boundaries of the board.

The loop that begins on line 16 and ends on line 33 asks the user for the initial location of the snowman and creates a snowman at that location. It continues to execute until the user enters a valid initial (x, y) BoxedSnowman location: one that would position the entire snowman on the game board. The user-specified x and y coordinates, input and parsed on lines 17–22, are passed to the BoxedSnowman2 class's three-parameter constructor on line 26. Because line 26 is inside of a try block (that begins on line 24), if the setX or setY methods in the BoxedSnowman2 class invoked by its constructor throws an exception, line 26 will not complete its execution. As a result, the snowman is not created.

The thrown exception is caught on line 29; line 31 outputs the exception message, and the next loop iteration begins. An erroneous user input and the corresponding output are shown at the top of Figure 10.16. When the user enters a valid location for the snowman, line 26 places the address of the newly created snowman in the variable s1, and the truth value of the Boolean variable correctXY used on line 16 is set to true (line 27), which terminates the loop. Line 35 causes the draw call back method to execute, and line 43 displays the snowman on the game board (Figure 10.16c).

Lines 46–83 implement the game environment's keyStruck call back method, which is used to move the snowman around the game board. Inside of its switch statement that begins on line 52, lines 57, 63, 69, and 75 invoke the BoxedSnowman2 class's set methods to move the snowman when one of the cursor control keys is struck. If these methods determine that the new x or y coordinate passed to them is invalid, they do not change the snowman's location and terminate after throwing a RuntimeException object.

Because the set method invocations are coded inside a try-catch construct (lines 50–82), the thrown exception is caught on line 79. Its message is unwrapped and placed in the String object message (line 81). When the keyStruck method ends, the draw call back method executes, and line 42 outputs the thrown error message to the top of the game board (Figure 10.16d). The next time a key is struck, the object message is set to the empty string on line 48, which causes the draw call back method to eliminate the message after a valid snowman motion.

```
1    import edu.sjcny.gpv1.*;
2    import java.awt.*;
3    import javax.swing.*;
4
5    public class ThrowingExceptions extends DrawableAdapter
6    { static ThrowingExceptions ge = new ThrowingExceptions();
7      static Game board gb = new Game board(ge, "THROWING EXCEPTIONS");
8      static BoxedSnowman2 s1;
9      static String message = "";
10
11     public static void main(String[] args)
12     { String s;
13       boolean correctXY = false;
14       int x, y;
15
```

```
16      while(correctXY == false) //x or y is not valid
17      { s = JOptionPane.showInputDialog("enter the snowman's " +
18                                          "X coordinate");
19        x = Integer.parseInt(s);
20        s = JOptionPane.showInputDialog("enter the snowman's " +
21                                          "Y coordinate");
22        y = Integer.parseInt(s);
23
24        try
25        {
26          s1 = new BoxedSnowman2(x, y, Color.BLUE);//exception produced?
27          correctXY = true;
28        } //end try
29        catch(RuntimeException e)
30        {
31          JOptionPane.showMessageDialog(null, e.getMessage());
32        } //end catch
33      } //end while
34
35      showGame board(gb);
36    }
37
38    public void draw(Graphics g)
39    {
40      g.setColor(Color.BLACK);
41      g.setFont(new Font("Arial", Font.BOLD, 18));
42      g.drawString(message,  120, 50);
43      s1.show(g);
44    }
45
46    public void keyStruck(char key)
47    { int newX, newY;
48      message = "";
49
50      try
51      {
52        switch (key)
53        {
54          case 'L':
55          {
56            newX = s1.getX() - 2;
57            s1.setX(newX); //could cause an exception
58            break;
59          }
60          case 'R':
61          {
62            newX = s1.getX() + 2;
63            s1.setX(newX); //could cause an exception
64            break;
```

```
65              }
66          case 'U':
67          {
68             newY = s1.getY() - 2;
69             s1.setY(newY); //could cause an exception
70             break;
71          }
72          case 'D':
73          {
74             newY = s1.getY() + 2;
75             s1.setY(newY); //could cause an exception
76          }
77        }
78      } //end try
79      catch(RuntimeException e)
80      {
81         message = e.getMessage();
82      } //end catch
83    }
84  }
```

Figure 10.15
The application **ThrowingExceptions**.

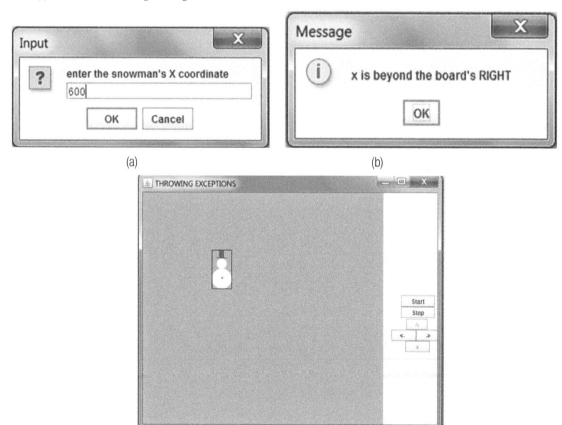

(a)

(b)

(c)

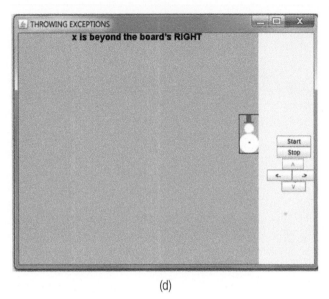

(d)

Figure 10.16

Output produced by the application **ThrowingExceptions**.

10.5 DEFINING EXCEPTION CLASSES

A new exception class can be defined by extending an existing exception class. Defining and using new exception classes in our programs makes them more readable and easier to understand because the names we give to them can be more representative of the error that caused the exception to be thrown. For example, if we defined an exception class named OffBoardException and used it on line 41 of Figure 10.14 and line 29 of Figure 10.15, the reason for throwing and catching the exception would be self-evident.

The concepts involved in and the syntax used to extend exception classes are the same concepts and syntax that apply to extending non-exception classes discussed in Chapter 8. The child class inherits all of the methods and data members in its inheritance chain, which includes the getMessage method defined in the class Throwable.

> **NOTE** *The child of a checked exception class is always a checked exception class.*
> *The child of an unchecked exception class is always an unchecked exception class.*

Figure 10.17 presents the definition of the exception class OffBoardException, which is an exception class because it extends RuntimeException and is an unchecked exception class because RuntimeException is an unchecked exception class. The brevity of its code is typical of most non-API exception classes and can be used as a template for defining other exception classes. Both of its constructors simply invoke the RuntimeException class's constructor. The message passed to the class's one-parameter constructor (line 7) is passed to its parent's constructor, which wraps it around the object it creates. The inherited default message is the null string. This class could be used everywhere the RuntimeException class is used in Figures 10.14 and 10.15.

```
1    public class OffBoardException extends RuntimeException
2    {
3      public OffBoardException()
4      {
5        super();
6      }
7      public OffBoardException(String message)
8      {
9        super(message);
10     }
11   }
```

Figure 10.17
The non-API exception class **OffBoardException**.

Catch Block Ordering

The application DefinedExceptionClass, shown in Figure 10.18, demonstrates the order in which exception objects in the same inheritance chain must be caught, whether they are API classes or defined exception classes. The catch clause that catches an OffBoardException object (line 13) is coded before the clause that catches its parent class's RuntimeException object (line 19), which is coded before the clause that catches its parent class's Exception object (line 25).

The correct ordering of the catch blocks is up the inheritance chain of the exception objects from child to ancestors. This implies that when one of the catch blocks in a try-catch construct catches a Throwable exception object, that catch clause must be coded last. The ordering is a consequence of the polymorphic feature of inheritance. Because a parent type parameter can point to (reference) a child, a catch clause that catches an instance of a super class will also catch an exception object in a class that inherits directly or indirectly from it. Coding the catch blocks of a try-catch construct in any other order produces a translation error because the catch blocks that catch the child class exceptions have been rendered unreachable.

The method test, coded on lines 32–48 of Figure 10.18, throws exception objects when it is passed the value 1, 2, or 3. It is invoked on line 11 inside a try block that begins on line 9 and is passed the loop variable of the for loop that begins on line 7. This causes it to throw one of three different types of exceptions. Because one of the exceptions is a checked exception (an instance of the class Exception on line 36), the method's signature (line 32) contains a throws clause.

The order of the catch clauses coded on lines 13–29 is consistent with the inheritance chain of the exception class OffBoardException (Figure 10.17), which inherits from the class Runtime-Exception, which inherits from the class Exception (Figure 10.1). These catch clauses output the message attached to the objects they catch, proceeded by annotation particular to each catch clause (Figure 10.19). The messages are created on lines 36, 40, and 45.

```
1    import java.io.IOException;
2
3    public class DefinedExceptionClass
4    {
5      public static void main(String[] args)
6      {
7        for(int i=1; i<=3; i++)
8        {
9          try
10         {
11           test(i);
12         }
13         catch(OffBoardException e) //a child of RuntimeException
14         {
15           System.out.print("Caught by the OffBoardException " +
16                              "catch block: ");
17           System.out.println(e.getMessage());
18         }
19         catch(RuntimeException e) //a child of Exception
20         {
21           System.out.print("Caught by the RuntimeException " +
22                              "catch block: ");
23           System.out.println(e.getMessage());
24         }
25         catch(Exception e) //a child of throwable
26         {
27           System.out.print("Caught by the Exception catch block: ");
28           System.out.println(e.getMessage());
29         }
30       }
31     }
32     public static void test(int path) throws Exception
33     {
34       if(path == 1) //throw an Exception object
35       {
36         throw new Exception("a message attached to an Exception object");
37       }
38       if(path == 2) //throw a RuntimeException object
39       {
40         throw new RuntimeException("a message attached to a " +
41                                     "RuntimeException object");
42       }
43       if(path == 3) //throw an OffBoardException object
```

```
44        {
45            throw new OffBoardException("a message attached to an " +
46                                        "OffBoardException object");
47        }
48     }
49  }
```

Figure 10.18
The application **DefinedExceptionClass**.

```
Caught by the Exception catch block: a message attached to an Exception object

Caught by the RuntimeException catch block: a message attached to a RuntimeException object

Caught by the OffBoardException catch block: a message attached to an OffBoardException object
```

Figure 10.19
The output produced by the application **DefinedExceptionClass**.

10.6 CHAPTER SUMMARY

One very important programming goal is to produce reusable methods, and the concept of exceptions helps us achieve this goal. It gives us the ability to defer the decision as to what to do when an error occurs during the execution of a method to the invoker of the method. This extends the reusability of a method because the action to take when an error occurs is usually application dependent. One application may choose to terminate the program, while another application may re-invoke the method after giving the user a chance to correct an erroneous input.

Under Java's implementation of exceptions, the invocation of a method that could detect an error is coded inside the `try` clause of a `try-catch` construct, and the clause is immediately followed by one or more `catch` clauses. Each `catch` clause has a parameter list with one parameter whose type is the API class `Throwable` or one of its descendants. The type used in each parameter list must be different.

When the method detects an error, it executes a `throw` statement, which terminates the execution of the method and the invoker's `try` clause. The `throw` statement includes an exception object in the class `Throwable`, or one of its descendants, that contains information about the error. This object is passed to the `catch` clause that contains a parameter in the exception object's class or one of its ancestors. The code block of that, and only that, `catch` clause then executes to perform the application-dependent processing associated with this type of error.

Instances of the class `Throwable` and each of its subclasses contain default error information, which can be overwritten when these exception objects are created by passing a string to the classes' constructors. The code within the `catch` clauses can invoke the `getMessage` method on the exception object passed to them to fetch the string containing the exception error information.

The API classes `Exception` and `Error` are the two direct subclasses of `Throwable`. The class `Error` and all of its descendants are unchecked exception classes, while the `Throwable` and

`Exception` classes are checked exception classes. Conditions that cause instances of the `Error` class or its descendants to be thrown are considered abnormal and are best processed by the Java Runtime Environment. The method that contains the `try-catch` construct must catch a thrown checked exception, or the method must inform the translator that it will intentionally ignore the error via a `throws` clause added to its signature. If a thrown checked exception is not caught within an application, the runtime environment terminates the program and outputs the exception object's error information.

A `finally` clause can be used to implement tasks that should be performed after a `try-catch` block is completed. It is coded immediately after the last catch block, and it always executes. It must be coded after the `try` clause when there are no `catch` clauses associated with the `try` clause.

When designing an algorithm for a method, we should always consider what could go wrong and include a strategy in the algorithm to detect the error. Usually, the Boolean condition of an `if` statement is used to detect an error, and the `if` statement's code block creates and throws an exception object. A new exception class can be defined by extending an existing exception class. Defining and using new exception classes in our programs makes them more readable and easier to understand because the name we give to the class can be more representative of the error that caused the exception to be thrown. All of these design issues contribute to the development of readable, more reusable and maintainable software.

Knowledge Exercises

1. True or false:
   a) An important programming design goal is to produce an error-free program.
   b) Dividing a large program into smaller classes and testing each class guarantees that errors will not occur at runtime.
   c) All uncaught exception objects are caught and handled by the Java Runtime Environment.
   d) The class `Throwable` has one direct subclass: `Exception`.
   e) Abnormal conditions that cause an instance of the class `Error` to be thrown are best processed by the Java Runtime Environment.
   f) The class `Exception` is an unchecked exception class, and the class `Error` is a checked exception class.
   g) An exception object is an instance of the class `Throwable` or one of its subclasses.
   h) The API exception classes cannot be extended.
   i) Any method that throws a checked exception must include a `throws` clause in its signature.
   j) If a method throws an exception, the method invoking it must contain a `try-catch` block.
   k) The code block of a `finally` clause always executes.
   l) If the methods invoked inside a `try` block do not throw an exception, the program skips the `catch` block(s).
   m) A `try-catch` construct can also be used to identify and process data as well as to detect errors.

n) The child of an unchecked exception class is always an unchecked exception class.

o) Some methods in the API classes throw exceptions.

2. Mention at least three things that might cause a runtime error or an exception in a program.

3. When would you choose to throw a checked rather than an unchecked exception?

4. Name a class you would extend to create an unchecked exception class.

5. Name a class you would extend to create a checked exception class.

6. Explain in some detail what happens when an error, such as division by zero, occurs in a Java program.

7. Tell whether each of these exceptions or errors is checked or unchecked:
   a) `IOException`
   b) `RunTimeException`
   c) `EOFException`
   d) `ArithmeticException`
   e) `NullPointerException`
   f) `AnnotationFormatError`
   g) `IndexOutOfBoundsException`
   h) `VirtualMachineError`

8. Explain the difference between the `throws` clause and the `throw` statement. Give an example of how each one is used.

9. Explain how you would fetch the string containing a caught exception object's error information.

Programming Exercises

1. Write a program that creates a three-element array and asks the user which element of the array should be output. Use a `try-catch` block to recover from an attempt to output an array element whose index is not 0, 1, or 2. Inform the user that an erroneous input was made, output the exception object's error information, and give the user an unlimited number of opportunities to correct the error. Do not use an `if` statement in this program.

2. Repeat Exercise 1 and include a separate method that is passed the array and the input index and performs the output. This method should use an `if` statement to detect an erroneous index and throw an unchecked exception containing the message: *The range of the index must be between 0 and 2.*

3. Repeat Exercise 2, modifying the method so it throws a checked exception in a new exception class named `InvalidIndexException`.

4. Repeat Exercise 2, modifying the method so it throws a checked exception in a new exception class named `IndexTooLowException` when the array index passed to the method is too low, and throws a checked exception in a new exception class named `IndexTooHighException` when the array index passed to the method is too high.

5. Write a program to output the number of operators contained within a valid arithmetic expression input by the program user. Use a `try-catch` construct to count the operators. Hint: the `parseDouble` method throws an exception when it is passed anything other than a string that represents a valid real number or a valid integer.

6. Write a static method named `inputInt` within a class named `ValidNumericInput` that displays the prompt passed to it in an input dialog box, accepts an integer input from the user, and returns the parsed integer. If the user does not enter a valid integer, or if the user clicks OK or Cancel without making an entry, the method throws an exception in the programmer-defined exception class `BadIntegerEntry`. The thrown exception object will contain a message indicating which event caused the exception: no entry or non-integer entry. Use the method in an application that gives the user an unlimited number of opportunities to enter two valid integers by invoking the method inside a `try-catch` construct coded inside a loop. Each time an erroneous input is made, the application will output the thrown exception object's error message before re-invoking the method. Note: a no-entry Cancel click returns `null`, and a no-entry OK click returns the empty string `""`.

7. Write a program to accept a sentence from the keyboard terminated by a new line. Use the `Integer` class's `parseInt` method to locate all the integers. Then, write them to the disk file *numbers.txt* (don't specify a path) one number per line in the order in which they appear in the sentence. After storing the integers in the disk file, ask the user which of the numbers to delete from the file via an invocation of the `inputInt` method described in Exercise 6. When the method throws an exception, the application should tell the program user which mistake (no-entry or non-integer entry) occurred and ask for another entry. Before terminating, the application should read the modified contents from the file and output them to the system console.

Enrichment

1. Read the API documentation on the class `Throwable` and its two direct subclasses.

2. Investigate how to determine from the API online documentation if an API method throws and exception and what exception it throws.

3. Investigate how the language C++ implements the concept of exceptions.

GRAPHICAL USER INTERFACES

11.1 *Overview*. *480*

11.2 *Enhancing Dialog Boxes*. *482*

11.3 *Creating a Graphical User Interface*
for an Application. *487*

11.4 *Event Processing* *500*

11.5 *Layout Managers*. *522*

11.6 *Applets*. *531*

11.7 *Chapter Summary* *544*

In this chapter

In this chapter, we will learn how to create more user-friendly and informative dialog boxes and how to build and incorporate graphical user interfaces (GUIs) into our programs. The use of these point-and-click interfaces makes interacting with a program more user friendly. Java provides two packages, the Abstract Window Toolkit (AWT) and Swing, to facilitate the development of dialog boxes and GUIs.

Principles for designing a GUI interface will be explained and illustrated as will the use of a GUI-builder worker class to create a window, add the GUI components to the window, and perform the processing associated with the user's interaction with its components. These components include panels, buttons, text fields, labels, and tool tips. Various layout managers, used to organize the components, will be compared.

Methods called event handlers will be discussed. These methods are invoked by the Java Runtime Environment (JRE™) when an event, such as a mouse click or a mouse drag, is performed on the GUI. We will learn how to write these event handler methods and how to register the methods with the Runtime Environment. The use of paint event handler methods to draw two-dimensional graphical objects on a GUI component will also be discussed.

Finally, these graphical concepts will be applied to Web-based programs called *applets*. We will discuss how to write applets, the basics of HTML code used to download and launch an applet in a Web browser, and some security issues associated with applets.

After successfully completing this chapter you should:

* Be able to create and use dialog boxes that are more informative and user friendly

- Know how to design and implement GUIs that contain panels, text fields, buttons, labels, and tool tips using Java's AWT and Swing packages
- Be familiar with top-level containers, containers, and atomic GUI components and their role in graphical interfaces
- Understand the advantages of using a GUI-builder worker class to construct a graphical interface and how to implement these classes
- Know the three (or sometimes four) step process for adding components to a container
- Understand how to write event handler methods to process mouse, keyboard, timer, and paint events that occur on a GUI
- Know how to register event handler methods with the Java Runtime Environment so they are invoked when the specific events occur
- Be able to distinguish between applications and applets and be able to implement an applet and launch it in a Web browser
- Understand security issues associated with applets and Java's role in these issues

11.1 OVERVIEW

A graphical user interface is a means of interacting with a program. Most often referred to using the acronym GUI (pronounced "goo-ee"), its design goal is to make the use of a program self-evident. GUIs are a much more user friendly than the original command-based interaction scheme in which a program would issue a text-based prompt that generically amounted to "what would you like to do?" and the user responded by typing a command such as "tax program."

Developed during the late 1970s, graphical interfaces were initially used to communicate with the operating system, but their power and ease of use was quickly adopted into all of the applications run on a system. Wherever possible, text-based prompts are replaced with icons, and keyboard input is replaced with mouse clicks, audio commands, and touch screen/pad input.

Just as graphical road signs succinctly communicate information to motorists, GUI objects, called *components,* permit us to quickly navigate our way through a program. The features of each of these components, which include clickable buttons, check boxes, radio buttons, scroll bars, sliders, and menu bars, to name a few, facilitate particular I/O functions that are common to most programs. Figure 11.1 shows some of the more commonly used components.

While the use of GUIs has reduced the time and effort required to interact with a program, incorporating a GUI into a program can significantly increase the time and effort required to develop it. In reaction to this, many integrated development environments provide a GUI-builder feature that allows the programmer to rapidly develop the interface. It is built by selecting commonly used GUI components from a graphical display, dragging them to a position on a panel that will become the user interface, and then setting features associated with them such as their color, size, text type, and visibility. As the programmer builds the interface, the IDE adds the code to the program that creates and displays the components and adds empty methods to the program that will execute when the user interacts with the components. The programmer then adds the code to perform the processing associated with the components to these methods.

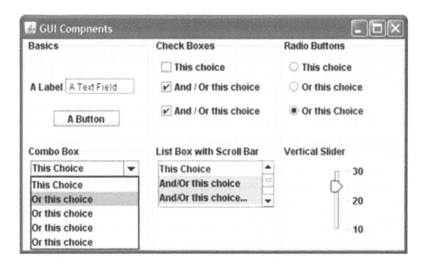

Figure 11.1
Commonly used GUI components.

The AWT and Swing Packages

The Java code generated by these GUI builders relies heavily on the classes that are part of the API AWT and Swing packages. Both of these packages are part of the Java Foundation Classes (JFC), a set of classes that support the development of graphical interfaces. The AWT package was part of the API before the Swing package was added to it. The Swing package both duplicated and extended the range of the types of GUI components available in the AWT package to include file and color-chooser dialog boxes and provided additional features such as tool tips and the ability to interact with the GUI in a drag-and-drop mode. All Swing components are designed to be 100% cross-platform compatible.

Java applications that use components in the Swing package are less dependent on the graphical features of the platform's operating system on which the application is run. For example, minor differences in the components' appearance (or look) and the change in their appearance when the user interacts with them (their feel) that are platform dependent can be eliminated, or the look and feel of the components can be made to emulate the platform on which the application is running.

In addition, Swing component classes are written in Java and do not contain any platform-specific code. For that reason, they are referred to as *lightweight* components, to distinguish them from the subset of *heavyweight* components that are "weighed down" by (i.e., contain) platform-specific code, and always emulate the look and feel of the platform on which they are running. Most applications use GUI components that are instances of classes in the API Swing (`javax.swing`) package.

11.2 ENHANCING DIALOG BOXES

Input and message dialog boxes are graphical user interfaces used to perform I/O with the program user. In addition to the versions of the showInputDialog and showMessageDialog methods discussed in Chapter 2, the JOptionPane class provides several overloaded versions of these methods and other methods that can be used to provide more informative and user-friendly dialog boxes. The default icon and title displayed in the dialog boxes can be changed, the dialog boxes can be displayed in the middle of a specified window such as the game board's window, and a default input or a set of input selections can be displayed in an input dialog box.

Table 11.1 presents a summary of the overloaded versions of the showInputDialog and showMessageDialog methods, with their signatures given in its left column. The check marks

Table 11.1
Options for Displaying Input and Message Dialog Boxes

Method	Default Input	Specify Window	Title	Icon	Input Choices
Input Dialog Boxes					
showInputDialog(Object prompt)					
showInputDialog(Object prompt, Object defaultInput)	√				
showInputDialog(Component window, Object prompt)		√			
showInputDialog(Component window, Object prompt, Object defaultInput)	√	√			
showInputDialog(Component window, Object prompt, String title, int messageIcon)		√	√	√	
showInputDialog(Component window, Object prompt, String title, int messageIcon, Icon icon, Object[] selectionValues, Object initialSelectionValue)	√	√	√	√	√
Message Dialog Boxes					
showMessageDialog(Component window, Object message)		√			
showMessageDialog(Component window, Object message, String title, int messageIcon)		√	√	√	

in the columns to the right identify the features of each version of the methods. The top section of the table presents the input dialog methods, and the message dialog methods are presented in the bottom section. The signatures of the methods that have been used up to this point in the textbook are shown at the beginning of the two sections of the table. All of the input dialog box methods return a reference to a `String` object except for the last one shown in the top portion of the table, which returns an `Object` reference.

The parameter `window` in the signatures of the message-box methods and last four input-box methods could be passed a reference to a GUI component such as a window. When it is, the dialog box is displayed in the center of the component. If the parameter is passed a `null` value, the dialog box is displayed in the center of the program window that invoked the method. To display it in the center of the game board window, the method would be passed the `GameBoard` object `gb` as shown on line 12 of the application `CenteredMsgBox`, shown in Figure 11.2. The output it produces is shown in Figure 11.3.

Normally, the `prompt` and `defaultInput` parameter used in the input dialog method signatures shown in the Table 11.1 are passed a `String` object. The `defaultInput` is displayed in the text area of the input box when it appears on the monitor. It can be changed (overtyped) by the program user. The argument passed to the parameter `title` (used in fifth and last rows of the table) is displayed in the title bar at the top of the dialog box. The parameter `message` in the message dialog method signatures is normally passed a `String` object or any object that contains a `toString` method. The parameter `icon` in the sixth row of the table is used to pass a programmer-defined instance of the `Icon` class to the method.

```
1    import edu.sjcny.gpv1.*;
2    import javax.swing.JOptionPane;
3
4    public class CenteredMsgBox extends DrawableAdapter
5    {
6      static CenteredMsgBox ge = new CenteredMsgBox();
7      static GameBoard gb = new GameBoard(ge, "My Game");
8
9      public static void main(String args[])
10     {
11       showGameBoard(gb);
12       JOptionPane.showMessageDialog(gb, "A Messages Box Centered " +
13                                        "in the Game Board Window");
14       showGameBoard(gb);
15     }
16   }
```

Figure 11.2
The application CenteredMsgBox.

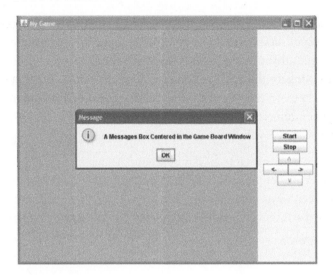

Figure 11.3
The output produced by the application **CenterMsgBox**.

The methods in Table 11.1 whose signatures contain the parameter messageIcon can be passed any of five static constants defined in the class JOptionPane. This parameter is used to specify which one of five predefined icons will be displayed on the left side of a dialog box. Table 11.2 gives the names of the constants, their integer value, and the icons that are associated with each of them. The methods in Table 11.1 whose signatures do not contain the parameter messageIcon always display the default icons identified parenthetically in the rightmost column of the table. An integer literal between -1 and 3 inclusive (one of the five constants' values) can alternately be passed to this parameter.

Table 11.2
The **JOptionPane** Class's Predefined Dialog Box Icon Constants and Icons

Constant Name	Value	Icon	Common Icon Use
PLAIN_MESSAGE	-1	none	Other defined icons are inappropriate: no icon is displayed
ERROR_MESSAGE	0	⊗	An error or problem has occurred
INFORMATION_MESSAGE	1	ⓘ	For your information (message dialog box default)
WARNING_MESSAGE	2	⚠	Consider possible ramifications
QUESTION_MESSAGE	3	?	A reply to the prompt is requested (input dialog box default)

The last method shown in the input portion of the Table 11.3 implements all the features presented in that table. In this version of the method the default input is actually designated to be one of a valid set of inputs contained in an array passed to the method's selectionValues parameter. The designation of the default value is performed by passing one of the elements of the array to the parameter initialSelectionValue. The elements of the array can be String objects, instances of a class that contains a toString method, or several other options that will be discussed later in this chapter. If a null value is passed to the parameter selectionValues, the user can overstrike the displayed default value; otherwise, the user can only select one of the objects in the array which are displayed in a drop-down box.

The application EnhancedDialogBoxes presented in Figure 11.4 demonstrates the use of all of the features implemented by the overloaded dialog box methods presented in Table 11.1, except centering the dialog box in a GUI component (which was demonstrated in the application presented in Figure 11.2). The dialog box outputs produced by the program are shown in Figure 11.5.

The word *ERROR* passcd to the second parameter of the method invoked on line 12 of Figure 11.4 appears in the title area of the message box it outputs (Figure 11.5a). This message box also contains the non-default Error icon, whose number (0) is passed to the method's third parameter using the static constant JOptionPane.ERROR _ MESSAGE.

Line 15 displays an input dialog box containing the default input, *Sophomore,* as shown in Figure 11.5b. The default value is passed to its second parameter on line 16.

The method invoked on line 19 displays the input dialog box that is shown in Figure 11.5c. The box contains the title *Standing* passed to the method's third parameter on line 21 and the Question icon because the numeric literal 3 is passed to its fourth parameter. The default input *Junior* is also displayed in the text area of the input box because the third element of the array, defined on lines 7 and 8, is passed to the method's last parameter on line 24. The null value passed to the method on line 22 indicates that a user programmer-defined icon is not passed to the method.

Figure 11.5d shows the input box displayed to its left after the user clicks the box's down arrow to display the valid input choices passed to the method on line 23. The coercion on line 19 is necessary because the method invoked on that line returns an Object reference variable that contains the address of the user-selected object contained in the array passed to it on line 23.

```
1    import javax.swing.JOptionPane;
2
3    public class EnhancedDialogBoxes
4    {
5      public static void main(String[] args)
6      {
7        String[] inputOptions = {"Freshman", "Sophomore",
8                                 "Junior", "Senior" };
9        String s1, s2;
10
11       // Titled message box with an error icon
```

```
12      JOptionPane.showMessageDialog(null, "The Disk I/O Failed", "ERROR",
13                              JOptionPane.ERROR_MESSAGE);
14      // Input box with a default input
15      s1 = JOptionPane.showInputDialog("Enter your Class Standing",
16                              "Sophomore");
17
18      // A Non-default icon titled Input box, a valid set of inputs
19      s2 = (String) JOptionPane.showInputDialog(null, "Select your " +
20                              "class standing",
21                              "Standing", 3,
22                              null,
23                              inputOptions,
24                              inputOptions[2]);
25
26      System.out.println(s1 + " " + s2);
27  }
28 }
```

Figure 11.4
The application **EnhancedDialogBoxes**.

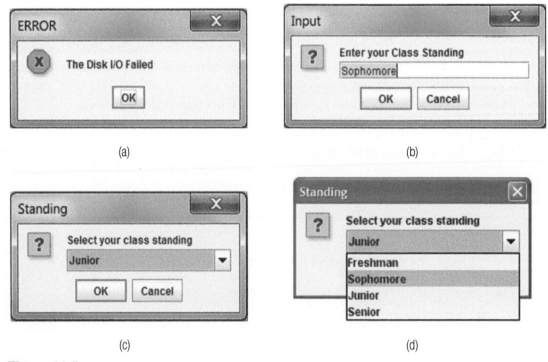

(a)

(b)

(c)

(d)

Figure 11.5
The output produced by the application **EnhancedDialogBoxes**.

11.3 CREATING A GRAPHICAL USER INTERFACE FOR AN APPLICATION

Graphical user interfaces are created by declaring an instance of a top-level container class and then adding GUI components to it. Top-level container classes in the Swing package include JWindow, JFrame, JApplet, and JDialog. The class JFrame extends the capabilities of its parent of the class Window by adding a title bar that contains the window management icons (minimize, resize, and close), an optional title, and the ability to drag the window. Figure 11.6 shows the inheritance chain of the Swing top-level containers.

Non-Web based GUI applications use JFrame as their top-level GUI container because it has the look and feel of a program window. Web based applications, referred to as applets, use JApplet as their top-level container. The class JDialog is used as the top-level container for GUI components that are to be part of a sub-window. Input and message dialog boxes are instances of this class. All top-level containers have a *content pane*, which is the area of the window that will contain the GUI components particular to an application.

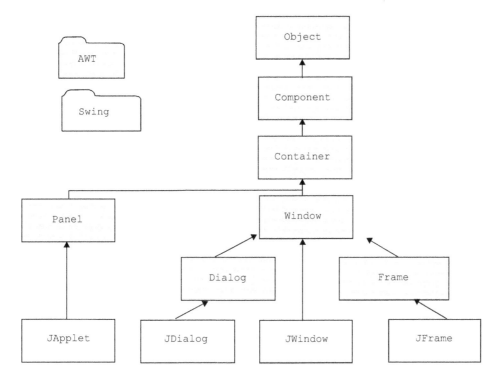

Figure 11.6
The inheritance chain of the top-level swing containers.

11.3.1 The Content Pane

Figure 11.7 shows two JFrame instances, one with a menu bar (left window) and one without a menu bar (right window). The content panes are the yellow portions of the windows. When a JFrame window is created, its outer width and height (in pixels) is specified. Within these outer dimensions, there is a rectangular border that is, by default, 4 pixels wide. A 26-pixel-high title bar is positioned directly below the top portion of the border, and a 23-pixel-high menu bar can be added to the window directly below the title bar. The remaining area of the window determines the width and height of the content pane, which are the window's dimensions minus the surrounding boarders, title bar, and menu bar.

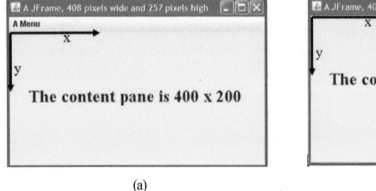
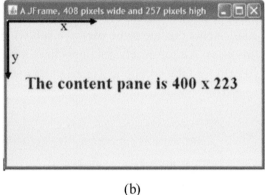

(a)   (b)

Figure 11.7
Two JFrame windows 408 pixels wide and 257 pixels high.

For example, the windows in Figure 11.7 are both 408 pixels wide and 257 pixels high. The left window's content pane is 400 pixels wide (408 minus the left and right border widths) and 200 pixels high (257 minus the top border, title bar, menu bar, and bottom border heights). The right window's content pane is 223 pixels high because the height of the menu bar (23 pixels) in the window to its left is now part of the content pane.

The origin of the coordinate system used to position components added to the content pane is located at the upper-left corner of the content pane. The positive x direction is to the right, and the positive y direction is downward. The text shown on the two content panes in Figure 11.7 was added at the same (x, y) locations. Because the origin of the content pane in the window without the menu bar is higher in the window, the text appears closer to the top of the window.

11.3.2 Creating and Displaying a Program Window

The one-parameter constructor of the JFrame class is used to create a program window. The string parameter passed to it is displayed on the left side of the window's title bar. Alternately, the default (no-parameter) constructor can be used to create a window with no title. Once created, the size of the window must be specified, and then the window must be made visible. The following code fragment creates the 708 x 434 pixel window shown in Figure 11.8, which is displayed with its upper left corner at the default location (0, 0) on the monitor.

```
JFrame appWindow = new JFrame("A GUI Window");
appWindow.setSize(708, 434); //content pane is 700 x 400
appWindow.setVisible(true);
```

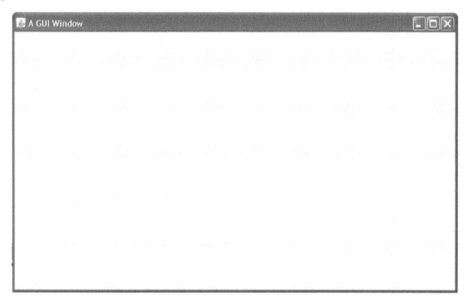

Figure 11.8
A program window.

Normally, three additional methods are invoked when a window is created. One method is used to reposition the upper left corner of the window from its default (0, 0) monitor location, and the second method is used to change the color of the content pane (which defaults to light gray). The third method is used to direct the Runtime Environment to terminate the program when the user closes the window. The default is to continue the program's execution.

The signatures of these three methods, the `JFrame` constructors, and the methods `setSize` and `setVisible`, and one additional method are shown in Table 11.3. All of the methods in the table are non-static methods, and all but the last one are members of the `JFrame` class. The last method is a member of the class `Component`.

Table 11.3
Methods Used to Create and Display a Window

Method Signature	Function
`JFrame();`	Construct a window with no title
`JFrame(String windowTitle)`	Construct a window with the title `windowTitle`
`setSize(int width, int height)`	Sets the width of the window to `width` pixels and the height of the window to `height` pixels
`setVisible(boolean isVisible)`	Displays the window on the monitor when `isVisible` is true

(Contd.)

Method Signature	Function
setLocation(int x, int y)	Positions the upper left corner of the window to pixel location (x, y) of the monitor
setDefaultCloseOperation(int action)	Specifies the action to be taken when the window is closed; action: 3 terminates the program
getContentPane()	Returns a Container reference to the window's content pane
setBackground(Color paneColor);	Sets the color of the window's content pane to paneColor, a Component class method

The application GUIWindow shown in Figure 11.9 creates and displays the window shown in Figure 11.10. Line 10 positions the upper left corner of the window 100 pixels below and to the right of the upper left corner of the monitor. Line 11 sets the color of the content pane to pink by invoking the setBackground method on the content-pane object whose address is returned from the getContentPane method. The JFrame class inherits this method from the Component class.

The argument passed to the setDefaultCloseOperation invoked on line 12 is a static constant defined in the JFrame class used to specify the action to be taken when the window is closed. When used in this context, the application is terminated when its window, referenced by appWindow, is closed. Although the value of the constant (three) could have been coded as a numeric literal, the use of the constant (EXIT _ ON _ CLOSE) makes the line more readable and is considered good programming practice.

If line 12 were eliminated from the program, the Java Runtime Environment would still consider the program active, even though the window has been closed and the main method has ended. One result of this would be that the IDE used to execute the program would still consider the program to be running. We will learn more about this in Chapter 14 when we study the concept of *threads*.

```
1     import javax.swing.*;
2     import java.awt.Color;
3
4     public class GUIWindow
5     {
6       public static void main(String[] args)
7       {
8         JFrame appWindow = new JFrame("A GUI Window");
9         appWindow.setSize(698, 443);
10        appWindow.setLocation(100, 100);
11        appWindow.getContentPane().setBackground(Color.PINK);
```

```
12        appWindow.setDefaultCloseOperation(JFrame.EXIT_ON_CLOSE);
13        appWindow.setVisible(true);
14   }
15 }
```

Figure 11.9
The application **GUIWindow**.

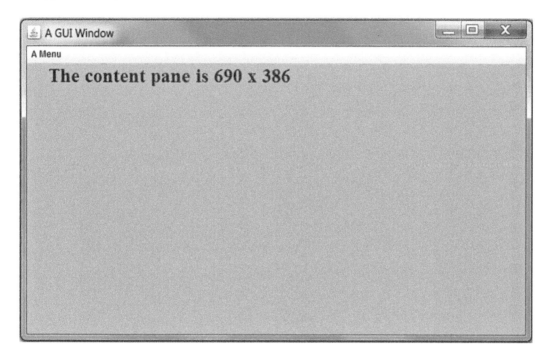

Figure 11.10
The window produced by the application **GUIWindow**.

GUI-Builder Worker Classes

Consistent with the concept of divide-and-conquer, most often the building of the user interface is not performed in the main method, but rather, it is relegated to one or more worker classes. This is particularly useful when the application will contain one or more windows because each window can be built by a separate worker class. For this reason, it is the approach taken by IDE's that contain drag-and-drop GUI builders.

Line 5 of the application GUIWindowBuilder, shown in Figure 11.11, creates the same window as the application shown in Figure 11.9, but this time, the window is an instance of the worker class WindowBuilder shown in Figure 11.12. The worker class extends the class JFrame, but it does not add any data members or methods. It simply contains a constructor: lines 6–15 of Figure 11.12.

Line 8 of the worker class invokes JFrame's one-parameter constructor to construct the window, passing it the string to be displayed in the window's title bar, then lines 10–15 set the window's size, location, color, close action, and visibility. This is the identical code used on lines 9–13 of the application shown in Figure 11.9, except that the methods are invoked on the window created on line 8 of the constructor. The invocation on lines 10–14 of Figure 11.12 could have been preceded by the keyword `this` followed by a dot to more clearly indicate that they were being invoked on this object that was created on line 8, but the coding shown in the figure is more commonly used.

```
1    public class GUIWindowBuilder
2    {
3      public static void main(String[] args)
4      {
5        WindowBuilder appWindow = new WindowBuilder("A GUI Window");
6      }
7    }
```

Figure 11.11
The application **GUIWindowBuilder**.

```
1    import javax.swing.*;
2    import java.awt.*;
3
4    public class WindowBuilder extends JFrame
5    {
6      public WindowBuilder(String title)
7      {
8        super(title);
9
10       setSize(698, 443);
11       setLocation(100, 100);
12       getContentPane().setBackground(Color.PINK);
13       setDefaultCloseOperation(JFrame.EXIT_ON_CLOSE);
14       setVisible(true);
15     }
16   }
```

Figure 11.12
The class **WindowBuilder**.

Depending on the application, the GUI-builder worker class may include one or more overloaded constructors to allow the client to specify not only the window's title, but also its size, location, color, close action, and visibility.

The coding style of relegating the task of creating a GUI window to a separate worker class that extends `JFrame` will be used in the remainder of this chapter.

11.3.3 Adding GUI Components to a Window

The Swing package contains a rich assortment of GUI components, some of which are shown in Figure 11.1, that can be added to a window. While there is some overlap in the roles that they play in the I/O process, each component has been designed to facilitate a particular I/O function.

For example, the functionality of radio buttons makes them the best components to use to acquire one choice from a small set of mutually exclusive choices.

The most common components used in GUI interfaces are buttons, text fields, labels, check boxes, radio buttons, and combo boxes. Table 11.4 lists the constructor methods used to create these components grouped by their intended functionality and gives a brief description of the I/O function they were designed to facilitate.

Table 11.4
Commonly Used Java Swing GUI Components

Component Constructors	Targeted Use
Input Components	
`JCheckBox(String text)` `JCheckBox(String text, boolean selected)`	Select one or more inputs from a group of suggested inputs by clicking a box
`JRadioButton(String text)` `JRadioButton(String text, boolean selected)`	Select one input from a group of suggested inputs by clicking a button
`JComboBox(E[] items)`	Select one input from a group of suggested inputs by clicking an item
Input or Output Component	
`JTextField(String text)`	Keyboard input, String output
Annotation or Output Component	
`JLabel(String text)`	Annotate a window including placing prompts at text boxes; String output to the window
Initiate Processing Component	
`JButton(String text)`	Execute instructions associated with the click of the button
Collect Other Related Components and 2D Graphics Components	
`JPanel()` `JPanel(LayoutManager layout)`	Group other related components and draw 2D shapes

The names of all of the Swing component class names begin with a capital J. They are all direct or indirect descendants of the class `JComponent`, whose inheritance chain is shown in Figure 11.13. The only exceptions to this are the top-level component classes, previously discussed in this chapter, whose inheritance chains are shown in Figure 11.6.

Just as the top-level components can contain other components, some non-top-level components can also contain other components. A `JPanel` is an example of this type of component, while buttons and text fields are designed to be **atomic** components.

> **Definition**
>
> **Atomic** components are GUI components that cannot contain other components.

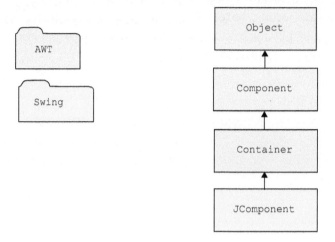

Figure 11.13
The `JComponent` class's inheritance chain.

Designing the Interface

Before adding a GUI component to a window, it is very useful to make a quick sketch of the interface that includes all of the components to be added and their position in the window. The choice of which components to add is based on the I/O requirements of the program and the component's targeted use listed in Table 11.4. As noted in the table, the `JTtextField` component can be used for both input and output.

If the program involves a series of inputs that should be entered in a particular order, adding input components to the window from left to right and top to bottom in order of entry enhances the friendliness of the interface. A sketch of an adding machine GUI is shown in Figure 11.14. Its level of detail is typical of that contained in a design sketch.

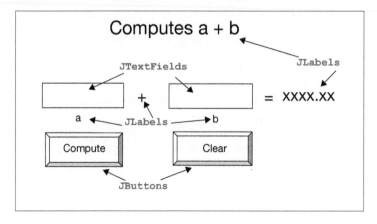

Figure 11.14
The GUI design for an adding machine.

Adding the Components

When an IDE is being used that has a GUI-builder feature, the program's window appears in the GUI builder. The components are added to the window by simply selecting them from a list of components, and then dragging them to their position in the window. Their size is typically adjusted by dragging resizing handles, and properties such as font color, font size, and initial visibility are specified via a menu of properties appropriate to each component.

While the particulars of GUI builders vary from one IDE to another, they all provide a rapid way of selecting, positioning, locating, and sizing an application's GUI components. Perhaps more importantly, while this process is being performed, the GUI builder adds the code to the application that creates, locates, and displays the components. It also adds templates for the code that responds to the runtime interaction with the components. These features greatly reduce the time to develop an application's GUI, which is the reason an IDE with a GUI builder should always be used when developing an application that has a graphical user interface.

Java also provides several *layout managers* that can facilitate the tedious process of locating components in a window when an IDE with a GUI builder is not available, but their use is limited to the development of simple IDEs. We will discuss layout managers in Section 11.5.

In the remainder of this section, we will become familiar with the methods used to construct, locate, size, and add components to a window and some of the methods used to adjust their properties. Invocations to these methods are added to our application when the interface is created with an IDE GUI builder. Even when the invocations are generated by the IDE, knowledge of these methods and their use is essential to altering the generated code and to completing the code templates added to the application.

A three or (for radio buttons) four step coding process is used to add a component to a window or to other non-atomic containers such as a `JPanel` object:

1. Create the component object
2. Specify the component's properties such as size, location, font style, tool tip, and visibility
3. Add mutually exclusive radio buttons to a common button group
4. Add the component to the window or non-atomic container

The more commonly used constructors used in step 1 of this process to create the components described in Table 11.4 are given in that table. The string passed to these constructors and the array passed to the combo box's constructor become the annotation that will appear on, within, or next to the component. For example, the following statement creates a button with the text *Click Me* displayed on it, and a text field with the text *Hamburger* displayed in it. The component's size must be wide enough to accommodate the width of the text, or the text will not be displayed:

```
JButton aButton = new JButton("Click Me");
JTextField entree = new JTextField ("Hamburger");
```

Table 11.5 gives the methods used in steps 2 and 4 of the process to specify a component's properties and add the component to a window or some other non-atomic container. The techniques and methods used in step 3 to group mutually exclusive radio buttons will be discussed in Chapter 12, as will the development of interfaces that contain check boxes and radio buttons. The `Component` and `Container` classes contain `get` methods for each of their `set` methods presented in the Table 11.5. All `JComponents` are visible by default.

Table 11.5
Methods Used to Specify a Component's Properties and Add it to a Container

Method Signature	Description
`JComponent` and `Component` Class Methods Invoked on Components	
`setToolTipText(String tip)`	Adds the tool tip `tip` to the component, displayed when the mouse pointer hovers over it
`setBounds(int x, int y,` `       int width, int height)`	Sets the component's location to (x, y) and its width and height to `width` and `height`
`setLocation(int x, int y)`	Sets the component's location to (x, y)
`setSize(int width, int height)`	Sets the component's width and height to `width` and `height`
`setText(String newText)`	Changes the text displayed on the component to `newText`
`setVisible(boolean visible)`	The component is visible when `visible` is passed the value `true`, invisible when passed `false`
`setFont(Font fontStyle)`	Sets the font style of the container or component that invoked the method to `fontStyle`
`Container` Class Methods	
`setLayout(LayoutManager layout);`	Sets the container's layout to `layout`, to specify location/size of components: `layout = null`
`add(Component theComponent)`	Adds `theComponent` to the container or component that invoked the method

When coded inside the constructor of a GUI-builder worker class, such as the one shown in Figure 11.12, the following code fragment adds a 300-pixel-wide by 30-pixel-high `JLabel` to the GUI that contains the text *Computes a + b*. The upper left corner of the text is located on the window's content pane at (120, 0), and the font type, style, and size of the displayed text is Sherif, bold, 24 point.

```
setLayout(null);
JLabel description = new JLabel("Computes a + b");
description.setBounds(120, 0, 300, 30);
description.setFont(new Font("Sherif", Font.BOLD, 24));
add(description);
```

The `null` value passed to the invocation of the `setLayout` method permits the use of the `setBounds` method to size and locate a component. Once invoked, all components subsequently added to the window can be positioned and sized using the `setBounds` or `setLocation` and `setSize` methods. The use of a non-atomic component's layout manager to size and position components added to it will be discussed in Section 11.5.

The following code fragment, when coded inside the constructor of a GUI-builder worker class, adds a 90-pixel-wide by 25-pixel-high JButton to the GUI. The button contains the text *Clear* and contains a tool tip. The upper left corner of the button is located at (235, 110). The fragment assumes that the setLayout method has been invoked and passed a null value before the code executes.

```
JButton clear = new JButton("Clear");
clear.setLocation(235, 110);
clear.setsize(90, 25);
clear.setToolTipText("Clears a, b and the sum");
add(clear);
```

The setLocation and setSize methods were used to locate and size the button simply to demonstrate the use of these methods. When both the location and the size of a component are being set, one invocation of the setBounds method is the preferred programming style.

The worker class AddingMachineGUI, shown in Figure 11.15, builds the graphical user interface, shown in Figure 11.16, whose design is shown in Figure 11.14. The application Adding-Machine, shown in Figure 11.17, creates an instance of this interface on line 8, sets its default close operation on line 9, and makes the interface visible on line 10. The last two tasks could have been performed by the GUI-builder class as they were in the class presented in Figure 11.12. The removal of these window initialization tasks from the GUI-builder class is often employed when more than one GUI is used in a program.

The code of the class AddingMachineGUI (Figure 11.15) follows the four-step process (without step 3 because the GUI does not contain radio buttons) discussed in this section to add the GUI components to the window it creates. The coding style used performs a step of the process on all of the components before moving on to the next step. Step 1 for all components is performed on lines 18–27, step 2 for all components is performed on lines 30–46, and step 4 is performed on lines 49–58.

Within each step, the components are processed in the order in which they appear in the GUI design, starting at the top and moving from left to right. Consistent with this approach, line 18 constructs the descriptive label that appears at the top of the GUI design, line 19 constructs the text field that is below it and to its left, line 20 constructs the label that contains the plus sign to the right of this text box, etc.

This coding style makes the program more readable and facilitates the coding process by reducing the number of iterations used to properly locate the components in the window. In addition, it is consistent with the requirements of one of the layout managers discussed later in this chapter and is the coding style often used in the code generated by an IDE's drag-and-drop GUI builder.

The class extends JFrame on line 4 of Figure 11.15 because it is going to create a window with a title bar containing a title and window management icons. All of the code to create the window and add the components to it is written inside the constructor. Line 12 constructs the window by invoking JFrame's one-parameter constructor and passing it the parameter title declared on line 10. As the comments at the end of the lines 12 and 13 state, all subsequent invocations of methods on unnamed objects operate on the window created on line 12.

Lines 13 and 14 specify the size of the window and the location of the upper left corner of the window when it is displayed on a monitor. Line 15 permits the programmer to take control of the sizing and positioning of the GUI components away from the JFrame's default layout manager. The remaining three sections of code create the GUI components, specify their properties, and add them to the JFrame window. The variables that reference the components are declared as class-level variables on lines 6–8 to allow methods that will be added to the class in the next section of this chapter to access the components.

```java
1    import javax.swing.*;
2    import java.awt.*;
3
4    public class AddingMachineGUI extends JFrame
5    {
6      JLabel description, plus, equals, sum, a, b;
7      JTextField aValue, bValue;
8      JButton compute, clear;
9
10     public AddingMachineGUI(String title)
11     {
12       super(title);        //Creates the window. All subsequent invocations
13       setSize(500, 250); //on an unnamed object operate on this window.
14       setLocation(200, 100);
15       setLayout(null);
16
17       //Step 1 create the components
18       description = new JLabel("Computes a + b");
19       aValue = new JTextField();
20       plus = new JLabel("+");
21       bValue = new JTextField();
22       equals = new JLabel("=");
23       sum = new JLabel("x,xxx.xx");
24       a = new JLabel("a");
25       b = new JLabel("b");
26       compute = new JButton("Compute");
27       clear = new JButton("Clear");
28
29       //Step 2 specify the component's properties
30       description.setBounds(120, 0, 300, 30);
31       description.setFont(new Font("Sherif", Font.BOLD, 24));
32       aValue.setBounds(60, 50, 100, 30);
33       plus.setBounds(190, 50, 20, 30);
34       plus.setFont(new Font("Sherif", Font.BOLD, 20));
35       bValue.setBounds(230, 50, 100, 30);
36       equals.setBounds(350, 50, 20, 30);
37       equals.setFont(new Font("Sherif", Font.BOLD, 20));
38       sum.setBounds(380, 50, 100, 30);
39       sum.setFont(new Font("Sherif", Font.BOLD, 20));
40       a.setBounds(105, 75, 20, 30);
41       a.setFont(new Font("Sherif", Font.BOLD, 20));
```

```
42        b.setBounds(275, 75, 20, 30);
43        b.setFont(new Font("Sherif", Font.BOLD, 20));
44        compute.setBounds(65, 110, 90, 25);
45        clear.setBounds(235, 110, 90, 25);
46        clear.setToolTipText("Clears a, b and the sum");
47
48        //Step 4 add the component to the container (Step 3 not relevant)
49        add(description);
50        add(aValue);
51        add(plus);
52        add(bValue);
53        add(equals);
54        add(sum);
55        add(a);
56        add(b);
57        add(compute);
58        add(clear);
59     }
60  }
```

Figure 11.15
The class **AddingMachineGUI**.

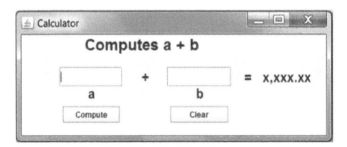

Figure 11.16
The graphical user interface created by the class **AddingMachineGUI**.

```
1   import javax.swing.*;
2   import java.awt.*;
3
4   public class AddingMachine
5   {
6     public static void main(String[] args)
7     {
8       AddingMachineGUI calculator = new AddingMachineGUI("Calculator");
9       calculator.setDefaultCloseOperation(JFrame.EXIT_ON_CLOSE);
10      calculator.setVisible(true);
11    }
12  }
```

Figure 11.17
The application **AddingMachine**.

11.4 EVENT PROCESSING

After the graphical interface is built, the next step in the GUI programming process is to identify the components in the interface that require application-dependent processing to be performed when the user interacts with them. For our adding machine, these would be the *Compute* and *Clear* buttons. When the compute button is clicked, the two text field entries are added, and the result is output. A click of the Clear button should clear the text boxes and the output sum.

In GUI jargon, when the user interacts with a component on the interface, we say that an *action* has been performed on the interface, or that an *event* has occurred. A click on one of our buttons is an example of an event. Other examples include the completion of an entry into a text box denoted by the striking of the Enter key, the movement of the mouse pointer over the window, or simply a click into a text box.

GUI events are detected by the Java Runtime Environment and some of them are dealt with, or processed, with no effort on the programmer's part. For example, when the user of a program's GUI interface clicks into one of its text fields, the insertion point cursor (*caret*) appears in the text field. This event is processed, or handled, by the code of API methods associated with the text field. When the click event occurs, the Runtime Environment executes a process to notify these methods that the event has occurred. After being notified of the event, they execute and display the insertion caret in the text field. Other sections of code associated with the text field subsequently handle keystroke events by displaying a typed character in the text field, and moving the caret to the right.

Events such as a click into a text box can be handled by the API methods because the action to be taken (display the caret at the position of the click) when the event occurs are part of the predefined look and feel of the GUI component. These application-independent GUI events are always processed by API methods. Other GUI events that occur on an application's interface, such as the clicking of the *Compute* button on our adding machine's interface, require the application programmer to process the event because the action to be taken is unique to this particular application.

More accurately, the application programmer partially processes these types of events because most often some processing that is part of the look and feel of the component also needs to be performed. For example, when the user clicks the *Compute* button of our adding machine, the API responds to the event by executing code that makes the button appear to have been depressed because this is part of a predefined look and feel of a button. Then, the application performs the processing particular to it: add two numbers together and display the result.

To initiate application-dependent processing when a GUI event occurs, the Java event-handling process permits the application programmer to add methods written as part of the application to the list of methods notified, or more accurately, executed, when the event occurs. We say that the programmer can add to the list of methods that are *listening* for the event to occur, and these methods are generically referred to as *event handlers*. Figure 11.18 illustrates this concept and the event processing execution path it produces.

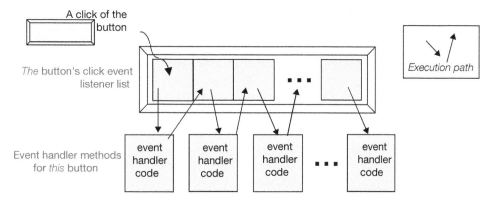

Figure 11.18
Java's event-processing process.

The process can be thought of as the execution of a switch statement, without any break statements, that executes all of its cases. Adding a method to a GUI component's event listener list would then be analogous to adding a case clause to the switch statement that invokes a method (the event handler method) to perform the processing for that case.

NOTE   *Each component object added to the interface has its own event listener list.*

11.4.1 Implementing Event Handler Methods

Because the application-dependent event handler methods we code are invoked within API methods that are part of each GUI object added to the interface, the signatures of the methods have to be defined within the API implementation. The set of API interfaces whose names end in *Listener* defines the signatures of the application-dependent event handler methods invoked when a GUI event occurs.

Table 11.6 presents the names of some of the more commonly used listener interfaces and the names and parameter lists of the event handler methods they define. They are all void methods, and in most cases, the names of the methods imply the events that they handle. The most obvious exception to this is the signature of the `actionPerformed` method at the top of the table. The events it handles, as well as those handled by the other methods presented in the table, are summarized in the middle column. The check mark in the rightmost column of the table indicates that the interface on that row has an *adapter* class associated with it. Adapter classes will be discussed in Section 11.4.4.

Table 11.6
Several API Listener Interfaces and Commonly Used Event Handler Methods they Define

Event Handler Interfaces and Their Void Method(s)	Events Handled	Adapter Class
`ActionListener` **Interface Method**		
`actionPerformed(ActionEvent e)`	A button click, a timer time out, or Enter key strike into a text field	
`FocusListener` **Interface Methods**		
`focusGained(FocusEvent e)`	A clickable component (e.g., a button or a text box) is clicked	
`focusLost(FocusEvent e)`	Another clickable component is clicked	
`KeyListener` **Interface Methods**		√
`keyPressed(KeyEvent e)`	A key is pressed	
`keyReleased(KeyEvent e)`	A key is released	
`keyTyped(KeyEvent e)`	A key is typed (pressed and released)	
`MouseListener` and `MouseMotionListener` **Methods**		√
`mouseClicked(MouseEvent e)`	A mouse click on a GUI component	
`mousePressed(MouseEvent e)`	A mouse button is pressed down on a GUI component	
`mouseDragged(MouseEvent e)`	Left mouse button is held down and the mouse is moved on a component	
`mouseReleased(MouseEvent e)`	A mouse button is released	

The application-dependent processing to be performed when a particular event occurs is coded inside an implementation of the event handler method that handles that event. The name, signature, and interface of the method can be determined be searching the middle column of Table 11.6 for the event to be handled. For example, to perform some processing whenever a key is typed, the processing would be coded inside the keyTyped method whose signature is defined in the KeyListener interface. The following code fragment counts the number of times the mouse is clicked.

```
public static int numOfClicks = 0;
public void mouseClicked(MouseEvent e)
{
  numOfClicks++;
}
```

The heading of a class that contains the implementation of an event handler method must contain an implements clause indicating that it implements the method's interface. This class is usually coded as an *inner* class of the class that declared the GUI component, although the method can be coded in same class that declared the GUI component.

It is good programming practice that the name of the inner class implies the component and the event its method handles or listens for. Consistent with this practice, its name usually ends with the word *Handler* or *Listener*. For example: `ComputeClickHandler` or `ComputeClickListener` would be good names for an inner class that contained an event handler that performs the processing associated with a click event on a button object named `compute`.

11.4.2 Registering the Event Handler

To complete the process of implementing an event handler, the event handler method must be added to, or *registered* with, the list of methods invoked when the event occurs. As indicated in Figure 11.18, the list is called a *listener list*, and each GUI component added to an application's interface maintains its own listener list.

To add an event handler method to the listener list maintained in a particular GUI component object, a method is invoked whose name begins with *add* followed by the name of the interface that defined the signature of the method: for example, `addMouseListener` or `addActionListener`. The method is invoked on the GUI component object and passed an instance of the class that contains the code of the event handler method. This invocation is said to *register* the event handler in the component's listener list.

The following code fragment adds (registers) the `actionPerformed` method coded in the inner class `ComputeClickHandler` in the listener list of the `JButton` object named `compute`:

```
ComputeClickHandler click = new ComputeClickHandler();
compute.addActionListener(click);
```

This two-step process of registering an event handler method with a GUI component is summarized below:

1. Create an instance of the inner class that implements the event handler method
2. Invoke the method `addNameOfTheInterface` on the GUI component passing it the object created in step 1

A more concise coding of this two-step process uses an anonymous object to register the event handler method, as shown in the following code fragment:

```
compute.addActionListener(new ComputeClickHandler());
```

When the event handler method is not coded inside an inner class, the event handler method is registered by passing the keyword `this` to the method invoked in step 2, as shown in the following code fragment:

```
compute.addActionListener(this);
```

Summary of the Process to Implement an Event Handler

The following four step process is used to implement an event handler method.

1. Use the middle column of Table 11.6 to determine the API method that handles the event

2. Add that method to an inner class that implements the method's interface, which is identified above the method in Table 11.6

3. Add the instructions to perform the event handling processing to the method

4. Add the method to (register it with) the listener list of the GUI component on which the event will occur: *guiComponent*.add*InterfaceName* (*innerClassObject*) ;

> **NOTE** *All of the interface's methods must be implemented in the class. Some of the implementations can contain an empty code block.*

Having gained an understanding of events and event handler methods, we will conclude this section with incorporating the event process into our adding machine GUI builder worker class (Figure 11.15), and a discussion of the `getSource` method.

Completion of the Adding Machine Application

The class `AddingMachineGUIV2`, shown in Figure 11.19, adds two button click event handler methods to the class `AddingMachineGUI` shown in Figure 11.15 and registers them with the GUI's button objects. One method adds two inputs and outputs the sum with two digits of precision, and the other method clears the inputs and the computed sum. The program's window after the user enters two inputs and clicks the *Compute* button is shown in Figure 11.20a, and Figure 11.20b shows the window after a subsequent click of the *Clear* button.

The inner classes `ComputeClickHandler` and `ClearClickHandler` (lines 67–82 and 83–91, respectively) are the two event handler classes. Each class implements the API interface `ActionListener` (lines 67 and 83) because they will handle a button click event. The middle column of Table 11.6 was used to determine that the inner classes would have to implement the interface `ActionListener` to handle the user button click events, and to determine that the name of the event handler methods would have to be `actionPerformed`.

`ComputeClickHandler`'s implementation of the interface's `actionPerformed` method (lines 69–81) computes and displays the sum of the user inputs when the `compute` button is clicked because it is added to (registered with) that object's listener list on line 51. This registration is performed on line 51 by passing an anonymous instance of the event handler's class `ComputeClickHandler` to the `addActionListener` method invoked on the `compute` object.

Similarly, line 52 adds the implementation of the `actionPerformed` method coded on lines 85–90 to the listener list of the `clear` button object by passing an anonymous instance of its class, `ClearClickHandler`, to the `addActionListener` method invoked on the `clear` object. Line 4 imports the event interfaces and classes used in the GUI builder class.

The revised code of the application `AddingMachine`, which is named `AddingMachineV2`, is shown in Figure 11.21. The program window declared on line 8 of the application is now an instance of the class `AddingMachineGUIV2`.

```
1    import javax.swing.*;
2    import java.awt.*;
3    import java.text.DecimalFormat;
4    import java.awt.event.*;
5
6    public class AddingMachineGUIV2 extends JFrame
7    {
8      JLabel description, plus, equals, sum, a, b;
9      JTextField aValue, bValue;
10     JButton compute, clear;
11
12     public AddingMachineGUIV2(String title)
13     {
14       super(title);     //Creates the window. All subsequent invocations
15       setSize(500, 250); //on unnamed object operate on this window.
16       setLocation(200, 100);
17       setLayout(null);
18
19       //Step 1 create the components
20       description = new JLabel("Computes a + b");
21       aValue = new JTextField();
22       plus = new JLabel("+");
23       bValue = new JTextField();
24       equals = new JLabel("=");
25       sum = new JLabel("x,xxx.xx");
26       a = new JLabel("a");
27       b = new JLabel("b");
28       compute = new JButton("Compute");
29       clear = new JButton("Clear");
30
31       //Step 2: specify the component's properties
32       description.setBounds(120, 0, 300, 30);
33       description.setFont(new Font("Sherif", Font.BOLD, 24));
34       aValue.setBounds(60, 50, 100, 30);
35       plus.setBounds(190, 50, 20, 30);
36       plus.setFont(new Font("Sherif", Font.BOLD, 20));
37       bValue.setBounds(230, 50, 100, 30);
38       equals.setBounds(350, 50, 20, 30);
39       equals.setFont(new Font("Sherif", Font.BOLD, 20));
40       sum.setBounds(380, 50, 100, 30);
41       sum.setFont(new Font("Sherif", Font.BOLD, 20));
42       a.setBounds(105, 75, 20, 30);
43       a.setFont(new Font("Sherif", Font.BOLD, 20));
44       b.setBounds(275, 75, 20, 30);
45       b.setFont(new Font("Sherif", Font.BOLD, 20));
46       compute.setBounds(65, 110, 90, 25);
47       clear.setBounds(235, 110, 90, 25);
48       clear.setToolTipText("Clears a, b and the sum");
```

```
49
50      // Register the event handler methods
51      compute.addActionListener(new ComputeClickHandler());
52      clear.addActionListener(new ClearClickHandler());
53
54      //Step 4: add the component to the container
55      add(description);
56      add(aValue);
57      add(plus);
58      add(bValue);
59      add(equals);
60      add(sum);
61      add(a);
62      add(b);
63      add(compute);
64      add(clear);
65    }
66    //Event handler inner classes and methods
67    public class ComputeClickHandler implements ActionListener
68    {
69      public void actionPerformed(ActionEvent e)
70      {
71        String s;
72        double a, b, result;
73        DecimalFormat f = new DecimalFormat("#,##0.00");
74
75        s = aValue.getText();
76        a = Double.parseDouble(s);
77        s = bValue.getText();
78        b = Double.parseDouble(s);
79        result = a + b;
80        sum.setText(f.format(result));
81      }
82    }
83    public class ClearClickHandler implements ActionListener
84    {
85      public void actionPerformed(ActionEvent e)
86      {
87        aValue.setText("");
88        bValue.setText("");
89        sum.setText("x,xxx.xx");
90      }
91    }
92 }
```

Figure 11.19
The class **AddingMachineGUIV2**.

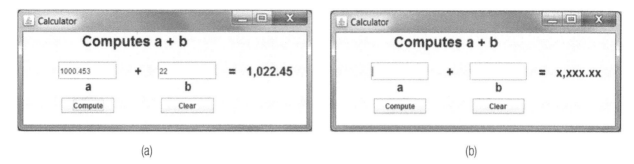

(a)   (b)

Figure 11.20
Output generated by the class **AddingMachineGUIV2**'s Compute and Clear button.

```
1     import javax.swing.*;
2     import java.awt.*;
3
4     public class AddingMachineV2
5     {
6       public static void main(String[] args)
7       {
8         AddingMachineGUIV2 calculator = new AddingMachineGUIV2("Calculator");
9         calculator.setDefaultCloseOperation(JFrame.EXIT_ON_CLOSE);
10        calculator.setVisible(true);
11      }
12    }
```

Figure 11.21
The application **AddingMachineV2**.

The getSource Method

When an event handler method is invoked, the argument passed to it contains information about the event, which includes the address of the GUI object involved in the event. For example, when the event handler that begins on line 69 of Figure 11.19 is invoked, the information passed to its parameter e contains the address of the object compute, declared on line 28 of the figure. This is the only object that could have been involved in the event because the object clear (declared on line 29) added the other implementation of the actionPerformed event handler to its listener list (line 52). As a result, the information passed to the parameter e was not used.

When an alternative coding style is used to implement the event handler, the information passed to the parameter e plays an essential role in the coding of the event handler. In this alternative approach, only one implementation of the event handler method is coded, and all of the objects on which this event could occur register that implementation into their listener list. Assuming the inner class containing the one event handler method implementation is named ButtonClickHandler, lines 51 and 52 of Figure 11.19 would become:

```
51        compute.addActionListener(new ButtonClickHandler());
52        clear.addActionListener(new ButtonClickHandler());
```

To discern which of the two buttons, `compute` or `clear`, was involved in a button click event, the GUI component object address contained in the information passed to the parameter e is compared to the addresses stored in the variables `compute` and `clear`. The method `getSource` in the `EventObject` class is used to fetch the address from the information passed to e. Figure 11.22 presents the code that would replace lines 67–82 and lines 83–92 of Figure 11.19 when this alternative implementation style is used. It presupposes that the previously discussed recoding of lines 51 and 52 has been performed.

The name of the (one) inner class whose heading is on line 67 of Figure 11.22 is now the generic name `ButtonClickHandler`, and the Boolean condition of the `if-else` clauses that begin on lines 75 and 84 use the `getSource` method to determine the object involved in the event. If the GUI contained more than two buttons, additional nested `if-else` clauses would be added to the method to process their click events.

```
67    public class ButtonClickHandler implements ActionListener
68    {
69      public void actionPerformed(ActionEvent e)
70      {
71        String s;
72        double a, b, result;
73        DecimalFormat f = new DecimalFormat("#,##0.00");
74
75        if(e.getSource() == compute)
76        {
77          s = aValue.getText();
78          a = Double.parseDouble(s);
79          s = bValue.getText();
80          b = Double.parseDouble(s);
81          result = a + b;
82          sum.setText(f.format(result));
83        }
84        else if(e.getSource() == clear)
85        {
86            aValue.setText("");
87            bValue.setText("");
88            sum.setText("x,xxx.xx");
89        }
90      }
91    }
92  }
```

Figure 11.22
An alternative coding style of the event handlers that begin on line 67 of Figure 11.19.

11.4.3 Paint Events, JPanels, and Two-Dimensional Graphics

A *paint event* is a generic term for any event that causes a graphical object to be drawn or redrawn. The most obvious paint events are the initial display of an application's GUI window and maximizing a window after it has been minimized. A more subtle paint event is continuously redrawing a window as it is dragged across the monitor.

To display a window on the monitor, the window (JFrame) object and all of the components added to it (JButton objects, JTextFields objects, etc.) have to be drawn, as do any two-dimensional (2D) shapes that were drawn in the window by the application using the methods in the Graphics class. To accomplish this, each component has a paint event handler, or call back method, that is invoked when a paint event occurs. The names of these event handlers typically begin with the word *paint*, for example paintComponents, paintComponent, and paint.

When they are invoked, these methods are passed a Graphics object, which they use to render (draw) the component. The Graphics object passed to the JPanel class's paintComponent call back method can be used to draw 2D graphics shapes defined in the Graphics class on a JPanel object. To accomplish this, we simply add a class to our application that extends JPanel and overrides its paintComponent method. Then, the panel is added to the application's window. The drawing of the 2D graphics is done inside the overridden version of the paintComponent method.

For example, the following code fragment would be added to a class that extends JPanel to draw a filled red rectangle 70 pixels wide by 30 pixels high, whose upper left corner is at (300, 200). The parent (JPanel) class's overridden method should always be invoked as the first line child's version of the method.

```java
public void paintComponent(Graphics g)
{
  super.paintComponent(g);
  g.setColor(Color.RED);
  g.fillRect(300, 200, 70, 30);
}
```

The class BoxedSnowmanV3, shown in Figure 11.23, extends the class JPanel and overrides its paintComponent method on lines 19–34. The overridden version of the method uses the Graphics object g passed to it to invoke the drawing methods of the Graphic class on lines 22–33.

The application Graphics2D shown in Figure 11.24 produces the output shown in Figure 11.25. The application does not import the game environment to perform the graphics displayed in its window. Instead it declares an instance of the class BoxedSnowmanV3, shown in Figure 11.24 on line 10, named s1 and adds this extended JPanel GUI component (line 11) to the JFrame window created on line 8. Every time the JFrame window is drawn or redrawn, the Java Runtime Environment invokes the JPanel component's paintComponent method to redraw component s1, just as it would do for any other GUI component that is added to a JFrame. Because the method is overridden, the 2D shapes are drawn or redrawn.

> **NOTE** *When one component is added to a JFrame, by default, it occupies JFrame's entire content pane.*

The paintComponent method begins by invoking JPanel's overridden version of the method on line 21. As previously mentioned, this should always be the first line of the overridden version of the method. Lines 22–31 draw a snowman with a rectangle around it, and lines 32–33 change the font from its default value and draw the string shown at the top of the application's window.

The difference between this graphical output and the graphical outputs produced by programs that use the game environment is that the method that performs the 2D graphics (lines 19–34 of Figure 11.23) is invoked by the Java Runtime Environment rather than the game environment.

There is also a subtle but very important difference between the BoxedSnowmanV3 class shown in Figure 11.23 and the BoxedSnowman class shown in Figure 4.4, which was part of an application that imported the game environment. The names of the set and get methods on lines 35–50 of Figure 11.23 have been changed from the names setX, getX, setY, and getY used in Figure 4.4. The get method names were changed because the BoxedSnowman class inherits methods named getX and getY from the JPanel class. Because these methods could be invoked by the Runtime Environment to determine the location of the JPanel when a paint event occurs, they should not be overridden. The names of the snowman's set and get methods were changed to setXS, getXS, setYS, and getYS for consistency and readability.

```java
1    import java.awt.*;
2    import javax.swing.*;
3
4    public class BoxedSnowmanV3 extends JPanel
5    {
6      private int x = 8;
7      private int y = 30;
8      private Color hatColor = Color.BLACK;
9      private int dx = 0;
10     private int dy = 0;
11     private int time = 0;
12
13     public BoxedSnowmanV3(int initalX, int initalY, Color hatColor)
14     {
15       x = initalX;
16       y = initalY;
17       this.hatColor = hatColor;
18     }
19     public void paintComponent(Graphics g)
20     {
21       super.paintComponent(g);
22       g.setColor(hatColor);
23       g.fillRect(x + 15, y, 10, 15); //hat
24       g.fillRect(x + 10, y + 15, 20, 2); //brim
25       g.setColor(Color.WHITE);
```

```
26        g.fillOval(x + 10, y + 17, 20, 20); //head
27        g.fillOval(x, y + 37, 40, 40); //body
28        g.setColor(Color.RED);
29        g.fillOval(x + 19, y + 53, 4, 4); //button
30        g.setColor(Color.BLACK);
31        g.drawRect(x, y, 40, 77); //inscribing rectangle
32        g.setFont(new Font("Sherif", Font.BOLD, 20)); //time format
33        g.drawString("Time: " + time, 300, 50); //time
34     }
35     public int getXS()
36     {
37        return x;
38     }
39     public void setXS(int newX)
40     {
41        x = newX;
42     }
43     public int getYS()
44     {
45        return y;
46     }
47     public void setYS(int newY)
48     {
49        y = newY;
50     }
51  }
```

Figure 11.23
The class **BoxedSnowmanV3**.

```
1     import javax.swing.*;
2     import java.awt.*;
3
4     public class Graphics2D extends JFrame
5     {
6       public static void main(String[] args)
7       {
8         JFrame window = new JFrame("Graphics");
9         window.setDefaultCloseOperation(JFrame.EXIT_ON_CLOSE);
10        BoxedSnowmanV3 s1 = new BoxedSnowmanV3(315, 165, Color.BLUE);
11        window.add(s1);
12        window.setSize(708, 434);
13        window.setVisible(true);
14      }
15  }
```

Figure 11.24
The application **Graphics2D**.

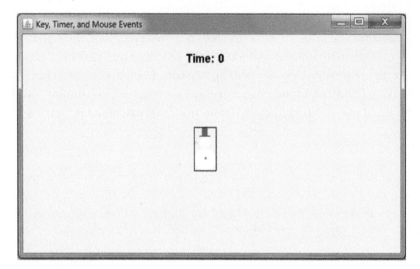

Figure 11.25
The output produced by the application **Graphics2D**.

11.4.4 Mouse, Keyboard, and Timer Events

Many of the GUI components included in the API respond to mouse-click events and keyboard events such as the pressing or typing of a key. The most obvious examples of this are radio-button event handlers and check-box event handlers that change the appearance of these components when they are clicked. Another example is the appearance of the caret in a text field when it is clicked, and the subsequent display of typed characters in the text field to the left of the caret. The GUI support in the API includes implementations of these non-application-dependent event handlers and their registrations.

Just as GUI components respond to these events to maintain their look and feel, there is often the need for an application to respond to a mouse or keyboard event in an application-dependent manner. Application-dependent processing of a JButton click event has already been discussed in this chapter. Other mouse events, such as the dragging of the mouse or clicking on a portion of the application's window that does not contain a GUI atomic component may be an important event in a particular application. For example, a mouse-drag event could be used to move the snowman shown in Figure 11.25 to another location in the program window, or a key-typed event such as typing the cursor control (arrow) keys could be used to move the snowman around the window. Similarly, a timer-tick event is certainly an important event to many applications that are time dependent.

In this section, we will learn how to incorporate mouse, keyboard, and timer events into any Java application. Although we have reacted to some of these events in our game programs, the details of the timer, keyboard, and mouse event handler implementations and their registration was performed by the game environment. Essentially, in the remainder of this section, we will gain insights into how this was accomplished by the game environment, so we can process these events in any application we write.

Keyboard and mouse events are processed within an application using the techniques discussed in Sections 11.4.1 and 11.4.2. An event handler method, whose signature is defined in an API interface, is implemented, and the method is added to (registered in) a list of methods invoked when the event occurs. The application-specific processing to be performed when the event occurs is coded into the event handler method. Timer events are processed in a similar way, but the syntax of registering the event handler is slightly different from that discussed in Section 11.4.2.

Mouse Events

There are eight mouse events associated with event handler methods whose signatures are defined in the API interfaces `MouseListener`, `MouseMotionListener`, and `MouseWheelListener`. The signatures of the eight methods and the interfaces that define them are given below, and four of the more commonly used methods are also described in Table 11.6.

```
void mouseClicked(MouseEvent e)      //defined in MouseListener
void mouseEntered(MouseEvent e)      //    "        "        "
void mouseExited(MouseEvent e)       //    "        "        "
void mousePressed(MouseEvent e)      //    "        "        "
void mouseReleased(MouseEvent e)     //    "        "        "
void mouseDragged(MouseEvent e)      //defined in MouseMotionListener
void mouseMoved(MouseEvent e)        //    "        "        "
void MouseWheelMoved(MouseEvent e)   //defined in MouseWheelListener
```

The names of the methods are representative of the mouse events they handle (the events that cause them to be invoked). The `mouseEntered` and `mouseExited` methods are invoked when the mouse cursor enters and exits the perimeter of a GUI component on which the event is registered.

To perform application-dependent processing when a mouse event occurs, the worker class that defines the GUI implements the relevant mouse event handler method and registers it using the `addMouseListener`, `addMouseMotionListener`, or `addMouseWheelListener` methods. The application-dependent processing is coded inside the method's code block. If the API interface that defines the method's signature contains multiple signature definitions, as the interfaces `MouseListener` and `MouseMotionListener` do, all the methods defined in the interface must be implemented in the worker class or within one of its inner classes. These additional implementations can contain empty code blocks. To avoid coding the additional methods and their empty code blocks, the class can extend the API `MouseAdapter` class instead of implementing one of the three mouse listener interfaces.

Event Handler Adapter Classes

An adapter class is a class that implements all the methods defined in one or more interfaces and provides empty implementations of the methods defined in the interface(s). The advantage of this is that their child classes inherit the empty implementations and can then simply implement, or more accurately, override the methods that handle the events of interest to them. For example, if only mouse-released events were to be processed by a GUI class, it would only have to override the `mouseReleased` method if it extended the API adapter class `MouseAdapter`, instead of implementing the entire `MouseListener` interface.

> **NOTE** *It is good programming style to end the name of an adapter class with the word Adapter.*

Many of the API interfaces that define multiple method signatures have adapter classes associated with them. The class mouseAdapter implements all eight mouse event handler methods. Because a class can only inherit from one class, most often the extension of an adapter class is performed by an inner class, and the relevant event handler methods are overridden within it.

The code fragment shown below registers an implementation of a mouse-entered event handler that outputs the message *Button b1 was Entered* every time the mouse pointer enters the boundaries of the JButton object b1.

```java
JButton b1 = new JButton("Enter Test");
b1.addMouseListener(new MouseHandler()); //register the event handler

public class MouseHandler extends MouseAdapter
{
  public void mouseEntered(MouseEvent e) //only method implemented
  {
    System.out.println("Button b1 was Entered");
  }
}
```

The argument passed to the mouse event handler method's parameter e is the address of a MouseEvent object. All eight of the mouse event handler methods are passed a reference to an instance of this class. The class contains several methods that can be used to obtain information related to the mouse event. For example the (x, y) position of the mouse when the event occurred can be determined by invoking the class's getX and getY methods on the object e references. The button on the mouse that was pressed can be determined from the integer returned from the method getButton(), and the number of mouse clicks performed on an GUI component can be determined from the integer returned from the method getClickCount(). The GUI component object on which the mouse event occurred can be determined by invoking MouseEvent's inherited method getSource().

The following code fragment outputs the location at which the mouse cursor entered the boundaries of the JButton object b1:

```java
JButton b1 = new JButton("Enter Test");
b1.addMouseListener(new MouseHandler()); //register the event handler

public class MouseHandler extends MouseAdapter
{
  public void mouseEntered(MouseEvent e) //only method implemented
  {
    System.out.println("Button b1 was Entered at pixel location (" +
                  e.getX() + ", " + e.getY() + ")");
  }
}
```

Keyboard Events

There are three keyboard events associated with event handler methods whose signatures are defined in the API interface `KeyListener`. These signatures are presented in Table 11.6 and described below:

```
void keyPressed(KeyEvent e)
void keyReleased(KeyEvent e)
void keyTyped(KeyEvent e)
```

The `keyPressed` event handler method is invoked whenever a key is struck, and the `keyReleased` method is invoked when the key is released. In addition, the `KeyTyped` method is invoked whenever a *non*-action key is struck (i.e., a key-typed event does *not* occur when an *action* key is struck). The action keys include the Shift, Num Lock, End, Home, Caps Lock, function keys, arrow keys, etc.

Whenever a non-action key is held down, it repeatedly generates a key-pressed event followed by a key-typed event. If the key held down is an action key, only key-pressed events are generated. In either case, when the key is released, a single key-released event occurs.

A class that services a key event must implement all three methods defined in the API interface `KeyListener` or extend the adapter class `KeyAdapter`. Key event handler methods are registered using the `addKeyListener` method. The argument passed to the parameter of the three mouse event handler methods is the address of a `KeyEvent` object. This object's class contains several methods that can be used to determine the key that caused the keyboard event. The method `getKeyChar()` returns the character generated by the non-action keys (lower and upper case). The returned character can be used to determine which non-action key has been struck. The following key event handler performs its output when the key P is typed:

```java
public void keyTyped(KeyEvent e)
{
  if(e.getKeyChar == 'P' || e.getKeyChar == 'p')
  {
    System.out.println("The P key was struck");
  }
}
```

When action keys are struck, they can be identified using the `getKeyCode` method in the class `KeyEvent`. It returns the integer key code of the key struck. This integer can be passed to the class's static `getKeyText` method, which returns a string that describes the key's code: e.g., "Right" for the right arrow key. The strings associated with each of the action keys can be easily identified by including the following statement inside an implementation of a `keyPressed` event handler method, assuming the variable `e` is the name of the method's parameter:

```java
System.out.println(KeyEvent.getKeyText(e.getKeyCode()));
```

The game environment passes the first character of the strings associated with the action keys to its call back method `keyStruck` (e.g., 'R' when the right arrow key is struck).

Keyboard Focus

For a component to respond to a keyboard event, it must have the keyboard's focus, which can be thought of as assigning (or attaching) the keyboard to a GUI component. Generally speaking, only one component in an application can have the keyboard's focus at any given time. When a component has the keyboard's focus, the key event handler methods registered in the component's event listener list will be executed when a key event occurs.

The `requestFocusInWindow` method, inherited from the `JComponent` class, is invoked on a `Swing` component to transfer the application's input focus to the component in a platform-independent way. For the transfer to take place, the component must have already been added to the application (i.e., has been rendered, is visible, etc.). To ensure that this has taken place when the keyboard focus is requested, the invocation should be made from within an overwritten version of the `addNotify` method, which is invoked when a component is added to an application. `Swing` components inherit this method from the `JComponent` class.

The code fragment shown in Figure 11.26 would be added to the `BoxedSnowmanV3` class shown in Figure 11.23 to register an implementation of a key event handler that outputs *Key Pressed* to the system console followed by the text generated by the key whenever a key is pressed.

```
addKeyListener(new KeyHandler()); //add keyPressed to listener list

public void addNotify()//invoked when component is added to application
{
  super.addNotify(); //invokes JComponent's addNotify method
  requestFocusInWindow(); //obtains the keyboard's focus
}

public class KeyHandler extends KeyAdapter
{
  public void keyPressed(KeyEvent e)
  {
    System.out.println("Key Pressed");
    System.out.println(KeyEvent.getKeyText(e.getKeyCode()));
  }
}
```

Figure 11.26
Code to add a key-pressed event handler to a GUI component class.

Timer Events

A timer event is an event produced by an object in the class API class `Timer`. It can be likened to the bell sounding on an egg timer after its time interval has expired. The time interval of a `Timer` object is the first argument passed to the constructor when the object is created. This integer value specifies the time interval in milliseconds (e.g., 1000 for a one-second interval). The constructor's second parameter is used to register the timer event handler method, which must be an instance of a class that implements the method `actionPerformed`. The signature of this method is defined in the `ActionListener` interface and given at the top of Table 11.6. A `Timer` object's interval begins with an invocation of the class's `start` method, and the timer generates an action event at the end of subsequent timer intervals (ticks).

The code fragment shown in Figure 11.27 simulates a three-minute egg timer that outputs *The egg is cooked* to the system console after three minutes have elapsed from the time when the `start` method is invoked on the timer object `eggTimer`.

```
int interval = 1000 * 60 * 3; //3 minutes (1,000 ms * 60 sec * 3 min)
Timer eggTimer = new Timer(interval, new EggTimerHandler());

eggTimer.start(); //the eggTimer's time interval begins

public class EggTimerHandler implements ActionListener
{
  public void actionPerformed(ActionEvent e) //Timer's event handler
  {
    System.out.println("The egg is cooked");
  }
}
```

Figure 11.27
Implementing a timer object and processing its timer event.

The code fragment shown in Figure 11.27 produces a line of output every three minutes because, by default when a timer's time interval expires, it is restarted. To stop this process, the `Timer` class's `stop` method is invoked. For example, to cook one egg, the following line of code would be added to the end of the `actionPerformed` method's code block shown in Figure 11.27:

```
eggTimer.stop(); //stops eggTimer from generating timer events
```

Alternately, the `Timer` class's `setRepeats` method can be passed the value `false` before the timer is started to prevent the timer from generating more than one timer event. The `setDelay` method in the `Timer` class can be used to delay the restarting of a running timer after a time event has occurred.

The class `BoxedSnowmanV4` shown in Figure 11.28 demonstrates the processing of timer, mouse, and keyboard events. It adds a timer event handler, a key event handler, and five mouse event handlers to the `BoxedSnowmanV3` class shown in Figure 11.23. These event handlers are coded as lines 57–61 and 67–106 in Figure 11.28. Lines 1–56 of that figure are the original version of the class with six (highlighted) lines added to it. The application `MouseKeyboardAndTimer-Events` shown in Figure 11.29 creates an instance of a boxed snowman on line 10 and adds the object (line 11) to the `JFrame` window it creates on line 8. Finally, it displays the window (line 13), which is shown in Figure 11.30a.

The number of seconds since the program has been launched is displayed at the top of the window. The program user can reposition the snowman in the window by dragging it to a new location

(Figure 11.30b), clicking its new window position (Figure 11.30c), or moving it right by pressing the keyboard's right arrow action key (Figure 11.30d).

The event handler `actionPerformed`, coded on lines 57–61 of the class shown in Figure 11.28, processes the timer events generated by the timer declared on line 13 and started on line 23. The timer's increment, passed to the constructor on line 13, is 1000 milliseconds (1 second) and the keyword `this`, passed to the constructor's second parameter, registers the `actionPerformed` method coded in this class as the timer's event handler. The class's heading (line 5) indicates that it implements the `ActionListener` interface.

After each timer event which is separated by one second, line 59 of the timer event handler increments the variable `time` and line 39 outputs the elapsed time to the top of the application's window (Figure 11.30b). The invocations of the `repaint` method on lines 60, 75, 85, and 96 have been added to the event handler methods to force a repainting of the class's `JPanel` at the end of their execution. These invocations cause the overridden version of the `paintComponent` method (lines 25–40) to execute.

All the mouse event handlers are coded inside the inner class `MouseHandler` that begins on line 79, and they are registered in the `JPanel`'s listener list on lines 20 and 21 using an anonymous instance of the inner class. When the left mouse button is pressed to initiate the dragging of the snowman to a new position, the `mousePressed` event handler coded on lines 87–91 executes. It computes the x and y separation (`dx` and `dy`) between the snowman's upper left corner (`xS`, `yS`) and the mouse pointer's current location returned from the invocations `e.getX()` and `e.getY()`.

As the mouse is dragged, the `mouseDragged` event handler, coded on lines 81 to 86, is continually invoked. It subtracts the x and y separations (`dx` and `dy`) from the current position of the mouse pointer to determine the new location of the snowman's upper left corner. This gives the appearance that the snowman is being dragged by the mouse pointer. Figure 11.30b shows the snowman's position ten seconds after the game began and after the mouse was pointed at the snowman and dragged to the upper left portion of the window.

When the mouse is clicked, the `mouseClicked` event handler, coded on lines 92–97, executes. It sets the location of the upper left corner of the snowman to the location of the mouse pointer on lines 94–95. This gives the appearance that the snowman has jumped to the clicked location. Figure 11.30c shows the snowman's position 15 seconds after the game began and after the mouse was clicked in the lower right portion of the window.

Whenever the mouse pointer enters or exits the boundaries of the `BoxedSnowmanV4` JPanel, which was added to the application's window (line 11 of Figure 11.29) and occupies its entire content pane, the `mouseEntered` or `mouseExited` event handler methods (Figure 11.28, lines 98–105) execute. Lines 100 and 104 then produce the output *Entered* or *Exited* on the system console. The system console output, shown at the bottom of Figure 11.30, was produced by moving the mouse cursor on to the window's content pane after the program was launched, then moving it off the pane.

The `addNotify` method that begins on line 62 in Figure 11.28 is invoked when the application adds the `BoxedSnowmanV4` object `s1` to the program's window. Line 65 transfers the application's input focus to the object's JPanel. Subsequent key-pressed events then invoke the event key handler keyPressed (lines 69–77), which is coded inside the inner class KeyHandler (lines 67-78). The event handler is registered with the JPanel's listener list on line 22. The method uses the string returned from the KeyEvent class's getKeyText method, invoked on line 71, to determine if the right arrow action key has been pressed (line 72). When the key is pressed, the code on line 74 moves the snowman three pixels to the right. The lower portion of Figure 11.30 shows the position of the snowman 15 seconds after the game began (Figure 11.30c) and after the right arrow action key has been held down for four seconds (Figure 11.30d).

```
1     import java.awt.*;
2     import javax.swing.*;
3     import java.awt.event.*;
4
5    public class BoxedSnowmanV4 extends JPanel implements ActionListener
6    {
7       private int xS = 8;
8       private int yS = 30;
9       private Color hatColor = Color.BLACK;
10      private int dx = 0;
11      private int dy = 0;
12      private int time = 0;
13      private Timer aTimer = new Timer(1000, this);
14
15      public BoxedSnowmanV4(int initalX, int initalY, Color hatColor)
16      {
17        xS = initalX;
18        yS = initalY;
19        this.hatColor = hatColor;
20        addMouseListener(new MouseHandler());
21        addMouseMotionListener(new MouseHandler());
22        addKeyListener(new KeyHandler());
23        aTimer.start();
24      }
25      public void paintComponent(Graphics g)
26      {
27        super.paintComponent(g);
28        g.setColor(hatColor);
29        g.fillRect(xS + 15, yS, 10, 15);  // hat
30        g.fillRect(xS + 10, yS + 15, 20, 2);  // brim
31        g.setColor(Color.WHITE);
32        g.fillOval(xS + 10, yS + 17, 20, 20); // head
33        g.fillOval(xS, yS + 37, 40, 40);  // body
34        g.setColor(Color.RED);
35        g.fillOval(xS + 19, yS + 53, 4, 4);  //button
36        g.setColor(Color.BLACK);
37        g.drawRect(xS, yS, 40, 77); // inscribing rectangle
38        g.setFont(new Font("Sherif", Font.BOLD, 20));
```

```
39        g.drawString("Time: " + time, 300, 50);
40    }
41    public int getXS()
42    {
43       return xS;
44    }
45    public void setXS(int newX)
46    {
47     xS = newX;
48    }
49    public int getYS()
50    {
51       return yS;
52    }
53    public void setYS(int newY)
54    {
55       yS = newY;
56    }
57    public void actionPerformed(ActionEvent e)
58    {
59       time++;
60       repaint();
61    }
62    public void addNotify()
63    {
64       super.addNotify();
65       requestFocusInWindow();
66    }
67    public class KeyHandler extends KeyAdapter
68    {
69      public void keyPressed(KeyEvent e)
70      {
71        String key = KeyEvent.getKeyText(e.getKeyCode());
72        if(key.equals("Right"))
73        {
74          xS = xS + 3;
75          repaint();
76        }
77      }
78    }
79    public class MouseHandler extends MouseAdapter
80    {
81      public void mouseDragged(MouseEvent e)
82      {
83        xS = e.getX() - dx;
84        yS = e.getY() - dy;
85        repaint();
86      }
87      public void mousePressed(MouseEvent e)
```

```
 88          {
 89            dx = e.getX() - xS;
 90            dy = e.getY() - yS;
 91          }
 92          public void mouseClicked(MouseEvent e)
 93          {
 94            xS = e.getX();
 95            yS = e.getY();
 96            repaint();
 97          }
 98          public void mouseEntered(MouseEvent e)
 99          {
100            System.out.println("Entered");
101          }
102          public void mouseExited(MouseEvent e)
103          {
104            System.out.println("Exited");
105          }
106        }
107  }
```

Figure 11.28
The class **BoxedSnowmanV4**.

```
 1     import javax.swing.*;
 2     import java.awt.*;
 3
 4     public class MouseKeyboardAndTimerEvents extends JFrame
 5     {
 6       public static void main(String[] args)
 7       {
 8        JFrame window = new JFrame("MOUSE, KEYBOARD, AND TIMER EVENTS");
 9         window.setDefaultCloseOperation(JFrame.EXIT_ON_CLOSE);
10         BoxedSnowmanV4 s1 = new BoxedSnowmanV4(315, 165, Color.BLUE);
11         window.add(s1);
12         window.setSize(708, 434);
13         window.setVisible(true);
14       }
15     }
```

Figure 11.29
The application **MouseKeyboardAndTimerEvents**.

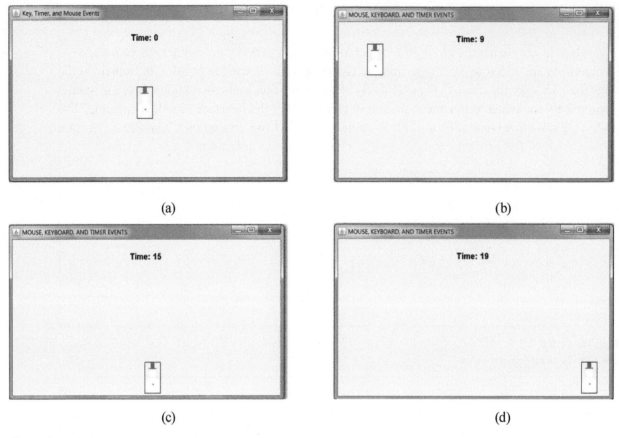

(a)

(b)

(c)

(d)

Console output:

Entered

Exited

Figure 11.30

The window and console output produced by the application **MouseKeyboardAndTimerEvents**.

11.5 LAYOUT MANAGERS

Java provides three *layout managers* that can facilitate the tedious process of locating components in a window when an IDE with a GUI builder is not available. By default they manage the placement and sizing of the components added to a JPanel or JFrame container. Their names are border layout, flow layout, and grid layout. Each layout manager uses a different approach to position and size the components added to a container.

Components are added to the container using the Container class's add method discussed in Section 11.3.3. The method is overloaded, and the version of the method used depends on the layout manager being used to position and size the components. The following code fragment uses the one-parameter version of the method to add the string annotation *Computes a + b* to a GUI that is using its default border layout manager to position and size components:

```
JLabel description = new JLabel("Computes a + b");
add(description);
```

When layout managers are used to build a graphical interface, most often the GUI's atomic components are added to JPanels, and the layout manager is used to position the panels in the interface. This greatly extends the usefulness of the layout managers. In addition, because atomic components are centered in panels, the use of panels makes the interface visually appealing. The following code fragment adds a JLabel containing the string annotation *Computes a + b* to a JPanel named panel1, and then panel1 is added to the GUI interface:

```
// Add a JLabel to a JPanel, and the JPanel to a GUI
JPanel panel1 = new JPanel();
JLabel description = new JLabel("Computes a + b");
panel1.add(description); //add the JLabel to the JPanel panel1
add(panel1); //add panel1 to the GUI
```

The positioning and sizing processes performed by the layout managers are implemented in the API classes BorderLayout, FlowLayout, and GridLayout. JPanels and JFrame objects store a reference to an object in one of these classes whose methods are used by the layout manager to size and locate the components added to them.

11.5.1 Designating the Layout Manager

By default, a JPanel uses *flow* layout and a JFrame uses *border* layout. These defaults can be overridden, or grid layout can be selected by invoking the Container class's setLayout method on a JPanel or JFrame object and passing it an instance of the layout manager class to be used to position the components added to the container. For example, the following code fragment sets the layout manager of a JPanel to border layout, overriding its default flow layout. Normally, a nameless object is passed to the method.

```
JPanel myPanel = new JPanel();
myPanel.setLayout(new BorderLayout()); //use border layout
```

To take control of the positioning and sizing of components within a container, a null value is passed to setLayout's parameter. When this is done, the components added to the container are positioned and sized using invocations to the setBounds, setsize, and setLocation methods, as discussed in Section 11.3.3.

```
// Programmer will specify the atomic components' size/location
JPanel myPanel = new JPanel();
myPanel.setLayout(null);
```

NOTE *A* null *or a non-default layout manager must be designated before components are added to an interface.*

While the use of a layout manager can facilitate the building of some GUI interfaces, it limits the programmer's ability to position and size the GUI components that make up the interface.

Table 11.7 summarizes the number of components, size, and positioning limitations imposed by the layout manager classes.

Table 11.7
Component Capacity, Size and Positioning Restrictions of the Layout Managers

Maximum Number of Components	Component Size	Positioning of Components
Border Layout (default layout manager for `JFrames` and applets: see Section 11.6)		
Five	The height and/or width of components are adjusted to fit the region to which they are assigned	Components are placed in one of five regions; the region assigned to each component is specified by the programmer, one component per region.
Flow Layout (default layout manager for `JPanels`)		
Unlimited	No restriction	Components are placed in rows in the order they are added to the container, beginning at the top left of the container. The row height is set to the largest component in the row.
Grid Layout		
Implied as the grid's rows × columns	All components are sized to the size of the cells	Components are placed in rows that contain cells, in the order they are added to the container, beginning with the top left cell, one item per cell. The number of rows and columns in the grid is specified by the programmer.

11.5.2 Border Layout

When the border layout is assigned to a container, it is divided into five regions named north, south, east, west, and center. The positioning of these regions in the container is shown in Figure 11.31. The font size of the text displayed in the south region of the figure was set larger than that of the text displayed in the other regions.

Figure 11.31
The positioning and sizing of the five border layout regions.

The height and width of the five components added to a container are adjusted in the following sequence, regardless of the order in which the program adds the components to the regions:

1. A component added to the north or south region maintains its height, and its width is the width of the container to which it is added

2. A component added to the east or west region maintains its width, and its height is set to the height between the north and south regions

3. The height and width of the component added to the center region is resized to fit between the other four regions

_____
NOTE

When using `BorderLayout`*:*
1. The width of the north and south regions are always equal
2. The height of the east, west, and center regions are always equal

The class `AddingMachineGUI3` shown in Figure 11.32 builds the GUI interface of the adding machine discussed in Section 11.3.3 using the border layout manager. The application `Border-Layout` shown in Figure 11.33 declares an instance of this class on line 8 of the figure and displays the graphical object on line 10. The application's GUI, built by the class `AddingMachineGUI3`, is shown in Figure 11.34. Although it is not identical to the GUI shown in Figure 11.16, which was built by the class `AddingMachineGUI` shown in Figure 11.15, the use of the border layout manager greatly facilitated the implementation of this GUI.

Because the atomic components of the GUI shown in Figure 11.34 are positioned in the upper, center, and lower areas of the interface, the border layout's north, center, and south regions were used in its implementation. In addition, because the center and lower areas contain multiple atomic components, `JPanels` were included to collect all three region's components.

The three `JPanels` used to collect the atomic components are declared on lines 9–11 of Figure 11.32, and line 18 designates that the border layout manager will be used to position them in the interface. Because the class extends `JFrame` (line 4), whose default layout manager is `BorderLay-out`, this line is not necessary; it is included as an example of how to specify the layout manager. The atomic components are added to the three panels on lines 43–53, and the panels are added to the border layout's north, center, and south regions (lines 54–56).

Before the atomic components are added to the panels, the components are constructed (lines 21–31), and their properties are set (lines 34–40). Lines 23 and 26 use the one-parameter constructor of the `JTextField` class to specify the width of the text fields. The `JLabel` created on line 30 is added to the `panel3` on line 52, in between the `compute` and `clear` buttons, to provide some additional separation between them.

```
1    import javax.swing.*;
2    import java.awt.*;
3
4    public class AddingMachineGUI3 extends JFrame
5    {
6      JLabel description, a, plus, b, equals, sum, centerSpace;
```

```
7        JTextField aValue, bValue;
8        JButton compute, clear;
9        JPanel panel1 = new JPanel();
10       JPanel panel2 = new JPanel();
11       JPanel panel3 = new JPanel();
12
13       public AddingMachineGUI3(String title)
14       {
15         super(title);
16         setSize(475, 150);
17         setLocation(200, 100);
18         setLayout(new BorderLayout());
19
20         //create the atomic components
21         description = new JLabel("Computes a + b");
22         a = new JLabel("a");
23         aValue = new JTextField(5);
24         plus = new JLabel("   +   ");
25         b = new JLabel("b");
26         bValue = new JTextField(5);
27         equals = new JLabel("   =   ");
28         sum = new JLabel("x,xxx.xx");
29         compute = new JButton("Compute");
30         centerSpace = new JLabel("      ");
31         clear = new JButton("    Clear    ");
32
33         //specify the component's properties
34         description.setFont(new Font("Sherif", Font.BOLD, 24));
35         plus.setFont(new Font("Sherif", Font.BOLD, 20));
36         equals.setFont(new Font("Sherif", Font.BOLD, 20));
37         sum.setFont(new Font("Sherif", Font.BOLD, 20));
38         a.setFont(new Font("Sherif", Font.BOLD, 20));
39         b.setFont(new Font("Sherif", Font.BOLD, 20));
40         clear.setToolTipText("Clears a, b and the sum");
41
42         //add the components to the window or non-atomic container
43         panel1.add(description);
44         panel2.add(a);
45         panel2.add(aValue);
46         panel2.add(plus);
47         panel2.add(b);
48         panel2.add(bValue);
49         panel2.add(equals);
50         panel2.add(sum);
51         panel3.add(compute);
52         panel3.add(centerSpace);
53         panel3.add(clear);
54         add(panel1, BorderLayout.NORTH);
```

```
55        add(panel2, BorderLayout.CENTER);
56        add(panel3, BorderLayout.SOUTH);
57    }
58 }
```

Figure 11.32
The class **AddingMachineGUI3** that uses the **BorderLayout** manager.

```
1    import javax.swing.*;
2    import java.awt.*;
3
4    public class BorderLayout
5    {
6      public static void main(String[] args)
7      {
8        AddingMachineGUI3 calculator = new AddingMachineGUI3("BORDER LAYOUT");
9        calculator.setDefaultCloseOperation(JFrame.EXIT_ON_CLOSE);
10       calculator.setVisible(true);
11     }
12 }
```

Figure 11.33
The application **BorderLayout**.

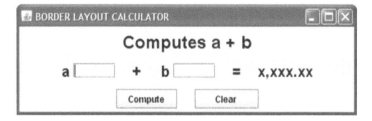

Figure 11.34
The application **BorderLayout's** graphical user interface.

11.5.3 Flow Layout

When flow layout is assigned to a container, it is divided into rows, with all rows being the width of the window's content pane. Each row's height is set to the height of the tallest component in the row. Figure 11.35 shows a GUI built using the flow layout. Five components were added to it after setting its layout manager to `FlowLayout`:

```
setLayout(new FlowLayout());
```

Beginning with the top row, components are positioned in the rows from left to right in the order in which they are added to the container. The row height is adjusted to the height of the tallest component in it, and the components are centered within the row. When a row fills up, the next component is added to the row below it. If the window height cannot accommodate all the rows necessary to display the components, they are not shown or are partially shown. If a single component is too wide for a row, it is only partially displayed.

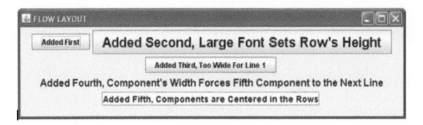

Figure 11.35
A GUI built using the **FlowLayout** manager.

The class FlowLayoutGUI, shown in Figure 11.36, builds the graphical interface shown in Figure 11.35 using the flow layout manager. Line 15 is needed to change the container's layout manager to flow layout because the class extends JFrame whose default manager is BorderLayout.

Following our GUI-building coding process, the atomic components are constructed in Figure 11.35 (lines 18–24), their properties are set (lines 27–29), and then they are added to the JFrame (lines 32–36). The application FlowLayout shown in Figure 11.37 declares an instance of this class on line 8 and displays the window on the monitor (line 10).

```
1    import javax.swing.*;
2    import java.awt.*;
3
4    public class FlowLayoutGUI extends JFrame
5    {
6      JButton first, second, third;
7      JLabel fourth;
8      JTextField fifth;
9
10     public FlowLayoutGUI(String title)
11     {
12       super(title);
13       setSize(650, 180);
14       setLocation(200, 100);
15       setLayout(new FlowLayout()); //Override the default BorderLayout
16
17       //Step 1 create the components
18       first = new JButton("Added First");
19       second = new JButton("Added Second, Large Font Sets Row's Height");
20       third = new JButton("Added Third, Could Not Fit on Row 1");
21       fourth = new JLabel("Added Fourth, Component's Width Forces " +
22                           "Fifth Component to the Next Row");
23       fifth = new JTextField("Added Fifth, Components are Centered " +
24                              "in the Rows");
25
26       //Step 2 specify the component's properties
27       second.setFont(new Font("Sherif", Font.BOLD, 22));
```

```
28        fourth.setFont(new Font("Sherif", Font.BOLD, 16));
29        fifth.setFont(new Font("Sherif", Font.BOLD, 14));
30
31        //Step 4 add the components to the container (Step 3 is skipped)
32        add(first);
33        add(second);
34        add(third);
35        add(fourth);
36        add(fifth);
37    }
38  }
```

Figure 11.36
The class `FlowLayoutGUI`.

```
1    import javax.swing.*;
2    import java.awt.*;
3
4    public class FlowLayout
5    {
6      public static void main(String[] args)
7      {
8        FlowLayoutGUI flowWindow = new FlowLayoutGUI("FLOW LAYOUT");
9        flowWindow.setDefaultCloseOperation(JFrame.EXIT_ON_CLOSE);
10       flowWindow.setVisible(true);
11     }
12 }
```

Figure 11.37
The application `FlowLayout`.

11.5.4 Grid Layout

The grid layout manager establishes a grid of cells arranged in rows and columns within a container. The number of rows and columns are specified by arguments passed to the `GridLayout` class's two–parameter constructor when the layout manager is specified:

```
setLayout(new GridLayout(4, 2)); //4 rows, 2 columns: eight cells
```

Every cell has the same height and width, which is set by the layout manager. The grid of cells always fills up the container, and the height and width of the cells are set to accommodate this. For example, a 4 x 2 grid would result in a cell height of one-quarter of the container height and a cell width of one-half the container width.

Components are added to the grid beginning with the cell in the upper left corner of the grid proceeding across a row before moving to the next row. If a component added to the grid is too large to fit into a cell, it is only partially displayed. Unused cells appear in the background color of the container.

Figure 11.38 shows a GUI interface built using a 3 x 2 grid layout. Five components were added to the JFrame container. The three buttons were added first, followed by a label and a text field. When the label's size is larger than the size of the cells because of its large font size and the length of its text.its text, the bottom of its text is truncated, and an ellipsis is shown to indicate that the remainder of its text could not be displayed. The cell in the lower-right corner of the grid was not used.

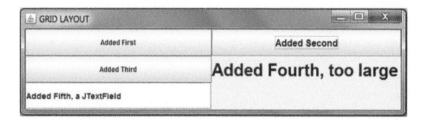

Figure 11.38
A GUI built using the **GridLayout** manager.

The class GridLayoutGUI shown in Figure 11.39 builds the graphical interface shown in Figure 11.38 using the grid layout manager. Line 15 changes the container's layout manager to GridLayout because the class extends JFrame, whose default manager is BorderLayout. Line 15 also specified the number of rows (three) and the number of columns (two) in the grid. The application GridLayout shown in Figure 11.40 declares an instance of this class on line 8 and displays the window on the monitor (line 10).

```
1    import javax.swing.*;
2    import java.awt.*;
3
4    public class GridLayoutGUI extends JFrame
5    {
6       JButton first, second, third;
7       JLabel fourth;
8       JTextField fifth;
9
10      public GridLayoutGUI(String title)
11      {
12         super(title);
13         setSize(650, 100);
14         setLocation(200, 100);
15         setLayout(new GridLayout(3, 2));
16
17         //Step 1 create the components
18         first = new JButton("Added First");
19         second = new JButton("Added Second");
20         third = new JButton("Added Third");
21         fourth = new JLabel("Added Fourth, too large");
```

```
22       fifth = new JTextField("Added Fifth, a JTextField");
23
24       //Step 2 specify the component's properties
25       second.setFont(new Font("Sherif", Font.BOLD, 16));
26       fourth.setFont(new Font("Sherif", Font.BOLD, 30));
27       fifth.setFont(new Font("Sherif", Font.BOLD, 14));
28
29       //Step 4  add the components to the container
30       add(first);
31       add(second);
32       add(third);
33       add(fourth);
34       add(fifth);
35     }
36   }
```

Figure 11.39
The class `GridLayoutGUI`.

```
1    import javax.swing.*;
2    import java.awt.*;
3
4    public class GridLayout
5    {
6      public static void main(String[] args)
7      {
8        GridLayoutGUI gridWindow = new GridLayoutGUI ("GRID LAYOUT");
9        gridWindow.setDefaultCloseOperation(JFrame.EXIT_ON_CLOSE);
10       gridWindow.setVisible(true);
11     }
12   }
```

Figure 11.40
The application `GridLayout`.

11.6 APPLETS

The programs we have written up to this point in the textbook are called applications. Applications are intended to run from your desktop, and once launched, they run autonomously, that is, outside the scope of another program. Another type of Java program is an applet, which is a program intended to run from within another program called an *applet container.* Typically, the applet container program is a Java-enabled Web browser because Java applets are intended to perform tasks associated with Web pages that are beyond the capabilities of the language used to define Web page content: HyperText Markup Language (HTML). These tasks include handling mouse events, displaying GUI components, and performing calculations.

HTML is a scripting language used to create Web pages and launch applets within a Web browser.

The Java Development Kit (JDK) contains an applet container program referred to as the *applet viewer*, which can also be used to run applets. It was included in the JDK to facilitate the testing of applets during their development. Applets, like applications, are developed using an integrated development environment, and most IDEs run applets from inside the JDK's applet viewer.

When we use a browser to visit a Website, the HTML document associated with the Website is downloaded to our computer from the Website's server. The browser interprets the text of the document to build and display the Web page. If the HTML document contains a reference to a Java applet, the translated bytecodes of the applet are downloaded from the Web server's disk, and then they are executed on our computer.

To prevent an executing applet from performing malicious activities, such as writing to its hard drive, on the computer on which it is running, the designers of Java restricted the range of the Java instruction set that can be included in an applet program. An attempt to execute restricted instructions contained in an applet results in a runtime error, whether is being run from within a Web browser or the applet viewer. During the development of an applet, restricted instructions that were unintentionally included in it are identified and removed during the testing phase. This Java-enforced level of security imposed on applets makes them safe to download and run from within a Web browser.

NOTE *Web browsers will download Java applets but not Java applications.*

11.6.1 Developing an Applet

To create an applet, we write an applet class and an HTML document that contains a reference to the class. When the applet container (i.e., a Web browser or the applet viewer) processes the HTML document, it creates an instance of the applet class and initiates its execution by invoking several of its methods.

Applet containers can only create instances of classes that extend the class `Applet` or its child class `JApplet`, which means that all applet classes that we code must extend one of these classes. Unlike application programs that begin their execution with the first executable statement in the method `main`, applet programs begin their execution with the first executable statement in a method named `init`. When an applet is launched, the applet container invokes this method, followed by the method `start`, and then the method `paint`. The method `paint` is reinvoked whenever the applet needs to be redisplayed.

Applets usually perform some of their processing inside overridden versions of these three inherited methods. Applets, like `JPanels`, are containers. They can be used to add a GUI interface to a Web page using the techniques previously discussed in this chapter or to add graphics to a Web page using the same drawing techniques used to add graphics to an application.

Figure 11.41 contains the code of the applet class CH11HelloWebWorld that produces the window, shown in Figure 11.42, when launched within the applet viewer container. The HTML document processed by the applet container is shown in Figure 11.43.

The class CH11HelloWebWorld is an applet because it extends the class Applet on line 4. It overrides its inherited paint method on lines 6–13. The applet container invokes this method to draw the applet, passing it a Graphics object in the same way as the paintComponent method discussed in Section 11.4.3 is invoked to draw a JPanel. Line 8 invokes the parent's version of the method, passing it the Graphics object g. This should always be the first executable statement in the overridden version of the method. The object g, passed to the method by the applet container, is used on lines 9–12 to perform the applet's graphical output.

```
1    import java.awt.*;
2    import java.applet.*;
3
4    public class CH11HelloWebWorld extends Applet
5    {
6      public void paint(Graphics g)
7      {
8        super.paint(g);
9        g.setFont(new Font("Sherif", Font.BOLD, 16));
10       g.drawString("Hello Web World", 170, 130 );
11       g.setColor(Color.BLUE);
12       g.fillOval(200, 140, 70, 70);
13     }
14   }
```

Figure 11.41
The applet **CH11HelloWebWorld**.

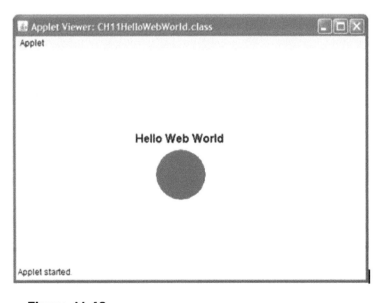

Figure 11.42
The output produced by the applet **CH11HelloWebWorld** running in the applet viewer.

```
1    <html>
2        <title>
3             Hello Applet
4        </title>
5        <body>
6             <applet code = "CH11HelloWebWorld.class"
7                             width = "500"
8                             height = "300">
9             </applet>
10       </body>
11   </html>
```

Figure 11.43
The HTML document that launches the applet **CH11HelloWebWorld**.

11.6.2 HTML Document Basics

The HTML document shown in Figure 11.43 would be used by an applet container to download and launch the applet shown in Figure 11.41. Like all HTML documents, it consists of instructions, called *elements*, describing how to display a Web page. The elements are enclosed within *tags*, which are enclosed in angle brackets and come in pairs. Pairs end with the same characters, which are part of the HTML scripting language. The second tag in a pair begins with a forward slash indicating the end of an instruction or section; the first tag in a pair does not begin with a slash. For example, the tags <html> and </html> that appear on lines 1 and 11 of Figure 11.43 are a pair. All HTML documents begin with the first tag of this pair and end with the pair's second tag. The remainder of the document in Figure 11.43 consists of a title element (lines 2–4) followed by a body element (lines 5–10) that contains an applet element (lines 6–9).

The title element contains the text of the Web page's title that will be displayed in a Web browser's window, in this case, *Hello Applet*. When the applet is launched from the applet viewer, the title is not displayed. The body element is meant to contain text and other HTML elements that will be displayed on the Web page. The body of the document shown in Figure 11.43 simply contains an applet element that references the class of our applet and sets the size of the applet when it is displayed by an applet container.

The first tag of the applet element contains the name of the applet's bytecode file and its extension. This is followed by the designation of the width and height of the applet: 500 and 300 on lines 7 and 8. The closing angle bracket for the first tag of the applet element is at the end of line 8. If the path name is not specified in front of the applet's file name, the file is assumed to be in the same folder as the HTML document. The tag on line 9 ends the applet element.

The generalized format of an applet element is shown below. The highlighted portions of it are application dependent:

```
<applet code = "CH11HelloWebWorld.class" width = "500" height = "300">
</applet>
```

The applet can be centered within the Web page by placing it inside center tags:

```
<body>
    <center>
            <applet code = "CH11HelloWebWorld.class"
                        width = "500"
                        height = "300">
            </applet>
    </center>
</body>
```

The use of indentation and new lines in the HTML documents is simply to improve the document's readability.

In addition to the applet element, text to be can displayed on the Web page by including it in the body element. There are several HTML tags that can be embedded in the text to control its formatting (e.g., its size, position, font style) the details of which are beyond the scope of this book.

11.6.3 The Applet Execution Path

The execution path of an applet is dictated by a protocol that is used by applet containers to launch, redisplay, and close an applet. The progression of steps contained in this protocol is often referred to as an applet's *life cycle*. The protocol includes a definition of the signatures of an applet's init, start, paint, stop, and destroy methods in the Java API classes Applet and Container, and a definition of when the applet container will invoke these methods. Table 11.8 shows the signature of these methods and their role in the life cycle of an applet. Overriding these methods within an applet class, to perform processing consistent with their intended use, produces a properly functioning applet.

Table 11.8
Methods Invoked by Applet Containers

When Invoked by the Applet Container	Intended Use
`public void init()`	
Invoked once: when the applet is launched	Perform initialization tasks normally relegated to a constructor, such as declaring and initializing class level variables, building the applet's GUI, registering event handlers, and creating threads (see Chapter 14)
`public void start()`	
Invoked after the init method and each time the Web page is revisited	Perform tasks that are associated with revisiting the Web page containing the applet, such as starting/restarting animation timers

(Contd.)

When Invoked by the Applet Container	Intended Use
`public void paint()`	
Invoked after the `init` and `start` methods and whenever the applet needs to be redisplayed, for example, when the applet container is minimized and then maximized	Repaint the applet; perform 2D graphics in applet classes that extend the class `Applet`
`public void stop()`	
Invoked when the Web page is left and before the destroy method is invoked	Perform tasks that are associated with leaving the Web page containing the applet, such as stopping animation timers
`public void destroy()`	
Invoked once when the applet is removed from memory, e.g., closed	Deallocate resources allocated to the applet

11.6.4 Incorporating GUIs and Two-Dimensional Graphics into Applets

Applets are containers. The `Applet` and `JApplet` classes both have the class `Container` in their inheritance chain. This gives them the ability to contain GUI components, process events, and draw 2D shapes on GUI interfaces using the same techniques and syntax discussed previously in this chapter to incorporate these features into `JPanels` and `JFrames`. An applet's default layout manager is `BorderLayout`.

Two-Dimensional Graphics in a `JApplet`

In Figure 11.41, we coded an applet to draw graphical text and a 2D shape (a filled oval) on a Web page. The applet's class extended the class `Applet` and performed its drawing inside an overridden version of the `paint` method. If the class extended the class `JApplet`, another approach to performing 2D graphics would be taken. The drawing would be performed inside a class that extends `JPanel` using an overridden version of the `paintComponent` method, and an instance of that class would be added to the applet. If this is not done, the graphics are not redrawn as part of the redrawing of the Web page.

The applet `CH11HelloWebWorldV2`, shown in Figure 11.44, presents a revised version of the `HelloWebWorld` applet shown in Figure 11.41. This version of the applet extends the class `JApplet` and performs its 2D graphics by declaring an instance of the class `GraphicsPanel` (lines 6 and 10), shown in Figure 11.45, and adding it to the applet (line 11 in Figure 11.44). The `GraphicsPanel` class extends `JPanel`, overrides its `PaintComponent` method on lines 6–13, and performs the drawing inside of it.

The HTML document processed by the applet container to generate the Web page shown in Figure 11.46 is the same as the document shown in Figure 11.43, except that line 3 would been probably be changed to `Hello Applet V2`, and line 6 has to be changed to:

```
<applet code = "CH11HelloWebWorldV2.class"
```

As indicated in Table 11.8, the overridden version of the `init` method shown in Figure 11.44 performs tasks normally relegated to constructors in application programs.

```
1    import java.awt.*;
2    import javax.swing.*;
3
4    public class CH11HelloWebWorldV2 extends JApplet
5    {
6      GraphicsPanel aPanel;
7
8      public void init()
9      {
10        aPanel = new GraphicsPanel();
11        add(aPanel);
12      }
13   }
```

Figure 11.44
The applet **CH11HelloWebWorldV2**.

```
1    import java.awt.*;
2    import javax.swing.*;
3
4    public class GraphicsPanel extends JPanel
5    {
6      public void paintComponent(Graphics g)
7      {
8        super.paintComponent(g);
9        g.setFont(new Font("Sherif", Font.BOLD, 16));
10        g.drawString("Hello Web World", 170, 130 );
11        g.setColor(Color.BLUE);
12        g.fillOval(200, 140, 70, 70);
13      }
14   }
```

Figure 11.45
The class **GraphicsPanel**.

Figure 11.46
The Web page containing the applet **CH11HelloWebWorldV2**.

GUI Components and Event Handling

A GUI interface for a Web page is built using the same techniques used to build a GUI interface for an application, which were previously discussed in this chapter, with one exception. Instead of building the interface and coding and registering the event handlers inside of a class that extends `JPanel` or `JFrame`, this processing is done in an applet class that becomes an element in the Web page's HTML document.

Tasks that would have been performed by a constructor when implementing a GUI class for an application, such as declaring GUI components, adding them to the interface, registering event handler methods, and specifying a layout manager are performed inside the applet's `init` method. GUI components can be positioned in the interface using the applet's default layout manager `BorderLayout`, or the layout manager can be changed using the `setLayout` method to `FlowLayout`, `GridLayout`, or set to `null` to use the `sizeSize`, `setLocation`, and `setBounds` methods to position the components. As is the case with applications, event handlers are coded as methods registered in listener lists, but now their code is placed inside the applet class or within inner classes added to it.

An example of building a graphical interface for a Web page is illustrated in Figure 11.47; it presents the applet `GuessingGame`, which builds the interface and implements the game. When the applet is launched its interface, shown in Figure 11.48, appears on the Web page.

Initially, the numbers 1 through 8 are displayed on a pair of buttons randomly selected from the 16-button grid positioned at the top of the applet's GUI. After studying the arrangement of the numbers, the player clicks the *Begin* button, and the numbers are hidden. The object of the game is to reveal all of the number pairs with a minimum number of clicks. To accomplish this, the player repeatedly attempts to click a pair of buttons whose numbers match. When a correct match is clicked, the number pair remains visible. When an incorrect match is clicked, the number pair remains visible for two seconds, an error count is incremented, and then numbers are hidden. The game continues until all the pairs of numbers have been revealed.

The applet consists of four major sections: the class-level variable declarations (lines 9–22), the `init` method (lines 24–55), three worker methods (lines 57–93), and the event handlers (lines 96–169).

The `init` method (lines 24–55), invoked by the applet container program to launch the applet, is used to build the GUI and initialize the game. A two-second (2,000 millisecond) timer is declared on line 22, and its second argument adds the timer event handler coded on lines 158–169 to its listener list. Line 28 changes the applet's default `BorderLayout` to a five-row by four-column `GridLayout`. Lines 17 and 26 create a `JButton` array named *cell*. Each time through the `for` loop that begins on line 40, a new button is created (line 42), the click event handler method defined on lines 114–156 is added to its listener list (line 44), and the button is added to a cell of the GIU's grid (line 45).

Lines 49–52 build the bottom row of the grid by adding two buttons, `begin` and `reset`, and two labels, `errors` and `nunberOfErrors`. The `actionPerformed` event handler method defined on lines 98–111 is added to these buttons' listener lists on lines 36–37. Line 31 invokes the setHorizontalAlignment method passing it the static constant RIGHT to position the errors and numberOfErrors labels, which were added to the bottom row of the grid, next to each other. Finally, line 54 of the init method invokes the worker method intializeGame (lines 57–67), to generate (line 59) and display (line 64) a randomly placed set of numbers on the 16 button grid.

The generateNumbers method, invoked on line 59 of the intializeGame method to initialize (line 54) and rest (line 109) the game, generates when the *Reset* button is clicked, generates and places the eight number pairs into the array values (lines 76–79), and then they are randomly swapped within the array (lines 80–84). The loop that begins on line 62 of the intializeGame method sets each button's text to one of these 16 randomized values by passing their setText method the string version of an element of the array (line 64). Line 64 uses the arrays cell and values as parallel arrays, as do the loops that process a pair of button clicks (lines 122 and 137).

```
1    import java.awt.*;
2    import java.applet.*;
3    import javax.swing.*;
4    import java.util.Random;
5    import java.awt.event.*;
6
7    public class GuessingGame extends JApplet implements ActionListener
8    {
9      boolean firstClick = true;
10     int firstClickValue = 0;
11     int firstClickIndex = 0;
12     int secondClickIndex = 0;
13     int errorCount = 0;
14     boolean correct = false;
15     int[] values = new int[16];
16     JButton b = new JButton();
17     JButton[]cell;
18     JLabel errors = new JLabel("Errors: ");
19     JLabel numberOfErrors = new JLabel("0");
20     JButton begin = new JButton("Begin");
21     JButton reset = new JButton("Reset");
22     Timer timer1 = new Timer(2000, new TimerHandler());
23
24     public void init()
25     {
26       cell = new JButton[16]; //the number buttons
27
28       setLayout(new GridLayout(5, 4)); //override default BorderLayout
29
30       //set properties of GUI compoments
31       errors.setHorizontalAlignment(JLabel.RIGHT);
32       errors.setFont(new Font("Serif", Font.BOLD, 30));
33       numberOfErrors.setFont(new Font("Serif", Font.BOLD, 30));
34
```

```
35        //add event handlers to listener lists
36        begin.addActionListener(new BeginResetHandler());
37        reset.addActionListener(new BeginResetHandler());
38
39        //create number buttons, set properties, register event handlers
40        for(int i = 0; i < 16; i++)
41        {
42          cell[i] = new JButton("0");
43          cell[i].setFont(new Font("Serif", Font.BOLD, 40));
44          cell[i].addActionListener(this);
45          add(cell[i]);
46        }
47
48        //add the lower buttons and labels
49        add(begin);
50        add(errors);
51        add(numberOfErrors);
52        add(reset);
53
54        intializeGame();
55      }
56
57      public void intializeGame()
58      {
59        generateNumbers();
60        numberOfErrors.setText("0");
61        errorCount = 0;
62        for(int i = 0; i < 16; i++)
63        {
64          cell[i].setText(Integer.toString(values[i]));
65          cell[i].setForeground(Color.BLACK);
66        }
67      }
68
69      public void generateNumbers() //generate buttons' numbers
70      {
71        Random rn = new Random();
72        int number = 0;
73        int cellNumber = 0;
74        boolean done;
75
76        for(int i = 1; i <= 16; i++) //all number buttons
77        {
78          values[i-1] = i % 8 + 1; //place numbers 1->8 twice
79        }
80        for(int i = 0; i < 16; i++) //all number buttons
81        {
82          number = rn.nextInt(15);
83          swap(values, i, number); //swap button value with a random button
```

```
84        }
85     }
86
87     public void swap(int[] array, int indx1, int indx2)
88     {
89       int temp;
90       temp = array[indx1];
91       array[indx1] = array[indx2];
92       array[indx2] = temp;
93     }
94
95     //event handlers *************************************
96     public class BeginResetHandler implements ActionListener
97     {
98       public void actionPerformed(ActionEvent e)
99       {
100        if(e.getSource() == begin) // start the game
101        {
102          for(int i = 0; i < 16; i++)
103          {
104            cell[i].setText(" "); //hide the numbers
105          }
106        }
107        else //generate and a new game
108        {
109          intializeGame();
110        }
111      }
112    }
113
114    public void actionPerformed(ActionEvent e) //number buttons' handler
115    {
116      if(firstClick) //show the number
117      {
118        for(int i = 0; i<16; i++) //all number buttons
119        {
120          if(e.getSource() == cell[i]) //button clicked found
121          {
122            cell[i].setText(Integer.toString(values[i]));
123            firstClick = false;
124            firstClickValue = values[i];
125            firstClickIndex = i;
126            break;
127          }
128        }
129      }
130      else //second click processing
131      {
```

```
132            timer1.start(); //two seconds
133            for(int i = 0; i<16; i++) //all number buttons
134            {
135              if(e.getSource() == cell[i]) //button clicked found
136              {
137                cell[i].setText(Integer.toString(values[i]));
138                firstClick = true;
139                secondClickIndex = i;
140                if(firstClickValue == values[i]) //correct match
141                {
142                  correct = true;
143                  cell[firstClickIndex].setForeground(Color.BLUE);
144                  cell[secondClickIndex].setForeground(Color.BLUE);
145                }
146                else //incorrect match
147                {
148                  correct = false;
149                  errorCount++;
150                  numberOfErrors.setText(Integer.toString(errorCount));
151                }
152                break;
153              } // end if
154            }   // end for
155          }   // end else
156        }
157
158        public class TimerHandler implements ActionListener
159        {
160          public void actionPerformed(ActionEvent e) //Timer's event handler
161          {
162            if(correct == false) //no match
163            {
164              timer1.stop(); //after a two second pause
165              cell[firstClickIndex].setText(" "); //hide the numbers
166              cell[secondClickIndex].setText(" ");
167            }
168          }
169        }
170 }
```

Figure 11.47
The applet **GuessingGame**.

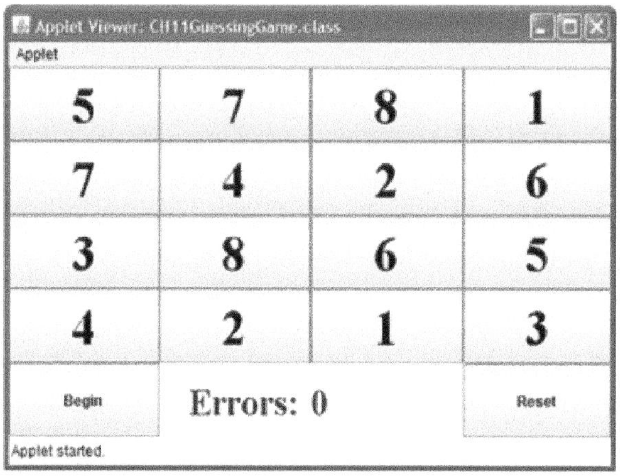

Figure 11.48
The GUI produced by the applet `GuessingGame`.

11.6.5 Portability and Security Issues

When designing a GUI interface for an applet, the highest level of portability across Web browsers is achieved when AWT components, rather than Swing components, are used in the interface. Alternately, the portability of Swing-based GUI applets can be extended across the range of available browsers by installing a Java plugin on the computer on which the browser is running. The plugin is freely available and is part of the JDK.

Although AWT GUI components used in applets offer more browser portability, Swing provides a richer complement of components. The more commonly used Swing components, such as labels, buttons, text fields, and check boxes do have AWT counterparts, but several Swing components (e.g., radio buttons) do not have an AWT counterpart. The AWT component class names do not include the leading `J` used in the Swing class names. For example, the name of the AWT button class is `Button`, and the name of the AWT label class is `Label` (Swing's class names are `JButton` and `JLabel`).

In addition to the difference in the names of the component classes, the names of some of the Swing and AWT methods used to perform common operations on GUI components are also different. For example, the Swing methods `setText` and `getText` can be used to change and fetch the annotation on a `JButton`. Their AWT counterparts are the methods `setLabel` and `getLabel`.

The applet shown in Figure 11.47 extends the class `JApplet` on line 7, and its graphical interface is built entirely with Swing components. The applet's portability can be extended by making it a child of the `Applet` class (extending `Applet` instead of `JApplet`), eliminating the `J` that begins all of the GUI component class names used in the applet, and changing the `setText` method invocations (e.g., on line 64) to invocations of the AWT `Button` class's `setLabel` method.

Often, it is desirable to allow an applet to perform certain operations that are beyond the range of those performed by the default Java instruction subset that can be included in an applet, such as installing Web-based software updates to a program stored on in a computer's hard drive. To accomplish this, applet developers obtain a digital security certificate from a certificate authority organization, which is attached to the applet. Before a certified applet is run inside a Web browser, information about the applet's developer and the restricted operation it will perform is announced to the user, and the user is asked if the developer is a trusted source. An acknowledgement of trust in the developer permits the applet to run and gain access to various resources of the user's computer, such as its hard drive, that would normally be restricted.

11.7 CHAPTER SUMMARY

The overloaded versions of the `showInputDialog` and `showMessageDialog` methods in the `JOptionPane` class can be used to display more informative and user-friendly dialog boxes then those versions used in previous chapters. A dialog box's default icon can be replaced with one of four other selections, its default title can be changed, and the window within which it is centered can be specified. In addition, a default input or a set of valid inputs from which to choose can be displayed in an input dialog box.

User-friendly graphical interfaces are incorporated into a program by adding a worker class that contains the code to build the interface. The program declares an instance of the class and makes it visible. Ordinarily, the worker class either extends `JFrame` for non-Web-based programs or the `JApplet` for Web-based programs. These API classes are referred to as top-level containers. The worker class contains code to create and add instances of `JButton`, `JTextField`, and `JLabels` to a container after setting their visibility, annotation, color, font, and size properties and their location within the container. An instance of the class `Timer` can be added to a container. Its time interval is set when it is created, and it is initiated by invoking the `start` method on the timer object.

A flow layout manager can be used to facilitate the positioning and sizing of components within a container. A container's default `FlowLayout` manager can be changed by invoking the `setLayout` method on the container or nullified by passing the method a `null` value. Some integrated development environments have a GUI-builder feature that generates the worker class as the programmer drags and drops GUI components onto a container and selects their properties from lists and dialog boxes.

The GUI-builder worker class also contains code to perform processing as the user interacts with the interface or when a timer's interval expires. These interactions are called events, and the code is placed inside call back methods referred to as event handlers. The signatures of these methods are defined in a group of API interfaces, three of which are named `ActionListener`, `KeyListener`, and `MouseMotionListener`. The methods defined in these three interfaces are invoked when a button is clicked, a key is typed, the mouse is clicked or dragged, or a time interval expires.

Event handler methods are associated with particular components in the GUI by registering them with the component via an invocation of methods such as `addActionListener`, `addKey-Listener`, and `addMouseMotionListener` passing them an instance of the class in which the event handler method is coded. In the case of a `Timer` object, the instance of the event handler's class is passed to the `Timer` object's constructor when it is created. The event handlers can be part of the GUI-builder worker class or an inner class defined within it. The heading of a class that contains the implementation of the event handler method must contain an `implements` clause indicating that it implements the method's interface. Alternately, the class can extend one of the API adapter classes that provide empty implementations of some of the API listener interfaces. The component on which an event occurred can be identified by invoking the `getSource` method on the argument passed to the event handler method, or the key struck on a keyboard can be determined by invoking the `getKeyCode` method on the argument.

A paint event is any event that causes a graphical object to be drawn or redrawn, such as maximizing a window after it has been minimized. When these events occur, a call back method is invoked by the Java Runtime Environment, which can be overridden to draw shapes on a GUI. These method names begin with the word "paint" (for example, `paintComponent`) and are ordinarily overridden in a separate drawing worker class. Then, an instance of the class is declared within the program (e.g., the method `main`), and the `add` method is invoked on the program's GUI-builder object (its window) to add the instance to it.

In addition to application programs, Java also supports applets, which run from within another program, such as a Web browser or applet viewer. Applet containers create instances of classes that extend the class `Applet` or its child class `JApplet`. Unlike application programs that begin their execution with the first executable statement in the method `main`, applet programs begin their execution with the first executable statement in a method named `init`. The applet container invokes this method when it launches the applet, followed by invocations of the methods `start` and `paint`. It invokes the method `stop` to suspend the applet and `destroy` to terminate the applet. Applets like `JPanels` are containers, and they can be used to add a GUI interface or 2D shapes to a Web page using the same techniques used to add a GUI and shapes to applications.

Applets are considered to be both portable and secure. The highest level of portability across Web browsers is achieved when AWT components, rather than Swing components are used. Security is provided for Java applets by restricting some of the functions they can perform and by attaching a digital security certificate to the applet.

Knowledge Exercises

1. True or false:
   a) GUI stands for Grand Unified Interaction.
   b) Although they take longer to develop, GUIs reduce the time and effort needed to interact with a program.
   c) To create a graphical user interface, declare an instance of a top-level container class object and add the GUI components to it.
   d) A paint event causes a graphical object to be drawn or redrawn.
   e) Check boxes permit multiple selections to be made.
   f) Multiple components in an application can have the keyboard's focus at the same time.

g) Java applications and applets both begin executing in their `main` method.

h) An enhanced dialog box can be used to display several valid inputs from which a user can choose.

i) The default layout manager for `JFrames` is the grid layout manager.

j) The border layout manager specifies five regions for the components.

k) The north and south regions of the border layout are always the width of the window.

l) All the cells of the grid layout have the same height and width.

m) Java applets are considered to be both portable and secure.

2. Give a statement that asks a person for his or her age using a dialog box containing an information message icon and the title *Happy Birthday*.

3. Name at least three GUI components and explain their usual uses.

4. Give the code to:
   a) Make the `JButton b1` disappear
   b) Relocate `JButton b2` to location (200, 400)
   c) Change the text displayed in `JTextBox tb1` to *Correct*
   d) Create a `JButton` named `b3` whose annotation is *Click Here*
   e) Change the text of `JLabel lb1` to *The Answer is Yes*
   f) Add the `JButton b4` to the `JPanel p1`
   g) Make the size of `JTextBox tb2` 100 pixels wide and 50 pixels high
   h) Attach the tool tip *Click After Entering a Number* to `JButton b5`

5. Name the five regions of the border layout and describe their location, height and width.

6. Name and describe the three layout managers that Java provides.

7. Give the code to:
   a) Allow components to be positioned and sized in the `JPanel p1` using the `setBounds` method
   b) Change a `JPanel p2`'s layout manager to `BorderLayout`

8. Sketch the position of five components (c1, c2, c3, c4, and c5) as each layout manager would present them after they were added to a container in the order c1 through c5. Clearly state your assumptions, where necessary, regarding the width and placement of the components.

9. Give the code to display a 600 x 800-pixel red window from within the method `main` without the use of a GUI-builder worker class.

10. What is the result of omitting the `setDefaultCloseOperation` when creating a window?

11. Explain the purpose of event handlers.

12. Give the name of the event handler that processes a click on a `JButton` object.

13. Three `JButton` objects named `b1`, `b2`, and `b3` are registered with the same event handler. Give the code in the event handler method to output *Button 2* when `b2` is clicked.

14. What are the three keyboard hander methods defined in the API `KeyListener` interface, and what events do they handle?

15. What are adapter classes, and what is the advantage of a class extending them?

16. What does it mean to say that a component must have the keyboard's focus?

17. How can a component get the keyboard's focus?

18. What are some of the differences between the AWT and Swing GUI packages?

19. State one advantage of using the classes in the AWT package over the classes in the Swing package, and vice versa.

20. Discuss the major difference between Java applications and applets.

21. How do Java applets provide security and portability?

Programming Exercises

1. Write a program with a GUI that allows the user to input the length and width of a rectangle. The GUI will have three buttons. When one of the buttons is clicked, the area of the rectangle is displayed in square feet. When the second button is clicked, the perimeter of the rectangle is displayed. When the third button is clicked, the GUI is restored to the condition it was in when the program was launched. Each button will have its own event handler.

2. Modify the program in Exercise 1 so one event handler performs the calculations, and the restoration for the GUI to its launch condition is performed by a second event handler.

3. Modify the program in Exercise 2 to include an additional input for the cost of carpet per square foot and a fourth button to calculate and display the cost of the carpet.

4. Write a GUI application whose window's title is *Favorite Color* and is initially blue. When a button on the interface is clicked, an enhanced dialog box is displayed from which the user can choose a color from among eight colors. When the OK button on the dialog box is clicked, the background of the window should change to the selected color.

5. Create a program to display a GUI window with the following features: its size is 400 x 450 pixels, and its location is 100, 100. The window title is *Surprise!* The window should contain a button labeled *Press Here*. When the button is pressed, the background color should change to your favorite color and a circle (or a smiley face) should appear.

6. Write a program using a GUI with three buttons, labeled *RED*, *YELLOW* and *BLUE*, which cause a filled rectangle to be drawn in the appropriate color when pressed.

7. Write a GUI application that will react to a mouse-click event by displaying the x and y coordinates of the position in the window where the mouse was clicked.

8. Create a GUI window with a mouse and a piece of cheese drawn on it, each at a random location. The keyboard directional arrow keys can be used to move the mouse to the piece of cheese.

9. Expand the application described in Exercise 8 so the cheese can be dragged around the window to the mouse.

10. Write a GUI application called `StopWatch` that displays the minutes and seconds that have elapsed since the interface's Start button was clicked. When the interface's Reset button is clicked, the elapsed time should return to zero, and the timer should stop. Each button should have its own event handler.

11. Design and implement a four-function GUI calculator with buttons for the digits from 0 to 9 and the arithmetic operations +, -, *, and /. The button for = should cause the operation to be performed and the result to be displayed in a text field. Also, include a Clear button to clear the calculator so another operation can be performed.

12. Write an applet named *Know Your Shapes* that displays a colorful circle, square, rectangle, and ellipse, each with a text field below it. After the user types the names of each shape in the text boxes and clicks the Done button, display *Correct* in the text fields in which the typed names are correct and the correct name of the shape in the text boxes in which the typed name is incorrect. After five seconds have elapsed, clear the text boxes and output *Try again* to the GUI.

Enrichment

Use Java's `Timer` object to create animation for a graphical object on a GUI interface.

References

Boese, Elizabeth Sugar. *An Introduction to Programming with Java Applets*. 3rd Ed. Sudbury, MA: Jones and Bartlett Publishers, 2010.

GRAPHICAL USER INTERFACES: A SECOND LOOK

12.1 *Borders Checkboxes and Radio Buttons* *550*

12.2 *Combo Boxes and Lists* *563*

12.3 *Menus* *572*

12.4 *File Chooser and Color Chooser Dialog Boxes* *585*

12.5 *Chapter Summary* *590*

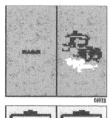
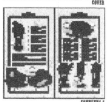

MENU DESIGN

In this chapter

In Chapter 11, we became familiar with the techniques used to create a GUI application's program window and add labels, buttons, and text fields to it, and how to respond to the user's interaction with these components via key strokes or mouse clicks and drags. In this chapter, we expand our knowledge of the other GUI component classes available in the API Swing package. Check boxes, radio buttons, combo boxes, and lists allow a user to select one or more inputs from a set of valid inputs. The procedure for adding a component to a window is expanded to include the grouping of radio buttons and the placement of titled borders around GUI components.

Menus are a common component of GUIs, and both drop-down and pop-up menus are discussed in this chapter, as are submenus and hot keys. In addition, the file-chooser and color-chooser dialog boxes used to facilitate disk I/O and color selection are presented in this chapter.

After successfully completing this chapter, you should:

- Be able to create and position check boxes, radio buttons, combo boxes, and lists and perform processing when the user selects inputs associated with these components
- Know how to enclose GUI components within titled borders and how to change the color, style, and thickness of borders
- Understand how to add scroll bars to combo boxes and lists
- Be able to assign hot keys to GUI components and perform processing in response to hot-key strokes
- Understand how to implement drop-down and pop-up menus and submenus and perform processing in response to menu selections
- Know how to use API defined dialog boxes to facilitate the input of file I/O paths, file names, and color selection

12.1 BORDERS CHECKBOXES AND RADIO BUTTONS

The GUI components check box and radio button are shown in the upper center and upper right portion of Figure 12.1. Groupings of check boxes and radio buttons are used to facilitate the selection of one or more inputs from a small set of valid inputs. When the user can select several of the inputs from the set, check boxes are used in the GUI. When the inputs are mutually exclusive, that is, only one of the valid inputs can be selected, radio buttons are used.

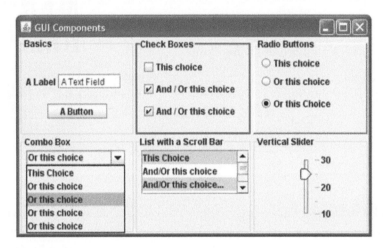

Figure 12.1
GUI components.

Ordinarily, a set of check boxes or a set of radio buttons is added to an instance of a `JPanel`, and then the panel is added to the window's content pane. This makes the check box set or radio button set easier to reposition in the window because only the panel's location needs to be changed, rather than changing the position of each of the boxes or buttons individually. In addition, the panel's border can be made visible to give the visual impression that the check boxes or buttons are part of a set, and a title can be added to the panel's border to provide additional information about the box or button set. This is the approach that was taken when the GUI illustrated in Figure 12.1 was built.

12.1.1 Borders

A border can be placed around any component that extends the class `JComponent`, although most often, the use of a border is associated with `JPanel` and `JLabel` components. This is done by invoking the `setBorder` method on the component and passing it the object returned from an invocation of one of the static methods in the `BorderFactory` class. These methods create most of the borders available in the API Swing package. The following code fragment was used to place the border containing the title *Basics* around the `JPanel` component p1 that contains the label, text field, and button on the top left side of Figure 12.1.

```
//Default light blue line border with a title
p1 = new JPanel();
p1.setBorder(BorderFactory.createTitledBorder("Basics"));
```

This one-parameter version of the `createTitledBorder` method creates a border drawn as a thin light blue line with the title displayed in the default position (i.e., the upper left corner of the border). The static method `createTitledBorder` is overloaded. All of the other versions of the method contain a `Border` type parameter, which is used to change the thickness, style, and color of the border, and some versions of the method contain parameters to change the title's vertical position, horizontal justification, and its font color and style.

In addition to the `createTitledBorder` method, the `BorderFactory` class contains static methods used to construct different styles of borders and specify the thickness and color of the border. These methods construct and return a `Border` object that describes the border, which is then passed to the overloaded versions of the `createTitledBorder` method. The following code fragment was used to create and place the thick red-colored line border around the `JPanel` that encloses the check boxes in Figure 12.1. The integer argument, 2, passed to the `BorderFactory` class's method `createLineBorder` changes the border thickness from the default value of 1 to 2:

```
//Double thick red colored line border with a title
p2 = new JPanel();
Border aBorder = BorderFactory.createLineBorder(Color.RED, 2);
p2.setBorder(BorderFactory.createTitledBorder(aBorder, "Check Boxes"));
```

Other border styles include an etched style, a beveled style, and a soft-beveled style. The `BorderFactory` class's `createBevelBorder` is used to change the style of the border from a line to a beveled appearance. The following code fragment was used to place the beveled border around the `JPanel` that encloses the radio buttons in Figure 12.1. The integer argument (0) passed to the `createBevelBorder` method specifies the type of bevel to use, in this case, raised:

```
//Raised beveled border with a title
p3 = new JPanel();
aBorder = BorderFactory.createBevelBorder(0);
p3.setBorder(BorderFactory.createTitledBorder(aBorder, "Radio Buttons"));
```

Borders can be created without titles by only passing the `setBorder` method a `Border` object returned from one of the `BorderFactory` class's static methods. The following code fragment places a raised beveled border with no embedded title around a `JPanel`:

```
//Double thick red colored line border, no title
p4 = new JPanel();
p4.setLayout(null);
p4.setBorder(BorderFactory.createBevelBorder(0););
```

12.1.2 Check Boxes

A grouping of check boxes is used on a GUI to facilitate the selection of one or more inputs from a small set of valid inputs. When the user clicks a check box, a check either appears in the check box or is removed from it. Using the techniques discussed in this section, check boxes are created, added to, and positioned in GUI containers. Processing can be initiated when the user checks or uncheckes them.

Creating Check Boxes

Check boxes are instances of the API class `JCheckBox` and can be created using the class's one (`String`) parameter constructor or the class's default constructor. The text that appears beside the check box when it is displayed is the string passed to the one-parameter constructor or the string passed to the class's `setText` method. The following code fragment creates the first two check boxes shown in the top center of Figure 12.1:

```
//Create check boxes and initialize their text.
JCheckBox cb1 = new JCheckBox("This choice");
JCheckBox cb2 = new JCheckBox();
ch2.setText(("And / Or this choice");
```

The `setText` method sets the text property of most GUI components that display text, and it can be used to initially set or to change the text associated with a component. As discussed in Chapter 11, the properties of atomic components and containers can be set and fetched using the methods shown in Table 11.5, which is recreated as Table 12.1 for convenience.

Table 12.1
Methods Used to Specify a Component's Properties and Add it to a Container

Method Signature	Description
`JComponent` and `Component` Class Methods Invoked on Components	
`setToolTipText(String tip)`	Adds the tool tip `tip` to the component, displayed when the mouse pointer hovers over it
`setBounds(int x, int y, int width, int height)`	Sets the component's location to (x, y) and its width and height to `width` and `height`
`setLocation(int x, int y)`	Sets the component's location to (x, y)
`setSize(int width, int height)`	Sets the component's width and height to `width` and `height`
`setText(String newText)`	Changes the text displayed on the component to `newText`
`setVisible(boolean visible)`	The component is visible when `visible` is passed the value `true`, invisible when passed `false`
`setFont(Font fontStyle)`	Sets the font style of the container or component that invoked the method to `fontStyle`
`Container` Class Methods	
`setLayout(LayoutManager layout);`	Sets the container's layout to `layout`, to specify location/size of components: `layout = null`
`add(Component theComponent)`	Adds `theComponent` to the container or component that invoked the method

By default, a check box is initially displayed unchecked (without a check mark). An additional Boolean argument can be passed to the JCheckBox class's one-parameter constructor to specify that the box will contain a check mark when it is initially displayed:

```
//Display a check in a check box
JCheckBox cb1 = new JCheckBox("Check box is checked", true);
```

Adding Check Boxes to Containers and Positioning Them

Check boxes are added to a GUI container using the add method, which is described at the bottom of Table 12.1. The following code fragment adds two check boxes to the JPanel container p1:

```
//Add two check boxes to a JPanel container
p1 = new JPanel();
JCheckBox cb1 = new JCheckBox("Hamburger");
JCheckBox cb2 = new JCheckBox("Taco");
p1.add(cb1);
p1.add(cb2);
```

Check boxes, like other components added to a container, are positioned within it using the techniques discussed in Chapter 11 (Section 11.3.3 when a layout manager is not used and Section 11.5 when a layout manager is used). When a layout manager is used, the check boxes will be positioned by the manager in the order in which they are added to the container.

If the container's layout manager has been set to null, the setBounds method described in Table 12.1 can be used to position and set the height and width of the component. The height and width passed to the method includes the box and its associated text. Alternately, the setLocation and setSize methods can be used to position a check box in the container and to specify its size.

The following code fragment was used to create the three check boxes shown in Figure 12.1 and the panel that contains them. The panel does not use a layout manager to position its components because the panel's setLayout method is passed a null value. This permits the use of the setBounds method to position and size the components added to it. The (x, y) position specified by the first two arguments sent to the method setBounds is relative to the upper left corner of the container (to which a component has been added).

```
// Position and size check boxes without using a layout manager
p2 = new JPanel();
p2.setLayout(null); //the default border manager is not used
Border aBorder = BorderFactory.createLineBorder(Color.RED, 2);
p2.setBorder(BorderFactory.createTitledBorder(aBorder, "Check Boxes"));

JCheckBox cb1 = new JCheckBox("This choice"); //initially unchecked
JCheckBox cb2 = new JCheckBox("And / Or this choice", true); //checked
JCheckBox cb3 = new JCheckBox("And / Or this choice", true); //checked

// Position and size the check boxes and their titles
cb1.setBounds(10, 30, 140, 20); //x, y, width, height
cb2.setBounds(10, 60, 140, 20);
cb3.setBounds(10, 90, 140, 20);
```

```
//Add them to the JPanel, p2
p2.add(cb1);
p2.add(cb2);
p2.add(cb3);
```

Determining a Check Box's Status

The status of a check box, checked or unchecked, can be determined by invoking the `isSlect-ed` method on it. The method returns the Boolean value `true` if the box is checked when the method is invoked, otherwise, it returns `false`. The following code fragment outputs `true` to the system console because check box `cb2` was created with a check in it:

```
//Determine if a check box is checked (its status)
JCheckBox cb2 = new JCheckBox("And / Or this choice", true);
if(cb2.isSelected() == true) //cb2 is checked
{
    System.out.println("true");
}
```

Check Box Events

In most applications that use check boxes, the interface contains a button that is clicked after the user checks one or more of the check boxes, and then the processing associated with the checked boxes is performed from within the button's event handler method, `actionPerformed`. When this is the case, the status of the check boxes is determined by invoking the `isSelected` method within the event handler method `actionPerformed`. The coding of this method and the techniques used to register it in the button's event handler list are those discussed in Section 11.4.

In applications where it is important to perform some processing *immediately after* a check box is checked, a check box event handler is implemented and registered with the check box's listener list. When the user checks or unchecks a check box, an item event occurs. The application can immediately perform some processing in response to this event by implementing the event handler method `itemStateChanged` inside the class that declared the check boxes or inside an inner class. In either case, the class's heading must indicate that it implements the interface `ItemListener`. The event handler's signature, which is given below, is the only signature defined within the interface `ItemListener`:

```
public void itemStateChanged(ItemEvent e)
```

The `itemStateChanged` method is added to the check box's event listener list by invoking the `addItemListener` method on the check box object and passing it the keyword `this`. When the method is implemented within an inner class, an instance of the inner class is declared and passed to the method.

The code fragment shown in Figure 12.2 outputs *Hamburger Selected* or *Hamburger Unselected* when the check box `cb1`, declared on line 9, is selected (checked) or unselected (unchecked). The code assumes that the event handler method `itemStateChanged` (lines 12–25) is written as shown (not coded inside of an inner class); which is why the keyword `this` is passed to the method invoked on line 10 to add the event handler method to cb1's event listener list. As indicated at the top of the figure, two imports must be included in the class's source file, and the class's heading must indicate that it implements the interface ItemListener.

```
1    //Two imports needed and an implements clause in the class' heading
2    import javax.swing.*;
3    import java.awt.event.*;
4
5      //Class heading and implements clause would be here
6      JCheckBox cb1; //class level variable
7
8        //coded in the class' constructor
9        cb1 = new JCheckBox("Hamburger");
10       cb1.addItemListener(this); //add event handler to cb1's list
11
12     public void itemStateChanged(ItemEvent e) //event handler method
13     {
14       if(e.getSource() == cb1) //cb1's box was clicked
15       {
16         if(cb1.isSelected() == true)
17         {
18           System.out.println("Hamburger Selected");
19         }
20         else
21         {
22           System.out.println("Hamburger Un-selected");
23         }
24       }
25     }
```

Figure 12.2
A code fragment that illustrates check box event handling without the use of an inner class.

12.1.3 Radio Buttons

Ordinarily, a radio button is grouped with other radio buttons into a mutually exclusive grouping because their most common use in GUIs is to facilitate the selection of one input from a small set of valid inputs. When the user clicks a radio button, a dot either appears on the button or is removed from it. Using the techniques discussed in this section, radio buttons can be created, added to, and positioned in GUI containers and made mutually exclusive. Processing is then initiated based on their selected or unselected status.

Creating Radio Buttons

A radio button is an instance of the API class JRadioButton and can be created using the class's one-parameter constructor or its default constructor. The text that appears beside the radio button when it is displayed is the string passed to the one-parameter constructor or the string passed to the class's `setText` method. The following code fragment creates the first two radio buttons shown in the top-right portion of Figure 12.1:

```
//Create radio buttons and initialize their text.
JRadioButton rb1 = new JRadioButton("This choice");
JRadioButton rb2 = new JRadioButton();
rb2.setText("Or this choice");
```

The `setText` method sets the text property of most GUI components that display text, and it can be used to initially set or to change the text associated with a component. The properties of radio buttons can be set and fetched using the methods shown in Table 12.1.

By default, a radio button is initially displayed unselected, without a center dot on it. A Boolean argument can be passed to the `JButton` class's two-parameter constructor to specify that the button will contain a dot (be selected) when the radio button is initially displayed.

```
//Display a dot in a radio button
JRadioButton rb3 = new JRadioButton("Button is selected", true);
```

Making Radio Buttons Mutually Exclusive

By default, a set of radio buttons are not mutually exclusive: one, several, or all of them could be selected at the same time. Because they are ordinarily used to choose one input from a set of mutually exclusive inputs, a set of radio buttons is designated to be mutually exclusive. When this designation is made, after one button in the set is selected, the previously selected button in the set is simultaneously deselected.

To designate a set of radio buttons to be mutually exclusive, the buttons are added to an instance of the class `ButtonGroup`. The following code fragment creates a mutually exclusive set of three radio buttons:

```
// Designate a set of radio buttons to be mutually exclusive
JRadioButton rb1 = new JRadioButton("This choice", true);
JRadioButton rb2 = new JRadioButton("Or this choice);
JRadioButton rb3 = new JRadioButton("Or this Choice");

// Create a radio button grouping
ButtonGroup bg1 = new ButtonGroup();

// Add buttons to the grouping bg1
bg1.add(rb1);
bg1.add(rb2);
bg1.add(rb3);
```

If several of the buttons in a mutually exclusive grouping were declared to be selected by passing the two-parameter constructor the value `true` when they are created, only the first button created will be selected when the group is initially displayed. A set of check boxes can be made mutually exclusive using this same technique: create a `ButtonGroup` object and then add the check boxes to the object. This is usually not done because it is contrary to the common inclusive use of check boxes in graphical interfaces.

Adding Radio Buttons to Containers and Positioning Them

Radio buttons are added to a GUI container using the add method, which is described at the bottom of Table 12.1. The following code fragment adds two mutually exclusive radio buttons to a JPanel container:

```
//Add two mutually exclusive radio buttons to a JPanel container
p1 = new JPanel();
JRadioButton rb1 = new JRadioButton("Hamburger");
JRadioButton rb2 = new JRadioButton("Taco");
ButtonGroup bg1 = new ButtonGroup();
bg1.add(rb1);
bg1.add(rb2);
p1.add(rb1);
p1.add(rb2);
```

Radio buttons, like other components added to a container, are positioned within it using the techniques discussed in Chapter 11 (Section 11.3.3 without a layout manager and Section 11.5 using a layout manager). When a layout manager is used, the radio buttons are positioned in the container by the manager in the order in which they are added to the container.

If the container's layout manager has been set to null, the setBounds method described in Table 12.1 can be used to position and set the height and width of the component and its associated text. Alternately, the setLocation and setSize methods, can be used to position a radio button in the container and to specify the height and width of the button and its associated text.

The following code fragment was used to create the three radio buttons shown in Figure 12.1, and the panel in which they are contained. The panel does not use a layout manager to position its components because the panel's setLayout method is passed a null value. This permits the use of the setBounds method to position and size the components added to it. The (x, y) position specified by the first two arguments sent to the method setBounds is relative to the upper left corner of the container to which a component has been added.

```
// Position and size radio buttons without using a layout manager
p3 = new JPanel();
p3.setLayout(null); //no border manager used
aBorder = BorderFactory.createBevelBorder(0);
p3.setBorder(BorderFactory.createTitledBorder(aBorder, "Radio Buttons"));

JRadioButton rb1 = new JRadioButton ("This choice");
JRadioButton rb2 = new JRadioButton ("Or this choice);
JRadioButton rb3 = new JRadioButton ("Or this choice", true);

ButtonGroup bg1 = new ButtonGroup();
bg1.add(rb1);
bq1.add(rb2);
bg1.add(rb3);

// Position and size the check boxes and their titles
rb1.setBounds(10, 30, 140, 20); //x, y, width, height
```

```
rb2.setBounds(10, 60, 140, 20);
rb3.setBounds(10, 90, 140, 20);

//Add them to the JPanel, p3
p3.add(rb1);
p3.add(rb2);
p3.add(rb3);
```

Determining a Radio Button's Status

The status of a radio button, selected or not selected, can be determined by invoking its `isSlected` method. The method returns the Boolean value `true` if the button is selected when the method is invoked, otherwise, it returns `false`. The following code fragment outputs `true` to the system console because the two-parameter constructor is passed the value `true` when the button is created:

```
//Determine if a radio button is selected
JRadioButton rb1 = new JRadioButton ("Radio button selected", true);
if(rb1.isSelected() == true) //rb1 is selected
{
   System.out.println("true");
}
```

Radio Buttons Events

In most applications that use radio buttons, the interface contains a `JButton` that is clicked after the user selects one of the radio buttons, and then the processing associated with the selection is performed from within the `JButton`'s event handler method, `actionPerformed`. When this is the case, the determination of which radio button in a group was selected is made by invoking the `isSelected` method on each of the buttons from within the `actionPerformed` method. The coding of this method and the techniques used to register it in the `JButton`'s event handler list were discussed in Section 11.4.

In applications where it is important to perform processing *immediately after* a radio button is selected, an event handler is implemented and registered with the radio button's listener list. The selection of a radio button generates an action event, which means the techniques used to perform processing when a radio button is selected are the same techniques used to perform processing when a `JButton` is clicked (discussed in Chapter 11). The application implements the event handler method `actionPerformed` inside the class that declared the radio button or within an inner class. In either case, the class's heading must indicate that it implements the interface `ActionListener`. The `actionPerformed` method's signature, which is given below, is the only signature defined within the interface `ActionListener`:

```
public void actionPerformed(ActionEvent e)
```

The method is added to the radio button's event listener list by invoking the `addActionListener` method on the radio button object and passing it the keyword `this`. When the method is implemented within an inner class, an instance of the inner class is declared and passed to the method.

The code fragment shown in Figure 12.3 outputs *Hamburger Selected* when the radio button `rb1`, declared on line 10, is selected, and it outputs *Taco Selected* when the radio button `rb2`, declared on line 12, is selected. The code assumes that the event handler method `actionPerformed` (lines 15–25) is not coded inside of an inner class; the keyword `this` is passed to the method invoked on lines 11 and 13 to add the event handler method to the buttons' event listener lists. As indicated at the top of the figure, two imports must be included in the class's source file, and the class's heading must indicate that it implements the interface `ActionListener`.

```
1    //Need two imports and an implements clause in the class' heading
2    import javax.swing.*;
3    import java.awt.event*;
4
5      //Class heading and implements clause would be here
6      JRadioButton rb1; //class level variables
7      JRadioButton rb2;
8
9        //coded in the class' constructor
10       rb1 = new JRadioButton("Hamburger");
11       rb1.addItemListener(this); //add event handler method to rb1's list
12       rb2 = new JRadioButton("Taco");
13       rb2.addItemListener(this); //add event handler method to rb2's list
14
15     public void actionPerformed(ActionEvent e)
16     {
17       if(rb1.isSelected() == true) //or e.getSource() == rb1 can be used
18       {
19         System.out.println("Hamburger Selected");
20       }
21       if(e.getSource() == rb2) //or rb2.isSelected() == true can be used
22       {
23         System.out.println("Taco Selected");
24       }
25     }
```

Figure 12.3
A code fragment that illustrates radio button event handling without the use of an inner class.

The GUI application `DollarMeal`, shown in Figure 12.4, illustrates the use of check boxes and radio buttons in a GUI application. It declares (on line 7) and displays (on line 9) an instance of the class GUI-builder worker class `MealMenu` shown in Figure 12.5. This class's constructor (lines 11–65) builds the GUI, shown in Figure 12.6a, which the user can use to order a meal. A typical order is shown in Figure 12.6b. A summary of the order is output to the system console (bottom of Figure 12.6) when the Place Order button is clicked at the bottom of the GUI.

The class `MenuMeal` extends `JFrame` and adds two panels (named p1 and p2, declared on lines 18 and 41) and a `JButton` (named `placeOrder`, defined on line 58) to the frame's content pane on lines 62–64. The layout managers of the content pane and the panels are set to `null` (lines 14, 19, and 42) to allow the panels and `JButton` to be positioned in the frame (lines 21, 44, and 59) and the panels' contents (check boxes and radio buttons) to be positioned inside of them using the `setBounds` method. The radio buttons and check boxes are created, located, and sized and then added to the panels on lines 23–38 and lines 46–56, respectively. The radio buttons are also added to a ButtonGroup to make then mutually exclusive (lines 31–34.).

The string order (declared on line 71) is output to the console on line 104 of the JButton's event handler actionPerformed (lines 68–105), which is added to the button's listener list on line 60. The method builds the output string using the check boxes' and radio buttons' isSelected method in a series of if-else and if statements to determine which of them have been selected (lines 73–103).

```
1    import javax.swing.*;
2
3    public class DollarMeal
4    {
5      public static void main(String[] args)
6      {
7        MealMenu window = new MealMenu();
8        window.setDefaultCloseOperation(JFrame.EXIT_ON_CLOSE);
9        window.setVisible(true);
10     }
11   }
```

Figure 12.4
The application **DollarMeal**.

```
1    import javax.swing.*;
2    import java.awt.event.*;
3
4    public class MealMenu extends JFrame implements ActionListener
5    {
6      JPanel p1, p2;
7      JRadioButton hamburger, taco, blt;
8      JCheckBox cheese, ketchup, napkins;
9      JButton placeOrder;
10
11     public MealMenu()
12     {
13       super("Dollar Meals");
14       setLayout(null);
15       setSize(303, 200);
16
17       //Build the radio button entree panel
18       p1 = new JPanel(); //declare the panel
19       p1.setLayout(null);
20       p1.setBorder(BorderFactory.createTitledBorder("Entree"));
21       p1.setBounds(5, 10, 140, 110); //locate and size the panel
22
23       hamburger = new JRadioButton("Hamburger", true); //declare buttons
24       taco = new JRadioButton("Taco");
25       blt = new JRadioButton("BLT Sandwich");
26
27       hamburger.setBounds(10, 20, 120, 20); //locate and size the buttons
```

```
28        taco.setBounds(10, 50, 120, 20);
29        blt.setBounds(10, 80, 120, 20);
30
31        ButtonGroup bg1 = new ButtonGroup(); //group the buttons
32        bg1.add(hamburger);
33        bg1.add(taco);
34        bg1.add(blt);
35
36        p1.add(hamburger); //add the buttons to the panel
37        p1.add(taco);
38        p1.add(blt);
39
40        //Build the check box extras panel
41        p2 = new JPanel(); //declare the panel
42        p2.setLayout(null);
43        p2.setBorder(BorderFactory.createTitledBorder("Extras"));
44        p2.setBounds(150, 10, 140, 110); //locate and size the panel
45
46        cheese = new JCheckBox("Cheese"); //declare the check boxes
47        ketchup = new JCheckBox("Ketchup");
48        napkins = new JCheckBox("Napkins");
49
50        cheese.setBounds(10, 20, 120, 20); //locate and size the check boxes
51        ketchup.setBounds(10, 50, 120, 20);
52        napkins.setBounds(10, 80, 120, 20);
53
54        p2.add(cheese); //add the check boxes to the panel
55        p2.add(ketchup);
56        p2.add(napkins);
57
58        placeOrder = new JButton("Place Order"); //declare the JButton
59        placeOrder.setBounds(80, 130, 120, 30); //locate and size it
60        placeOrder.addActionListener(this); //register the event handler
61
62        add(p1); //add the panels and the JButton to the content pane
63        add(p2);
64        add(placeOrder);
65      }
66
67      //Place order button handler
68      public void actionPerformed(ActionEvent e)
69      {
70        int extras = 0;
71        String order = "";
72
73        if(hamburger.isSelected() == true)
74        {
75          order = order + "Hamburger ";
76        }
```

```
77        else if(taco.isSelected() == true)
78        {
79          order = order + "Taco ";
80        }
81        else if(blt.isSelected() == true)
82        {
83          order = order + "BLT sandwich ";
84        }
85        if(cheese.isSelected() == true)
86        {
87          order = order + " and cheese";
88          extras++;
89        }
90        if(ketchup.isSelected() == true)
91        {
92          order = order + " and ketchup";
93          extras++;
94        }
95        if (napkins.isSelected() == true)
96        {
97          order = order + " and napkins";
98          extras++;
99        }
100       if(extras == 0)
101       {
102         order = order + " no extras";
103       }
104       System.out.println(order);
105    }
106 }
```

Figure 12.5
The class **MealMenu**.

(a)

(b)

Console output:

Taco and cheese and napkins

Figure 12.6
The GUI of the application **DollarMeal**, a user input, and the corresponding console output.

12.2 COMBO BOXES AND LISTS

The GUI components combo boxes and lists are shown in the lower left and lower center portion of Figure 12.1. These components are similar to a set of radio buttons and a set of check boxes in that they are used to facilitate the selection of one or more inputs from a set of valid inputs. When the number of elements in the set is small, most GUI designers use radio buttons and check boxes to present the selection alternatives. When the set contains a large number of elements, combo boxes and lists are the preferred components because they can include a scroll bar to permit the user to view the alternative selections without taking up a large portion of the program's window. Table 12.2 summarizes the terminology, features, and common uses of the GUI components combo boxes and lists.

Table 12.2
Terminology and Features of Combo Boxes and Lists

Combo Box	List
Element name	
An item	A value
Most Common Use	
Select one item from a set of valid items	Select one or more values from a set of valid values
Elements specified as	
An array containing the items	An array containing the values
Elements can be changed from their initial values during the program's execution	
No	Yes
Instance of	
`JComboBox` class	`JList` class
Scrollable	
Yes	Yes
User selection technique	
Click an item	Click an item, Control-Click for multiple items, or Shift-Click for an interval of items
User could type an input that is not an element	
Yes	No

The elements displayed in a combo box are called *items*, and those displayed in a list are called *values*. Only one item can be selected from a combo box, which makes it the component of choice for selecting one item from a large set of mutually exclusive items. A list is normally used when one or more values can be selected. The ability to select one or more values from a list is its default mode, but this can be restricted to a sequential set of values or only one value.

A single element in a combo box or list is selected by clicking it, which causes the previously selected item (or items, in the case of a list) to be simultaneously deselected. Multiple non-sequential values in a list can be selected by clicking them while holding down the Ctrl (control) key on the keyboard. Multiple sequential values in a list can be selected by clicking the first value in the sequence then holding down the Shift key and clicking the last value in the sequence. Table 12.3 summarizes the methods used to create and operate on combo boxes and lists and to service click events on them.

Table 12.3
Methods That Perform Common Combo Box and List Operations

Combo Box Named `aBox`	List Named `aList`
Creation	
`JComboBox aBox;` `aBox = new JComboBox(itemArray);`	`JList aList;` `aList = new JList(valueArray);`
Fetch the index, or the item selected, or the first value in sequential order selected	
`int i = aBox.getSelectedIndex();` `Object item=aBox.getSelectedItem();`	`int i = aList.getSelectedIndex();` `Object value = aList.getSelectedValue();`
Fetch all selections	
Not applicable	`int[] i = aList.getSelectedIndices();` `Object[] values = getSelectedValues();`
Add a scroll bar	
`aBox.setMaximumRowCount(aLowCount);`	`aList.setVisibleRowCount(aLowCount);` `JScrollPane sp= new JScrollPane(aList);`
Change displayed elements	
Not permitted	`aList.setListData(newValueArray);`
Permit User to type a new element	
`aBox.setEditable(true);`	Not permitted
Event handling	

Interface: `ActionListener`
Event handler:
   `actionPerformed(ActionEvent e)`
Register event handler using:
   `addActionListener`
	Interface: `ListSelectionListener`
	Event handler:
	   `valueChanged(ListSelectionEvent e)`
	Register event handler using:
	   `addListSelectionListener`

Creating Combo Boxes and Lists

A combo box is an instance of the class `JComboBox`, and a list is an instance of the class `JList`. The elements displayed in both types of instances are placed in an array passed to their class's one-parameter constructor when they are created. They maintain the index that was associated with them in the array passed to the JComboBox and JList constructors and are displayed in ascending index order. The following code sequence creates a combo box and a list that displays the days of the week beginning with Sunday. The list will display all seven days, the combo box will display the seven days when the arrow at the top of it is clicked.

```
//Create a Combo Box and a List that display the days of the week
String days = {"Sunday", "Monday", "Tuesday", "Wednesday",
                "Thursday", "Friday", "Saturday"};

JComboBox aBox = new JComboBox(days);
JList aList = new JList(days);
```

Fetching the Selected Item and Value(s)

The index of the item selected in a combo box, or the *lowest* index of the values selected in a list, can be fetched by invoking the components' getSelectedIndex method. Alternately, the item selected in a combo box or the value with the lowest index selected in a list can be fetched using the getSelectedItem and the getSelectedValue methods, respectively. Both of these methods return a reference to an Object, which must be cast into the type of the reference variable to which it is assigned. Assuming the program user selected Wednesday in the combo box and selected Monday and Thursday in the list, the following code sequence would output two lines to the system console containing *3 Wednesday* followed by *1 Monday*:

```
//Fetch the item and first value selected in a combo box and list
String days = {"Sunday", "Monday", "Tuesday", "Wednesday",
                "Thursday", "Friday", "Saturday"};
int comboIndex, listIndex;
String item, value;

JComboBox aBox = new JComboBox(days);
JList aList = new JList(days);

//After the user makes selections, the following code is executed
comboIndex = aBox.getSelectedIndex();
item = (String) aBox.getSelectedItem();
listIndex = aList.getSelectedIndex();
value = (String) aList.getSelectedValue();

System.outprintln(comboIndex +  " " + item);
System.outprintln(listIndex +  " " + value);
```

The indices of all of the values selected in a list can be fetched by invoking the getSelectedIndices method on the component object. All of the selected values can be fetched by invoking the getSelectedValues method on the component object. Both methods return the address of an array. The indices are returned in an integer array, and the values are returned in an array of Object references. Assuming the program user selected Monday and Thursday in the list, the following code sequence would output two lines to the system console: *1 Monday* followed by *4 Wednesday*. The output would not depend on the order in which the user made the selections.

```
//Fetch all indices and values selected from a list
String days = {"Sunday", "Monday", "Tuesday", "Wednesday",
               "Thursday", "Friday", "Saturday"};
int[] listIndices;
String[] values;
JList aList = new JList(days);

//After the user makes selections, the following code is executed
listIndices = aList.getSelectedIndices();
values = (String) aList.getSelectedValues();

for(int i = 0; i < values.length; i++)
{
   System.out.println(listIndices[i] + " " + values[i]);
}
```

Adding a Vertical Scroll Bar

A combo box can be, and a list is normally, displayed with a vertical scroll bar on their right side, which is used to scroll through the set of valid inputs. The techniques used to select and fetch elements from these components do not change when scroll bars are incorporated into them.

The `setMaximumRowCount` method is invoked on a combo box object to set the number of items displayed at one time *and* to add a scroll bar to its right side. This one invocation is all that is required to add a scroll bar to a combo box, as shown in following code fragment, which creates a combo box with a scroll bar that displays four days of the week at a time:

```
//Add a scroll bar to a combo box
String days = {"Sunday", "Monday", "Tuesday", "Wednesday",
               "Thursday", "Friday", "Saturday"};

JComboBox aBox = new JComboBox(days);
aBox.setMaximumRowCount(4); //four sequential items displayed at a time
```

When the component is a list, two steps are required. The `setVisibleRowCount` method is invoked on the list object and passed the number of items to be displayed at one time in the component. Then, an instance of a `JScrollPane` is created, and the list object is passed to the class's one-parameter constructor. The `JScrollPane` object, not the list (`JList`) object, is subsequently added to the GUI container. The following code fragment creates a list with a scroll bar that displays four days of the week at a time:

```
String days = {"Sunday", "Monday", "Tuesday", "Wednesday",
               "Thursday", "Friday", "Saturday"};

JList aList = new JList(days);
JPanel aPanel = new JPanel();

aList.setVisibleCount(4); //four sequential items displayed at a time
JScrollPane aScrollableList = new JScrollPane(aList);
aPanel.add(aScrollableList);
```

If a layout manager is not used to position the scroll pane in the container (e.g., the `JPanel`'s layout manager is set to `null`), the `setVisibleCount` method is not invoked to set the number of items displayed at one time. Instead, the height of the `JScrollPane` object, required to display the desired number of rows, is passed to the invocation of the `setBounds` method used to position and size the scroll pane object within the container, as shown below:

```
//Position and size the scroll pane object
String days = {"Sunday", "Monday", "Tuesday", "Wednesday",
               "Thursday", "Friday", "Saturday"};

JList aList = new JList(days);
JPanel aPanel = new JPanel();
aPanel. setLayout(null);

JScrollPane aScrollableList = new JScrollPane(aList);
aScrollableList.setBounds(10, 20, 120, 80); //80 displays 4 values
aPanel.add(aScrollableList);
```

The application `ExpandedDollarMeal`, shown in Figure 12.7, is a modified version of the application `DollarMeal` presented in Figure 12.4. It declares (line 8) and displays (line 10) an instance of the class `ExpandedMealMenu` shown in Figure 12.8. This class's constructor (lines 17–52) builds the GUI shown on the left side of Figure 12.9. A typical meal order is shown on the right side of the figure. When the button at the bottom of the interface is clicked, a summary of the order is output to the system console (bottom of Figure 12.9).

In a similar way to the class `MealMenu` shown in Figure 12.5, the `ExtendedMealMenu` class extends `JFrame` and adds two panels (named `p1` and `p2`, declared on lines 24 and 35) and a `JButton` (named `placeOrder`, defined on line 45) to the frame's content pane on lines 49–51. The layout managers of the content pane and the panels are set to `null` (lines 20, 25, and 36) to allow the panels to be positioned in the frame (lines 27 and 38) and the panels' contents (a combo box and a list) to be positioned inside of them using the `setBounds` method.

The class `ExtendedMealMenu` uses a combo box with a scroll bar to display the expanded number of entrees (seven), defined on lines 7–9, and a list with a scroll bar to display and the expanded number of extras (nine), defined on lines 10–12. These arrays are passed to the constructors used to create the combo box `entree` on line 29 and list `extrasList` on line 40; then the combo box and the list are located, sized, and added to the panels on lines 30–32 and lines 41–43, respectively. Line 30 adds a scroll bar to the combo box that scrolls through four items at a time. Line 41 adds the list to a `JScrollPane` object. The location and size of the scroll pane is set on line 42. The last argument, 80, sent to the invocation of the `setBounds` method on this line, is a height sufficient to display four values in the now-scrollable list, which is added to the panel (`p2`) on line 43.

The console output is produced on lines 59–66 of the `JButton`'s event handler `actionPerformed` (lines 55 67), which is added to the button's listener list on line 47.

Lines 59 and 60 use the combo box's `getSelectedIndex` and `getSelectedItem` methods to output the selected entrée's index and name. The array of selected extras returned from the `JList` class's `getSelectedValues` method on line 62 is output to system console inside the for loop that begins on line 63. The array reference variable `extrasOrderedArray` is declared on line 57 to be an array of `Object` references, because the `getSelectedValues` method returns a reference to an array of objects.

```
1    import javax.swing.*;
2
3    public class ExpandedDollarMeal
4    {
5      public static void main(String[] args)
6      {
7        String title = "Expanded Dollar Meal";
8        ExpandedMealMenu window = new ExpandedMealMenu(title);
9        window.setDefaultCloseOperation(JFrame.EXIT_ON_CLOSE);

10       window.setVisible(true);
11     }
12   }
```

Figure 12.7
The application **ExpandedDollarMeal**.

```
1    import javax.swing.*;
2    import java.awt.event.*;
3
4    public class ExpandedMealMenu extends JFrame implements ActionListener
5    {
6      JPanel p1, p2;
7      String[] entreeItems = {"Hamburger", "Taco", "BLT Sandwich",
8                              "Nachos", "Chicken Soup", "Hot Chili",
9                              "Salad"};
10     String[] extrasValues = {"Cheese", "Ketchup", "Napkins", "Mustard",
11                              "Mayonnaise", "Salsa", "Paper Plate",
12                              "Utensils", "Water"};
13     JComboBox entree;
14     JList extrasList;
15     JButton placeOrder;
16
17     public ExpandedMealMenu(String title)
18     {
19       super(title);
20       setLayout(null);
21       setSize(303, 200);
22
23       //Build the entree panel
24       p1 = new JPanel(); //declare the panel
25       p1.setLayout(null);
26       p1.setBorder(BorderFactory.createTitledBorder("Entree"));
```

```
27        p1.setBounds(5, 10, 140, 110); //locate and size the entree panel
28
29        entree = new JComboBox(entreeItems);
30        entree.setMaximumRowCount(4);
31        entree.setBounds(10, 20, 120, 20);
32        p1.add(entree);
33
34        //Build extras panel
35        p2 = new JPanel(); //declare the panel
36        p2.setLayout(null);
37        p2.setBorder(BorderFactory.createTitledBorder("Extras"));
38        p2.setBounds(150, 10, 140, 110); //locate and size the extras panel
39
40        extrasList = new JList(extrasValues);
41        JScrollPane aScrollableList = new JScrollPane(extrasList);
42        aScrollableList.setBounds(10, 20, 120, 80); //80 displays 4 values
43        p2.add(aScrollableList);
44
45        placeOrder = new JButton("Place Order"); //declare the JButton
46        placeOrder.setBounds(80, 130, 120, 30); //locate and size it
47        placeOrder.addActionListener(this); //register its event handler
48
49        add(p1); //add the panels and the JButton to the content pane
50        add(p2);
51        add(placeOrder);
52    }
53
54    //Place order button handler
55    public void actionPerformed(ActionEvent e)
56    {
57      Object[] extrasOrderedArray;
58
59      System.out.print("\nEntree Number " + entree.getSelectedIndex() +
60                        ": " + entree.getSelectedItem() );
61
62      extrasOrderedArray = extrasList.getSelectedValues();
63      for(int i = 0; i < extrasOrderedArray.length; i++)
64      {
65        System.out.print(", " + extrasOrderedArray[i]);
66      }
67    }
68 }
```

Figure 12.8
The class **ExpandedMealMenu**.

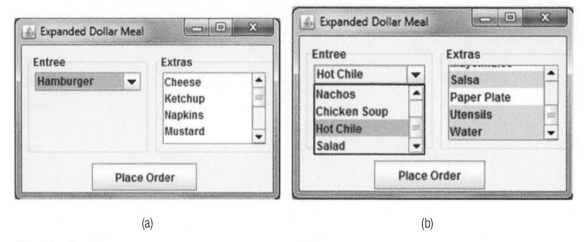

(a)   (b)

Console Output:

Entree Number 5: Hot Chili, Salsa, Utensils, Water

Figure 12.9
The GUI of the application **ExpandedDollarMeal**, a user input, and the corresponding console output.

The values initially displayed in a JList object, which are passed to the class's constructor when the list is created, can be changed. To do this, the method setListData is invoked on the JList object and passed an array containing the list's new values. The following line of code displays the objects contained in the array newValueArray in the JList object aList:

```
aList.setListData(newValueArray);
```

An Editable Combo Box

Each JComboBox object has a Boolean data member isEditable whose default value is false. When the data member's value is set to true using the class's setEditable method, a text box is displayed at the top of the combo box, as shown in Figure 12.10a. This now-editable combo box retains all the functionality of the un-editable version discussed in this section, and it also allows the user to type an item into the text box. The item typed does not have to be one of the items passed to the one-parameter constructor when the combo box was created.

For example, if the user were to type *Ham Sandwich* into the text box, the combo box would appear as shown in Figure 12.10b. The item typed in the text box would be returned from the next invocation of the box's getSelectedItem method, unless one of the other items in the combo box is selected before it is invoked.

The window shown in Figure 12.10a was produced by the application ExpandedDollarMeal (Figure 12.7) after the following line of code was added to the class ExpandedMealMenu (Figure 12.8) just before line 32:

```
entree.setEditable(true);
```

(a)   (b)

Console Output

Entree Number -1: Ham Sandwich, Mustard

Figure 12.10
The GUI of the application **ExpandedDollarMeal** with an editable combo box added to it.

The console output at the bottom of Figure 12.10 was produced after the user typed *Ham Sandwich* in the text box and clicked "Mustard" and the Place Order button in the window on the right side of the figure. Because *Ham Sandwich* is not one of the items in the array `entreeItems` (lines 7–9 of Figure 12.8) passed to `JComboBox`'s one-parameter constructor when the combo box was created, the index returned from the method `getItemSelected` is -1 (as shown at the bottom of Figure 12.10).

Combo Box and List Event Handling

When an item is selected in a combo box, an *action event* occurs; when a value is selected in a list, a *list selection event* occurs. In most applications, we do not respond to either of these events individually because the GUI usually contains a `JButton` object that is clicked after the user has interacted with all of the other input components on the interface. That was the case in the application `ExpandedValueMeal`, in which the user clicked the Place Order button after the meal selection was made. Until that button was clicked, the user could change the selections made in both the combo box and the list. The servicing of the button-click action event was performed by the event handler coded on lines 55–67 of the `ExpandedMealMenu` class presented in Figure 12.8, and this event handler was registered in the button's listener list on line 47 of that class.

To service either a combo-box item selection or a list value selection at the time the selection is made, we implement event handlers and register them with the components' listener lists. The techniques used to perform this are the same techniques used in Figure 12.8, which were discussed in Section 11.4:

1. Implement the event handler's interface by coding the event handler method whose signature is defined in the interface

2. Register the method with the components' event listener list.

In the case of a combo box action event, the interface and the method used to register the event are the same as those used to service a `JButton` click action event:

1. The interface is `ActionListener`;
2. The signature of the event handler is `actionPerformed(ActionEvent e)`
3. The method used to register the event is `addActionListener`, which is invoked on the `JComboBox` object and passed an instance of the class in which the event handler is coded

In the case of a list selection event, the interface and methods use to service the event are:

1. The interface is `ListSelectionListener`;
2. The signature of the event handler is `valueChanged(ListSelectionEvent e)`;
3. The method used to register the event is `addListSelectionListener`, which is invoked on the `JList` object and passed an instance of the class in which the event handler is coded

The names of these interfaces and methods are summarized at the bottom of Table 12.3. The methods previously discussed to fetch the index or element selected, which are also summarized in Table 12.3, are used inside the combo box and list event handler methods to identify and process the selection.

12.3 MENUS

A menu is a GUI component used to obtain one of several valid inputs from the program user. In this way, menus are similar to combo boxes. The advantage menus have over combo boxes and the other GUI components we have discussed is that they can be used to present a wide variety of valid inputs while occupying a relatively small portion of the program's window. In addition, because their placement in the window does not vary from one application to another, they present an input interface that is more familiar to the user.

The Java API supports two types of menus: drop-down menus and pop-up menus. Drop-down menus are positioned in a menu bar whose location in the window is platform dependent, and pop-up menus remain invisible until the user performs a platform-dependent mouse action or key action. The most common position for a menu bar is just below the window's title bar, and the most common mouse action to expose a pop-up menu is a right-button mouse click. We will begin our discussion of menus with drop-down menus contained in a menu bar.

12.3.1 Drop-Down Menus

The program widow in Figure 12.11a was generated on a platform that places the menu bar just below the window's title bar. The menu-bar object contains one drop-down menu object on its left side that has the string "A Menu" associated with it. The user has clicked this menu object to expose the menu's four drop-down objects and then clicked the last of these objects to expose another drop-down menu containing three more objects. Figure 12.11b gives the API classes of the objects that make up the program's menu, displayed in Figure 12.11a. These classes are `JMenuBar`, `JMenu`, and `JMenuItem`. The two submenu objects shown in Figure 12.11a are instances of the class `JMenu`.

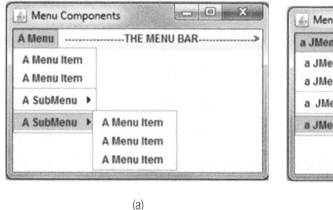
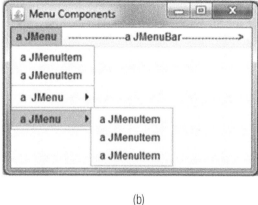

(a)   (b)

Figure 12.11
Drop-down menu components and their API classes.

The `JMenuItem` objects within a drop-down menu are the terminal components of the menu. These items are the set of valid inputs. The user selects one of these inputs by clicking it, which generates an action event just as clicking a `JButton` object generates an action event. The processing associated with the selected menu item is performed within the `actionPerformed` event handler method whose signature is defined in the interface `ActionListener`.

Building a Drop-Down Menu System

Generally speaking, a drop-down menu system consisting of a menu bar containing one or more drop-down menus is added to an instance of a `JFrame` using the following four step process. The code fragments used to illustrate each step of the process were used to create the menu system shown in Figure 12.12. These fragments would be added to the constructor of a GUI-builder worker class that extends the class `JFrame`.

1. Create a menu bar object, which is an instance of `JMenuBar`, and add it to the `JFrame` instance using the `JFrame` class's method `setJMenuBar`

    ```
    //Add the MenuBar
    JMenuBar aMenuBar = new JMenuBar(); //create the menu bar
    setJMenuBar(menuBar); //add the menu bar to the JFrame
    ```

2. Create drop-down menu objects, which are instances of `JMenu`, and add them to the menu bar object by invoking the `add` method on them; the drop-down menu's string annotation, which is passed to `JMenu`'s constructor, appears on the menu bar from left to right in the order in which the menus are added to the menu bar

    ```
    //Add two drop down menus to the menu bar
    JMenu dropDownMenu1 = new JMenu("Dollar"); //create menu
    JMenu dropDownMenu2 = new JMenu("Deluxe"); //create menu
    aMenuBar.add(dropDownMenu1); //add a menu to the menu bar
    aMenuBar.add(dropDownMenu2); //add a menu to the menu bar
    ```

3. For each drop-down menu added to the menu bar, repeatedly create and add either an instance of

   a) A clickable terminal menu item, which is an instance of the class JMenuItem:

   ```
   JMenuItem saladItem = new JMenuItem("Salad"); //create items
   JMenuItem soupItem = new JMenuItem("Chicken Soup");
   dropDownMenu1.add(saladItem);
   dropDownMenu1.add(soupItem);
   ```

   or

   b) A submenu, which is an instance of the class JMenu

   ```
   JMenu subMenu1 = new JMenu("Sandwich"); //create submenu
   JMenu subMenu2 = new JMenu("Mexican"); //create submenu
   dropDownMenu1.add(subMenu1); //add the 1st submenu to the menu
   dropDownMenu1.add(subMenu2); //add the 2nd submenu to the menu
   ```

   The menu items and submenus appear from top to bottom on the drop-down menu in the order in which they are added.

4. Repeat Step 3 for all the submenus; ordinarily, only a set of terminal items are added to the submenus

   ```
   JMenuItem subItem1 = new JMenuItem("Hamburger"); //create item
   JMenuItem subItem2 = new JMenuItem("BLT"); //create item
   subMenu1.add(subItem1);
   subMenu1.add(subItem2);
   ```

Figure 12.12
A drop-down menu system that contains two submenus.

Menu Separator Bars

Separator bars are added to a drop-down menu to visually group related elements. There are two separator bars in the drop-down menu shown in Figure 12.12: one above the *Sandwich* submenu and one below it. The JMenu method addSeparator is invoked on a drop-down JMenu menu object to add a separator bar to the menu. Menu items, menu separators, and submenus appear from top to bottom within the drop-down menu in the order in which they are added. The two menu separators in Figure 12.12 were added to the drop-down menu `dropDownMenu1` using the following code fragment:

```
//Add menu separator bars
dropDownMenu1.add(saladItem); //add to the menu as 1st item
dropDownMenu1.add(soupItem); //add to the menu as 2nd item
dropDownMenu1.addSeparator();
JMenu subMenu1 = new JMenu("Sandwich"); //create submenu
dropDownMenu1.add(subMenu1); //add the submenu to the menu
dropDownMenu1.addSeparator();
```

Menu Mnemonics

A mnemonic is a keyboard event that is designated to be equivalent to the user clicking a GUI component such as a menu item or a button. Other names for mnemonics are *shortcut keys* or *hot keys*. The designation is made by invoking the `setMnemonic` method on the component. The method is overloaded and can be passed either a single character or one of the keyboard key codes defined in the class `KeyEvent` as a static integer constant. Every key on the keyboard, and its shifted version, has a unique key-code constant associated with it. For example, the constant static VK_2 is associated with an unshifted 2 key keystroke, and the constant VK_AT is associated with a shifted @ key keystroke. (VK stands for virtual key.)

When a hot key is designated to be equivalent to clicking a GUI component, striking it when the component is visible is equivalent to clicking the component. In addition, the first occurrence of the key's character in the string associated with the component (the string passed to the constructor when the component is created) is underlined on the menu. The following code fragment designates the S and C keys to be hot keys for the *Salad* and *Chicken Soup* menu items displayed in Figure 12.12:

```
//Designate Hot Keys
JMenuItem saladItem = new JMenuItem("Salad");
JMenuItem soupItem = new JMenuItem("Chicken Soup");
dropDownMenu1.add(saladItem);
dropDownMenu1.add(soupItem);
saladItem.setMnemonic('S');
soupItem.setMnemonic('C');
```

JMenuItem Object Action Events

When the user clicks a `JMenuItem` object or presses a hot key associated with the object, an action event occurs. The processing to be performed when this event occurs is coded in the event handler method `actionPerformed` whose signature is defined in the interface `ActionListener`. The event handler method is added to the `JMenuItem` object's listener list by invoking the method `addActionListener` on the object and passing the method an instance of the class in which the event handler is coded.

The application `Menus`, shown in Figure 12.13, declares (line 8) and displays (line 10) an instance of the class `MenuBarBuilder` shown in Figure 12.14. This class extends `JFrame`, adds a menu bar to the frame (lines 21–22), and then adds the drop-down menu shown on the top left and right sides of Figure 12.15 to the menu bar (lines 25–26). The console output shown at the bottom of the figure was produced by the application after the user selected *Nachos* from the menu, as shown in Figure 12.15b.

The drop-down menu is created by the method `buildDollarMenu` (lines 30–82 of Figure 12.14) that returns a reference to an instance of a `JMenu`. This method is invoked on line 25 of the class's constructor, and the returned drop-down menu is added to the menu bar on line 26. It is good coding practice to build each drop-down menu added to a menu bar in a separate method because it makes our code more readable and easier to maintain.

Line 33 declares the `JMenu` object `dollarMenu` that will be returned by the method on line 81. Lines 36–47 create the drop-down menu's two items and two submenus (lines 36–39) and adds these four objects and two separators to the `dollarMenu` object (lines 42–47). The code on lines 50–54 creates five submenu items and then adds these five objects to the two submenu objects (lines 57–61).

Lines 64–70 designate hot keys for each of the menu's seven menu selections (`JMenuItem` instances). Lines 73–79 register an action event handler method into each of these instances' listener lists by invoking the `addActionListener` method on each instance and passing it an instance of the inner class `dollarMenuListener`.

The event handler method `actionPerformed` (lines 86–98) is coded within the inner class (lines 84–99). It invokes the `getSource` method on the `ActionEvent` object passed to the method (lines 90–96) to determine which menu item the user selected in Figure 12.15b. In the interest of brevity, a series of one-line `if` statements are used to make the determination and set the selection into the string `entree` declared on line 88. This string is output on line 97 of the event handler method.

```
1    import javax.swing.*;
2
3    public class Menus
4    {
5      public static void main(String[] args)
6      {
7        String title = "Expanded Dollar Meal Menu";
8        MenuBarBuilder window = new MenuBarBuilder(title);
9        window.setDefaultCloseOperation(JFrame.EXIT_ON_CLOSE);

10        window.setVisible(true);
11      }
12    }
```

Figure 12.13
The application **Menus**.

```
1     import javax.swing.*;
2     import java.awt.event.*;
3
4     public class MenuBarBuilder extends JFrame
5     {
6        //Menu item references
7        private JMenuItem saladItem;
8        private JMenuItem chickenSoupItem;
9        private JMenuItem bLTSubItem;
10       private JMenuItem hamburgerSubItem;
11       private JMenuItem tacoSubItem;
12       private JMenuItem nachosSubItem;
13       private JMenuItem chiliSubItem;
14
15       public MenuBarBuilder(String title)
16       {
17          super(title);
18          setSize(303, 200);
19
20          //Step 1: Create and add the menu bar to the JFrame
21          JMenuBar menuBar = new JMenuBar();
22          setJMenuBar(menuBar);
23
24          //Step 2: Create and add the menus to the menu bar
25          JMenu dropDownMenu = buildDollarMenu();
26          menuBar.add(dropDownMenu);
27       }
28
29       //Step 3: Create and add the items and the submenus to the menu
30       public JMenu buildDollarMenu() //Builds and returns the dollar menu
31       {
32          //Create the drop down menu
33          JMenu dollarMenu = new JMenu("Dollar");
34
35          //Create the menu items and submenus
36          saladItem = new JMenuItem("Salad");
37          chickenSoupItem = new JMenuItem("Chicken Soup");
38          JMenu sandwichSubMenu = new JMenu("Sandwich");
39          JMenu mexicanSubMenu = new JMenu("Mexican");
40
41          //Add the menu items, submenus, and separators to the menu
42          dollarMenu.add(saladItem);
43          dollarMenu.add(chickenSoupItem);
44          dollarMenu.addSeparator();
45          dollarMenu.add(sandwichSubMenu);
46          dollarMenu.addSeparator();
47          dollarMenu.add(mexicanSubMenu);
48
49          //Create submenu items
```

```
50      bLTSubItem = new JMenuItem("BLT");
51      hamburgerSubItem = new JMenuItem("Hamburger");
52      tacoSubItem = new JMenuItem("Taco");
53      nachosSubItem = new JMenuItem("Nachos");
54      chiliSubItem = new JMenuItem("Chili");
55
56      //Add the submenu items to the submenus
57      sandwichSubMenu.add(hamburgerSubItem);
58      sandwichSubMenu.add(bLTSubItem);
59      mexicanSubMenu.add(tacoSubItem);
60      mexicanSubMenu.add(nachosSubItem);
61      mexicanSubMenu.add(chiliSubItem);
62
63      //Assign mnemonics to the menu items
64      saladItem.setMnemonic('S');
65      chickenSoupItem.setMnemonic('C');
66      bLTSubItem.setMnemonic('B');
67      hamburgerSubItem.setMnemonic('H');
68      tacoSubItem.setMnemonic('T');
69      nachosSubItem.setMnemonic('N');
70      chiliSubItem.setMnemonic('L');
71
72      //Register event handlers
73      saladItem.addActionListener(new dollarMenuListener());
74      chickenSoupItem.addActionListener(new dollarMenuListener());
75      bLTSubItem.addActionListener(new dollarMenuListener());
76      hamburgerSubItem.addActionListener(new dollarMenuListener());
77      tacoSubItem.addActionListener(new dollarMenuListener());
78      nachosSubItem.addActionListener(new dollarMenuListener());
79      chiliSubItem.addActionListener(new dollarMenuListener());
80
81      return dollarMenu;
82    }
83
84    public class dollarMenuListener implements ActionListener
85    {
86      public void actionPerformed(ActionEvent e)
87      {
88        String entree = "";
89
90        if(e.getSource() == saladItem) entree = "Salad";
91        if(e.getSource() == chickenSoupItem) entree = "Chicken Soup";
92        if(e.getSource() == bLTSubItem) entree = "BLT Sandwich";
93        if(e.getSource() == hamburgerSubItem) entree = "Hamburger";
94        if(e.getSource() == tacoSubItem) entree = "Taco";
95        if(e.getSource() == nachosSubItem) entree = "Nachos";
96        if(e.getSource() == chiliSubItem) entree = "Chili";
97        System.out.println("Dollar Meal Entree: " + entree);
```

```
 98          }
 99     }
100  }
```

Figure 12.14
The class **MenuBarBuilder**.

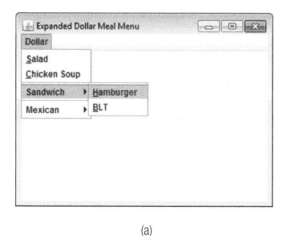
(a)

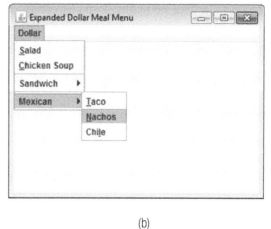
(b)

Console Output:
Dollar Meal Entree: Nachos

Figure 12.15
The GUI menu and output produced by the application Menus.

Menu Radio Button and Check Box Items

In addition to JMenuItem objects, check boxes and radio buttons can be added to drop-down menus and selected from the menu by the program user. These menu items are instances of the JCheckBoxMenuItem and JRadioButtonMenuItem classes, respectively. Figure 12.16 shows a drop-down menu that contains four check boxes and four mutually exclusive radio buttons.

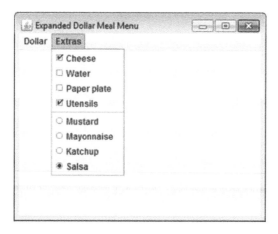

Figure 12.16
A GUI menu containing check boxes and radio buttons.

Once created, radio-button and check-box menu items are added to JMenu objects using the same techniques used to add JMenuItem objects to drop-down menus and submenus. The techniques used to perform the processing associated with their selection are also the same as the techniques used to process JMenuItem selections because radio-buttons and check-boxes added to menus generate action events when they are selected. Their event handler method is action-Performed whose signature is defined in the interface ActionListener, and the event handler method is registered by invoking the method addActionListener on the menu item.

The following code fragment, when added to the end of the constructor of the class shown in Figure 12.14, creates the drop-down menu shown in Figure 12.16 and adds it to the menu bar created on line 21 of Figure 12.14. It invokes the menu-builder method buildExtrasMenu shown in Figure 12.17, which builds the drop-down menu and returns its address.

```
JMenu extras = buildExtrasMenu();
menuBar.add(extras);
```

The method buildExtrasMenu would be included as a member method of the class MenuBarBuilder shown in Figure 12.14, as would an inner class named ExtrasMenuListener that implements the ActionListener interface. This inner class would contain the event handler actionPerformed registered with the radio buttons and check boxes on lines 35–42 of Figure 12.17. The declarations of the reference variables on lines 7–14 of that figure would be added to the class menuBarBuilder as class-level variables to make them accessible to the radio button and check box event handler.

```
1    public JMenu buildExtrasMenu() //Builds and returns the extras menu
2    {
3       //Create the menu object
4       JMenu extrasMenu = new JMenu("Extras");
5
6       //Create the menu items and submenus
7       cheeseItem = new JCheckBoxMenuItem("Cheese");
8       waterItem = new JCheckBoxMenuItem("Water");
9       paperPlateItem = new JCheckBoxMenuItem("Paper plate");
10      utensilItem = new JCheckBoxMenuItem("Utensils");
11      mustardItem = new JRadioButtonMenuItem("Mustard");
12      mayonnaiseItem = new JRadioButtonMenuItem("Mayonnaise");
13      katchupItem = new JRadioButtonMenuItem("Katchup");
14      salsaItem = new JRadioButtonMenuItem("Salsa");
15
16      //Create button group
17      ButtonGroup bg = new ButtonGroup();
18      bg.add(mustardItem);
19      bg.add(mayonnaiseItem);
20      bg.add(katchupItem);
21      bg.add(salsaItem);
22
23      //Add the menu items to the menu
24      extrasMenu.add(cheeseItem);
```

```
25     extrasMenu.add(waterItem);
26     extrasMenu.add(paperPlateItem);
27     extrasMenu.add(utensilItem);
28     extrasMenu.addSeparator();
29     extrasMenu.add(mustardItem);
30     extrasMenu.add(mayonnaiseItem);
31     extrasMenu.add(katchupItem);
32     extrasMenu.add(salsaItem);
33
34     //Register event handlers
35     cheeseItem.addActionListener(new ExtrasMenuListener());
36     waterItem.addActionListener(new ExtrasMenuListener());
37     paperPlateItem.addActionListener(new ExtrasMenuListener());
38     utensilItem.addActionListener(new ExtrasMenuListener());
39     mustardItem.addActionListener(new ExtrasMenuListener());
40     mayonnaiseItem.addActionListener(new ExtrasMenuListener());
41     katchupItem.addActionListener(new ExtrasMenuListener());
42     salsaItem.addActionListener(new ExtrasMenuListener());
43
44     return extrasMenu;
45  }
```

Figure 12.17
The method **buildExtrasMenu**.

12.3.2 Pop-Up Menus

A pop-up menu is a space-saving alternative to a menu-bar-based drop-down menu. Unlike drop-down menus, pop-up menus are associated with a particular component in a graphical interface, and they remain invisible until the user performs a platform-dependent mouse or keyboard action on the GUI component. The most common action on the component is a right mouse click.

Pop-up menus are instances of the class JPopupMenu and can be created using the class's default constructor:

```
//Create a pop-up menu object
JPopupMenu aMenu = new JPopupMenu();
```

The techniques discussed in the previous section used to add menu items, submenus, separators, and hot keys to drop-down menus are the same techniques used to add these elements to pop-up menus. Menu items, separators, and submenus are added to the pop-up menu object using the JPopupMenu class's add method, and hot keys are added using the class's setMnemonic method. The following code fragment creates the pop-up menu shown in Figure 12.18a:

```
//Create a pop-up menu and add three menu items to it
JPopupMenu aMenu = new JPopupMenu();

JMenuItem blue = new JMenuItem("Blue"); //create the menu items
JMenuItem red = new JMenuItem("Red");
JMenuItem green = new JMenuItem("Green");
```

```
aMenu.add(blue); //add the menu items to the pop-up menu
aMenu.add(red);
aMenu.add(green);

blue.setMnemonic('B'); //designate the hot keys
red.setMnemonic('R');
green.setMnemonic('G');
```

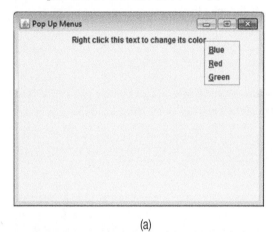
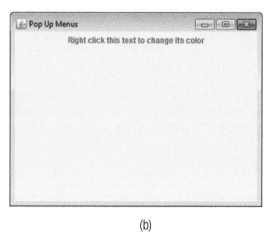

(a)   (b)

Figure 12.18

Windows produced by the application **PopUpMenu**.

To associate a pop-up menu with a GUI component, the setComponentPopupMenu method is invoked on the GUI component, and the pop-up menu object is passed to the method. When the user performs the platform-dependent action on the component (e.g., right clicking the component), the menu becomes visible. The last line of the following code fragment was used to associate the menu shown in Figure 12.18a with the JLabel displayed at the top of the window:

```
//Associate a pop-up menu with a GUI component
JPopupMenu aMenu = new JPopupMenu();

JMenuItem blue = new JMenuItem("Blue");
JMenuItem red = new JMenuItem("Red");
JMenuItem green = new JMenuItem("Green");

aMenu.add(blue);
aMenu.add(red);
aMenu.add(green);

blue.setMnemonic('B');
red.setMnemonic('R');
green.setMnemonic('G');

//Associate the pop-up menu with a JLabel object
JLabel aLabel = new JLabel("Right click this text to change its color");
aLabel.setComponentPopupMenu(aMenu);
```

Selecting a menu item from a pop-up menu generates an action event, just as selecting an item from a drop-down menu does. As previously discussed, action events are serviced by implementing the event handler method `actionPerformed` whose signature is defined in the interface `ActionListener`. The event handler method is registered with a menu item's listener list by invoking the `addActionListener` method on the menu item object. Assuming the event handler `actionPerformed` was implemented in the class that defined the menu item `blue`, the following code fragment would add the event handler to the item's listener list:

```
//Register a drop-down menu item selection event handler
JMenuItem blue = new JMenuItem("Blue");
blue.addActionListener(this);
```

The application shown in Figure 12.19 uses a pop-up menu to change the color of the text displayed at the top of its window. The Figure 12.18a shows the window after the application is launched and the user has right clicked the text. Figure 12.18b shows the program's window after the user has selected *Red* from the pop-up menu, either by clicking the word *Red* or striking its hot key, R. These actions change the color of the text to red.

The application's window (Line 8 of Figure 12.19) is an instance of the class `PopUpMenuWindow`, shown in Figure 12.20, which extends `JFrame`. The class's constructor builds the pop-up menu and adds it to the `JFrame`. The pop-up menu (`aMenu`) and its three menu items (`blue`, `red`, and `green`), are created on lines 9–12 of the figure. The menu items are added to the menu (lines 20–22), their hot keys are designated (lines 24–26), and the event handler method coded on lines 37–42 is registered with their listener lists on lines 28–30. Line 32 associates the pop-up menu `aMenu` with the `JLabel` created on line 7. Finally, line 33 adds the label to the `JPanel` created on line 19, and then line 34 adds the panel to the `JFrame`.

When the program user right clicks the text at the top of the program window and clicks a selection in the pop-up menu, lines 39–41 of the action event handler method `actionPerformed` changes the color of the displayed text.

```
1    import javax.swing.*;
2
3    public class PopUpMenu
4    {
5      public static void main(String[] args)
6      {
7        String title = "Pop Up Menus";
8        PopUpMenuWindow window = new PopUpMenuWindow(title);
9        window.setDefaultCloseOperation(JFrame.EXIT_ON_CLOSE);

10       window.setVisible(true);
11     }
12   }
```

Figure 12.19
The application **PopUpMenu**.

```
1    import javax.swing.*;
2    import java.awt.event.*;
3    import java.awt.Color;
4
5    public class PopUpMenuWindow extends JFrame implements ActionListener
6    {
7      JLabel aLabel = new JLabel("Right click this text to change its color");
8
9      JPopupMenu aMenu = new JPopupMenu();
10     JMenuItem blue = new JMenuItem("Blue");
11     JMenuItem red = new JMenuItem("Red");
12     JMenuItem green = new JMenuItem("Green");
13
14     public PopUpMenuWindow(String title)
15     {
16       super(title);
17       setSize(400, 300);
18
19       JPanel aPanel = new JPanel();
20       aMenu.add(blue);
21       aMenu.add(red);
22       aMenu.add(green);
23
24       blue.setMnemonic('B');
25       red.setMnemonic('R');
26       green.setMnemonic('G');
27
28       blue.addActionListener(this);
29       red.addActionListener(this);
30       green.addActionListener(this);
31
32       aLabel.setComponentPopupMenu(aMenu);
33       aPanel.add(aLabel);
34       add(aPanel);
35     }
36
37     public void actionPerformed(ActionEvent e)
38     {
39       if(e.getSource() == blue) aLabel.setForeground(Color.BLUE);
40       if(e.getSource() == red) aLabel.setForeground(Color.RED);
41       if(e.getSource() == green) aLabel.setForeground(Color.GREEN);
42     }
43  }
```

Figure 12.20
The class **PopUpMenuWindow**.

12.4 FILE CHOOSER AND COLOR CHOOSER DIALOG BOXES

The API Swing package provides three dialog boxes that can be used to facilitate commonly performed user tasks: specifying the path to a file to be opened or saved and specifying a color to be used in a graphics application. The `JFileChooser` class contains the methods that display file-open and file-save dialog boxes. The `JColorChooser` class contains the method that displays a dialog box containing a predefined palette of colors from which to choose and provides the ability to define a custom color.

12.4.1 File-Chooser Dialog Box

Figure 12.21a shows an Open file-chooser dialog box, and Figure 12.21b shows the Save file-chooser dialog box. Both dialog boxes are displayed by the application, `FileChoosers`, shown in Figure 12.22. The Open dialog box is displayed by line 15, which invokes the `showOpenDialog` method on the `JFileChooser` object `fc` created on line 14. Line 15 of the application does not complete execution until the user clicks the dialog box's Open or Cancel buttons or closes the dialog box. Until one of these events occurs, the user can browse the system's file structure to locate and select a file to be opened, or enter the name of the file into the File Name text field.

When a folder is selected by double clicking its name, the folder name appears in the Look In text field of the dialog box, and its subfolders are displayed. When a file is selected by clicking its name, the file name is displayed in the dialog box's File Name text field. After the Open or Cancel button is clicked, or the dialog box is closed, the `showOpenDialog` method returns an integer whose value is dependent upon which of these three events occurred. Line 15 of Figure 12.22 stores the returned integer in the variable `cancelApproveError`.

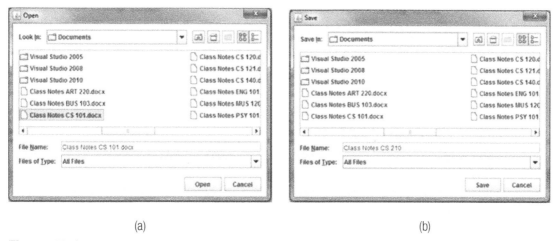

(a) (b)

Figure 12.21
File-chooser Open and Save dialog boxes.

Lines 16 and 23 compare this integer to two static integer constants `APPROVE _ OPTION` and `CANCEL _ OPTION` (defined in the `JFileChooser` class) to determine if the user clicked Open (line 16) or Cancel (line 23). When the user clicks the Cancel button, line 25 reports a record of that click to the system console. When neither button is clicked, line 29 reports that an error has occurred.

When the user clicks the Open button, line 19 places the address of the string returned from the File class's getPath method in the String variable path. This string, which contains the path to the file the user selected and the file's name, is output to the system console (lines 20–21) preceded by a line of annotation (the first two lines of output shown in Figure 12.23). Normally, the string path would be used to attach a Scanner object to the selected input file, as shown in the following code fragment:

```
File fileObject = new File(path);
Scanner fileIn = new Scanner(fileObject);
```

Lines 33–49 use a similar sequence of code to fetch a path and file name from the user in which to save information generated by the program. The only differences are that line 34 invokes the showSaveDialog method on the JFileChooser object fc to display the Save dialog box shown in Figure 12.21b, and the string referenced by the variable path on line 38 would be used to attach a PrintWriter object to the specified output file, as shown in the following code fragment:

```
FileWriter fileWriterObject = new FileWriter(path);
PrintWriter fileOut = new PrintWriter(fileWriterObject, false);
```

The last two lines of output shown in Figure 12.23 were produced by lines 39–40, after the user typed *Class Notes CS 210* in the text field of the dialog box shown in Figure 12.21b and clicked the Save button.

NOTE   *The default folder, shown in the **Look In** and **Save In** text fields of the Open and Save dialog boxes when they are initially displayed, is platform dependent.*

```
1    import javax.swing.*;
2    import java.io.*;
3
4    public class FileChoosers
5    {
6      public static void main(String[] args)
7      {
8        JFileChooser fc;
9        String path;
10       int cancelApproveError;
11       File file;
12
13       //Demonstrate the ***OPEN*** file dialog box
14       fc = new JFileChooser();
15       cancelApproveError = fc.showOpenDialog(null);
16       if(cancelApproveError == JFileChooser.APPROVE_OPTION) //Open clicked
17       {
18         file = fc.getSelectedFile(); //fetches file information
19         path = file.getPath(); //returns the path and file name
```

```
20          System.out.println("The path to the file to be opened is:\n" +
21                              path);
22        }
23        else if(cancelApproveError == JFileChooser.CANCEL_OPTION) //canceled
24        {
25          System.out.println("The user canceled the file open operation");
26        }
27        else //an error
28        {
29          System.out.println("An error has occurred");
30        }
31
32        //Demonstrate the ***SAVE*** file dialog box
33        fc = new JFileChooser();
34        cancelApproveError = fc.showSaveDialog(null);
35        if(cancelApproveError == JFileChooser.APPROVE_OPTION) //open clicked
36        {
37          file = fc.getSelectedFile();
38          path = file.getPath();
39          System.out.println("The path to the file to be written is:\n" +
40                              path);
41        }
42        else if(cancelApproveError == JFileChooser.CANCEL_OPTION) //canceled
43        {
44          System.out.println("The user canceled the file save operation");
45        }
46        else //an error
47        {
48          System.out.println("An error has occurred");
49        }
50      }
51    }
```

Figure 12.22
The application **FileChoosers**.

Console Output:
The path to the file to be opened is:
C:\Users\Bill\Documents\Class Notes CS 101.docx
The path to the file to be written is:
C:\Users\Bill\Documents\Class Notes CS 210

Figure 12.23
The output produced by the application **FileChoosers**.

12.4.2 Color-Chooser Dialog Box

The JColorChooser class's static method showDialog is used to display a color-chooser dialog box like the one shown in Figure 12.24a. The following code fragment was used to display it and to designate the color black as a default color choice. The second argument passed to the method is displayed at the top of the dialog box and is usually used as a user prompt.

```
//Display a color chooser dialog box.
Color aColor;
aColor = JColorChooser.showDialog(null, "Choose the Window's color",
                                  Color.BLACK);
```

The user has overridden the default color choice passed to the method's third parameter by selecting the pink swatch in the middle of the box's top row of color swatches. This selection is displayed in the grid labeled *Recent* in Figure 12.24a.

The Figure 12.24b shows the window of the application ColorChooser whose code is shown in Figure 12.25, after the user selected the color pink from the color-chooser dialog box it displays

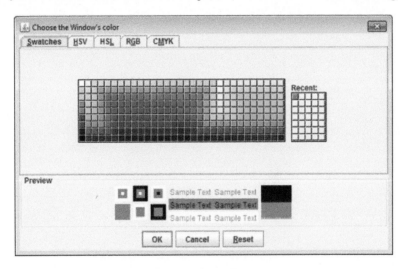

(a)

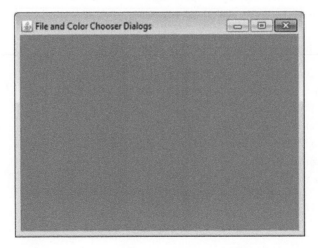

(b)

Figure 12.24

A **JFileChooser** dialog box and the **ColorChooser** application's program window.

and clicked OK. This application creates its window, which is an instance of a ColorChooser-Window, on line 8 of Figure 12.25 and makes it visible on line 10.

The constructor of the ColorChooserWindow class (lines 6–19 of Figure 12.26) displays a color-chooser dialog box (lines 15–16) and stores the address of the returned Color object that describes the color selected by the user (pink, in this case) in the variable aColor declared on line 12. Then, line 17 sets the background color of the JPanel (declared on line 11) to this color. Finally, line 18 adds the panel to the JFrame.

```
1    import javax.swing.*;
2
3    public class ColorChooser
4    {
5     public static void main(String[] args)
6     {
7       String title = "File and Color Chooser Dialogs";
8       ColorChooserWindow window = new ColorChooserWindow(title);
9       window.setDefaultCloseOperation(JFrame.EXIT_ON_CLOSE);
10      window.setVisible(true);
11     }
12   }
```

Figure 12.25
The application **ColorChooser**.

```
1    import javax.swing.*;
2    import java.awt.Color;
3
4    public class ColorChooserWindow extends JFrame
5    {
6      public ColorChooserWindow(String title)
7      {
8        super(title);
9        setSize(400, 300);
10
11       JPanel aPanel = new JPanel();
12       Color aColor;
13
14       //Obtain the background color of the window
15       aColor = JColorChooser.showDialog(null, "Choose the Window's color",
16                                        Color.BLACK);
17       aPanel.setBackground(aColor);
18       add(aPanel);
19     }
20   }
```

Figure 12.26
The class **ColorChooserWindow**.

12.5 CHAPTER SUMMARY

The GUI components check box, radio button, combo box, and list are used to select one or more inputs from a set of valid inputs. These components are instances of the classes `JCheckBox`, `JRadioButton`, `JComboBox`, and `JList`, respectively. Ordinarily, either a set of radio buttons or a combo box is used when the choices are mutually exclusive, and a set of check boxes or a list is used when this is not the case. Radio buttons are made mutually exclusive by adding them to an instance of the `ButtonGroup` class using the class's `add` method.

When the set of input choices is large, a combo box and a list are preferred over radio buttons and check boxes because the number of items they display at one time can be specified using the methods `setMaximumRowCount` for a combo box and `setVisibleCount` for a list. The method `setMaximumRowCount` adds a scroll bar to a combo box, and a scroll bar can be incorporated into a list object by passing it to the constructor of a `JScrollPane` object when the scroll pane is created. This permits the user to view a large number of selection choices within a small space on the program's window.

The annotation to be displayed next to a radio button or a check box is passed to the constructor invoked to create these objects. The elements, displayed in combo boxes and lists, are placed in an array that is passed to their class's one-parameter constructor when they are created. Multiple non-sequential values in a list can be selected by clicking them while holding down the Control key (Ctrl) on the keyboard. Multiple sequential values in a list can be selected by clicking the first value in the sequence, holding down the Shift key, and clicking the last value in the sequence. The ability to select one or more values from a list is its default mode, but this can be restricted to a sequential set of values or only one value.

Normally, a set of check boxes, a set of radio buttons, a combo box, or a list is added to an instance of a `JPanel`, and the panel is then added to the window's content pane. This makes the components easier to position in the window, and the panel's border can be made visible to give the impression that the boxes or buttons it contains are part of a set. The panel's `setBorder` method and the static methods of the `BorderFactory` class can be used to display and customize a panel's border and add an informative title. A border can be placed around any component that extends the class `JComponent`, although it is most often used to put a border around a `JPanel` or a `JLabel` object.

When it is important to perform processing immediately after a check box or radio button is selected/unselected, the event handler method `itemStateChanged` (for a check box defined in the interface `ItemListener`) and `actionPerformed` (for a radio button defined in the interface `ActionListener`) is implemented and registered in the component's listener list. The event handler can invoke the `getSource` method on the argument passed to the method's parameter to determine which component was selected/unselected, and the `isSelected` method can then be invoked on the component to determine its status (selected returns `true`). The selection made in a combo box or all the selections made in a list can be determined using the methods presented in Table 12.3, which also presents a method to change the values displayed in a list (`setListData`) and to make a combo box editable (`setEditable`).

The Java API supports two types of menus, drop-down menus (JMenu instances) and pop-up menus (JPopupMenu instances), which are used to construct a user friendly interface that presents a group of valid input items (JMenuItem, JCheckBoxMenuItem, and JRadioButtonItem instances) in a relatively small portion of the program's window. The annotation associated with these components is passed to their class's one-parameter constructor when they are created.

Drop-down menus are added to a menu bar (JMenuBar instance) whose location in the window is platform dependent. Pop-up menus are associated with other GUI components and remain invisible until the user performs a platform-dependent action (e.g., a right mouse click) on the associated component. The add method is invoked on a drop-down or pop-up menu object to add a menu item or a drop-down (sub) menu to them, and the addSeparator method is invoked on these menu objects to visually group their related elements. Hot keys can be added to menu items by invoking the setMnemonic method on them. When the user selects a menu item, an action event occurs. The event is serviced using the same techniques used to service action events on JRadioButton objects and JButton objects. The event handler is the method actionPerformed defined in the interface ActionListener.

In addition to these GUI components, the API Swing package also provides three dialog boxes that can be used to facilitate commonly performed user tasks: specifying the path to a file to be opened or saved and specifying a color to be used in a graphics application. The JFileChooser class in the Swing package provides methods to display file open and save dialog boxes, and the JColorChooser class provides a method to display a dialog box that contains a predefined palette of colors from which to choose a color and also provides the ability to define a custom color.

Knowledge Exercises

1. True or false:
   a) Radio buttons are commonly used to select one or more inputs from a set of valid inputs.
   b) Adding check boxes or radio buttons to a panel makes them easier to reposition.
   c) Combo boxes are used to make multiple selections from a set of valid inputs.
   d) Combo boxes or lists are used when the number of input choices is large.
   e) A scroll bar can be associated with a list to keep the size of the component small.
   f) A scroll bar cannot be associated with a combo box.
   g) Elements in a list are called items, elements in a combo box are called values.
   h) Multiple values can be selected from a list component at one time.
   i) Multiple items can be selected from a combo box at one time.
   j) The elements displayed in a list and or combo box are defined as an array of objects.
   k) GUI components can be made invisible.
   l) Combo boxes can be edited, allowing a user to type a choice into a text field.
   m) Lists can be edited, allowing a user to type a choice into a text field.
   n) Java supports drop-down but not pop-up menus.
   o) Hot keys or shortcut keys can be assigned using the setMnemonic method.
   p) Radio buttons and check boxes can be added to a menu.

592 ■ Programming Fundamentals Using Java

2. Give examples of when you would use a group of check boxes and when you would use a group of radio buttons.

3. State when you would use a combo box and when you would use a list.

4. Explain how:
   a) Radio buttons can be grouped together to make them mutually exclusive
   b) A border is added to a GUI component such as a `JPanel`
   c) A border's color and style can be changed from its default color and style

5. Compare and contrast the features of combo boxes and lists.

6. Explain one difference in the way that scroll bars are added to combo boxes and lists.

7. Discuss the differences between drop-down and pop-up menus.

8. What are two advantages of including menus in your applications?

9. What are mnemonics? Give an example of one.

10. Briefly explain the function of a `JFileChooser` object.

11. Briefly explain the function of a `JColorChooser` object.

12. Place the letter A, B, or C next to each of the components given below to designate the interface that defines the component's event handler method. The designations are:

   A: `ItemListener`
   B: `ListSelectionListener`
   C: `ActionListener`

   a) Check box   b) Radio button
   c) Combo box   d) List
   e) Menu item

13. Place the letter A, B, or C next to each of the components given below to designate the component's event handler method. The designations are:

   A: `actionPerformed`
   B: `itemStateChanged`
   C: `valueChanged`

   a) Check box   b) Radio button
   c) Combo box   d) List
   e) Menu item

14. Give the method used to:
   a) Determine if a check box is selected
   b) Determine if a radio button is selected
   c) Get the item selected in a combo box
   d) Get the index of the item selected in a combo box
   e) Get the indices of the all the values selected in a list

f) Get the first value selected in a list

g) Get all the values selected in a list

15. Give the class of each of the following components:

    a) Check box   **b)** Radio button

    c) Combo box   **d)** List

    e) Drop-down menu   **f)** Pop-up menu

    g) Menu item   **h)** Menu check box

    i) Menu radio button

16. Give the name of the method used to:

    a) Add a component to a `JPanel` object   **b)** Add a menu bar to a `JFrame` object

    c) Add a drop-down menu to a menu bar   **d)** Associate a pop-up menu to a component

    e) Add a hot key to a menu item   **f)** Add a check box to a menu

    g) Add a radio button to a menu   **h)** Display a file-save dialog box

    i) Display a choose-color dialog box

Programming Exercises

1. Design, write, and test a GUI application for the Speedy Cable Service. Include a menu to offer the user any combination of the following service options: basic, movie, sports, premium, and learning. When a user clicks the calculate button, the monthly charge for all of the services selected should be computed and output in a dialog box. (The costs are as follows: basic is $30, movie is $15, sports is $20, premium is $30, and learning is $12). Customers can also select high or regular definition for a fee of $10 or $5 respectively.

2. Using a GUI design, write and test an application for a bank that offers the user the following choices: make a deposit, make a withdrawal, and check the balance of an account from a drop down menu. Dialog boxes should be used for user input and output.

3. Colorful Sports Inc. just hired you to write a pop-up menu GUI application that their customers will use to order winter clothing from a selection of three custom-colored items they sell: shirts for $30, parkas for $150, and gloves for $15. The customer can select any or all of the items and can specify the size (small, medium, large, or extra large) for each item selected. Each item should have a hot key associated with it. When an item is selected, present the user with a dialog box from which he or she can select the color of the item. Provide a Place Order button that calculates and outputs the total cost to the GUI, including an 8% sales tax, the items ordered, and a swatch of the color of each item to the GUI. Include a Reset button on the GUI that clears the output and all of the selections that were made. Design the GUI.

4. Write the code and test the application described in Exercise 3.

5. Design a GUI for Sam's Sub Shop to allow users to place orders for heroes or subs. The selections should include (but are not limited to) the following items: the choice of bread (Italian, wheat, rye), one or more fillings (ham, cheese, turkey, tuna, lettuce, tomato, mayonnaise, and mustard), and one or more beverages (soda, water, and coffee). After the selections are made,

allow the user to click a button and view his or her order in a dialog box. Provide a Reset button that clears the output and all of the selections that were made.

6. Write a program to implement the design for Sam's Sub Shop in Exercise 5.

7. Design a GUI for the Tanya's Tour Trips travel agency that her customers can use to select the year, month, and day of the trip, the number of people traveling (up to four people), and a group of cities to be visited from a list of 30 cities. When the Book It button is clicked, the date of travel (mm/dd/yy) is output to the GUI along with a scrollable list of the cities to be visited. The GUI should also provide a Reset button that clears the output and all of the selections.

8. Write a program to implement the design for Tanya's Tour Trips in Exercise 7.

Enrichment

Investigate other GUI components, such as sliders, that are provided by the Java API.

GENERICS AND THE API COLLECTIONS FRAMEWORK

13.1 *Overview*. *596*

13.2 *Generic Methods* *596*

13.3 *Generic Classes* *611*

13.4 *The API Collections Framework*. *621*

13.5 *Chapter Summary* *637*

In this chapter

In this chapter, we extend our knowledge of methods and classes by incorporating the feature of generics into them. This will make the methods and classes we write more reusable and less error prone. A generic method can be passed arguments of any type, and the types of the data members of a generic class can be specified when an instance in the class is created. These powerful features can be used to write classes called data structures that can store, fetch, and process a set of any type of objects. Data structures such as lists, queues, stacks, sets, and hash maps will be discussed.

A set of highly reusable generic methods, interfaces, and classes make up the Java Collections Framework. The methods implement classic computer algorithms, and the classes implement commonly used techniques for efficiently processing large data sets. We will learn the functionality of these methods and classes and how to incorporate them into the programs we write. In addition, we will discuss two groupings of classes included in the framework and the advantages of the Map grouping that can be used to efficiently locate a particular object in a large data set by simply specifying a key value that has been associated with the object.

After successfully completing this chapter, you should:

- Know how generic classes and methods extend reusability and reduce runtime errors
- Understand the difference between a value parameter list and a type parameter list
- Be able to write generic classes and methods and use generic interfaces
- Know how to invoke generic methods and how to declare instances of generic classes
- Understand and be able to write and use overloaded generic methods

- Be able to use the methods in the Java Collections Framework in the programs you write, including the methods defined in the `Collections` class
- Understand the generic interface hierarchy defined in the Java Collections framework
- Create applications that use the generic data structures classes implemented in the framework
- Understand the differences between Lists, Sets, Queues and Priority Queues, and Maps and their implementations in the framework

13.1 OVERVIEW

Generics is a feature of programming languages that extends the reusability of methods and classes. It provides reusability by permitting the type of a method's parameters and returned value to be specified by the method's invoker and by permitting the type of a class's data members to be specified when an instance of the class is created. Thus, the use of generics makes it possible to write one sort method that can sort an array of *any* type of object passed to the method and to write one class that can store, fetch, delete, and process a set of objects of any type. In addition, the use of generics can also move certain type-checking errors from runtime to compile time, where they are easier to detect and eliminate.

Java supports generics and provides a syntax that can be used to implement methods and classes in a generic way. Using this powerful feature of the language, we can pass any type of argument into a generic method's parameter and specify the type of a generic class's data members and its methods' parameters. In addition, the Java API provides generic implementations of many of the classic algorithms used to efficiently process and store large data sets containing data of any type. These generic implementations are known as *collections*, and they comprise the Java collections framework.

In the first part of this chapter, we will become familiar with Java's implementation of generics, how to write generic methods and classes, and how to invoke generic methods and declare instances of generic classes. This will facilitate our understanding of the second part of the chapter in which we will become familiar with many of the methods, interfaces, and classes in Java's Collections Framework, all of which are implemented using generics.

13.2 GENERIC METHODS

When any method with a non-empty parameter list is invoked, values are passed into each of its parameters. These values are usually different for each invocation of the method, and they can be either primitive values or the address of an object (reference values). The parameter list, enclosed in parentheses at the end of the method's signature, can be thought of as a list of values that will be passed to the method or a *value* parameter list. This list contains the name of each parameter and the type of the value that will be passed to it. When the value passed to the method is a primitive value, the type is a primitive type. When the value passed to the method is a reference value, the address of an object, the type is a class name.

Generic methods are passed values just like non-generic methods. What makes them different from non-generic methods is that at least one of the parameters in their value parameter list can be passed a reference to an instance of *any* class. A specific class name is not coded for this parameter. Instead, a *type placeholder* is coded in the value parameter list as the parameter's class name, and the placeholder is included in a *type* parameter list section of the method's signature.

```
public static <T> void outputAnyObject(T theObject)
```

Type parameter lists are coded just to the left of the method's returned type. They are a list of the type placeholders used in the method's parameter list, separated by commas, and the list is enclosed in angle brackets. For example: `<T>` or `<T1, T2>`. Good coding style dictates that place-holder names begin with a capital letter and be as brief as possible. All of the type placeholders used in a method's value parameter list must be included in the method's type parameter list.

For example, the first signature shown below could be used for a generic method that outputs an instance of any class, and the second signature could be used for a method that outputs two instances of any class:

```
public static <T> void outputAnyObject(T theObject)
public static <T> void outputAnyTwoObjects(T object1, T object2)
```

The type placeholders that appear in a method's signature can be used within the code body of the method. Often, they are used to declare local reference variables within the methods that can refer-ence instances of the class of the parameter of which they are a part.

The signatures of generic methods can also include non-generic types. For example, the fol-lowing signature could be used for a generic method that outputs an instance of any class a given number of times (i.e., `nTimes`):

```
public static <T> void outputNTimes(T theObject, int nTimes)
```

The following signature could be used for a method that outputs two objects, possibly of two dif-ferent classes, a given number of times:

```
public static <T1, T2> void outputNTimes2(T1 obj1, T2 obj2, int nTimes)
```

NOTE *The primitive types (`int`, `double`, `char`, etc.) cannot be passed to generic param-eter types.*

Only object references can be passed to generic parameter types. To pass a primitive value to a parameter whose type is a generic placeholder, it must be wrapped inside an instance of a primitive wrapper class (e.g., `Integer`, `Double`, `Char`, etc.). As we will see, this can be performed by the autoboxing feature of Java.

Generic Returned Types

In a non-void generic method, one of the type placeholders can be used to designate the re-turned type. For example:

```
public static <T1, T2> T2 output2Objects(T1 object1, T2 Object1)
```

In this case, T2 is the returned type, and the method would have to return the address of an object whose class is the same as the class of the second argument passed to it. To return an object that is the same type as the first parameter, the returned type would be changed to T1. Generic methods can return primitive values and non-generic reference variable types, just as non-generic methods can, by coding their specific type as the method's return type.

The application GenericParameters shown in Figure 13.1 contains a generic method output2Objects (lines 18–24) that outputs two objects of any type sent to it and returns the object passed to its second parameter. The method is invoked twice within the application. In the first invocation of the method (line 12), the arguments are two primitive variables, amount and price, declared on lines 5 and 6. Because primitives cannot be passed to generic parameters, these two arguments are autoboxed, and then the address of the Integer and Double objects are passed to the method's parameters.

NOTE *Primitive arguments are autoboxed into wrapper objects before they are passed to generic parameters.*

Similar autoboxing is performed on the first argument of the second invocation (line 13), which is a primitive char variable declared on line 7. The second argument in this invocation is an instance of the class Student, shown in Figure 13.2, which is declared on line 8. Before the application ends, lines 14 and 15 of Figure 13.1 output the generic method's returned values. The program's output is shown in Figure 13.3.

The declarations on lines 5–7 of the application could have declared amount, price, and initial to be three wrapper objects and initialized them using the wrapper classes's constructors as shown below. Although the coding of the invocation statements would not change, this would eliminate the need for the autoboxing. The declarations on lines 5–7 are considered to be better programming style.

```
Integer amount = new Integer(45);
Double price = new Double(567.89);
Character initial = new Character('P');
```

The type parameter list in the signature of the generic method output2Objects (line 18) includes two generic placeholders: T1 and T2. These placeholders are used in the method's parameter list as the types of the objects passed to it. The placeholder T2 is also used as the method's returned type because that is the generic type of the method's second parameter that is returned on line 23.

Lines 20 and 21 output the objects passed to the method to the system console using implicit invocations of the toString method. During the first invocation of the generic method (line 12), the toString methods of the Integer and Double classes are invoked because this invocation passes these autoboxed types into the method's type placeholders. Similarly, during the second invocation of the method (line 13), the toString methods of the Character class and Student class (lines 12–16 of Figure 13.2) are invoked. If the Student class did not contain a toString method, the toString method inherited from the class Object would have been invoked.

The object returned on line 12 of Figure 13.1 is an instance of the wrapper class Double. Its assignment to the primitive double variable returnedPrice declared on line 9 is valid because Java's autounboxing feature unwraps the value stored inside the object before the assignment is made.

```
1   public class GenericParameters
2   {
3     public static void main(String[] args)
4     {
5       int amount = 45;
6       double price = 567.89;
7       char initial = 'P';
8       Student s1 = new Student(19, "Sam Jones");
9       double returnedPrice;
10      Student returnedStudent;
11
12      returnedPrice = output2Objects(amount, price);
13      returnedStudent - output2Objects(initial, s1);
14      System.out.println(returnedPrice);
15      System.out.println(returnedStudent);
16    }
17
18    public static <T1, T2> T2 output2Objects(T1 object1, T2 object2)
19    {
20      System.out.println(object1);
21      System.out.println(object2 + "\n");
22
23      return object2;
24    }
25  }
```

Figure 13.1
The application **GenericParameters**.

```
1   public class Student
2   {
3     int age;
4     String name;
5
6     public Student(int age, String name)
7     {
8       this.age = age;
9       this.name = name;
10    }
11
12    public String toString()
13    {
```

```
14      String s;
15      return s = "age " + age + " name " + name;
16    }
17  }
```

Figure 13.2
The class **Student**.

```
45
567.89

P
age 19 name Sam Jones

567.89
age 19 name Sam Jones
```

Figure 13.3
The output produced by the application **GenericParameters**.

13.2.1 Overloading Generic Methods

As discussed in Chapter 3, overloaded methods are a set of methods defined in a class that have the same name and different parameter lists. When the translator encounters an invocation of an overloaded method in a set of non-generic methods, it seeks a version of that method whose parameters match the invocation's arguments. This version of the method is invoked when the program executes the invocation statement. If a match cannot be found, a translation error is generated.

NOTE   *Generic methods can be included in a set of overloaded methods.*

Generic methods can overload non-generic methods and other generic methods. When generic methods are included in a set of overloaded methods, the translator seeks a version of the method that *best fits* the argument list in the method invocation statement. To determine a best fit, the translator follows a set of protocols. The protocols do *not* take into consideration the order in which the overloaded methods are coded. If a best fit cannot be found that is consistent with the protocols, a translation error is generated.

The methods shown in Figure 13.4 can be used to illustrate three of these best-fit protocols. The figure contains four overloaded versions of the method IdentifyYourself, each of which has two parameters. Version 1, shown at the top of the figure, is non-generic. The other three versions are generic. As we will discover, the best-fit protocols do not permit all four of these methods to be included in a set of overloaded methods.

When the method IdentifyYourself is invoked and passed two *integer primitive* arguments, Version1 could be executed because it has two integer parameters. The other three versions of the method could also be executed because one argument (in the case of Version 2) or both of the arguments (in the case of Versions 3a and 3b) could be autoboxed and the `Integer` wrapper object(s) could then be passed to the methods' parameters. The best-fit protocol in this case results in Version 1's execution because the types in its parameter list (`int`) are an exact match with the two integer arguments passed to it.

When the method is invoked and the first argument passed to it is an object and the second is an integer primitive value, Version 2 could be invoked. Version 3a could also be invoked because the second argument could be autoboxed, and the resulting `Integer` wrapper object could then be passed to the method's second parameter. It turns out that Version 3b could also be invoked, even though its parameter list implies that the two objects passed to it must be of the same type, `T`. The best-fit protocol in this case results in Version 2's execution because the type of its second parameter, `int`, is an exact match for the second argument passed to the method.

```
// Version 1
public static void IdentifyYourself(int a, int b)
{
      System.out.println("Version 1 was invoked");
}


// Version 2
public static <T> void IdentifyYourself (T a, int b)
{
      System.out.println("Version 2 was invoked");
}


// Version 3a
public static <T1, T2> void IdentifyYourself (T1 a, T2 b)
{
      System.out.println("Version 3a was invoked");
}


// Version 3b
public static <T> void IdentifyYourself (T a, T b)
{
      System.out.println("Version 3b was invoked");
}
```

Figure 13.4
A set of overloaded methods.

Best-fit protocols do not allow Versions 3a and 3b to be in the same class because both can accept two object instances of the same type or different types. When coded in the same class, an attempt to invoke `IdentifyYourself` and pass it two objects results in a translation error, indicating that the invocation is ambiguous (could be serviced by either version of the method). The coding of Version 3a is preferred over Version 3b.

The application `GenericOverloading`, shown in Figure 13.5, includes the first three overloaded versions of `IdentifyYourself` presented in Figure 13.4. The invocations of the method on lines 5–8 and the output produced by the program (Figure 13.6) demonstrate the translator's best-fit selection protocols. The coding order of the methods has been reversed to demonstrate that the best-fit protocols do not consider the order in which the methods appear in the class.

In the interest of brevity, lines 6–8 pass the method nameless instances of the classes Integer and Double, and the Student class (shown in Figure 13.2).

```
1    public class GenericOverloading
2    {
3      public static void main(String[] args)
4      {
5        IdentifyYourself(1, 2); //int, int: Version 1
6        IdentifyYourself(new Integer(10), 2); //object, int: Version 2
7        IdentifyYourself(2, new Double(20.3)); //int, object: Version 3a
8        IdentifyYourself(new Integer(10), new Student(19, "Evie")); //V3a
9      }
10
11     // Version 3a
12     public static <T1, T2> void IdentifyYourself(T1 a, T2 b)
13     {
14       System.out.println("Version 3a was invoked");
15     }
16
17     // Version 2
18     public static <T> void IdentifyYourself(T a, int b)
19     {
20       System.out.println("Version 2 was invoked");
21     }
22
23     // Version 1
24     public static void IdentifyYourself(int a, int b)
25     {
26       System.out.println("Version 1 was invoked");
27     }
28   }
```

Figure 13.5
The application **GenericOverloading**.

```
Version 1 was invoked
Version 2 was invoked
Version 3a was invoked
Version 3a was invoked
```

Figure 13.6
The output produced by the application **GenericOverloading**.

13.2.2 Arrays as Generic Parameters and Returned Values

As is the case for non-generic methods, any parameter in a generic method's parameter list can be a reference to an array object. By specifying the parameter's type to be one of the generic placeholders included in the method's type parameter list followed by an open and closed brace, the address of any array of objects can be passed to the parameter. The following generic method signature could be used for a method that outputs the contents of a non-primitive type array and returns one of its elements.

```
public static <T> T outputArray(T[] anArray)
```

The pair of brackets that follow the placeholder in the method's signature indicate that the address of an array will be passed to the method's parameter.

The application `GenericsArrayParameters`, shown in Figure 13.7, contains a generic method named `outputArray` (lines 24–33) that outputs the contents of the array of objects passed to it to the system console. The method also returns one element of the array whose index is specified by the invoker. Any array to be output can be passed to the method's first parameter, *except* for an array of primitive values. Java autoboxing feature will not convert an array of primitives passed to the method to an array of wrapper class objects. The output produced by the program is shown in Figure 13.8.

The method's signature (line 24) contains two parameters, `anArray` and `elementReturned`, and includes one generic placeholder, `T`, in its type parameter list. This placeholder is used as the type of the method's first parameter. It is also used as the method's generic returned type because an element of the array will be returned by the method. The method's `for` loop (lines 26–29) outputs all of the array elements using an implicit invocation of the `toString` method, and line 32 returns the array element whose index is passed to the method's second parameter. The application invokes the method three times, passing it a different array each time.

The first two invocations pass the method the array of wrapped integer values (line 15) and an array of wrapped real numbers (line 16), declared and initialized on lines 5 and 6 respectively. These arrays cannot be declared as arrays of primitive values because Java will not autobox an array of primitive values before passing it to a generic array parameter. The values contained in the returned `Integer` and `Double` objects are autounwrapped and assigned to the primitive variables `intReturned` and `doubleReturned`.

An array of `Student` objects, whose class is defined in Figure 13.2, is passed to the method on line 17. The address of the student object returned from this invocation is assigned to the reference variable `studentReturned` declared on line 10. Lines 19–21 produce the last three outputs, which are the contents of the two returned wrapper objects and the returned `Student` object.

```
1    public class GenericsArrayParameters
2    {
3      public static void main(String[] args)
4      {
5        Integer[] intArray  = {10, 20, 30, 40, 50};
```

```
6          Double[] doubleArray = {11.1, 22.2, 33.3, 44.4};
7          Student[] studentArray = new Student[2];
8          int intReturned;
9          double doubleReturned;
10         Student studentReturned;
11
12         studentArray[0] = new Student(19, "Sam Jones");
13         studentArray[1] = new Student(20, "Nora King");
14
15         intReturned = outputArray(intArray, 3); //autounbox the returned
16         doubleReturned = outputArray(doubleArray, 2); //int and double
17         studentReturned = outputArray(studentArray, 1);
18
19         System.out.println(intReturned);
20         System.out.println(doubleReturned);
21         System.out.println(studentReturned);
22     }
23
24     public static <T> T outputArray(T[] anArray, int elementReturned)
25     {
26       for(int i = 0; i < anArray.length; i++)
27       {
28         System.out.println(anArray[i]);
29       }
30       System.out.println();
31
32       return anArray[elementReturned];
33     }
34 }
```

Figure 13.7
The application **GenericArrayParameters**.

```
10
20
30
40
50

11.1
22.2
33.3
44.4
```

```
age 19 name Sam Jones
age 20 name Nora King


40
33.3
age 20 name Nora King
```

Figure 13.8
The output produced by the application **GenericArrayParameters**.

Returning Generic Arrays

As discussed in Chapter 6, when a non-generic array is returned from a method the type of the array followed by a set of brackets (e.g., Student[ ]) replaces the keyword void in the method's signature, and a return statement that includes the array's name is coded in the method.

The same syntax is used to return a generic array from a generic method, except that the type of the array is replaced with one of the generic placeholders used in the method's signature. For example, the following method signature could be used in a method that returns a generic array whose type was the same as the first argument passed to the method:

```
public static <T1, T2> T1[] returnArray(T1[] anArray, T2 anObject)
```

The array returned would be the one whose name is included in a return statement executed within the method.

The generic method shown in Figure 13.9 swaps the first two elements of the array passed to it and returns the modified array to the invoker. As previously mentioned, the array passed to the method cannot be an array of primitive values. Line 3 of the method creates a generic local variable named temp whose type is the type placeholder used to specify the type of the array passed to the method.

```
1     public static <T> T[] swap0and1(T[] anArray)
2     {
3       T temp;
4
5       temp = anArray[0];
6       anArray[0] = anArray[1];
7       anArray[1] = temp;
8
9       return anArray;
10    }
```

Figure 13.9
A generic method that returns an array.

13.2.3 Copying a Generic Array

Although local generic variables can be declared inside a generic method, limits are imposed on the creation of generic arrays inside a generic method. The syntax used to create a non-generic array inside a method, which could be used to hold a copy of another non-generic array, cannot be used to create a generic array. The following declaration produces a compile time *generic array creation* error if T is a generic placeholder:

```
T[] copy = new T[100]; //not allowed
```

The good news is that a copy of a generic array can be created within a generic method using the Arrays class's copyOf method that was discussed in Chapter 6, and the copy can then be modified and returned from the method. Another alternative is that an array-like instance of the class ArrayList can be created, modified, and returned from a generic method. The ArraysList class will be discussed later in this chapter (Section 13.3.1), as will the correct syntax for creating a generic array that is not a copy of another generic array.

Lines 29–39 of the application ReturningGenericArrays, shown in Figure 13.10, is a generic method named invertArray that copies any type of array passed to it and then returns a modified version of the array to the method's invoker. The returned array contains the elements of the array passed to the method with their order reversed (first to last becomes last to first). The output produced by the program is shown in Figure 13.11.

Line 31 of the method declares a generic array reference variable named copy using the placeholder T1 that appears in the method's signature (line 29). The Arrays class's copyOf method is used on line 33 to create a duplicate of the array passed to the method and assign its address to the variable copy. The code of the for loop that begins on line 34 then copies the object references from the original array (anArray) into the newly created array (copy) in reverse order. Line 38 returns the array created inside the method to the invoker.

The first time the method is invoked (line 14), it is passed the Integer wrapper array declared on line 7. The second invocation (line 15) passes the method the array of objects declared on lines 9–11. This array is created by initializing it to three nameless Student objects whose class is shown in Figure 13.2.

The arrays returned from the method invocations are output inside the two for loops that begin on lines 17 and 23. The first of these loops outputs the contents of the original and reverse order Integer arrays, iArray and iArrayReturned, side by side (top part of Figure 13.11). The second loop repeats this process for the Student arrays sArray and sArrayReturned (bottom part of Figure 13.11).

```
1    import java.util.Arrays;
2
3    public class ReturningGenericArrays
4    {
5      public static void main(String[] args)
6      {
7        Integer[] iArray= {1,2,3,4};
```

```
8          Integer[] iArrayReturned;
9          Student[] sArray = {new Student(17, "Robert"),
10                             new Student(20, "Carol"),
11                             new Student(16, "Maggie")};
12         Student[] sArrayReturned;
13
14         iArrayReturned = invertArray(iArray);
15         sArrayReturned = invertArray(sArray);
16
17       for(int i = 0; i < iArray.length; i++) //all the Integer Objects
18       {
19         System.out.println(iArray[i] + "\t" + iArrayReturned[i]);
20       }
21       System.out.println();
22
23       for(int i = 0; i < sArray.length; i++) //all the Student Objects
24       {
25         System.out.println(sArray[i] + "\t" + sArrayReturned[i]);
26       }
27     }
28
29     public static <T1> T1[] invertArray(T1[] anArray)
30     {
31       T1[] copy;
32
33       copy = Arrays.copyOf(anArray, anArray.length);
34       for(int i = 0; i < copy.length; i++)
35       {
36         copy[i] = anArray[copy.length - 1 - i];
37       }
38       return copy;
39     }
40   }
```

Figure 13.10
The application `ReturningGenericArrays`.

```
1  4
2  3
3  2
4  1

age 17 name Robert  age 16 name Maggie
age 20 name Carol   age 20 name Carol
age 16 name Maggie  age 17 name Robert
```

Figure 13.11
The output produced by the application `ReturningGenericArrays`.

13.2.4 Operating on Generic Objects

As we have already seen, one way to perform processing on an object is to invoke a worker method. For example, to fetch the private integer data member named x of an instance of a Snowman object named s1, we could invoke the class's getX method on the object to perform the work of fetching the variable's contents:

```
Snowman s1 = new Snowman();
int x = s1.getX();
```

When the translator processes this invocation, it searches the object's class and its inheritance chain for a method named getX that has an empty parameter list and returns an integer. If it finds a method with this signature, the translation continues. Otherwise, the translation ends in a *cannot find symbol method getX( )* error.

Now consider the case when the s1 is a generic parameter in the signature of a generic method, and the invocation of the getX method is issued from within the generic method, as shown in this code fragment:

```
public static <T> boolean collision(T s1, T s2)
{
  int x1 = s1.getX()
         :
}
```

In this case, the translation of the method will end in a *cannot find symbol method getX( )* translation error, even if the class of the argument passed to s1 contains a getX method. The object s1's class is specified to be the generic type placeholder T in the method's parameter list, so now there is no relationship between the parameter s1 and the Snowman class, or any other class. The translator cannot look into T to locate the method getX; it is simply a generic placeholder.

To remedy this problem, the author of the generic method collision would include an extends clause inside the type parameter list of the generic method's signature that included the name of an interface that defines the getX method's signature. Assuming the name of the interface is Detectable, the modified signature of the generic method would be:

```
public static < T extends Detectable <T> > boolean collision(T s1, T s1)
```

The extends clause added to the method's signature directs the translator to look into the interface Detectable to verify the getX method's signature, and only objects whose classes implement this interface can be passed to this method.

> **NOTE** *The keyword* extends *is always used in a type parameter list to identify an interface. The keyword* implements *is not used.*

The class of any object passed to the method would have to implement the interface Detectable(i.e., include an implements clause in its heading, and an implementation of a getX method whose signature is defined in that interface). If it did not implement the interface, the translator would issue the error message. In the case when two Snowman objects were passed to the method, the error message would indicate that the method *could not be applied to (Snowman, Snowman)*.

The application `OperatingOnGenericObjects` shown in Figure 13.12 contains a generic method named `min` (lines 15–26) that returns the address of the smallest object in an array of objects passed to it. The work of comparing two elements of the array is performed by a worker method named `compareTo`, which is invoked on an element of the generic array (line 20) and passed a reference (defined on line 17) to an element of the array. An `extends` clause involving the array's generic placeholder `T` has been added to the method's signature (line 15) to permit the translator to look into an interface named `Comparable` to verify the signature of the `compareTo` method invoked on line 20. The syntax `<T>` that follows the name of the interface specifies that an object in the class `T` will be passed to the `compareTo` method. The result is that only objects whose classes implement this interface can be passed to the method `min`, and the object passed to the `compareTo` method on line 12 must be a reference to the type of object passed to the method `min`.

Several API classes including the `String` class and the primitive wrapper classes, which include the `Integer` class, implement the interface `Comparable`. It is left up to the implementer of the interface to decide what it means for an object in the implementing class to be equal to, greater than, or less than another instance of the class. As would be expected, the `Integer` class compares two `Integer` objects numerically.

The class `StudentV2` (shown in Figure 13.13) also implements the interface `Comparable`. The inclusion of `<StudentV2>` at the end of the `implements` clause in the class's heading designates that its version of the `compareTo` method must be passed a `StudentV2` instance. Line 20 effectively compares the ages of two instances of the class numerically.

The method `min`, invoked on line 11 of Figure 13.12, is passed the array of `Integer` objects declared on line 5, and the returned minimum object is then output to the system console (Figure 13.14). During this invocation of the method, the `Integer` class's implementation of `compareTo` is invoked on line 20 because the type of `anArray` is `Integer`. In the second invocation of the method `min` (line 12), the method is passed the `StudentV2` array, defined on lines 6–9 of Figure 13.12, which causes line 20 to invoke the `compareTo` method on lines 18–21 of Figure 13.13. The returned minimum `StudentV2` object returned from `min` is then output to the system console (Figure 13.14).

```
1    public class OperatingOnGenericObjects
2    {
3      public static void main(String[] args)
4      {
5        Integer[] iArray= {110, 36, 78, 43, 23, 83, 34, 24};
6        StudentV2[] sArray = {new StudentV2(18, "Sam"),
7                              new StudentV2(32, "Carol"),
8                              new StudentV2(16, "Maggie"),
9                              new StudentV2(25, "James")};
10
11       System.out.println("iArray minimum is: " + min(iArray));
12       System.out.println("sArray minimum is: " + min(sArray));
13     }
14
```

```
15    public static <T extends Comparable<T>> T  min(T[] anArray)
16    {
17      T minimum = anArray[0];
18      for(int i = 1; i < anArray.length; i++)
19      {
20        if(anArray[i].compareTo(minimum) < 0)
21        {
22          minimum = anArray[i];
23        }
24      }
25      return minimum;
26    }
27  }
```

Figure 13.12
The application `OperatingOnGenericObjects`.

```
1    public class StudentV2 implements Comparable<StudentV2>
2    {
3      private int age;
4      private String name;
5
6      public StudentV2(int age, String name)
7      {
8        this.age = age;
9        this.name = name;
10     }
11
12     public String toString()
13     {
14       String s;
15       return s = "age " + age + " name " + name;
16     }
17
18     public int compareTo(StudentV2 s1)
19     {
20       return age - s1.age;
21     }
22  }
```

Figure 13.13
The class `StudentV2`.

```
iArray minimum is: 23
sArray minimum is: age 16 name Maggie
```

Figure 13.14
The output from the application `OperatingOnGenericObjects`.

13.3 GENERIC CLASSES

A generic class is a class whose heading contains a type parameter list, which is used to specify the type of one or more of its data members. They are widely used in the implementation of data structures. The class can contain both non-generic and generic methods that use the type place-holders included in the class's type parameter list. The type parameter list is coded immediately after the class's name. For example:

```
public class AGenericClass <T1, T2, T3>
```

If a generic class extends another class and/or implements an interface, the `extends` and `implements` clauses are added to the method's heading after its type parameter list. For example, the heading of a generic class named `Employee` that was a subclass of `Person` could be:

```
public class Employee <T> extends Person implements Comparable<Employee>
```

The following statement declares an instance of this class using its two parameter constructor:

```
Employee s1 = new Employee <Integer> (45323, "Ryan");
```

The `<Integer>` included in the declaration is called a *type argument list*. A type argument list is enclosed in angle brackets and consists of a list of one or more class names separated by commas (e.g., `<Integer, String, Integer>`). It is coded immediately before the arguments passed to the class's constructor. The type argument list must include one class name for each type parameter included in the class's heading.

When an instance of a generic class is declared, the class names in the type argument list of the declaration are matched with the type parameters in the class's heading, one for one in the or-der in which they appear. These class names are effectively substituted for the type placeholders wherever they are used in the class's code. For example, when the object `s1` is declared on line 3 of the `main` method shown at the top of Figure 13.15, the class `String` is effectively substituted for the placeholder `T` on lines 3 and 6 of the class `StudentV3` shown in the bottom portion of the figure. As a result, `s1`'s data member `id` is a reference to a `String` object, and the first parameter passed to the class's constructor on line 3 of the `main` method must be a `String` (*CS103* on line 3 of `main`).

Similar substitutions are made when the object `s2` is declared on line 4 of the `main` method. Because the type argument list on that line contains the class `Integer`, `s2`'s data member `id` will be a reference to an `Integer` object, and the first argument passed to the class's constructor on line 4 of the `main` method must be an instance of an `Integer`. In this case, it is the nameless `Integer` wrapper containing a `10`. The integer literal `10` could be substituted for the nameless object passed to the constructor on line 4, because it would be autoboxed before it was passed to the constructor's first parameter.

```
1    public static void main(String[] args)
2    {
3      AStudentV3 s1 = new AStudentV3 <String>("CS103", "Tom");
4      AStudentV3 s2 = new AStudentV3 <Integer>(new Integer(10), "Ryan");
5    }
```

```
1    public class AStudentV3 <T>
2    {
3      private T id;
4      private String name;
5
6      public StudentV3(T id, String name)
7      {
8        this.id = id;
9        this.name = name;
10     }
11   }
```

Figure 13.15
A generic class and a **main** method that declares two instances of the class.

When an instance of a generic class is declared, a type argument list should always be included in the declaration immediately before the arguments passed to the class's constructor, as shown on lines 3 and 4 of the main method in Figure 13.15. Its inclusion provides Java type checking and is considered good programming practice.

The type argument list can also be included between the class name and the variable name on the left side of an object declaration statement. When used, this list must match the argument list that appears on the right side of the declaration. For example, lines 3 and 4 of the main method shown in Figure 13.15 would become:

```
AStudentV3 <String> s1 = new AStudentV3 <String>("CS103", "Tom");
AStudentV3 <Integer> s2 = new AStudentV3 <Integer>(new Integer(10),"Ryan");
```

The inclusion of the argument list in front of the variable names effectively extends the type checking Java performs. A subsequent attempt to assign the reference variable s1, whose id data member was specified to be a string, to s2, whose id data member is an instance of an Integer (e.g., s2 = s1), results in an *incompatible types* translation error. This level of translation-time type checking is usually desirable. Although the following two declarations are also syntactically correct, they are considered unsafe from a type-checking viewpoint.

```
//******** Unsafe generic object declarations ********//
AStudentV3 <String> s1 = new AStudentV3("CS103", "Tom");
AStudentV3 s2 = new AStudentV3("CS103", "Tom");
```

The application GenericClasses, shown in Figure 13.16, declares four type-safe instances of the generic class StudentV3 shown in Figure 13.17. The output produced by the program is shown in Figure 13.18. Each StudentV3 object has an identification (ID) number and a name. The type of the ID is declared to be generic on line 3 of Figure 13.17 by coding the placeholder T, included in the class's heading, as the type of the data member id. The class's constructor also uses the type parameter T as the type placeholder for its first parameter.

The three object declarations on lines 6–8 of Figure 13.16 use the preferred type-safe two-argument list syntax to declare one object with a String type ID (line 6), and two Integer type ID objects (lines 7 and 8). A fourth object is declared on line 9 using the type-safe one-argument list syntax. The types of the first argument passed to the constructors invoked on lines 6–9 are consistent with the class names these lines pass to the StudentV3 class's type parameter list (when autoboxing is considered). The four objects are output on lines 13–16 using an implicit invocation of the generic class's toString method (lines 11–15 of Figure 13.17). When lines 14–16 of Figure 13.16 execute, the Integer class's toString method is invoked implicitly on line 14 of Figure 13.17 to add the IDs of objects s2, s3, and s4 to the string s.

The reference variable s5 declared in line 10 of Figure 13.16 can only reference a StudentV3 object whose id data member is a string because its declaration includes a String type parameter. The reference variable s5 declared on line 11 can reference any StudentV3 object because it does not include a type parameter list. Type-safe assignments are performed on these variables on lines 18 and 19, and then the objects they reference are output on lines 20 and 21.

Line 23 of Figure 3.16 invokes the StudentV3 class's compareTo method to compare the object s5 references to the object s6 references. This method (lines 16–19 of Figure 13.16) compares the name data members of two StudentV3 instances: the object that invoked it and the object passed to its parameter. To make the comparison, the method invokes a compareTo method on line 18. Because the name data members used in the invocation are strings, the String class's compareTo method is invoked. The returned value is seven because the first letter in s5's name (the *T* in *Tom*) is seven characters beyond the first letter of s6's name (the *M* in *Maggie*). This retuned value is the last output shown in Figure 13.17.

```
1    public class GenericClasses
2    {
3      public static void main(String[] args)
4      {
5        Integer id = new Integer(1672);
6        StudentV3 <String> s1 = new StudentV3 <String>("Sci103", "Tom");
7        StudentV3 <Integer> s2 = new StudentV3 <Integer>(1672,"Maggie");
8        StudentV3 <Integer> s3 = new StudentV3 <Integer>(45323, "Ryan");
9        StudentV3 s4 = new StudentV3 <Integer>(53812, "Logan");
10       StudentV3 <String> s5 = null;
11       StudentV3 s6 = null;
12
13       System.out.println(s1);
14       System.out.println(s2);
15       System.out.println(s3);
16       System.out.println(s4 + "\n");
17
18       s5 = s1; //Safe
```

```
19        s6 = s2; //Safe
20        System.out.println(s5);
21        System.out.println(s6);
22
23        System.out.println(s5.compareTo(s6));
24    }
25 }
```

Figure 13.16
The application **GenericClasses**.

```
1    public class StudentV3 <T> implements Comparable<StudentV3>
2    {
3      private T id;
4      private String name;
5
6      public StudentV3(T id, String name)
7      {
8        this.id = id;
9        this.name = name;
10     }
11     public String toString()
12     {
13       String s;
14       return s = "ID: " + id + "; Name: " + name;
15     }
16     public int compareTo(StudentV3 s)
17     {
18        return name.compareTo(s.name);
19     }
20   }
```

Figure 13.17
The class **StudentV3**.

```
ID: Sci103; Name: Tom
ID: 1672; Name: Maggie
ID: 45323; Name: Ryan
ID: 53812; Name: Logan

ID: Sci103; Name: Tom
ID: 1672; Name: Maggie
7
```

Figure 13.18
The output produced by the application **GenericClasses**.

13.3.1 Generic Data Structure Classes

A data structure is an object that can store a larger set of objects, such as 10,000 `Student` objects, in a way that facilitates the operations that will be performed on them. Common operations are fetching and updating an object. An array is a data structure that is part of every programming language, and we have used this data structure to store objects such as `Snowmen` and strings. Other common data structures are stacks, queues, linked lists, trees, and hashed structures. These data structures are usually implemented as generic classes so that, like an array, they can be used to store a set of any type of object. In this section, we use the data structure queue to illustrate the nuances of implementing a generic data structure class.

A queue can be thought of as a fair waiting line that has a *front or head* and *rear or tail* end. When an object is added to a queue, it is added at the end, or rear, of the queue. When an object is fetched from the queue, the object at the front of the queue is fetched *and* deleted from the queue. This process of adding and fetching objects is referred to as a First In First Out (FIFO) process: the first object added to the data structure is the first object fetched (and deleted) from the data structure. The add operation is called `enqueue` (*en*ter the *queue*), and the fetch/delete operation is called `dequeue` (*de*part from the *queue*).

Queues are used by applications that process objects, once and only once, in the order they are received. Print requests to a shared printer are stored in a queue, as is information about airplane objects waiting for their turn to land on a busy runway, as are processes waiting to be run by an operating system.

A Non-generic Queue

The class `Queue` shown in Figure 13.19 is a non-generic array-based implementation of a queue that can only store `StudentV4` objects whose class is shown in Figure 13.20. The class `Queue` contains a constructor (lines 11–15), an `enQueue` method (lines 17–30), and a `deQueue` method (lines 32–46). The implementation of these methods make the class a *circular* queue because lines 27 and 42 reposition the front and rear of the queue back to zero to prevent them from exceeding the bounds of the array. The application `NonGenericQueueApp`, shown in Figure 13.21, declares a `Queue` object (line 5) and then adds (enqueue), fetches/deletes (dequeue), and outputs several `StudentV4` objects. The output produced by the program is shown in Figure 13.22.

The queue implementation shown in Figure 13.19 is array based. It stores the object passed to the `enqueue` method on line 17 in an array of `StudentV4` objects named `data`, declared on lines 9 and 14. The `dequeue` method returns an element of this array on line 44.

The size of the array is passed to the class's constructor (line 11) and stored in the data member `size` (line 13). The `enqueue` method returns `false` (line 21) when the queue is full, as determined by line 19, and the `dequeue` method returns `null` (line 37) when the queue is empty, as determined by line 35. The remaining implementation details are not relevant to our discussion and are typically discussed in a data structures textbook.

The application shown in Figure 13.21 creates an instance of a `Queue` on line 5 that can store a maximum of four `StudentV4` objects. Then it creates four objects and invokes the `enqueue` method to store them in the queue (lines 8–15). An attempt to store a fifth object in the queue (lines 16–18) returns `false` (the first output shown in Figure 13.22, produced by lines 17–18). The other five outputs shown in Figure 13.22 are produced by the five invocations of the `dequeue` method inside the `for` loop that begins on line 20 of Figure 13.21. The fifth invocation returns `null` because the queue is empty.

```
1 // A Non-Generic Queue. It can only queue StudentV4 Objects
2
3   public class Queue
4   {
5     private int size;
6     private int numOfNodes = 0;
7     private int front = 0;
8     private int rear = 0;
9     private StudentV4[] data;
10
11    public Queue(int n)
12    {
13      size = n;
14      data = new StudentV4[n];
15    }
16
17    public boolean enQueue(StudentV4 newItem) //add a StudentV4 object
18    {
19      if(numOfNodes == size) //the queue is full
20      {
21        return false;
22      }
23      else //add the object to the structure
24      {
25        numOfNodes = numOfNodes + 1;
26        data[rear] = newItem;
27        rear = (rear + 1) % size;
28        return true;
29      }
30    }
31
32    public StudentV4 deQueue( ) //fetch and delete a StudentV4 object
33    {
34      int frontLocation;
35      if(numOfNodes == 0) //the queue is empty
36      {
37        return null;
38      }
39      else //return an object from the structure
40      {
41        frontLocation = front;
42        front = (front + 1) % size;
```

```
43              numOfNodes = numOfNodes - 1;
44              return data[frontLocation];
45          }
46      }
47  }
```

Figure 13.19
The class `Queue`.

```
1   public class StudentV4 implements Comparable <StudentV4>
2   {
3     private int id;
4     private String name;
5
6     public StudentV4(int id, String name)
7     {
8       this.id = id;
9       this.name = name;
10    }
11
12    public String toString()
13    {
14      String s;
15      return s = "ID: " + id + "; Name: " + name;
16    }
17
18    public int compareTo(StudentV4 s)
19    {
20      return name.compareTo(s.name);
21    }
22  }
```

Figure 13.20
The class `StudentV4`.

```
1   public class NonGenericQueueApp
2   {
3     public static void main(String[] args)
4     {
5       Queue aQueue = new Queue(4);
6       StudentV4 aStudent;
7
8       aStudent = new StudentV4(1, "Nora");
9       aQueue.enQueue(aStudent);
10      aStudent = new StudentV4(2, "Logan");
11      aQueue.enQueue(aStudent);
12      aStudent = new StudentV4(3, "Evie");
13      aQueue.enQueue(aStudent);
14      aStudent = new StudentV4(4, "Ryan");
```

```
15          aQueue.enQueue(aStudent);
16          aStudent = new StudentV4(5, "Skyler"); //queue already full
17          System.out.println("Fifth enqueue successful? " +
18                              aQueue.enQueue(aStudent));
19
20          for(int i=1; i <= 5; i++) //one more than the queue's capacity
21          {
22             System.out.println(aQueue.deQueue());
23          }
24       }
25   }
```

Figure 13.21
The application **NonGenericQueueApp**.

```
Fifth enqueue successful? false
ID: 1; Name: Nora
ID: 2; Name: Logan
ID: 3; Name: Evie
ID: 4; Name: Ryan
null
```

Figure 13.22
The output produced by the application **NonGenericQueueApp**.

A Generic Queue Implementation

When implementing a generic data structure, one that can store objects of any class, it's a good idea to implement it as a non-generic version of the structure, such as the implementation shown in Figure 13.19, then, after it is tested and verified, convert it to a generic implementation. This approach is consistent with the concept of divide and conquer.

The class `GenericQueue`, shown in Figure 13.23, is the generic version of the class `Queue` shown in Figure 13.19. The code in the two figures can be compared line by line to find the changes made to produce the generic version, indicated by the yellow highlights in Figure 13.23. The first step in this conversion process is to add a generic parameter list <T> to the generic version's heading (line 3 of Figure 13.19) and then use this as a placeholder to eliminate the occurrences of the class name `StudentV4` from the class. This class name appears on lines 9, 14, 17, and 32 of the non-generic version. The new versions of lines 17 and 32 in Figure 13.23 simply substitute the generic placeholder `T` for the class name.

Lines 9 and 14 allocate the array `data` in the non-generic version. There are two options here, neither of which is as obvious as the changes made on to lines 17 and 32. The complication stems from the fact that Java does not permit the declaration of a generic array.

The most obvious change to the two lines, which is shown below, is not valid because Java does not support the use of a generic placeholder in the creation of an array. The new version of line 14 produces a *generic array creation* translation error.

```
9     private T[] data;
14    data = new T[n] //generic array creation is not allowed
```

Because all Java classes inherit from the class `Object` and since polymorphism allows parents to point to children, the following innovative change to line 14 eliminates the *generic array creation* translation error:

```
9     private T[] data;
14    data = (T[]) new Object[n]  //object can point to any class instance
```

The coercion on line 14 is necessary because line 9 declares data as a reference to an array of type `T`. We could proceed in this way and complete the conversion with the following change to line 26, but the changes made to line 14 are considered type-unsafe:

```
26 data[rear] = (T) newItem;
```

The better type-safe approach is to substitute an instance in the API generic class `ArrayList` for the array declared on lines 9 and 14. Taking this approach, the new versions of these lines are shown on lines 9 and 14 of Figure 13.23. Because the variable `data` now references an `ArrayList` object, the invocations of this class's `add` and `get` methods replace the array element accesses on lines 26 and 44 of the non-generic version of the queue in the type-safe conversion of the class shown in Figure 13.23. These two changes complete the generic conversion of the class `Queue`.

```
1     import java.util.ArrayList;
2
3     public class GenericQueue <T>
4     {
5       private int size;
6       private int numOfNodes = 0;
7       private int front = 0;
8       private int rear = 0;
9       private ArrayList <T> data;
10
11      public GenericQueue(int n)
12      {
13        size = n;
14        data = new ArrayList <T> (size);
15      }
16
17      public boolean enQueue(T newItem)
18      {
19        if(numOfNodes == size) //the queue is full
20        {
21          return false;
22        }
23        else //add the object to the structure
24        {
25          numOfNodes = numOfNodes + 1;
```

```
26            data.add(rear, newItem);
27            rear = (rear + 1) % size;
28            return true;
29        }
30    }
31
32    public T deQueue( ) //fetch and delete an object
33    {
34        int frontLocation;
35        if(numOfNodes == 0) //the queue is empty
36        {
37            return null;
38        }
39        else
40        {
41            frontLocation = front;
42            front = (front + 1) % size;
43            numOfNodes = numOfNodes - 1;
44            return data.get(frontLocation);
45        }
46    }
47 }
```

Figure 13.23
The class **GenericQueue**.

The application GenericQueueApp shown in Figure 13.24 is the same application presented in Figure 13.21, except that it declares a generic queue object on line 5. Both of these applications produce the same output, which is shown in Figure 13.22. The use of the type argument list at the end of the declaration on line 5 of Figure 13.23 ensures that only StudentV4 instances will be stored in the queue. An attempt to enqueue another type object into the queue, aQueue, declared on that line, will result in a *cannot find symbol method enqueue* translation error.

Because the class GenericQueue is generic, the application could have declared a second instance of this class to queue 100 Snowman objects using the following declaration:

GenericQueue <Snowman> snowmanQueue = **new** GenericQueue <Snowman> (100);

```
1   public class GenericQueueApp
2   {
3     public static void main(String[] args)
4     {
5       GenericQueue <StudentV4> aQueue = new GenericQueue <StudentV4> (4);
6       StudentV4 aStudent;
7
8       aStudent = new StudentV4(1, "Nora");
9       aQueue.enQueue(aStudent);
10      aStudent = new StudentV4(2, "Logan");
```

```
11          aQueue.enQueue(aStudent);
12          aStudent = new StudentV4(3, "Evie");
13          aQueue.enQueue(aStudent);
14          aStudent = new StudentV4(4, "Ryan");
15          aQueue.enQueue(aStudent);
16          aStudent = new StudentV4(5, "Skyler"); //queue already full
17          System.out.println("Fifth enqueue successful? " +
18                              aQueue.enQueue(aStudent));
19
20          for(int i=1; i <= 5; i++) //one more that the queue's capacity
21          {
22             System.out.println(aQueue.deQueue());
23          }
24       }
25    }
```

Figure 13.24
The application `GenericQueueApp`.

13.4 THE API COLLECTIONS FRAMEWORK

Programs often process information that is comprised of a collection of instances of one class. For example, a process that stores the maintenance work orders for an apartment complex, stores transcripts of all of the students at a college, or searches employee personnel records for a particular employee's phone number. To facilitate the storage and processing of information groups such as these (i.e., work orders, transcripts, and personnel records), the Java API provides *collection classes*. A single instance of one of these classes, a *collection object*, can store an entire information group.

The class `GenericQueue`, shown in Figure 13.23, is an example of a generic collection class. One instance of this class could store all of the maintenance work orders for an apartment complex, a second instance could store the transcripts of all of the students at a college, and a third instance could be used to store a company's employee records. Like our `GenericQueue` class, the API collection classes are generic, and they are therefore highly reusable.

While a queue collection object would be a perfect choice for storing work requests because of its first-in-first-out characteristic, this same characteristic (especially the deletion associated with first-out) makes a queue instance a poor choice for a transcript collection or an employee record collection. In recognition of the fact that any one collection class is not ideally suited for all applications, the Java API implements a variety of the most useful types of collection classes. This variety includes a set, priority queue, linked list, hash map, and several other collection-class implementations. These classes are part of the API *Collections Framework*. The framework also includes:

- A set of interfaces that define the generic signatures of methods common to groups of collection classes, such as the methods `add` and `remove` that add an item to and delete an item from a collection

- A set of static generic methods contained in the class `Collections` that implement algorithms that efficiently perform common operations on collections such as `sort`, `binarySearch`, `min`, and `max` whose names imply their functionality

13.4.1 Framework Interfaces

There are eight core collection interfaces, shown in blue in Figure 13.25, that are divided into two groups: those that extend the interface Map and those that extend the interface Collection. The core interface Map is not a sub-interface; it does not extend another interface. The other seven core interfaces are sub-interfaces; they directly extend an interface.

The significance of the inheritance chains shown in the figure is that a class that implements one of the core interfaces must implement all of the methods whose signatures are contained in it and in its parent interfaces. In addition, any method that can operate on an instance of a class that implements a parent interface can also operate on an instance of a class that implements one of the parent's child interfaces.

All of the core interfaces are generic. As shown next to their names in Figure 13.25, they include one or two type parameters in their type parameter lists to represent the type of the information stored in the collection. The type parameter list of the interface Collection, and all of its sub-interfaces, contains one type parameter. An object stored in the API collection classes that implement these interfaces is called an *element*. The type parameter lists of the interfaces Map and SortedMap include two parameter types. The object pairs stored in a collection class that implements Map or SortedMap are called a *key* and a *value*.

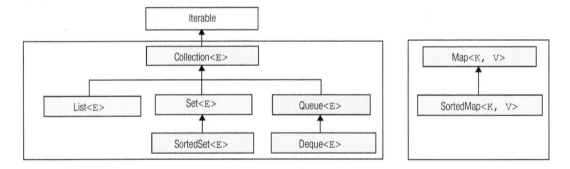

Figure 13.25
The core interfaces of the Java collections framework (shown in blue).

NOTE   *Classes that implement the core framework interfaces are called collection classes*

13.4.2 Framework Algorithms: The Collections Class

The Collections class implements *algorithms* that efficiently perform common operations on the objects contained in a collection. The class contains 52 static methods, most of which are passed an instance of a class that implements a specific framework core interface or an extension of one of these interfaces. Some of the frequently used methods are shown in Table 13.1. The methods in the top portion of the table can only be invoked on objects whose class implements the interface List. The methods in the bottom portion of the table can be invoked on objects whose class implements the interface Collection. The use of these methods will be demonstrated within the applications and classes presented in the remainder of this chapter.

Table 13.1
Collections Class Methods

Method	Description
Operate on collection objects whose class implements `List`	
`binarySearch`	Returns the index of a specified element
`copy`	Copies one list's elements into another
`indexOfSubList`	Returns the index of the first occurrence of a specified sublist of elements
`replaceAll`	Replaces all occurrences of a specified element with a specified element
`sort`	Sorts the list's elements using their overridden `compareTo` method
`swap`	Swaps the position of two elements whose indices are specified
Operate on a collection object whose class implements `Collection`	
`addAll`	Adds all specified elements, or all elements of an array, to a collection
`disjoint`	Determines if two collections contain at least one element in common
`frequency`	Determines the number of occurrences of a specified element
`max`	Returns the smallest of the elements using their overridden `compareTo` method
`min`	Returns the largest of the elements using their overridden `compareTo` method

13.4.3 The `LinkedList` and `ArrayList` Classes

The API Framework classes `LinkedList` and `ArrayList` implement the `List` interface. An instance of a class that implements this interface can contain duplicate objects in its collection. In addition, the objects in the collection have a *sequential ordering* imposed upon them from zero to one less than the number of elements in the collection. As a result, objects stored in a class that implements the interface `List` can easily be processed sequentially based on their location in the list. The `ArrayList` and `LinkedList` classes implement many of the same interfaces, so they share many of the same methods, including the ability to be operated upon by the methods in the `Collections` class.

Objects are added to a collection class that implements the interface `List` by passing them to the `add` method defined in the interface. The one-parameter version of the method appends the object to the collection. The two-parameter version of the method is passed an object and an integer (index), which becomes the new element's location in the collection. The location of the element previously at that position, and the locations of all of the elements beyond it, are increased by one. The `add` method effectively inserts the new element in between two existing elements. Instances of the `ArrayList` class and the `LinkedList` class expand to accommodate the number of elements added to the collection, and elements are not deleted when they are fetched.

Having already used the `ArrayList` class in the implementation of our generic queue at the end of Section 13.3.1 (Figure 13.23), we will use an instance of `LinkedList` in the remainder of this section to become more familiar with many of the methods these two classes share. The following code fragment adds three `StudentV4` objects to the `LinkedList` instance `underGrads`:

```
// Create a linked list and add the elements to it
LinkedList <StudentV4> underGrads = new LinkedList<StudentV4>();
StudentV4 s1 = new StudentV4(2071, "Dana");
StudentV4 s2 = new StudentV4(8129, "Annie");
StudentV4 s3 = new StudentV4(6142, "Nadia");

undergrads.add(s1);
undergrads.add(s2);
undergrads.add(1, s3); //s3 is added in between s1 and s2
```

The `get` and `remove` methods are passed an integer, which is the location of the element to be fetched or removed from the collection. When an element is removed, the locations of all of the elements beyond it are decreased by one. An overloaded version of the `remove` method is passed a reference to the object to be removed, and the `getLast` method returns a reference to the element with the highest index. The last two lines of the following code fragment remove s3 from the linked list `underGrads` and outputs object s2's information twice.

```
// Delete and fetch elements of a linked list
LinkedList <StudentV4> underGrads = new LinkedList<StudentV4>();
StudentV4 s1 = new StudentV4(2071, "Dana");
StudentV4 s2 = new StudentV4(8129, "Annie");
StudentV4 s3 = new StudentV4(6142, "Nadia");

undergrads.add(s1);
undergrads.add(s2);
undergrads.add(1, s3); //s3 is added in between s1 and s2

undergrads.remove(1); //deletes s3 from the linked list
System.out.println(undergrads.get(1)); //fetches the element 1, now s2
System.out.println(undergrads.getLast()); //fetches the last element, s2
```

The application `LinkedListApp`, shown in Figure 13.26, demonstrates the use of a `LinkedList` generic collection object to store and output student transcript objects. The transcripts are instances of the class `Transcripts` shown in Figure 13.27. Each transcript contains three data members: `name`, `gpa`, and `creditsEarned`, defined on lines 3–5 of that figure. The application also demonstrates the use of many of the `Collections` class's methods listed in Table 13.1 and the use of an iterator, which is a time-efficient way of processing sequential elements in a `LinkedList`. The output produced by the program is shown in Figure 13.28.

Line 10 of the application shown in Figure 13.26 is a type-safe declaration of a genetic `LinkedList` collection object named `underGrads` that can store a collection of `Transcripts` objects. Any attempt to add anything other than a `Transcripts` instance to this collection results in a translation error. The objects created on lines 11–14 are added to the collection using the `LinkList` class's `add` method on lines 16–19. Because the overloaded version of the method that is passed a specific location at which to insert the elements is not used, the new elements, `t1`, `t2`, `t3`, and `t4`, occupy locations zero through three respectively.

Line 25 outputs the objects by invoking the `LinkList` class's `get` method inside the `for` loop that begins on line 23. The method is passed the loop variable, `i`, as the location of the element to be fetched. The annotation produced by line 22, and the four lines of output produced by line 25, are shown at the top of Figure 13.28. The `LinkLink` class's `size` method is used in the `for` statement on line 23 to terminate the loop.

Lines 28–57 use the `Collections` class's static methods to process the elements of the list. The elements of the collection of `Transcript` are sorted by invoking the `Collections` class's `sort` method on line 30 and passing it the collection object `underGrads`. The `sort` method orders and relocates the elements within the collection object's first four locations, then lines 31–34 output them in element-location order (the second group of outputs shown in Figure 13.28). Examining these lines, we see that the transcripts have been sorted in ascending order based on the value of the students' GPA.

The API documentation of the `Collections` class indicates that its `sort` methods sorts in "ascending order, according to the *natural ordering* of its elements." This is another way of stating that the `sort` method invokes the `compareTo` method defined in the interface `Comparable` as part of its sorting algorithm, and it is left to the designer of the class of the list's elements (in our case, the class `Transcripts`) to decide what it means to say one element is less than another. Once this decision has been made, the `compareTo` method is implemented in a way that reflects the decision.

NOTE *The class of the objects being sorted using the `Collections` class's `sort` method, must implement the interface `Comparable` or a translation error is generated.*

In this case, it was decided that one transcript is less than another if its GPA is lower, and the coding of the `compareTo` method on lines 21–27 of Figure 13.27 reflects that decision.

Consistent with the description of the `compareTo` method in the interface `Comparable`, the method returns a negative number on line 26 if the object that invoked it is less than the object passed to it, (otherwise it returns a positive number for greater than and zero for equal). The implements clause included in the heading of the class indicates that the `compareTo` method will be passed a reference to a `Transcripts` instance. Omitting the parameter list in the implements cause on line 1 of Figure 13.27 would result in a translation error on that line and line 30 of Figure 13.26.

Lines 38 and 39 of Figure 13.26 invoke the `Collections` class's `max` and `min` methods that return a reference to the maximum and minimum elements in the collection. These methods also invoke the `Transcripts` class's `compareTo` method to compare two elements, so they return a reference to the elements in the collection with the highest and lowest GPA (the third group of outputs in Figure 13.28).

Lines 42–48 of Figure 13.26 produce the fourth group of outputs shown in Figure 13.28. Before the output is performed, line 44 invokes the `Collections` class's `replaceAll` method. The method is passed the `LinkedList` collection object `underGrads` and the two `Transcript` objects `t1` and `t2`. This causes all occurrences of `t1` in the collection to be replaced with `t2` (in this case, just one replacement is made).

Line 52 uses the `Collections` class's `binarySearch` method to find and output the current location of object `t4`, which at this point is the second element (location 1 in the collection). Line 57 invokes the `swap` method to swap the first (location 0) and the last (location 3) elements in the collection. The collection is then output within the `while` loop that begins on line 59 that uses an iterator to traverse and output the list.

```
1    import java.util.LinkedList;
2    import java.util.Collections;
3    import java.util.List;
4    import java.util.ListIterator;
5
6    public class LinkedListApp
7    {
8      public static void main(String[] args)
9      {
10       LinkedList <Transcripts> underGrads = new LinkedList<Transcripts>();
11       Transcripts t1 = new Transcripts("Dana", 3.5, 45);
12       Transcripts t2 = new Transcripts("Carol", 3.8, 45);
13       Transcripts t3 = new Transcripts("Alice", 1.7, 22);
14       Transcripts t4 = new Transcripts("Bob", 2.6, 120);
15
16       underGrads.add(t1); //Add the transcripts to the list
17       underGrads.add(t2);
18       underGrads.add(t3);
19       underGrads.add(t4);
20
21       //Output the transcripts sequentially
22       System.out.println("\nAll transcripts in order of entry");
23       for(int i = 0; i < underGrads.size(); i++)
24       {
25          System.out.println(underGrads.get(i));
26       }
27
28       //The Collections class's sort method
29       System.out.println("\nAll transcripts in sorted order by GPA");
30       Collections.sort(underGrads);
31       for(int i = 0; i < underGrads.size(); i++)
32       {
33          System.out.println(underGrads.get(i));
34       }
35
36       //The Collections class's min and max methods
37       System.out.println("\nHighest GPA is " +
38                          Collections.max(underGrads));
```

```
39        System.out.println("Lowest GPA is " + Collections.min(underGrads));
40
41        //The Collection class's replaceAll method
42        System.out.println("\nAll transcripts replacing "+
43                            "Dana's transcript with Carol's transcript");
44        Collections.replaceAll(underGrads, t1, t2);
45        for(int i = 0; i < 4; i++)
46        {
47          System.out.println(underGrads.get(i));
48        }
49
50        //The Collections class's binarySearch method
51        System.out.println("\nt4, Bob, is currently at location " +
52                            Collections.binarySearch(underGrads, t4));
53
54        //Use of an iterator
55        System.out.println("\nAll transcripts output using an iterator " +
56                            "after locations 0 and 3 were swapped");
57        Collections.swap(underGrads,0, 3);
58        ListIterator <Transcripts> anIterator = underGrads.listIterator(0);
59        while (anIterator.hasNext())
60        {
61          System.out.println(anIterator.next());
62        }
63      }
64  }
```

Figure 13.26

The application **LinkedListApp**.

```
1    public class Transcripts implements Comparable <Transcripts>
2    {
3      String name;
4      double gpa;
5      int creditsEarned;
6
7      public Transcripts(String name, double gpa, int creditsEarned)
8      {
9        this.name = name;
10       this.gpa = gpa;
11       this.creditsEarned = creditsEarned;
12     }
13
14     public String toString()
15     {
16       return "name: " + name +
17              "; gpa: " + gpa +
18              "; credits earned: " + creditsEarned;
```

```
19      }
20
21    public int compareTo(Transcripts aTranscript)
22    {
23      //Defines the natural order of transcripts
24      int gpa1 = (int) (gpa * 100);
25      int gpa2 = (int) (aTranscript.gpa * 100);
26      return gpa1 - gpa2;
27    }
28  }
```

Figure 13.27
The class `Transcripts`.

All transcripts in order of entry
name: Dana; gpa: 3.5; credits earned: 45
name: Carol; gpa: 3.8; credits earned: 45
name: Alice; gpa: 1.7; credits earned: 22
name: Bob; gpa: 2.6; credits earned: 120

All transcripts in sorted order by GPA
name: Alice; gpa: 1.7; credits earned: 22
name: Bob; gpa: 2.6; credits earned: 120
name: Dana; gpa: 3.5; credits earned: 45
name: Carol; gpa: 3.8; credits earned: 45

Highest GPA is name: Carol; gpa: 3.8; credits earned: 45
Lowest GPA is name: Alice; gpa: 1.7; credits earned: 22

All transcripts replacing Dana's transcript with Carol's transcript
name: Alice; gpa: 1.7; credits earned: 22
name: Bob; gpa: 2.6; credits earned: 120
name: Carol; gpa: 3.8; credits earned: 45
name: Carol; gpa: 3.8; credits earned: 45

t4, Bob, is currently at location 1

All transcripts output using an iterator after locations 0 and 3 were swapped
name: Carol; gpa: 3.8; credits earned: 45
name: Bob; gpa: 2.6; credits earned: 120
name: Carol; gpa: 3.8; credits earned: 45
name: Alice; gpa: 1.7; credits earned: 22

Figure 13.28
The output produced by the application `LinkedListApp`.

Iterators

An iterator is an object that can be used to move through (traverse) an ordered list, usually in a forward (increasing element location) direction or in a backward (decreasing element location) direction. The iterator's class ordinarily contains methods that can fetch, add, and remove the list element just after or just before the iterator's current location and determine if there is an element just before and just after the iterator's current location. The API class `ListIterator` provides all of these methods.

An iterator's current location is always either between two elements of a list, just before the first element, or just after the last element. Figure 13.29 shows the five possible iterator positions for a collection that contains four elements. The `ListIterator` class's `hasPrevious` method returns `false` when the iterator is positioned before the first element in the list, and its `hasNext` method returns `false` when the iterator is positioned after the last element in the list. Otherwise, they return `true`. The method `next` returns the element to the iterator's right *and* then advances the iterator one position to the right. The method `previous` returns the element to the iterator's left and then advances the iterator one position to the left.

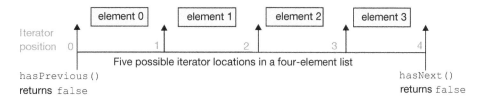

Figure 13.29
Positions of a list iterator.

Line 58 of Figure 13.26 invokes the `LinkedList` class's `listIterator` method, which creates and returns an instance of the class `ListIterator`. The method is passed the iterator position 0, which, as shown in Figure 13.29, positions the iterator before the first element in the list. The iterator object `anIterator`, declared and initialized on line 58, is used to invoke the `hasNext` method in the Boolean condition of the `while` loop that begins on line 59. The output statement on line 61 of the loop outputs all of the elements of the list by invoking the iterator's `next` method inside the `println` method, which returns the address of the next element of the array and advances the iterator.

The use of an iterator in a `while` loop is a more time-efficient way to traverse a list than the other output traversals that use `for` loops in the application `LinkedListApp` (e.g., lines 45-48). The reason it is more efficient is that the iterator maintains its position in the list after each iteration of the loop, which means it only has to advance one element during the next iteration. In contrast each iteration of the application's `for` loops that do not use an iterator begins at the first element of the list. As a result, the number of elements the `for` loops have to traverse to output the *last* element in the list is the same number of elements traversed by the `while` loop to output *all* of the elements in the list.

13.4.4 The `HashSet`, `TreeSet`, and `LinkedSet` Classes

The framework collection classes `HashSet`, `TreeSet`, and `LinkedSet` implement the interface `Set`. An instance of a class that implements `Set` cannot contain duplicate objects in its collection, as determined by the implementation of the `equals` method in the objects' class. For example if the elements in the collection were the Major League Baseball teams, an attempt to use the class's `add` method to include a duplicate team object in the collection would result in a non-operation, and the `add` method would return `false`.

These three classes do not contain a `get` method for fetching elements from the collection. They do have a method named `iterator` that can be used to attach an iterator to an instance of these classes, which is used in the following code fragment to fetch and output all of the elements of the `TreeSet` object `ts`. An instance of a `TreeSet` maintains its elements in a sorted order, and a traversal of it using an iterator returns the elements in ascending order. The following code fragment outputs *4 7 22* to the system console:

```
TreeSet <Integer> ts = new TreeSet<Integer>();

ts.add(22); //Autoboxing
ts.add(4);
ts.add(7);

Iterator anIterator = ts.iterator();
while (anIterator.hasNext())
{
  System.out.print(anIterator.next() + " ");
}
```

Instances of the `HashSet`, `TreeSet`, and `LinkedSet` classes expand to accommodate the number of elements added to the collection. Elements can be removed using the classes's `remove` method. Several of the `Collections` class's methods, such as `max`, `min`, `addAll`, and `disjoint` can be used to process elements in these three collection classes. The class `LinkedSet` extends `HashSet`.

13.4.5 The `ArrayDeque` and `PriorityQueue` Classes

The framework collection classes `ArrayDeque` and `PriorityQueue` implement the interfaces `Deque` and `Queue`, respectively. An instance of these classes can contain duplicate objects in its collection. In addition, the objects in the collection have a first-in-first-out ordering imposed upon them. As a result, the methods implemented in these classes to add and remove objects are not passed an integer index to specify the new element's location in the collection.

Instances of these classes would be good candidates for collecting the maintenance work orders of an apartment complex. Ordinarily work orders, such as polishing doorknobs, eliminating rats running around the kitchen, replacing a light, and toilets backing up, are added in the order in which they are received. Obviously, some of these are more urgent than others.

Each class adds its own embellishment to the first-in-first-out ordering of a traditional queue collection. The class `ArrayDeque` has a method named `add` that adds a new element to the end or rear of the collection, and a method named `remove` that removes an element from the front of the collection. When elements are added to the collection with the `addFirst` method and removed with the `remove` method, the collection object emulates a *last-in-first-out* collection (called a *stack*).

The `PriorityQueue` class's first-in-first-out ordering would be more accurately described as first in - with the highest priority - first out, in that the elements are maintained in a priority ordering. An element's priority is determined by the natural ordering of the objects as defined by their class's implementation of the `compareTo` method specified in the interface `Comparable`. The collection object uses the integer returned from the `compareTo` method as the element's priority. Normally, one of the element's data members is used to designate the element's priority and is then used to determine the integer returned from the implementation of the `compareTo` method. The element with the lowest natural ordering has the highest priority (e.g., a priority of 1 is higher than a priority of 2).

The application `Queues`, shown in Figure 13.30, demonstrates the use of the `ArrayDeque` and `PriorityQueue` classes to collect maintenance work orders that are objects in the class `WorkOrder` (Figure 13.31). An instance of a `WorkOrder` contains three data members: an apartment number, a description of the work to be performed, and a priority declared on lines 3–5 of the class. The output produced by the application is shown in Figure 13.32.

The application `Queues` (Figure 13.30) declares an instance of `ArrayDeque` named `tasks` on line 7, which specifies that all of the collection's elements will be `WorkOrder` instances. Lines 10–13 uses the class's `add` method to add four new work orders to the collection, which are then dequeued using the `remove` method and output (line 18) inside the `while` loop that begins on line 28. The loop's Boolean condition uses the `ArrayDeque`'s `size` method to determine when all of the work orders have been removed from the queue. This method returns the number of elements in the collection. As shown in the top of Figure 13.32, the work orders are fetched and output by lines 16–19 in the chronological order in which the work orders were added to the collection `tasks` on lines 10–13.

To remedy the fact that the use of the `tasks` collection has the maintenance man polishing a door knob while rats are running around the apartment complex and toilets are backing up, the `PriorityQueue` object `ptasks` is declared on line 8 of the application. The work orders are added to this collection on lines 23–26 in the same chronological order in which they were added to the `tasks` collection (lines 10–13). The work orders in the `ptasks` collection are fetched and output on line 32 inside a `while` loop (line 30) that duplicates the loop used to output the `tasks` collection (line 16).

This time, the output is prioritized by the value of the work orders' data member `priority`. The two highest priority work orders, given a priority of 1 on lines 24 and 26 when they were added to the collection, are output before the two lower priority work orders. The *Rats running around the kitchen* work order is placed in front of the *Toilet backing up* work order on the queue because it was added to the queue chronologically before the toilet maintenance request. Even though the

Polish doorknob work order was the first order added to the `ptasks` collection (line 23), it is fetched by line 32 after the two priority 1 work orders and the priority 7 work order within the collection because it has a lower priority: 10.

To define the natural ordering of `WorkOrder` objects, lines 20–23 of the `WorkOrder` class (Figure 13.31) implements the `compareTo` method. The integer returned from this method is used in the manner described in the `Comparable` interface by a `PriorityQueue` collection object to determine its elements' priority ordering. The method is passed a `WorkOrder` object as designated in the implements clause in the class's heading. The implements clause, which includes a type parameter list consistent with the method's parameter list on line 20, must be included in the class's heading.

```java
1    import java.util.*;
2
3    public class Queues
4    {
5      public static void main(String[] args)
6      {
7        ArrayDeque <WorkOrder> tasks = new ArrayDeque<WorkOrder>();
8        PriorityQueue <WorkOrder> ptasks = new PriorityQueue<WorkOrder>();
9
10       tasks.add(new WorkOrder("1C", "Polish door knob.", 10));
11       tasks.add(new WorkOrder("8A", "Rats running around kitchen.", 1));
12       tasks.add(new WorkOrder("8A", "Replace light bulb in hall.", 7));
13       tasks.add(new WorkOrder("12B", "Toilet backing up.", 1));
14
15       System.out.println("Work Orders Non-prioritized by an ArrayQueue");
16       while(tasks.size() != 0)
17       {
18         System.out.println(tasks.remove());
19       }
20
21       System.out.println();
22
23       ptasks.add(new WorkOrder("1C", "Polish door knob.", 10));
24       ptasks.add(new WorkOrder("8A", "Rats running around kitchen.", 1));
25       ptasks.add(new WorkOrder("8A", "Replace light bulb in hall.", 7));
26       ptasks.add(new WorkOrder("12B", "Toilet backing up.", 1));
27
28       System.out.println("Work Orders Prioritized by " +
29                            "a PriorityQueue");
30       while(ptasks.size() != 0)
31       {
32         System.out.println(ptasks.remove());
33       }
34     }
35   }
```

Figure 13.30
The application **Queues**.

```
1   public class WorkOrder implements Comparable <WorkOrder>
2   {
3     String apartmentNumber;
4     String description;
5     int priority;
6
7     public WorkOrder(String location, String description, int priority)
8     {
9       apartmentNumber = location;
10      this.description = description;
11      this.priority = priority;
12    }
13
14    public String toString()
15    {
16      return "Apartment " + apartmentNumber +
17             ", " + description;
18    }
19
20    public int compareTo(WorkOrder aWorkOrder)
21    {
22      return priority - aWorkOrder.priority;
23    }
24  }
```

Figure 13.31
The class **WorkOrder**.

```
Work Orders Non-prioritized by an ArrayQueue
Apartment 1C, Polish doorknob.
Apartment 8A, Rats running around kitchen.
Apartment 8A, Replace light bulb in hall.
Apartment 12B, Toilet backing up.

Work Orders Prioritized by a PriorityQueue
Apartment 8A, Rats running around kitchen.
Apartment 12B, Toilet backing up.
Apartment 8A, Replace light bulb in hall.
Apartment 1C, Polish doorknob.
```

Figure 13.32
The output produced from the application **Queues**.

13.4.6 The HashMap, TreeMap, and LinkedHashMap Classes

The framework collection classes HashMap and LinkedHashMap implement the interface Map, and the TreeMap class implements the Map and SortedMap interfaces. Instances of these classes store objects, called *values*, which are paired (associated) with another object called a *key*.

Each value object must be associated with a unique key object. The values stored in these collection classes are analogous to the elements stored in the collection classes previously discussed in this chapter. They are instances of *any* class.

When a key and a value pair are added to the collection using the class's `put` method, the key and the associated value are passed to the method. This establishes the key and value association. A value is fetched from the collection by invoking the class's `get` method and passing it the key associated with the value to be fetched. The following code fragment declares a `TreeMap` collection object named `patientInfo` whose keys are Strings and whose values are instances of the class `Patient` shown in Figure 13.33. It adds the object value `p1` and its associated string key *Jones* to the collection and then outputs the value after it is fetched from the collection by passing the key *Jones* to the `TreeMap` class's `get` method.

```
TreeMap<String, Patient> patientInfo = new TreeMap<String, Patient>();
Patient p1 = new Patient("Tom Jones", "2/3/1989", "643 976-4545");

//Save the key and value pair in the collection
patientInfo.put("Jones", p1);

//Fetch and output the value whose key is "Jones"
System.out.println(patientInfo.get("Jones"));
```

The output produced by the code fragment's implicit invocation of the `Patient` class's `toString` method (lines 13–16 of Figure 13.33) is shown below:

name Tom Jones, DOB: 2/3/1989, Cell Number: 643 976-4545

Fetching a value from a collection by specifying a key associated with the value is the most commonly used mode of accessing values stored in a collection and is a feature supported by the API classes that implement the `Map` interface.

Instances of the classes `HashMap`, `TreeMap`, and `LinkedHashMap` expand beyond their initial default capacity to accommodate the number of values added to them. From a speed viewpoint, a `HashMap` collection object affords the best performance, followed closely by `TreeMap` instances. A `TreeMap` collection object imposes a sorted order on the values in the collection, and a `Linked-HashMap` collection object maintains the order in which the values were added to collection. A `HashMap` collection object imposes a pseudorandom order on the values. The class of keys associated with the values added to a `TreeMap` collection object must implement the interface `Comparable` to define the natural ordering of the keys stored in the collection object.

```
1    public class Patient
2    {
3      String name;
4      String DOB;
5      String cellNumber;
6
7      public Patient(String name, String DOB, String cellNumber)
8      {
```

```
9         this.name = name;
10        this.DOB = DOB;
11        this.cellNumber = cellNumber;
12    }
13    public String toString()
14    {
15      return name + ", \tDOB: " + DOB + ", \tCell Number: " + cellNumber;
16    }
17 }
```

Figure 13.33
The class **Patient**.

The application TreeMapApp, shown in Figure 13.34, demonstrates the use of a TreeMap collection object named patientInfo (declared on line 8) to store a collection of Patient object values and the techniques used to fetch values from the collection and output the entire collection. A set of inputs and the resulting outputs produced by the program are shown in shown in Figure 13.35. The class Patient is shown in Figure 13.33.

Lines 17–20 of Figure 13.34 add the objects declared on lines 10–13 to the collection object patientInfo by passing its add method a string key and an associated value. The keys are the last names of the patients. Although a value's key need not be contained in the value's object, in this case, the value object does contain the last as well as the first name of the patient.

The sentinel loop that begins on line 26 and ends on line 41 is used to repeatedly fetch and display a patient's information, given the patient's last name. The user is prompted to enter a person's last name before the loop begins (lines 23–25) and at the end of every loop iteration (lines 38–40) via an input dialog box (Figure 13.35a). If the user clicks Cancel in response to the prompt, the showInputDialog method returns a null value, and the loop ends.

When the returned value is not null, the input string is passed to the collection object's get method on line 28. The get method returns the address of the value object in the collection associated with that string key or a null if the key is not associated with a value in the collection. When a null is returned, lines 31–32 inform the user that the person is not in the database (the collection). Otherwise, the person's information is output to a message dialog box on line 36 using an implicit invocation to the Patient class's toString method. A typical output is shown in Figure 13.35b.

When the while loop ends, the enhanced for loop that begins on line 44 fetches and outputs all of the value objects stored in the collection to the system console (shown in the bottom portion of Figure 13.35). The keys passed to the get method invoked on line 46 are sequentially accessed from the Set of keys returned from the collection object's keySet method invoked on the right side of line 44. The collection values are output in last-name sorted order because a TreeMap collection object maintains the key set in sorted order, and the set returned from the ketSet method reflects that ordering.

```
1    import java.util.TreeMap;
2    import javax.swing.*;
3
4    public class TreeMapApp
5    {
6      public static void main(String[] args)
7      {
8        TreeMap<String, Patient>patientInfo = new TreeMap<String, Patient>();
9        String lastName;
10       Patient p1 = new Patient("Tom Jones", "2/3/1989", "643 976-4545");
11       Patient p2 = new Patient("Amy Adams", "8/5/1991", "643 531-2283");
12       Patient p3 = new Patient("Norm Baum", "5/9/1945", "541 386-2371");
13       Patient p4 = new Patient("Ray Rondo", "2/6/1998", "643 736-2949");
14       Patient aPatient;
15
16       //Save the key and value pairs in the collection
17       patientInfo.put("Jones", p1);
18       patientInfo.put("Adams", p2);
19       patientInfo.put("Baum", p3);
20       patientInfo.put("Rondo", p4);
21
22       //Fetch and output a patient's value (object)
23       lastName = JOptionPane.showInputDialog("Enter a patient's last " +
24                                              "name \nClick Cancel " +
25                                              "to output all patients");
26       while(lastName != null) //not a Cancel click
27       {
28         aPatient = patientInfo.get(lastName);
29         if(aPatient == null) //key is not in collection
30         {
31           JOptionPane.showMessageDialog(null, "That person is not in" +
32                                              "our data base");
33         }
34         else //output the value
35         {
36           JOptionPane.showMessageDialog(null, aPatient);
37         }
38         lastName = JOptionPane.showInputDialog("Enter a patient's last " +
39                                              "name \nClick Cancel " +
40                                              "to output all patients");
41       }
42
43       //Output all patients
44       for (String key: patientInfo.keySet()) //all keys in the collection
```

```
45      {
46         aPatient = patientInfo.get(key);
47         System.out.println(aPatient);
48      }
49    }
50  }
```

Figure 13.34
The application `TreeMapApp`.

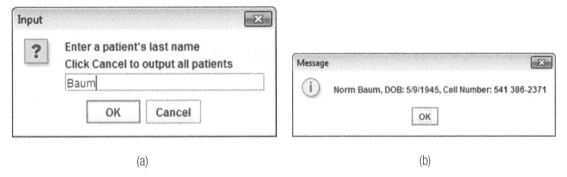

(a)   (b)

Console Output:
Amy Adams, DOB: 8/5/1991, Cell Number: 643 531-2283
Norm Baum, DOB: 5/9/1945, Cell Number: 541 386-2371
Tom Jones,   DOB: 2/3/1989, Cell Number: 643 976-4545
Ray Rondo,   DOB: 2/6/1998, Cell Number: 643 736-2949

Figure 13.35
An input and the outputs produced by the application `TreeMapApp`.

The following code fragment produces the same output as the enhanced `for` loop on lines 44–48 of Figure 13.34 when substituted for it. It uses an `Iterator` object to traverse the key set.

```
// Use of an iterator to traverse a TreeMap instance (i.e, patientInfo)
Set <String> keys = patientInfo.keySet();
Iterator anIterator = keys.iterator();

while (anIterator.hasNext())
{
  String k = (String) anIterator.next();
  System.out.println(patientInfo.get(k));
}
```

13.5 CHAPTER SUMMARY

Generic implementations of methods and classes extend their reusability, thereby reducing the time and cost required to develop a software product. A generic method is an implementation of an algorithm that can process any type object passed to one or more of its parameters. Within the method's parameter list, the names of the parameters are preceded by a generic type placeholder, such as `T` or `T1`, instead of the name of a specific class. When a primitive value is passed to a parameter that uses a generic placeholder, it is autoboxed, and the address of the wrapper object is passed to the method.

All of the placeholders used in the method's parameter list must appear in a generic parameter list included in the method's signature just before its returned type: e.g., `<T, T1>`. One of these placeholders can also take the place of a specific returned type within the method's signature, and the placeholders can be used within the method to declare reference variables that can reference the type of objects passed the method's generic parameters. When a wrapper class object is returned from a generic method, it is unboxed before it is assigned to a primitive value. The `copy` method in the `Arrays`' class or an instance of an `ArrayList` is used to copy generic arrays passed to a method because Java does not support the declaration of a generic array.

Using the syntax of generics, one method can be written that produces an annotated output of an array of any type of object passed to it, but in this case, the class of the objects contained in the array would have to include a `toString` method. The class of the objects passed to a generic method must indicate that it implements an interface that defines the signature of the methods invoked within the generic method to operate on the objects passed to it. Typically, they are API interfaces such as `Comparable` and `Cloneable`. Like non-generic methods, generic methods can be overridden and overloaded. The version of an invoked overloaded method is identified using a best-fit protocol involving the arguments and the method's parameter types.

Generic classes can contain generic methods, and generic placeholders can be used to specify the type of one or more of the class's data members. All of the placeholders used in the class must appear in a generic parameter list that is coded in the class's heading just after its class name. To maximize the type checking performed by the translator, the declaration of an instance of a generic class should include a generic parameter list that specifies the type of each of the class's placeholders for the object being declared. If the class implements an interface whose method signatures are generic, the class names passed to the type parameters of the class's implementation of the method should be included in its implements clause, for example:

```
className implements Comparable<theArgumentsClassName>.
```

The API collections framework contains a group of generic classes that implement many of the classic data structures used to efficiently store and process large data sets. These implementations include the classes `LinkedList`, `ArrayList`, `ArrayDeque`, `PriorityQueue`, and `Array-BlockingQueue`, whose items are sequentially accessed, and the classes `HashMap`, `TreeMap`, and `LinkedHashMap`, whose values are accessed by specifying an object, called a key, that is associated with an object when it is added to the data set. The `LinkedList` and `LinkedHashMap` classes provide the poorest performance from a speed viewpoint. The collections framework also includes several interfaces used by its generic classes and a class named `Collections` whose methods can perform common operations on the items and values stored in instances of its collection classes such as sorting, searching, swapping, and locating maximums and minimums.

Knowledge Exercises

1. True or False:
   a) Objects can be passed to parameters that use generic placeholders.
   b) Primitive values can be passed to generic parameters.
   c) The parameter lists of generic methods can include parameters of primitive types and/or class names.
   d) The placeholder used as a method's returned type must appear in the method's type parameter list.
   e) A type parameter list can include type placeholders that are not used in the method's parameter list.
   f) A generic method can declare a reference variable using one of its generic type placeholders.
   g) An array of any type of object can be passed to a parameter of a generic method.
   h) A generic method can declare an array of one of its generic types.
   i) Generic methods can be overloaded.
   j) Generic methods can be overridden.
   k) The syntax of the invocation statement used to invoke a non-generic method is the same syntax used to invoke a generic method.

2. Give the signature of a generic method:
   a) Named `output` that has two generic parameters and does not return a value
   b) Named `find` that has one generic parameter and two integer parameters and returns an integer
   c) Named `clone` that returns an instance of the object passed to its generic parameter
   d) Named `min` that is passed an array of any type of object and returns a reference to one of the array's elements

3. Give the statement(s) to make a copy of an array passed to a parameter named `values` whose generic placeholder is `T1`.

4. Give the signature of a generic method with one parameter that operates on the object passed to its parameter using a method with no parameters defined in the interface `Addable`.

5. True or False:
   a) Generic classes can contain generic methods.
   b) Generic classes can contain non-generic methods.
   c) The heading of a generic class must contain a generic parameter list.
   d) The type specification of a generic class's data members can be a generic placeholder.
   e) Generic classes can extend other classes.
   f) Generic classes can implement interfaces.

6. Give the heading of a generic class named `g6Class` whose code uses two generic placeholders.

7. Give the heading of a generic class named `g7Class` that implements the `compareTo` method defined by the interface `Comparable` to compare the object that invoked it to another `g7Class` object.

8. Give a type-safe declaration of an instance of the class `ArrayList` that will be used to store 200 `String` objects.

9. Give a type-safe declaration of a reference variable that can reference the object declared in Exercise 8.

10. True or False:

   a) The collections framework is part of the API.

   b) The collections framework contains many generic classes that implement data structures used to efficiently store large data sets.

   c) The items stored in an instance of the framework class `LinkedList` can be associated with a key.

   d) The `sort` method in the `Collections` class can be used to sort the values of an instance of the framework class `HashMap`.

   e) The values stored in an instance of the framework class `TreeMap` are maintained in sorted order based on the keys with which they are associated.

   f) An iterator can be used to sequentially traverse through the elements stored in the framework collection classes.

11. Give the name of a frameworks class you could use to store a data set whose elements would be fetched by specifying a value associated with a string such as *Mary Smith*.

12. Give the name of a frameworks class you could use to store a data set whose elements would be fetched on a first-in-first-out basis.

13. Give a type-safe declaration statement to declare an object in the class identified in Exercise 12 that will store values that are objects in the class `PhoneListing`.

Programming Exercises

1. Write a generic method that outputs the three objects passed to it to the system console, each on a separate line. Test it by passing it a `String`, `Double`, and `Integer` object. (Why are these three classes used in this programming exercise?)

2. Write an overloaded version of the method described in Programming Exercise 1 that adds an integer primitive parameter to the method's signature and outputs it, too. Test it by passing the method an `Integer`, `Double`, and `String` object and an integer primitive value.

3. Write a generic method that outputs the first of two different objects passed to it to the system console and returns the second object passed to it. Test it by passing it a `String` and an `Integer` object and then outputting the returned object.

4. Write a generic method that returns the larger of two objects of the same type passed to it. Test it by passing it two `String` objects and two `Integer` objects. Then output the returned objects

to the system console. (Why are the `String` and `Integer` classes used in this programming exercise?)

5. Write a generic method that sorts and outputs an array of objects passed to it to the system console, each on a separate line. Test it by passing it an array of `Integer` objects.

6. Expand the method described in Programming Exercise 5 so it also makes a copy of the sorted array and returns it. Test your method by outputting the returned array.

7. Write a generic data structure class named `arrayDS` that uses an `ArrayList` object to store any type of object passed to its `insert` method and returns the object whose index is passed to its `fetch` method. Test the class by declaring a type-safe instance of the class that can store a set of salaries: `Double` objects. Then, accept a given number of salaries and insert them into the data structure. When the input is complete, ask the user for the item number to fetch from the data structure and output it to the system console.

8. Expand Programming Exercise 7 to include two additional lines of output that contains the maximum and minimum salaries in the data structure. Use the methods in the framework `Collections` class to determine the salaries to be output.

9. Declare a type-safe data structure instance of the framework class `HashMap` whose keys are `String` objects (a person's name) and whose value is a `Double` object (the person's weight). Then accept a given number of persons' names and weights and insert them into the data structure. Fetch back the weight of the person whose name is input by the user, and output it to the system console. Finally, use an iterator to output the names and weights of all the objects in the data structure, one person per line.

Enrichment

Investigate the new features of Java 8, especially the use of lambda expressions and generics.

Investigate the differences between a deque and a queue.

References

Horstmann, Cay. *Java SE 8 for the Really Impatient*. Upper Saddle River, NJ: Pearson, 2014.

MULTITHREADING AND CONCURRENCY

14.1 *Overview* *644*

14.2 *Creating and Initiating Threads* *645*

14.3 *Thread States* *649*

14.4 *The Producer-Consumer Problem* *652*

14.5 *Solutions to the Producer Consumer Problem* *660*

14.6 *The Synchronized Statement* *673*

14.7 *Chapter Summary* *677*

In this chapter

In this chapter, we will learn the techniques used to divide a program into two or more independent execution paths, called *threads*, and how to share information between them. Using these techniques, one of a program's threads can perform a time-consuming calculation on a set of inputs while another thread is accepting the next set of inputs. We will learn that modern operating systems can give the impression that threads are in concurrent execution or actually execute them concurrently.

We will discuss the problems associated with threads sharing data, the techniques and Java constructs used to avoid these problems, and the meaning of the term *thread safe* used in the description and implementation of several Java API classes such as the generic collection class `ArrayBlocking-Queue`. We will learn how to write methods and classes that are thread safe using Java's synchronized method construct and its `synchronized` statement.

The Java syntax used to implement thread classes, create thread objects, and initiate and terminate their execution will be presented. We will learn that threads have a lifetime, and that during this lifetime, a Java thread exists in one of six states. The restrictions imposed on a thread while in these states, and the events that cause threads to transition from one state to another, will be discussed. During this discussion, we will be introduced to methods such as `wait`, `sleep`, and `notify`, which a programmer can use to transition a thread from one state to another.

After successfully completing this chapter, you should:

- Understand what threads are, how they are used, and how they can share information
- Know how to divide a program into one or more threads or execution paths

- Understand the six transition states of threads
- Be able to implement thread classes, create thread objects, and initiate and terminate threads
- Understand the concepts of concurrency and synchronization and how to create thread safe classes
- Be able to explain the Producer-Consumer synchronization problem connected with threads and its solution
- Know how to use thread safe Java API classes within a multithreaded application

14.1 OVERVIEW

In computer science, *concurrency* is the concept of executing several programs, or several parts of a program, at the same time or giving the user the impression that they are being executed at the same time. For example, one program may be displaying and updating the time of day while another program is playing a music video available on a Website. In addition, one part of the music program could be downloading the video from the Website while another part of that program is playing the part of the video already downloaded.

Concurrently executing programs, such as a time-of-day program and a program that plays music videos are often referred to as *processes*. Concurrently executing parts of a process, such as the two parts of a music video program that downloads and simultaneously plays the video, are referred to as *threads*. Figure 14.1 shows two processes in concurrent execution. Even what appears to be a single program running on a computer system could be a process with a set of simultaneously executing threads. In fact, when we consider the support every program receives from the operating system and the Java Runtime Environment, every Java program is a process with multiple threads.

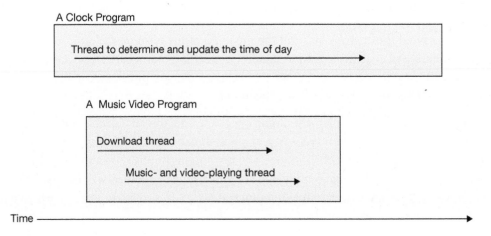

Figure 14.1
A single-thread and a double-thread process.

A thread can be considered to be an execution path through a program, and the programs discussed up to this point in the text should be thought of as having one thread. This thread, called the *main thread*, contains the code of the method `main`, and it is created and started by the Java Runtime Environment when the program is launched. As we will see, the main thread can create and start other threads. The creation and starting of threads, and the sharing of information and system resources among them, are the topics of concurrent (*multitasking*) programming.

Actual and Perceived Concurrency

For a thread to be in execution, the address of one of its instructions must be stored in the instruction register of a CPU in order for the instruction to be interpreted (decoded) and executed by the CPU's data path. As a result, two or more threads can only execute concurrently if the system they are running on has more than one CPU or the system's CPU contains multiple data paths, called cores. A system that has one CPU containing one data path can give the impression that several threads are executing simultaneously by sharing the CPU's processing time among threads.

Threads that share a CPU's data path are each given a quantum (or "time slice") of CPU time based on a scheduling algorithm, which is platform or operating system dependent. Fortunately, the speeds of modern computers permit a significant number of instructions, often in the millions, to execute during a time quantum. In addition, the time interval between the quanta is small enough to give the system user the perception that all of the threads are being executed without interruption. This is analogous to our perception that an incandescent light bulb does not blink 120 times a second when powered by 60 cycle current.

14.2 CREATING AND INITIATING THREADS

There are three ways to create and initiate the execution of a thread. All of them involve coding a class that includes a method named `run` defined in the interface `Runnable`. When a thread is allocated its first quantum of CPU time, its execution begins with the first executable statement in the method `run`. This method is to a thread as the method `main` is to an application. The thread's algorithm is coded in this method.

Defining a Thread's Class

A thread class's heading must either indicate that it implements the interface `Runnable` or extends the class `Thread` (which implements the interface `Runnable`). Figure 14.2 shows a thread class named `ExtendsThread` that extends the class `Thread`, and Figure 14.3 shows a class named `ImplementsRunnable` that implements the interface `Runnable`. As shown in Figure 14.2, the first executable statement in the constructor of a class that extends `Thread` should be an invocation of its parent's constructor. Both classes implement the method `run`, defined in the interface `Runnable`, and contain the `String` data member `name` that is initialized to the string passed to the class's constructor.

```
1    import javax.swing.*;
2
3    public class ExtendsThread extends Thread
4    {
5      private String name;
6
7      public ExtendsThread(String name)
8      {
9        super();
10       this.name = name;
11     }
12
13     public void run() //A thread's entry point
14     {
15       System.out.println(name + " is executing");
16
17       String answer  = JOptionPane.showInputDialog("What is 23 + 57 ?");
18       if(answer.equals("80"))
19       {
20         System.out.println("Correct, 23 + 57  = 80");
21       }
22       else
23       {
24         System.out.println("Incorrect, 23 + 57  = 80");
25       }
26     }
27  }
```

Figure 14.2
The class **ExtendsThread** that extends the class **Thread**.

```
1    public class ImplementsRunnable implements Runnable
2    {
3      private String name;
4      private int nLines;
5
6      public ImplementsRunnable(String name)
7      {
8        this.name = name;
9      }
10
11     public void run() //A thread's entry point
12     {
13       System.out.println(name + " is executing");
14     }
15  }
```

Figure 14.3
The class **ImplementsRunnable** that implements the interface **Runnable**.

Initiating a Thread's Execution

The code of the `main` method creates an object in the thread's class. The next step is to initiate this object's execution from within the `main` method, which makes the thread eligible for a quantum of CPU time. The way this is done depends on whether the thread class's heading indicates that it extends the class `Thread` or implements the interface `Runnable`.

If the class extends the class `Thread` and is named `ExtendsThread` (as in Figure 14.2), the following code fragment would be used in the `main` method to create the `Thread` instance `thread1` and make the thread eligible for a quantum of CPU time:

```
//Create and initiate a thread whose class extends Thread
ExtendsThread thread1 = new ExtendsThread("thread1");
thread1.start();
```

We will learn more about the `Thread` class's `start` method in the next section. When any thread is granted its first quantum of CPU computing time, its execution begins with the first executable statement in its `run` method.

If the thread's class implements the class `Runnable` (as in Figure 14.3), there are two alternative approaches to initiate the thread's execution. Assuming the thread class is named `ImplementsRunnable`, the following code fragment would be used in the `main` method to create the `Thread` instance `thread1` and make the thread eligible for a quantum of CPU time. It creates a `Runnable` object and passes it to the one-parameter constructor of the `Thread` class.

```
// Create and initiate a thread whose class implements Runnable
ImplementsRunnable runnableObj = new ImplementsRunnable("thread2");
Thread thread1 = new Thread(runnableObj);
thread1.start();
```

The alternate technique when the thread class implements the interface `Runnable` is to not explicitly declare the `Thread` instance or initiate its execution. This approach uses the concept of an *executor service* to create the thread and manage the initiation and execution of the thread. Using this approach, we can reduce the amount of overhead associated with creating multiple threads because an executor maintains an expandable pool of threads, each of which can be assigned or *reassigned* to a `Runnable` object.

The following code fragment illustrates this approach. It invokes the `Executors` class's static method `newCachedThreadPool` to create an executor service referenced by `threadLauncher`. This object maintains a thread pool and is capable of adding threads to the pool and assigning runnable objects to existing threads. Its `execute` method assigns the `Runnable` object passed to its parameter (in our case, an instance of the class `ImplementsRunnable`) to one of the threads in its pool and initiates its execution.

```
ImplementsRunnable runnableObj = new ImplementsRunnable("thread3");
ExecutorService threadLauncher = Executors.newCachedThreadPool();
threadLauncher.execute(runnableObj); //initiate thread1 as runnableObj
```

The application `CreatingThreads`, shown in Figure 14.4, creates and initiates three threads using the three techniques discussed in this section. The output produced by the threads is shown in Figure 14.5.

The first thread, created on line 8, is an instance of the class ExtendsThread shown in Figure 14.2, which as its name implies, extends the class Thread. The second thread is created on line 12 by passing the object created on line 11, runnableObj1, to Thread's one-parameter constructor. The object runnableObj1 is an instance of the class ImplementsRunnable shown in Figure 14.3, which implements the class Runnable. These two threads are initiated on lines 19 and 20 of Figure 14.4.

To initiate the third thread, another instance of the class ImplementsRunnable (Figure 14.3) is created on line 15, the instance runnableObj2. Line 23 passes this object to the execute method invoked on threadLauncher: the object created on line 16 that contains a thread pool. The invocation of execute on line 23 causes a thread to be added to this thread pool, the object runnableObj2 is associated with the thread, and the thread is initiated.

These three threads and the main thread will share CPU time during the program's execution. As soon as a thread receives a quantum of computing time, the first statement in its run method (lines 15 and 13 of Figures 14.2 and 14.3, respectively) output the thread's name data member to the system console. The output sequence shown in the lower portion of Figure 14.5 indicates that the main method ended before any of the threads were granted a quantum of computing time. The output also indicates that thread1 was granted a quantum of computing time before thread2, which was granted a quantum of computing time before the third thread. The last console output shown at the bottom of the figure was generated after the user entered 80 in the input dialog box displayed by thread1 (shown in the upper portion of the figure) and then clicked OK. At this point, the other two threads had already completed their execution.

```
1    import java.util.concurrent.*;
2
3    public class CreatingThreads
4    {
5      public static void main(String[] args)
6      {
7        // create a thread
8        ExtendsThread thread1 = new ExtendsThread("thread1");
9
10       // create a runnable object and then a thread
11       ImplementsRunnable runnableObj1 = new ImplementsRunnable("thread2");
12       Thread thread2 = new Thread(runnableObj1); //creates a thread
13
14       // create a runnable object and a thread pool
15       ImplementsRunnable runnableObj2 = new ImplementsRunnable("thread3");
16       ExecutorService threadLauncher = Executors.newCachedThreadPool();
17
18       // initiate the threads
19       thread1.start(); //initiates thread 1
20       thread2.start(); //initiates thread 2
21
22       // assign a runnable object to a thread in the thread pool
```

```
23          threadLauncher.execute(runnableObj2);
24
25          threadLauncher.shutdown();
26
27          System.out.println("main method has completed its execution");
28      }
29  }
```

Figure 14.4
The application `CreatingThreads`.

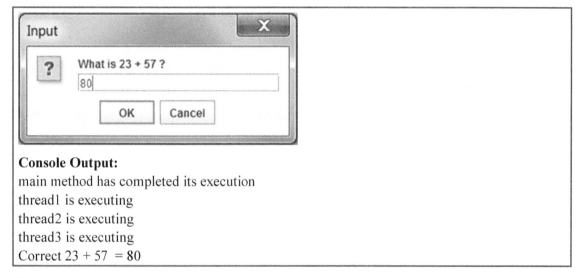

Figure 14.5
An input to the application `CreatingThreads` and the outputs generated by it.

14.3 THREAD STATES

The time from when a thread object is created until it no longer exists is called a thread's *lifetime*. During its lifetime, a thread is in one of six Java-defined states within the Java Virtual Machine. The names of the six states are: new, runnable, blocked, waiting, timed waiting, and terminated. Figure 14.6 shows these states and the possible transitions from one state to another depicted by the arrows in the figure. The green arrows indicate that the thread is becoming more likely to being granted a quantum of computing time.

14.3.1 The New, Runnable, and Terminated States

As shown on the left side of Figure 14.6, when a thread is created, it enters the new state. It remains there until it is initiated by the method `start` or the method `execute` (e.g., lines 19 and 23 of Figure 14.4, respectively). Once initiated, it enters the runnable state. Only threads that are in the runnable state can be assigned a quantum of CPU computing time by the operating system. When the thread completes its execution, it enters the terminate state. All system resources allocated to a task that is in this state are reclaimed, and the task ceases to exist (shown in the lower right side of Figure 14.6).

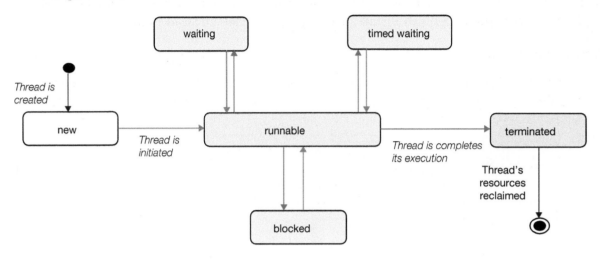

Figure 14.6
Transitions among the six states of a thread during its life.

Threads that are in the runnable state can be assigned a quantum of computing time by the operating system. The algorithm used to select which of the threads in the runnable state receives the next quantum of CPU time is platform dependent and is normally based on a priority assigned to the thread. The higher the task's priority, the more likely it is to receive a quantum of computing time when it is in the runnable state. Round-robin scheduling is a common algorithm used by operating systems to assign a quantum of computing time to tasks of equal priority while they are in the runnable state. Figure 14.7 shows this process for three tasks of equal priority named thread1, thread2, and thread3.

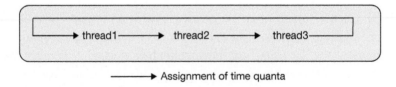

→ Assignment of time quanta

Figure 14.7
Round-robin scheduling of three threads in the runnable state.

By default, Java assigns the newly created thread the priority of the thread that created it. When an application's main method is created, its priority is set to the Thread class's static integer constant, NORM _ PRIORITY, which is midway between the class's constants MAX _ PRIORIY and MIN _ PRIORITY. This default priority value can be changed by invoking the Thread class's set-Priority method and passing it a new priority within the range of the static constants Thread. MAX _ PRIORITY to Thread.MIN _ PRIORITY, inclusive.

14.3.2 The Blocked, Waiting, and Timed Waiting States

Most threads over their lifetime transfer between the runnable state into the waiting, timed waiting, or blocked states several times. These transitions can be initiated by various events, such as the thread performing I/O or by threads invoking methods that initiate the transfer.

The Blocked State

After a thread has issued a request for input (e.g., displayed an input prompt to the user and is waiting for the completion of the input), it is moved from the runnable state into the blocked state because it cannot continue its execution until the input is complete. This transfer from the runnable state into the blocked state and back again, shown in the bottom center of Figure 14.8, is associated with the initiation and completion of a pending input or output event.

A thread can also enter the blocked state if it contains a Java concurrency construct called a *synchronized code block*, and it cannot enter the code block because a warning, called a *lock,* has been issued indicating it is unsafe to execute the code. For example, if the task of a thread's synchronized code block was to increase the pressure inside a storage tank, another thread whose task was to determine if the tank's pressure sensor was functional could issue a lock until it determined that the sensor was functional. Synchronized code blocks are also used to prevent one thread from changing shared data while another thread is reading it.

The transition from the runnable state to the blocked state and back again, initiated by a locked and then unlocked synchronized code block, is also depicted in the bottom center portion of Figure 14.8. We will learn more about synchronized code blocks and locks later in this chapter.

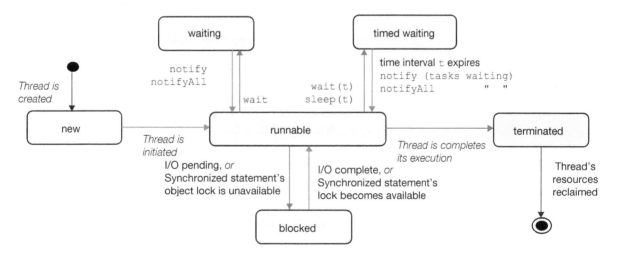

Figure 14.8
Actions and events that transition a thread from the runnable state and back again.

The Waiting and Timed Waiting States

A thread moves from the runnable state to the waiting or timed waiting state when it, or another thread, invokes the `wait` method on the thread. It can also enter the timed waiting state when the `sleep` method is invoked on it. These state transitions are shown in the top center portion of Figure 14.8.

When a thread in the runnable state invokes the `wait` method and does not pass it an argument, the thread enters the waiting state. A thread that does not have all the system resources it needs to complete its algorithm, such as when a piece of data or a resource it needs is not yet available, will enter the waiting state via an invocation of the no-parameter version of the method `wait`. The thread will reenter the runnable state when another thread *notifies* it or notifies all of the threads waiting for the data item or resource, that the data item or resource is available via an invocation of the `notify` or `notifyAll` methods. This transition back to the runnable state is depicted at the top-left portion of Figure 14.8.

When a thread in the runnable state invokes the `wait` method or the `Thread` class's static method `sleep` and passes it an integer argument, the thread enters the timed waiting state for that number of milliseconds. When the time period expires, the thread returns to the runnable state, as shown in the top right portion of Figure 14.8. A thread that cannot perform its task until a known period of time passes can use either the `sleep` or the `wait` method to exit the runnable state. The following code fragment would be used by a task to remove itself from the runnable state for one second (i.e., 1000 milliseconds):

```
Thread.sleep(1000);
```

Threads placed in the timed waiting state with an invocation to `wait` also exit the state when an invocation to the `notify` or `notifyAll` method is made by some other thread. If a thread was willing to wait for up to one minute for a piece of data that was not yet available, and then proceed with or without the data item, it would do so using the following code fragment:

```
int t = 1000 * 60; //one minute = 60,000 milliseconds
wait(t); //in the timed waiting state
```

Concurrent algorithms that use the methods `wait`, `sleep`, `notify`, and `notifyAll` to perform state transitions are quite common, however, an error-free implementation of these algorithms can be rather elusive. As a result, Java provides several levels of support to facilitate their use. Armed with an understanding of how to create threads, thread states, and the events and methods that initiate transitions between states, we are now ready to expand our concurrency knowledge base by implementing a classic concurrent algorithm: the Producer-Consumer algorithm, which if not properly implemented results in the Producer-Consumer problem.

14.4 THE PRODUCER-CONSUMER PROBLEM

The Producer-Consumer problem is a classic concurrency synchronization problem that arises when one thread is producing (i.e., generating) a resource that another task is consuming (i.e., using). For example, one thread is computing a data value that another thread outputs to the system console after combining it with other data values. The word consumer is used in the name of the problem because an assumption of the problem is that once the resource (e.g., a data item) is obtained by the thread that uses it, the thread that produced it no longer needs to maintain a record of it. (This situation was made famous by the Pac-Man game.)

In object oriented programming, data is shared between threads using an object whose address is known to both the producer and consumer threads. The shared resource is typically a data member of the object whose class implements a `set` method the producer method invokes and a `get` method the consumer thread invokes. The object is referred to as a *buffer object*, or more simply a *buffer*, because it is a holding area for the shared resource. A *bounded buffer* is a buffer object that can hold a specified number of shared items. An object in the API class `ArrayBlockingQueue`, which we will learn more about later in this chapter, can be used as a bounded buffer to safely share data between producer and consumer tasks.

Instances of the class `Buffer`, shown in Figure 14.9, can buffer an integer data item in the data member `sharedData`, defined on line 3. The single thread application `BufferDemo`, shown in Figure 14.10, uses the `Buffer` object `aBuffer` to store three integer data items it alternately produces (stores in the buffer's data member) on line 10 and then consumes (fetches) and outputs on lines 13–14. The output generated by the program is shown in Figure 14.11.

```
1    public class Buffer
2    {
3       private int sharedData;
4
5       public Buffer()
6       {
7
8       }
9
10      public void setData(int dataItem)
11      {
12         sharedData = dataItem;
13      }
14
15      public int getData()
16      {
17         return sharedData;
18      }
19   }
```

Figure 14.9
The class **Buffer**.

```
1    public class BufferDemo
2    {
3       public static void main(String[] args)
4       {
5          private Buffer aBuffer = new Buffer();
6          private int dataItem;
7
8          for(int i = 1; i <= 3; i++)
9          {
```

```
10              aBuffer.setData(i); //produce a data item
11              System.out.println("Produced " + i);
12
13              dataItem = aBuffer.getData(); //consume a data item
14              System.out.println("Consumed " + dataItem);
15          }
16      }
17  }
```

Figure 14.10
The application **BufferDemo**.

```
Produced 1
Consumed 1
Produced 2
Consumed 2
Produced 3
Consumed 3
```

Figure 14.11
The output produced by the application **BufferDemo**.

Although the application Buffer does produce and consume integer data items stored in a Buffer object, it does not illustrate the producer and consumer problem because the buffer is not shared between two threads. The main thread is the only thread in the application. It does not simulate a producer thread performing a second write to the buffer before a consumer thread is issued a quantum of computing time to read the first item written to the buffer. In this single thread example, once line 10 of Figure 14.10 executes, it cannot execute again until line 13 executes.

There is one case when this single thread producer-consumer application could degenerate into a producer-consumer problem: if lines 10 and 11 of Figure 14.10 were switched with lines 13 and 14. In this case, the consumer would be consuming its first data item before the producer produced it, and the last data item produced (3) would not be consumed. Figure 14.12 shows the application's output when lines 10–11 and lines 13–14 are switched. As shown in the figure, the first item consumed is the default value of the buffer object's integer data member sharedData, 0, which is not a produced value, and the last data item consumed is 2. The data item 3 is not consumed.

```
Consumed 0
Produced 1
Consumed 1
Produced 2
Consumed 2
Produced 3
```

Figure 14.12
The output produced by the application **BufferDemo** when lines 10–11 are switched with lines 13–14.

While this error in the application would be easily discovered and rectified because the erroneous output is repeatable and the producer and consumer are in the same thread (`main`'s thread), this type of problem is much more difficult to avoid, discover, and rectify when the producer and consumer are in different threads or in entirely different applications. The complications include the fact that the output becomes less repeatable or predictable in a multithreaded version of the application, and the producer and/or consumer's time quantum could expire before their invocations of the `set` and `get` methods complete execution.

To illustrate these complications, the producer and consumer tasks, lines 10–11 and 13–14 of Figure 14.10, have been transferred into two different classes named `Producer` and `Consumer`, shown in Figures 14.13 and 14.14, respectively. These classes implement the interface `Runnable`, so instances of these classes can be used to separate the producer and consumer tasks into two separate threads.

When a `Producer` object is created, the class's constructor (line 8 of Figure 14.13) is passed an instance of the class `Buffer` whose code is shown in Figure 14.9. The address of the `Buffer` class object is stored in the data member `sharedData` declared on line 5. The producer tasks coded as lines 24 and 25 are inside a `for` loop (lines 15–26) that executes ten times. The loop variable, `i`, is passed to the shared `Buffer` object's `setData` method on line 24. A producer object will produce the values 1 to 10 in ascending order.

Line 19 invokes the `Thread` class's static method `sleep` to move the `Producer` object into the timed waiting state for a random time period of up to ten milliseconds. This is to simulate a random number of time quanta expiring during the processing required to produce the shared data item, `i`. The `Random` object `delay` used to generate the time increment passed to the `sleep` method is declared on line 6. The `sleep` method can throw a checked `InterruptedException` object, which is why it is coded inside a `try-catch` construct (lines 17–23).

The code block of the class `Consumer`, shown in Figure 14.14, is similar to that of the `Producer` class's code block. The most obvious difference is that producer tasks (lines 24–25 of Figure 14.13) have been replaced by the consumer tasks (lines 28 and 29 of Figure 14.14). In addition to this change, before the consumers `run` method ends, it invokes the method `outputConsumed-Summary` (line 35). This method outputs two lines of statistics that summarize the performance of a `Consumer` thread. The two arrays it uses to store the statistics are declared on lines 6 and 7 and updated each time through the run method's `for` loop on lines 32 and 33.

```
1    import java.util.Random;
2
3    public class Producer implements Runnable
4    {
5      private Buffer sharedData;
6      private Random delay = new Random();
7
8      public Producer(Buffer sharedData)
9        {
```

```
10        this.sharedData = sharedData;
11      }
12
13    public void run()
14    {
15      for(int i = 1; i <= 10; i++)
16      {
17        try
18        {
19          Thread.sleep(delay.nextInt(10) + 1); //simulate data processing
20        }
21        catch(InterruptedException e)
22        {
23        }
24        sharedData.setData(i);
25        System.out.println("Produced " + i);
26      }
27    }
28  }
```

Figure 14.13
The class **Producer**.

```
1     import java.util.Random;
2
3     public class Consumer implements Runnable
4     {
5       private Buffer sharedData;
6       private int[] timesConsumed = new int[10];
7       private boolean[] consumedData = new boolean[10];
8
9       public Consumer(Buffer sharedData)
10      {
11        this.sharedData = sharedData;
12      }
13
14      public void run()
15      {
16        Random delay = new Random();
17        int dataItem;
18
19        for(int i = 1; i <= 10; i++)
20        {
21          try
22          {
23            Thread.sleep(delay.nextInt(10) + 1); //simulate data fetch
24          }
```

```
25          catch(InterruptedException e)
26          {
27          }
28          dataItem = sharedData.getData();
29          System.out.println("Consumed " + dataItem + " <---");
30
31          //record consumed statistics
32          consumedData[dataItem - 1] = true;
33          timesConsumed[dataItem - 1]++;
34        }
35        outputConsumedSummary();
36    }
37
38    private void outputConsumedSummary() //outputs final statistics
39    {
40      try
41      {
42        Thread.sleep(5000);
43      }
44      catch(InterruptedException e)
45      {
46      }
47      System.out.print("Consumed data: ");
48      for(int i = 1; i <= 10; i++)
49      {
50        if(consumedData[i-1] == true)
51        {
52          System.out.print(" " + i);
53        }
54      }
55      System.out.print("\nTimes consumed:");
56      for(int i = 1; i <= 10; i++)
57      {
58        if(consumedData[i-1] == true)
59        {
60          System.out.print(" " + timesConsumed[i-1]);
61        }
62      }
63    }
64  }
```

Figure 14.14
The class **Consumer**.

The application PCThreadProblems presented in Figure 14.15 declares an instance of a Producer and a Consumer object on lines 10 and 11, passing their constructors the shared Buffer object declared on line 8. Then, lines 13–15 associate these runnable objects with threads and initiate them. The output produced by two successive executions of the application is shown on the left and right sides of Figure 14.16. Line numbers were added to the figure to facilitate its discussion.

If there were no producer-consumer problems, both columns of output would be the same as the output shown in Figure 14.17, in which all of the values produced are immediately followed by the value being consumed. Each value produced (the values 1 through 10) is consumed once and only once, as indicated by the summary at the bottom of the figure. As the summary at the bottom of each column of Figure 14.16 indicates, not all of the data produced by the two executions of the application PCThreadProblems were consumed. On the left side of the figure, only the values 1, 3, 5, 6, and 7 were consumed, with 1 being consumed twice and 3 and 6 being consumed three times each. Similar problems occurred during the second execution of the application, as shown on the right side of the figure.

These problems occur in this producer-consumer multithreaded application because the producer and consumer are not waiting for each other to complete their tasks. Whenever either thread receives a quantum of computing time, it produces or consumes as many values as it can, without any consideration of whether or not the other thread has consumed or produced a value. Referring to lines 13–15 of the left column of Figure 14.16, the consumer thread was able to consume the same value (6) from the buffer three times before the producer thread could produce the value 7 (line 16). In some cases, the producer thread was able to produce several values before the consumer thread was able to consume them, as shown on lines 7–9 of the right column in Figure 14.16.

The obvious remedy is for the producer to produce a value and not produce another value until the consumer consumes the value. Similarly, once the consumer consumes a value, it should not consume another value until the producer produces another value. This process is referred to as synchronizing the producer and consumer tasks. Synchronizing these tasks assures that the producer and consumer will alternate their access to the buffer, as depicted in Figure 14.17.

```
1    import java.util.concurrent.ExecutorService;
2    import java.util.concurrent.Executors;
3
4    public class PCThreadProblems
5    {
6      public static void main(String[] args)
7      {
8        Buffer aBuffer = new Buffer();
9
10       Producer producerThread = new Producer(aBuffer);
11       Consumer consumerThread = new Consumer(aBuffer);
12
13       ExecutorService launcher = Executors.newCachedThreadPool();
14       launcher.execute(producerThread);
15       launcher.execute(consumerThread);
16
17       launcher.shutdown();
18     }
19   }
```

Figure 14.15
The application **PCThreadProblems**.

```
1       Produced 1                              Produced 1
2       Consumed 1 <---                         Consumed 1 <---
3       Consumed 1 <---                         Produced 2
4       Produced 2                              Consumed 2 <---
5       Produced 3                              Produced 3
6       Consumed 3 <---                         Consumed 3 <---
7       Consumed 3 <---                         Produced 4
8       Consumed 3 <---                         Produced 5
9       Produced 4                              Produced 6
10      Produced 5                              Consumed 6 <---
11      Consumed 5 <---                         Produced 7
12      Produced 6                              Produced 8
13      Consumed 6 <---                         Consumed 8 <---
14      Consumed 6 <---                         Produced 9
15      Consumed 6 <---                         Consumed 9 <---
16      Produced 7                              Consumed 9 <---
17      Consumed 7 <---                         Produced 10
18      Produced 8                              Consumed 10 <---
19      Produced 9                              Consumed 10 <---
20      Produced 10                             Consumed 10 <---
21      Consumed data:   1 3 5 6 7             Consumed data:   1 2 3 6 8 9 10
22      Times consumed: 2 3 1 3 1              Times consumed: 1 1 1 1 1 2 3
        First Execution                         Second Execution
```

Figure 14.16

The output produced by two successive executions of the application **PCThreadProblems**.

```
Produced 1
Consumed 1 <---
Produced 2
Consumed 2 <---
Produced 3
Consumed 3 <---
Produced 4
Consumed 4 <---
Produced 5
Consumed 5 <---
Produced 6
Consumed 6 <---
Produced 7
Consumed 7 <---
Produced 8
Consumed 8 <---
Produced 9
Consumed 9 <---
Produced 10
Consumed 10 <---
Consumed data:   1 2 3 4 5 6 7 8 9 10
Times consumed: 1 1 1 1 1 1 1 1 1 1
```

Figure 14.17

A problem-free producer-consumer output.

14.5 SOLUTIONS TO THE PRODUCER CONSUMER PROBLEM

One approach to solving producer-consumer problems revealed by the application shown in Figure 14.15 is to replace the Buffer class instance declared on line 8 of Figure 14.15 with an instance of a synchronized API collection class. These classes are said to be thread safe. API collection classes that are thread safe do not allow a consumer to consume unless a producer has produced and vice-versa.

We will discuss this approach after we discuss and implement changes to the Buffer class that would make it thread safe. In this thread safe buffer implementation, the wait and notify methods and a Java lock are used to synchronize a producer's and consumer's access to the shared data object. The changes we will make to the Buffer class are effectively what we would see if we looked "under the hood" of the API's implementations of its thread safe collection classes.

14.5.1 Synchronizing a Buffer Class: Synchronized Methods

The changes we will make to the Buffer class to make it thread safe involve modifications to the class's setData and getData methods that are based on the following three synchronization criteria:

- Its getData method should have a way of determining if a *new* data item has been written to the buffer and only return a value when this is the case
- The setData method should have a way of determining if the data item currently in the buffer has been *consumed* and only overwrite the data item when this is true
- When one method is in execution, the other method should not be allowed to begin execution; that is, they should not be permitted to execute concurrently, they should be mutually exclusive

The first two criteria will involve adding two Boolean data members to the Buffer class, which we will name writeable and readable. These variables will be used by the setData and getData methods to determine if they should write to, or read from, the buffer. The setData method will write to the buffer when writeable is true, and the getData method will read from the buffer when readable is true.

Before the methods end their execution, they will reverse the truth values of the two variables:

- setData will set readable to true to indicate to getData that it can read from the buffer, and it will set writeable to false to remind itself that it cannot write to the buffer
- getData will set writeable to true to indicate to setData that it can write to the buffer, and it will set readable to false to remind itself that it cannot read from the buffer

The code fragments shown in Figure 14.18 illustrate these ideas but should be considered pseudocode. They will be modified when incorporated into the revised Buffer class because they do not satisfy our third criteria: when one method is in execution, the other method should not be allowed to begin execution.

setData method	getData method
1 `if(writeable == true)`	1 `if(readable == true)`
2 `{`	2 `{`
3 `  //write the buffer's data member`	3 `  writeable = true;`
4 `  writeable = false;`	4 `  readable = false;`
5 `  readable = true;`	5 `  //return buffer's data member`
6 `}`	6 `}`

Figure 14.18
Pseudocode of the first two producer-consumer synchronization criteria.

The need for the third criterion is more easily understood in the context of the first two criteria, which are expressed in Figure 14.18. Consider the case when the code fragment of the `getData` method shown on the right side of the figure has just completed line 3, setting `writeable` to `true`. If at this point the `setData` method was allowed to execute, the Boolean condition on line 1 (on the left side of figure) would evaluate to `true`, and line 3 would write a new value into the buffer. Here's the problem: line 5 of the `getData` method has not yet executed to return the value that was just overwritten. Allowing this situation to occur results in a lost data item, i.e., a produced data item that is not consumed. Other execution-sequence scenarios result in the other equally unacceptable outcome: a data item is consumed twice. It is often critical that the execution of a portion of a thread's code not be interrupted once it begins. This section of code is referred to as a *critical section*.

Java provides a remedy for this situation by allowing us to declare methods to be synchronized. When two or more methods in a class are declared synchronized and one of the methods is in execution, the other method(s) cannot begin execution. A thread that attempts to initiate the execution of a second synchronized method enters the waiting state. Declaring the `setData` and `getData` methods to be synchronized would solve the lost data item problem we cited previously. When the methods are synchronized after the `getData` method sets `writeable` to `true` on line 3 (right side Figure 14.18), the `setData` method cannot begin its execution until line 5 of the `getData` method executes and returns the now non-overwritten data value to its invoker. The producer thread that invoked the `setData` method would enter the waiting state.

There are two subtle, but remaining pieces to the puzzle that the following two questions expose:

- How does the producer thread that was moved to the waiting state when it invoked `setData` while `getData` was in execution return to the runnable state?
- What if the `getData` method is invoked while `readable` is `false`, in which case its `return` statement (line 5 of Figure 14.18) is unreachable? (The Java version of the pseudocode produces a translation error.)

The solution to the first remaining piece of the puzzle is that the `getData` method invokes either the `notify` method (or `notifyAll` method) just before it ends. This moves one (or all) of the threads that invoked methods synchronized to the `getData` method from the waiting state to the runnable state. In our case, the `setData` method would then begin its execution when the operating system granted the thread that invoked it a CPU time quantum. A similar modification, an invocation of the method `notify` or `notifyAll`, must be added to the `setData` method.

The solution to the second remaining piece of the puzzle (what if the `getData` method is invoked while `readable` is `false`, in which case its return statement is unreachable) also has to do with a thread entering the waiting state. In this case, the thread that invoked the `getData` method effectively places itself into the waiting state to pause its execution until `readable` becomes `true`. (i.e., the `wait` method is invoked inside the `getData` method). The thread will return to the runnable state when a thread that invoked the `setData` method issues an invocation to `notify` or `notifyAll`. A similar modification has to be made to the thread that invokes the `setData` method.

Synchronizing the `setData` and `getData` methods also prevents another facet of the producer-consumer problem from occurring: *deadlock*. Deadlock occurs when two or more threads, which share resources, are all waiting for each other to complete and none of them can proceed. The situation is analogous to north bound and east bound cars at the stop signs of an intersection with their drivers waiting for each other to proceed, or north and south bound cars are waiting for each other at a one lane bridge. To see when this would occur in non-synchronized methods, let us once again consider the case when the code fragment of the `getData` method shown on the right side of Figure 14.18 has just completed line 3, setting `writeable` to `true`. If at this point, the `setData` method was allowed to execute and run to completion, line 4 of the method would set `writeable` back to `false`. After the method ended, the `getData` method would continue its execution at line 4, and `readable` would be set to `false`. Now both `writeable` and `readable` are `false` and neither method can execute.

> **NOTE** *When writeable data is being shared between two or more threads, the access to the data must be synchronized.*

Synchronized Methods

Methods are declared synchronized by including the keyword `synchronized` in their signature. The execution of a class's synchronized methods is mutually exclusive, and a lock analogy is used to explain the transfer of execution from one synchronized method to another.

One lock is shared by all of the synchronized methods, and initially it is available to all of the synchronized methods. When a synchronized method is invoked by a thread, it must first acquire the lock for it to begin execution. Once acquired, the lock effectively locks out all invocations of other synchronized methods issued by threads. When an invocation is issued by a thread and the lock is not available (i.e., another synchronized method has previously acquired the lock), the thread enters the waiting state until the method in execution surrenders the lock. A method implicitly surrenders the lock when it invokes the `wait` method, the `notify` method, or the `notifyAll` method.

The Synchronized Buffer Class SynchronizedBuffer

The class `SynchronizedBuffer`, shown in Figure 14.19, is the thread safe version of the class `Buffer` presented in Figure 14.9. It uses synchronized methods and other concepts discussed in this section to eliminate the producer-consumer problems resulting from the use of the `Buffer` class by the application `PCThreadProblems` (Figure 14.15).

The `SynchronizedBuffer`'s revised `setdata` and `getData` methods begin on lines 12 and 31 of Figure 14.19, respectively. Their signatures include the keyword `synchronized`, which declares them to be synchronized methods and making their executions mutually exclusive. Lines 25–27 of the `setData` method and lines 45–47 and line 49 of the `getData` method are analogous to lines 3–5 on the left and right sides of Figure 14.18, respectively. This is the portion of the methods that access the shared buffer and reverse the truth values of the Boolean variables `writeable` and `readable` declared on lines 4 and 5 of Figure 4.19.

The `while` statements at the beginning of these methods (lines 16 and 36), use the variables `writeable` and `readable` in their Boolean conditions. When these variables are `false`, the methods place themselves in the waiting state by invoking the `wait` method (lines 18 and 38). This surrenders the lock and also prevents the `return` statement on line 49 from being unreachable.

The variable `readable` is initialized to `false` on line 5. This guarantees that if a consumer thread executes before a producer thread and the `getData` method acquires the lock, it will execute the `wait` statement on line 38, surrender the lock, and enter the waiting state. Then, when a producer thread executes and invokes the `setData` method, the method can acquire the lock. Because `writeable` is initialized to `true` on line 4, the producer method's execution proceeds to completion (lines 25–28) producing a data item, reversing the truth values of the Boolean variables, and finally invokes `notifyAll` to surrender the lock.

After `notifyAll` is invoked, the consumer task will reenter the runnable state, and its pending invocation of `getData` can reacquire the lock. Because the `setData` method set `readable` to `true`, the `getData` proceeds to completion. Before it ends, it reverses the truth value values of the Boolean conditions, invokes `notifyAll`, and returns the consumed data item its invoker.

Instead of the `getData` method returning the buffer's data item `sharedData` on line 49, it returns the contents of the local variable `dataItem`. This local variable was assigned `sharedData`'s value on line 47. This is done because the invocation to `notifyAll` has to be coded before the `return` statement on line 49, or it will be unreachable. Here's the problem: once `notifyAll` is invoked, the producer thread could execute and invoke the `setData` method. Because `writeable` has already been set to `true` (line 45) the `setData` method will execute to completion and overwrite the contents of the variable `sharedData` before line 49 executes. If this happened and line 49 returned the variable `sharedData`, the *new* data item written would be returned, and a data item would be lost. By returning the variable `dataItem`, the `getData` method correctly returns the potentially overwritten data item.

```
1    public class SynchronizedBuffer
2    {
3      int sharedData;
4      private boolean writeable = true;
5      private boolean readable = false;
6
```

```
7       public SynchronizedBuffer()
8       {
9
10      }
11
12      public synchronized void setData(int dataItem)
13      {
14        try
15        {
16          while(writeable == false)
17          {
18            wait();
19          }
20        }
21        catch(InterruptedException e)
22        {
23        }
24
25        sharedData = dataItem;
26        writeable = false;
27        readable = true;
28        notifyAll();
29      }
30
31      public synchronized int getData()
32      {
33        int dataItem;
34        try
35        {
36          while(readable == false)
37          {
38            wait();
39          }
40        }
41        catch(InterruptedException e)
42        {
43        }
44
45        writeable = true;
46        readable = false;
47        dataItem = sharedData;
48        notifyAll();
49        return dataItem;
50      }
51  }
```

Figure 14.19
The class **SynchronizedBuffer**.

In the interest of completeness, the changes to the original Producer and Consumer classes (presented in Figures 14.13 and 14.14) necessary for them to share data via an instance of the class

SynchronizedBuffer are given as highlighted lines of code in Figures 14.20 and 14.21. Aside from their class names being changed to ProducerV2 and ConsumerV2, the only changes to these classes are the substitutions of the SyncronizedBuffer class's name for the Buffer class's name. One similar highlighted substitution was made on line 8 of the application PCThreadSync presented in Figure 14.22, which is a modification of the application PCThreadProblems presented in Figure 14.15.

A typical output produced by the application PCThreadSync is given in Figure 14.23. As shown in the two-line summary at the bottom portion of the figure, the synchronization techniques incorporated into the shared buffer object have resulted in every produced data item (the integers 1 through 10) being consumed once and only once.

```
1    import java.util.Random;
2
3    public class ProducerV2 implements Runnable
4    {
5      private SynhronizedBuffer sharedData;
6      private Random delay = new Random();
7
8      public ProducerV2(SynchronizedBuffer sharedData)
9      {
10        this.sharedData = sharedData;
11     }
12
13     public void run()
14     {
15       for(int i = 1; i <= 10; i++)
16       {
17         try
18         { //simulate data processing
19           Thread.sleep(delay.nextInt(10) + 1);
20         }
21         catch(InterruptedException e)
22         {
23         }
24         sharedData.setData(i);
25         System.out.println("Produced " + i);
26       }
27     }
28   }
```

Figure 14.20
The class **ProducerV2** that uses a **SynchronizedBuffer** object.

```
1    import java.util.Random;
2
3    public class ConsumerV2 implements Runnable
4    {
```

```java
5      private SynhronizedBuffer sharedData;
6      private int[] timesConsumed = new int[10];
7      private boolean[] consumedData = new boolean[10];
8
9      public ConsumerV2(SynhronizedBuffer sharedData)
10     {
11        this.sharedData = sharedData;
12     }
13
14     public void run()
15     {
16        Random delay = new Random();
17        int dataItem;
18
19        for(int i = 1; i <= 10; i++)
20        {
21          try
22          {
23            Thread.sleep(delay.nextInt(10) + 1); //simulate data fetch
24          }
25          catch(InterruptedException e)
26          {
27          }
28          dataItem = sharedData.getData();
29          System.out.println("Consumed " + dataItem + " <---");
30
31          //record consumed statistics
32          consumedData[dataItem - 1] = true;
33          timesConsumed[dataItem - 1]++;
34        }
35        outputConsumedSummary();
36     }
37
38     private void outputConsumedSummary() //output final statistics
39     {
40        try
41        {
42          Thread.sleep(5000);
43        }
44        catch(InterruptedException e)
45        {
46        }
47        System.out.print("Consumed data: ");
48        for(int i = 1; i <= 10; i++)
49        {
50          if(consumedData[i-1] == true)
51          {
52            System.out.print(" " + i);
53          }
```

```
54        }
55        System.out.print("\nTimes consumed:");
56        for(int i = 1;  i <= 10;  i++)
57        {
58          if(consumedData[i-1] == true)
59          {
60            System.out.print(" " + timesConsumed[i-1]);
61          }
62        }
63      }
64  }
```

Figure 14.21
The class **ConsumerV2** that uses a **SynchronizedBuffer** object.

```
1    import java.util.concurrent.ExecutorService;
2    import java.util.concurrent.Executors;
3
4    public class PCThreadSync
5    {
6      public static void main(String[] args)
7      {
8        SynchronizedBuffer aBuffer = new SynchronizedBuffer();
9
10        ProducerV2 producerThread = new Producer V2(Buffer);
11        ConsumerV2 consumerThread = new Consumer V2(aBuffer);
12
13        ExecutorService launcher = Executors.newCachedThreadPool();
14        launcher.execute(producerThread);
15        launcher.execute(consumerThread);
16
17        launcher.shutdown();
18      }
19  }
```

Figure 14.22
The application **PCThreadSync**.

```
Produced 1
Consumed 1 <---
Consumed 2 <---
Produced 2
Consumed 3 <---
Produced 3
Produced 4
Consumed 4 <---
Produced 5
Consumed 5 <---
Produced 6
```

```
Consumed 6 <---
Produced 7
Consumed 7 <---
Produced 8
Consumed 8 <---
Produced 9
Produced 10
Consumed 9 <---
Consumed 10 <---
Consumed data:  1 2 3 4 5 6 7 8 9 10
Times consumed: 1 1 1 1 1 1 1 1 1 1
```

Figure 14.23
The output produced by the application **PCThreadSync**.

One remaining issue concerning the output that is revealed in the first two highlighted lines output at the top portion of the Figure 14.23 should be discussed. Based on these outputs, it appears that data item 2 was consumed before it was produced. This was not the case.

What actually happened was that after data item 2 was produced by the producer thread's second invocation of the setData method (line 24 of Figure 14.20) and the setData method invoked notifyAll on line 28 of Figure 4.19, the consumer thread was brought from the waiting state to the runnable state. At that point, the producer thread's time quantum must have expired before line 25 of Figure 14.20 could execute and produce its output: *Produced 2*.

The next time quantum must have been awarded to the consumer thread, and its invocation of the getData method on line 28 of Figure 14.21 ran to completion consuming data item 2. The consumer thread's time quantum still had not expired, so line 29 of Figure 14.21 executed producing the puzzling output: *Consumed 2*.

When the producer thread was finally awarded a CPU time quantum, it continued where it left off when its previous time quantum had expired and executed line 25 of Figure 14.20, producing the output *Produced 2*. It was not the process of consuming and producing that was reversed; rather, it was the outputs that announce these events that were reversed. No data was lost. This same set of events occurred after data item 3 was produced, as evidenced by the third and fourth highlighted lines in Figure 14.23.

The remedy would be to perform the output inside of the synchronized methods setData and getData. This was purposely not done in order to reinforce the point that statements (such as these output statements) that need to be synchronized should be implemented inside synchronized methods and to illustrate the uncertainty of two sequential instructions (e.g., lines 24–25 of Figure 14.20 executing without interruption in a multithreaded application.

14.5.2 The API ArrayBlockingQueue Class

The API generic class ArrayBlockingQueue can be used as a producer consumer buffer. It is a synchronized thread safe implementation of a queue, which means that the solutions to the producer-consumer problems discussed in this chapter have been incorporated into the class.

A queue is a collection whose elements are maintained in a first-in-first-out order, which makes instances of this class well suited for use as a producer-consumer buffer. The first data item added to the buffer is the first item returned (and removed) from the buffer. The buffer stores references to objects because the class is a generic class. An instance of this class effectively performs all of the synchronization functionality of instances of the class `SynchronizedBuffer` shown in Figure 14.19.

The class's constructor is passed an integer parameter, which is the maximum number of elements that can be stored in the buffer at one time. The buffer is actually an array of reference variables, and this array-based queue is implemented as a circular queue. When used as a producer-consumer buffer, it is usually more efficient to increase the size of the buffer (the array) beyond one element, especially when the time between productions and consumptions can vary by a significant amount of time, because the producer and the consumer tasks do not have to alternate. That is, the producer could produce several items while the consumer is processing the first item.

The class's `put` method is invoked by the producer thread to add a data item, passed to it, to the rear of the queue. When the `put` method is passed a primitive value, the value is autoboxed before being added to the buffer. If the buffer is full when the `put` method is invoked, the method waits until an element becomes available (i.e., an item is consumed), and then the new item is added to the buffer.

The class's `take` method is invoked by the consumer thread to fetch a data item's address from the front of the queue and remove it from the buffer. If the buffer is empty when it is invoked, the method waits until an object is added to the buffer (i.e., an item is produced), and then its address is returned and deleted from the buffer.

The application `PCThreadSyncAPI`, shown in Figure 14.24, is a modified version of the synchronized producer-consumer multithreaded application presented in Figure 14.22. This version uses an instance of the API `ArrayBlockingQueue` as a data buffer. Figure 14.25 shows a typical output produced by its producer and consumer threads, which are now instances of the classes shown in Figures 14.26 and 14.27.

The changes to the application class shown in Figure 14.22 are highlighted in Figure 14.24. They include the change to declaration of the shared buffer object on lines 9 and 10, and the changes to the names of the producer and consumer classes on lines 11 and 12. The invocation of the constructor on line 10 is passed an `Integer` type argument because the buffer will store autoboxed integers. It is also passed a buffer size of one to make the application consistent with the application shown in Figure 14.22.

The producer and consumer classes shown in Figures 14.20 and 14.21 have been modified to reflect the change in the class of the shared buffer object. The modified versions of these classes are shown in Figures 14.26 and 14.27 and have been renamed `ProducerV3` and `ConsumerV3`. The type of the shared buffer object declared on line 6 of these classes has been changed to the `Array-BlockingQueue`, as has the type of their constructors' parameter (lines 9 and 10 in Figures 14.26 and 14.27, respectively).

Line 21 of the `ProducerV3` class invokes the `ArrayBlockingQueue` class's `put` method to add a data item to the buffer, and line 25 of the `ConsumerV3` class invokes the class's `take` method to fetch a data item from the buffer. The data item address returned from the `take` method is coerced into the `Integer` reference variable `dataItem` declared on line 18 of the consumer thread's class because the `take` method is generic and its returned type is `Object`.

The application does not include an implementation of a synchronized buffer class. That implementation was done for us by the author of the API `ArrayBlockingQueue` class.

```
1    import java.util.concurrent.ExecutorService;
2    import java.util.concurrent.Executors;
3    import java.util.concurrent.ArrayBlockingQueue;
4
5    public class PCThreadSyncAPI
6    {
7      public static void main(String[] args)
8      {
9        ArrayBlockingQueue <Integer> aBuffer;
10       aBuffer = new ArrayBlockingQueue <Integer> (1);
11       ProducerV3 producerThread = new ProducerV3(aBuffer);
12       ConsumerV3 consumerThread = new ConsumerV3(aBuffer);
13
14       ExecutorService launcher = Executors.newCachedThreadPool();
15       launcher.execute(producerThread);
16       launcher.execute(consumerThread);
17
18       launcher.shutdown();
19     }
20  }
```

Figure 14.24
The application **PCThreadSyncAPI**.

```
Produced 1
Consumed 1 <---
Produced 2
Consumed 2 <---
Consumed 3 <---
Produced 3
Produced 4
Consumed 4 <---
Produced 5
Consumed 5 <---
Produced 6
Consumed 6 <---
Produced 7
Consumed 7 <---
Produced 8
```

```
Consumed 8 <---
Consumed 9 <---
Produced 9
Produced 10
Consumed 10 <---
Consumed data:  1 2 3 4 5 6 7 8 9 10
Times consumed: 1 1 1 1 1 1 1 1 1 1
```

Figure 14.25
Output produced by the application **PCThreadSyncAPI**.

```
1    import java.util.Random;
2    import java.util.concurrent.ArrayBlockingQueue;
3
4    public class ProducerV3 implements Runnable
5    {
6      ArrayBlockingQueue <Integer> sharedData;
7      Random delay = new Random();
8
9      public ProducerV3(ArrayBlockingQueue <Integer> sharedData)
10     {
11       this.sharedData = sharedData;
12     }
13
14     public void run()
15     {
16       for(int i = 1; i <= 10; i++)
17       {
18         try
19         { //simulate data processing
20           Thread.sleep(delay.nextInt(10) + 1);
21           sharedData.put(i);
22           System.out.println("Produced " + i);
23         }
24         catch(InterruptedException e)
25         {
26         }
27       }
28     }
29   }
```

Figure 14.26
The class **ProducerV3** that uses an API **ArrayBlockingQueue** object as a buffer

```java
1    import java.util.Random;
2    import java.util.concurrent.ArrayBlockingQueue;
3
4    public class ConsumerV3 implements Runnable
5    {
6      ArrayBlockingQueue <Integer> sharedData;
7      int[] timesConsumed = new int[10];
8      boolean[] consumedData = new boolean[10];
9
10     public  ConsumerV3(ArrayBlockingQueue <Integer> sharedData)
11     {
12       this.sharedData = sharedData;
13     }
14
15     public void run()
16     {
17       Random delay = new Random();
18       Integer dataItem = 0;
19
20       for(int i = 1; i <= 10; i++)
21       {
22         try
23         {
24           Thread.sleep(delay.nextInt(10) + 1); //simulate data fetch
25           dataItem = (Integer) sharedData.take();
26           System.out.println("Consumed " + dataItem + " <---");
27         }
28         catch(InterruptedException e)
29         {
30         }
31
32         //record consumed statistics
33         consumedData[dataItem - 1] = true;
34         timesConsumed[dataItem - 1]++;
35       }
36       outputConsumedSummary();
37     }
38
39     private void outputConsumedSummary()
40     {
41       try
42       {
43         Thread.sleep(5000);
44       }
45       catch(InterruptedException e)
46       {
47       }
48       System.out.print("Consumed data: ");
49       for(int i = 1; i <= 10; i++)
```

```
50     {
51        if(consumedData[i-1] == true)
52        {
53           System.out.print(" " + i);
54        }
55     }
56     System.out.print("\nTimes consumed:");
57     for(int i = 1; i <= 10; i++)
58     {
59        if(consumedData[i-1] == true)
60        {
61           System.out.print(" " + timesConsumed[i-1]);
62        }
63     }
64   }
65 }
```

Figure 14.27
The class `ConsumerV3` that uses an API `ArrayBlockingQueue` object as a buffer.

14.6 THE SYNCHRONIZED STATEMENT

The synchronized statement is an alternative way of synchronizing a thread's access to a shared data item, which in this case, must be an object. The statement begins with the keyword `synchronized`, followed by a set of parentheses that enclose the thread's name for the shared data item, which is followed by a statement block as shown below:

```
synchronized (sharedObject)
{
    //one or more statements
}
```

In order for a thread to execute the statements contained in the code block, it must acquire a lock that Java associates with the shared object. If another thread has already acquired the lock, a thread that unsuccessfully attempted to acquire the lock enters the blocked state, as shown in the lower center portion of Figure 14.8. The lock is released when the synchronized statement block of the thread with the lock completes its execution. At that point, all threads that entered the blocked state because they could not acquire the shared object's lock return to the runnable state.

A thread does not have to acquire the lock to execute the methods of the shared data object when the invocation statement is not inside a synchronized statement's code block. This implies that the synchronized statement only restricts access to a shared data object's methods when at least two threads contain synchronized statements involving that object. In contrast, the *synchronized-method* construct discussed in the previous section prohibits all threads from executing any of the synchronized methods of an object until the threads acquire the object's lock. An understanding of this is fundamental to knowing how to use these two alternative synchronization features of the Java language and the restrictions they impose.

> *Synchronized methods within a class cannot be executed concurrently, they are mutually exclusive.*

NOTE *Similarly, a synchronized statement on a shared object prevents threads that contain the same synchronized statement from concurrently executing the code block associated with their statement. The code blocks are mutually exclusive.*

The application `SynchronizedStatement`, shown in Figure 14.28, demonstrates the use of the `synchronized` statement to produce an accurate count of the number of transactions made on an ATM system that has two ATM locations. Each ATM machine's transactions are processed by a separate thread in this multithreaded application. When the total number of transactions made on the ATM system reaches a maximum, which in the interest of brevity has been set to three, both ATM machines on the system are shut down.

The two `Runnable` objects (ATM1 and ATM2) created on lines 9 and 10 of the application, are instances of the class `AtmTransaction` shown in Figure 14.29. When created, they are passed an instance of the buffer class `Counter` (Figure 14.30) declared on line 8 of the application. The two ATM threads share the `Counter` instance and use its methods to count the total number of transactions made on the ATM system.

Figure 14.31 shows two sets of outputs produced by the program. The output on the left side of the figure shows the two machines being shut down after three transactions have been made on the system. The output on the right side of the figure exhibits a producer-consumer problem: each ATM machine has performed three transactions for a total of six transactions. This output was produced when the synchronized statement on line 19 of Figure 14.29 was eliminated from the `AtmTransactions` class's `run` method.

The loop that begins on line 14 of Figure 14.29 simulates the threads' processing transactions at the ATM machines with which they are associated. The synchronized code block that begins on line 19 accomplishes the thread synchronization. When one of the ATM threads begins the code block's execution, the execution of the other thread in this class cannot proceed past line 19 until the execution of the code block, which ends on line 29, is complete.

Lines 25–28 increments the transaction `Counter` object shared by the threads. Line 26 moves the thread to the timed waiting state to simulate the thread's time quantum expiring between the fetching of the counter's value (line 25) and the incrementing and setting of it (line 27). When the thread's wait time interval expires and it is granted another CPU time quantum, the current transaction count is incremented, set, and then output to the system console (lines 27 and 28). While one ATM thread is in the timed waiting state, it still holds the lock on the shared data object, and the other thread cannot enter the synchronized statement's code block. This causes the sequence of fetching, incrementing, and setting the shared data item to be uninterruptible. The code to actually process a transaction (e.g., dispense funds) would replace the comment on line 34.

When the number of transactions performed on the ATM system reaches three, as determined by the `if` statement on line 21, the `break` statement (line 23) ends the loop, and the shutdown message is output by line 36. When the `synchronized` statement on line 19 is eliminated (i.e., commented out), the unsynchronized thread execution produces six transactions before the ATM system is shut down, as shown on the right side of Figure 14.31. The line-by-line unsynchronized execution sequence of the threads that produces the first two outputs (1 and 1) is shown in Figure 14.32. As the highlighted portions of the figure indicate, due to the simulated expiration of ATM 1's time quantum (line 26 in the top-left portion of the figure), ATM 2's thread is allowed to fetch the counter's value (line 25 in the top-right of the figure) before ATM 1's thread can write the incremented value to the shared counter (line 27 in the middle-left of the figure). The result is that each ATM increments a count of 0 and outputs a 1 (middle-left and bottom-right portions of the figure).

```
1    import java.util.concurrent.ExecutorService;
2    import java.util.concurrent.Executors;
3
4    public class SynchronizedStatement
5    {
6      public static void main(String[] args)
7      {
8        Counter shared = new Counter();
9        AtmTransaction ATM1 = new AtmTransaction(shared);
10       AtmTransaction ATM2 = new AtmTransaction(shared);
11
12       ExecutorService launcher = Executors.newCachedThreadPool();
13
14       launcher.execute(ATM1);
15       launcher.execute(ATM2);
16
17       launcher.shutdown();
18     }
19   }
```

Figure 14.28
The application **SynchronizedStatement**.

```
1    public class AtmTransaction implements Runnable
2    {
3      private Counter shared;
4
5      public AtmTransaction(Counter shared)
6      {
7        this.shared = shared;
8      }
9
10     public void run()
11     {
12       int count;
13
14       while(true)
15       {
```

```
16          //use of a synchronized statement
17          try
18          {
19            synchronized(shared) //increments the transaction counter
20            {
21              if(shared.getCounter >= 3) //reached transaction limit
22              {
23                break;
24              }
25              count = shared.getCounter();
26              Thread.sleep(10); //simulate end of time quantum
27              shared.setCounter(count + 1);
28              Counter.outputCounter();
29            }
30          }
31          catch(InterruptedException e)
32          {
33          }
34          //code to process a transaction would be coded here
35        }
36        System.out.println("An ATM is shutting down");
37      }
38    }
```

Figure 14.29
The class **AtmTransaction**.

```
1    public class Counter
2    {
3      private static int counter = 0;
4
5      public int getCounter()
6      {
7        return counter;
8      }
9
10     public void setCounter(int value)
11     {
12       counter = value;
13     }
14
15     public static void outputCounter()
16     {
17       System.out.println(counter);
18     }
19   }
```

Figure 14.30
The class **Counter**.

```
1                                1
2                                1
3                                2
An ATM shutting down             2
An ATM shutting down             3
                                 An ATM shutting down
                                 3
                                 An ATM shutting down
With Synchronization             Without Synchronization
```

Figure 14.31
Output produced by the application **AtmTransaction**.

ATM 1 Thread	ATM 2 Thread
Lines 15-21	
Line 25 count=0=shared.getCounter();	
Line 26 Entered timed waiting state	
	Lines 15-21
	Line 25 count=0=shared.getCounter();
	Line 26 Entered Timed waiting state
Line 27 shared.setCounter(0 + 1);	
Lines 28 Output: 1	
Lines 15-21	
Line 25 count=1=shared.getCounter();	
Line 26 Enter timed waiting state	
	Line 27 shared.setCounter(0 + 1);
	Lines 28 Output: 1

Figure 14.32
SynchronizedStatement's thread-execution sequence when the synchronized statement is eliminated from the **AtmTransaction** class.

NOTE
Synchronized statements are used inside of classes that extend Runnable *to synchronize the invocations of a shared object's methods.*
Synchronized methods are used inside a shared object's class to synchronize invocations to the shared object's methods.

14.7 CHAPTER SUMMARY

Programs can be divided into a two or more independently executing parts called threads. Threads are instances of a class that implements the interface Runnable or a class that extends the class Thread (which implements the interface Runnable). These objects are typically created, and their execution is initiated from within the program's main method. Once initiated, their execution begins with the first executable statement in their run method, whose signature is defined in the interface `Runnable`.

During the lifetime of a thread, which is the time between when the thread is created and when it is terminated, it exists in one of six Java states named new, runnable, blocked, waiting, timed waiting, and terminated. When a thread object is created, it enters the new state, and when it completes its execution, it enters the terminated state. The remainder of its lifecycle is spent in the other four states. Threads that are in the runnable state can be assigned a quantum of execution time by the operating system, and the algorithm used to assign threads in the runnable state a quantum of commuting time is platform dependent. Events, such as performing input or output, can cause threads to transition out of and back into the runnable state, as can invocations of the methods `notify`, `notifyAll`, `wait`, and `sleep`.

Threads can share data and communicate with each other via the data members of an object, which is referred to as a shared data buffer object. The address of the buffer object is passed to the threads' constructor when they are created, and the threads access the data using the buffer class's `set` and `get` methods or equivalent methods. When the shared data is writeable, such as in the producer-consumer problem, a variety of problems can develop that do not occur in single threaded applications. The Java synchronized method construct and Java's `synchronized` statement can be used to avoid these problems.

When the `set` and `get` methods are coded as synchronized methods, and a thread attempts to initiate their execution before a previously initiated execution of them is completed, the thread is removed from the runnable state and placed in the waiting state. The thread is returned to the runnable state when the `set` or `get` method in execution issues an invocation to the `notify` or `notifyAll` method at the end of its execution. When the synchronized statement is used, the threads sharing the buffer object place their invocations of the `set` and `get` methods inside the synchronized statement's code block. When a thread's execution path attempts to execute the statements within the code block while another thread's synchronized statement's code block is in execution, the thread is moved from the runnable state to the blocked state. It is returned to the runnable state when the processing performed by the statements in the code block of the synchronized statement in execution is completed.

An instance of an API class that is designated to be thread safe can be used as a data buffer object to share data among threads in a safe, problem-free way. The generic class `ArrayBlockingQueue`, which is part of the collections framework, is thread safe. When a buffer object in this class is shared by two or more producer and consumer threads the producer threads are blocked from overwriting objects in the buffer that have not been consumed, and the consumer threads are blocked from fetching objects from the buffer that have not been produced or have been previously consumed. In addition, the buffer can be specified to hold more than one item, which can improve the performance of a producer-consumer application.

Knowledge Exercises

1. True or False:
   a) All Java programs contain at least one thread.

b) Programs with multiple threads must be run on a system that has more than one CPU.

c) The scheduling algorithm used to assign a CPU to a thread is platform dependent.

d) Two threads can never be in execution at the same time.

e) A thread's class must implement the Java API class `Runnable`.

f) The method `start` can be used to initiate the execution of a thread.

g) A thread's class does not have to contain a method named `run`.

h) Once a thread begins its execution, it always continues to execute until it completes its execution.

2. If you wanted a thread to output the message *Thread1 is executing* as soon as it begins executing, where would you code the output statement?

3. Give the states a Java thread can be in during its lifetime.

4. In which state must a Java thread be for it to receive a quantum of execution time?

5. Give the method(s) invoked to place a thread in the waiting state.

6. Give the method(s) invoked to place a thread in the timed waiting state.

7. Give two ways a thread could enter the waiting state.

8. Give two ways a thread could enter the blocked state.

9. True or false:
   a) A thread can place itself into the waiting state.
   b) A thread can remain in the waiting state indefinitely.
   c) When a thread leaves the blocked state, it enters the waiting state.
   d) A thread can be in two states at the same time.
   e) A thread in the terminated state can return to the runnable state.
   f) After a thread's execution is initiated, it enters the new state.
   g) Once a thread leaves the runnable state, it cannot return to that state.
   h) The invocation `wait(3)` places a thread in the timed waiting state for three seconds.

10. Give the code to:
    a) Create and initiate the execution of a thread whose class `Output` extends the class `Thread`.
    b) Create and initiate the execution of a thread whose class `Input` implements the interface `Runnable`.
    c) Accomplish Exercise 9c using an executor service.

11. Explain the producer and consumer problem and some of the solutions to it.

12. Define the term thread safe in the context in which it is used in the API documentation.

13. Give the two features of Java that can be used to synchronize the access to a shared buffer object.

14. True or false:

   a) A producer thread reads data from a shared buffer.

   b) If threads sharing a data item only fetch its value, there is no need to synchronize access to it.

   c) All of the API classes are thread safe.

   d) The API class `ArrayBlockingQueue` is thread safe.

   e) When a class that is thread safe is used to share data among threads, deadlock cannot occur.

Programming Exercises

In the following exercises, do not use an API class to share data between threads unless explicitly told to do so.

1. Give a thread safe invocation of the `getY` method on the shared buffer object `xyLocation` that is an instance of a non-thread safe class.

2. A thread safe class can be used to share its string data member `title` among concurrent threads. Give the code of the class's `setTitle` method.

3. Write a program that creates and launches a thread that outputs the string *Happy Birthday Nadia* a given number of times to the system console, one output per line. The number of times to perform the output will be input by the program user via a message dialog box and passed to the thread class's one-parameter constructor.

4. Write a program that creates and launches two threads that output their names a given number of times to the system console, one output per line. Their names and the number of times to output their names will be input by the program user via a message dialog box and passed to the thread class's two-parameter constructor. The two threads should be instances of the same class and launched after all the user I/O is complete. Use the program to demonstrate, via the program's output, that threads share a CPU's computing time.

5. Repeat Exercise 2, but this time, the threads should be instances of two different classes, and the thread that produces the most output should complete its output before the other thread begins its output, regardless of the order in which the threads are launched. Verify the correctness of your program when one of the threads produces a large amount of output by reversing the order in which the threads are launched.

6. Write a program that computes and outputs two terms of the Fibonacci sequence whose term numbers are input by the program user, each term being calculated concurrently by a separate thread. After accepting the two inputs, the application will create and launch the threads. The thread class should invoke the recursive method given below to perform the calculation. Use the program to discover a set of inputs that causes the first thread launched to complete its execution first and a set of inputs that causes the second thread launched to complete its execution first.

```
public static long fibonacci(long n)
{
    if(n==1 || n==2)
```

```
  {
    return 1;
  }
  else
  {
    return(fib(n-1) + fib(n-2));
  }
}
```

7. Write a program that repeatedly asks the user to enter an integer via a message box and outputs the integer to the system console, until the user enters -1. The input and output should be performed by two separate threads. After each output, the output thread should enter the timed waiting state for a random amount of time between 1 and 20 seconds. Examine the output to be sure that every number input is output when you enter the inputs as rapidly as possible.

8. Write a program that repeatedly computes and outputs the nth term of the Fibonacci sequence, with the term number being input by the program's user, until the user enters -1. The main method will launch two threads: one that performs the input and another that calculates and outputs the value of the term to the system console. Examine the output to make sure that there is an output for every input when the term numbers are input as rapidly as possible and the term numbers are in the range of 30–50. The calculation/output thread should invoke the method given in Exercise 6 to compute the value of the Fibonacci term. Perform the synchronization using synchronized methods in the buffer class.

9. Repeat Exercise 8 using synchronized statements.

10. Repeat Exercise 8 using an instance of the API `ArrayBlockingQueue` class as a shared data buffer. The buffer should only hold one data item. Which approach is less work and therefore more efficient?

11. Repeat Exercise 10 using an instance of the API `ArrayBlockingQueue` class that can hold four shared data items. Discover the range of Fibonacci term numbers for which this sized buffer noticeably improves the program's performance and explain why this is the case.

Enrichment

1. Investigate classical synchronization problems such as the Dining Philosophers problem and the Readers-Writers problem.

2. Explore other thread synchronization techniques used in hardware or software.

3. Find other examples of synchronization in everyday problems, such as accessing a shared database.

4. Look for other synchronization problems such as the Sleeping Barber problem and explain how these are similar to problems presented in this chapter.

References

Silberschatz, Abraham, et al. *Operating System Concepts*, 9th Ed. New York: John Wiley and Sons, 2013.

DESCRIPTION OF THE
GAME ENVIRONMENT

A.1 OVERVIEW OF THE GAME ENVIRONMENT

The game environment is comprised of the interface `Drawable` and the two classes `DrawableAdapter` and `GameBoard`. To use the game environment in an application, the interface and these two classes must be included as part of the application (see Appendix B).

Figure A.1 shows a Java application that displays the game environment's window shown in Figure A.2. It assumes the game environment package `edu.sjcny.gpv1` has been added to the system's CLASSPATH variable. If the alternate approach described in Appendix B and in the *IDE Specific Tools* subfolder contained on the book's DVD, which does not require a change in the system's CLASSPATH variable, was used to incorporate the game environment into the application's project, the import statement may not be necessary.

```
1   import edu.sjcny.gpv1.*; //May not be necessary
2   public class GameWindowDemo extends DrawableAdapter
3   {
4     static GameWindowDemo ga = new GameWindowDemo();
5     static GameBoard gb = new GameBoard(ga, "The Game's Title");
6
7     public static void main(String[] args)
8     {
9        showGameBoard(gb);
10    }
11 }
```

Figure A.1
The application **GameWindowDemo** that displays the game environment window.

As shown on line 2 of Figure A.1, game programs that use the game environment must extend the class `DrawableAdapter` and declare a static class level instance of the application's class using the default (no-parameter) constructor, as shown on line 4. Then, an instance of the class `GameBoard` is declared, passing the constructor the class level instance of the application's class and the title of the game (line 5). Finally, the `showGameBoard` method in the `DrawableAdapter` class is invoked from within the `main` method (line 9) and passed the `GameBoard` object declared on line 5. This method displays the application's window shown in Figure A.2.

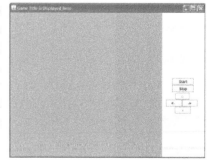

Figure A.2
A game application's window.

The Game Window

As shown in Figure A.2, a game application's window contains six buttons on its right side. The large pink panel to the left of the buttons is called the game board. Game piece objects are displayed on the game board. The color of the game board can be changed by invoking the API Component class's setBackground method on the GameBoard object (declared on line 5 of Figure A.1) and passing it the new board color (an instance of an API Color class object).

Timers and Timer Methods

In addition to the six buttons, a GameBoard object has three timers associated with it. These begin ticking when the game's player clicks the game window's Start button, and they stop ticking when the game window's Stop button is clicked. The GameBoard class contains methods (subprograms) that the programmer can invoke to stop and start a timer, and a method to change the rate at which a timer ticks. These methods are invoked on the GameBoard object declared on line 5 of Figure A.1. Section A.2.1 gives the signatures and a description of each of these methods. By default, the tick rates of the timers (named 1, 2, and 3) are once every second, once every half second, and once every quarter second, respectively.

Each timer has a call back method, or subprogram, associated with it, which the game environment invokes every time the timer ticks. The names of the methods, which are described in Section A.2.3, are timer1, timer2, and timer3. The class DrawableAdapter contains empty implementations of the methods. If the programmer includes (overrides) these methods in a game program, the game environment will invoke (or "call back") the programmer's versions of the methods after every tick of the timers. Java code placed inside of these methods can be used to keep track of a game's time and to animate objects on the game board.

Game Player Action Methods

There are eight other call back methods in the game environment, which are described in Section A.2.3. Seven of these are invoked by the game environment when the game player performs input actions common to most games. Four of these are associated with the game window's left, right, up, and down buttons, one is associated with the keyboard, and two are associated with the mouse. Empty implementations of the methods are coded in the class DrawableAdapter. If the programmer includes (overrides) these methods in a game program, the game environment invokes (calls back) the programmer's overridden version of the methods every time the game player clicks a directional button, presses a keyboard key, or drags or clicks the mouse on the game board.

The eighth call back method in this group of methods is associated with redrawing the game window. It is called by the game environment every time the game window needs to be redrawn (e.g., is minimized and then restored) and every time the seven game player input action call back methods or the three timer call back methods complete their execution. An empty implementation of this method is also included in DrawableAdapter class.

Game Window Coordinate System

The game window has a Cartesian coordinate system associated with it as shown in Figure A.3. The coordinate system's origin is in the upper left corner of the game window, with the positive x direction to the right and the positive y direction downward. The height and width of the top and left borders of the window place the upper left corner of the game board at (5, 30). The game window can be sized by using the last two parameters of the game board's four-parameter constructor to specify the coordinates of the lower right corner of the game board, which defaults to (500, 500).

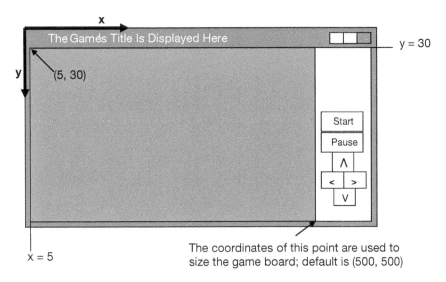

Figure A.3
The game environment coordinate system.

A.2 DESCRIPTION OF THE GAME ENVIRONMENT'S CLASSES AND INTERFACE

The game environment is comprised of two classes, named `GameBoard` and `DrawableAdapter`, and one interface named `Drawable`.

A.2.1 The GameBoard Class

The class `GameBoard` contains two constructors. One creates a default-sized game board with a programmer specified title, and the other adds the ability to specify the game board's size. A game application must construct a static `GameBoard` object and pass it a static instance of the application's class (see lines 4 and 5 of Figure A.1). Assuming the static instance of the application class was named `ga`, the following line of code creates the `GameBoard` instance `qb` with a default game board size, 500 x 500 pixels:

```
static GameBoard gb = new GameBoard(ga, "The Game's Title");
```

The GameBoard object can be used within the game application class to invoke the class's other three methods that are used to set the time increment of any of the GameBoard object's three timers and to start and stop these timers. The following invocation stops timer 2:

```
gb.stopTimer(2);
```

Constructors

public GameBoard(Object app, String windowTitle)

This method constructs a GameBoard object, defaulting to the coordinates of the lower right corner of the game board to (500, 500).

Parameters:

> app is an instance of the application's class.
> windowTitle will be displayed as the title of the application's window in its title bar.

public GameBoard(Object app, String windowTitle,
                     int xMaxValue, **int** yMaxValue)

This method constructs a GameBoard object whose lower-right corner is specified by the last two arguments passed to it.

Parameters:

> app is an instance of the application's class.
> windowTitle will be displayed as the title of the application's window in its title bar.
> xMaxValue is the x-pixel coordinate of the lower-right corner of the game board.
> yMaxValue is the y-pixel coordinate of the lower-right corner of the game board.

Methods

public void setTimerInterval(**int** timerNumber, **int** interval)

This method sets the interval of one of the game environment's three timers. The default increments for the timers are 1000ms (1 second) for timer 1, 500ms (1/2 second) for timer 2, and 250 ms (1/4 second) for timer 3.

Parameters:

> timerNumber is the number of the timer (1, 2, or 3) whose interval is being set.
> interval is the time between ticks of the timer in milliseconds (e.g., 1000 = 1 second).

public void startTimer(**int** timerNumber)

This method starts the timer whose number (1, 2, or 3) is passed to it. While the timer is ticking, the timer's call back method (timer1, timer2, or timer3) will be executed on each subsequent tick of the timer. Ticking is stopped when the game player clicks the game board's Pause button or when the GameBoard class's stopTimer method is invoked. Ticking is restarted when the Start button is clicked or this method is reinvoked.

Parameters:

timerNumber designates the timer to be started: 1, 2, or 3.

public void stopTimer(**int** timerNumber)

This method stops the timer whose number (1, 2, or 3) is passed to it. After this method is invoked, clicking the game board's Start button will *not* restart the timer. The timer's call back method (timer1, timer2, or timer3) will not be executed until the timer is started again via an invocation of the startTimer method, which will also reactivate the game board's Start button.

Parameters:

timerNumber designates the timer to be stopped: 1, 2, or 3.

A.2.2 The DrawableAdaper Class

A game program's class must extend the class DrawableAdaper (as on line 2 of Figure A.1). It provides empty implementations of the eleven call back methods defined in the game package interface Drawable. A description of these eleven methods is given in Section A.2.3. In addition, it provides a method that displays an instance of a GameBoard object passed to it (line 9 of Figure A.1).

Methods of the Class DrawableAdapter

public static void showGameBoard(GameBoard gb)

This method displays the game program's window. Normally, it is invoked as the last statement in the game program's main method.

Parameters:

gb is the application's GameBoard object.

A.2.3 The Interface Drawable

The interface Drawable defines eleven call back methods invoked by the game environment. They are coded (as required) in the game application's class (the class that contains the method main). They are used to service various actions by the game's player (e.g., a mouse click or drag, a keystroke, or a button click), and to perform processing such as animation every time a game environment's timer ticks.

The call back method draw is invoked by the game environment when the game window has to be redrawn (e.g., it is dragged to a new location) and after any of the other ten call back methods complete their execution.

Call Back Methods

`public void` draw(Graphics g)

This method is invoked when the game application window is initially displayed or needs to be redisplayed and each time one of the other ten call back methods complete their execution.

Parameters:

g is an instance of the API class Graphics attached to the game board, which is passed into this method when it is invoked by the game environment. It can be used to draw two-dimensional shapes on the game board by invoking the methods in the Graphics class.

`public void` timer1()

This method is invoked every time timer 1 ticks. The timer ticking can be started or stopped by invoking the GameBoard class's startTimer and stopTimer methods, respectively. If the timer is ticking, it is stopped whenever the Stop button in the game's window is clicked and restarted whenever the Start button in the game's window is clicked.

`public void` timer2()

This method is invoked every time timer 2 ticks. The timer ticking can be started or stopped by invoking the GameBoard class's startTimer and stopTimer methods, respectively. If the timer is ticking, it is stopped whenever the Stop button in the game's window is clicked and restarted whenever the Start button in the game's window is clicked.

`public void` timer3()

This method is invoked every time timer 3 ticks. The timer ticking can be started or stopped by invoking the GameBoard class's startTimer and stopTimer methods, respectively. If the timer is ticking, it is stopped whenever the Stop button in the game's window is clicked and restarted whenever the Start button in the game's window is clicked.

`public void` leftButton()

This method is invoked whenever the Left button in the game's window is clicked.

`public void` rightButton()

This method is invoked whenever the Right button in the game's window is clicked.

`public void` upButton()

This method is invoked whenever the Up button in the game's window is clicked.

`public void` downButton()

This method is invoked whenever the Down button in the game's window is clicked.

`public void` keyStruck(**char** key)

This method is invoked whenever a key on the keyboard is struck. If the key is held down, the method is continually invoked until the key is released.

Parameters:

key contains the upper case version of the character that was struck. The cursor control keys return 'L', 'R', 'U' or 'D' when the left, right, up, or down arrows are struck.

public void mouseClicked(int x, int y, int buttonPressed)

This method is invoked whenever a mouse button is clicked.

Parameters:

x and y are the game board coordinates of the mouse cursor location at the time the mouse was clicked.

buttonPressed contains a 1 if the left mouse button was clicked or a 3 if the right mouse button was clicked.

public void mouseDragged(int x, int y)

This method is continually invoked while the mouse is being dragged.

Parameters

x and y are the game board coordinates of the mouse cursor location at the time the method is invoked.

USING THE GAME
ENVIRONMENT PACKAGE

The game environment can be easily used within the Eclipse, NetBeans, and JCreator IDEs without changing the operating system's CLASSPATH variable by following the IDE-specific directions listed below. Alternately, the package `edu.sjcny.gbvl`, which is in the `Package` subfolder of the `Game Environment\Class, Package and JAR file` folder on the DVD that accompanies this text can be stored on your system and added to its CLASSPATH variable. Then, the following import statement can be used to incorporate the game environment into a game application:

```
import edu.sjcny.gpvl.*;
```

NON-CLASSPATH ALTERING IDE-SPECIFIC INSTRUCTIONS

Eclipse IDE
Method 1: Import the Eclipse project template

1. Create a folder and bring up Eclipse into that folder.
2. Import the project `EclipseGameTemplate7` into the folder.
   - Click File - Import – General - Existing Projects into Workspace – Next
   - Browse to the DVD folder:
     ```
     Game Environment\IDE Specific Tools\Eclipse\Workspace
     ```
     and click the `EclipseGameTemplate7` template folder, then click OK
   - Check the box next to *Copy Projects Into Workspace*, then click Finish
3. Open the project `EclipseGameTemplate7` and add the program-specific code to it.

Method 2: Add the game environment JAR file or its classes to a new Eclipse project

Either the JAR file `gameEnvironment.jar` contained in the folder `GameJAR` or the classes contained in the `GameClasses` folder can be added to any existing Eclipse project and its build path. Both of these folders are in the `Game Environment\IDE Specific Tools\Eclipse` subfolder on the DVD that accompanies this textbook. To add them to an existing Eclipse project's build path:

1. Launch Eclipse in the existing project's workspace
2. Locate and copy the folder `GameJAR` or `GameClasses`
3. Right click the project node in Eclipse's Package Explorer view pane, then click Paste
4. Right click the project node in the Package Explorer view pane, then click Properties - Java Build Path - Libraries
   (a) To add the `gameEnvironment.jar` file, click "Add JAR's..." and locate and check the `gameEnvironment.jar` JAR file, click OK, click OK

    (b) To add the `GameClasses` folder, click "Add Class Folder" and locate and check the `GameClasses` folder, click OK, click OK

NetBeans IDE

1. Create a folder with a name relevant to the program being developed
2. Copy the NetBeans project `NBGameTemplate7` located in the `Game Environment\IDE Specific Tools\NetBeans` subfolder on the DVD that accompanies this textbook and paste it into the folder created in Step 1
3. Open the project `NBGameTemplate7` and add the program-specific code to it

JCreator IDE

Method 1

1. Create a folder with a name relevant to the program being developed
2. Copy the JCreator project `JCGameTemplate7` located in the `Game Environment\IDE Tools\JCreator` subfolder on the DVD that accompanies this textbook and paste it into the folder created in Step 1
3. Open the project `JCGameTemplate7` and add the program-specific code to it

Method 2

1. Create a JCreator project
2. Copy and paste the folder `edu` (i.e., the package `edu.sjcny.gpv1`, contained in the `Game Environment\IDE Tools\JCreator` subfolder on the DVD that accompanies this book, into the project's class folder
3. Include the following import statement in the application:

```
import edu.sjcny.gpv1.*;
```

ASCII TABLE

Decimal	Octal	Hex	Binary	Char	Description
000	000	000	00000000	NUL	(null)
001	001	001	00000001	SOH	(start of Heading)
002	002	002	00000010	STX	(start of text)
003	003	003	00000011	ETX	(end of text)
004	004	004	00000100	EOT	(end of transmission)
005	005	005	00000101	ENQ	(enquiry)
006	006	006	00000110	ACK	(acknowledge)
007	007	007	00000111	BEL	(audible bell)
008	010	008	00001000	BS	(backspace)
009	011	009	00001001	HT	(horizontal tab)
010	012	00A	00001010	LF	(line feed, new line)
011	013	00B	00001011	VT	(vertical tab)
012	014	00C	00001100	FF	(form feed)
013	015	00D	00001101	CR	(carriage return)
014	016	00E	00001110	SO	(shift out)
015	017	00F	00001111	SI	(shift in)
016	020	010	00010000	DLE	(data link escape)
017	021	011	00010001	DC1	(device control 1)
018	022	012	00010010	DC2	(device control 2)
019	023	013	00010011	DC3	(device control 3)
020	024	014	00010100	DC4	(device control 4)
021	025	015	00010101	NAK	(negative acknowledge)
022	026	016	00010110	SYN	(synchronous idle)
023	027	017	00010111	ETB	(end of trans. block)
024	030	018	00011000	CAN	(cancel)
025	031	019	00011001	EM	(end of medium)
026	032	01A	00011010	SUB	(substitute)
027	033	01B	00011011	ESC	(escape)
028	034	01C	00011100	FS	(file separator)
029	035	01D	00011101	GS	(group separator)
030	036	01E	00011110	RS	(record separator)
031	037	01F	00011111	US	(unit separator)
032	040	020	00100000	SP	(space)
033	041	021	00100001	!	

(Contd.)

Decimal	Octal	Hex	Binary	Char	Description
034	042	022	00100010	"	
035	043	023	00100011	#	
036	044	024	00100100	$	
037	045	025	00100101	%	
038	046	026	00100110	&	
039	047	027	00100111	'	
040	050	028	00101000	(	
041	051	029	00101001	)	
042	052	02A	00101010	*	
043	053	02B	00101011	+	
044	054	02C	00101100	,	
045	055	02D	00101101	-	
046	056	02E	00101110	.	
047	057	02F	00101111	/	
048	060	030	00110000	0	
049	061	031	00110001	1	
050	062	032	00110010	2	
051	063	033	00110011	3	
052	064	034	00110100	4	
053	065	035	00110101	5	
054	066	036	00110110	6	
055	067	037	00110111	7	
056	070	038	00111000	8	
057	071	039	00111001	9	
058	072	03A	00111010	:	
059	073	03B	00111011	;	
060	074	03C	00111100	<	
061	075	03D	00111101	=	
062	076	03E	00111110	>	
063	077	03F	00111111	?	
064	100	040	01000000	@	
065	101	041	01000001	A	
066	102	042	01000010	B	
067	103	043	01000011	C	
068	104	044	01000100	D	
069	105	045	01000101	E	
070	106	046	01000110	F	
071	107	047	01000111	G	
072	110	048	01001000	H	
073	111	049	01001001	I	
074	112	04A	01001010	J	

Decimal	Octal	Hex	Binary	Char	Description
075	113	04B	01001011	K	
076	114	04C	01001100	L	
077	115	04D	01001101	M	
078	116	04E	01001110	N	
079	117	04F	01001111	O	
080	120	050	01010000	P	
081	121	051	01010001	Q	
082	122	052	01010010	R	
083	123	053	01010011	S	
084	124	054	01010100	T	
085	125	055	01010101	U	
086	126	056	01010110	V	
087	127	057	01010111	W	
088	130	058	01011000	X	
089	131	059	01011001	Y	
090	132	05A	01011010	Z	
091	133	05B	01011011	[	
092	134	05C	01011100	\	
093	135	05D	01011101	]	
094	136	05E	01011110	^	(caret)
095	137	05F	01011111	_	(underscore)
096	140	060	01100000	`	
097	141	061	01100001	a	
098	142	062	01100010	b	
099	143	063	01100011	c	
100	144	064	01100100	d	
101	145	065	01100101	e	
102	146	066	01100110	f	
103	147	067	01100111	g	
104	150	068	01101000	h	
105	151	069	01101001	i	
106	152	06A	01101010	j	
107	153	06B	01101011	k	
108	154	06C	01101100	l	
109	155	06D	01101101	m	
110	156	06E	01101110	n	
111	157	06F	01101111	o	
112	160	070	01110000	p	
113	161	071	01110001	q	
114	162	072	01110010	r	
115	163	073	01110011	s	

(Contd.)

Decimal	Octal	Hex	Binary	Char	Description
116	164	074	01110100	t	
117	165	075	01110101	u	
118	166	076	01110110	v	
119	167	077	01110111	w	
120	170	078	01111000	x	
121	171	079	01111001	y	
122	172	07A	01111010	z	
123	173	07B	01111011	{	
124	174	07C	01111100	|	(vertical bar)
125	175	07D	01111101	}	
126	176	07E	01111110	~	(tilde)
127	177	07F	01111111	DEL	(delete)

JAVA KEY WORDS

Java Keywords				
abstract	default	if	private	this
assert[2]	do	implements	protected	throw
boolean	double	import	public	throws
break	else	instanceof	return	transient
byte	enum[3]	int	short	try
case	extends	interface	static	void
catch	final	long	strictfp[1]	volatile
char	finally	native	super	while
class	float	new	switch	
continue	for	package	synchronized	

1: added in version 1.2
2: added in version 1.4
3: added in version 5.0

JAVA OPERATORS AND
THEIR RELATIVE PRECEDENCE

1 is highest precedence

Operator	Description	Precedence	Operator	Description	Precedence
postfix operators		1	*equality operators*		7
++	postfix increment		==	is equal to	
−−	postfix decrement		!=	is not equal to	
unary operators		2	*bitwise* AND		8
++	prefix increment		&	bitwise AND	
−−	prefix decrement		*bitwise exclusive* OR		9
+	leading plus		^	exclusive OR	
−	leading minus		*bitwise inclusive* OR		10
!	logical not		|	inclusive OR	
~	Bitwise complement		*logical* AND		11
multiplicative operators		3	&&	conditional AND	
*	multiplication		*logical* OR		12
/	division		||	conditional OR	
%	remainder		*ternary*		13
additive operators		4	?:	conditional	
+	addition		*assignment*		14
−	subtraction		=	assignment	
shift operators		5	+=	addition assignment	
<<	shift left		−=	subtraction assignment	
>>	shift right		*=	multiplication assignment	
>>>	unsigned shift right		/=	division assignment	
relational operators		6	%=	remainder assignment	
<	less than		&=	bitwise AND assignment	
<=	less than or equal to		^=	bitwise exclusive OR assignment	
>	greater than		|=	bitwise inclusive OR assignment	
>=	greater than or equal to		<<=	bitwise left shift assignment	
instanceof	class comparator		>>=	bitwise right shift assignment	
			>>>=	bitwise unsigned right shift assign	

USING THE GAME
GLOSSARY OF PROGRAMMING TERMS

Abstract class A class that includes the keyword abstract in its signature and cannot be instantiated; it is used during the design process to collect data members and methods common to several classes

Aggregated class A class that contains at least one data member that references an object

Aggregation The concept of referencing objects from a class's data members

Algorithm A step-by-step solution to solving a problem or task that a computer system can execute

Applet A Java program that runs from within another program, which is typically a Web browser; it has restrictions placed on its instruction set consistent with this execution mode's need for enforced security

Applet container program The program, typically a Web browser, within which an applet runs; the container invokes the methods that are part of the applet's lifecycle

Applet lifecycle The period of time that begins when an applet's execution is initiated and ends when it is terminated; during this time period, the applet's container program invokes the applet methods `init`, `start`, `paint`, `stop`, and `destroy` to manage its execution

Application Programming Interface (API) A collection of packages containing interfaces and implementations of classes and data structures that can easily be incorporated into a Java program

Application software All non-operating system software, typically for use by human users

Argument A value passed to a method when it is invoked

Argument list A sequence of argument names separated by commas enclosed in a set of parentheses

Array An ordered collection of primitive or reference variables stored inside an object, which are sequentially associated with an integer beginning with zero; arrays are an implementation of the mathematical concept of subscripted variables

Array of objects An array of reference variables that contains the addresses of a set of instances of the same class

ASCII Table A specific tabulation of characters and control characters and the bit patterns used to represent them

Assignment The act of changing the contents of a variable

Atomic components Graphical user interface (GUI) components that cannot contain other components, such as text fields and buttons; most of the program user's interactions are with these components

Autoboxing A context-sensitive feature of Java in which primitive literals or variables are replaced with instances of wrapper classes that contain their values

Base case Part of the methodology of formulating recursive algorithms, which is a known or trivial solution to the problem

Base class A class that is inherited from, also known as a parent or super class

Binary numbers A number system based on two, as opposed to the decimal system, which is based on ten

Bit A single unit of storage that can assume two states, which are referred to as off and on, or zero and one or false and true

Boolean expression An expression involving relational and logic operators that evaluates to true or false

Buffer Memory used to temporarily store data during program execution

Byte A set of eight contiguous (adjacent) bits, often used to represent a single character in the Modern Latin (English) alphabet

Byte codes The translation of a program produced by the Java language translator into intermediate code

Central processing unit (CPU) Electronic circuitry that interprets and executes instructions; the CPU can perform arithmetic and logic operations, has the ability to skip or re-execute instructions based on the truth value of a logic operation, and contains a limited amount of storage called registers

Chain inheritance When the parent class of a class extends another class

Child class A class that inherits from (extends) another class; also known as a sub or derived class

Class A collection of variables and methods; a blueprint for an object

Class-level variable A variable defined within a class but outside of a method's code block

Cloning an object Creating a new instance of a class and (deep) copying the values of all of the data members of an existing instance of the class into the new instance

Code block A set of instructions enclosed with a set of open and close braces, { }

Collection A data structure that is accessed without specifying a key

Collections Framework of the API Part of the API that contains generically implemented data structures, methods that perform common operations on data elements, and a set of associated interfaces

Computer system A set of electronic circuits, mechanical devices and enclosures, and instructions that these devices execute to perform a task

Concatenation The act of appending one string to another

Concurrency Executing several programs, or several parts of a program, at the same time

Constructor A method in a class that is used to create an instance of a class and return its address; its name is the same as the class's name

Consumer A process that expends data

Content pane The portion of a widow or other top-level container that holds the visible components added to the container

Control of flow statement A statement that overrides the default sequential execution path of a program, such as a decision statement, a repetition (loop) statement, or a subprogram invocation

Counting algorithm An algorithm that counts by adding an increment to, or subtracting a counting increment from, the current value of a counter

Data members The variables defined within a class, class level variables

Data structure An organization of data within memory to facilitate its processing from a speed and memory requirements viewpoint

Deep comparison of two objects Comparing the values of one or more of the data members of an object to the corresponding data members of another instance of the class

Deep copy of an object Copying the values of one or more of the data members of an instance of a class into the corresponding data members of another instance of the class

Derived class A class that inherits from (extends) another class; also known as a child or subclass.

Deserializing objects The act of reassembling objects after they are read from a disk file

Dialog box A predefined pop-up graphical interface used to pause a program's execution until the program user acknowledges a message or performs an input

Divide and conquer Expressing or defining a complicated entity as a set of less complicated entities; for example, expressing the solution to a complex problem as the solutions to a set of simpler problems, or defining the data members of a complex class to be instances of less complicated classes

Dynamic binding Delaying the process of locating an invoked method until runtime

Dynamic programming A programming technique aimed at reducing execution time, which avoids repetitive processing by saving and then reusing prior processing results

Element One of the variables contained in an array or one object contained in a data structure

Enumerated type A user defined type created within a Java program by specifying its type name and allowable values within an `enum` statement

Event An asynchronous occurrence during a program's execution that can be used to redirect the execution path of a program

Event handler A method that is executed when an event occurs

Exception class The API class `Throwable` or a descendent of that class

Exception error message A string contained within an exception object that normally contains descriptive error information

Exception object An instance of the API class `Throwable`, or one of its decedents, which can be passed to a `catch` clause when an error is detected during the execution of a method

Exceptions A programming construct that promotes the reusability of methods by deferring the decision as to what action to take when an error condition is detected to the invoker of the method

Final class A class that cannot be a parent class; it cannot be extended

Flow chart A graphical representation of an algorithm

Fractal A mathematical or geometric object that has the property of self-similarity; that is, each part of the object is a smaller or reduced copy of itself

General solution Part of the methodology of formulating recursive algorithms; it is a solution to the original problem that uses the portion of the methodology known as the reduced problem

Generic class A class that contains generic methods and is coded in a way as to permit the type of its data members to be specified when an instance of the class is created

Generic method A method that can perform its algorithm on any type of objects passed to it

Generic parameter A parameter that can be passed an object of any type and whose type is specified using a type placeholder

Generic parameter list A list of the type placeholders, coded within a method's signature, that are used in the method's parameter list

Generics A programming concept that promotes reusability by permitting the type of a method's parameters and returned value to be specified by the method's invoker and permitting the type of a class's data members to be specified when an instance of the class is created

Get method A method used to fetch the values of a class's private data members

Graphical User Interface (GUI) A means of interacting with the program user via a point-and-click mode, as opposed to a text-based mode, aimed at facilitating the I/O process

Hypertext Markup Language (HTML) A scripting language for writing instructions to be downloaded and executed by a Web browser to build and display a Web page; the script can contain instructions to download and execute a Java applet

Index The integer associated with a variable in an array

Inheritance A programming concept in which a new class can contain all of the data members and methods of an existing class by simply including an `extends` clause in its heading

Inner class A class that is defined within another class

Input method A method normally named `input` that ordinarily permits the program user to input the values of all of an object's data members

Instance of a class A specific object in the class

Integrated Development Environment (IDE) A program used by a programmer to develop a software product; it contains a collection of tools (e.g., a syntax checker, translator, editor, file-management system) that facilitate the development process

Interface A Java construct used to specify the signatures of related methods that are implicitly abstract and/or a declaration of public constants that are implicitly static and final

Iterator An object that can be used to perform time-efficient processing on all of the data elements contained in any data structure that imposes an ordering on its data elements

Java Development Kit (JDK) A set of tools used to develop Java programs; these tools include the API classes, a debugger, a compiler, an interpreter, an applet viewer, a documentation generator, a disassembler, various linking, loading, and binding tools, and a runtime environment

Java Virtual Machine A virtual computer system whose programming language is Java byte codes

Key A value associated with a data element that can be used to refer to the element

Layout manager A predefined protocol for the sizing and positioning of components added to a GUI container

Listener list An association of events and their event-handler methods that is part of a GUI component object

Local variable A variable defined within a code block whose scope is limited to the instructions within the code block

Loop A sequence of instruction that is repeated a specified number of times or until a Boolean value becomes true or false

Map A set of data structures that associate a key with each data element stored in the structure; the key can be used to specify the data element on which to operate

Menu mnemonic A menu shortcut key (hot key) associated with a terminal menu item

Methods The subprograms defined within a class, a sequence of instructions that perform a particular task

Multidimensional array An array in which each variable of the array is associated with 2, 3, … indices, for example an array of rows and columns

Multiple inheritance When a class inherits from more than one class; this is not supported in Java

Multitasking Executing several threads of an application at the same time or giving the impression that they are executing at the same time

Nested loops Coding loops inside of loops

Nested statements Statements that are contained within another statement or another statement's statement block

Non-void method A method that returns a value, whose type is specified in the method's signature

Object A particular occurrence of a class that contains all of the class's non-static data members

Object oriented programming (OOP) An approach to programming (a programming paradigm) aimed at facilitating the development of programs that deal with objects, such as starships, people, or Web pages

One-dimensional array An array in which each variable of the array is associated with one index

Operating system software A program to manage the resources of a computer system and to permit a user of the system to interact with it, usually via a point-and-click interface

Overloading methods The act of writing two or more methods in the same class that have the same name but different parameter lists

Overriding a method Rewriting an inherited method using the exact same signature of the inherited method

Parallel arrays A use of multiple one-dimensional arrays in which the ith element of each array is associated with the same entity; for example, if Mary's age was stored in the second element of one array, then the rest of Mary's information would be stored in the second element of the other arrays

Parameter A variable that can receive a value (an argument) passed to a method when it is invoked

Parameter list A sequence of parameter names, each proceeded by its type, separated by commas, and enclosed in a set of parentheses

Parent class A class that is inherited from, also known as a super or base class

Parsing The act of changing a string into a numeric; also the act of separating a string into its component parts that are separated by a specified delimiter

Platform A particular CPU model and operating system

Platform independence The concept that the programmer's translation of a program can be transmitted to, and then run on, any computer system

Polymorphism The ability of one invocation to morph itself into an invocation of a parent's version of a method or any of its children's versions of the method; rooted in the fact that a parent reference variable can refer to an instance of a child class

Pop-up menu A space-saving alternative to a menu-bar-based drop-down menu that remains invisible until the user performs a platform-dependent mouse or keyboard action on a GUI component

Precedence rules A specification of the order in which to perform a set of operations

Primitive variable A variable that can store a numeric value, a Boolean value, or one character; the type used in its declaration is one of the primitive types

Primitive type The Java types `byte`, `short int`, `long`, `float`, `double`, `char`, and `boolean`

Priority queue A queue that associates a priority with each of its data elements; the elements assigned the highest priority are fetched and deleted (on a first-in-first-out basis) before those of lower priority

Private data member A data member of a class that cannot be directly accessed by methods that are not part of the class; `get` and `set` methods are used to fetch and change their values

Producer A process that generates data

Pseudorandom numbers Apparent, but not truly, random numbers

Public data members Data members of a class that can be directly accessed by methods that are not part of the class; they are accessed by coding their name preceded by either the name of an instance of the class or the class name, followed by a dot

Queue A data structure in which the data elements are fetched and deleted on a first-in-first-out basis

Random access memory (RAM) High-speed, high-cost storage physically located in close proximity to the central processing unit

Recursion The act of defining something in terms of itself

Recursive method A method that invokes itself or initiates a sequence of method invocations that eventually leads to an invocation of itself

Reduced problem Part of the methodology of formulating recursive algorithms, it is a problem similar to the original problem, usually between the original problem and the base case, usually closer to the original problem, and (when progressively reduced) becomes the base case for all versions of the original problem

Reference variable A variable that can store a memory address; the type used in its declaration is the name of a class

Registering an event handler The act of associating an event-handler method with a particular event that could be performed on a GUI component

Runtime the time during which the program is in execution

Scope of a variable or a method The range of a program's instructions within which a variable can be used or a method can be invoked

Sentinel loop A loop that ends on a particular value of the data it is processing or on a particular user input; for example, a negative deposit

Serializing objects The act of disassembling objects before writing them to a disk file so they can be recreated when they are read from the disk

Set methods Methods used to change the values of a class's private data members

Shallow comparison Comparing the contents of one variable to the contents of another variable using the equality (==) operator

Shallow copy Copying the contents of one variable into another using the assignment (=) operator

Shared buffer Memory used to temporarily share a data item among one or more threads

Show method A method named `show` that ordinarily outputs all of the data members of an object or draws the object

Signature of a method The first line of a method's code

Software engineer A computer professional that produces programs that are error free, within budget, on schedule, and satisfy the customers' current and future needs

States of a thread The six statuses a thread can assume from the time it is created to the time it is terminated

Static data member A class's data member that is designated to be shared by all instances of the class by including the keyword `static` in its declaration

Static method A method that is designated to be invoked by preceding the method name by the method's class name followed by a dot; they are intended to be methods that do not operate on instances of the class

String A finite sequence of characters

Subclass A class that inherits from (extends) another class, also known as a derived or child class

Super class A class that is inherited from, also known as a base and parent class

Swapping algorithm An algorithm that swaps the values contained in two variables

Synchronized buffer A buffer whose access is managed in a way that imposes protocols of proper access to the data on the threads that share the buffer

Syntax The rules for forming properly constructed program instructions; the grammar of a programming language

Text file A file whose information is intended to be characters and is therefore interpreted using the ASCII or Unicode tables; ordinarily the file extension `.txt` is appended to the file's name

Thread An independent execution path through a program

Token A component part of a string that is terminated by a specified delimiter, for example, a space

Tokenizing a string Extracting all of the tokens from a string

Top-level container The basic building block component of a graphical interface, which contains the other GUI components that make up the interface

`toString` method A method named `toString` whose task is to return the string representation of an object; ordinarily, the string contains the annotated values of all of an object's data members

Totaling or summation algorithm An algorithm that computes the sum of a set of numeric values by repeatedly adding each value to the subtotal of the values in the set that preceded it

Type placeholder Any valid identifier that is not the name of a class used within the application of which it is a part; a placeholder is used as a type of a generic parameter and can be used as a returned type

Unboxing A context-sensitive feature of Java in which an instance of a wrapper class object is replaced with the primitive value it contains

Unicode An expanded tabulation of characters and control characters and the bit patterns used to represent them

Universal modeling language (UML) diagram A graphical representation of a class that specifies the class's name, data members, and the signatures of its methods; it is used to design a class

Variable A named memory cell that can store a specific type of data item

Void method A method that does not return a value

Worker method A method that is invoked by another method to perform a specific task (work) for it; for example, fetching the value of one of an object's data members or drawing the object

Wrapper class An API class that contains non-static primitive data members of a particular type

USING THE ONLINE API DOCUMENTATION

The documentation of the Application Programing Interface (API) is available online. To access it, you can Google: *Java API documentation* and click the link that begins with `docs.oracle.com/javase`, such as the one shown below:

http://docs.oracle.com/javase/7/docs/api/

To quickly locate the documentation on a particular class, you can Google the class's name and then click the link to the class's documentation. The following link was displayed after Googling *Java Math class*:

http://docs.oracle.com/javase/7/docs/api/java/lang/Math.html

Clicking this link displays the information shown in Figure G.1, which is typical of the format of the documentation for any class. As shown in the figure, the class name is at the top of the documentation. Below it is the package that is imported into a class to gain access to the API class and its methods. This package name can be copied from the documentation and pasted into the class's file just before its class heading. It is preceded by the keyword `import` and followed by a semicolon.

Below the package name is the specification of the class's access and inheritance details. In the case of the `Math` class, this information indicates that the class's access is public, the class is final (which means it cannot be extended as a parent class), and its parent class is the class `Object`. Below that is a general description of the class.

Below the general descriptive information is a *Field Summary* (Figure G.2), which is a tabulation of the name and description of all of the data members contained in the class. This is followed by a *Method Summary*, which is a tabulation of the names of each method in the class and their parameter list followed a brief description of the method's functionality.

To the left of each data member's name in the Field Summary is its type, which may be preceded by the keyword `static`. Static data members are accessed by preceding their name with the name of the class followed by a dot. To the left of each method's name in the Method Summary is the method's returned type, which may be preceded by the keyword `static`. Static methods are invoked by preceding their name with the name of the class followed by a dot. Non-static methods are invoked by preceding their name with the name of an instance of the class followed by a dot.

More detained documentation on a data member or a method can be displayed by clicking the name of the data member in the Field Summary or the name of the method in the Method Summary. Figure G.3 was displayed when the method name `acos`, shown at the bottom of Figure G.2, was clicked.

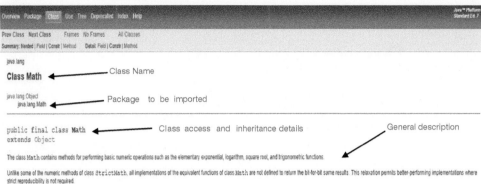

Figure G.1
The top portion of the online documentation of the **Math** class.

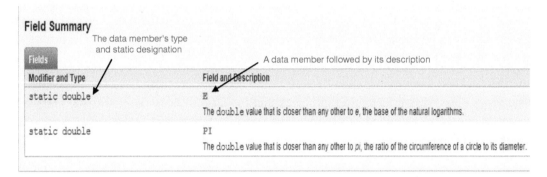

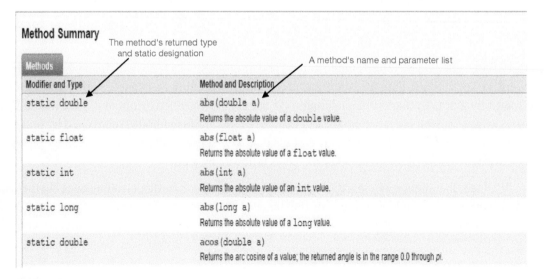

Figure G.2
The partial Field Summary and Method Summary of the API Math class.

acos

```
public static double acos(double a)
```

Returns the arc cosine of a value; the returned angle is in the range 0.0 through *pi*. Special case:
* If the argument is NaN or its absolute value is greater than 1, then the result is NaN.

The computed result must be within 1 ulp of the exact result. Results must be semi-monotonic.

Parameters:

a - the value whose arc cosine is to be returned.

Returns:

the arc cosine of the argument.

Figure G.3
Detailed documentation of the Math class's **acos** method.

SOLUTIONS TO SELECTED ODD KNOWLEDGE EXERCISES

CHAPTER 1

1. **(b)** The number of computers grew from 200 to 800 – a factor of 4

3. Operating systems (such as: Windows. Linux or Apple OS X) are the instructions used by the computer system to schedule tasks, to allocate memory and other system resources, to detect errors and to perform other computer system functions. Application software is commonly used by the human user, while system software is used by the computer system. Examples of application software include word processors, spreadsheets, mail readers, Web browsers, and game programs.

5. Both a and c are characteristics of secondary storage which is nonvolatile, has a very large capacity and is slower and cheaper than RAM.

7. **(a)** A device that is only used for output is a printer or a speaker.

   (c) Devices used for both input and output include touch screens, flash drives, floppy disks, and writable CDs, DVDs.

9. The computer as we know it today was the work of many people over hundreds of years, beginning with the development of early calculating machines: the abacus, the slide rule, Napier's bones and the Pascaline. The modern computer was based on the designs of Babbage, von Neumann, Mauchly, and Eckert. Lady Ada Lovelace and Grace Hopper were pioneers in the field of programming languages. Metcalfe and Boggs, Cerf and Kahn and Berners-Lee connected computers together into networks, the Internet and the World Wide Web, respectively.

11. **(b)** loses its contents if power is interrupted.

13. **(c)** chips, replacing the larger transistor circuits.

15. **(a)** First programmer - Lady Ada Augusta Byron, the Countess of Lovelace
    (b) Inventor of the Java programming language – James Gosling

17. Platform independence is the ability of software to run on any computer system or platform. Every manufacturer's chipset has its own unique machine language and therefore usually requires its own translating program to translate from source code instructions to its machine language. Java achieves platform independence by compiling the source code instructions into byte code, which is later translated on the end user's computer into its own specific machine code.

19. A class is a group of related data members and member methods. It is the template used to create an object. An object is a particular instance of a class. From one class we can create an unlimited number of objects or instances of the class, just as with a blueprint we can create many houses, or with a cookie cutter, we can create many batches of cookies.

21. **(a)** CPU – central processing unit   **(c)** I/O – input/output
    (e) JVM – Java virtual machine   **(g)** GUI- graphical user interface

23. **(d)** (5, 30) since it is 5 pixels to the left of the left boundary and 30 pixels below the top.

25. **(1)** character data, **(2)** translated instructions, and **(3)** numeric data.

27. **(a)** 01010011 = 83 in decimal   **(b)** 00101111 = 47 in decimal

CHAPTER 2

1. **(a)** False, the contents of the variable may change but the data type does not
   (c) False   **(e)** False

3. A variable is a named memory cell that stores one data item that can change during program execution. Primitive variables can store a single numeric data value, one character, or one Boolean truth value. Reference variables store (RAM) memory addresses.

5. (a) `boolean false`   **(c)** `double 0.0`

7. Numeric literals, containing decimals such as 19.5, are assumed to be type double. If a numeric literal is to be assigned to a `float` variable, the letter `f` for float, must be appended to the literal to inform the translator that a loss of precision is acceptable, otherwise an error results. (This is a correct declaration `float weight = 19.5f;`)

9. (a) `System.out.println("Sara Larson");`
   `System.out.println("Smalltown, USA");`

   (b) `System.out.println("Sara Larson" + "\n"Smalltown, USA");`

11.

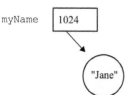

The `String` object at
memory address 1024

   `int distance = 675; String myName = "Jane";`

13. (a)   17 - 5 * 2 + 12 = 19   **(c)**   (48 + 12) / 12 + 18 * 2 = 41
   (d)   21 - 9 + 18 + 4 * 3.7 = 44.8

15. `double average = ((double)(55 + 57 + 60)) / 3;`

17. (a) True   **(b)** False, it is used for output
   (c) True   **(d)** False, it would return the empty string ("")
   (e) True

19. `sBalance = JOptionPane.showInputDialog("Type your current " + "checking account`
                                  `balance");`

21. `double  deposit;`
   `deposit = Double.parseDouble(sDeposit);`

CHAPTER 3

1. (a) True   **(b)**   False, it is the method signature
   (c) False   **(d)**   False, this method returns a value

3. (a)   The signature of a method that does not operate on an object must contain the keyword `static`.
   (c)   When we invoke a static method, we begin the invocation statement with the name of <u>the class</u> followed by a dot.

5. (a)   True
   (c)   False, the client method sends an argument into the worker method's parameter
   (e)   False, a method can only return a single value
   (g)   False
   (h)   False, value parameters

7. The statement following the statement that invoked the method executes next.

9. `static double checkAmount;`

11. (a)   `drawRect`   **(c)** `drawOval`
   (e)   `fillOval`, using the same value for the height and width

13. (a)   House is to object as blueprint is to class.
   (c)   The name of the graphic used to specify a class is a UML diagram.
   (e)   Member methods of a class are usually designated to have private access.

15. (a)   The address of the object `joe`

(c)

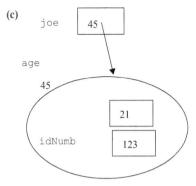

```
Person joe = new Person();
```

17. (a) `public CoffeeCup(int size, double price)`
`{   this.size = size;`
`    this.price = price;`
`}`

(b) `CoffeeCup cup1 = new CoffeeCup(8, 3.85);`
(c) `System.out.println(cup1);`
(d) `System.out.println(cup1.tostring());`
(e) CoffeeCup@456af2 (the address, 456af2, will probably be different)
(f) `g.drawString(cup1.toString(), 200, 250);`

19. `public void show(Graphics g)`
`{`
`    g.drawString("size is: " + size, 250, 250);`
`    g.drawString("price is: " + price, 250, 280;`
`}`

20.

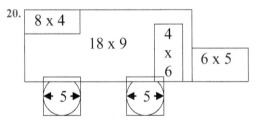

21. This might be a typical response based on the model given in Exercise 20

Component	Shape	Shape's X or Line's X₁ coordinate	Shape's Y Line's Y₁ coordinate	Width Line's X₂ coordinate	Height Line's Y₂ coordinate
window	rectangle	x	y	8	4
body	rectangle	x	y	18	9
door	rectangle	x + 14	y + 2	4	6
cab	rectangle	x + 18	y + 4	6	5
rear tire	circle	x + 3	y + 8	5	5
front tire	circle	x + 11	y + 8	5	5

23. (a) `this.total = total * 2;`
(c) `public void setTotal(int total)`
`{`
`  this.total = total;`
`}`

(e) `int currentTotal = myAccount.getTotal();`
`myAccount.setTotal(currentTotal * 2);`

(g) `public void toString()`
```
{
   System.out.println("The total is: " + total );
}
```

(i) `private`

25. **(a)** `static Starship largest(Starship ship1, Starship ship2);`
   (b) `ship1 = largest(ship1, ship2);`
   (c) The new color.
   (d) `public boolean sameModel(Starship ship1, Starship ship2);`
   (e) `isSame = sameModel(ship1, ship2);`

CHAPTER 4

1. **(a)** True   **(c)** False   **(e)** True

3. Method invocations and control-of-flow (or control) statements, such as decision and loops, alter the execution path.

5.
```
if (myBalance ==10.0)
{
   System.out.println(myBalance);
}
 else
{
   System.out.println("my balance is not 10.0");
}
```

7. **(a)** True

   (c) True, although it can be empty

   (e) True

   (g) True

9. **(a)** False, but it is good programming style to include a default statement

   (c) True

   (e) True

   (g) False, it can only be written as a switch statement if the selection statements are of the appropriate type

11.
```
if(item.equals("Hamburger"))
{
   System.out.println("You ordered a Hamburger.");
}
else if(item.equals("Taco"))
{
   System.out.println("You ordered a Taco.");
}
else if(item.equals("BLT"))
{
   System.out.println("You ordered a BLT sandwich.");
}
else
{
   System.out.println("You did not place a valid order.");
}
```

13. **(a)**
```
Scanner consoleIn = new Scanner(System.in);
System.out.println("Type the year of your birth: ");
int birthYear;
birthYear = consoleIn.nextInt();
```
(b)
```
Scanner consoleIn = new Scanner(System.in);
String name;
System.out.print("Enter your name: ");
name = consoleIn.nextLine();
```

15. **(a)** True   **(b)** False   **(c)** True

17. **(a)**
```
File fileObject = new File("e:/Dates.txt");
Scanner fileIn = new Scanner(fileObject);
int year;
year = fileIn.nextInt();
```
(b)
```
File fileObject = new File("e:/Names.txt");
Scanner fileIn = new Scanner(fileObject);
String name;
int age;
age = fileIn.nextInt();
fileIn.nextLine();   // to flush the buffer
name = fileIn.nextLine();
```

19.
```
import java.io.*;
public class DiskIO
{
   public static void main(String[] args) throws IOException
   {
      double myBalance =2567.00;
      double yourBalance = 3876.25;
      new // if file exists it will be deleted
      FileWriter fileWriterObject = new FileWriter("c:/Balances.txt");
      PrintWriter fileOut = new PrintWriter(fileWriterObject, false);

      fileOut.println(myBalance + " " + yourBalance);
      fileOut.close();
   }
}
```

21. `inputfile.close();`

CHAPTER 5

1. **(a)** False, it is possible for a while loop body not to execute at all

   (c) True   **(e)** False, it is a pretest loop

   (g) True   **(i)** True

   (k) False, when the Boolean condition becomes false.

   (m) True, since the loop is never entered the loop control variable is not changed

   (o) True

3.
```
int n;
int count =1;
int sum =0;
String instring;
instring = JOptionPane.showInputDialog("Type a number: " );
```

```
      n = Integer.ParseInt(instr);
      while(count <= n)
      {
        if (count % 2 ==0)      //number is even
        {
            sum = sum + count;
        }
        count++;
      }   //end while
      JoptionPane.showMessageDialog(null, "The sum of even integers " +
                              "from 1 to " + n + " is " + sum);
```

5. **(a)** The value of i is never equal to 20, so the loop never terminates.
   (b) Because the loop does not terminate the output statement after the loop is never reached and is not executed.

7. **(a)** Output: 8, 5, 2, -1
   (b)
```
      for (int x = 8; x >= -1; x = x - 3)
      {
        System.out.println(x);
      }
```

9.
```
   int trys = 0;
   int input;
   String sInput;
   do
   {
      trys++;
      sInput = JOptionPane.showInputDialog("Enter a number from 0 to 5");
      input = Integer.parseInt(sInput);
      if(input >= 0 && input <= 5)
      {
         JOptionPane.showInputDialog("Thanks for the valid input");
         break;
      }
      else
      {
         JOptionPane.showInputDialog("invalid input");
      }
   } while(trys < 3);
```

11. **(a)**
```
    int randomNumber;
    Random randomObject = new Random(); // uses time of day
    for(int i=1; i<=20;, i++)
    {
       randomNumber = randomObject.nextInt(501));

       System.out.print(randomNumber);
    }
```
   (c)
```
    int randomNumber;
    int min =7;
    int max =500;
    Random randomObject = new Random(2468); // uses seed
    for(int i=1; i<=20;, i++)
```

```
    {
        randomNumber = min + randomObject.nextInt(500 - min + 1);
        System.out.print(randomNumber);
    }
```

CHAPTER 6

1. (a) True   (c) True
  (e) True   (g) False, arrays can be multi-dimensional
  (i) True

3. An array element is a reference variable, while a non-array element may be a primitive or a reference variable. An array variable is able to store many elements, while a primitive variable only stores one. An array variable uses square brackets ([ ]) and an index to indicate the position of an element in the array, while a non-array variable does not.

5. (a) True   (c) False, `gameScores[99]`
  (e) False, 100   (g) `System.out.println(gameScores[99]);`

  (i)
```
int total = 0;
for(int i = 0; i <  gameScores.length; i++)
{
    total = total + gameScores[i];
}
System.out.println(total / gameScores.length);
```

7. (a) 45   (c) 4
  (e) y[4] = y[4] + 20.5;   (f) z = y[0] + y[1] +y[2];

9. (a)
```
String[] names = new String[50];
double[] weights = new double[50];
double[] targetWeights = new double[50];
```

  (c)
```
for(int i = 0; i < names.length; i++)
{
    if(names[i].equalsIgnoreCase("joe smith")
    {
        System.out.println(weight[i] + " " + targetWeight[i]);
    }
}
```

CHAPTER 7

1. (a) True   (c) True
  (e) False, a deep copy   (g) True

3. A shallow comparison compares reference variables or the addresses of two objects to determine if they refer to the same object or two different objects. A deep comparison compares the contents of the data members of two objects to determine if they are the same.

5. Explain the difference between a deep copy and a clone. A deep copy copies the values of the data members of one object into the data members of another object, using the `set` method. When an object is cloned, a new instance of the object's class is created, and the values of all of an existing object's data members are copied into the corresponding data members of the new object. There are now two objects instead of one.

7.
```
if(s1 != s2)
{
    System.out.println(" Two objects");
}
```

9. **(a)** *6*   **(c)** *Hello everyone*

    (e) *Hello*

11. Aggregation is combining objects so that the instance of one class is a field in another class. It establishes a "has a" relationship.

13. Use the API BigInteger class to create a BigInteger object.

```
BigInteger num1 =  new BigInteger ("123456789101112133456789");
```

15. Invoke the BigInteger multiply method on the BigInteger object. For example,

```
BigInteger num1 =  new BigInteger ("123456789101112133456789");
BigInteger num2 =  new BigInteger.valueOf(2);
BigInteger largenum = num1.multiply(num2);
```

17. **(a)** 2

    (b) `CarColor favoriteColor = CarColor.BLUE;`

    (c) `System.out.println(CarColor.BLUE + " " + favoriteColor.ordinal());`

CHAPTER 8

1. **(a)** False   **(c)** True
    (e) False, constructors are not inherited   **(g)** True
    (i) False, they are overloaded   **(k)** True
    (m) False, all we need are the class's byte codes

3. Reduced coding time: a parent class can collect functionality and data members common to several classes into one class so they need only be coded once in the parent class.

   Code reusability: A child can inherit all of the data members and methods of a previously developed class not coded as part of its program, and then add methods and data members or overwrite methods that are not suited for its applications.

5. Public: Child classes and client code have direct access. Protected: Child classes have direct access but not client code in a separate package. Private: Neither child classes nor client code have direct access.

7. `super.input();`

9. Declare the method to be final.

11. When you wanted to expand its parameter list.

13. An abstract class is used to collect all of the data members and methods that are common to two or more classes that will make up a program. The classes simply extend it, and then add the data members and methods specific to them to it.

15. `Transporter[] vehicles = new Transporter[200];`

17. An interface can contain the signatures of related methods that are implicitly abstract and/or declarations of public constants that are implicitly static and final. An advantage of an interface is that any class that implements the interface must implement all of the methods defined in the interface.

19. Include the `implements ManyMethods` clause in the adapter class's signature, and implement all 20 of the methods defined in the interface with empty code blocks.

CHAPTER 9

1. **(a)** True

    (c) False, usually the most difficult part is the discovery of the reduced problem

    (e) True, if the base case is not realized

    (g) False; typically they are slower than their loop base (iterative) counterparts because of the time required to transfer execution to the recursive invocations they make

3. The symbol with the number 5 to its left

5. Iterative: f1 = 1; f2 = 1; f3 = 1 + 1 = 2; f4 = 1 + 2 = 3; f5 = 2 + 3 = 5; f6 = 3 + 5 = 8;
          f7 = 5 + 8 = 13; f8 = 8 + 13 = 21;

   Non-iterative: f8 = f7 + f6 = (f6 + f5) + (f5 + f4) =
                  (f5 + f4) + (f4 + f3) + (f4 + f3) + (f3 + 1) =
                  (f4 + f3) + (f3 + 1) + (f3 + 1) + (1 + 1) + (f3 + 1) + (1 + 1) (1 + 1) + 1 =
                  (f3 + 1) + (1 + 1) + (1 + 1) + 1 + (1 + 1) + 1 + (1 + 1) + (1 + 1) + 1 +
                  (1 + 1) (1 + 1) + 1 =
                  (1 + 1) + 1 + (1 + 1) + (1 + 1) + 1 + (1 + 1) + 1 + (1 + 1) + (1 + 1) + 1 +
                  (1 + 1) (1 + 1) + 1 =
                  21

7. Dynamic programming

9. Base case: `if(m == n) return n;`
   Reduced problem: sum of the even integers from m-2 to n
   General Solution: m + the reduced problem

11. Because that is the base case, which halts the recursive invocations.

13. Combine the base case, reduced problem and general solution into a recursive algorithm, using a flow chart similar to the one shown in Figure 9.6

15. To move six rings: $2^6 - 1$ For ten rings: $2^{10} - 1$ For n rings: $2^n - 1$

CHAPTER 10

1. (a) True   (c) True
   (e) True   (h) False
   (j) False, but if the exception is a checked exception the method's signature must contain a `throws` clause
   (l) True   (n) False

3. When the error that caused the problem is a serious error, because the translator will then warn the programmer that a catch block to deal with the problem was not included in the program that invoked the method.

5. `Exception`

7. (a) Checked   (c) Checked
   (e) Unchecked   (g) Unchecked

9. Invoke the `getMessage` method on the exception object passed to the catch clause:

   `String error = e.getMessage();`

CHAPTER 11

1. (a) False, it stands for Graphical User Interface
   (c) True
   (e) True
   (g) False, applets do not
   (i) False, their default layout manager is border layout
   (k) True

3. Buttons are used to initiate processing; Radio buttons are used to select one item from a set of mutually exclusive items; Check boxes are used select to one or more items from a set of items.

5. North, west, center, east, and south

7. (a) `p1.setLayout(null);`   (b) `p2.setLayout(new BorderLayout());`

9. `JFrame aWindow = new JFrame("Exercise 9 Window Title");`
   `aWindow.setSize(600, 800);`

```
aWindow.getContentPane().setBackground(Color.RED);
aWindow.setDefaultCloseOperation(JFrame.EXIT _ ON _ CLOSE);
aWindow.setVisible(true);
```

11. Event handlers are overridden methods, whose signatures are predefined, and execute when a particular event they are associated with occurs on a GUI component.

13. Assuming e is the name of the parameter in the event handler's signature, the statement would be:

```
if(e.getSource() == b2) System.out.print("Button 2");
```

15. An adapter class is a class that implements all of the methods whose signatures are defined in an interface. The code blocks of the method implementations are usually empty. The advantage they offer is that a class that extends them only needs to implement the interface's methods that are relevant to its functionality.

17. The `requestFocusInWindow` method, inherited from the `JComponent` class, is invoked on a Swing component. The invocation is normally made from within an overwritten version of the `addNotify` method, which is invoked when a component is added to an application.

19. The highest level of portability across web browsers is achieved when `AWT` components are used. Swing classes are 100% cross-platform compatible, and cross platform look and feel differences can be eliminated when they are used.

21. Java restricts the range of the instruction set that can be included in an applet program. For example disk I/O instructions are not permitted.

CHAPTER 12

1. (a) False, they are normally used to select one input from a set of mutually exclusive inputs
   (c) False, only one selection can be made (e) True
   (g) False, vice versa   (i) False
   (k) True   (m) False
   (o) True

3. A combo box is used to select one item from a set of items; lists are used to select one or more values from a set of values.

5. Only one item can be selected from a combo box, one or more values can be selected from a list. The items in a combo box are displayed when the arrow in its drop-down button is clicked. A list is displayed with a scroll bar by default when the size of the list box is too small to display all of its values.

7. Drop-down menus display their selections when the user clicks them. Pop-up menus display their selections when the user performs a platform dependent mouse action or key action.

9. A mnemonic is a keyboard event that is designated to be equivalent to the user clicking a GUI component such as a menu item or a button. Other names for mnemonics are shortcut keys or hot keys.

11. A `JColorChooser` object is an API defined dialog box that can be used to facilitate the choice or creation of a color.

13. (a) A: `actionPerformed`   (b) A: `actionPerformed`
    (c) A: `actionPerformed`   (d) C: `valueChanged`
    (e) A: `actionPerformed`

15. (a) `JCheckBox`   (c) `JComboBox`
    (e) `JMenu`   (g) `JMenuItem`
    (i) `JRadioButtonMenuItem`

CHAPTER 13

1. (a) True   (c) False
   (e) False   (g) True
   (i) True   (k) True

3. `T1[] copy;`
`copy = Arrays.copyOf(values, values.length);`

5. (a) True   **(c)** True
   (f) True

7. `public class G7Class <T> implements Comparable<GClass>`

9. `ArrayList <String> s2;`

11. `HashMap`, or `TreeMap`, or `LinkedHashMap`

13. `PriorityQueue <PhoneListing> pl = new PriorityQueue <PhoneListing>();`

CHAPTER 14

1. (a) True, until the program it is part of ends
  (c) True
  (e) True, or they can extend the class `Thread` (which implements the interface `Runnable`).
  (g) False

3. New, runnable, waiting, timed waiting, blocked, and terminated

5. The wait method

7. The method invokes the `wait` method, or the method invokes the `sleep` method.

9. (a) True   **(c)** False
  (e) False   **(g)** False

11. The consumer task is using data generated by another task, the producer task. Two problems can occur. The producer generates a data item and overwrites a previously generated data item not yet processed by the consumer task, or the consumer reprocess a previously processed data item (or a data item containing a default value) because the producer has not generated a new data item.

13. Use synchronized methods or synchronized statements.

INDEX

@Override directive, 366

A

Access, 111, 173
    Private, 111
    Public, 111
actionPerformed Method, 503, 504
Aggregation, 329–337
    Concept of, 330
Algorithm, 5
American Standard Code for Information
    Interchange (ASCII), 30
    Extended, 31, 61
    Table, 693–696
Android Development Tools (ADT), 25
API Graphics class, 89–93
    Changing the Drawing Color, 89–90
    Drawing Lines, Rectangles, Ovals, and
        Circles, 90–93
Applet(s), 480, 531–544
    Container, 531
    Developing an, 532–534
    Execution path, 535–536
    HTML Document Basics, 534–535
    Incorporating GUIs and Two-Dimensional
        Graphics into, 536–543
        GUI Components and Event Handling,
            538–544
        Two-Dimensional Graphics in a
            JApplet, 536
    Portability and Security Issues, 543–544
    viewer, 532
Application Programming Interface
    (API), 19
Application software, 3
Array(s), 236
    Application programmer interface array
        support, 278–283

arraycopy Method, 278–279
    Arrays Class, 279–283
    Common array algorithms, 265–277
        Minimum or maximum value, 267–269
        Searching, 266–267
        Sorting, 269–277
    Use of the Minimum Value
        Algorithm, 277
    Use of the Search Algorithm, 276–277
    Use of the Selection Sort Algorithm, 277
    Concept of, 236–238
    Declaring, 238–241
        Dynamic allocation of, 239–241
    Deleting, modifying, and adding disk file
        items, 286–290
    Destination, 278
    Loops and, 241–243
    Multi-dimensional, 283–285
        Two-Dimensional, 284–285
        Initializing Two-Dimensional, 285
    Objects, 243–250
        Processing of an, 245–250
    Origin of, 236
    Parallel, 258–265
    Passing arrays between methods, 250–258
        Objects to a Worker Method, 253–257
        Primitives to a Worker Method, 251–252
        Returning an Array from a Worker Method,
            257–258
    Source, 278
ArrayBlockingQueue, 668
Artificial Intelligence, 8, 10
Atomic, 494

B

Babbage, Charles, 7
Backing-storage devices, 5
Berners-Lee, Tim, 12

Boolean (logical) expression(s), 138–144
  Comparing string objects, 143–144
            compareTo, 143
            compareToIgnoreCase, 143
    equalsIgnoreCase, 143
  Compound, 140–143
    AND (&&) and OR (||) operators,
        141–143
  Simple, 139–140
    Lexicographical or dictionary order, 139
    Relational and Equality Operators, 139
Borders, 550–551
Break and continue statements, 221–222
Buffer, 653
  bounded, 653
  object, 653
Byte of storage, 31

C

Calculations, 50–58
  Arithmetic Calculations and the Rules of
      Precedence, 50–52
    Mixed mode arithmetic, 51
    Integer division, 51
    Precedence Rules, 51
  Promotion and Casting, 54–56
    Mixed Mode Arithmetic Expressions, 55
  The Assignment Operator and Assignment
      Statements, 53–54
  The Math Class, 56–58
    Random numbers, 58
Call Back Methods, 688–689
Central Processing Unit (CPU), 4
Cerf, Vinton, 12
Check Boxes, 551
  Adding to Containers and Positioning Them,
      553–554
  Check box event, 554
  Creating, 552– 553
  Determining a status, 554
Choice expression, 161
Class, 22, 94
  Abstract super, 399
  Adapter, 405
  Aggregated, 329

Base, 355
Child, 354
Outer, 337
Parent, 354
  Invoking a, 361
  Invoking Child Class Methods, 372
Random, 224–227
Scanner, 169
  Input methods used in, 169
Super, 355
Classes, 19
  Abstract, 372–382
  Adapter, 353
  Adding methods to, 102–121
    Constructors and the Keyword this,
        107–109
    Private Access and the set/get Methods,
        109–116
    The show Method, 103–106
    The toString and input Methods, 116–121
  Class Code Template, 95–96
  Event Handler Adapter, 513
  Final, 383
  Inner, 337–340
  Locale, 202
    format, 202
    getCurrencyInstance, 202
  NumberFormat, 202
Code, 23
  Block, 76
  Driver, 24
Code-breaking machine, 8
Collections, 596
Color-Chooser Dialog Box, 587–589
  JColorChooser, 587
Combo Boxes and Lists, 563–572
  Adding a Vertical Scroll Bar, 566–570
  Creating, 564–565
  Editing a, 570–571
  Event handling, 571–572
  Fetching the Selected Item and Value(s),
      565–566
  Methods to perform operations, 564
  Terminology and features of, 563
Common Business Oriented Language
    (COBOL), 10

compareTo Method, 609
Components, 480
Computer system, 2–5
  Major component of a, 2
Concurrency, 644
  Actual, 645
  Perceived, 645
consoleIn Method, 169–172
Constructors, 97, 686
  Invoking a Parent Class, 361
  Overloading, 121–124
Control-of-flow or *control* statements, 138
Cost-effective approach, 18
Counting algorithm, 67–70
  A Counting Application: Displaying a
    Game's Time, 68–70
Critical section, 661

D

Data members, 20, 95
  Protected, 383–384
Debugging, 11
DecimalFormat class, 70
Deep Space Delivery game, 17
Default Locale, 203
Dequeue, 615
Dialog box output and input, 58–64
  Input Dialog Boxes, 60
  Message dialog boxes, 59–60
  Parsing Strings into Numerics, 60–64
    Numeric Wrapper Classes and, 61
Disk file I/O, 172–179
  Appending Data to an Existing
    Text File, 179
  Deleting, Modifying, and Adding File Data
    Items, 179
  Determining the Existence of a
    File, 175
  Sequential Text File Input, 173–175
  Sequential Text File Output, 175–178
do-while statement, 219–221
  Syntax of the, 219–221
  Common syntactical errors, 220
drawString Method, 64–65

E

Eclipse, 22
Electronic Delay Storage Automatic Calculator
  (EDSAC), 9
Electronic digital computer, 8
Electronic Discrete Variable Automatic
  Computer (EDVAC), 8
Electronic Numerical Integrator and Computer
  (ENIAC), 8
Element(s), 534, 622
End of File (EOF) character, 178
Enhanced for statement, 228–229
Enigma encoding Machine, 8
Enqueue, 615
Enumerated types, 343–345
    Enumeration, 343
      Syntax of, 345
      Three objects of, 345
Ethernet, 11
Event processing, 500–522
  Event handlers, 500
    addActionListener, 503
      addKey-Listener, 503
      addMouseMotionListener, 503
  GUI events, 500
  Implementing Event Handler Methods,
    501–503
  Mouse, Keyboard, and Timer Events,
    512–522
    Keyboard Focus, 516
  Paint Events, JPanels, and Two-Dimensional
    Graphics, 509–512
  Registering the Event Handler, 503–509
    Completion of the Adding Machine
      Application, 504
    getSource Method, 507
    listener list, 503
Exception(s), 179–185, 450–475
  An overview, 450–451
    Terminology, 450–451
  Classes and objects, 451–453
    Checked and unchecked, 452–453
  Creative error message, 466
  Defining classes, 472–475
    Catch Block Ordering, 473

Processing thrown, 453–464
  Non-error Checking Use of, 459–461
  Unwrapping Error Messages, 459
  The finally Clause, 461–464
  try-catch-finally construct, 461
Thrown checked, 453
Throw statement, 465
  Execution Path of, 466
Execution,
  path, 138
  sequential, 192

F

Flash drives, 5
Fibonacci sequence, 436
File-Chooser Dialog Box, 585–587
  JFileChooser, 585
Finally clause, 476
Formatting numeric output, 70
            A first pass, 70–71
  A second pass, 202–208
    Currency Formatting, 202–203
    The DecimalFormat Class: A Second
        Look, 204–208
Formula Translation (FORTRAN), 10
for Statement, 193–202
  A for Loop Application, 197–199
  Common coding errors, 194–194
  Syntax of the, 193–197
  The Totaling and Averaging Algorithms,
      200–202
Fractal(s), 437
  Geometric, 437
  Sierpinsky, 437

G

Game development environment, 26–30
  Changing the Game Board's Size, 29–30
  Creating and Displaying a Game Window
      and Its Title, 28–29
  Installing and Incorporating the Game
      Package into a Program, 28
  The Game Board Coordinate System, 27–28
  The Game Window, 26–27

Game environment, 683–689
  Description, 685–689
    DrawableAdaper Class, 687
    GameBoard class, 685–687
    interface Drawable, 687–689
  Glossary of programming terms, 701–707
  Overview, 683–685
    Game Window, 684
    Timers and Timer Methods, 684
    Game Player Action Methods, 684
    Game Window Coordinate System, 685
  Using the package, 691–692
Game theory, 9
Gates, Bill, 11
Generic(s), 596–637
  API collections framework, 621–637
    ArrayDeque and PriorityQueue Classes,
        630–633
    Framework Algorithms: The Collections
        Class, 622–623
    Framework interfaces, 622
    HashMap, TreeMap, and LinkedHashMap
        Classes, 633–637
  HashSet, TreeSet, and LinkedSet
      Classes, 630
    LinkedList and ArrayList Classes,
        623–629
  Classes, 611–621
    Generic Queue Implementation, 618
    Generic Data Structure, 615–621
    Non-generic Queue, 615
  Methods, 596–610
    Arrays as Generic Parameters and
        Returned Values, 603–610
    Copying an array, 606
    Operating on generic objects, 608–610
    Overloading, 600–602
    Returning arrays, 605
  Overview, 596
getKeyCode method, 515
get method, 113
Gosling, James, 11
Graphical text output, 64–67
  draw Call Back Method, 65–67
  drawString Method, 65
  setFont method, 67

Graphical User Interface (GUI), 337, 480–544
    Applets, 531–544
    Creating application for, 487–499
        Adding GUI Components to a Window, 492–499
        Commonly Used Java Swing GUI Components, 493
        Creating and Displaying a Program Window, 488–492
        Designing the Interface, 494
        GUI-Builder Worker Classes, 491–492
        JWindow, JFrame, JApplet, and JDialog, 487
        The content pane, 488
    Enhancing dialog boxes, 482–486
        showInputDialog Method, 482
        showMessageDialog Method, 482
    Event processing, 500–522
    Layout managers, 522–531
    Overview, 480–481
        Abstract Window Toolkit (AWT) and swing packages, 481

H

Handler or *Listener*, 503
Hard drives, 5
Hardware, 2
hasnext method, 629
History of computing, 5–13
    Computer generations, 9–10
        Fifth-Generation (Present and Beyond): Artificial Intelligence, Parallel Processing, Quantum Computing, 10
        First-Generation (1937–1946): Vacuum Tubes, 9
        Fourth-Generation (1971–present): Microprocessors and VLSI, 10
        Second-Generation (1947–1963): Transistors, 9–10
        Third-Generation (1964–1971): Integrated Circuits (IC) or "chips", 10
    Computers become a reality, 7–9

Early computer devices, 6
    More Notable Contributions, 11–12
    Smaller, Faster, Cheaper Computers, 12–13
Hollerith, Herman, 7
Hopper, Admiral Grace Murray, 11

I

if-else Statement, 150–158
    Detecting Collisions: Use of the if and else-if Statements, 154–158
If Statement, 144–150
    Using the, 146–150
Index, 236
Information passing, 79–89
    Class Level Variables, 85–89
    Parameters and arguments, 79–82
    Returned Values, 84–85
    Scope and Side Effects of Value Parameters, 82–84
Inheritance, 353–385
    Chain, 357
    Concept of, 354–355
    Design processing in, 372–385
        Making a Class Inheritance Ready: Best Practices, 384–385
    Implementing, 357–372
        Constructors and Inherited Method Invocations, 361–368
        Extending Inherited Data Members, 368–372
        Overriding Methods, 364–368
    Multiple, 357
    UML diagrams and language of, 355–357
        Establishing Parent-Child Relationship, 356
        Forms of, 357
        Parent-Child Relationship, 355
Inherited Method Invocation Syntax, 368
InputDialogBox method, 60
Input Method, 117
Input/output (I/O) devices, 3
Institute for Advanced Study (IAS), 9
Integrated Development Environment (IDE), 22–28, 41

Mobile-Device Application Development
Environments, 25–28
Iterator(s), 629
Interface(s), 353, 398–406
Idiosyncrasies concerning, 399
When to Define and Use an, 400–405
International Business Machine Corporation
(IBM), 7
Items, 563
itemStateChanged, 554

J

Java, 11
Application program template, 40–41
Keywords, 697
Operators and their relative precedence, 699
Platform independence and, 17–20
Java Application Programmer Interface,
19–20
Java Development Kit (JDK), 532
Java Runtime Environment (JRE), 20
Java Virtual Machine (JVM), *18*
JCheckBox Classes, 493, 552
JComboBox Class, 563
JList Class, 563
Jobs, Steve, 11
JOptionPane Method, 59, 84
JRadioButton, 493, 555

K

Kahn, Robert, 12
Key, 622
Knuth, Donald, 12

L

Layout manager(s), 522–531
Border Layout, 524–527
Designating the, 523–524
Component Capacity, Size and
Positioning Restrictions, 524
Flow Layout, 527–529
Grid Layout, 529–531
Leading zero, 204

Lifetime, 649
Lock, 651
Loop,
do-while, 220
post-test, 220
statements to use, 222–224

M

Member methods, 95
Memory storage schemes, 30–34
Representing Character Data, 30–31
Representing Numeric Data, 32–34
Representing Translated Instructions, 31–32
Menu(s), 572–584
Building a, 573–574
Drop-down, 572–573
JMenuItem Object Action Events, 575–579
Mnemonic, 575
Pop-up, 581–584
Radio Button and Check Box Items,
579–581
Separator bars, 574–575
Method(s), 20, 76–78
Abstract Parent, 382
Designing Parent Methods to Invoke Child,
382
Final, 367
Invoking a Parent's Version of an
Overwritten, 365
Methods invoking methods within their
class, 301–303
Motivation for writing, 76
Private class, 302–303
Public or protected methods,
Syntax of a, 76–78
Method Search Path, 368

N

Nested for loops, 208–211
CheckerBoard, 211
Nested if statement, 158–160
NetBeans, 22
nextDouble methods, 171, 230
nextInt Method, 225

New-line character, 178
Nonstatic void methods, 90
Notify Method, 660
notifyAll Method, 652

O

Object(s), 22
    Collection, 621
    Comparing, 303–306
        Deep Comparisons, 305–306
        Shallow Comparisons, 304–305
    Copying and cloning, 306–318
        Cloning objects, 309
        Deep Copies and Clones, 308–318
        Shallow copies, 307–308
    Creating, 96–98
        Constructor methods, 97–98
    Designing a graphical, 100–102
        Drawing an, 100–102
    Displaying an, 98–100
    Queue collection, 621
Object-oriented programming (OOP)
        languages, 11, 21–22, 93–94
    Class starship method, 21–22
        Create, draw and move, 22
    What Are Classes and Objects?, 93–94
Online API documentation, 709–711
Operating system software, 3
Overriding methods, 364–368
    Common things, 368
Overloading methods vs, 367

P

Packages, 19
Pac-Man game, 652
Parallel processing, 10
Pascaline, 6
Passing by value, 80
Passing Objects to and from Worker methods,
        125–128
                Passing Objects to Worker
        Methods, 125–127
                Returning an Object from a
        Worker Method, 127–128

Point-and-click interface, 337
pow method, 59, 79
Polymorphism, 353, 385–398
    getClass and getName method and the
                instanceof operator, 393–398
    Parent and Child References, 385–387
    Polymorphic array, 390–392
        advantages of, 392
    polymorphic invocation, 387–389
    Role in Parameter Passing, 392–393
print Method, 59
println Method, 59
Processes, 644
Processing large numbers, 340–343
    BigInteger Class, 341–343
    BigDecimal Class, 343
Producer-Consumer problem (PCP), 652–673
    Solutions to, 660–673
        ArrayBlockingQueue, 668–673
        Synchronizing a Buffer Class:
                Synchronized Methods, 660–668
        Pseudocode of the PCP, 661
Program specification, 13–17
    Specifying a game program, 15–17

Q

Quantum computing, 10

R

Radio buttons, 555–562
    Adding Buttons to Containers and
                Positioning Them, 557–558
    Creating, 555–556
    Determining the status of, 558
    Events, 558–562
    Making Buttons Mutually Exclusive, 556
Random access memory (RAM) or main
        memory, 3
Recursion, 418–444
    formulating and implementing recursive
        algorithms, 423–429
        Base Case, Reduced Problem, and
                General Solution, 423–425
        Implementing Algorithms, 425–427

Practice problems, 428–429
non-recursive, 419
problems with, 435–444
 Dynamic programming, 440–444
 when to use, 437–440
Recursive, 418
Towers of Hanoi problem, 429–434
 Base case, 430–431
 General solution, 432–433
 Implementation, 433–434
 Reduced problem, 432
 Statement of the Problem, 429–430
understanding a recursive method's
 execution path, 421–423
What is, 418–421
Run-time stack, 435

S

Scientific notation, 205
Sentinel value, 214
Serializing objects, 406–411
 object deserialization, 407
 object serialization, 407
Serialization, 353, 406
setBorder Method, 550
setColor Method, 89
setMaxRowCount Method, 590
set Method, 112
setTimerInterval Method, 686
setVisibleCount Method, 567
showGameBoard method, 66
showInputDialog method, 59, 84
showMessageDialog method, 59
Signature, 76
Sleep method, 652
Software, 3
engineer, 13
Software Development Kit (SDK), 25
Sqrt method, 64
Stack, 631
Static data members, 298–300
stopTimer Method, 687
String, 44

Class: A second look, 318–322
 Converting Strings to Characters, 319
 Creating Strings from Primitive Values,
 318–319
 Processing Strings, 319–322
 Formatting, 204
 Immutability, 112
 Objects, 48–50
Subscriber identification module (SIM)
 cards, 4
switch Statement, 160–168
 break statement, 164–168
 if-else statements and, 162
Synchronized code block, 651
Synchronized statement, 673–677
Syntax error, 23
System console output, 44–48
 Escape sequence, 45–48
 Comments and Blank Lines, 48
 String output, 44
 The Concatenation Operator and Annotated
 Numeric Output, 44–45

T

Thread(s), 644–652
 Creating and initiating, 645–649
 Defining class, 645–646
 Initiating the execution, 647–649
 Main, 645
 States, 649–652
 Blocked, Waiting, and Timed Waiting,
 651–652
 New, Runnable, and Terminated,
 649–650
Totaling or summation algorithm, 200
Trailing zero, 204
Transmission Control Protocol/Internet
 Protocol (TCP/IP), 11
Text document (TEX) typesetting system, 12
toString Method, 116
Turing, Alan, 8
Type argument list, 611

U

UNICODE table, 31
Unified modeling language (UML) diagram,
      94–95, 355
Universal automatic computer
      (UNIVAC 1), 10

V

Value parameters, 80
Value(s), 563, 622
Variables, 41–44
   Class Level, 85–89
      code block, 86
      local variable, 86
      swap methods, 87
   Primitive, 42–44
   Reference, 42, 48–50

Very-large-scale integration (VLSI), 10
void Method, 77, 117
von Neumann architecture, 9

W

wait Method, 651, 662
while Statement, 212–219
   Common coding errors, 213
   Detecting an End Of File, 217–219
   sentinel loop, 214–216
   Syntax of the, 212–213
World Wide Web Consortium (W3C), 12
Wrapper classes, 322–328
   Autoboxing and Unboxing, 324–325
   Characters, 326–328
   Class objects, 322–324
   Constants, 326